NAOKI URASAWA
with FUJIO PRODUCTIONS LTD.

夢 MUJIRUSHI 印
The Sign of Dreams

NAOKI URASAWA
with FUJIO PRODUCTIONS LTD.

夢印 MUJIRUSHI
The Sign of Dreams

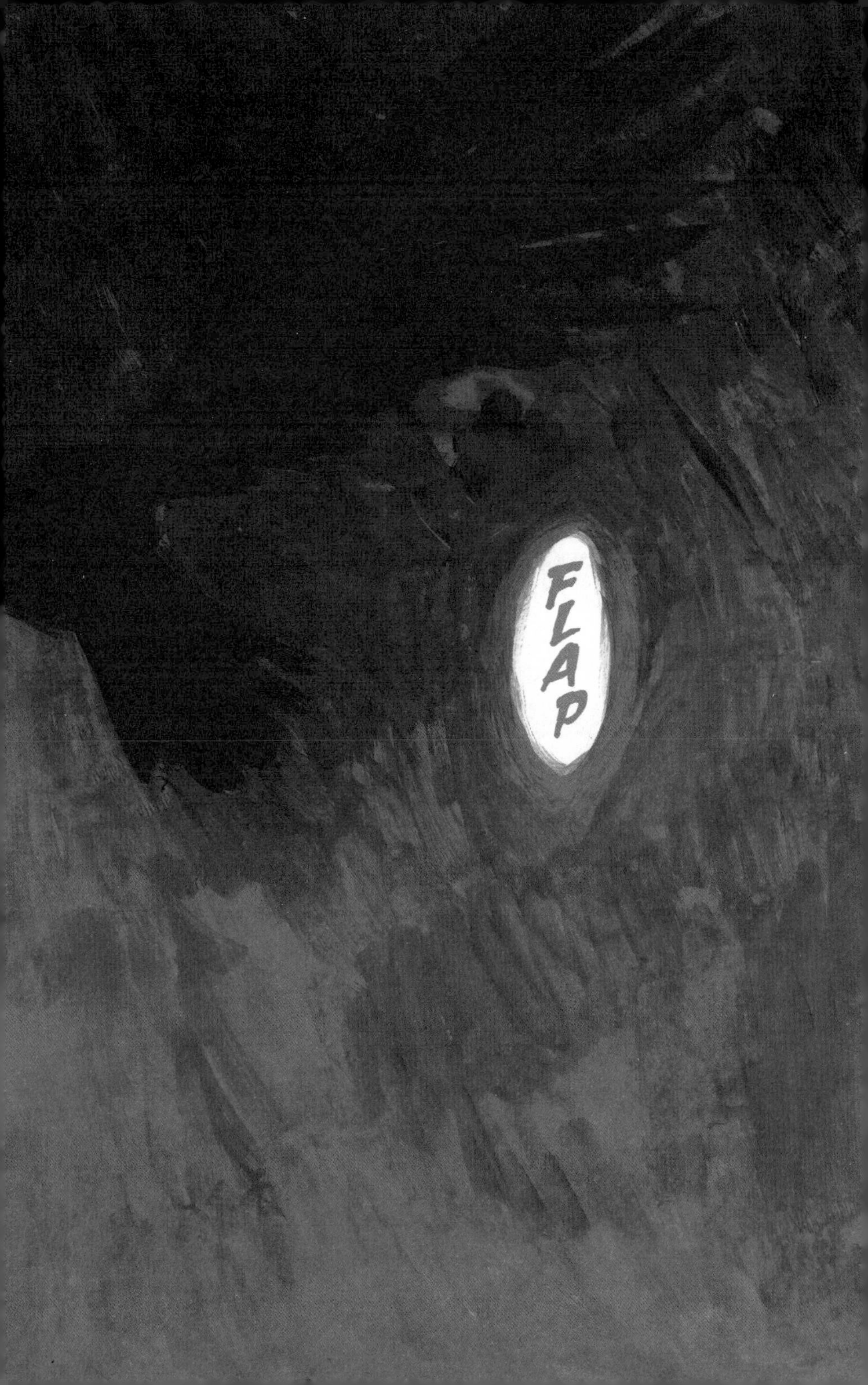
FLAP

contents

1er Sheeh! **Research Institute**

HM?

HOLD OUT YOUR HAND.

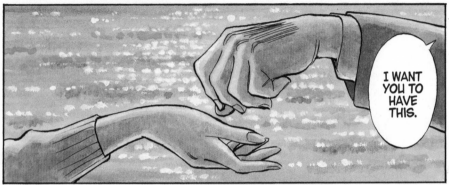

I WANT YOU TO HAVE THIS.

O-OH NO!

AGH!

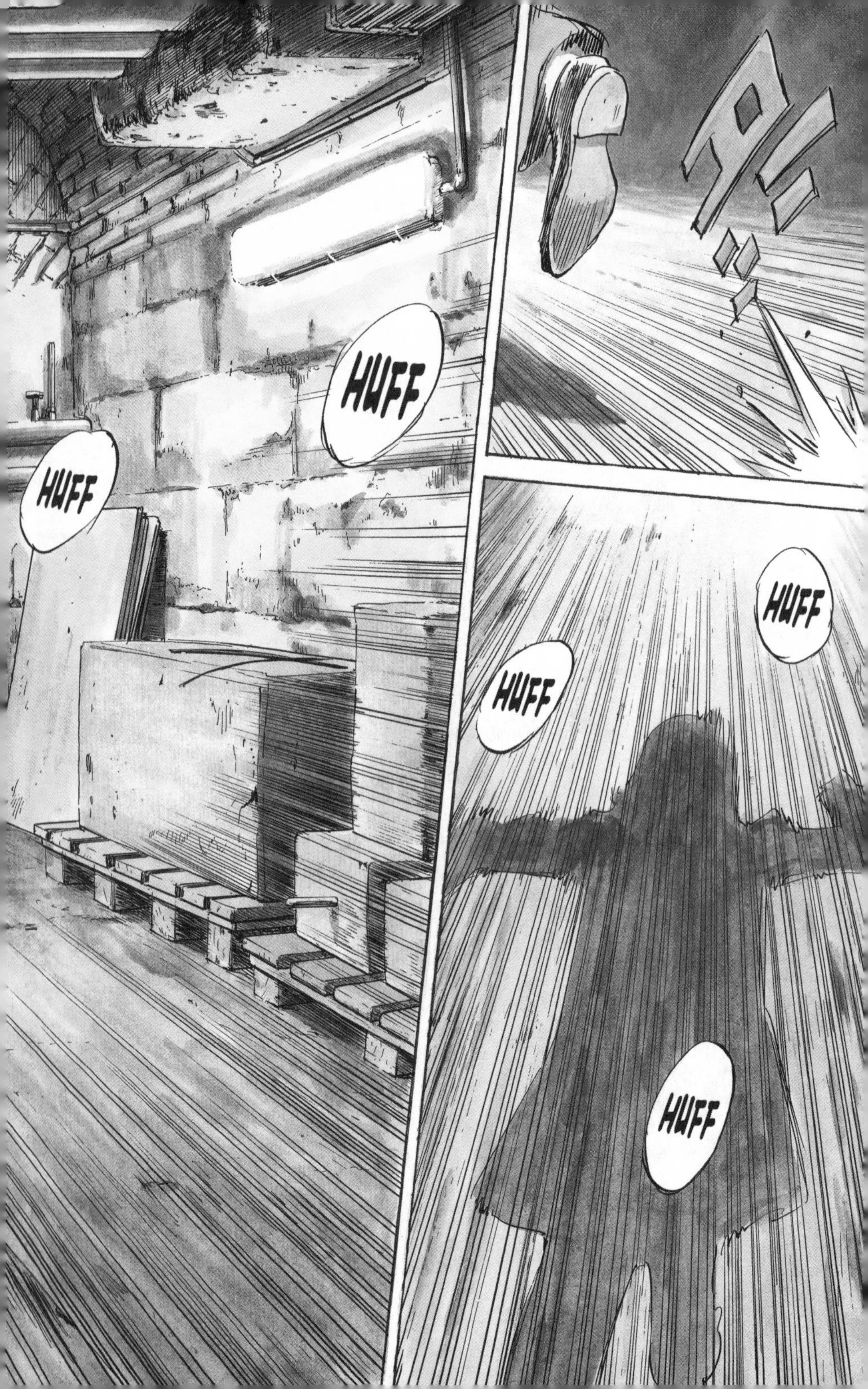
HUFF
HUFF
HUFF
HUFF
HUFF

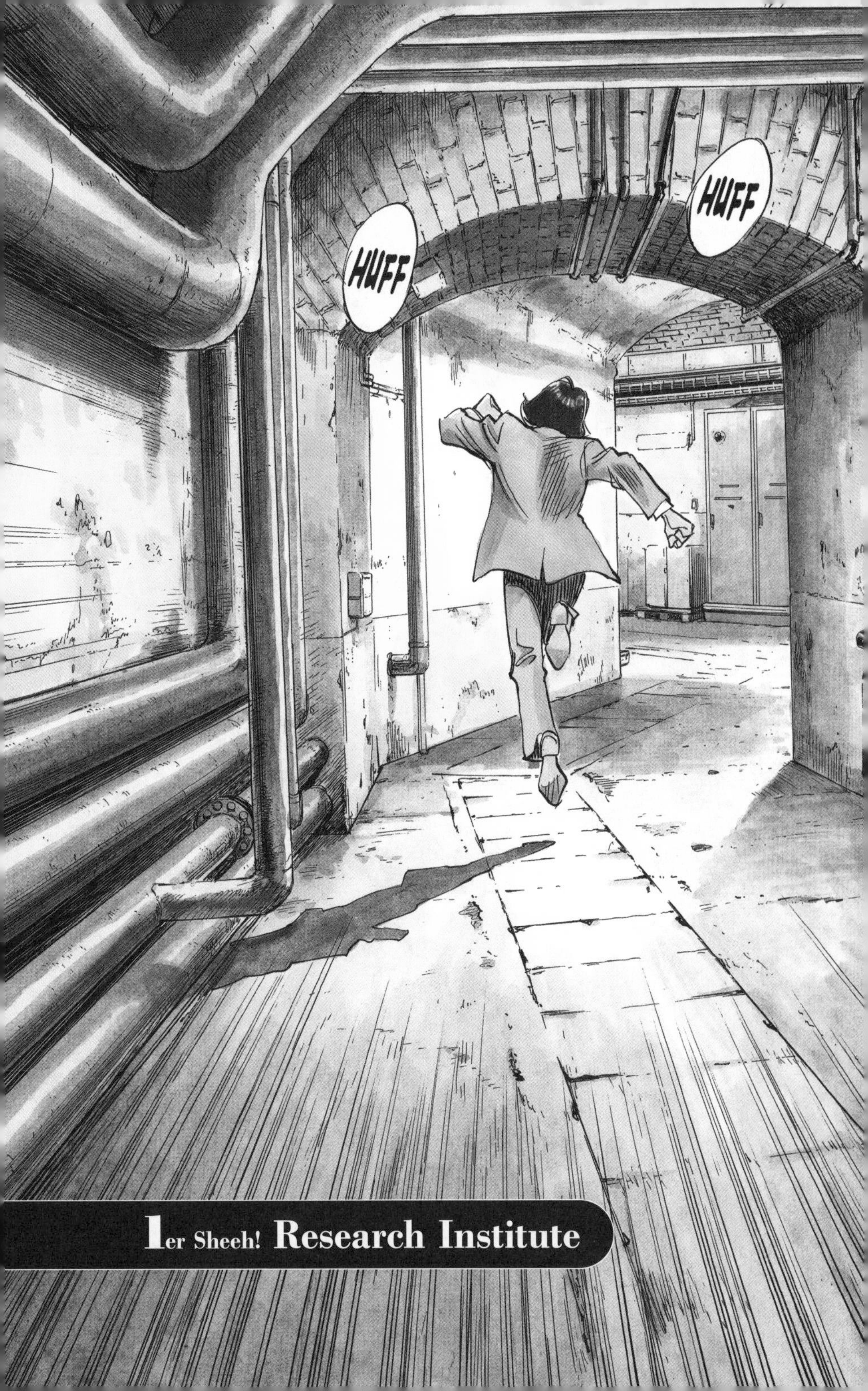
HUFF
HUFF

1er Sheeh! Research Institute

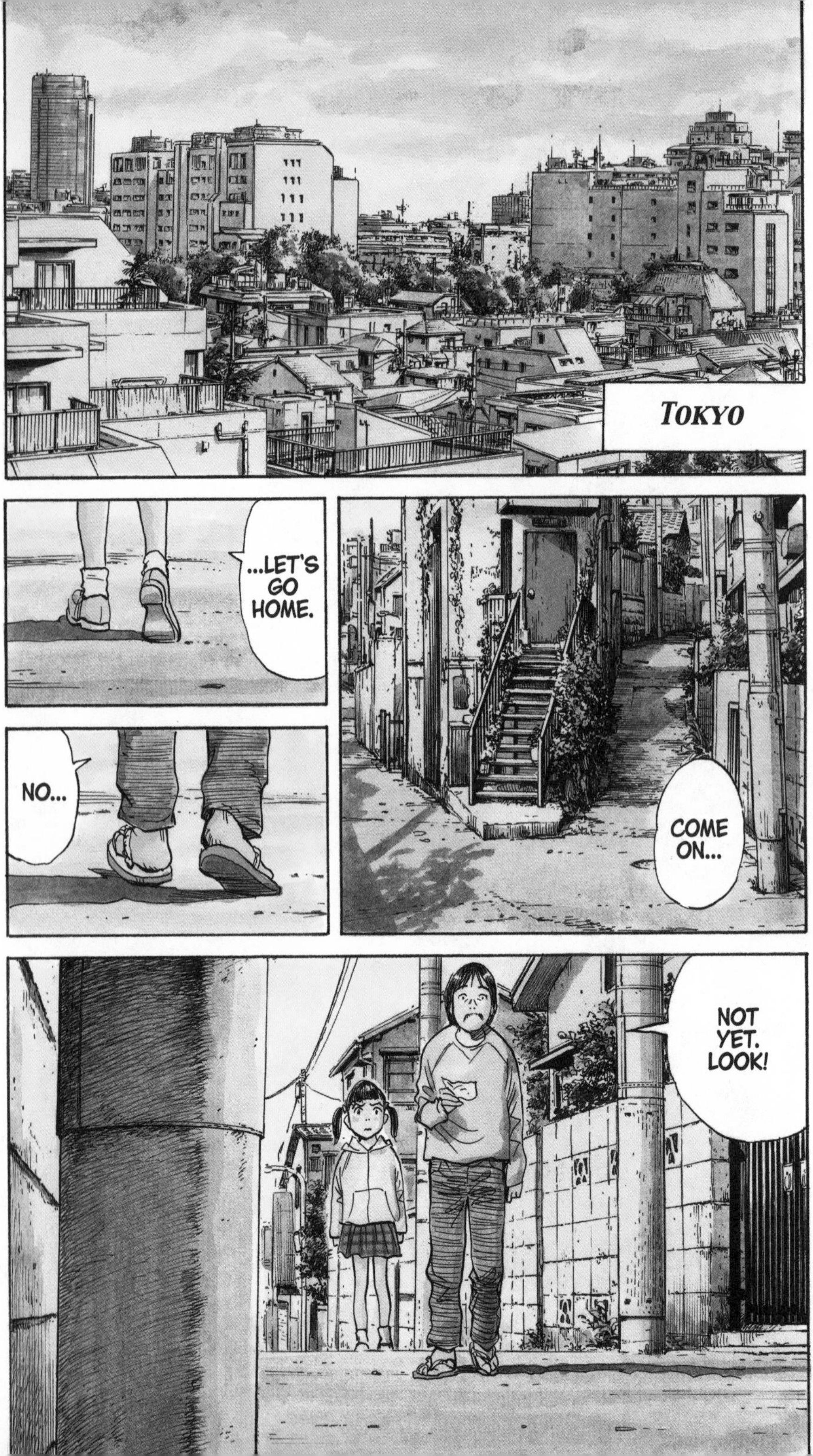
TOKYO
COME ON...
...LET'S GO HOME.
NO...
NOT YET. LOOK!

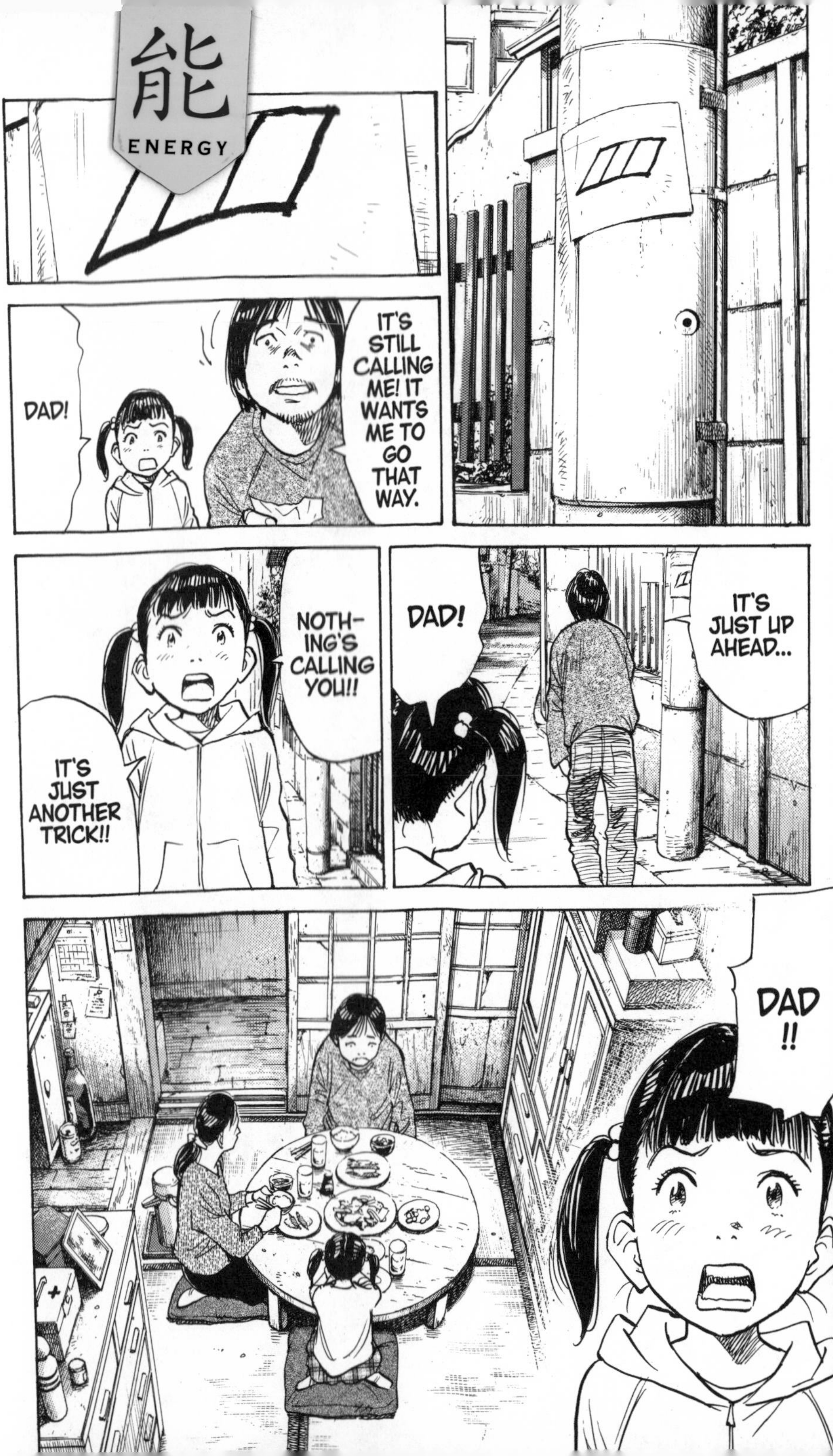
能
ENERGY
IT'S STILL CALLING ME! IT WANTS ME TO GO THAT WAY.
DAD!
IT'S JUST UP AHEAD...
DAD!
NOTHING'S CALLING YOU!!
IT'S JUST ANOTHER TRICK!!
DAD!!

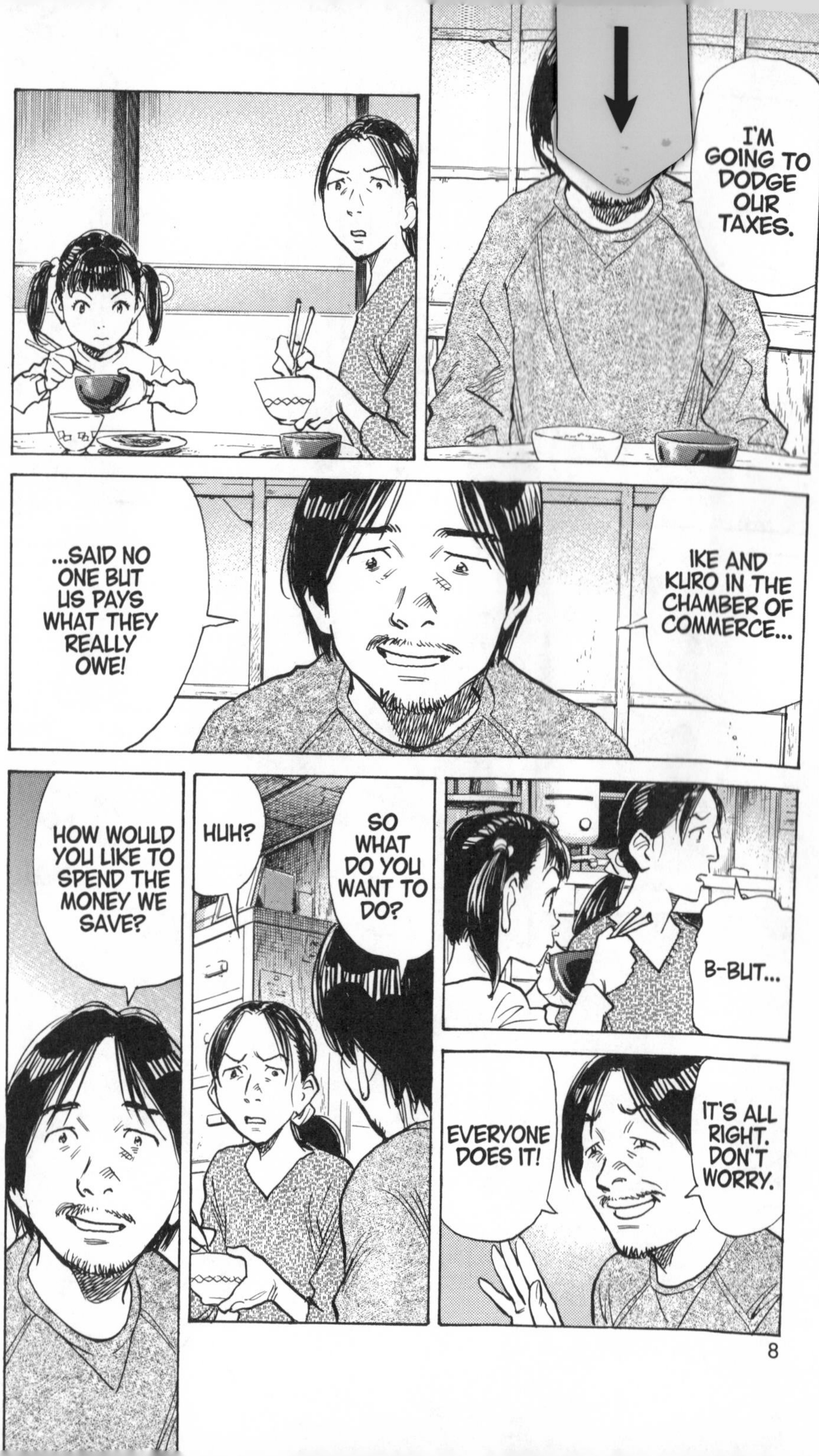
I'M GOING TO DODGE OUR TAXES.
IKE AND KURO IN THE CHAMBER OF COMMERCE...
...SAID NO ONE BUT US PAYS WHAT THEY REALLY OWE!
B-BUT...
IT'S ALL RIGHT. DON'T WORRY.
EVERYONE DOES IT!
SO WHAT DO YOU WANT TO DO?
HUH?
HOW WOULD YOU LIKE TO SPEND THE MONEY WE SAVE?

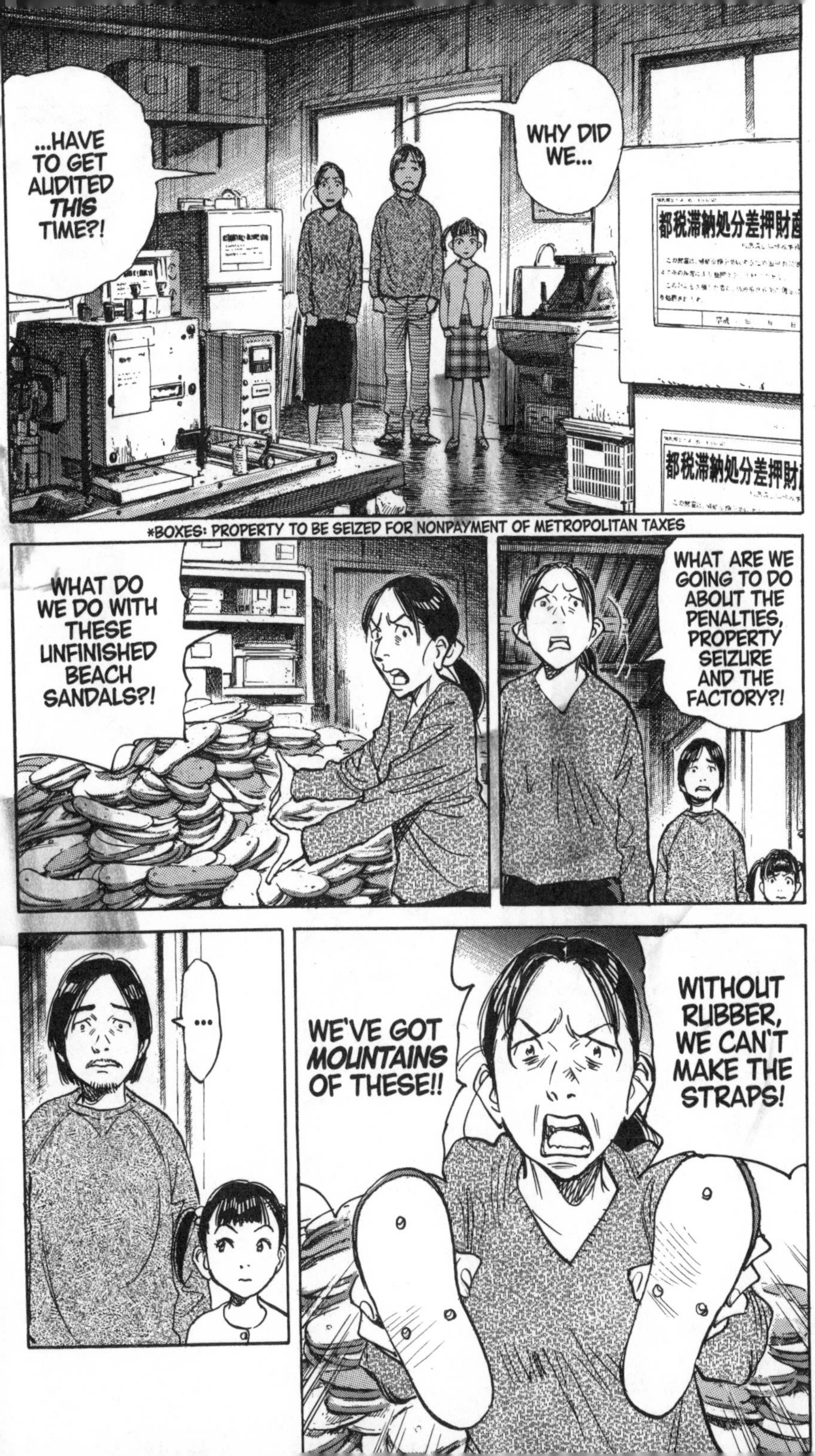
WHY DID WE...
...HAVE TO GET AUDITED THIS TIME?!
都税滞納処分差押財
都税滞納処分差押財
*BOXES: PROPERTY TO BE SEIZED FOR NONPAYMENT OF METROPOLITAN TAXES
WHAT ARE WE GOING TO DO ABOUT THE PENALTIES, PROPERTY SEIZURE AND THE FACTORY?!
WHAT DO WE DO WITH THESE UNFINISHED BEACH SANDALS?!
WITHOUT RUBBER, WE CAN'T MAKE THE STRAPS!
WE'VE GOT MOUNTAINS OF THESE!!
...

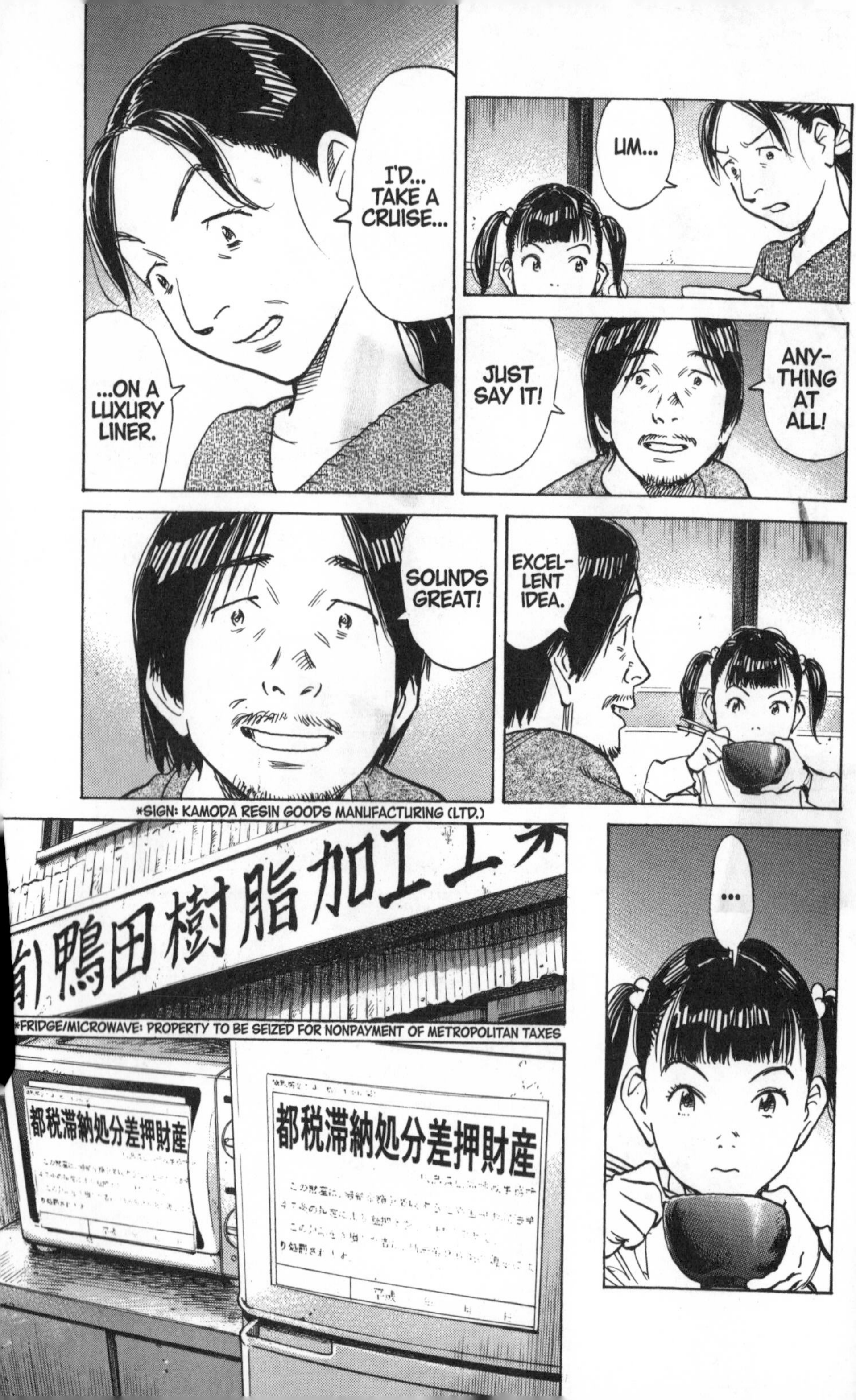
UM...
ANY-THING AT ALL!
JUST SAY IT!
I'D... TAKE A CRUISE...
...ON A LUXURY LINER.
EXCEL-LENT IDEA.
SOUNDS GREAT!
...
*SIGN: KAMODA RESIN GOODS MANUFACTURING (LTD.)
鴨田樹脂加工工
*FRIDGE/MICROWAVE: PROPERTY TO BE SEIZED FOR NONPAYMENT OF METROPOLITAN TAXES
都税滞納処分差押財産
都税滞納処分差押財産

DAD!

IT'S STILL CALLING ME! IT WANTS ME TO GO THAT WAY.

NOTH-ING'S CALLING YOU!!

IT'S JUST ANOTHER TRICK!!

DAD!

IT'S JUST UP AHEAD...

DAD!!

I'M GOING TO DODGE OUR TAXES.

...SAID NO ONE BUT US PAYS WHAT THEY REALLY OWE!

IKE AND KURO IN THE CHAMBER OF COMMERCE...

HOW WOULD YOU LIKE TO SPEND THE MONEY WE SAVE?

HUH?

SO WHAT DO YOU WANT TO DO?

B-BUT...

EVERYONE DOES IT!

IT'S ALL RIGHT. DON'T WORRY.

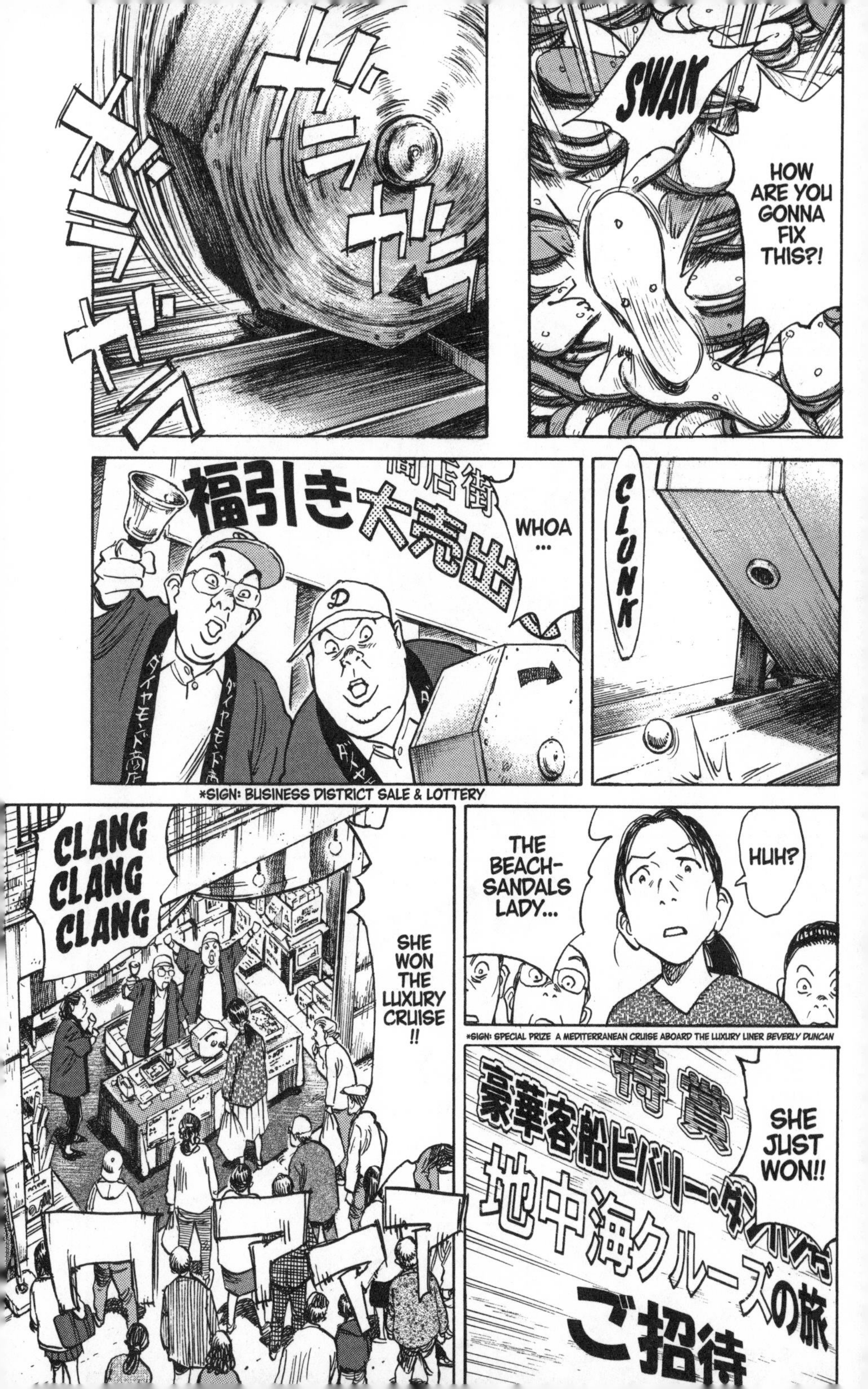
SWAK
HOW ARE YOU GONNA FIX THIS?!
CLUNK
WHOA ...
福引き大売出
商店街
*SIGN: BUSINESS DISTRICT SALE & LOTTERY
THE BEACH-SANDALS LADY...
HUH?
*SIGN: SPECIAL PRIZE A MEDITERRANEAN CRUISE ABOARD THE LUXURY LINER BEVERLY DUNCAN
特賞
豪華客船ビバリー・ダンカン号
地中海クルーズの旅
ご招待
SHE JUST WON!!
CLANG CLANG CLANG
SHE WON THE LUXURY CRUISE!!

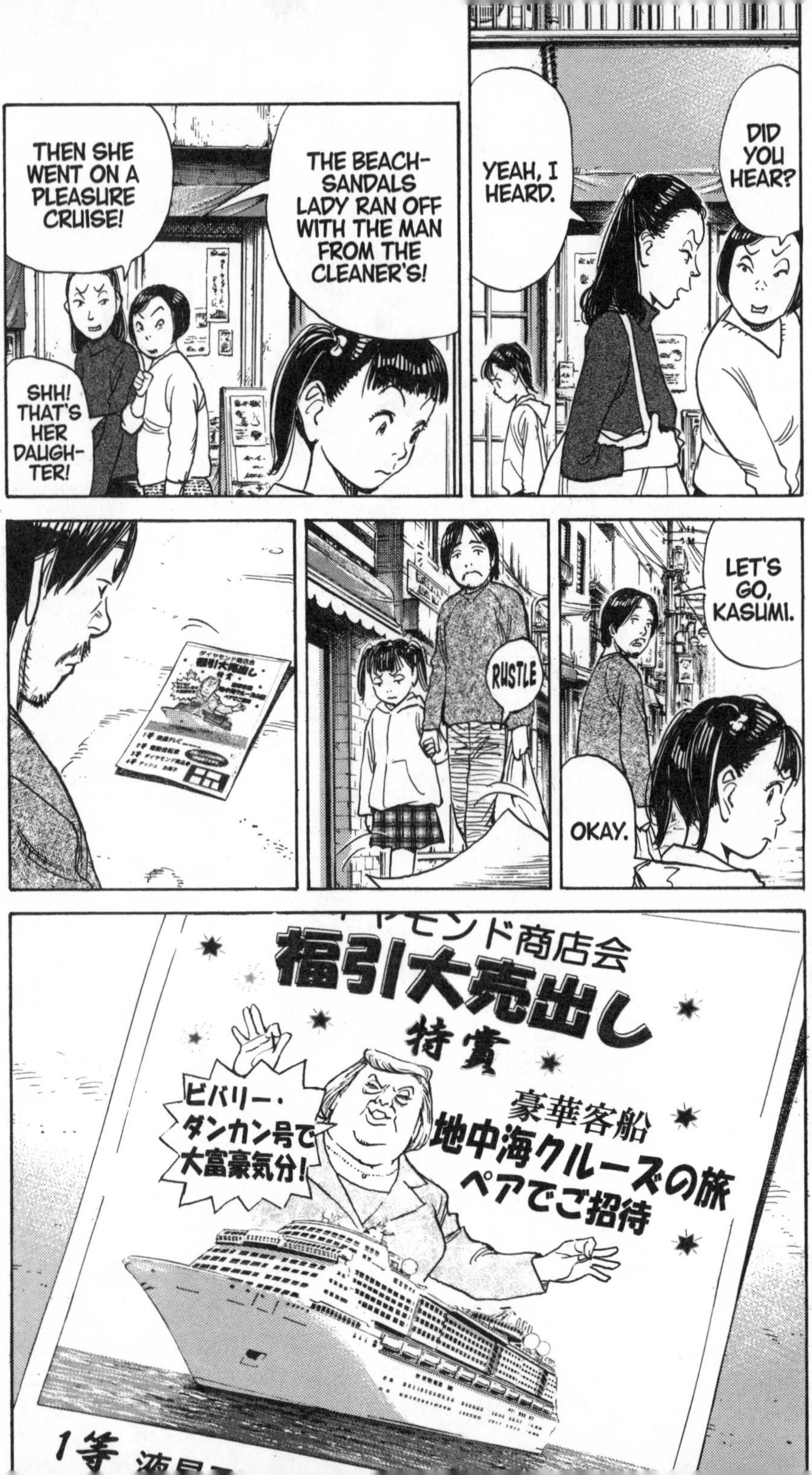
DID YOU HEAR?
YEAH, I HEARD.
THE BEACH-SANDALS LADY RAN OFF WITH THE MAN FROM THE CLEANER'S!
THEN SHE WENT ON A PLEASURE CRUISE!
SHH! THAT'S HER DAUGHTER!
LET'S GO, KASUMI.
OKAY.
RUSTLE
ヤモンド商店会
福引大売出し
特賞
豪華客船
地中海クルーズの旅
ペアでご招待
ビバリー・ダンカン号で大富豪気分!
1等

*FLYER: DIAMOND STORE ASSOCIATION SALE & LOTTERY SPECIAL PRIZE TWO TICKETS FOR A MEDITERRANEAN CRUISE ABOARD LUXURY LINER! FEEL LIKE A BILLIONAIRE ON THE BEVERLY DUNCAN!

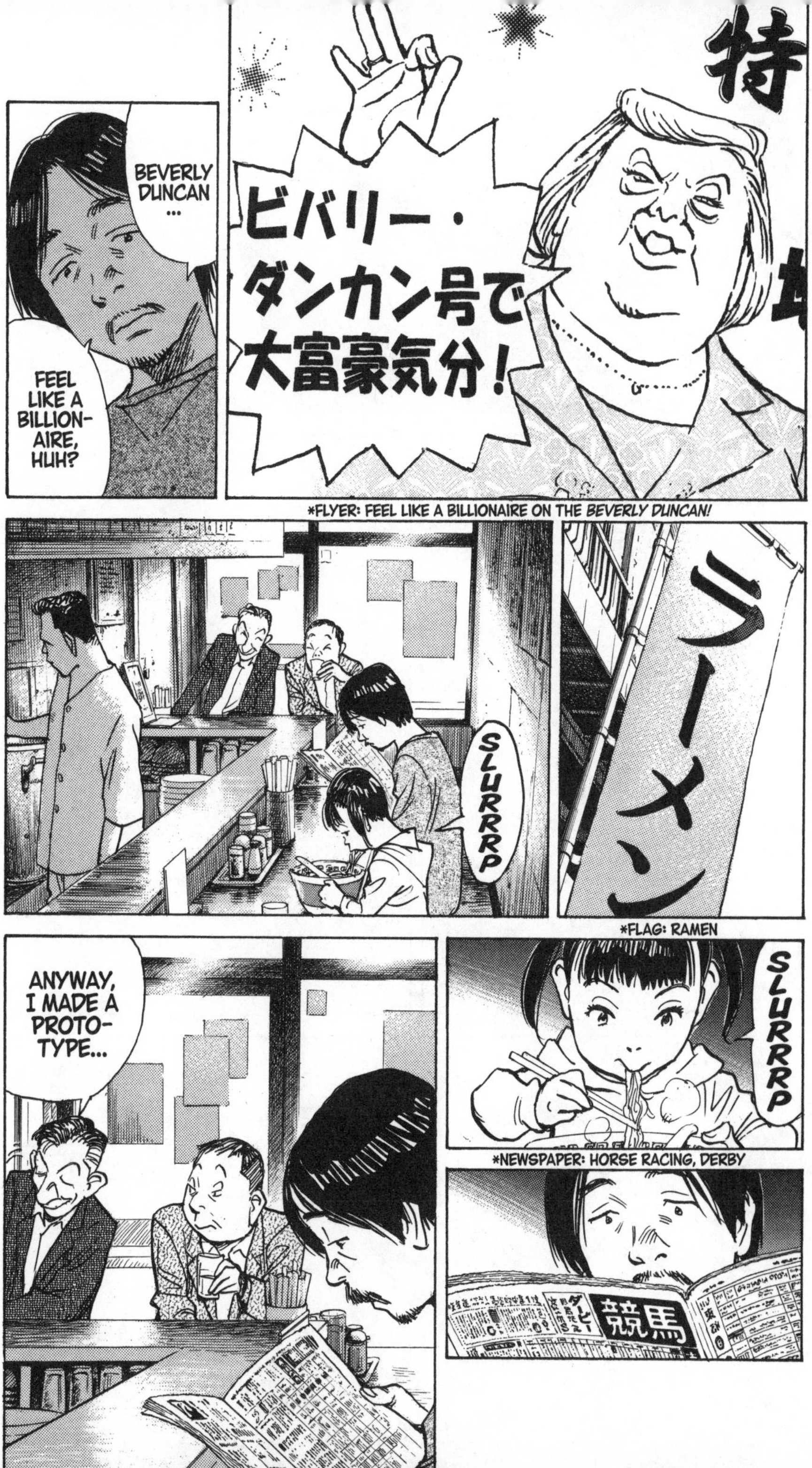
特
ビバリー・ダンカン号で大富豪気分！
BEVERLY DUNCAN ...
FEEL LIKE A BILLIONAIRE, HUH?
*FLYER: FEEL LIKE A BILLIONAIRE ON THE *BEVERLY DUNCAN!*
ラーメン
SLURRRP
*FLAG: RAMEN
SLURRRP
*NEWSPAPER: HORSE RACING, DERBY
競馬
ダービー
ANYWAY, I MADE A PROTOTYPE...

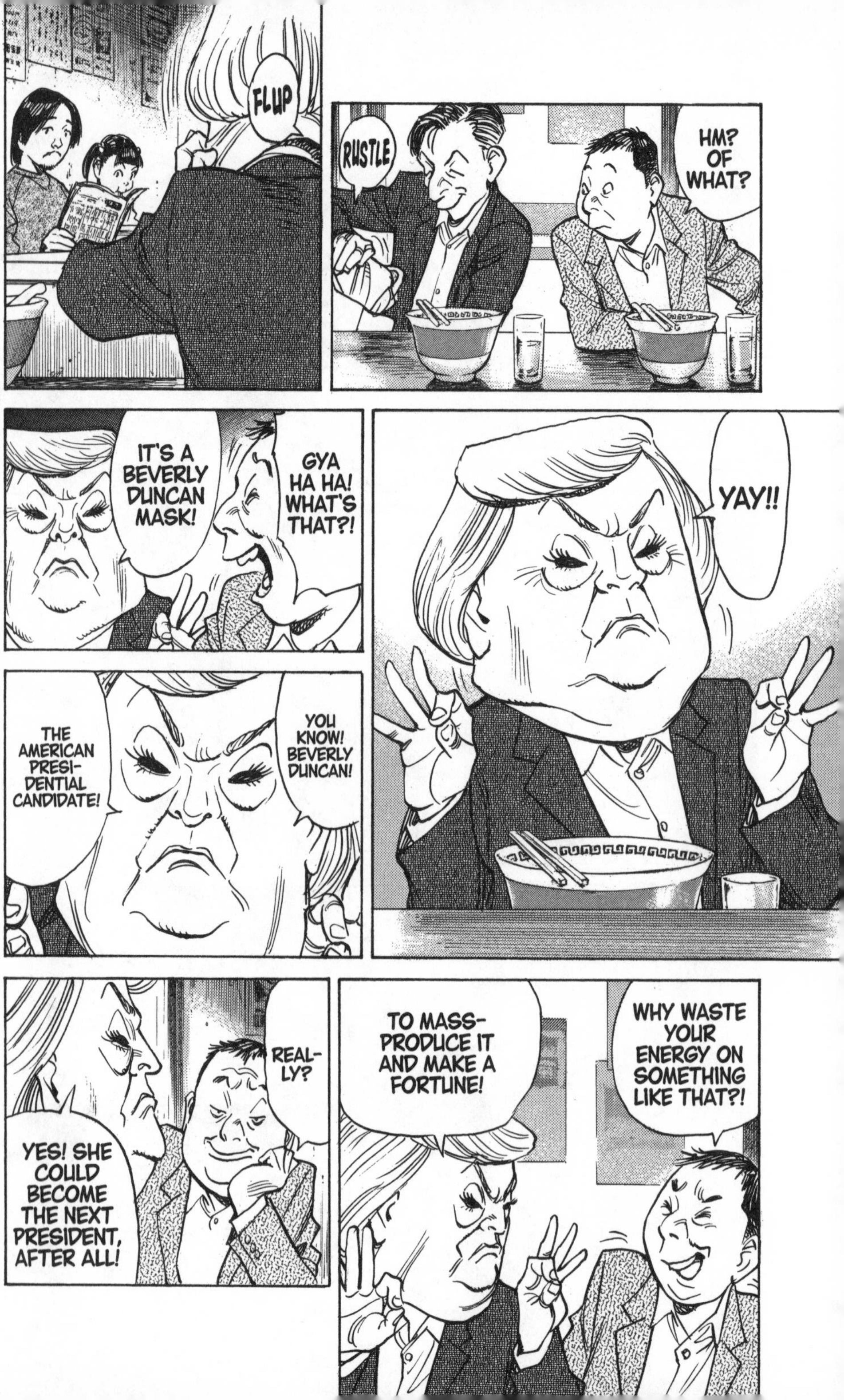
HM? OF WHAT?
RUSTLE
FLUP
YAY!!
GYA HA HA! WHAT'S THAT?!
IT'S A BEVERLY DUNCAN MASK!
YOU KNOW! BEVERLY DUNCAN!
THE AMERICAN PRESI-DENTIAL CANDIDATE!
WHY WASTE YOUR ENERGY ON SOMETHING LIKE THAT?!
TO MASS-PRODUCE IT AND MAKE A FORTUNE!
REAL-LY?
YES! SHE COULD BECOME THE NEXT PRESIDENT, AFTER ALL!

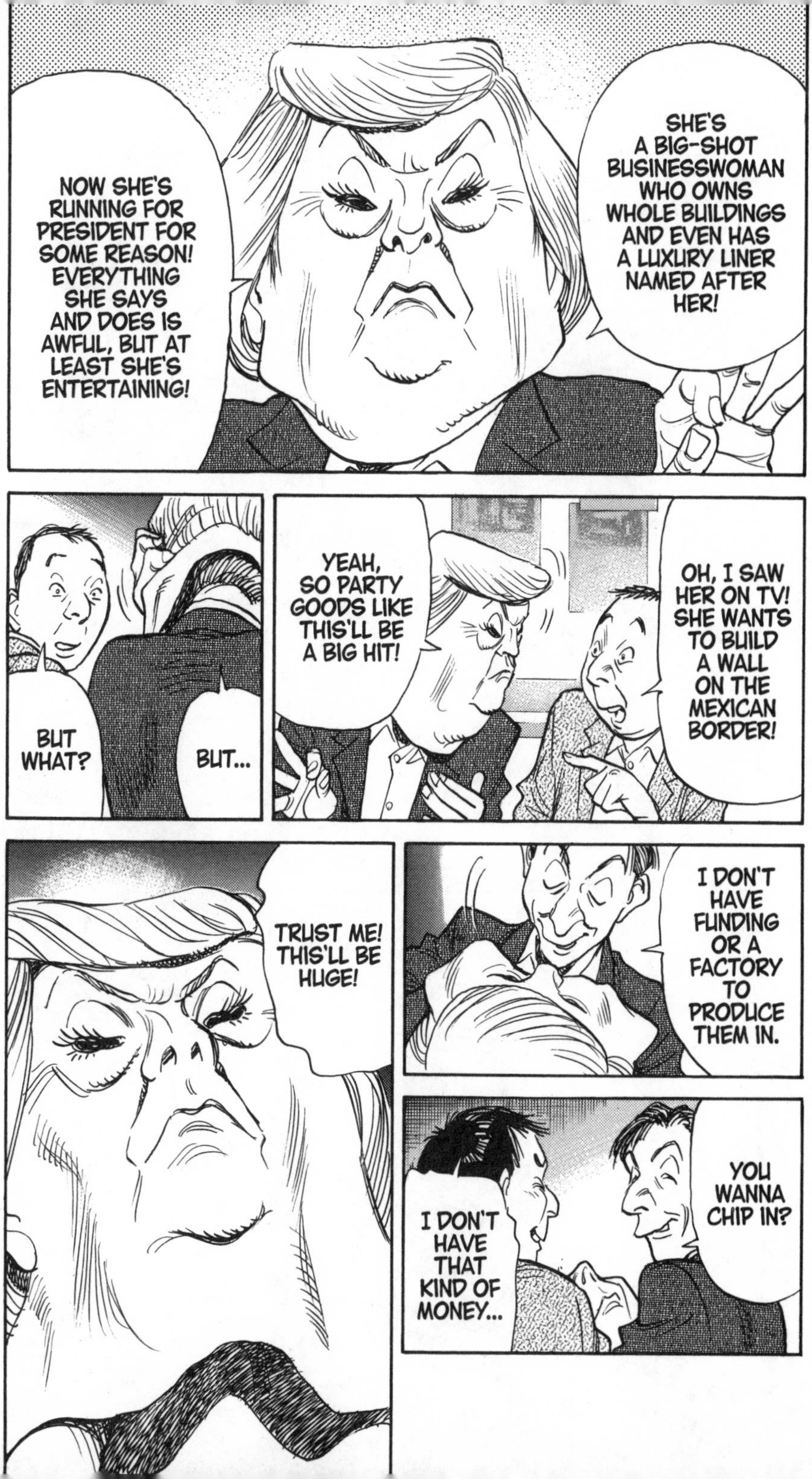
SHE'S A BIG-SHOT BUSINESSWOMAN WHO OWNS WHOLE BUILDINGS AND EVEN HAS A LUXURY LINER NAMED AFTER HER!
NOW SHE'S RUNNING FOR PRESIDENT FOR SOME REASON! EVERYTHING SHE SAYS AND DOES IS AWFUL, BUT AT LEAST SHE'S ENTERTAINING!
OH, I SAW HER ON TV! SHE WANTS TO BUILD A WALL ON THE MEXICAN BORDER!
YEAH, SO PARTY GOODS LIKE THIS'LL BE A BIG HIT!
BUT...
BUT WHAT?
I DON'T HAVE FUNDING OR A FACTORY TO PRODUCE THEM IN.
YOU WANNA CHIP IN?
I DON'T HAVE THAT KIND OF MONEY...
TRUST ME! THIS'LL BE HUGE!

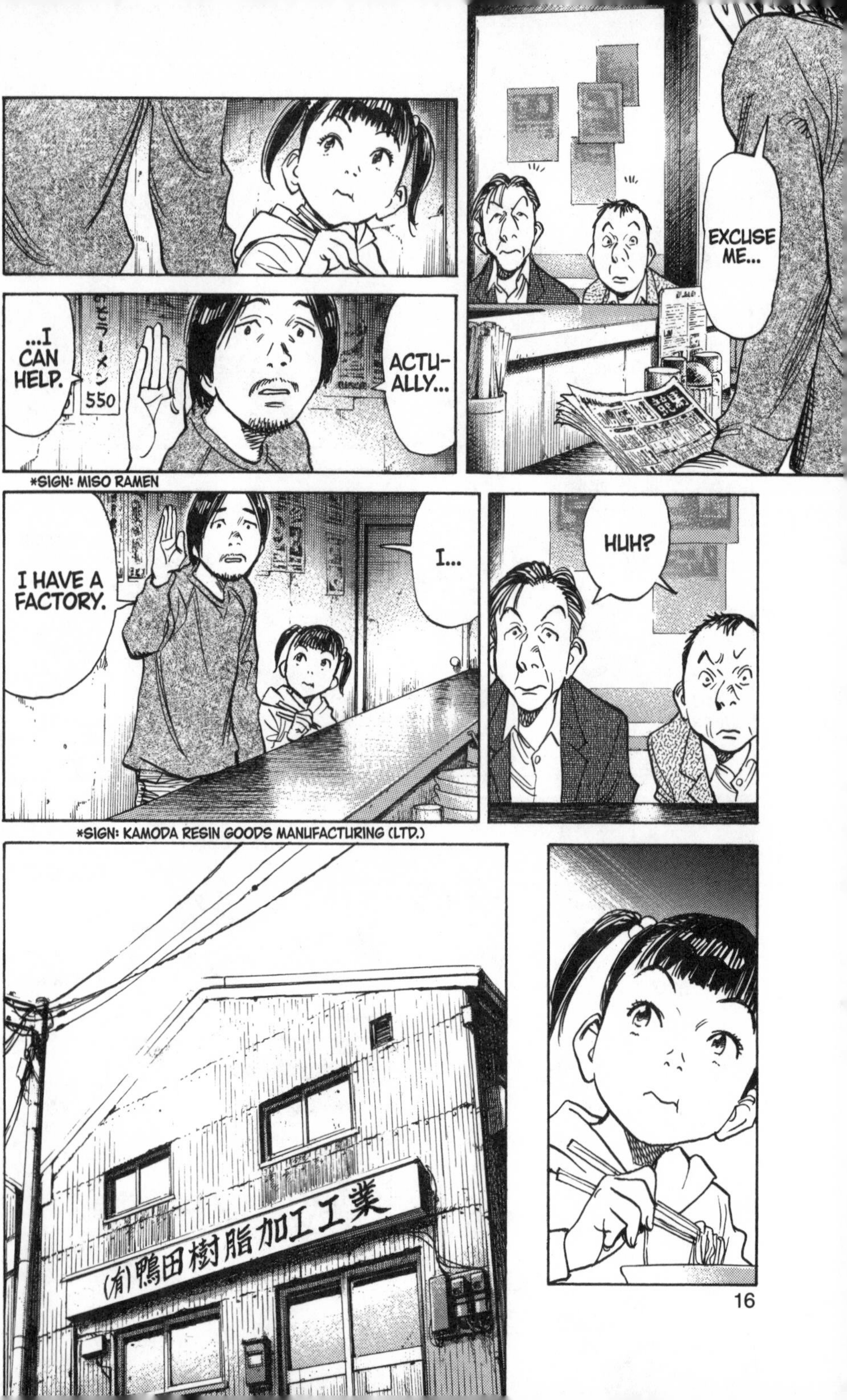
EXCUSE ME...
ACTU-ALLY...
...I CAN HELP.
*SIGN: MISO RAMEN
HUH?
I...
I HAVE A FACTORY.
*SIGN: KAMODA RESIN GOODS MANUFACTURING (LTD.)
(有)鴨田樹脂加工工業

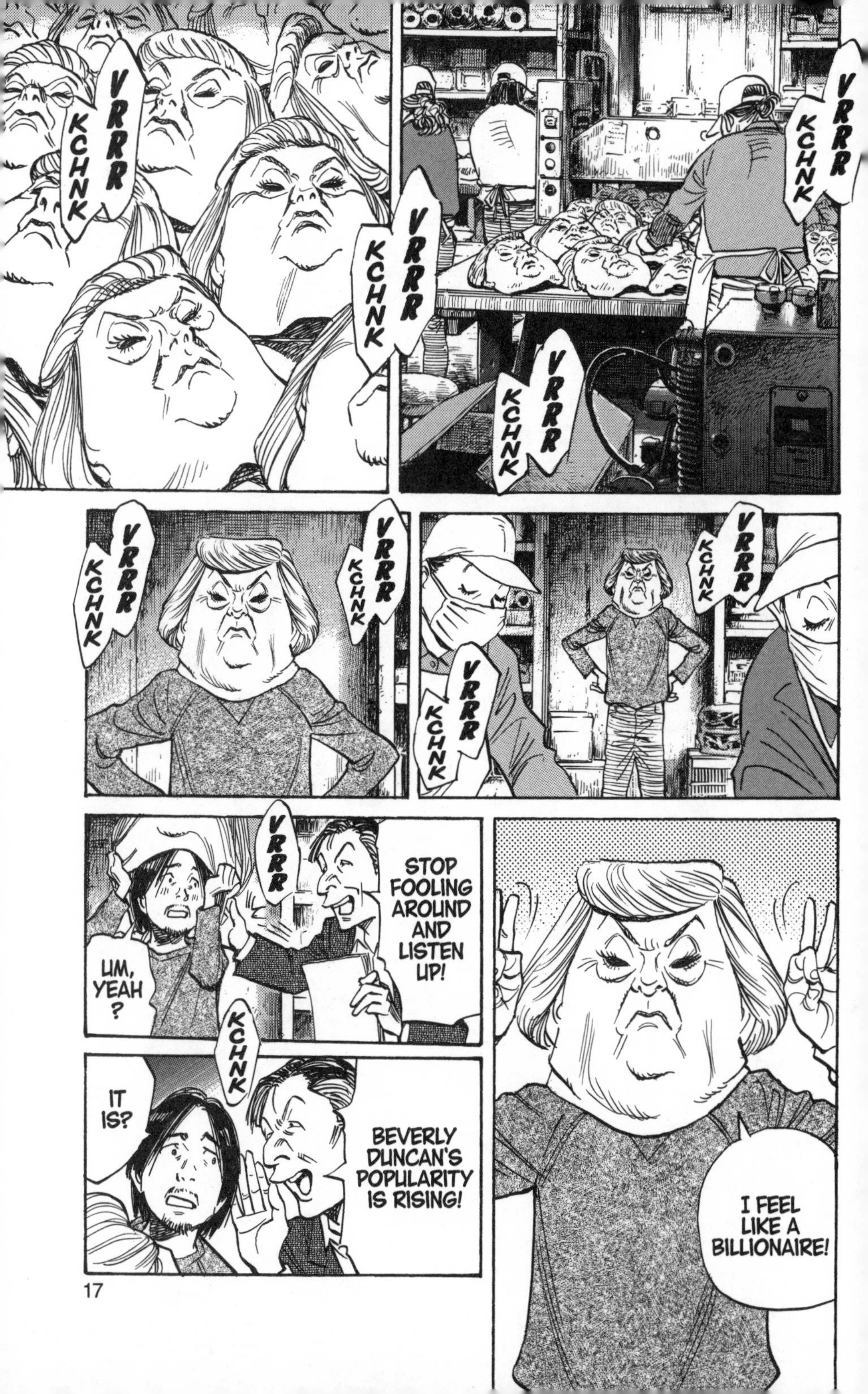
VRRR KCHNK
VRRR KCHNK
VRRR KCHNK
VRRR KCHNK
VRRR KCHNK
VRRR KCHNK
VRRR KCHNK
VRRR KCHNK
I FEEL LIKE A BILLIONAIRE!
STOP FOOLING AROUND AND LISTEN UP!
VRRR
UM, YEAH?
KCHNK
BEVERLY DUNCAN'S POPULARITY IS RISING!
IT IS?

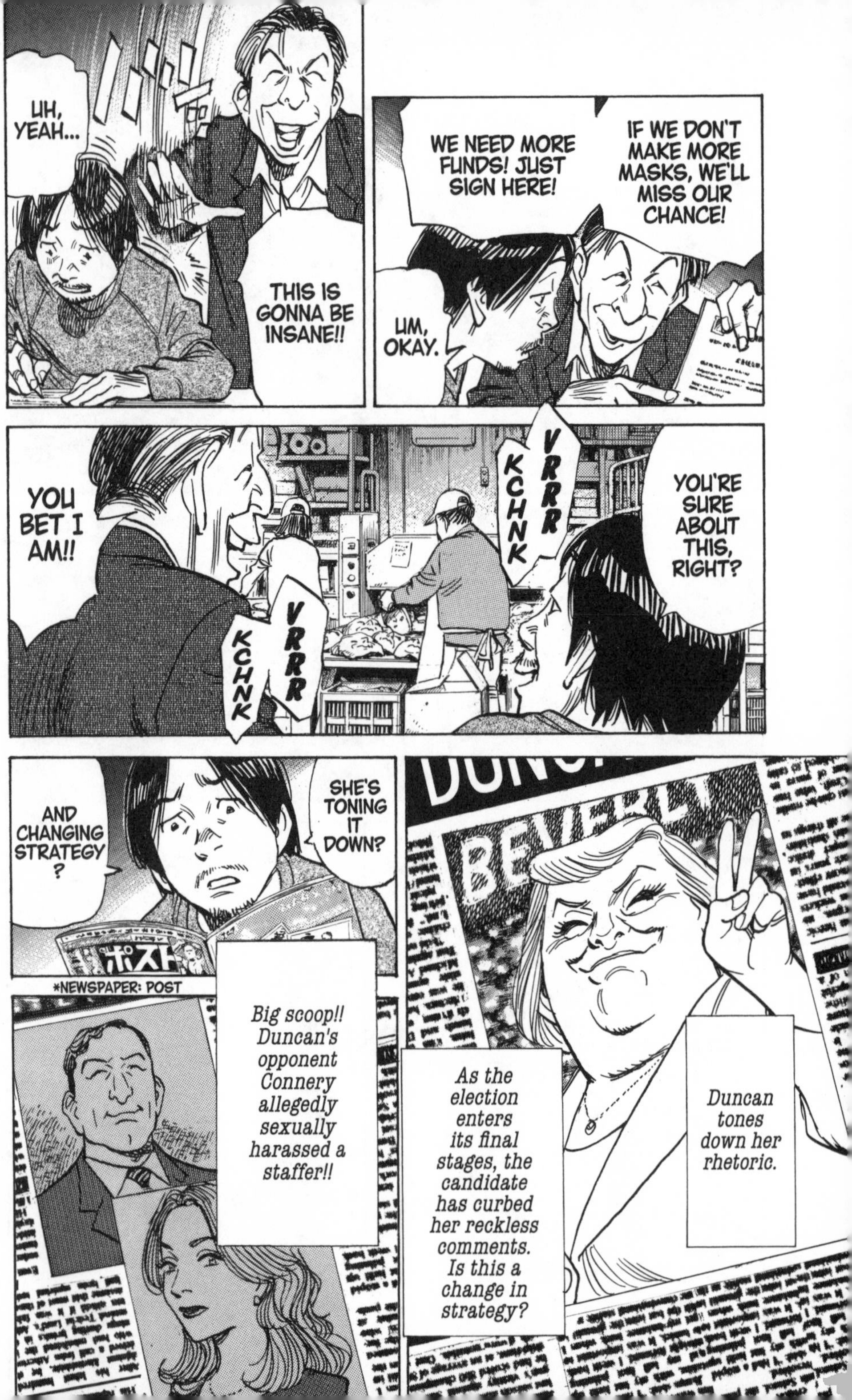
IF WE DON'T MAKE MORE MASKS, WE'LL MISS OUR CHANCE!
WE NEED MORE FUNDS! JUST SIGN HERE!
UM, OKAY.
THIS IS GONNA BE INSANE!!
UH, YEAH...
YOU'RE SURE ABOUT THIS, RIGHT?
VRRR
KCHNK
YOU BET I AM!!
VRRR
KCHNK
Duncan tones down her rhetoric.
As the election enters its final stages, the candidate has curbed her reckless comments. Is this a change in strategy?
SHE'S TONING IT DOWN?
AND CHANGING STRATEGY?
*NEWSPAPER: POST
Big scoop!! Duncan's opponent Connery allegedly sexually harassed a staffer!!

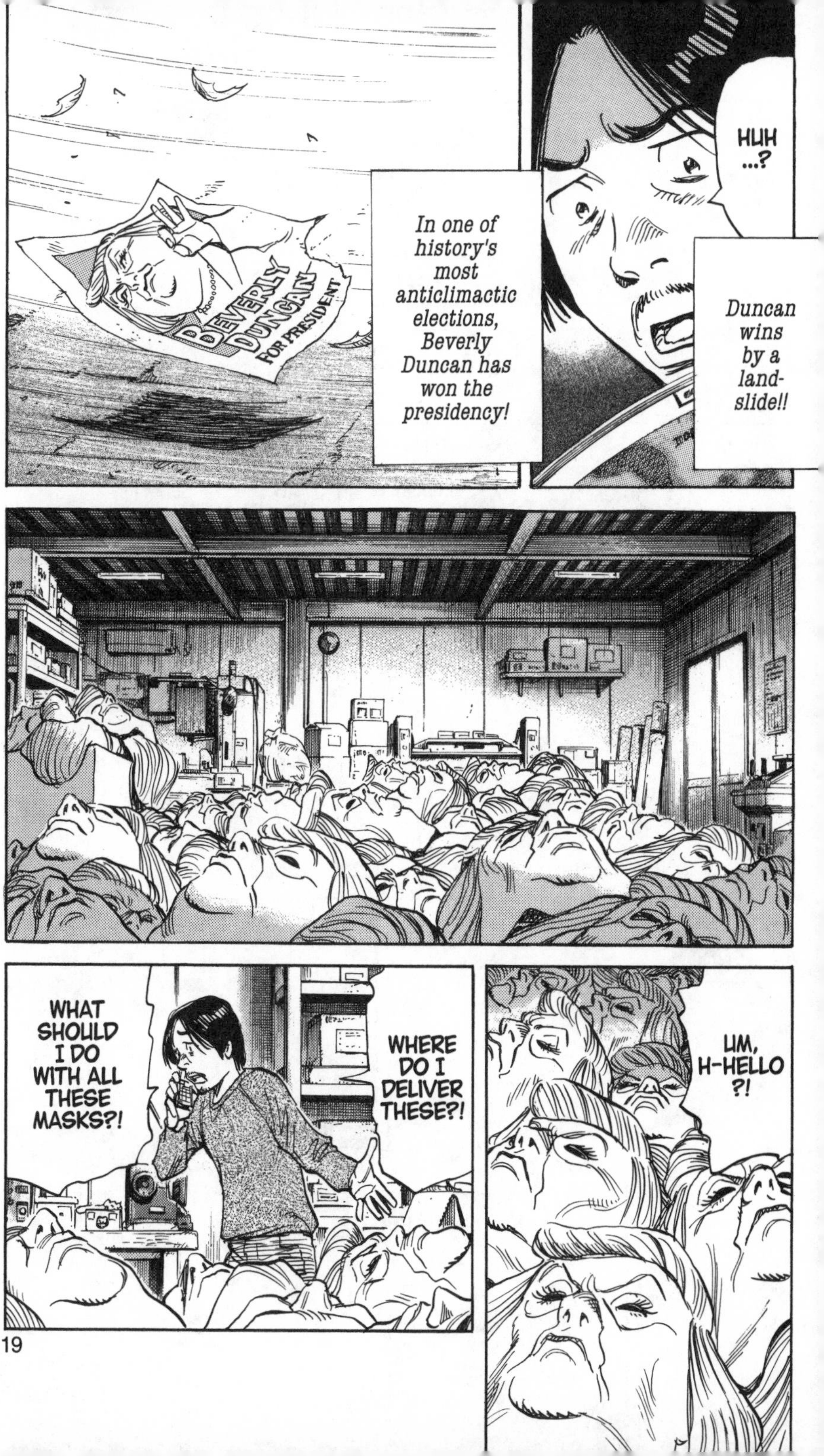
HUH ...?
Duncan wins by a landslide!!
BEVERLY DUNCAN FOR PRESIDENT
In one of history's most anticlimactic elections, Beverly Duncan has won the presidency!
UM, H-HELLO ?!
WHERE DO I DELIVER THESE?!
WHAT SHOULD I DO WITH ALL THESE MASKS?!

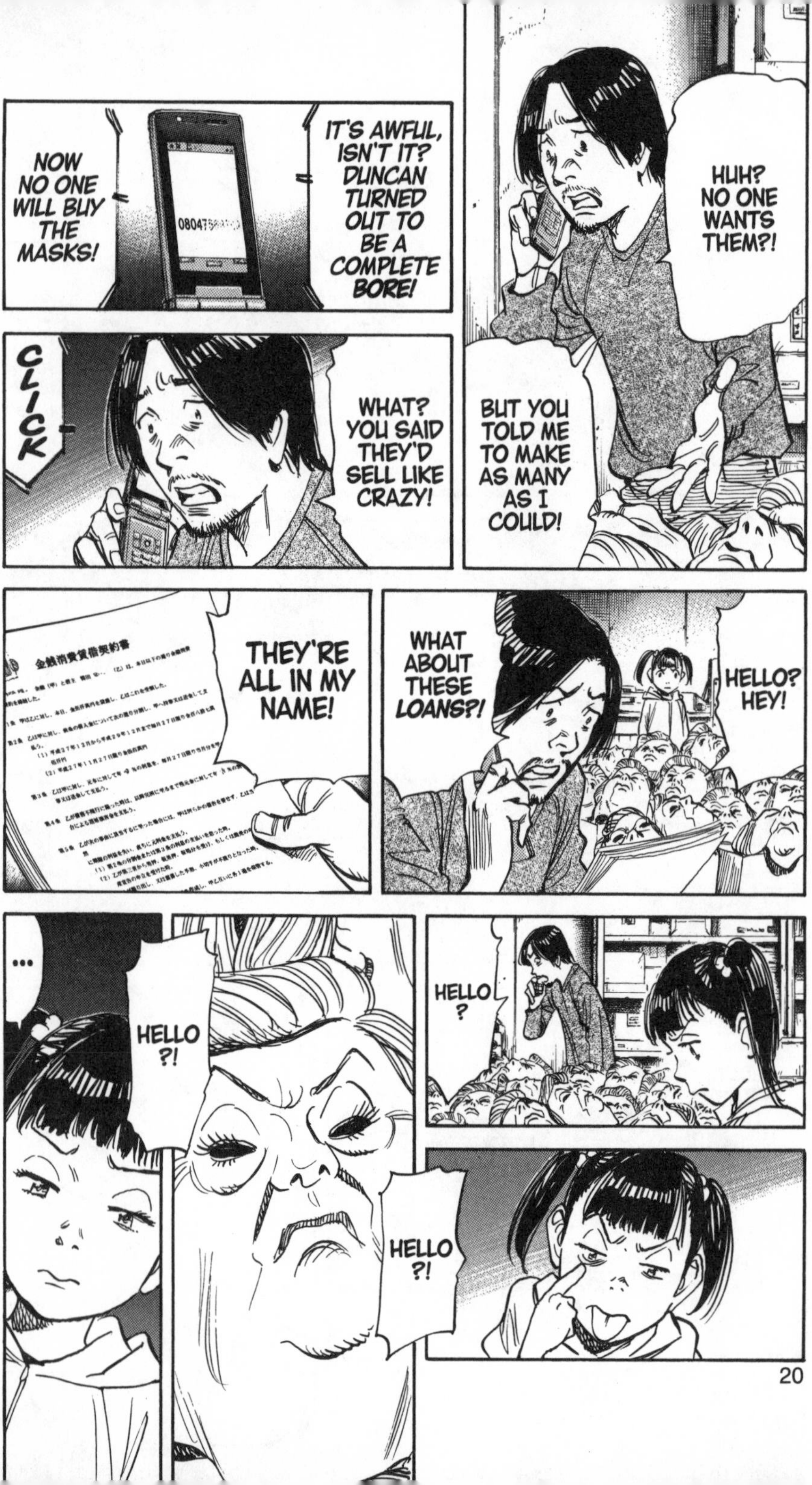
HUH? NO ONE WANTS THEM?!
BUT YOU TOLD ME TO MAKE AS MANY AS I COULD!
IT'S AWFUL, ISN'T IT? DUNCAN TURNED OUT TO BE A COMPLETE BORE!
NOW NO ONE WILL BUY THE MASKS!
08047
WHAT? YOU SAID THEY'D SELL LIKE CRAZY!
CLICK
HELLO? HEY!
WHAT ABOUT THESE LOANS?!
THEY'RE ALL IN MY NAME!
金銭消費貸借契約書
HELLO ?
HELLO ?!
HELLO ?!
...

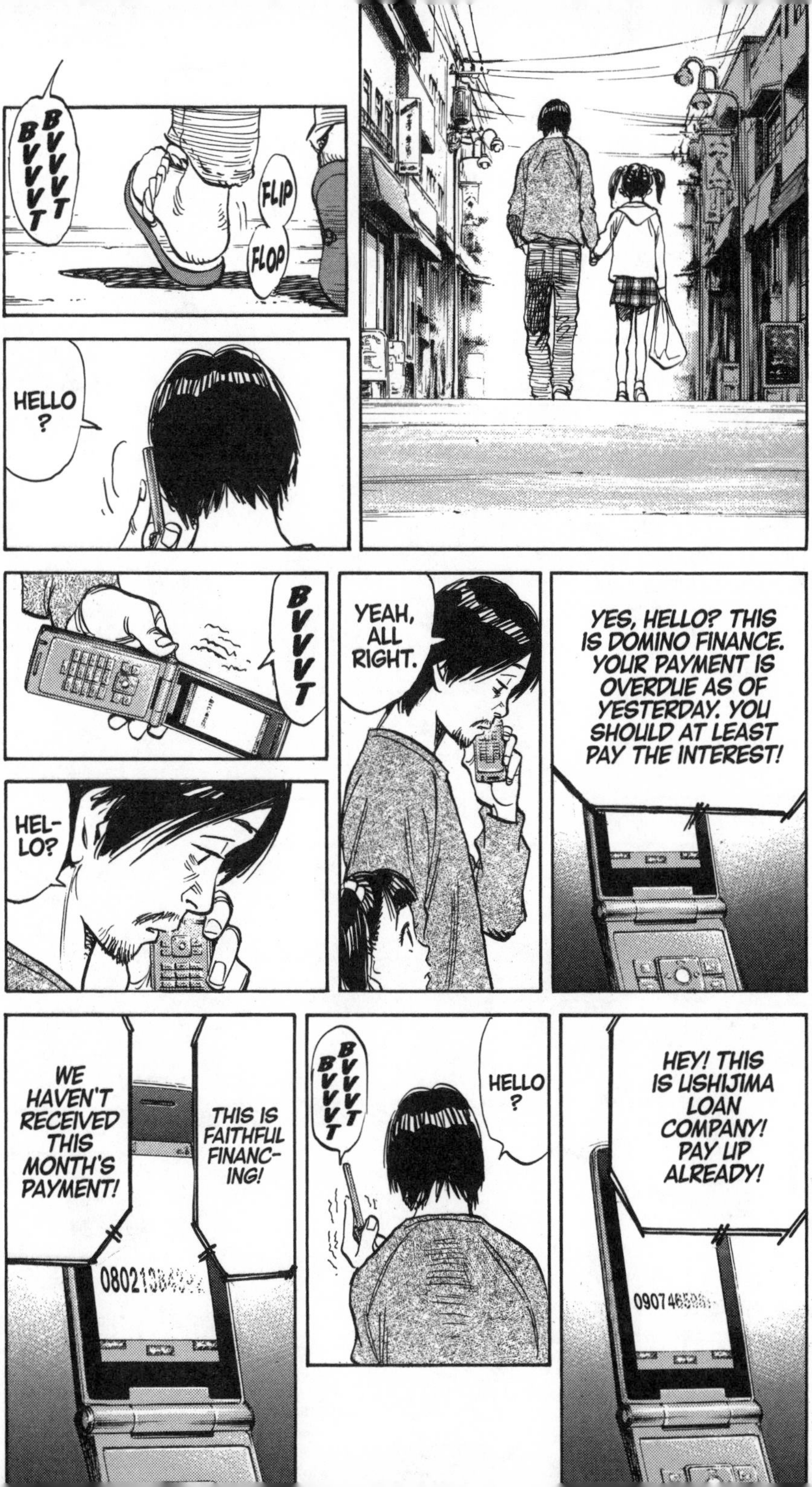
BVVVVT
BVVVVT
FLIP
FLOP
HELLO?
YES, HELLO? THIS IS DOMINO FINANCE. YOUR PAYMENT IS OVERDUE AS OF YESTERDAY. YOU SHOULD AT LEAST PAY THE INTEREST!
YEAH, ALL RIGHT.
BVVVVT
HEL-LO?
HEY! THIS IS USHIJIMA LOAN COMPANY! PAY UP ALREADY!
BVVVVT
BVVVVT
HELLO?
THIS IS FAITHFUL FINANC-ING!
WE HAVEN'T RECEIVED THIS MONTH'S PAYMENT!

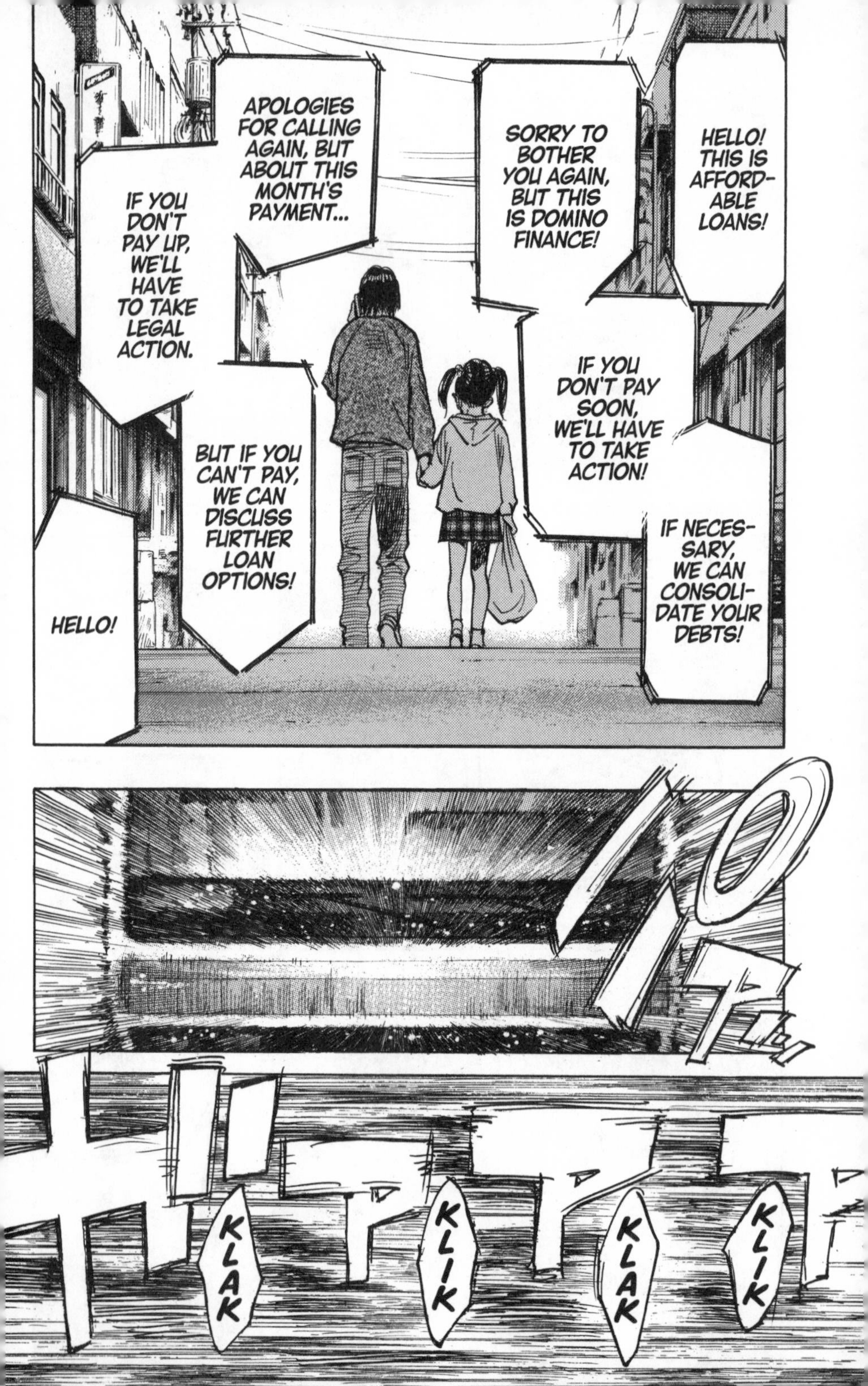
HELLO! THIS IS AFFORD-ABLE LOANS!
SORRY TO BOTHER YOU AGAIN, BUT THIS IS DOMINO FINANCE!
APOLOGIES FOR CALLING AGAIN, BUT ABOUT THIS MONTH'S PAYMENT...
IF YOU DON'T PAY UP, WE'LL HAVE TO TAKE LEGAL ACTION.
IF YOU DON'T PAY SOON, WE'LL HAVE TO TAKE ACTION!
BUT IF YOU CAN'T PAY, WE CAN DISCUSS FURTHER LOAN OPTIONS!
IF NECES-SARY, WE CAN CONSOLI-DATE YOUR DEBTS!
HELLO!
KLIK
KLAK
KLIK
KLAK

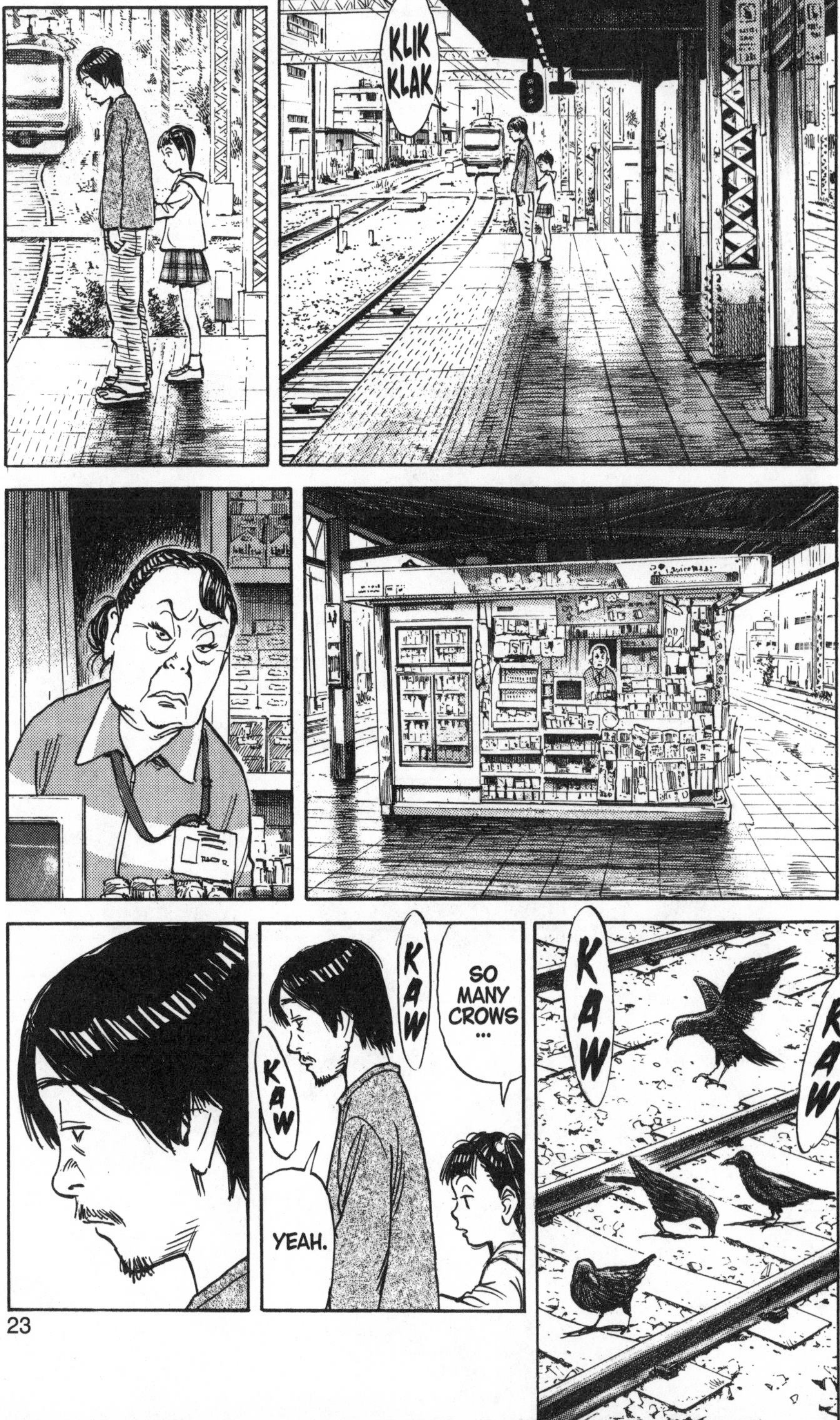
KLIK KLAK
KAW KAW
KAW KAW
SO MANY CROWS ...
KAW KAW
KAW KAW
YEAH.

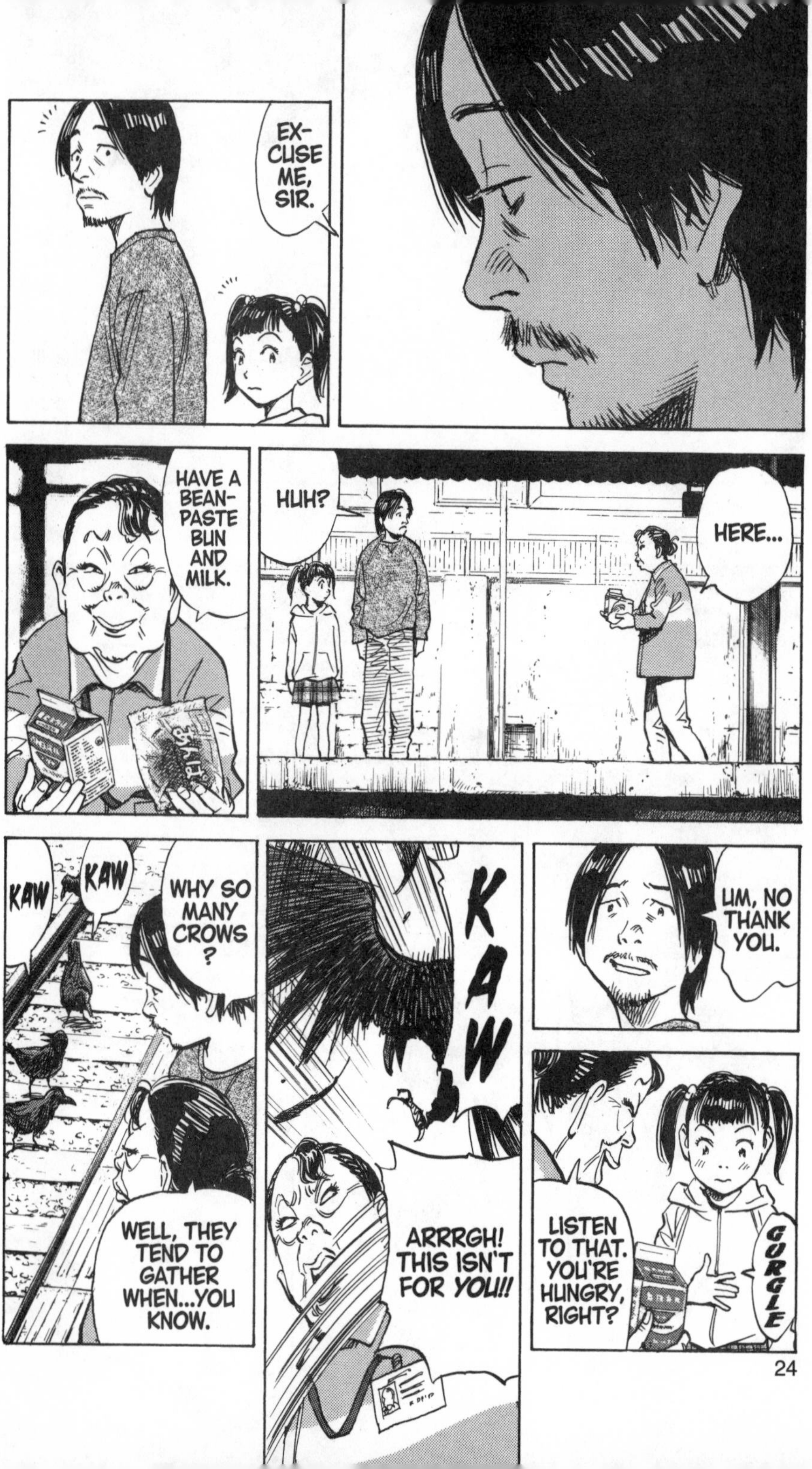
EX-CUSE ME, SIR.
HERE...
HUH?
HAVE A BEAN-PASTE BUN AND MILK.
UM, NO THANK YOU.
LISTEN TO THAT. YOU'RE HUNGRY, RIGHT?
GURGLE
KAW
KAW
ARRRGH! THIS ISN'T FOR *YOU*!!
KAW
KAW
WHY SO MANY CROWS?
WELL, THEY TEND TO GATHER WHEN...YOU KNOW.

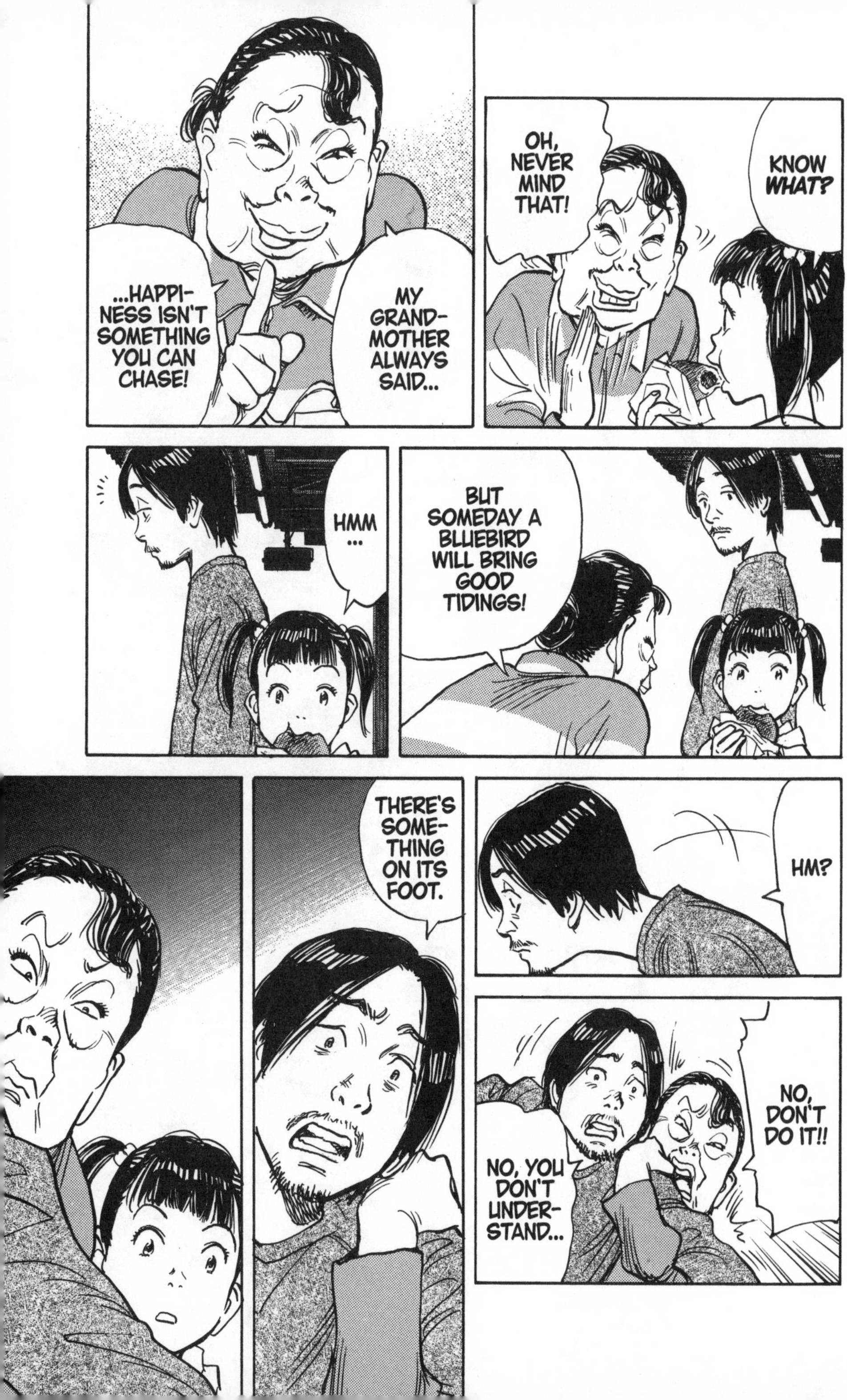
KNOW WHAT?
OH, NEVER MIND THAT!
MY GRAND-MOTHER ALWAYS SAID...
...HAPPI-NESS ISN'T SOMETHING YOU CAN CHASE!
BUT SOMEDAY A BLUEBIRD WILL BRING GOOD TIDINGS!
HMM ...
HM?
NO, DON'T DO IT!!
NO, YOU DON'T UNDER-STAND...
THERE'S SOME-THING ON ITS FOOT.

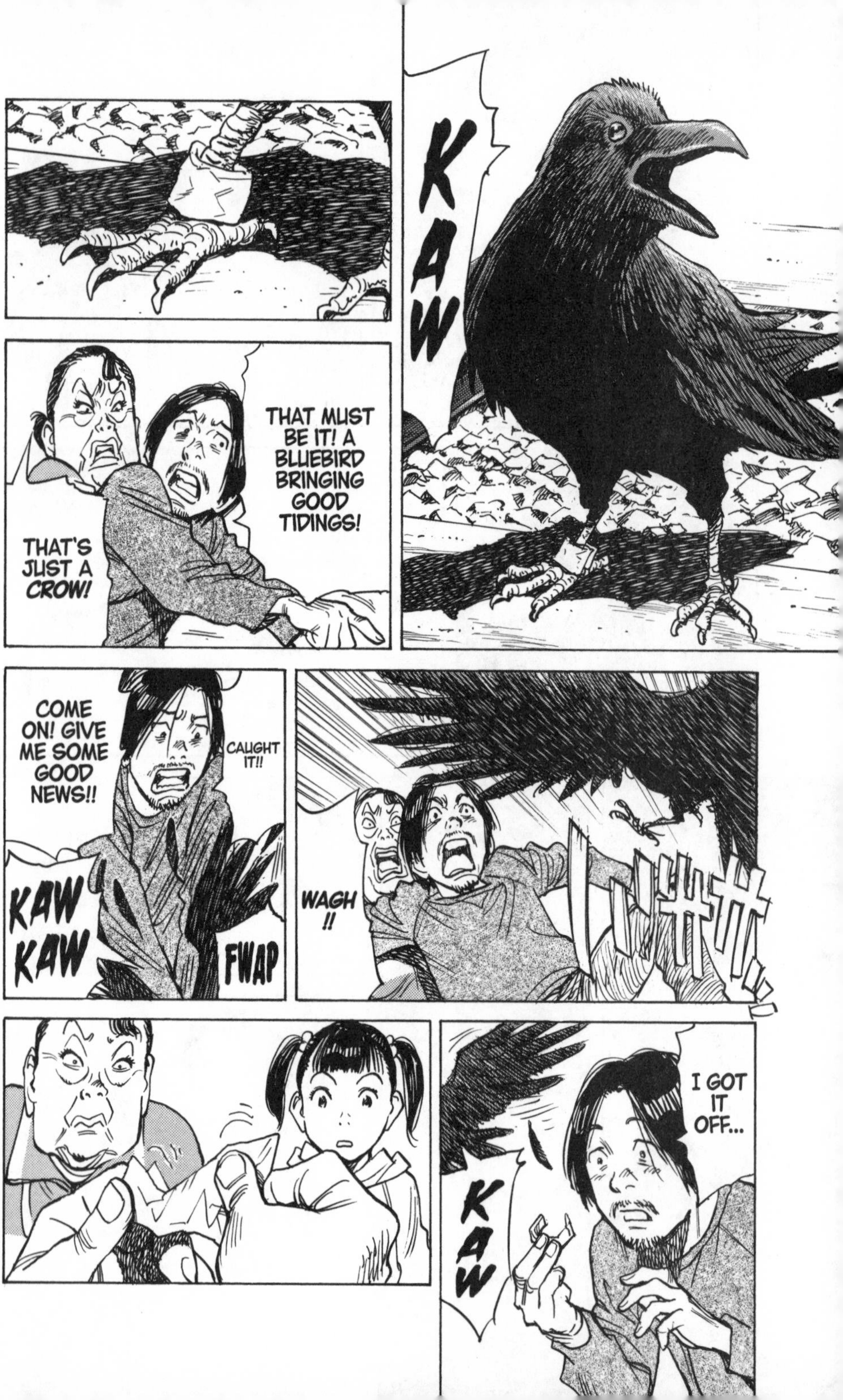
KAW KAW
THAT MUST BE IT! A BLUEBIRD BRINGING GOOD TIDINGS!
THAT'S JUST A *CROW!*
WAGH !!
CAUGHT IT!!
COME ON! GIVE ME SOME GOOD NEWS!!
FWAP
KAW KAW
I GOT IT OFF...
KAW

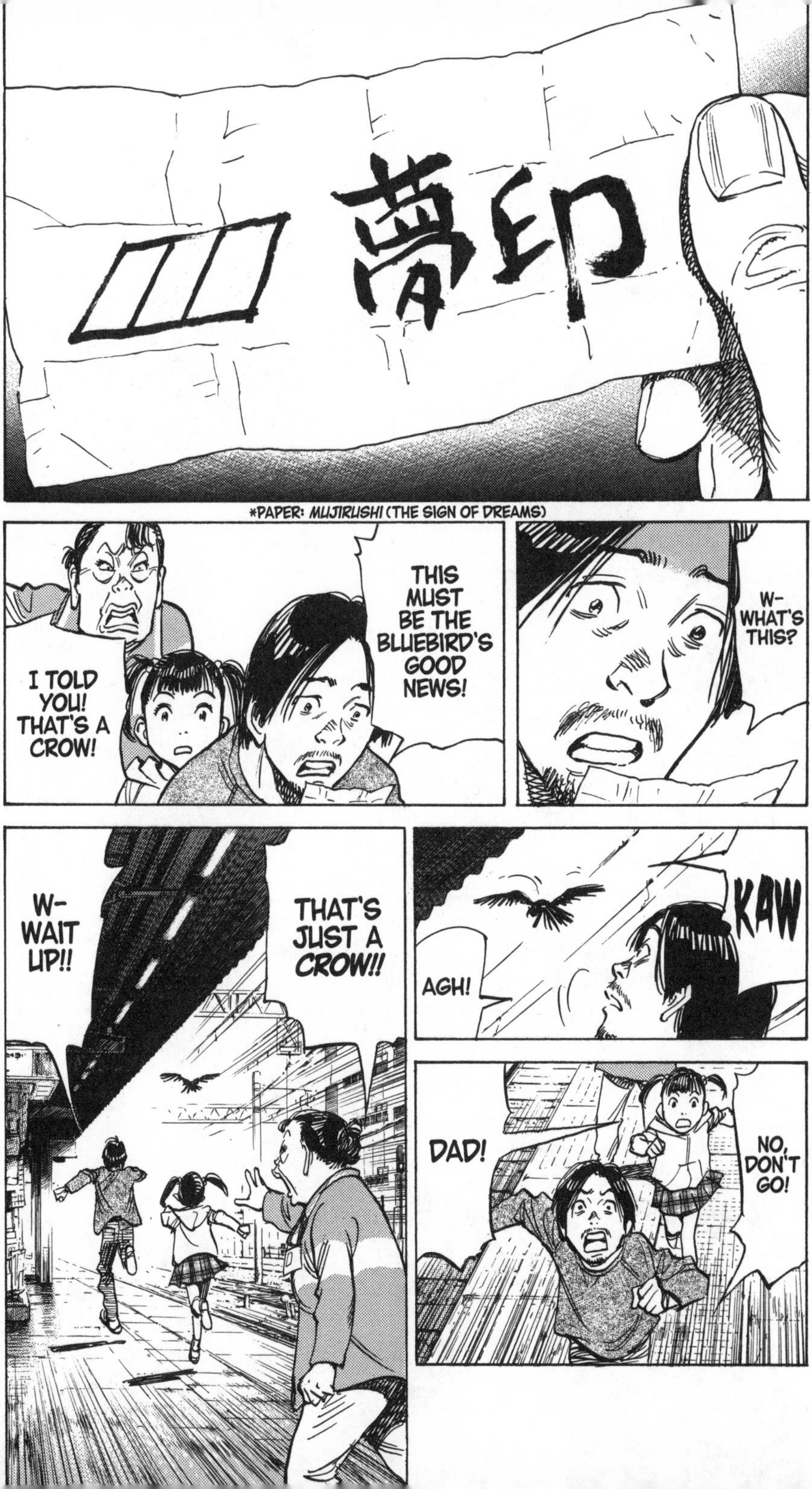
夢印
*PAPER: MUJIRUSHI (THE SIGN OF DREAMS)
W- WHAT'S THIS?
THIS MUST BE THE BLUEBIRD'S GOOD NEWS!
I TOLD YOU! THAT'S A CROW!
KAW
AGH!
NO, DON'T GO!
DAD!
THAT'S JUST A CROW!!
W- WAIT UP!!

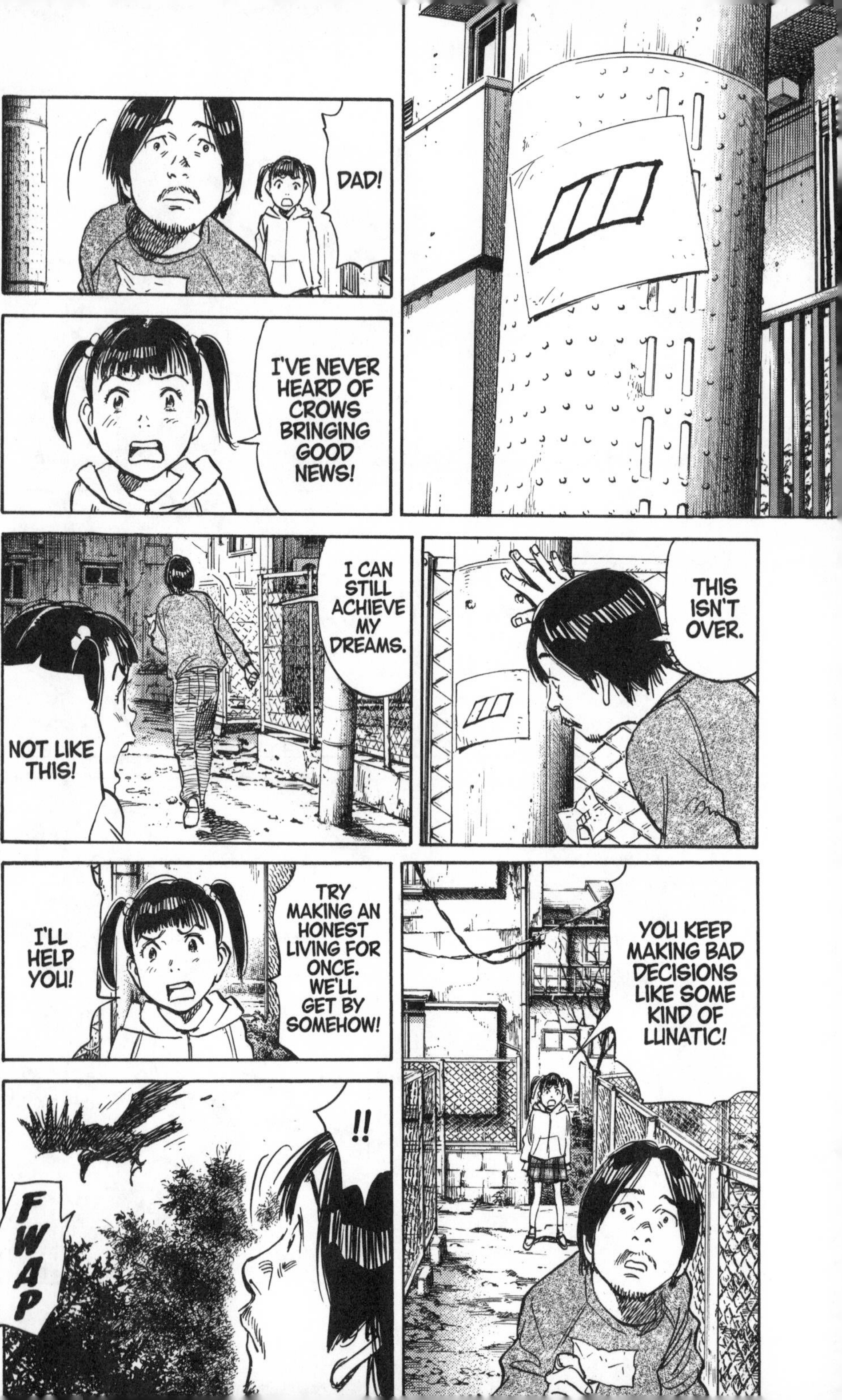
DAD!
I'VE NEVER HEARD OF CROWS BRINGING GOOD NEWS!
THIS ISN'T OVER.
I CAN STILL ACHIEVE MY DREAMS.
NOT LIKE THIS!
YOU KEEP MAKING BAD DECISIONS LIKE SOME KIND OF LUNATIC!
TRY MAKING AN HONEST LIVING FOR ONCE. WE'LL GET BY SOMEHOW!
I'LL HELP YOU!
!!
FWAP

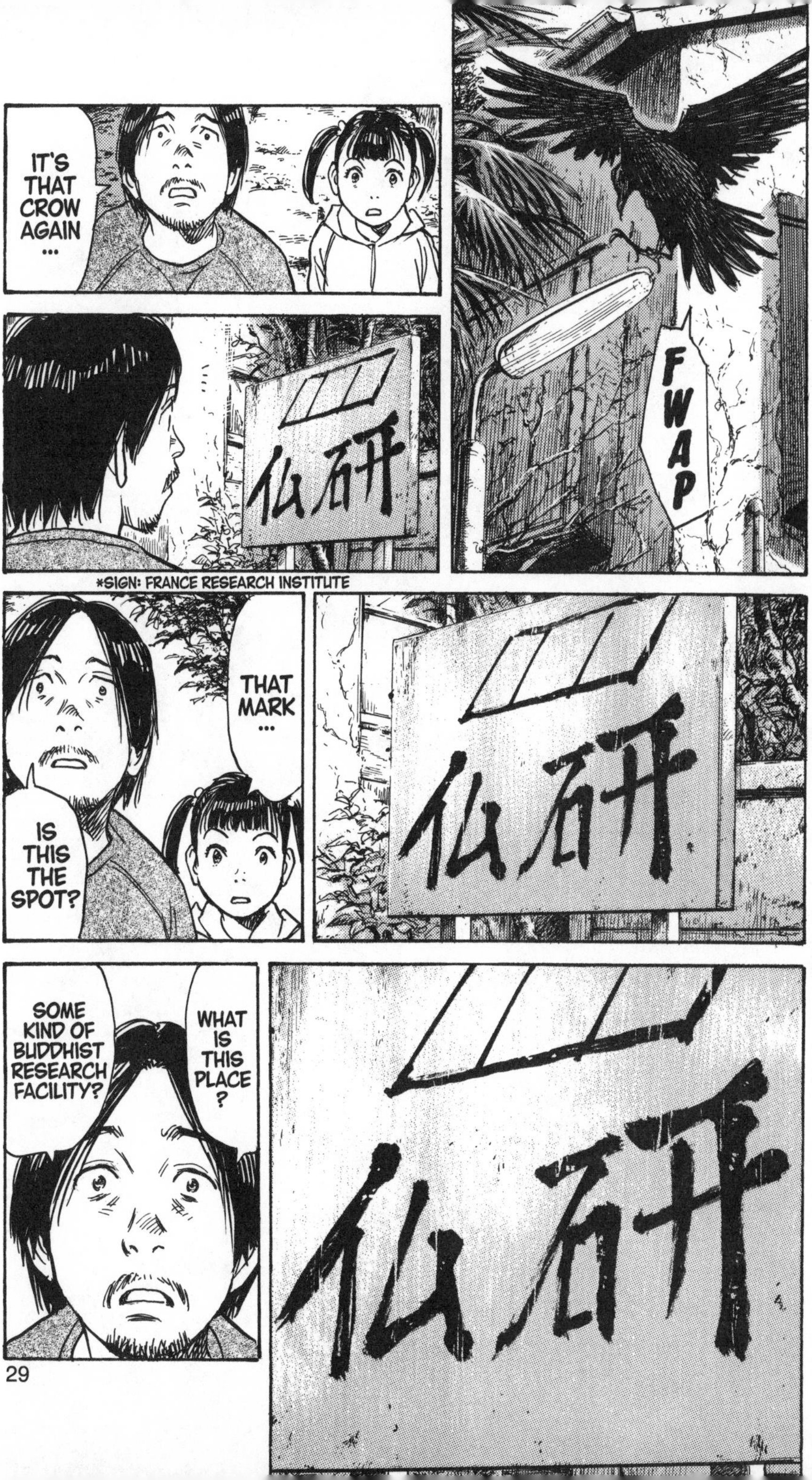
FWAP
IT'S THAT CROW AGAIN ...
仏研
*SIGN: FRANCE RESEARCH INSTITUTE
仏研
THAT MARK ...
IS THIS THE SPOT?
仏研
WHAT IS THIS PLACE ?
SOME KIND OF BUDDHIST RESEARCH FACILITY?

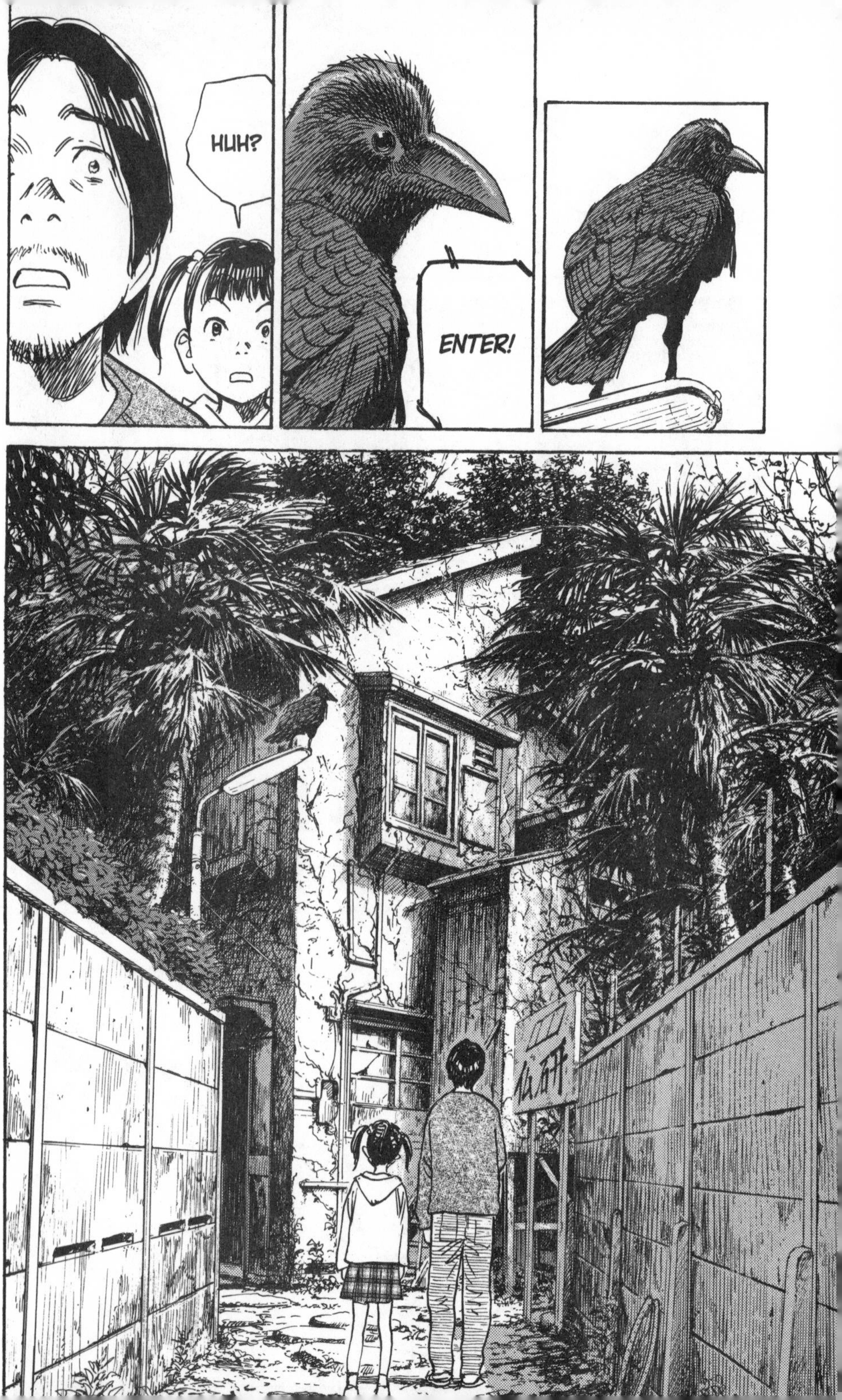
ENTER!
HUH?

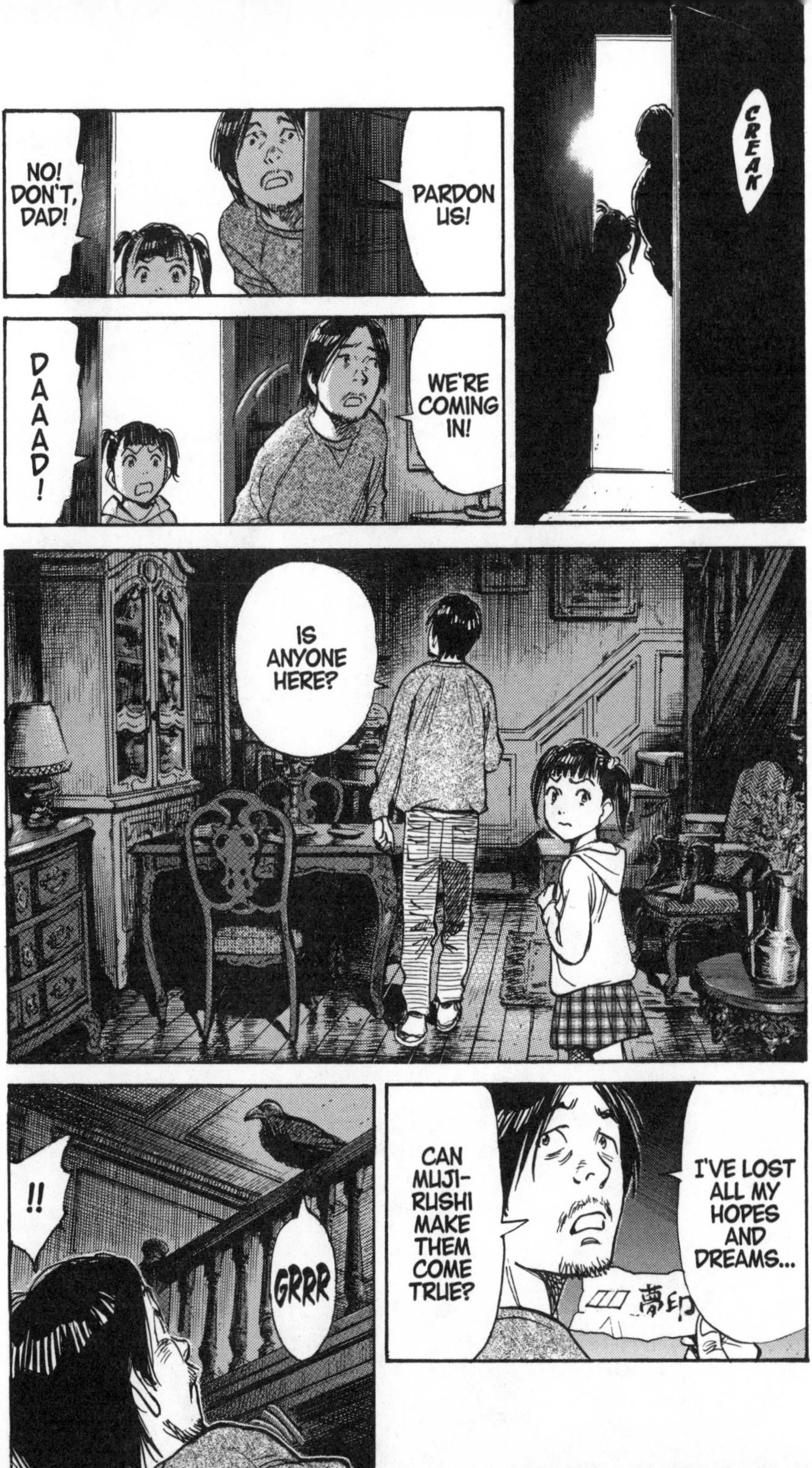
CREAK
PARDON US!
NO! DON'T, DAD!
WE'RE COMING IN!
DAAAAD!
IS ANYONE HERE?
I'VE LOST ALL MY HOPES AND DREAMS...
CAN MUJI-RUSHI MAKE THEM COME TRUE?
!!
GRRR

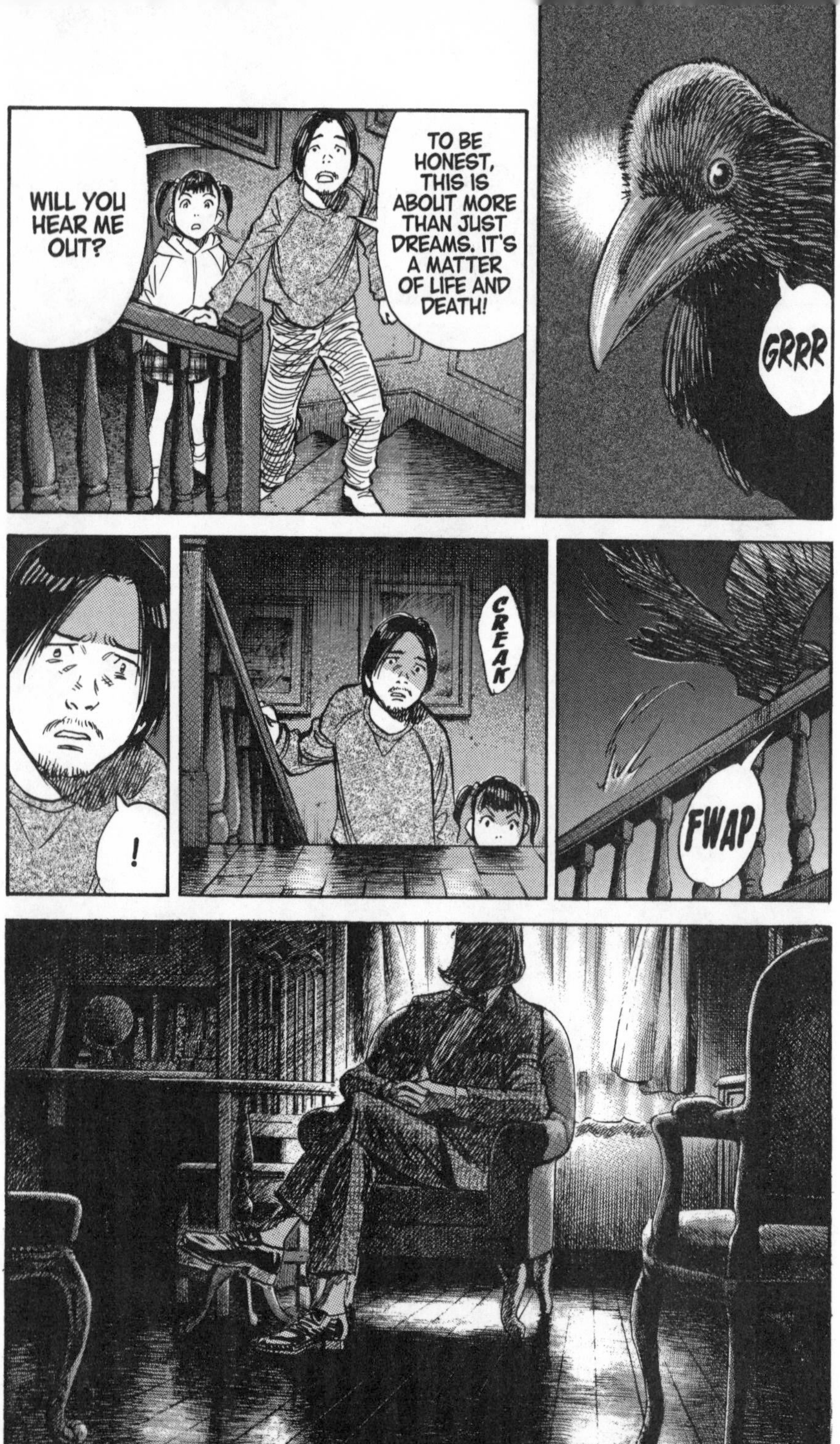
GRRR
TO BE HONEST, THIS IS ABOUT MORE THAN JUST DREAMS. IT'S A MATTER OF LIFE AND DEATH!
WILL YOU HEAR ME OUT?
FWAP
CREAK
!

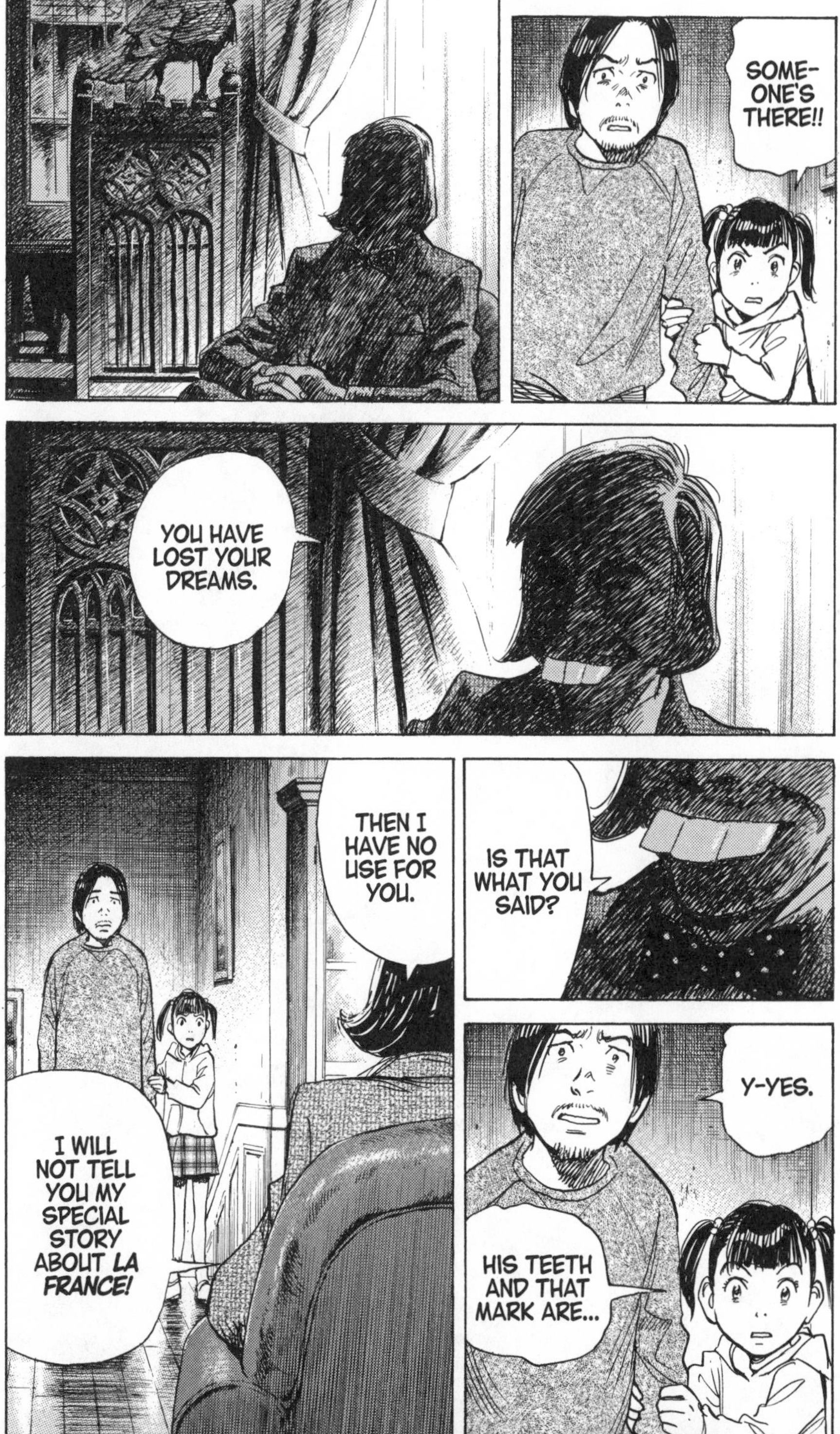
SOME-ONE'S THERE!!
YOU HAVE LOST YOUR DREAMS.
IS THAT WHAT YOU SAID?
Y-YES.
HIS TEETH AND THAT MARK ARE...
THEN I HAVE NO USE FOR YOU.
I WILL NOT TELL YOU MY SPECIAL STORY ABOUT LA FRANCE!

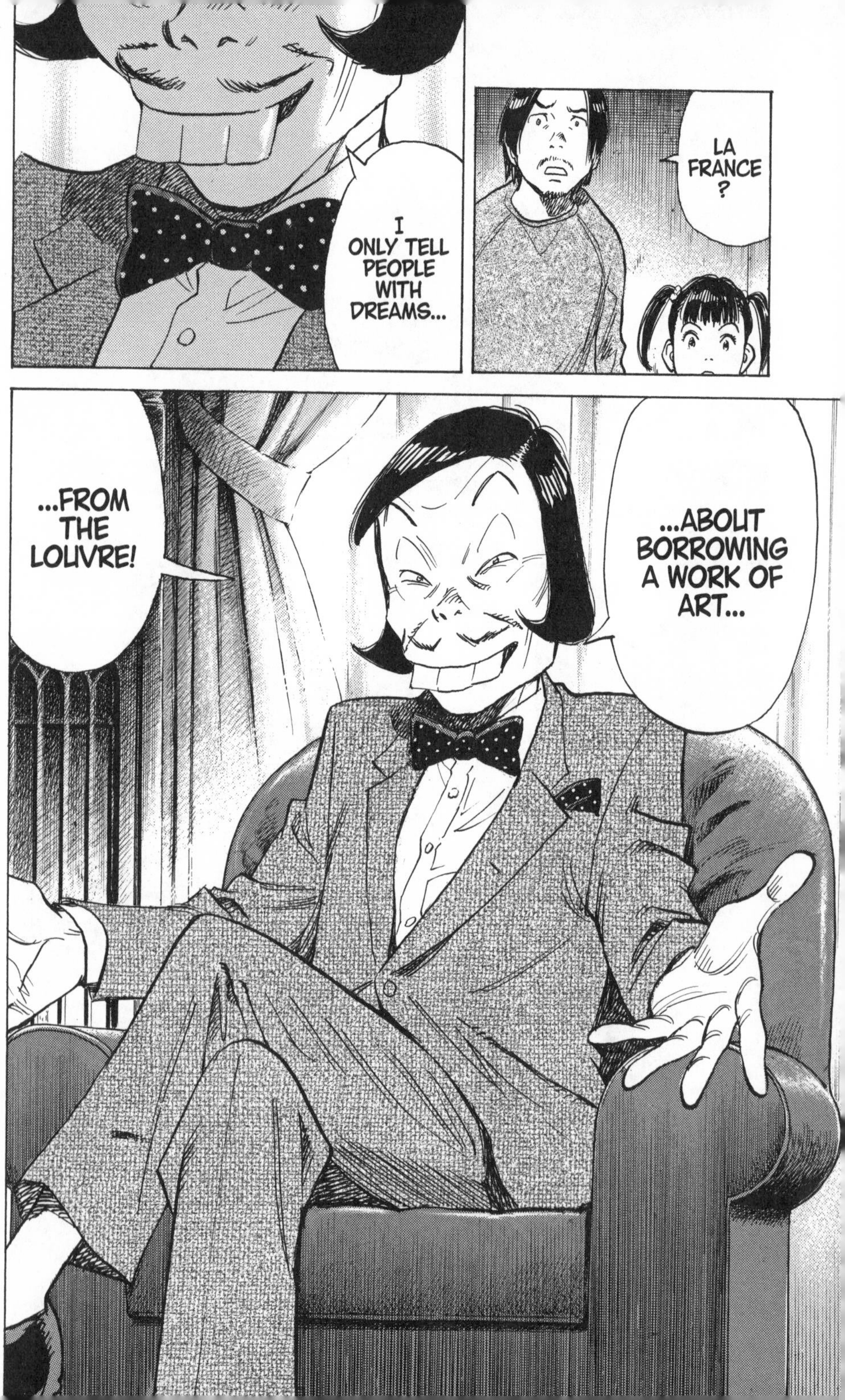
LA FRANCE?
I ONLY TELL PEOPLE WITH DREAMS...
...ABOUT BORROWING A WORK OF ART...
...FROM THE LOUVRE!

2ème Sheeh! City of Flowers

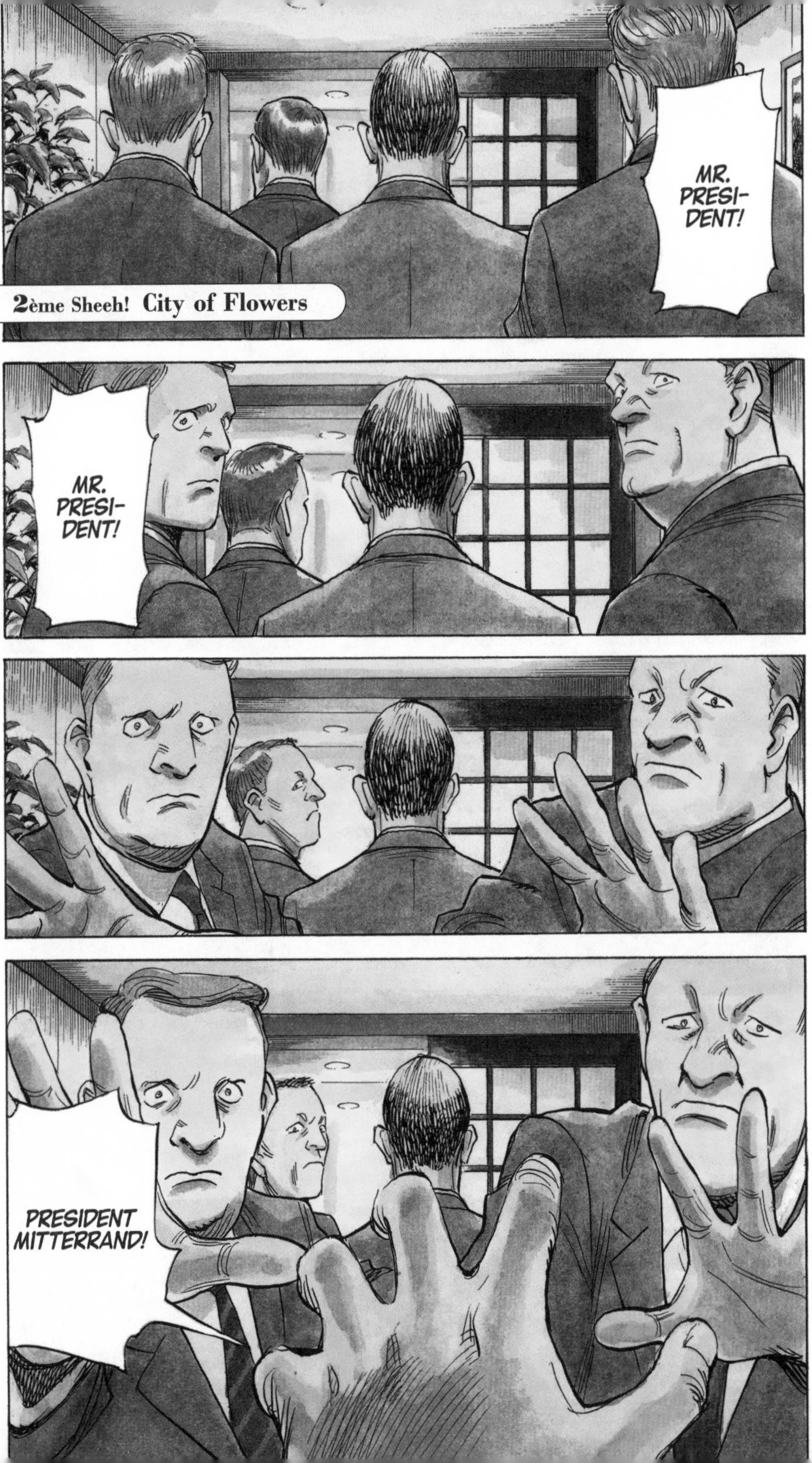
MR. PRESIDENT!
MR. PRESIDENT!
PRESIDENT MITTERRAND!

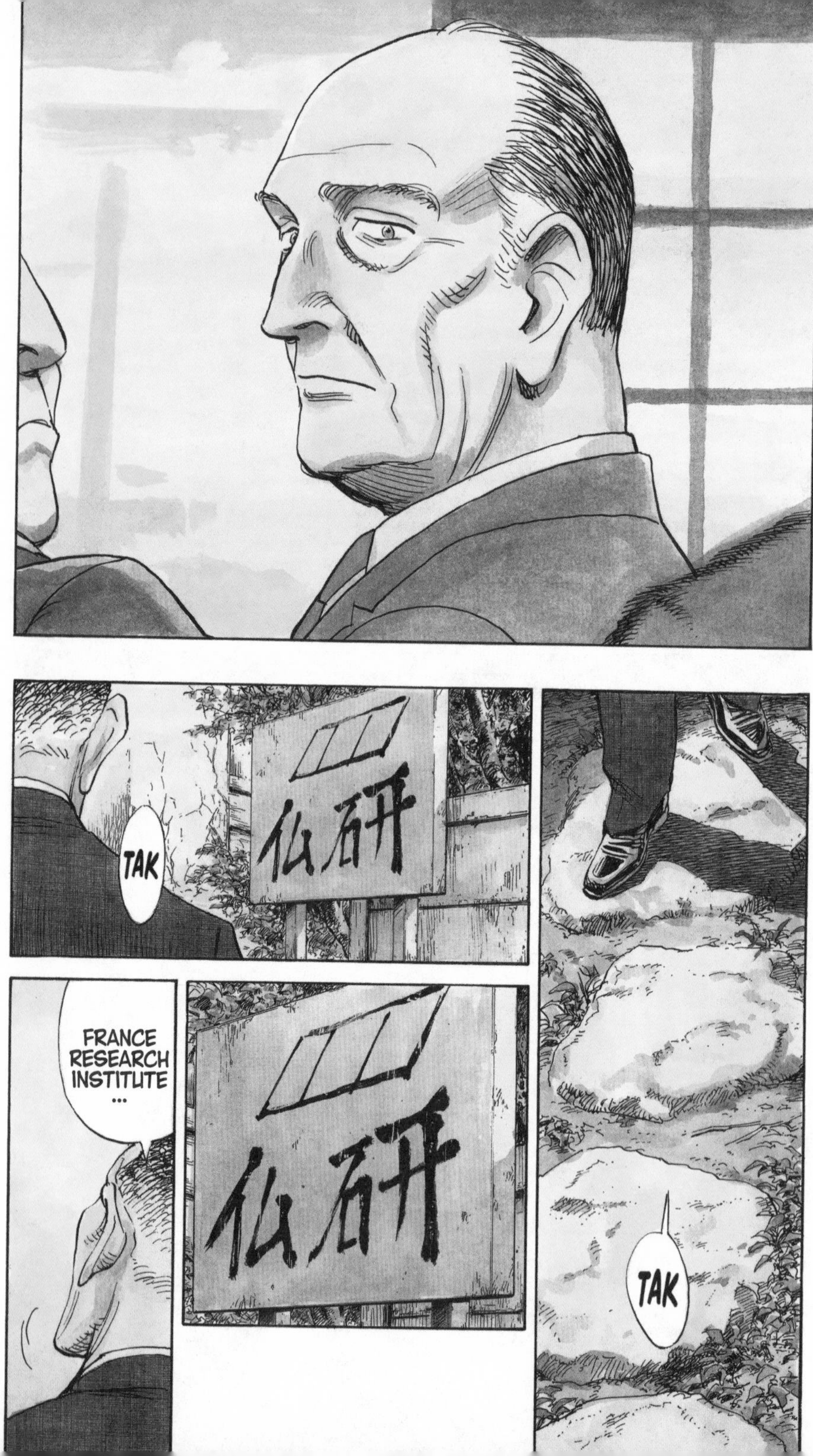
TAK
仏研
TAK
仏研
FRANCE RESEARCH INSTITUTE ...

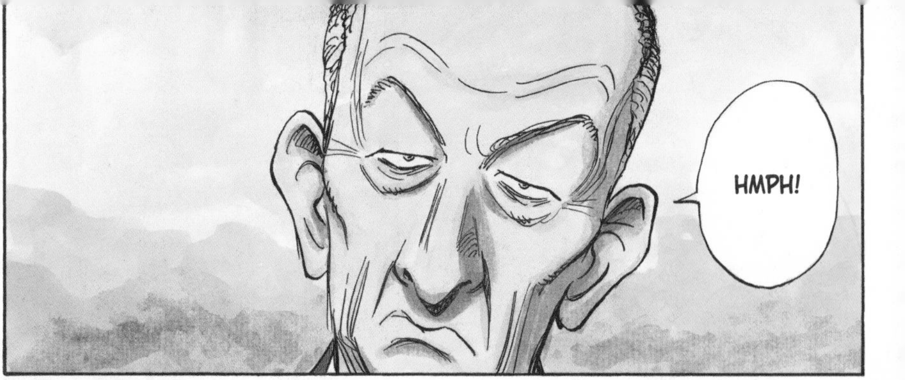
HMPH!

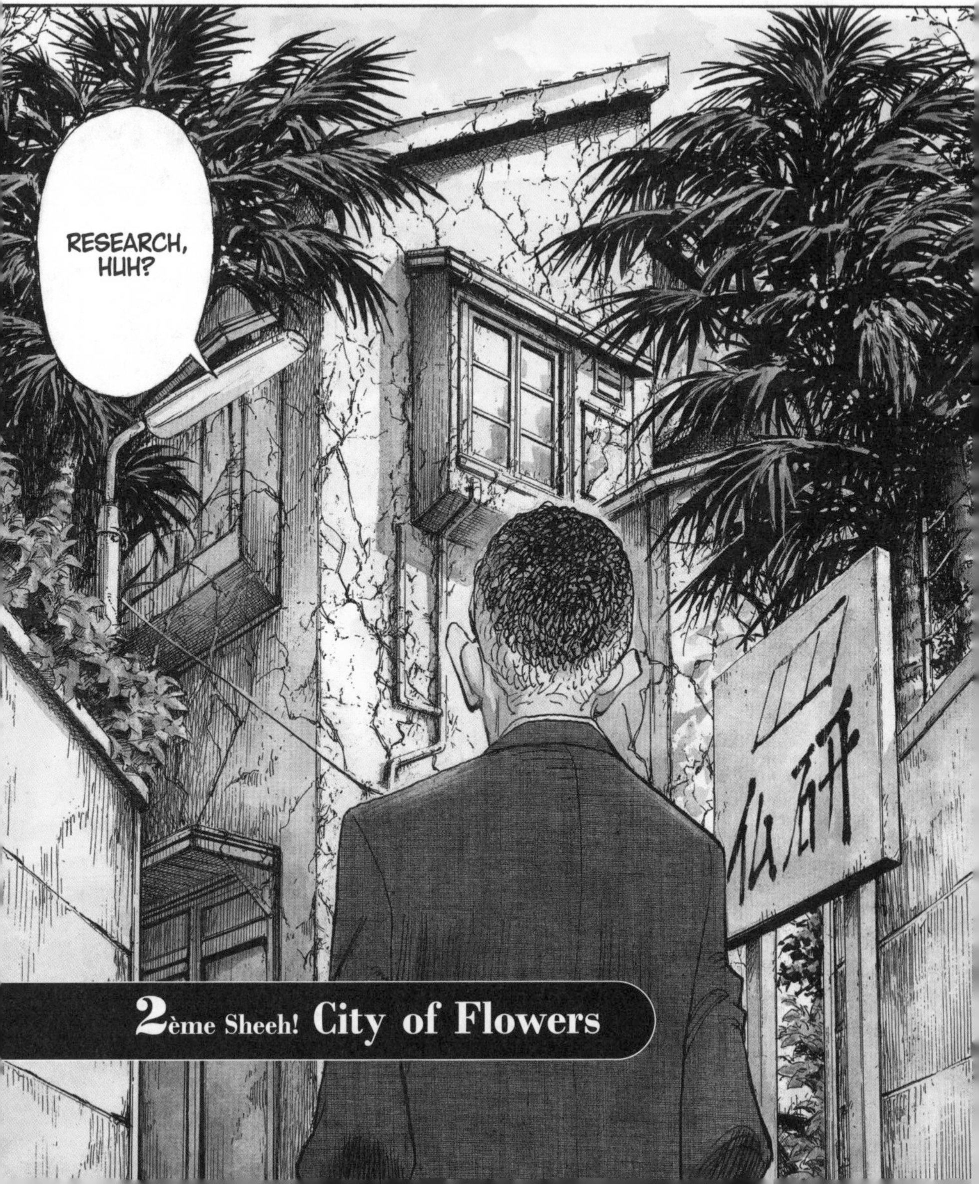
RESEARCH, HUH?
仙研

2ème Sheeh! City of Flowers

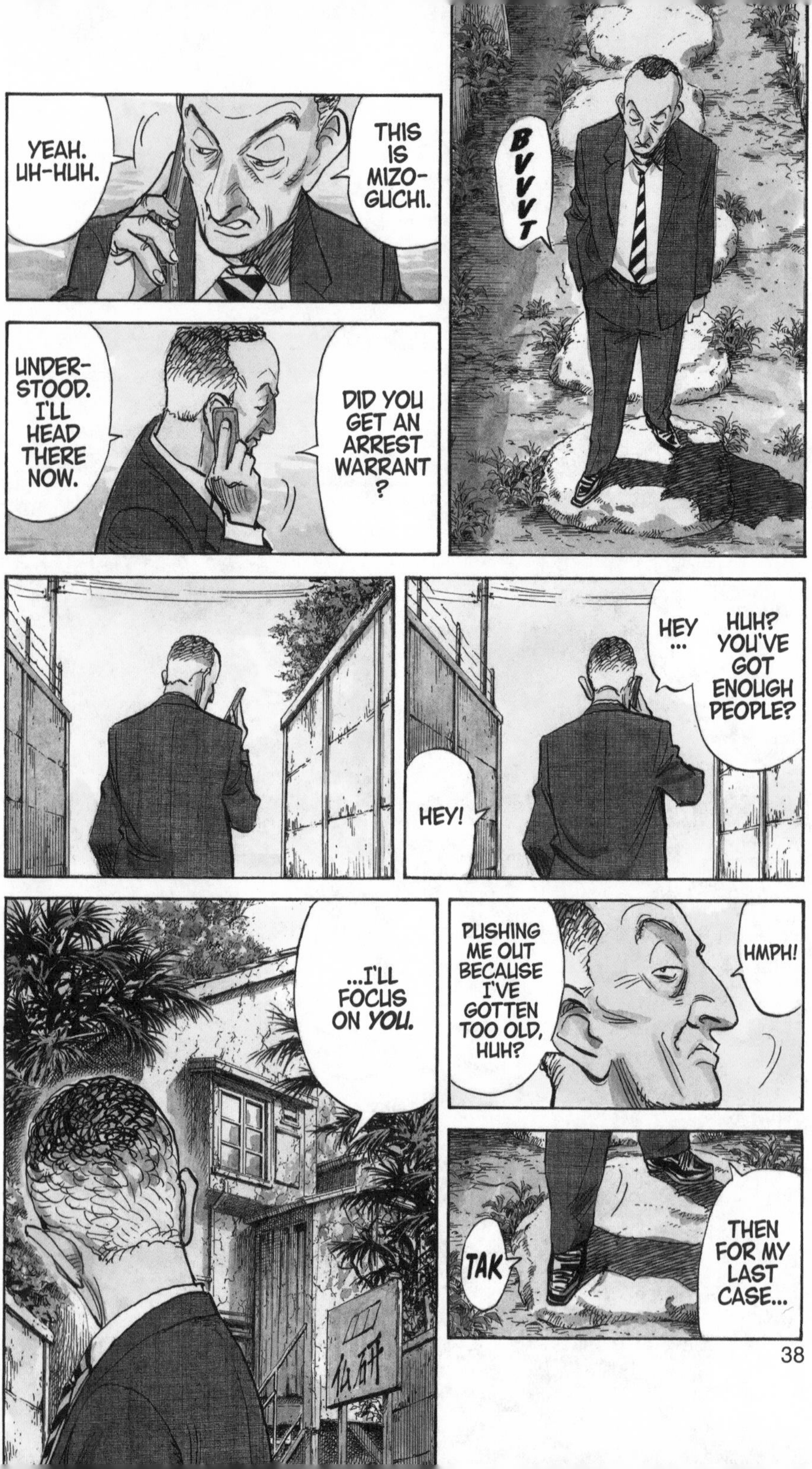
BVVVT
THIS IS MIZOGUCHI.
YEAH. UH-HUH.
DID YOU GET AN ARREST WARRANT?
UNDERSTOOD. I'LL HEAD THERE NOW.
HUH? YOU'VE GOT ENOUGH PEOPLE?
HEY...
HEY!
HMPH!
PUSHING ME OUT BECAUSE I'VE GOTTEN TOO OLD, HUH?
THEN FOR MY LAST CASE...
TAK
...I'LL FOCUS ON *YOU.*
仏研

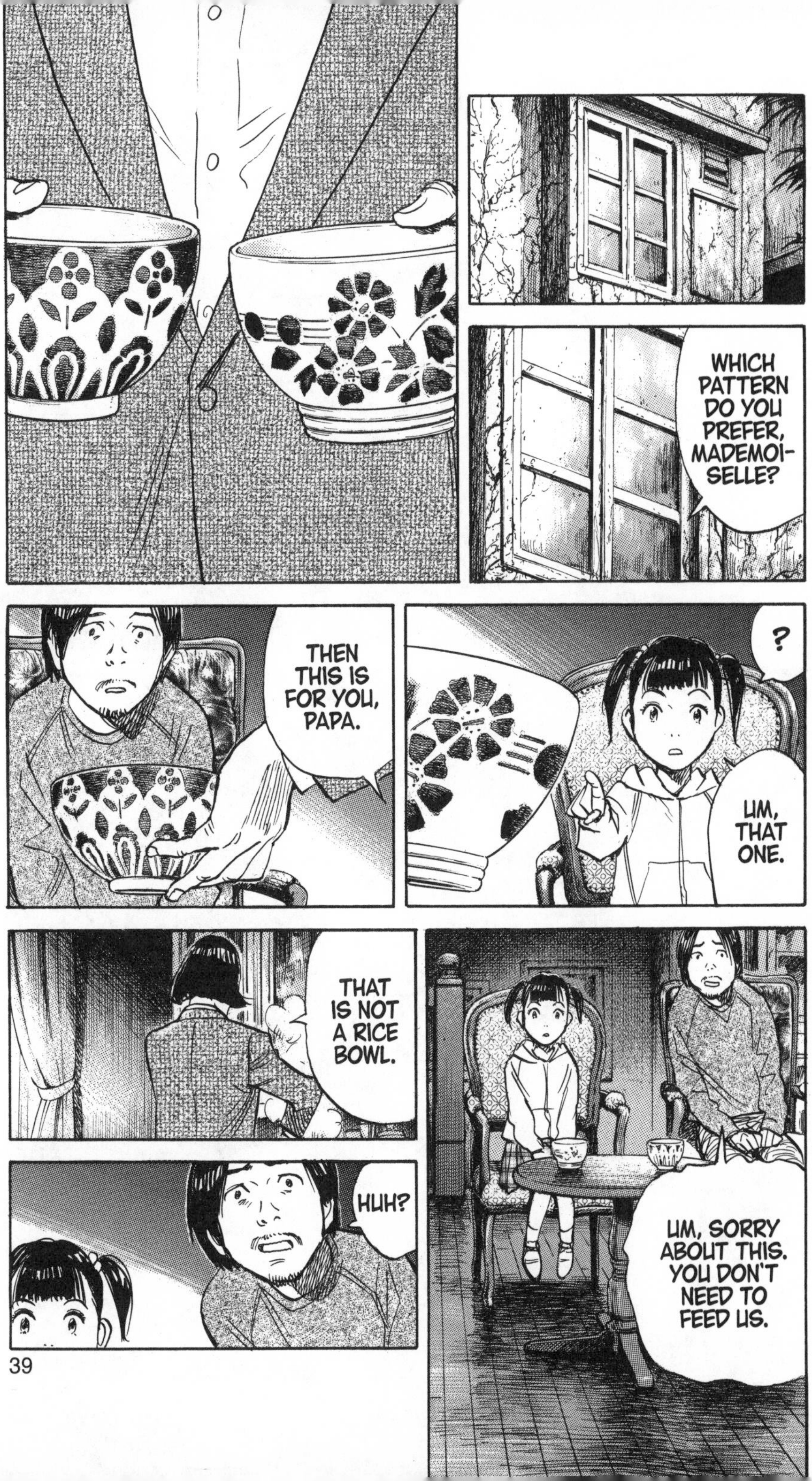
WHICH PATTERN DO YOU PREFER, MADEMOI-SELLE?
?
UM, THAT ONE.
THEN THIS IS FOR YOU, PAPA.
UM, SORRY ABOUT THIS. YOU DON'T NEED TO FEED US.
THAT IS NOT A RICE BOWL.
HUH?

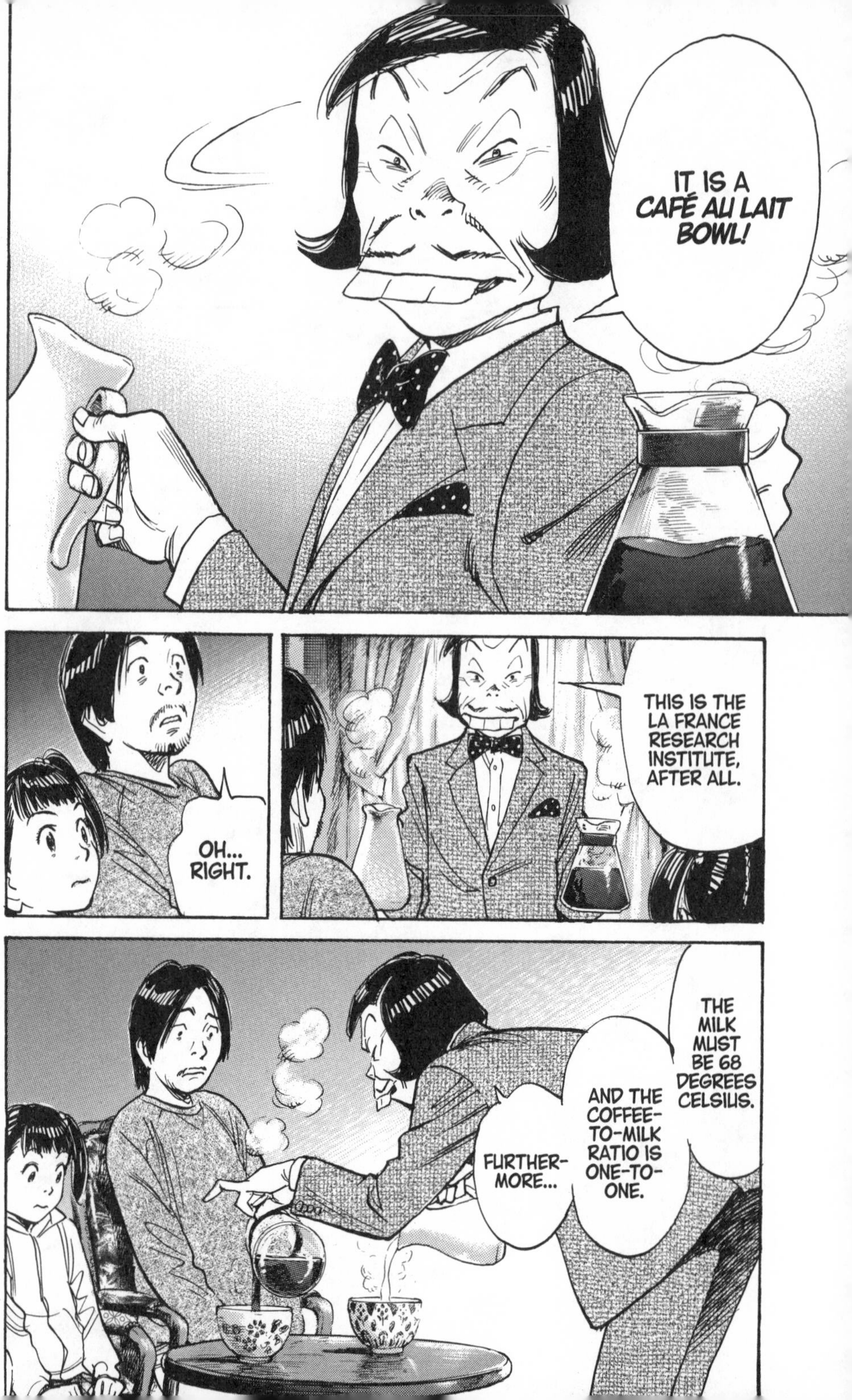
IT IS A CAFÉ AU LAIT BOWL!
THIS IS THE LA FRANCE RESEARCH INSTITUTE, AFTER ALL.
OH... RIGHT.
THE MILK MUST BE 68 DEGREES CELSIUS.
AND THE COFFEE-TO-MILK RATIO IS ONE-TO-ONE.
FURTHER-MORE...

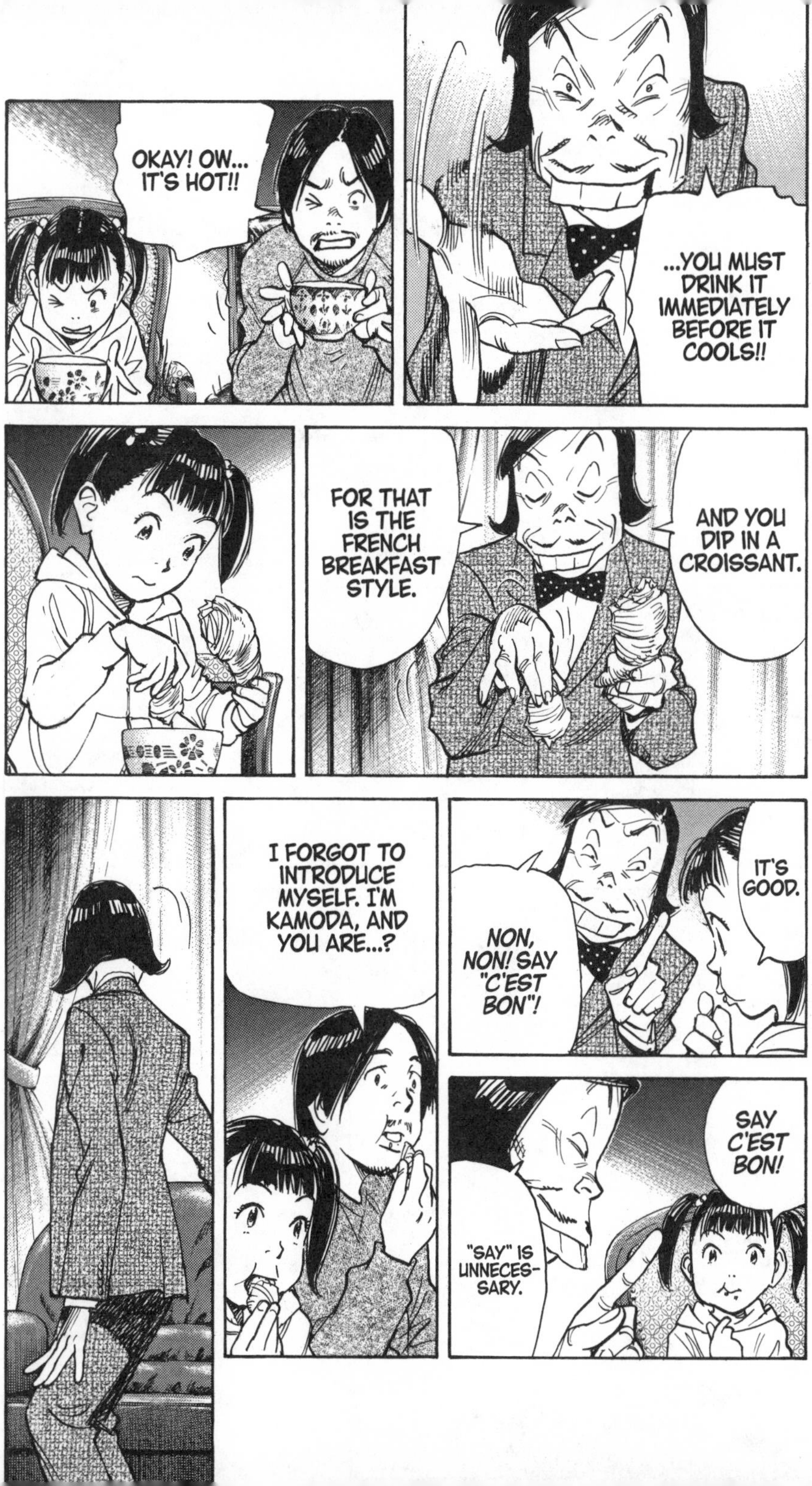
...YOU MUST DRINK IT IMMEDIATELY BEFORE IT COOLS!!
OKAY! OW... IT'S HOT!!
AND YOU DIP IN A CROISSANT.
FOR THAT IS THE FRENCH BREAKFAST STYLE.
IT'S GOOD.
NON, NON! SAY "C'EST BON"!
SAY C'EST BON!
"SAY" IS UNNECES-SARY.
I FORGOT TO INTRODUCE MYSELF. I'M KAMODA, AND YOU ARE...?

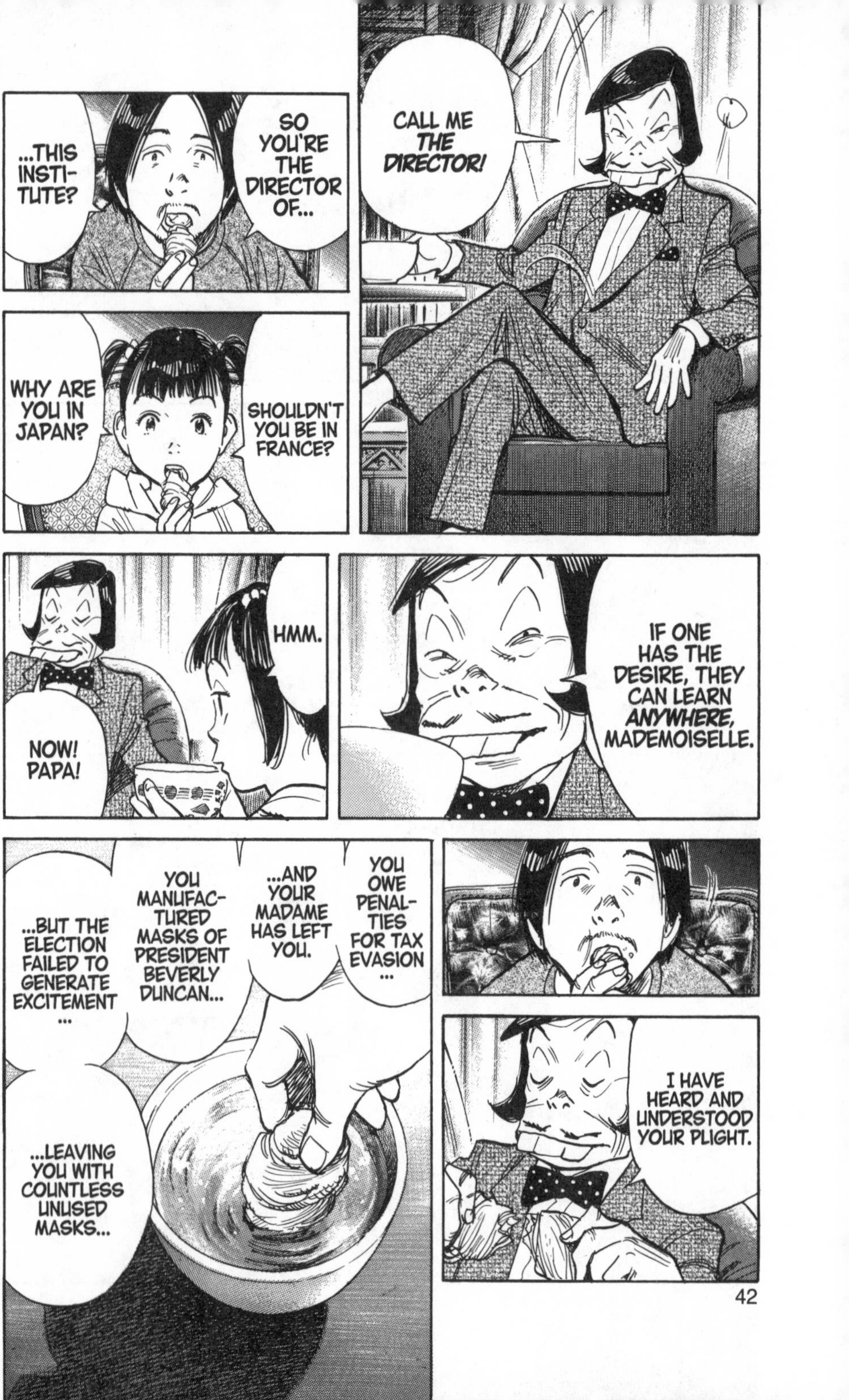
CALL ME *THE DIRECTOR!*
SO YOU'RE THE DIRECTOR OF...
...THIS INSTITUTE?
SHOULDN'T YOU BE IN FRANCE?
WHY ARE YOU IN JAPAN?
IF ONE HAS THE DESIRE, THEY CAN LEARN *ANYWHERE,* MADEMOISELLE.
HMM.
NOW! PAPA!
I HAVE HEARD AND UNDERSTOOD YOUR PLIGHT.
YOU OWE PENALTIES FOR TAX EVASION...
...AND YOUR MADAME HAS LEFT YOU.
YOU MANUFACTURED MASKS OF PRESIDENT BEVERLY DUNCAN...
...BUT THE ELECTION FAILED TO GENERATE EXCITEMENT...
...LEAVING YOU WITH COUNTLESS UNUSED MASKS...

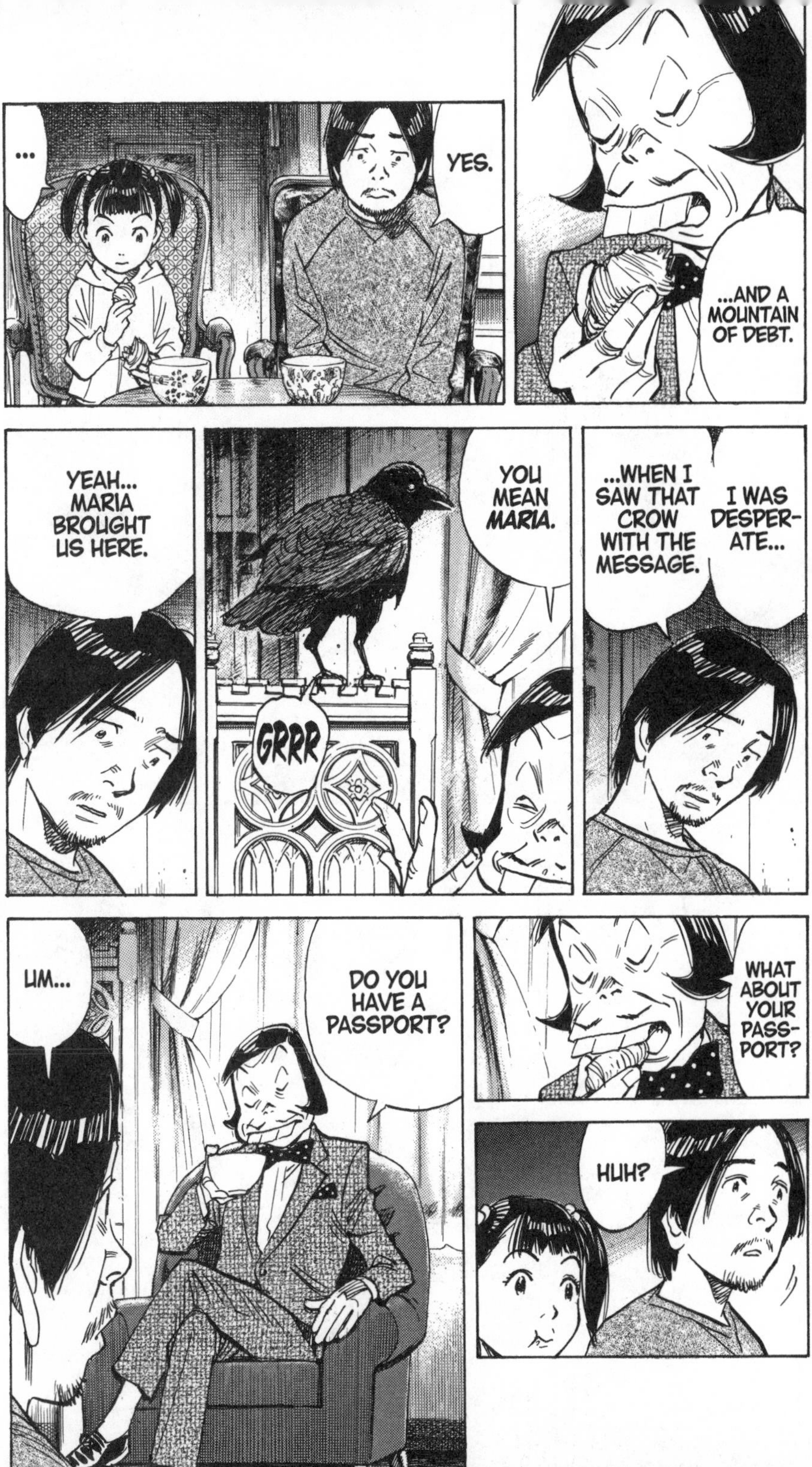
...AND A MOUNTAIN OF DEBT.
YES.
...
I WAS DESPER-ATE...
...WHEN I SAW THAT CROW WITH THE MESSAGE.
YOU MEAN *MARIA*.
GRRR
YEAH... MARIA BROUGHT US HERE.
WHAT ABOUT YOUR PASS-PORT?
HUH?
DO YOU HAVE A PASSPORT?
UM...

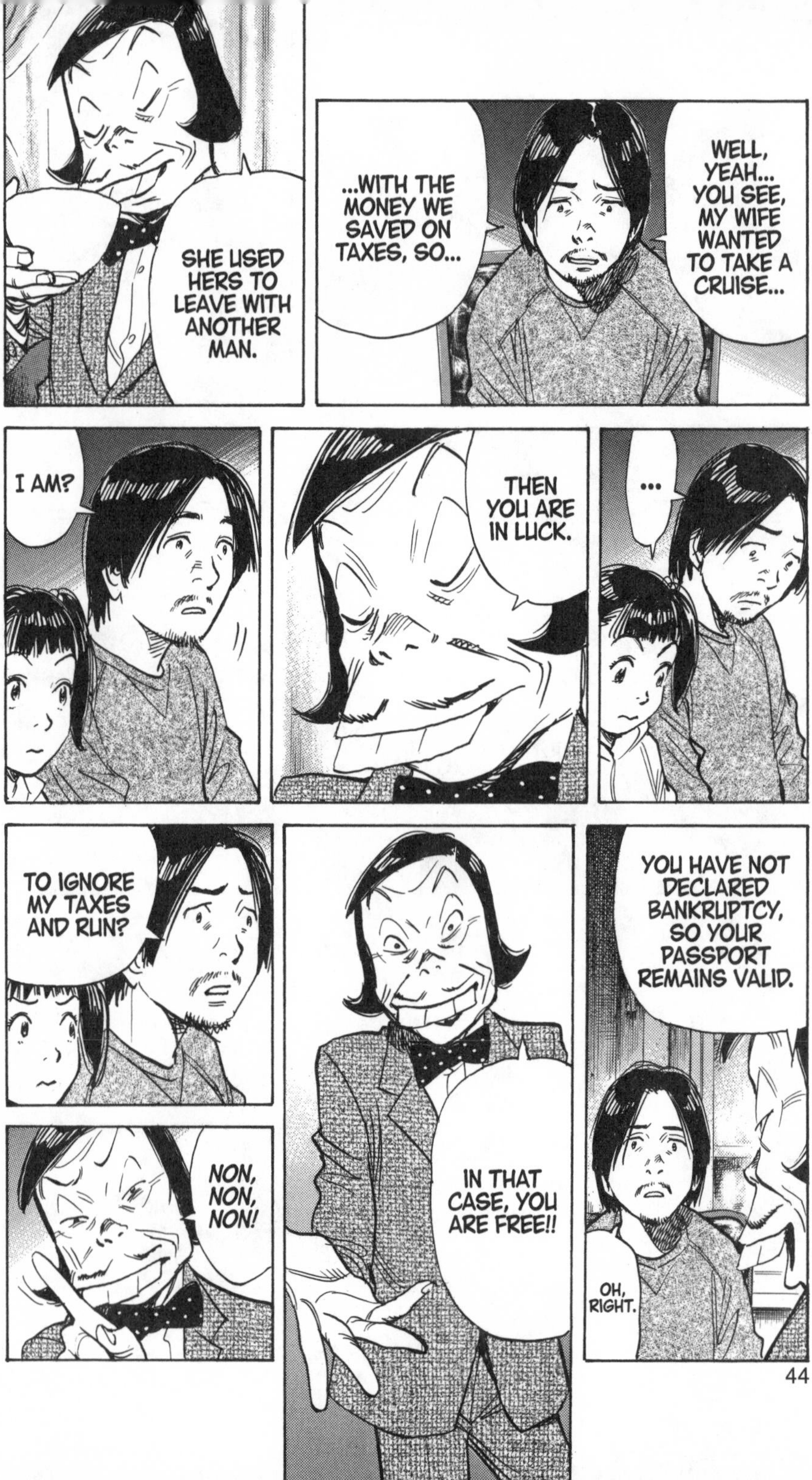
WELL, YEAH... YOU SEE, MY WIFE WANTED TO TAKE A CRUISE...
...WITH THE MONEY WE SAVED ON TAXES, SO...
SHE USED HERS TO LEAVE WITH ANOTHER MAN.
...
THEN YOU ARE IN LUCK.
I AM?
YOU HAVE NOT DECLARED BANKRUPTCY, SO YOUR PASSPORT REMAINS VALID.
OH, RIGHT.
IN THAT CASE, YOU ARE FREE!!
TO IGNORE MY TAXES AND RUN?
NON, NON, NON!

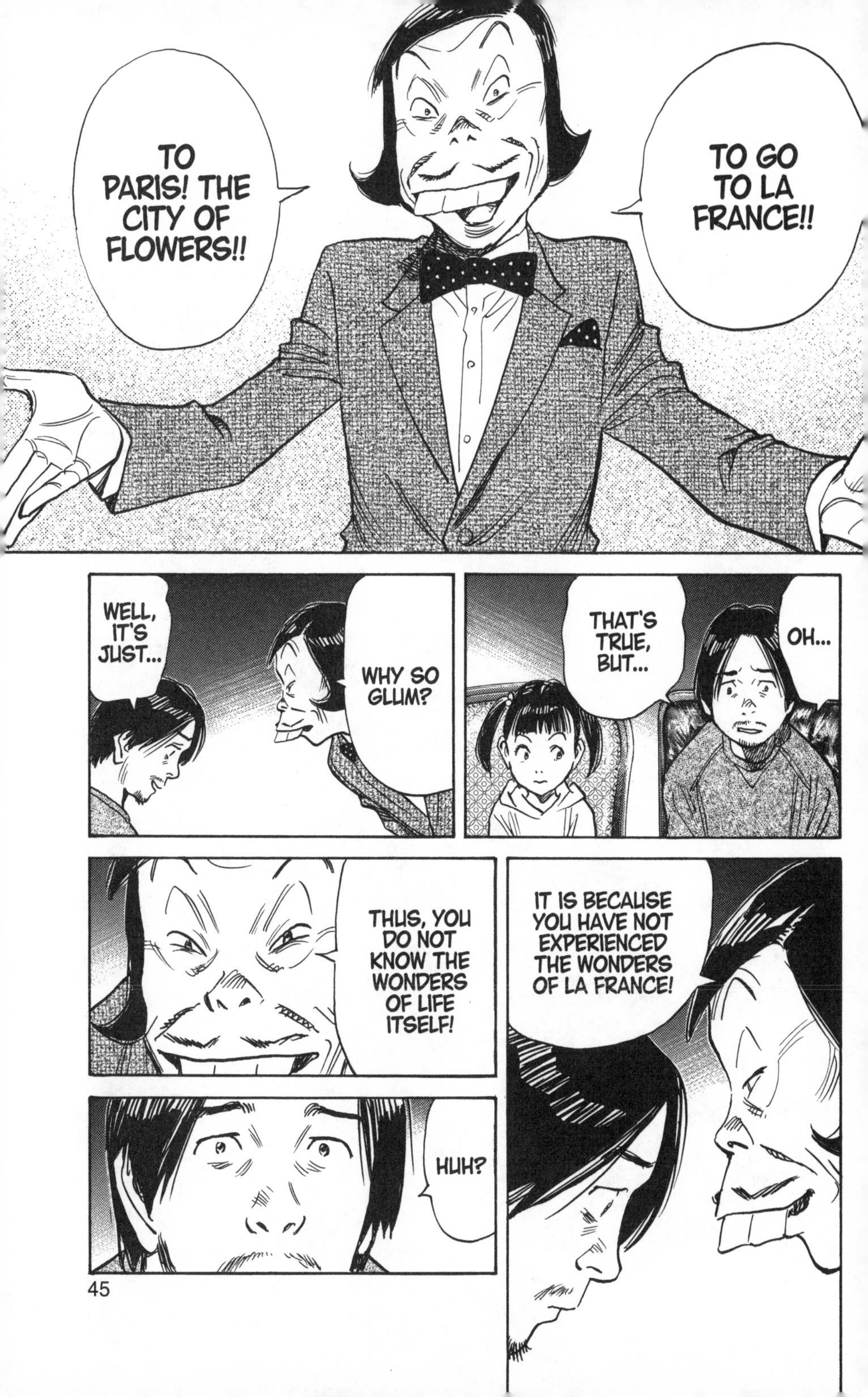
TO GO TO LA FRANCE!!
TO PARIS! THE CITY OF FLOWERS!!
OH...
THAT'S TRUE, BUT...
WHY SO GLUM?
WELL, IT'S JUST...
IT IS BECAUSE YOU HAVE NOT EXPERIENCED THE WONDERS OF LA FRANCE!
THUS, YOU DO NOT KNOW THE WONDERS OF LIFE ITSELF!
HUH?

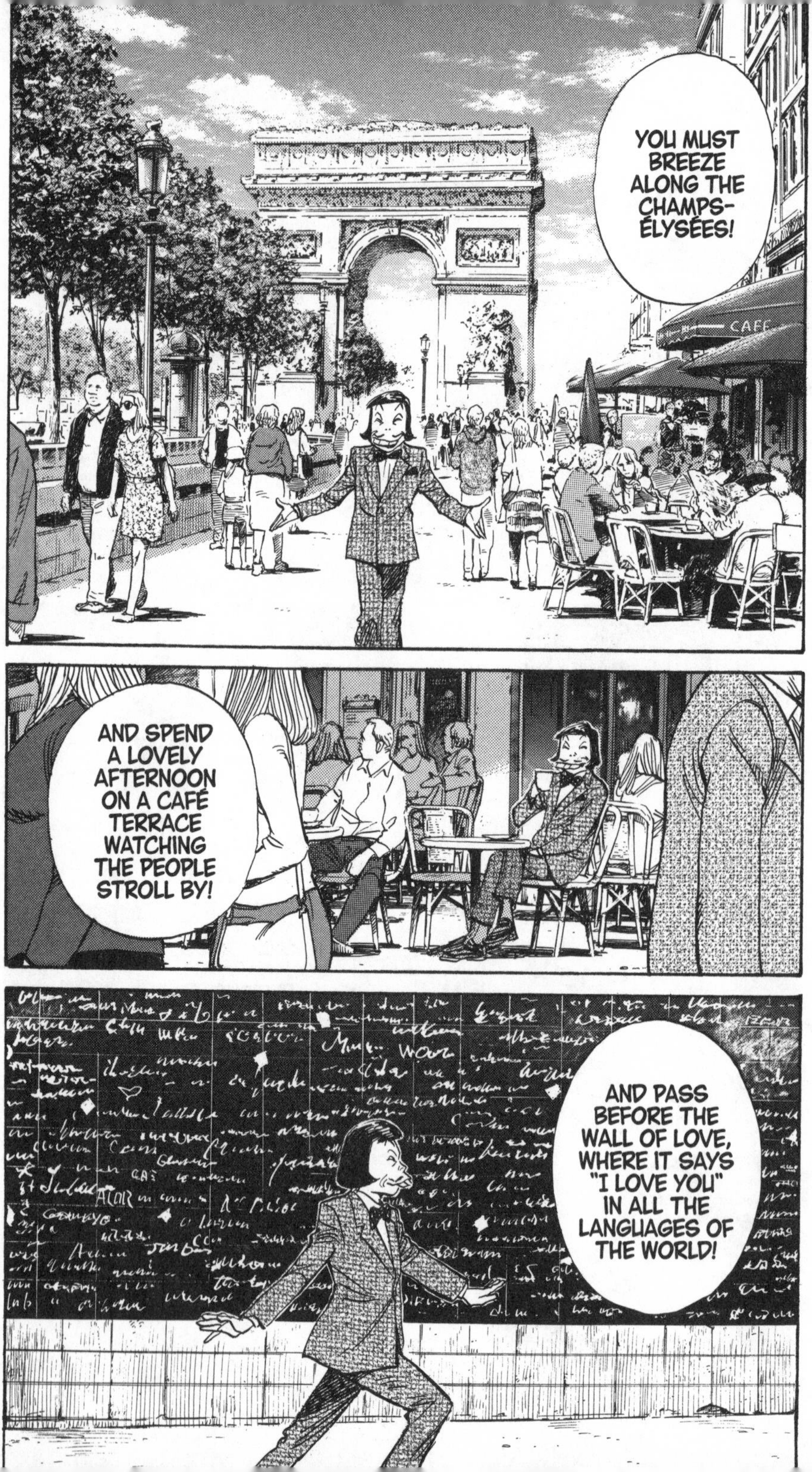
YOU MUST BREEZE ALONG THE CHAMPS-ÉLYSÉES!
CAFE
AND SPEND A LOVELY AFTERNOON ON A CAFÉ TERRACE WATCHING THE PEOPLE STROLL BY!
AND PASS BEFORE THE WALL OF LOVE, WHERE IT SAYS "I LOVE YOU" IN ALL THE LANGUAGES OF THE WORLD!

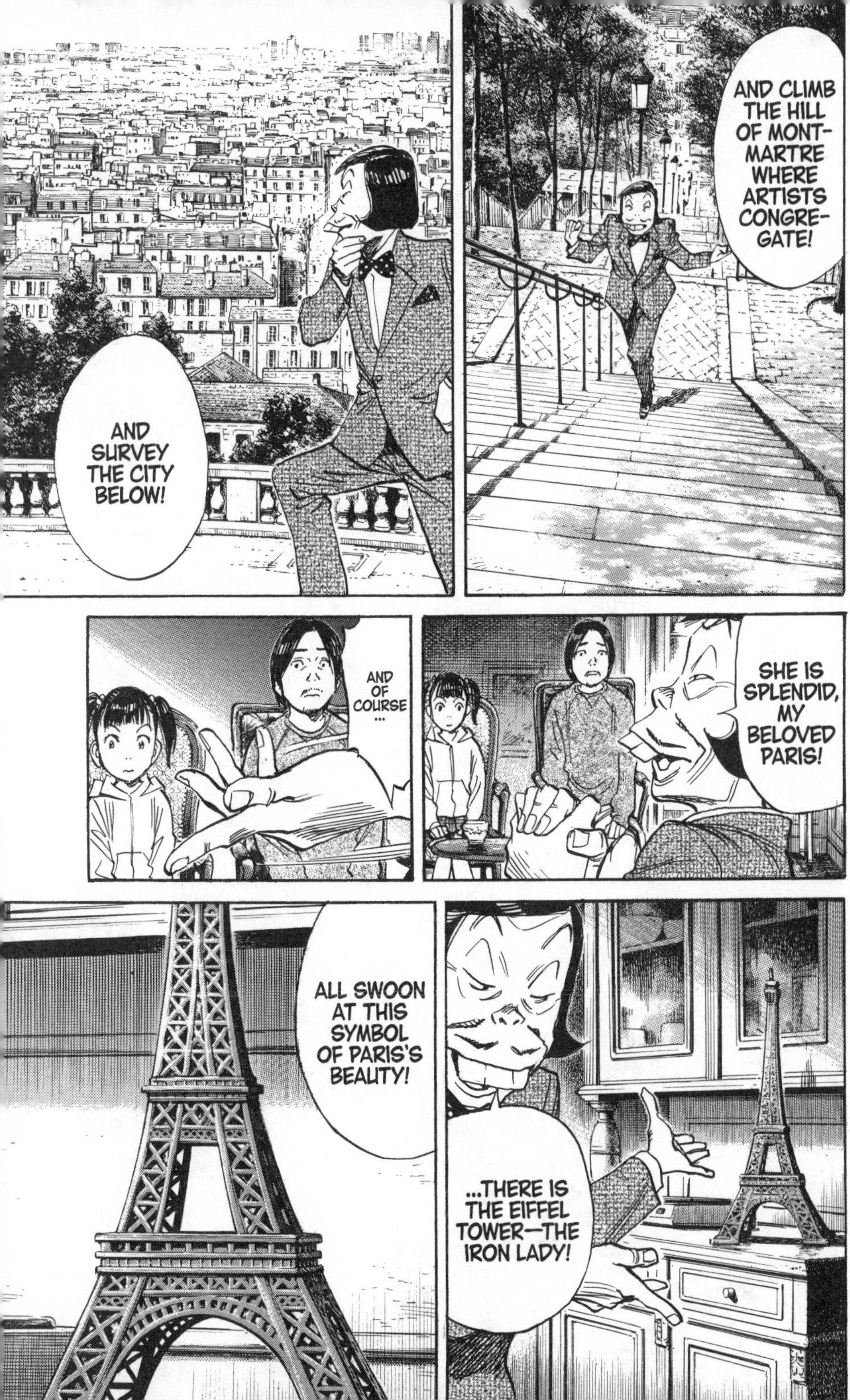
AND CLIMB THE HILL OF MONTMARTRE WHERE ARTISTS CONGREGATE!
AND SURVEY THE CITY BELOW!
SHE IS SPLENDID, MY BELOVED PARIS!
AND OF COURSE ...
...THERE IS THE EIFFEL TOWER—THE IRON LADY!
ALL SWOON AT THIS SYMBOL OF PARIS'S BEAUTY!

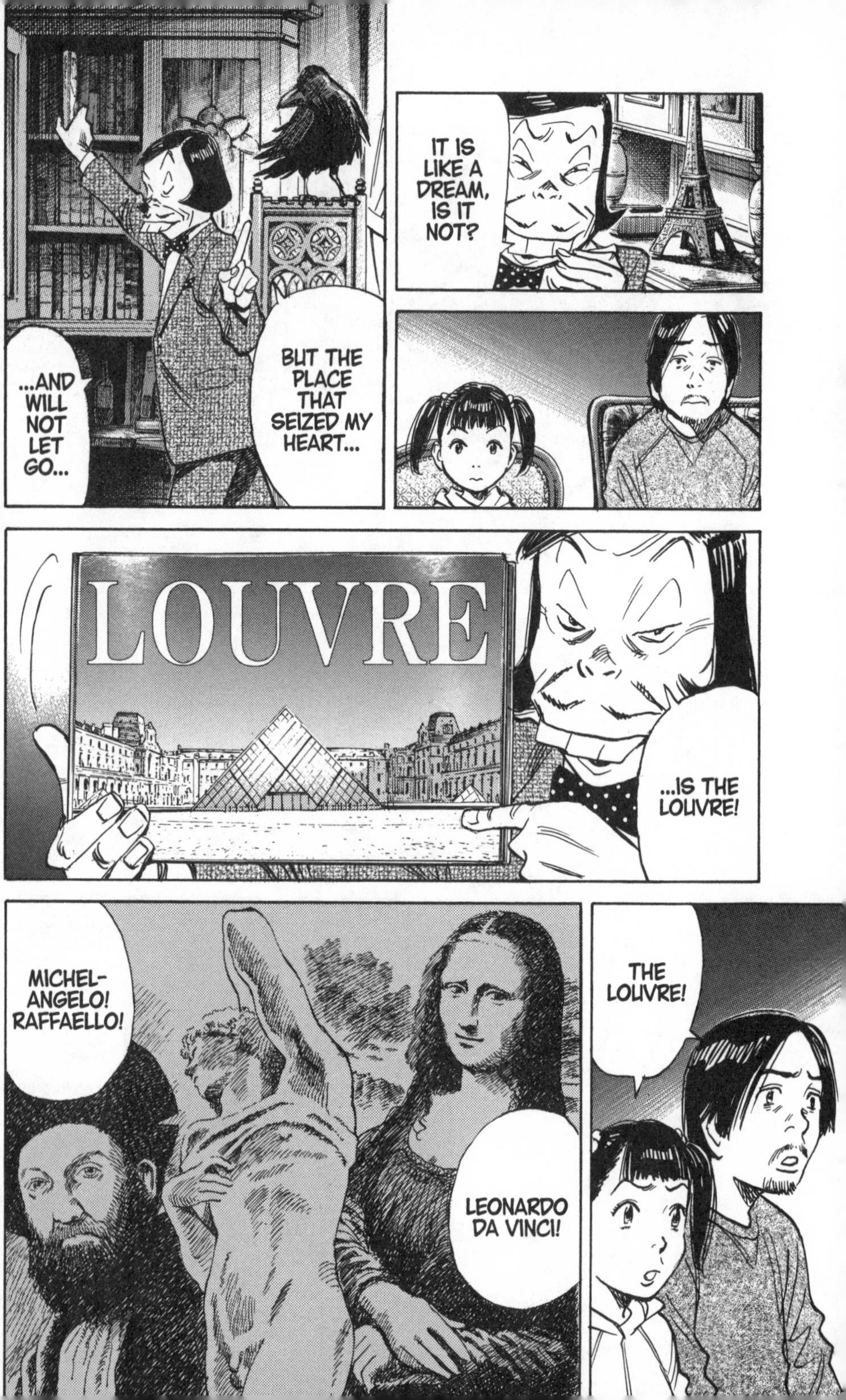
IT IS LIKE A DREAM, IS IT NOT?
BUT THE PLACE THAT SEIZED MY HEART...
...AND WILL NOT LET GO...
LOUVRE
...IS THE LOUVRE!
THE LOUVRE!
LEONARDO DA VINCI!
MICHEL-ANGELO! RAFFAELLO!

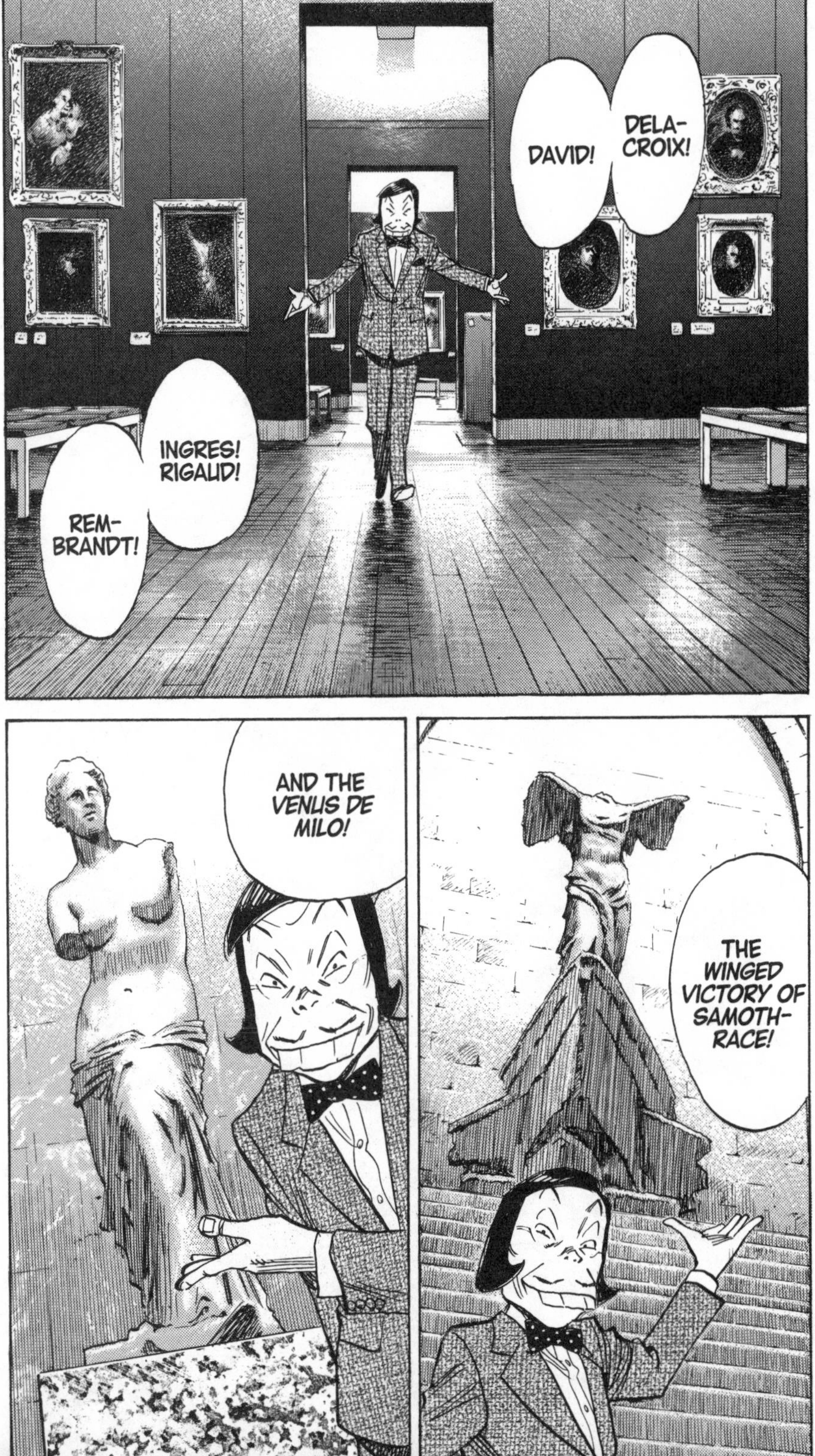
DELA-CROIX!
DAVID!
INGRES! RIGAUD!
REM-BRANDT!
THE WINGED VICTORY OF SAMOTH-RACE!
AND THE VENUS DE MILO!

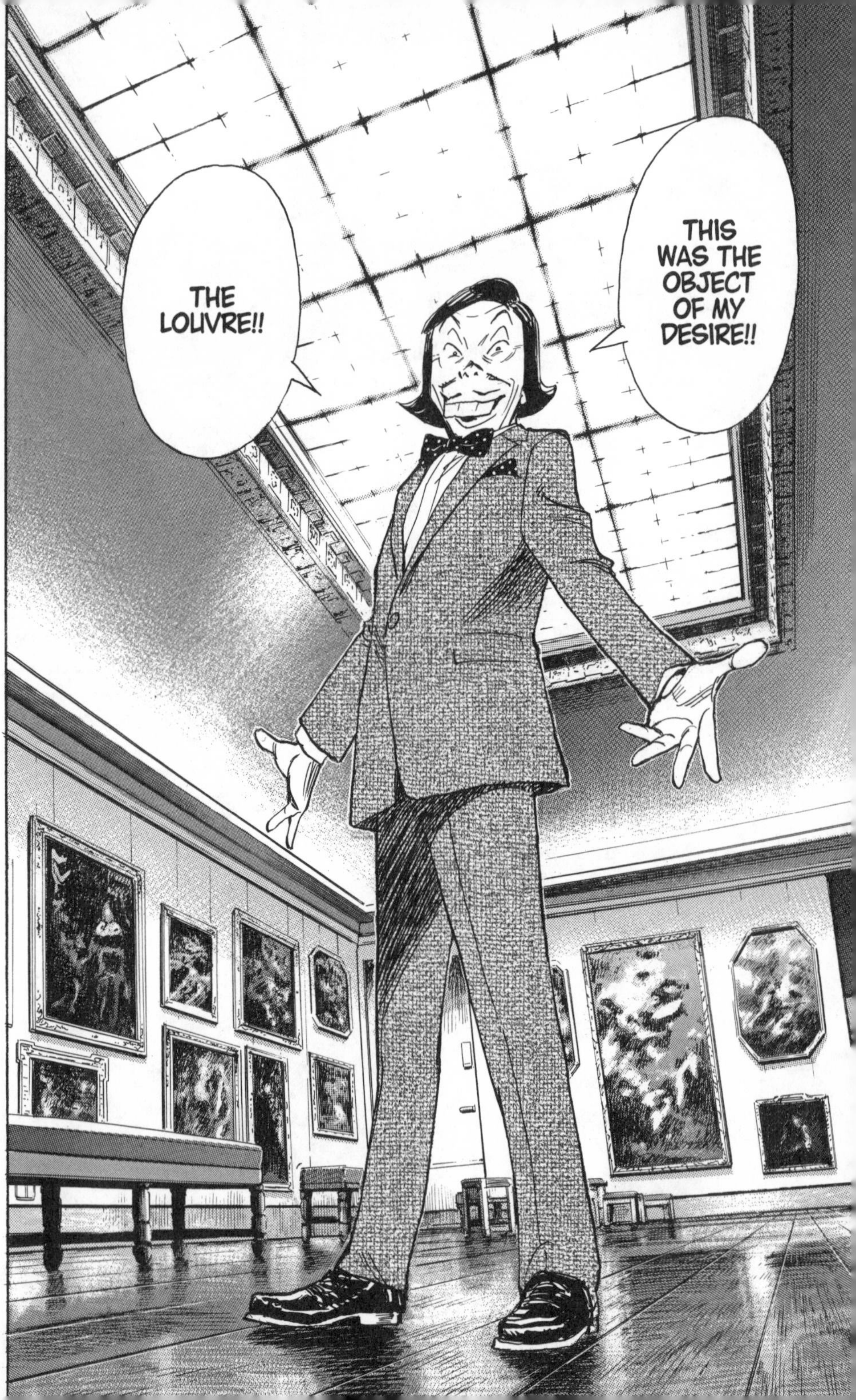
THIS WAS THE OBJECT OF MY DESIRE!!
THE LOUVRE!!

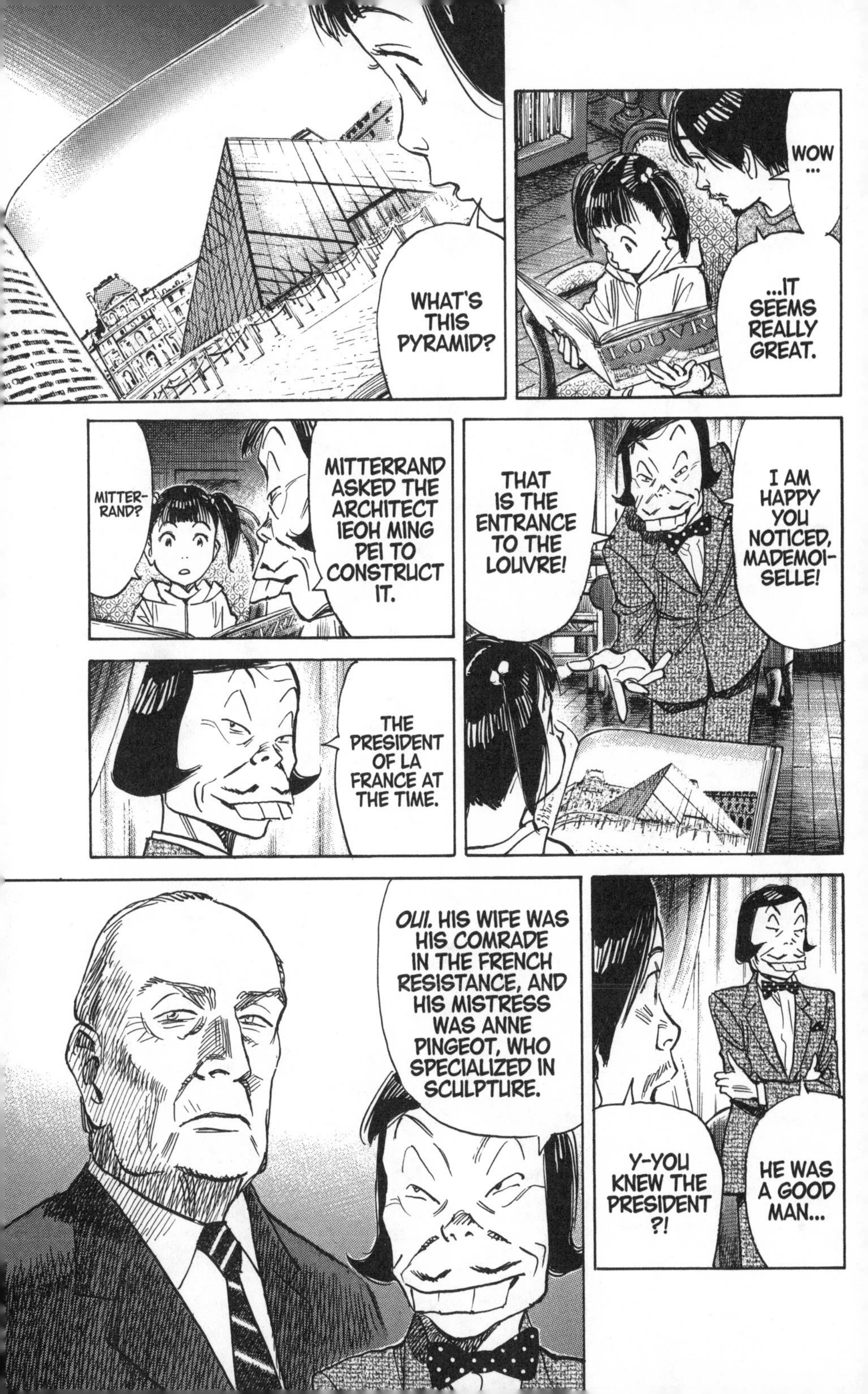
WOW ...
...IT SEEMS REALLY GREAT.
WHAT'S THIS PYRAMID?
I AM HAPPY YOU NOTICED, MADEMOISELLE!
THAT IS THE ENTRANCE TO THE LOUVRE!
MITTERRAND ASKED THE ARCHITECT IEOH MING PEI TO CONSTRUCT IT.
MITTER-RAND?
THE PRESIDENT OF LA FRANCE AT THE TIME.
HE WAS A GOOD MAN...
Y-YOU KNEW THE PRESIDENT ?!
OUI. HIS WIFE WAS HIS COMRADE IN THE FRENCH RESISTANCE, AND HIS MISTRESS WAS ANNE PINGEOT, WHO SPECIALIZED IN SCULPTURE.

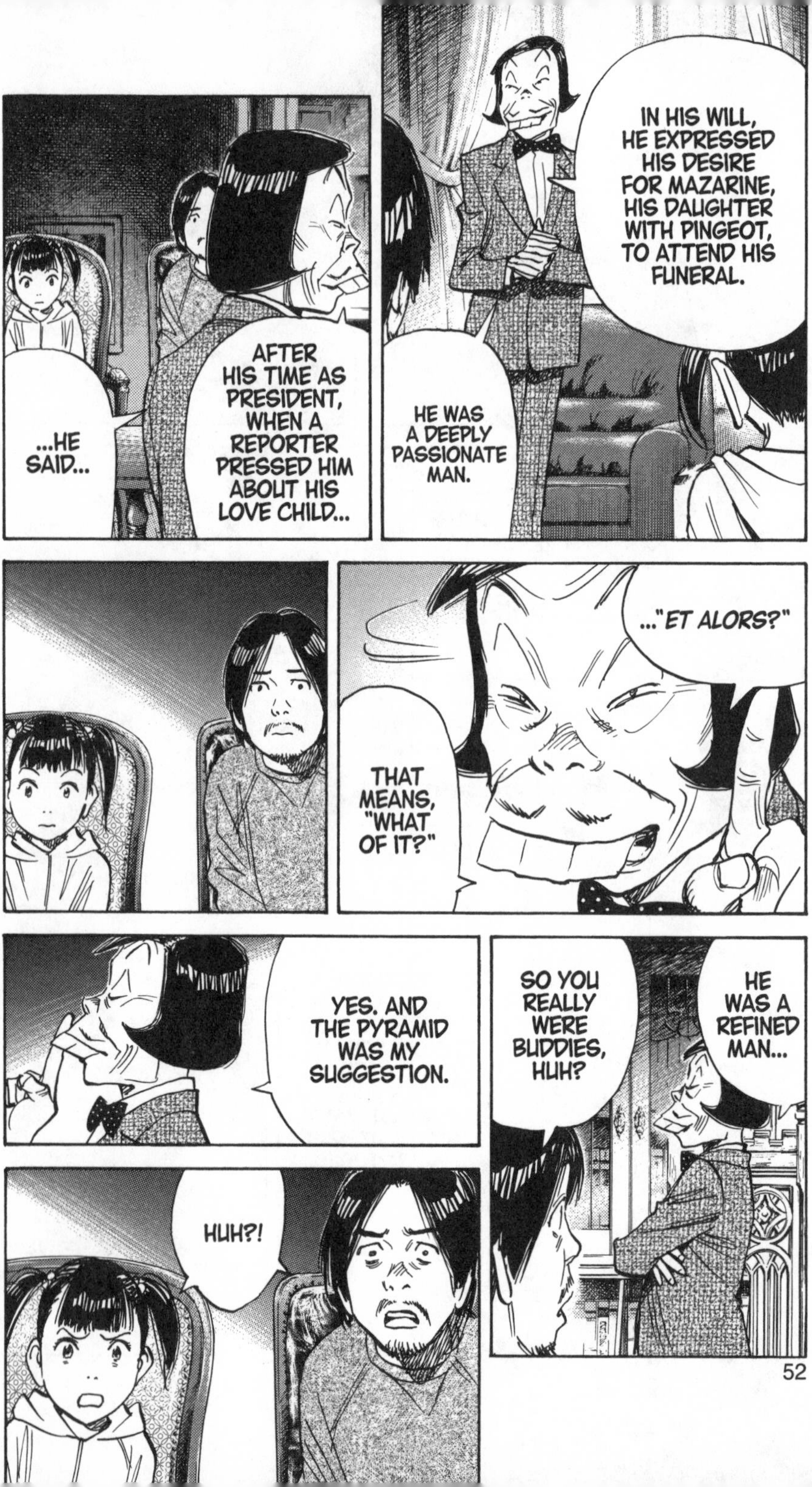
IN HIS WILL, HE EXPRESSED HIS DESIRE FOR MAZARINE, HIS DAUGHTER WITH PINGEOT, TO ATTEND HIS FUNERAL.
HE WAS A DEEPLY PASSIONATE MAN.
AFTER HIS TIME AS PRESIDENT, WHEN A REPORTER PRESSED HIM ABOUT HIS LOVE CHILD...
...HE SAID...
..."ET ALORS?"
THAT MEANS, "WHAT OF IT?"
HE WAS A REFINED MAN...
SO YOU REALLY WERE BUDDIES, HUH?
YES. AND THE PYRAMID WAS MY SUGGESTION.
HUH?!

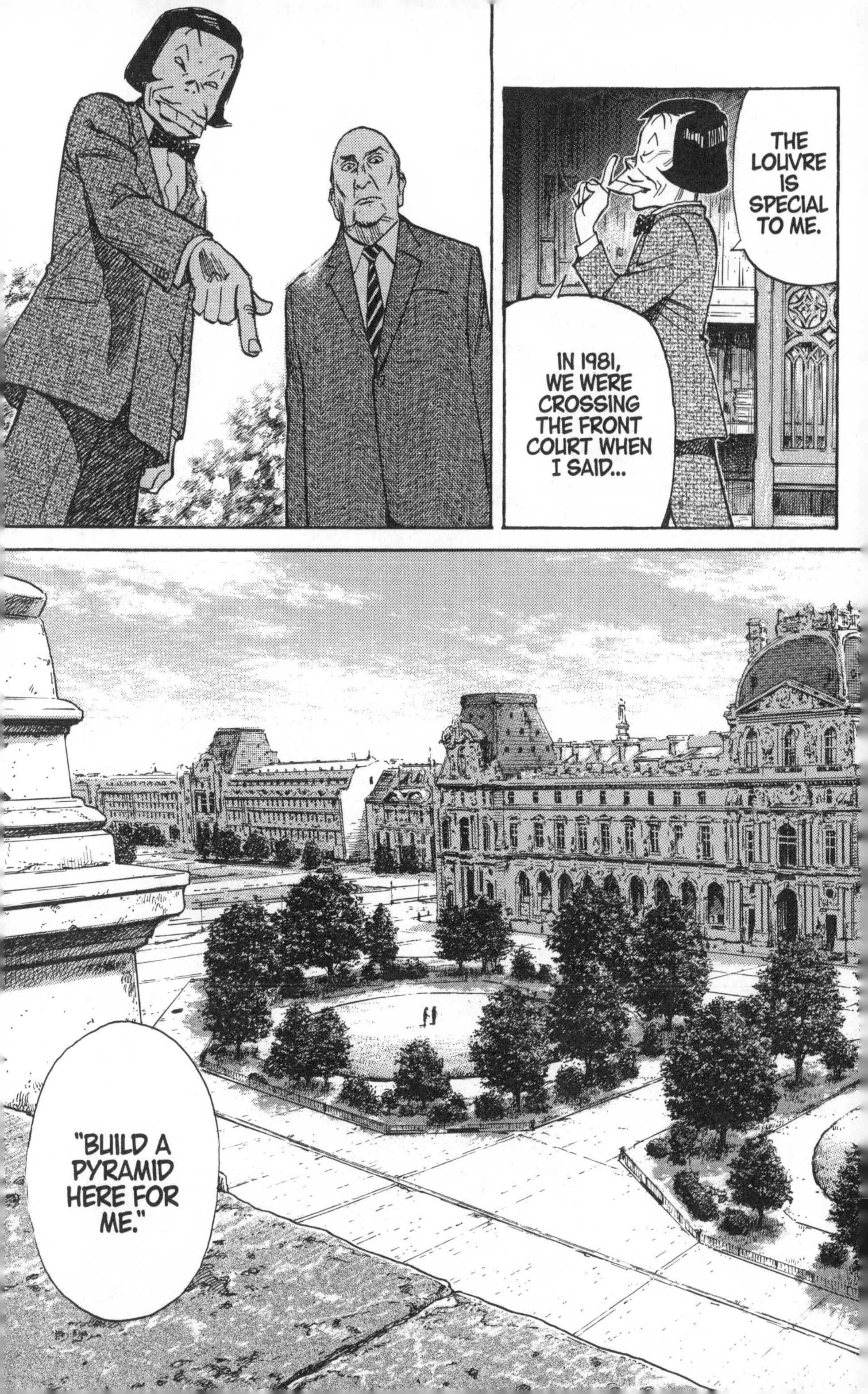
THE LOUVRE IS SPECIAL TO ME.
IN 1981, WE WERE CROSSING THE FRONT COURT WHEN I SAID...
"BUILD A PYRAMID HERE FOR ME."

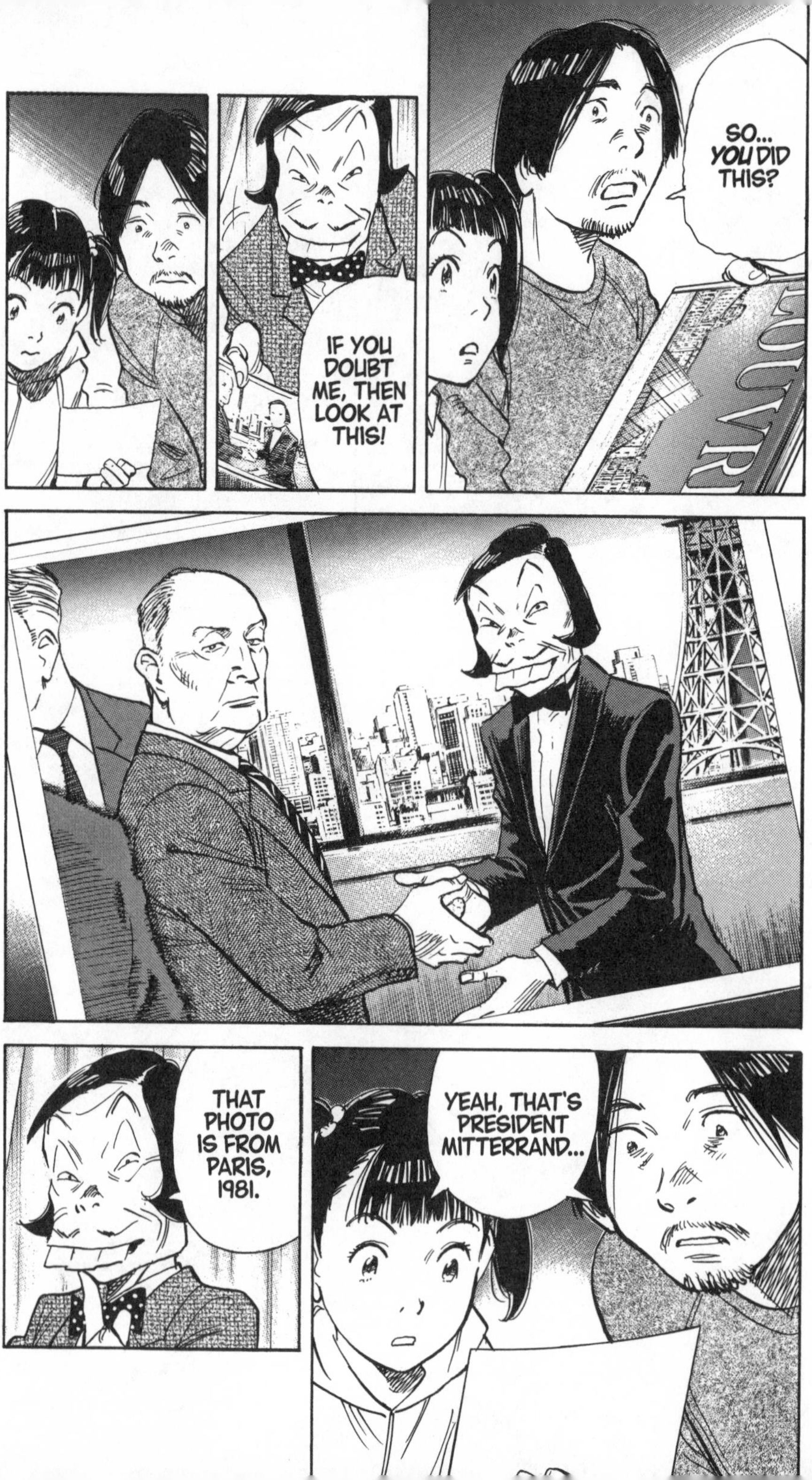
SO... YOU DID THIS?
IF YOU DOUBT ME, THEN LOOK AT THIS!
YEAH, THAT'S PRESIDENT MITTERRAND...
THAT PHOTO IS FROM PARIS, 1981.

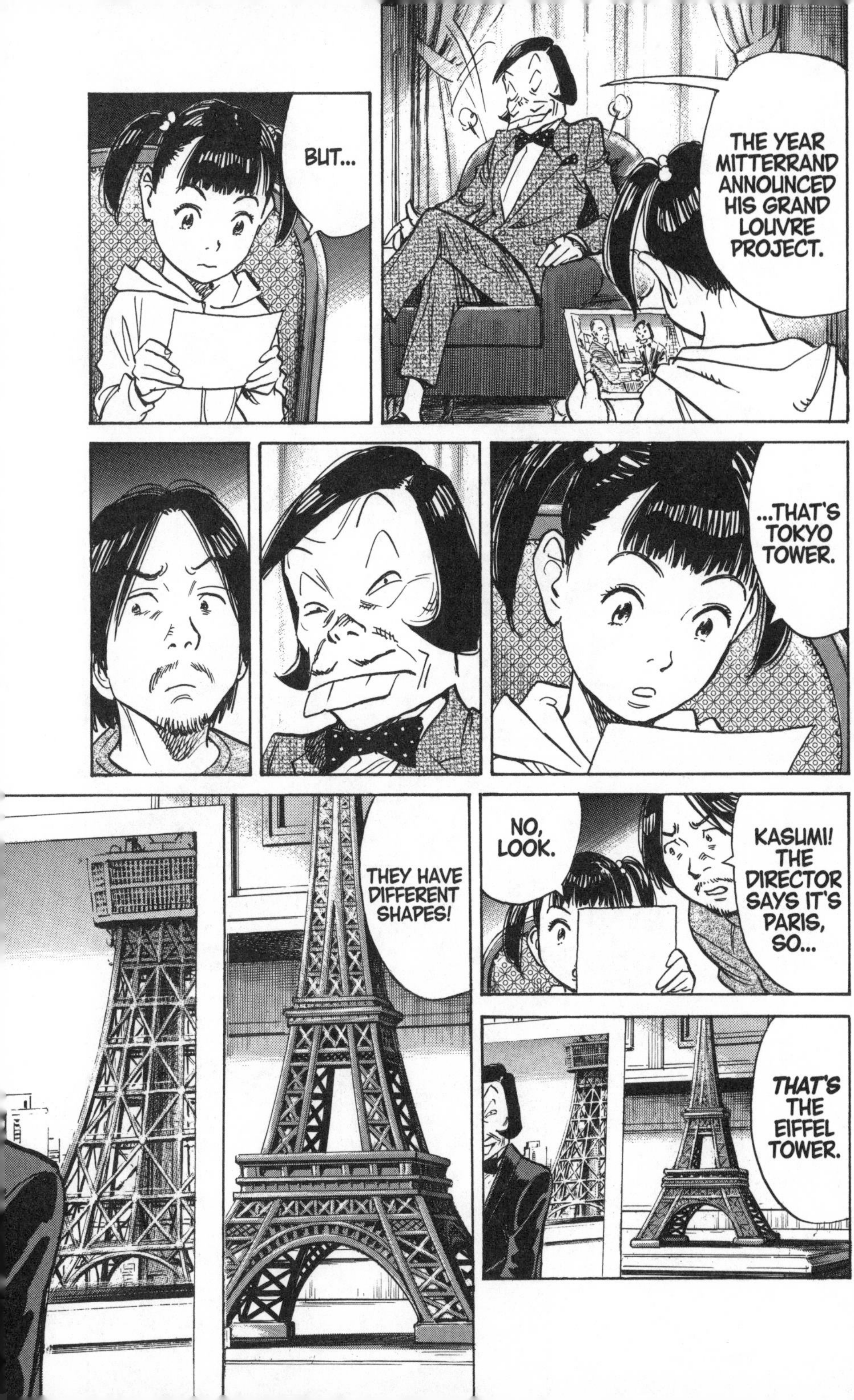
THE YEAR MITTERRAND ANNOUNCED HIS GRAND LOUVRE PROJECT.
BUT...
...THAT'S TOKYO TOWER.
KASUMI! THE DIRECTOR SAYS IT'S PARIS, SO...
NO, LOOK.
THAT'S THE EIFFEL TOWER.
THEY HAVE DIFFERENT SHAPES!

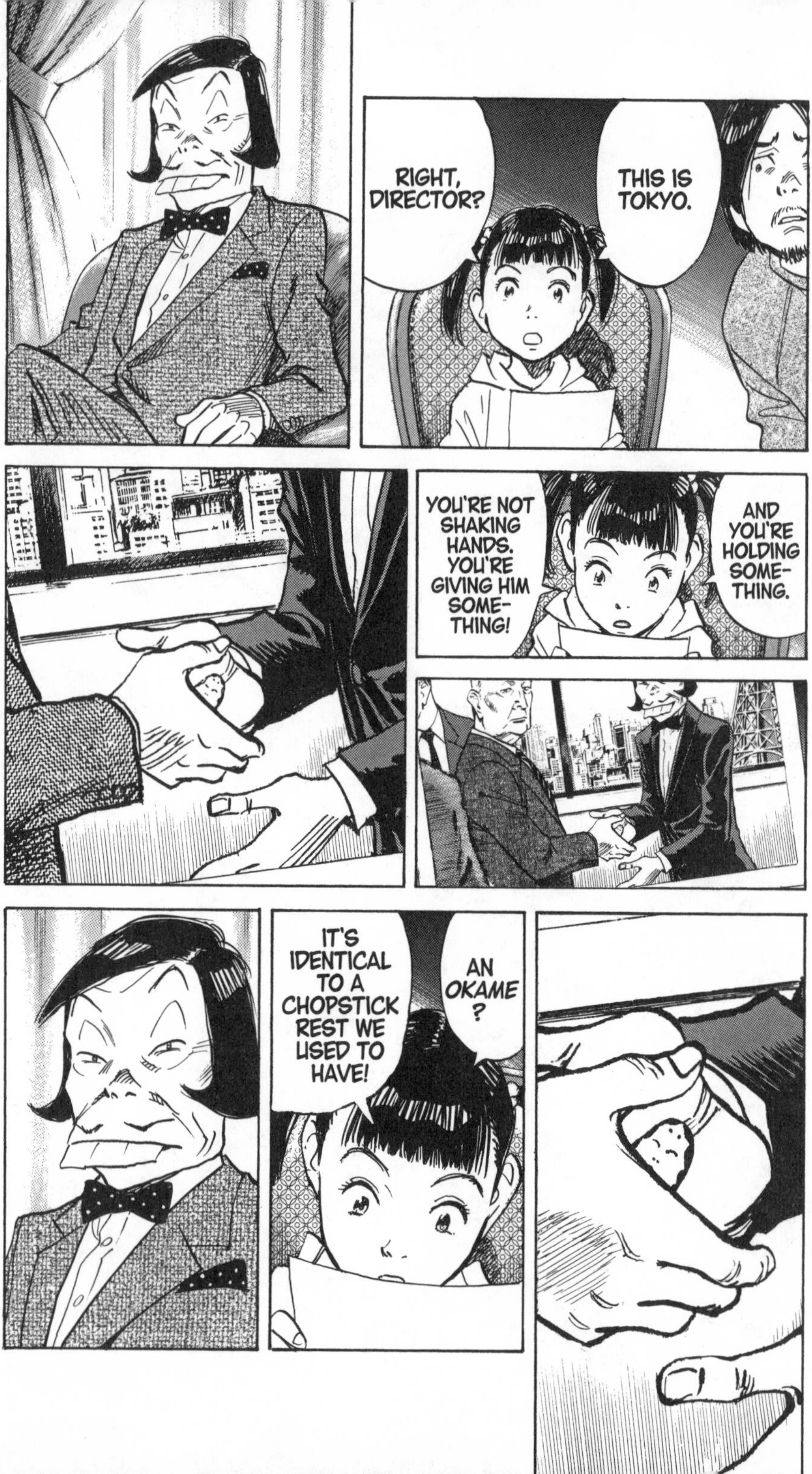
THIS IS TOKYO.
RIGHT, DIRECTOR?
AND YOU'RE HOLDING SOMETHING.
YOU'RE NOT SHAKING HANDS. YOU'RE GIVING HIM SOMETHING!
AN OKAME?
IT'S IDENTICAL TO A CHOPSTICK REST WE USED TO HAVE!

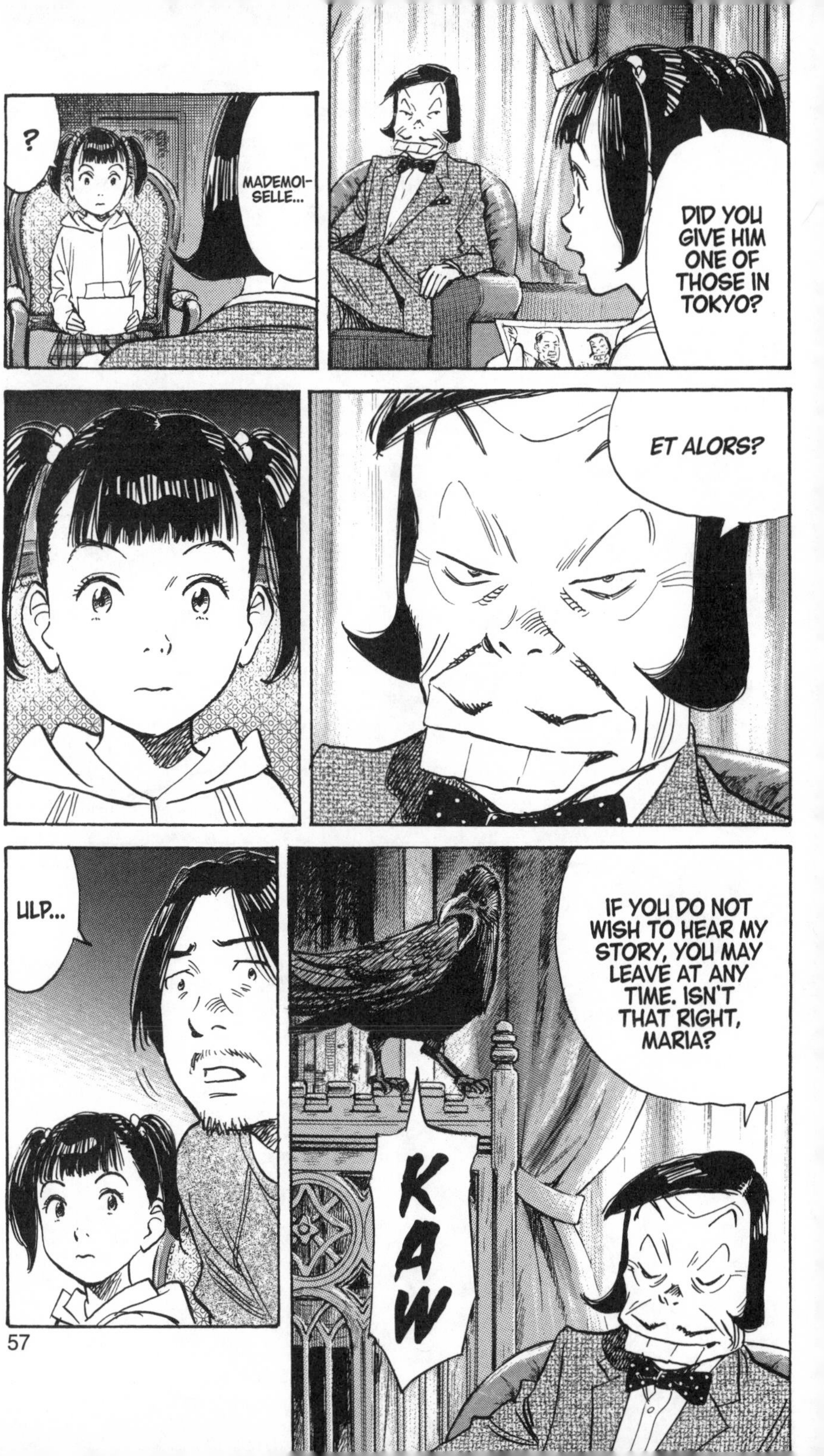
DID YOU GIVE HIM ONE OF THOSE IN TOKYO?
MADEMOI-SELLE...
?
ET ALORS?
IF YOU DO NOT WISH TO HEAR MY STORY, YOU MAY LEAVE AT ANY TIME. ISN'T THAT RIGHT, MARIA?
KAW
ULP...

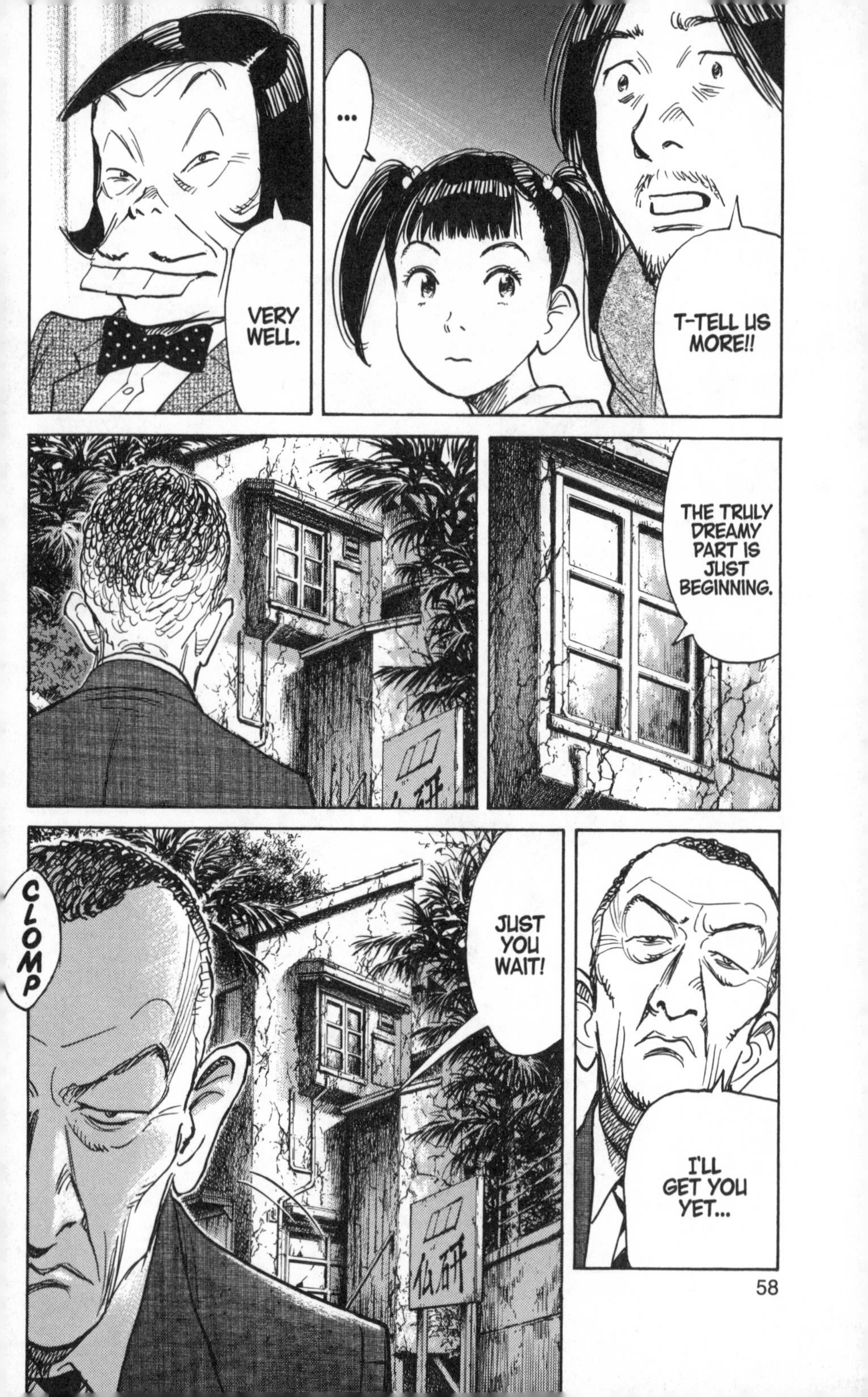
...
T-TELL US MORE!!
VERY WELL.
THE TRULY DREAMY PART IS JUST BEGINNING.
I'LL GET YOU YET...
JUST YOU WAIT!
仏研
CLOMP

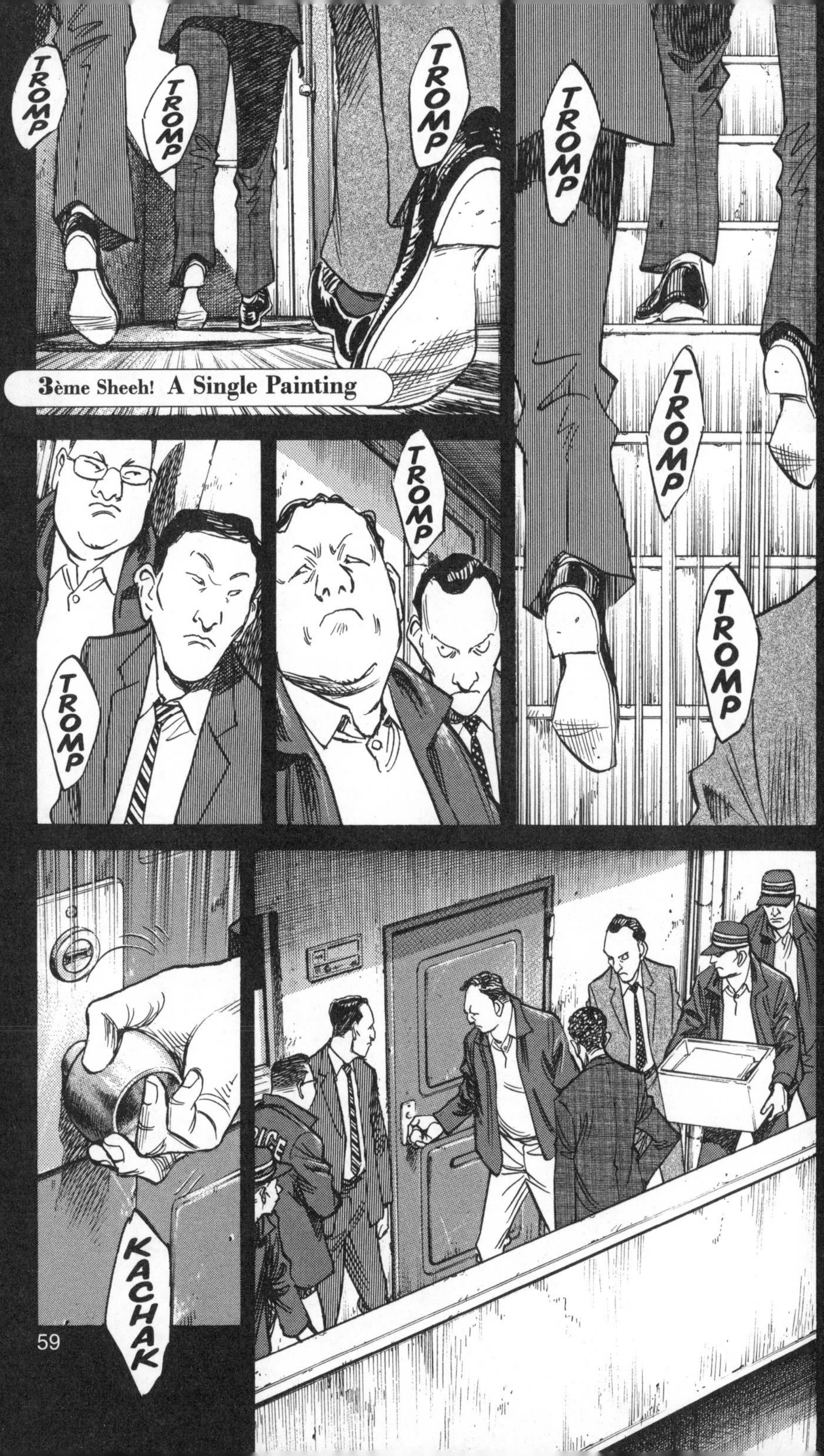
TROMP
TROMP
TROMP
TROMP
TROMP
TROMP
3ème Sheeh! A Single Painting
TROMP
TROMP
KACHAK

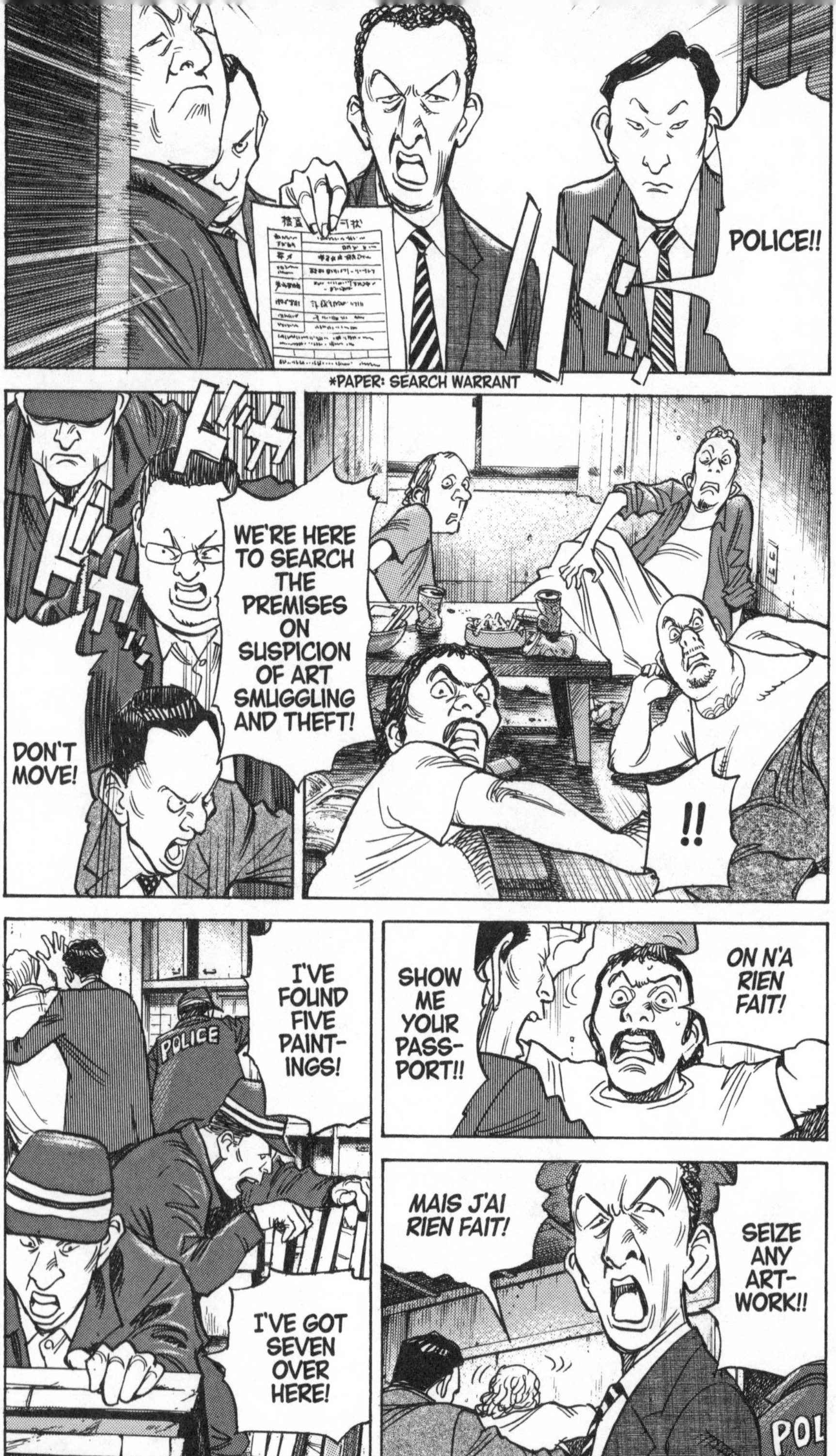
POLICE!!
*PAPER: SEARCH WARRANT
!!
WE'RE HERE TO SEARCH THE PREMISES ON SUSPICION OF ART SMUGGLING AND THEFT!
DON'T MOVE!
ON N'A RIEN FAIT!
SHOW ME YOUR PASSPORT!!
SEIZE ANY ARTWORK!!
MAIS J'AI RIEN FAIT!
POL
I'VE FOUND FIVE PAINTINGS!
POLICE
I'VE GOT SEVEN OVER HERE!

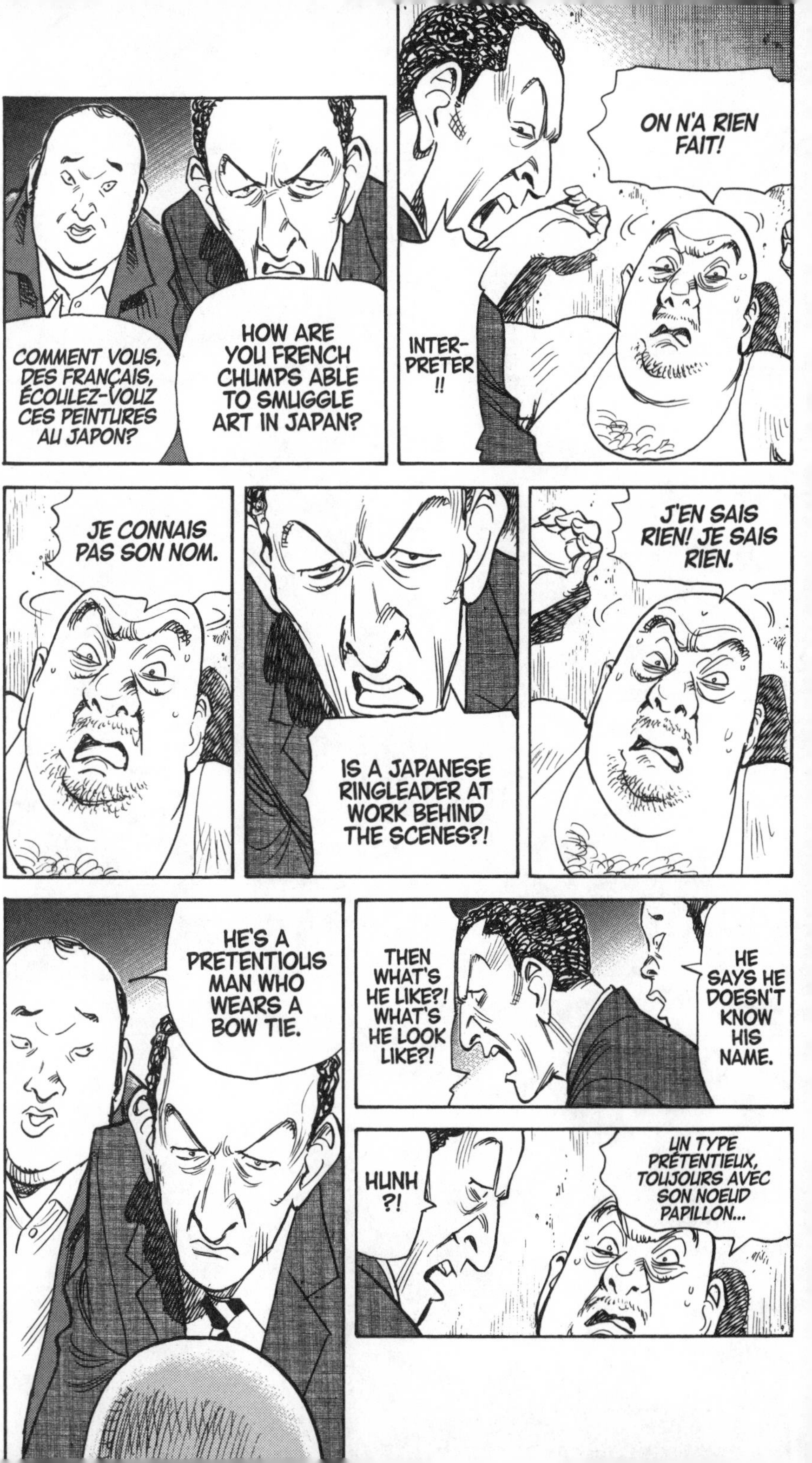
ON N'A RIEN FAIT!
INTER-PRETER!!
HOW ARE YOU FRENCH CHUMPS ABLE TO SMUGGLE ART IN JAPAN?
COMMENT VOUS, DES FRANÇAIS, ÉCOULEZ-VOUZ CES PEINTURES AU JAPON?
J'EN SAIS RIEN! JE SAIS RIEN.
IS A JAPANESE RINGLEADER AT WORK BEHIND THE SCENES?!
JE CONNAIS PAS SON NOM.
HE SAYS HE DOESN'T KNOW HIS NAME.
THEN WHAT'S HE LIKE?! WHAT'S HE LOOK LIKE?!
UN TYPE PRÉTENTIEUX, TOUJOURS AVEC SON NOEUD PAPILLON...
HUNH?!
HE'S A PRETENTIOUS MAN WHO WEARS A BOW TIE.

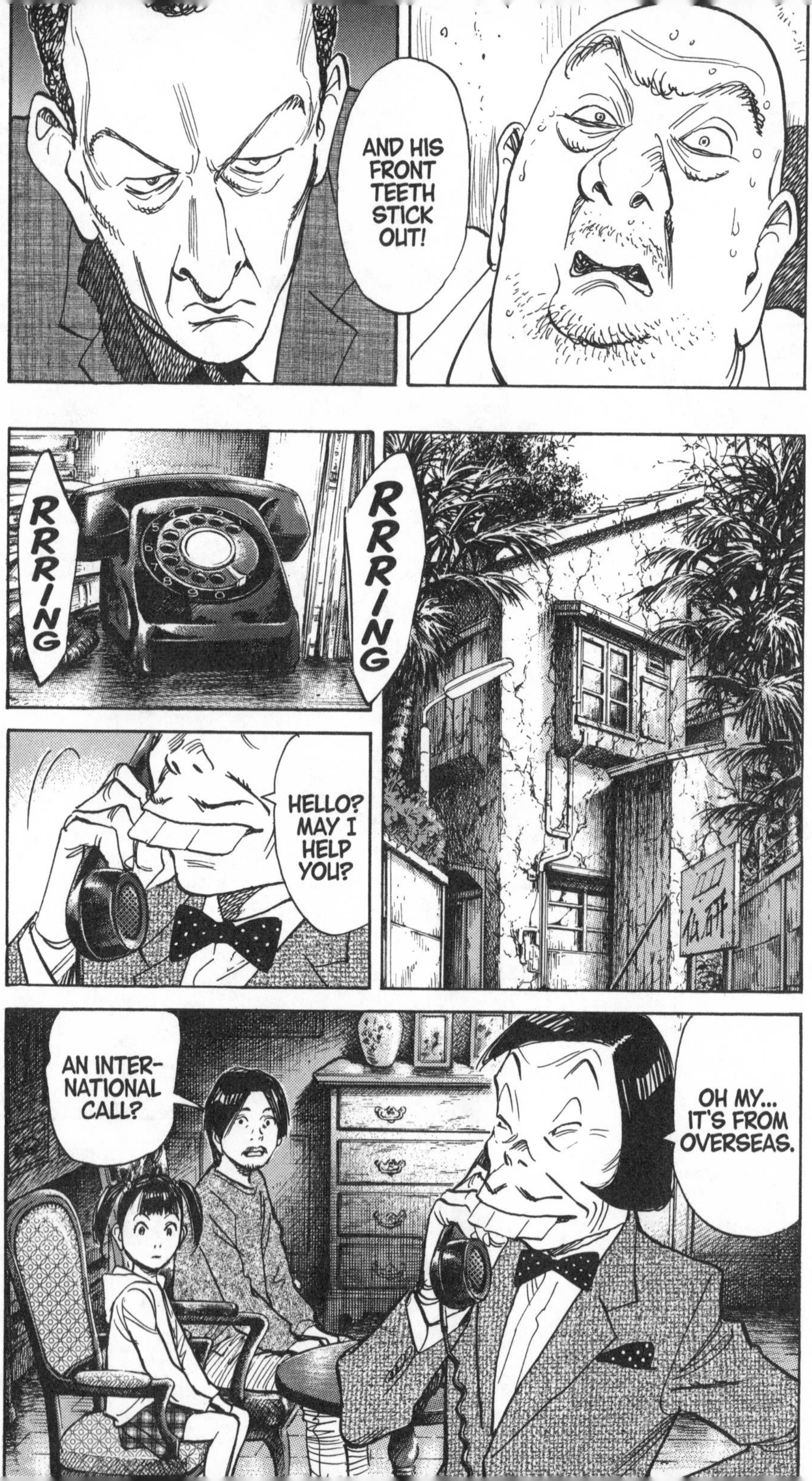
AND HIS FRONT TEETH STICK OUT!
RRRING
RRRING
HELLO? MAY I HELP YOU?
OH MY... IT'S FROM OVERSEAS.
AN INTER-NATIONAL CALL?

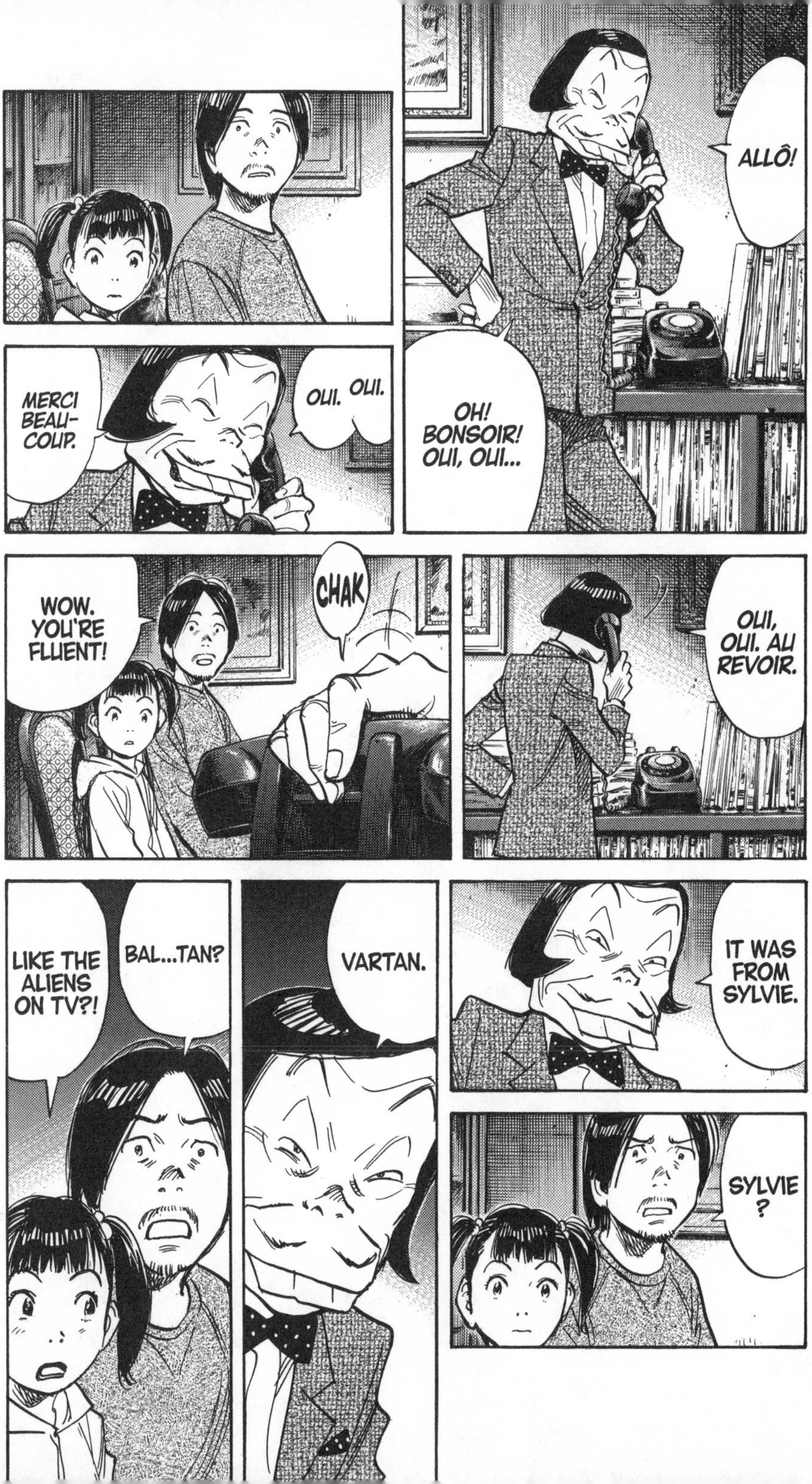
ALLÔ!
OH! BONSOIR! OUI, OUI...
OUI. OUI.
MERCI BEAU-COUP.
OUI, OUI. AU REVOIR.
CHAK
WOW. YOU'RE FLUENT!
IT WAS FROM SYLVIE.
SYLVIE?
VARTAN.
BAL...TAN?
LIKE THE ALIENS ON TV?!

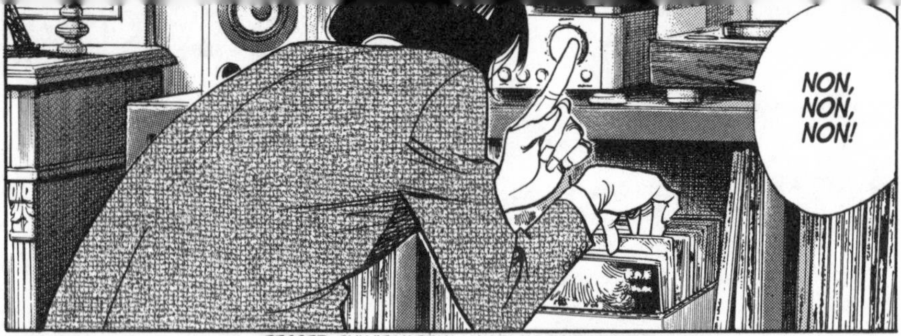
NON, NON, NON!

*RECORD: SYLVIE VARTAN, *ANATA NO TORIKO* (YOUR CAPTIVE)

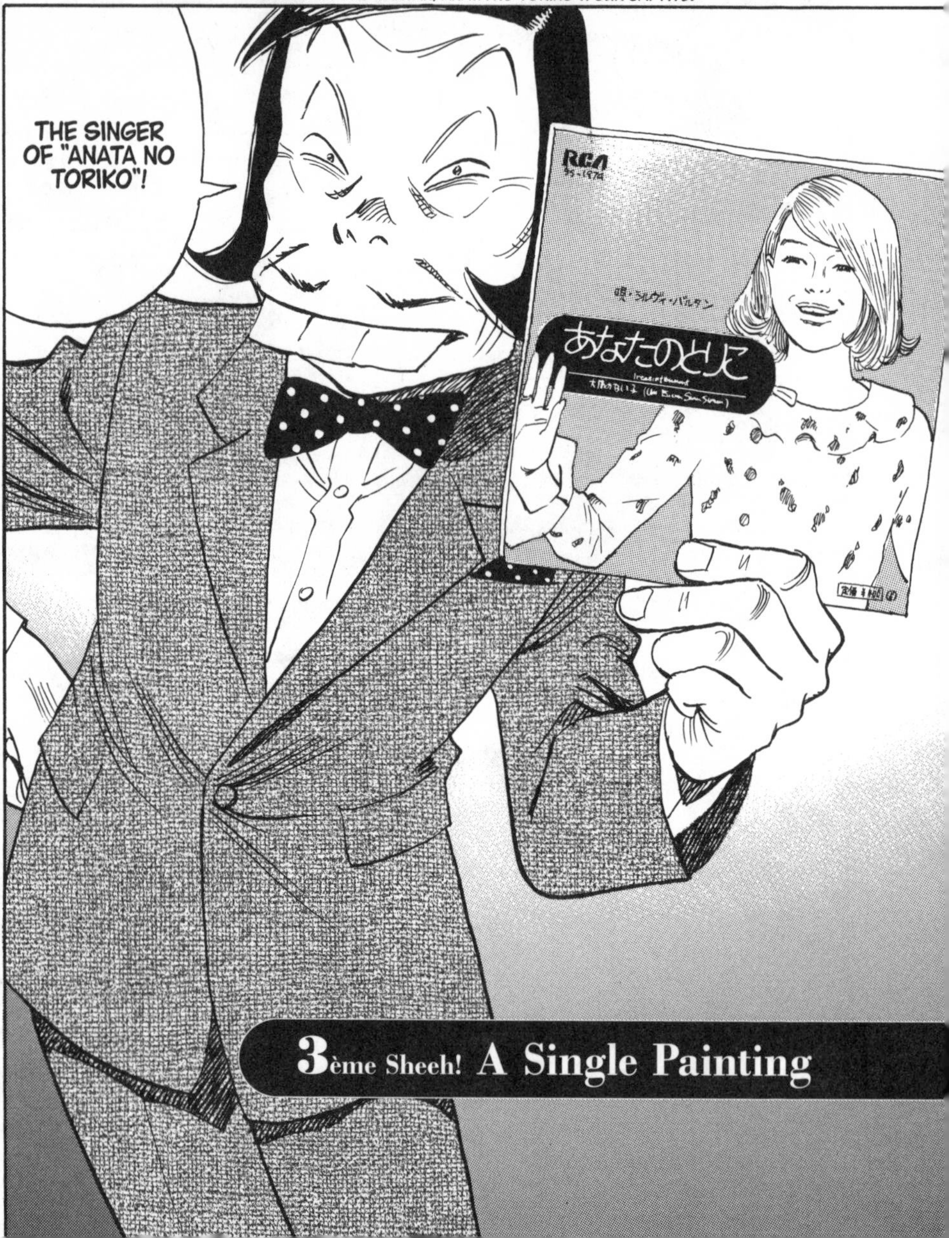
THE SINGER OF "ANATA NO TORIKO"!
RCA
3ème Sheeh! A Single Painting

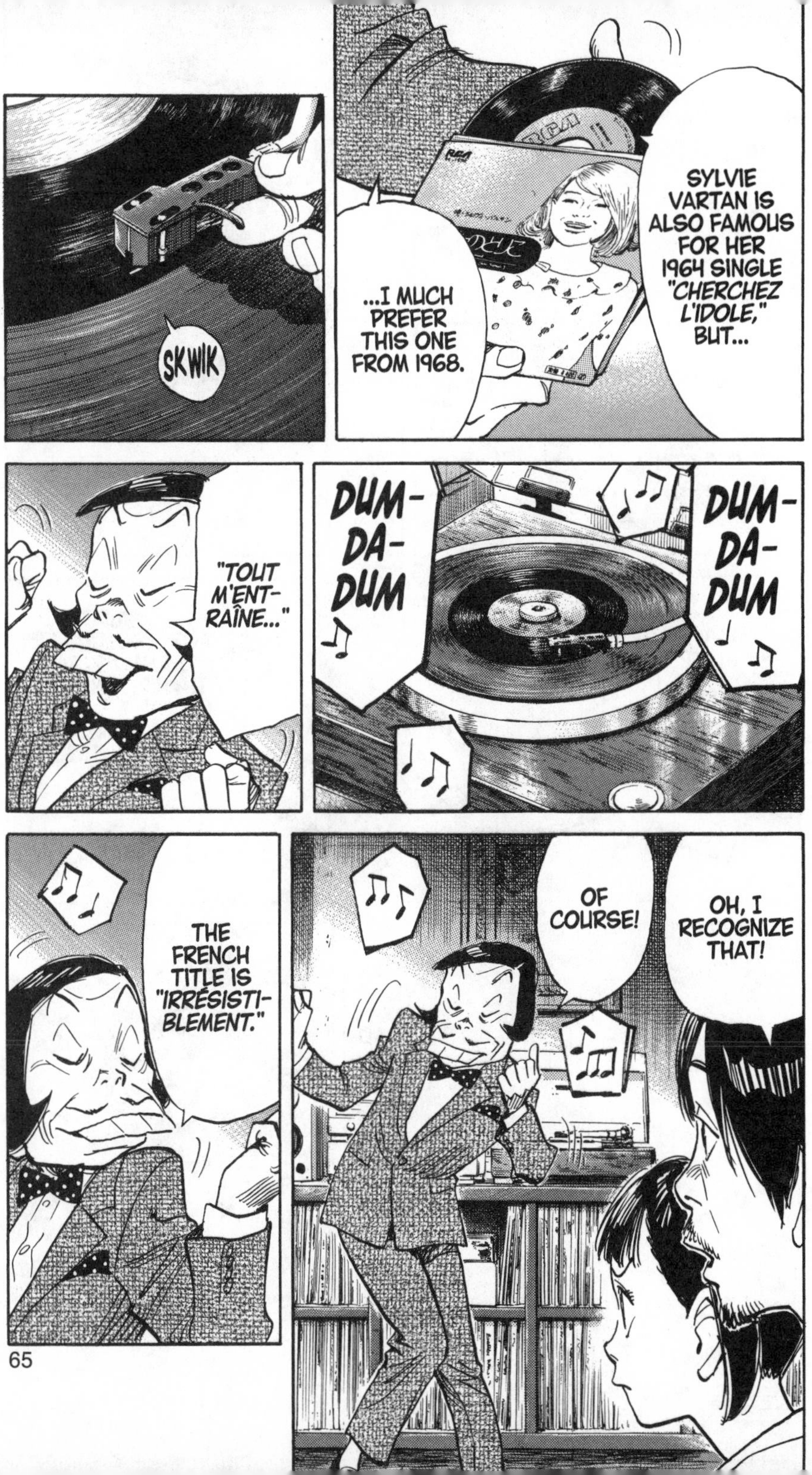
SYLVIE VARTAN IS ALSO FAMOUS FOR HER 1964 SINGLE "CHERCHEZ L'IDOLE," BUT...
...I MUCH PREFER THIS ONE FROM 1968.
SKWIK
DUM-DA-DUM
DUM-DA-DUM
"TOUT M'ENTRAÎNE..."
OH, I RECOGNIZE THAT!
OF COURSE!
THE FRENCH TITLE IS "IRRÉSISTIBLEMENT."

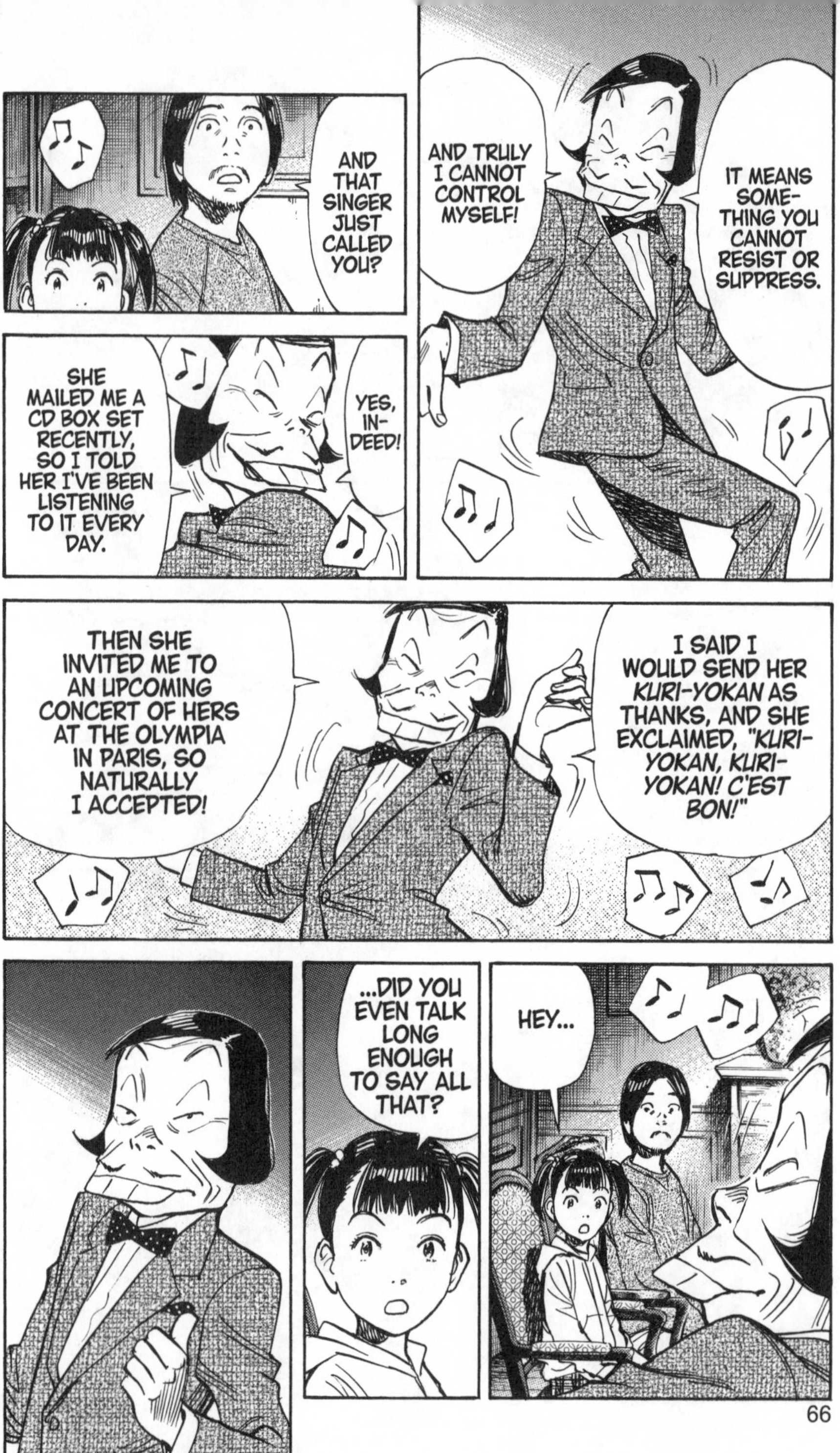
IT MEANS SOMETHING YOU CANNOT RESIST OR SUPPRESS.
AND TRULY I CANNOT CONTROL MYSELF!
AND THAT SINGER JUST CALLED YOU?
YES, INDEED!
SHE MAILED ME A CD BOX SET RECENTLY, SO I TOLD HER I'VE BEEN LISTENING TO IT EVERY DAY.
I SAID I WOULD SEND HER KURI-YOKAN AS THANKS, AND SHE EXCLAIMED, "KURI-YOKAN, KURI-YOKAN! C'EST BON!"
THEN SHE INVITED ME TO AN UPCOMING CONCERT OF HERS AT THE OLYMPIA IN PARIS, SO NATURALLY I ACCEPTED!
HEY...
...DID YOU EVEN TALK LONG ENOUGH TO SAY ALL THAT?

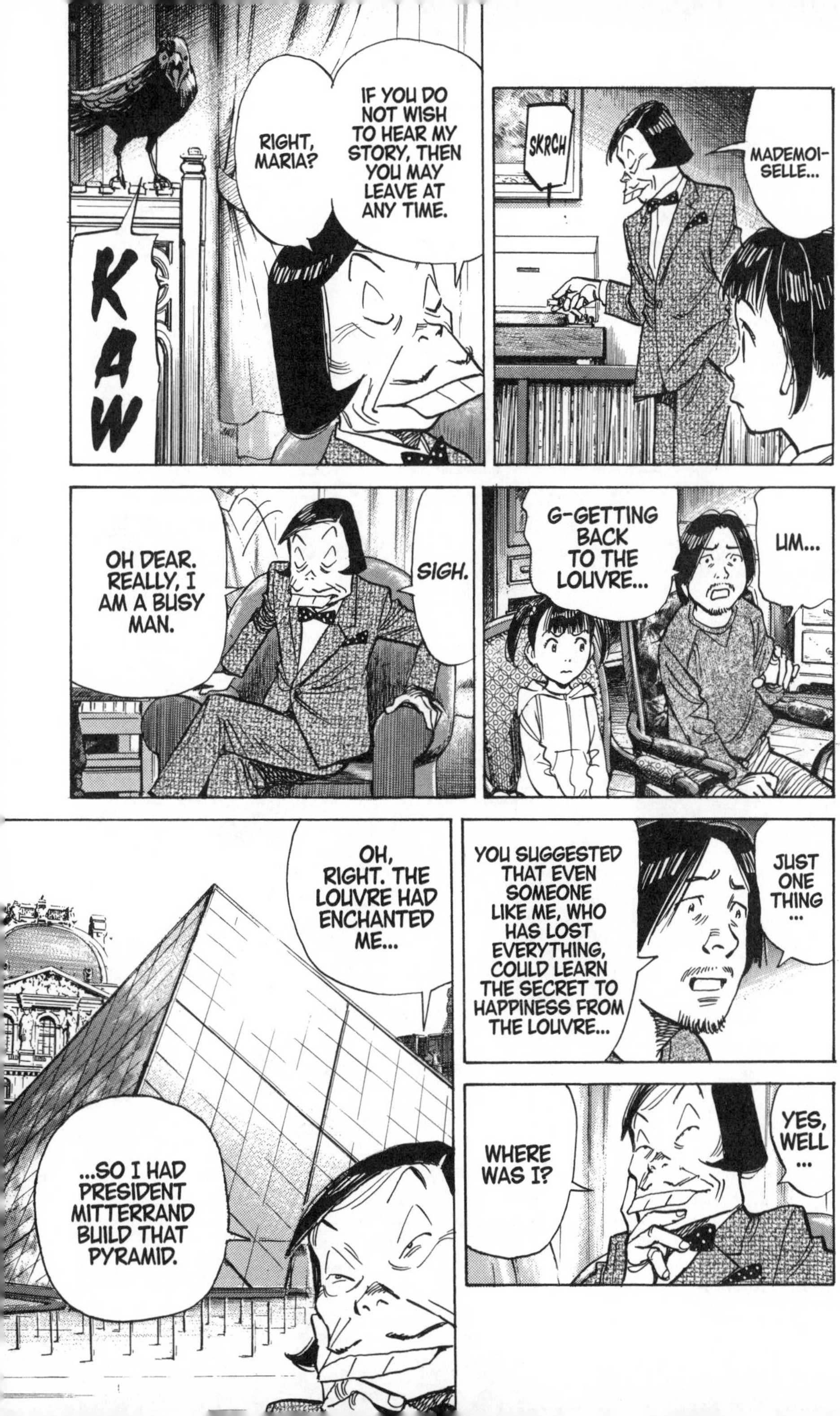
MADEMOISELLE...
SKRCH
IF YOU DO NOT WISH TO HEAR MY STORY, THEN YOU MAY LEAVE AT ANY TIME.
RIGHT, MARIA?
KAW
UM...
G-GETTING BACK TO THE LOUVRE...
SIGH.
OH DEAR. REALLY, I AM A BUSY MAN.
JUST ONE THING...
YOU SUGGESTED THAT EVEN SOMEONE LIKE ME, WHO HAS LOST EVERYTHING, COULD LEARN THE SECRET TO HAPPINESS FROM THE LOUVRE...
YES, WELL...
WHERE WAS I?
OH, RIGHT. THE LOUVRE HAD ENCHANTED ME...
...SO I HAD PRESIDENT MITTERRAND BUILD THAT PYRAMID.

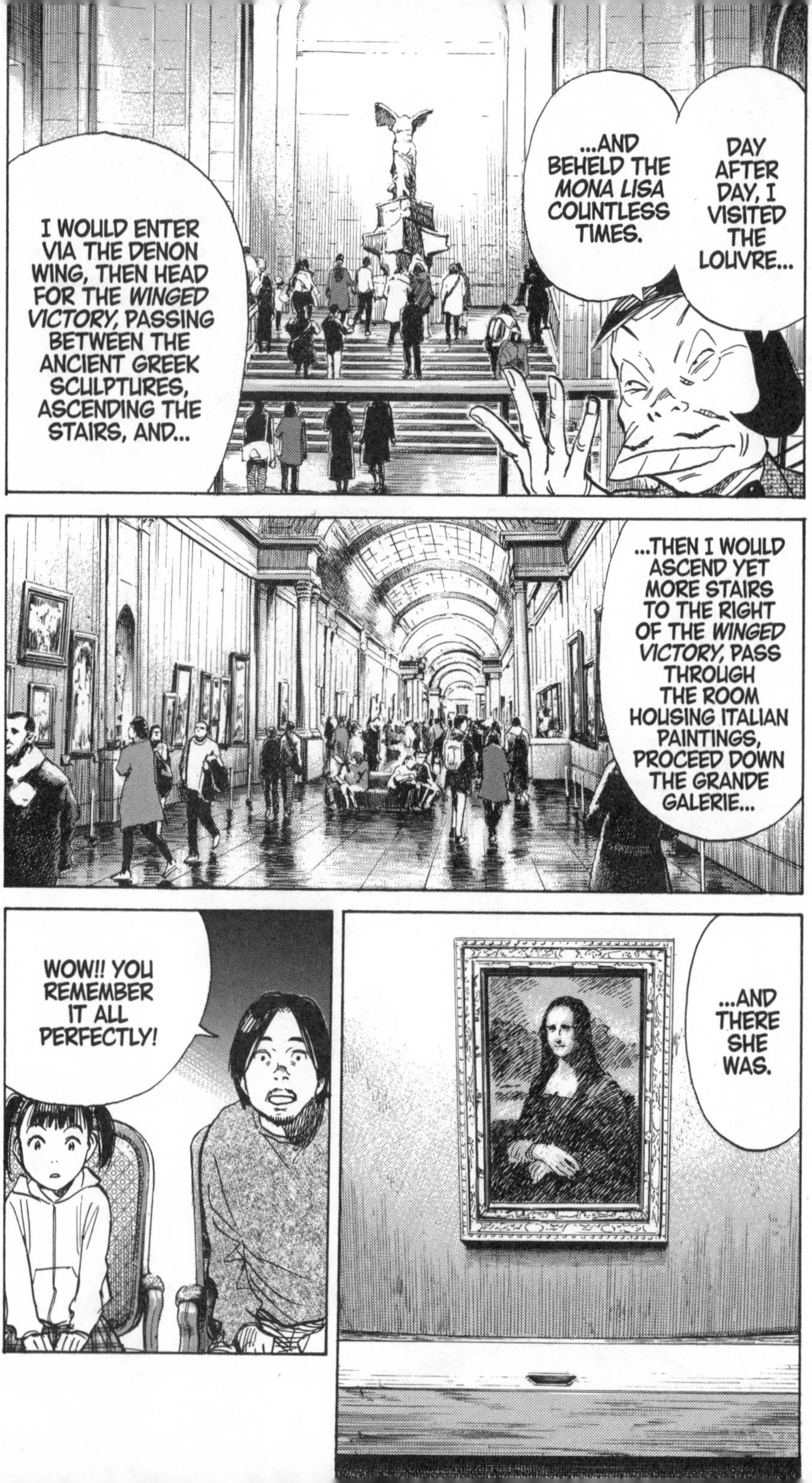
DAY AFTER DAY, I VISITED THE LOUVRE...
...AND BEHELD THE MONA LISA COUNTLESS TIMES.
I WOULD ENTER VIA THE DENON WING, THEN HEAD FOR THE WINGED VICTORY, PASSING BETWEEN THE ANCIENT GREEK SCULPTURES, ASCENDING THE STAIRS, AND...
...THEN I WOULD ASCEND YET MORE STAIRS TO THE RIGHT OF THE WINGED VICTORY, PASS THROUGH THE ROOM HOUSING ITALIAN PAINTINGS, PROCEED DOWN THE GRANDE GALERIE...
...AND THERE SHE WAS.
WOW!! YOU REMEMBER IT ALL PERFECTLY!

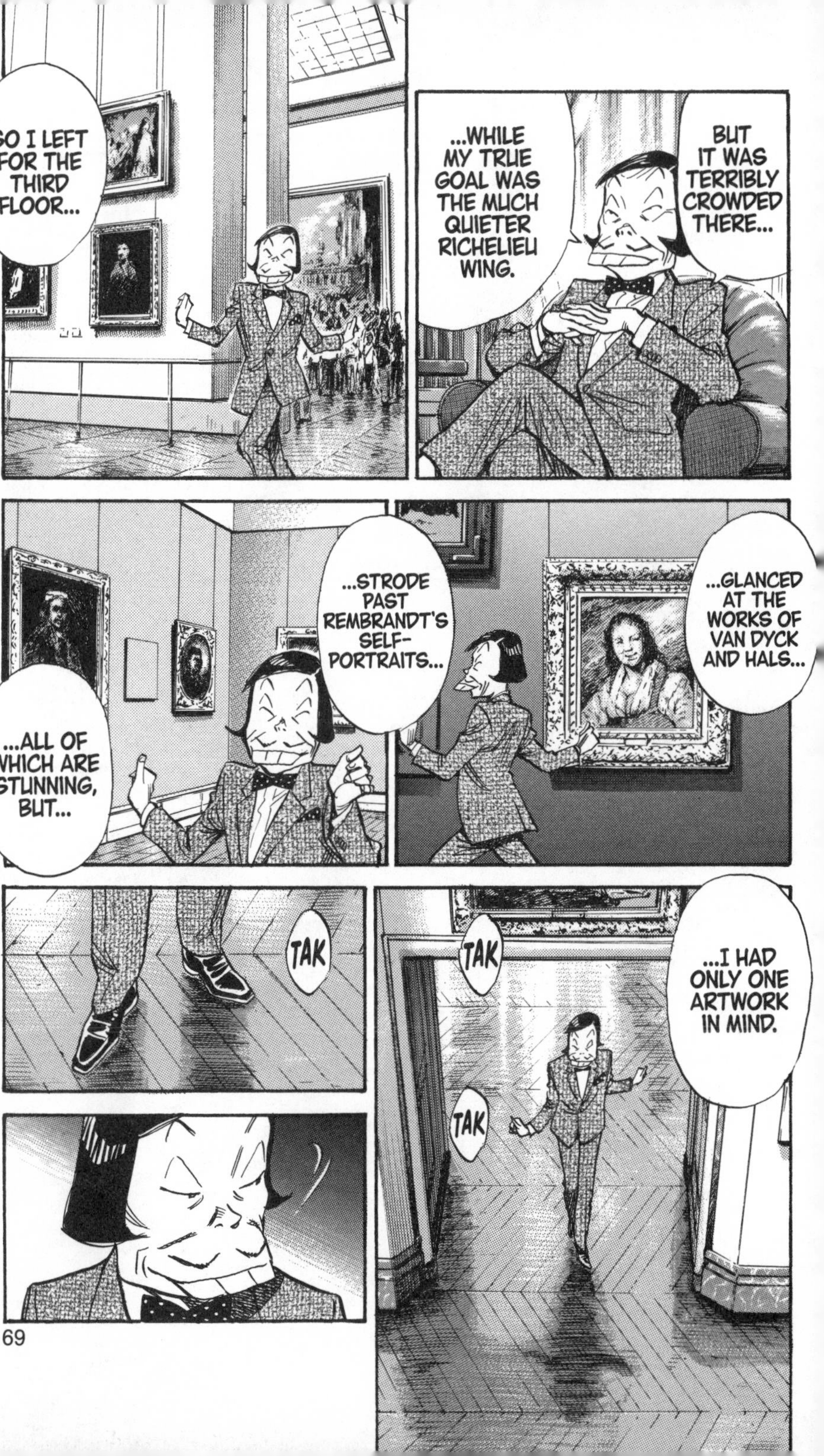
BUT IT WAS TERRIBLY CROWDED THERE...
...WHILE MY TRUE GOAL WAS THE MUCH QUIETER RICHELIEU WING.
SO I LEFT FOR THE THIRD FLOOR...
...GLANCED AT THE WORKS OF VAN DYCK AND HALS...
...STRODE PAST REMBRANDT'S SELF-PORTRAITS...
...ALL OF WHICH ARE STUNNING, BUT...
...I HAD ONLY ONE ARTWORK IN MIND.
TAK
TAK
TAK

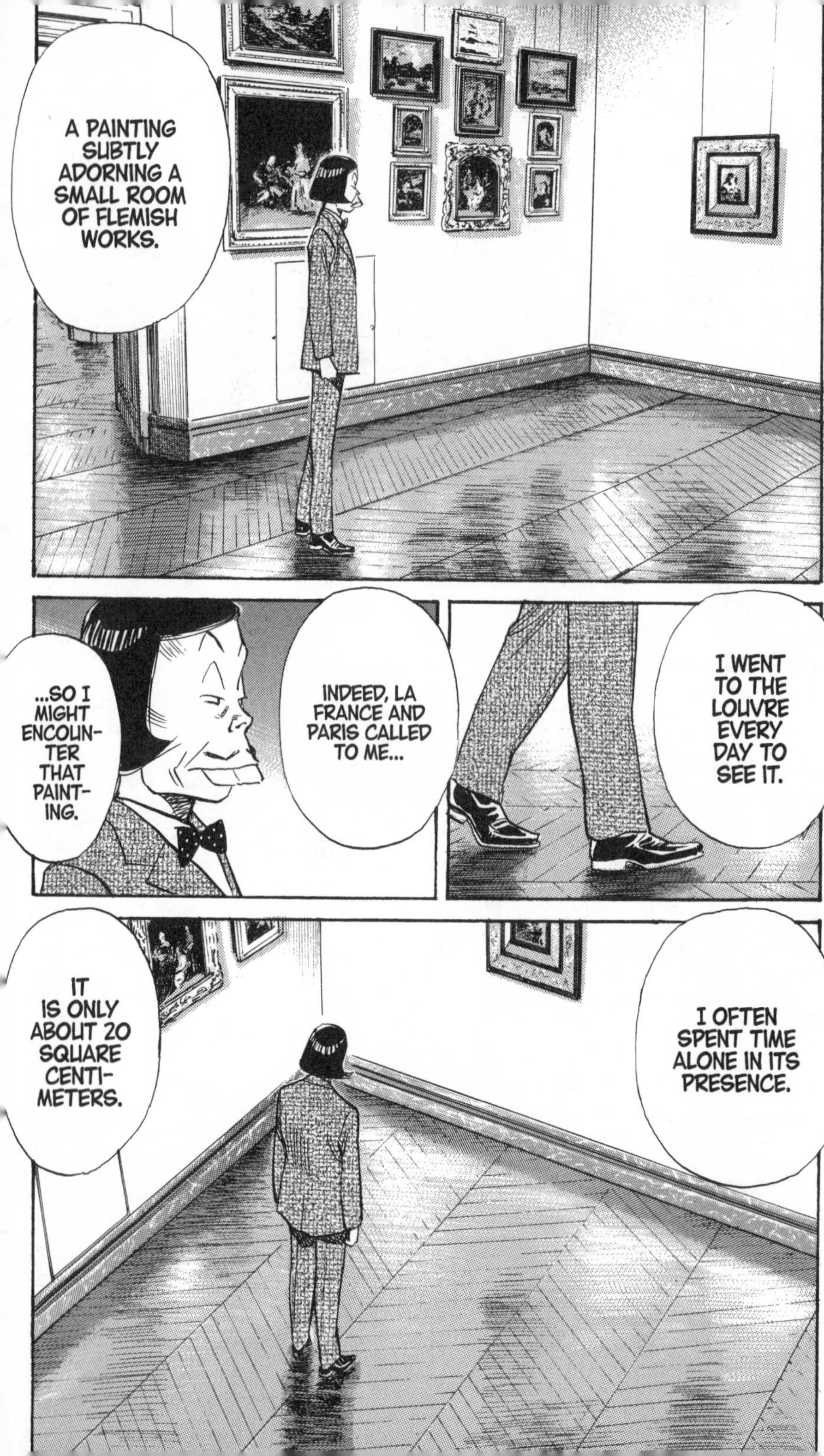
A PAINTING SUBTLY ADORNING A SMALL ROOM OF FLEMISH WORKS.
I WENT TO THE LOUVRE EVERY DAY TO SEE IT.
INDEED, LA FRANCE AND PARIS CALLED TO ME...
...SO I MIGHT ENCOUNTER THAT PAINTING.
I OFTEN SPENT TIME ALONE IN ITS PRESENCE.
IT IS ONLY ABOUT 20 SQUARE CENTIMETERS.

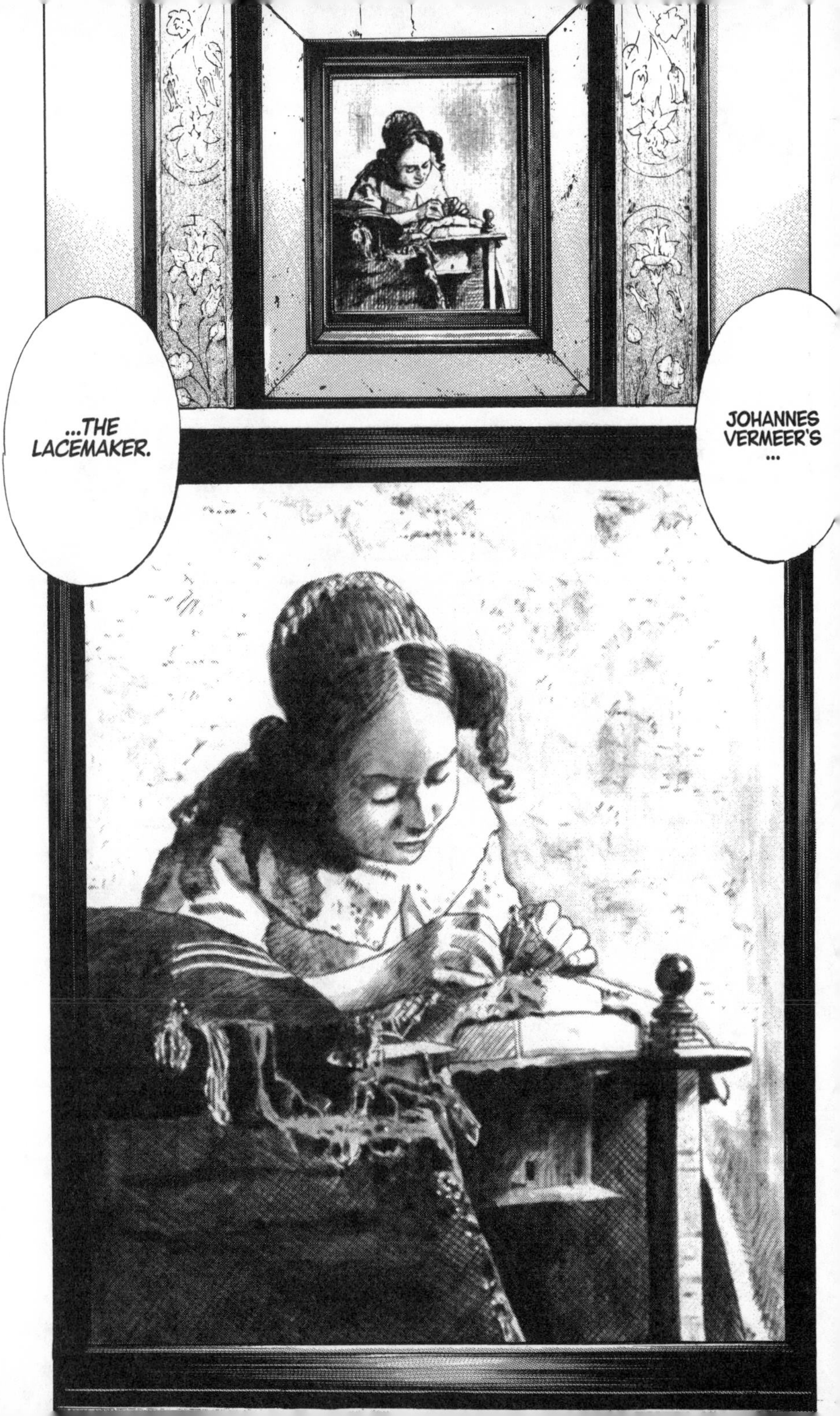
JOHANNES VERMEER'S ...
...THE LACEMAKER.

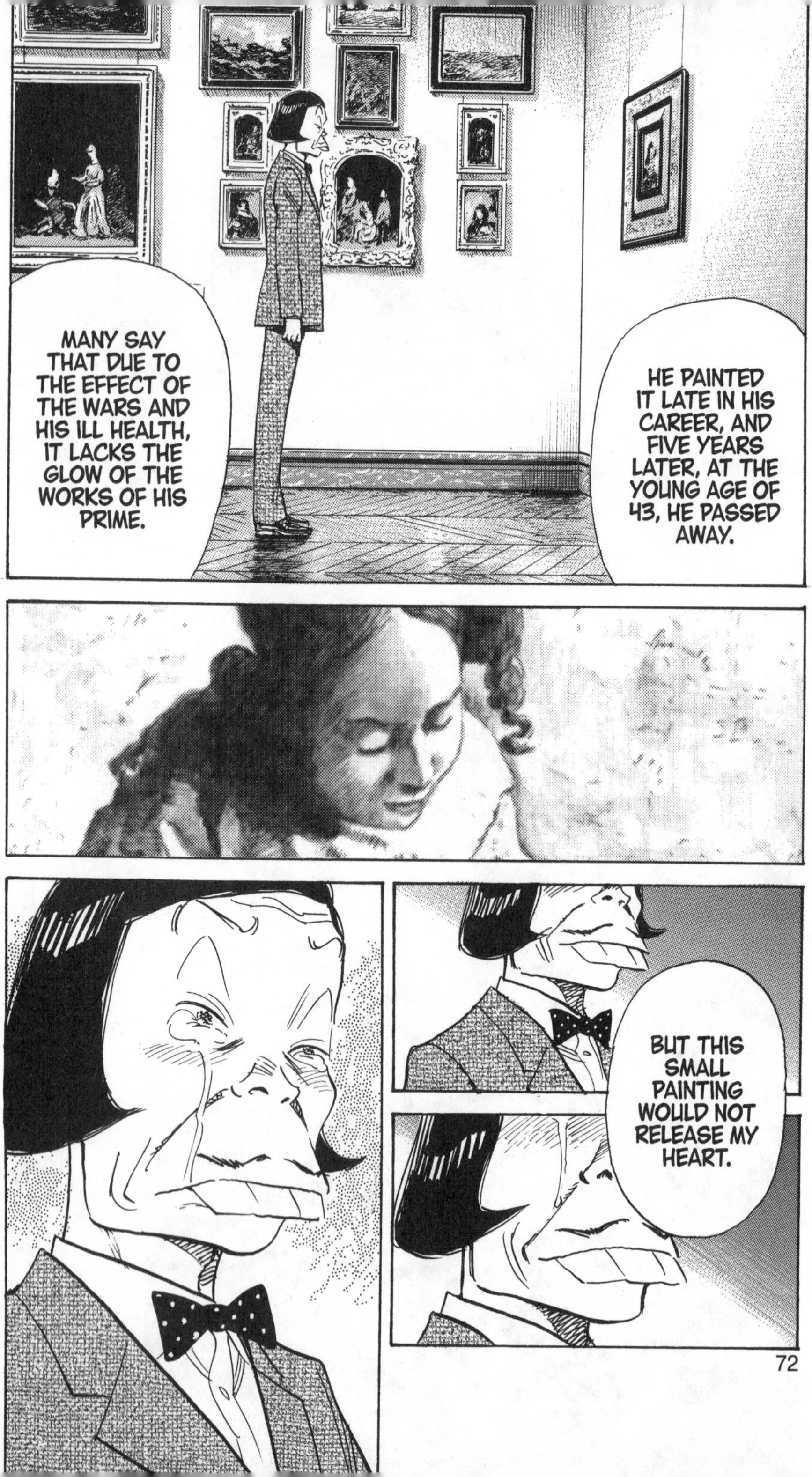
HE PAINTED IT LATE IN HIS CAREER, AND FIVE YEARS LATER, AT THE YOUNG AGE OF 43, HE PASSED AWAY.
MANY SAY THAT DUE TO THE EFFECT OF THE WARS AND HIS ILL HEALTH, IT LACKS THE GLOW OF THE WORKS OF HIS PRIME.
BUT THIS SMALL PAINTING WOULD NOT RELEASE MY HEART.

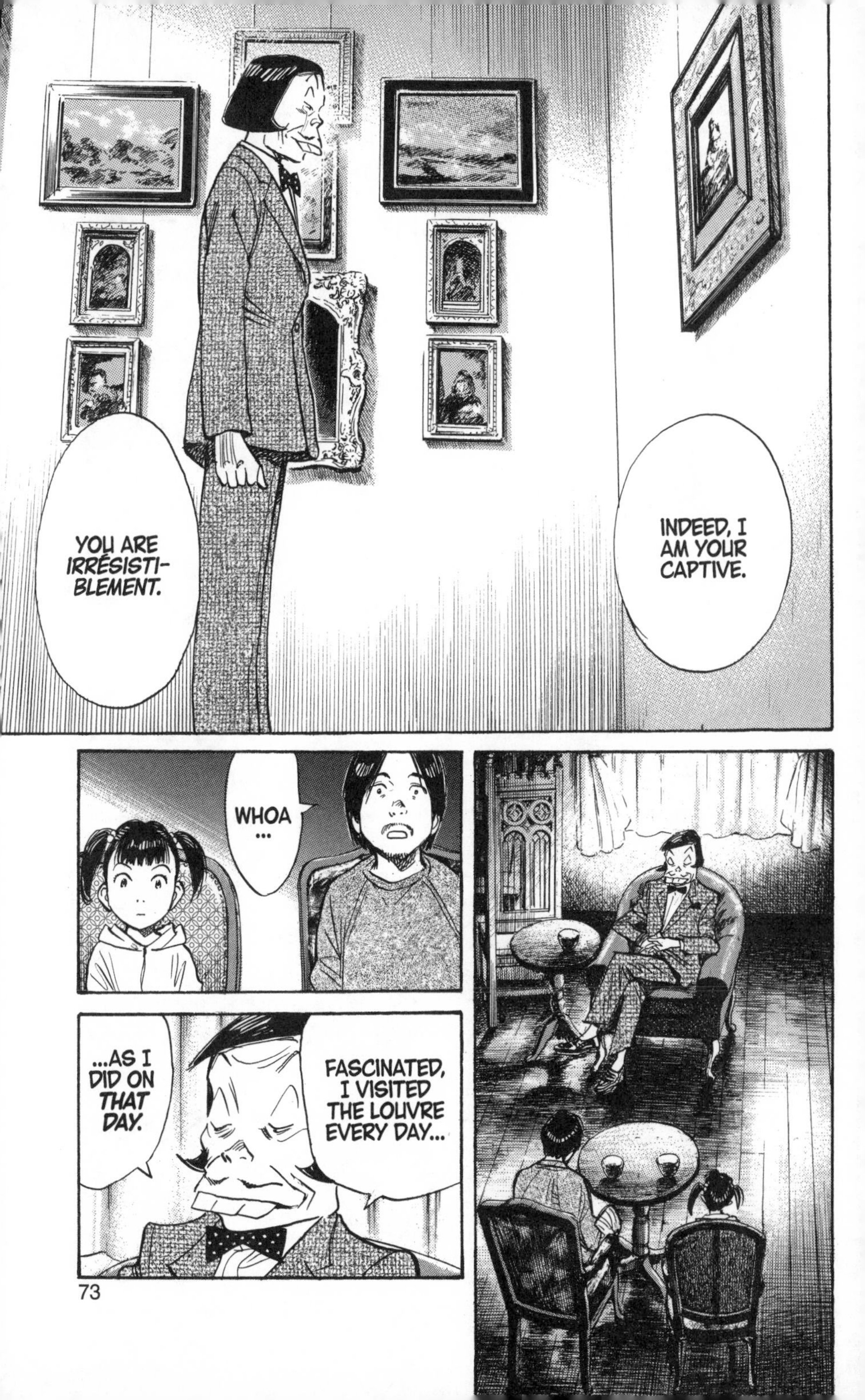
INDEED, I AM YOUR CAPTIVE.
YOU ARE IRRÉSISTIBLEMENT.
WHOA ...
FASCINATED, I VISITED THE LOUVRE EVERY DAY...
...AS I DID ON *THAT* DAY.

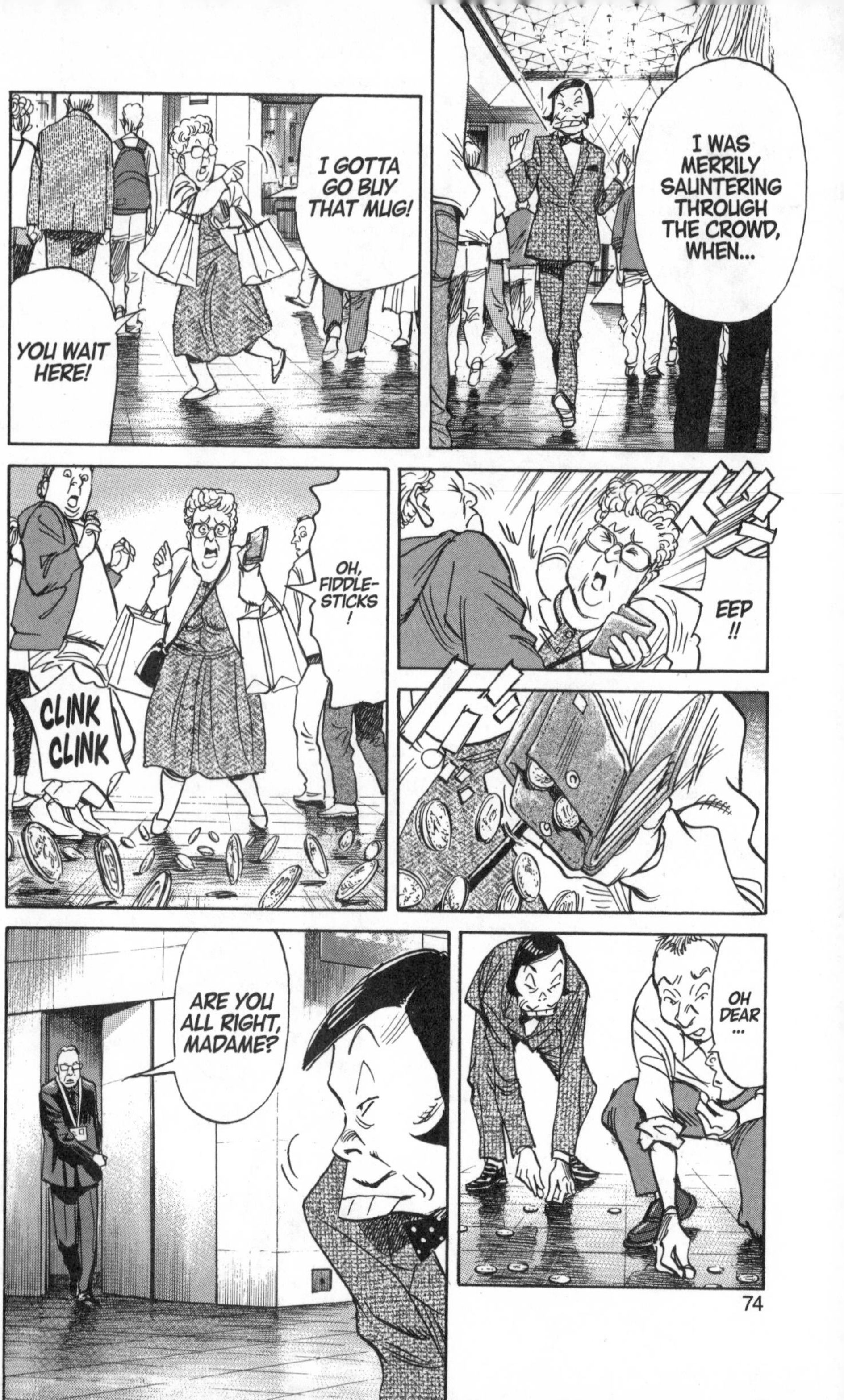
I WAS MERRILY SAUNTERING THROUGH THE CROWD, WHEN...
I GOTTA GO BUY THAT MUG!
YOU WAIT HERE!
EEP !!
OH, FIDDLE-STICKS!
CLINK CLINK
OH DEAR...
ARE YOU ALL RIGHT, MADAME?

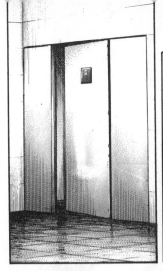

NO, I'M NOT ALL RIGHT! HUMF!

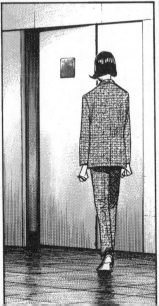

OH MY! SUCH GENTLEMEN! MERCI BEAUCOUP!

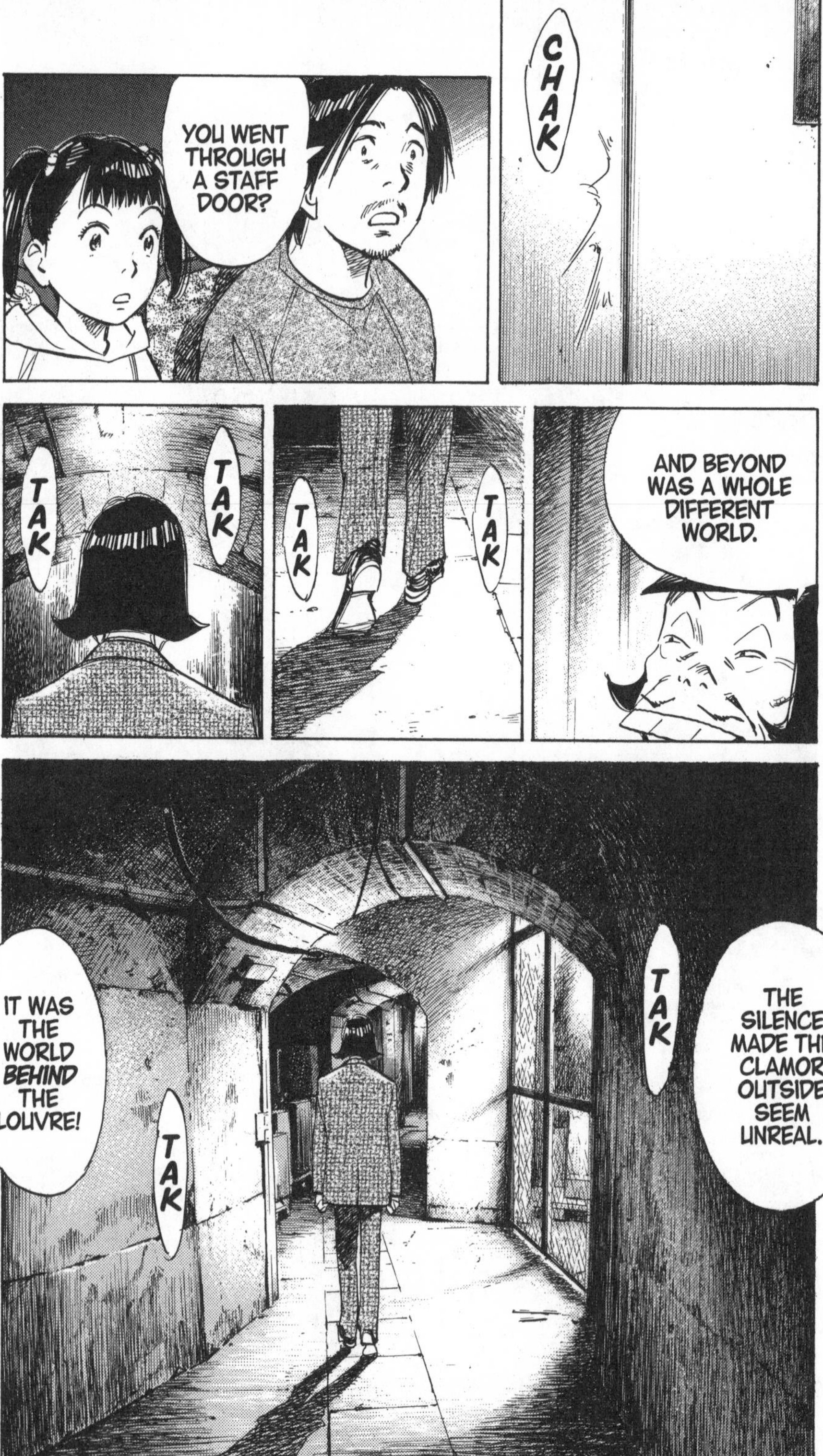
CHAK
YOU WENT THROUGH A STAFF DOOR?
AND BEYOND WAS A WHOLE DIFFERENT WORLD.
TAK
TAK
TAK
TAK
THE SILENCE MADE THE CLAMOR OUTSIDE SEEM UNREAL.
TAK
IT WAS THE WORLD BEHIND THE LOUVRE!
TAK

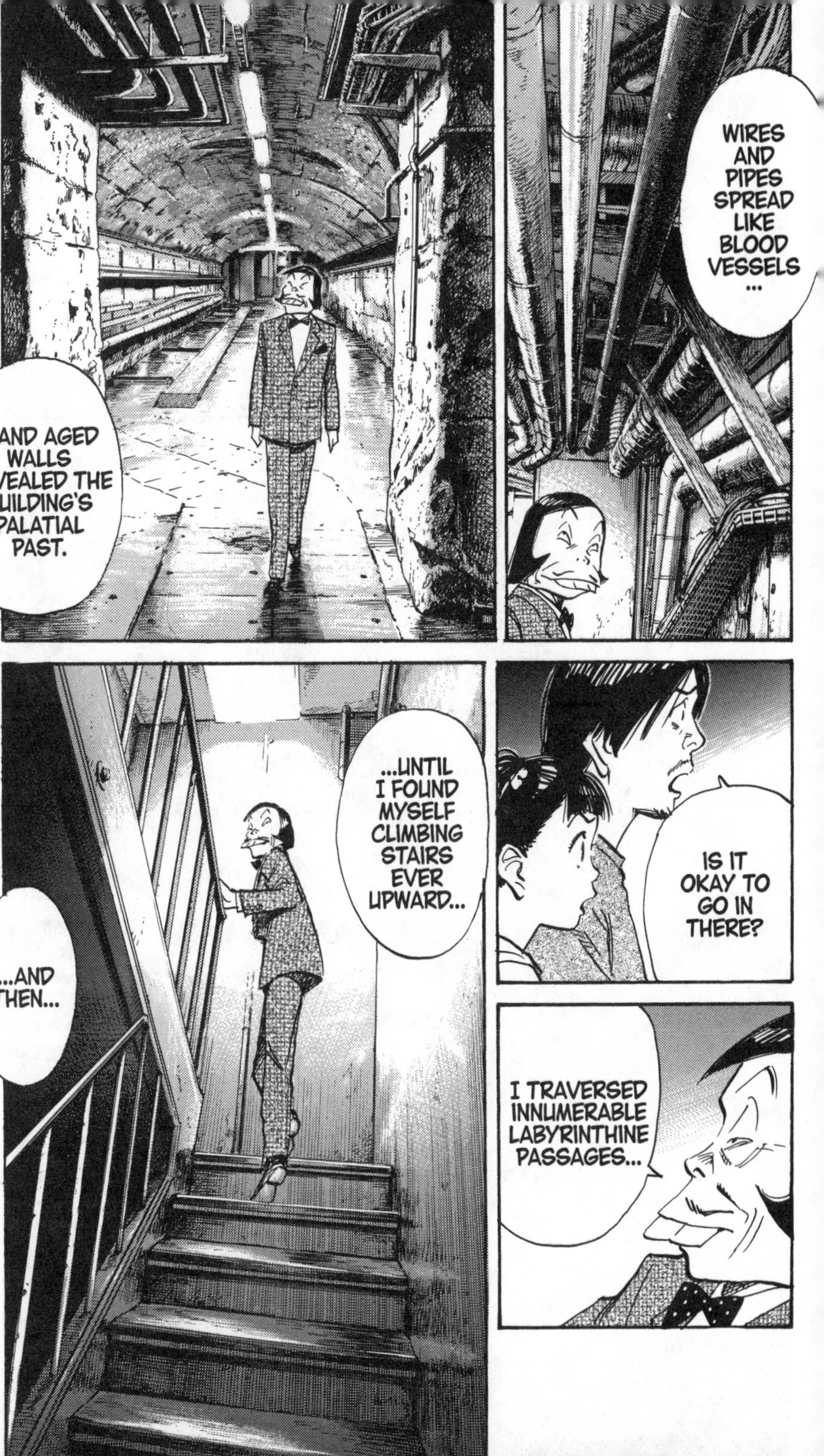
WIRES AND PIPES SPREAD LIKE BLOOD VESSELS ...
...AND AGED WALLS REVEALED THE BUILDING'S PALATIAL PAST.
IS IT OKAY TO GO IN THERE?
I TRAVERSED INNUMERABLE LABYRINTHINE PASSAGES...
...UNTIL I FOUND MYSELF CLIMBING STAIRS EVER UPWARD...
...AND THEN...

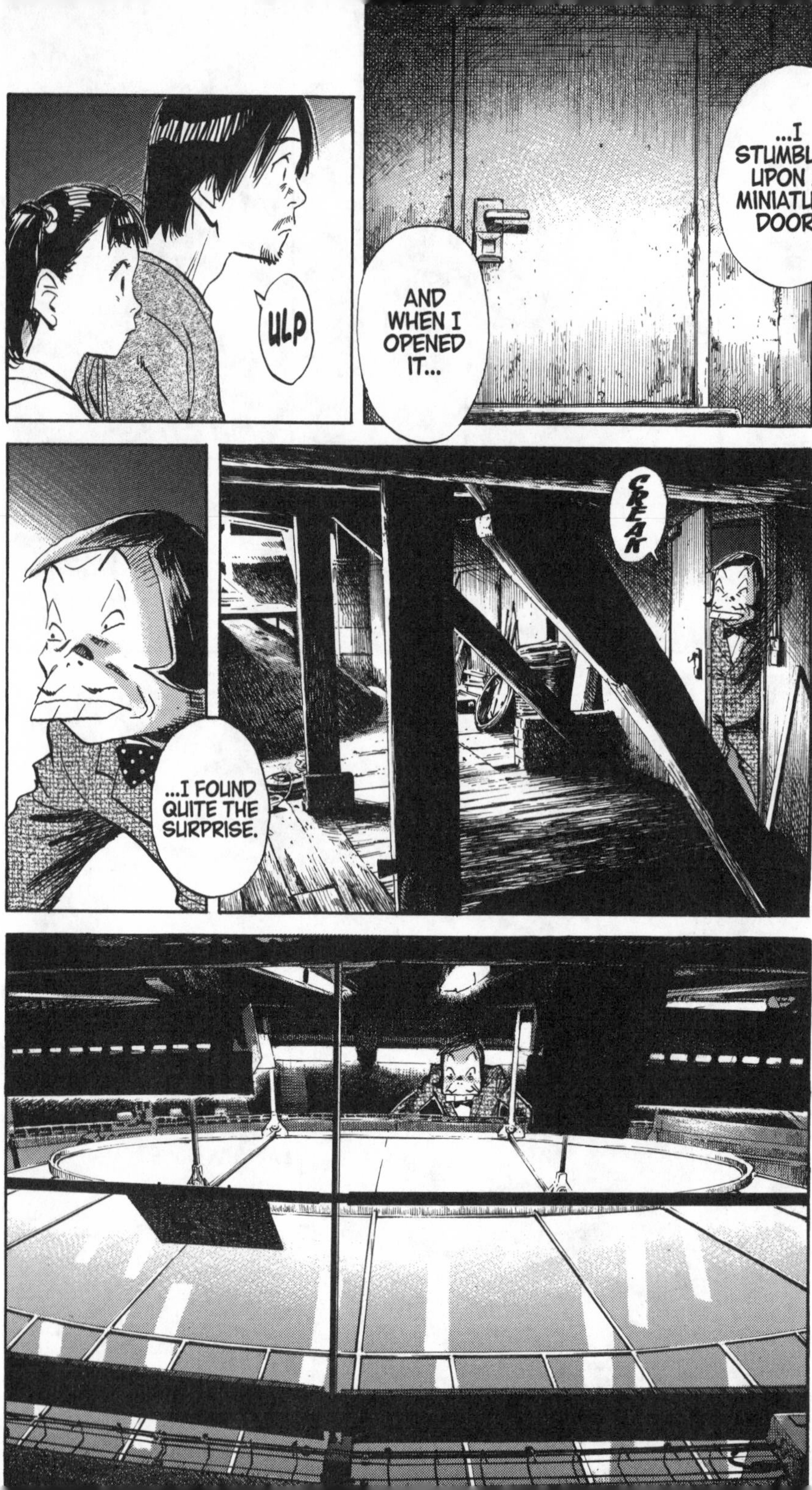
...I STUMBLED UPON A MINIATURE DOOR.
AND WHEN I OPENED IT...
ULP
CREAK
...I FOUND QUITE THE SURPRISE.

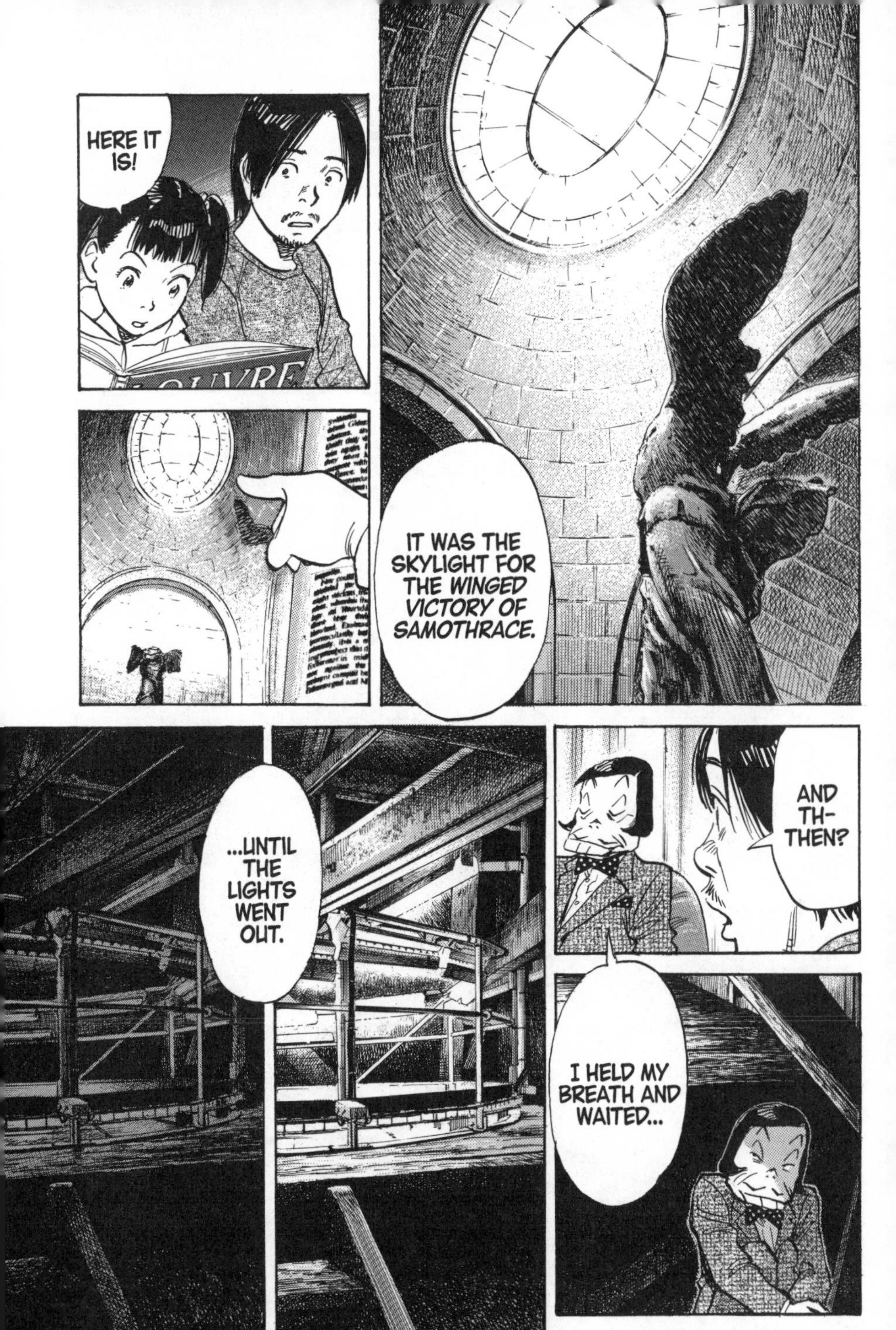
IT WAS THE SKYLIGHT FOR THE WINGED VICTORY OF SAMOTHRACE.
HERE IT IS!
AND TH-THEN?
I HELD MY BREATH AND WAITED...
...UNTIL THE LIGHTS WENT OUT.

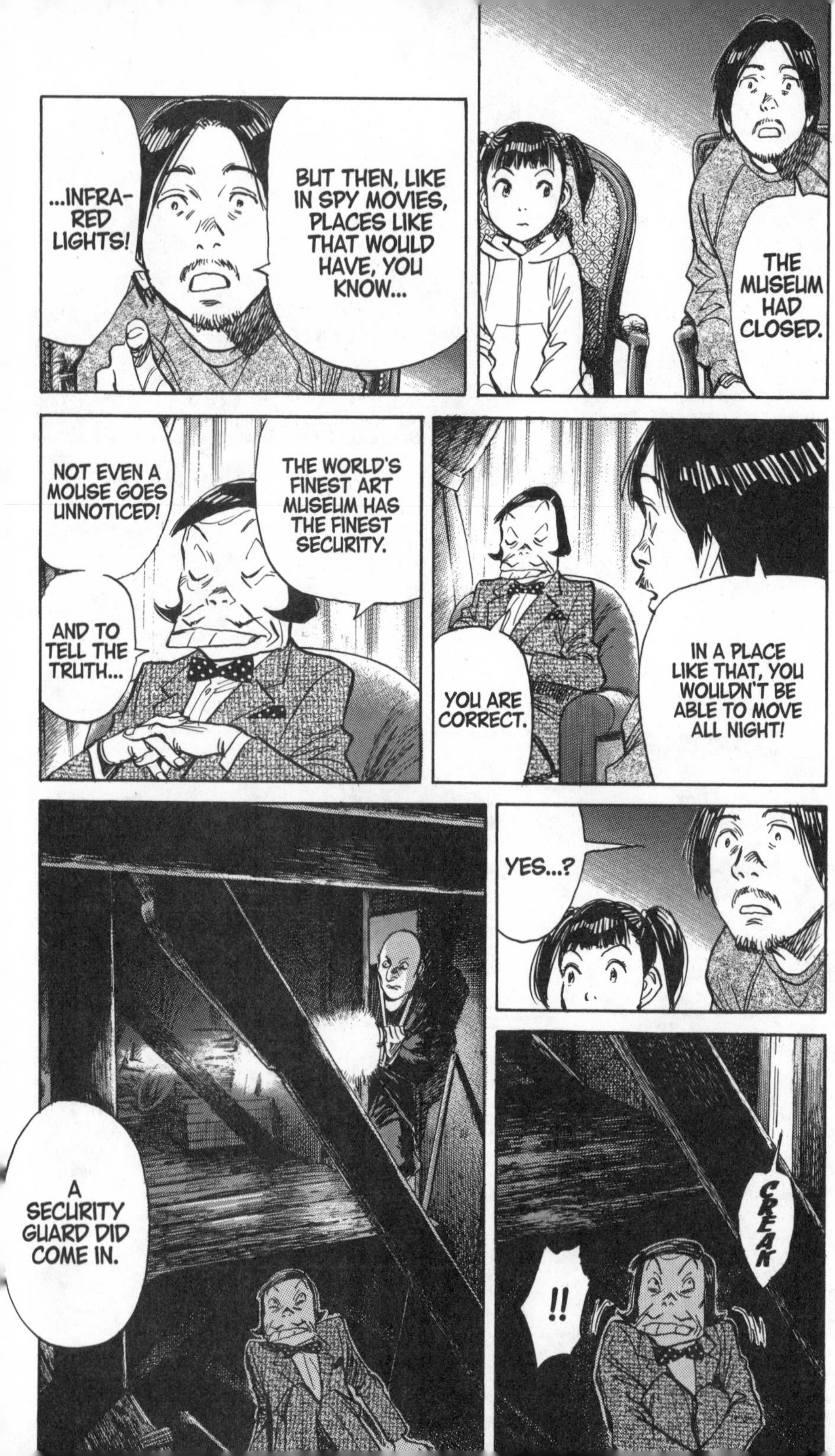
THE MUSEUM HAD CLOSED.
BUT THEN, LIKE IN SPY MOVIES, PLACES LIKE THAT WOULD HAVE, YOU KNOW...
...INFRA-RED LIGHTS!
IN A PLACE LIKE THAT, YOU WOULDN'T BE ABLE TO MOVE ALL NIGHT!
YOU ARE CORRECT.
THE WORLD'S FINEST ART MUSEUM HAS THE FINEST SECURITY.
NOT EVEN A MOUSE GOES UNNOTICED!
AND TO TELL THE TRUTH...
YES...?
CREAK
!!
A SECURITY GUARD DID COME IN.

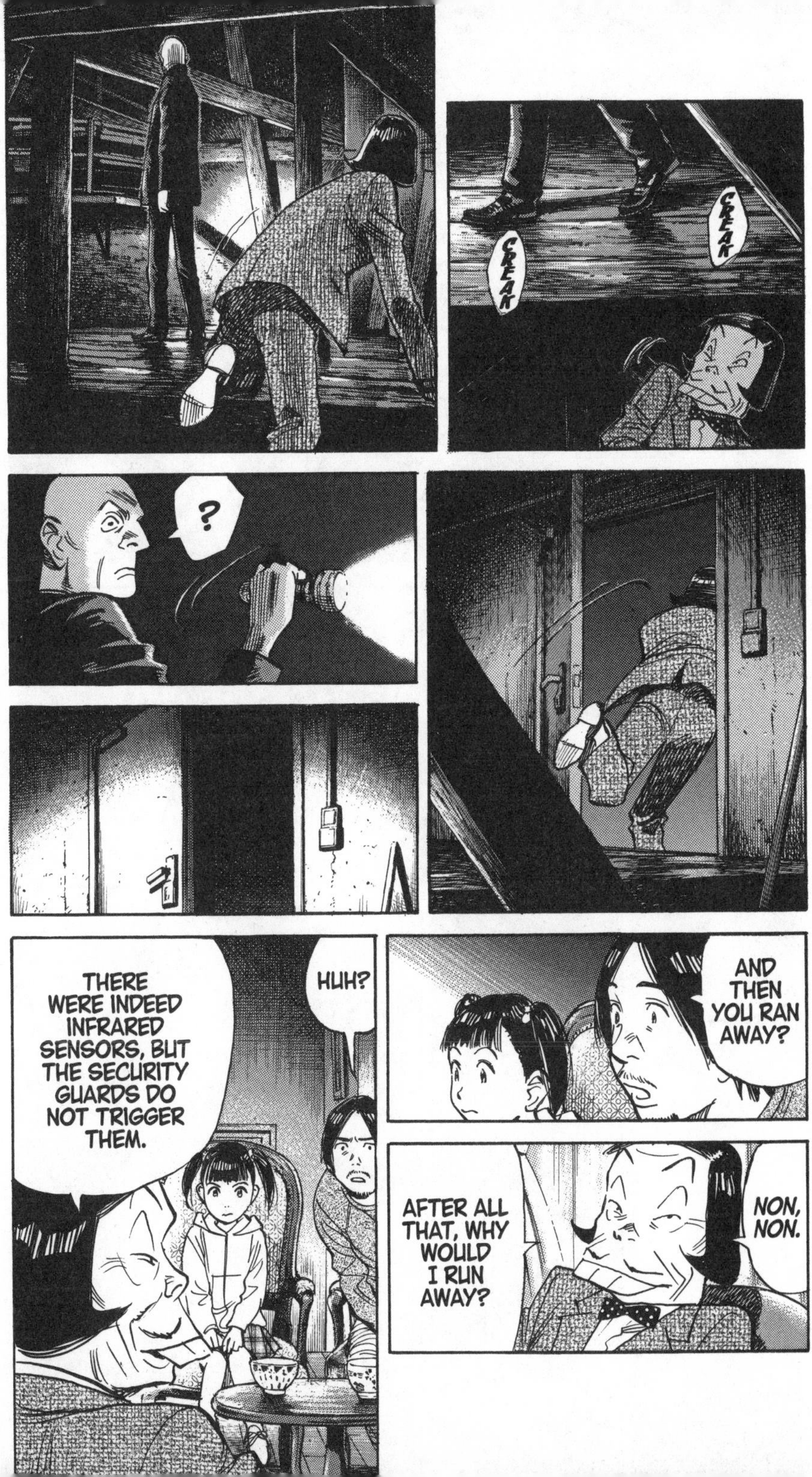
CREAK
CREAK
?
AND THEN YOU RAN AWAY?
NON, NON.
AFTER ALL THAT, WHY WOULD I RUN AWAY?
HUH?
THERE WERE INDEED INFRARED SENSORS, BUT THE SECURITY GUARDS DO NOT TRIGGER THEM.

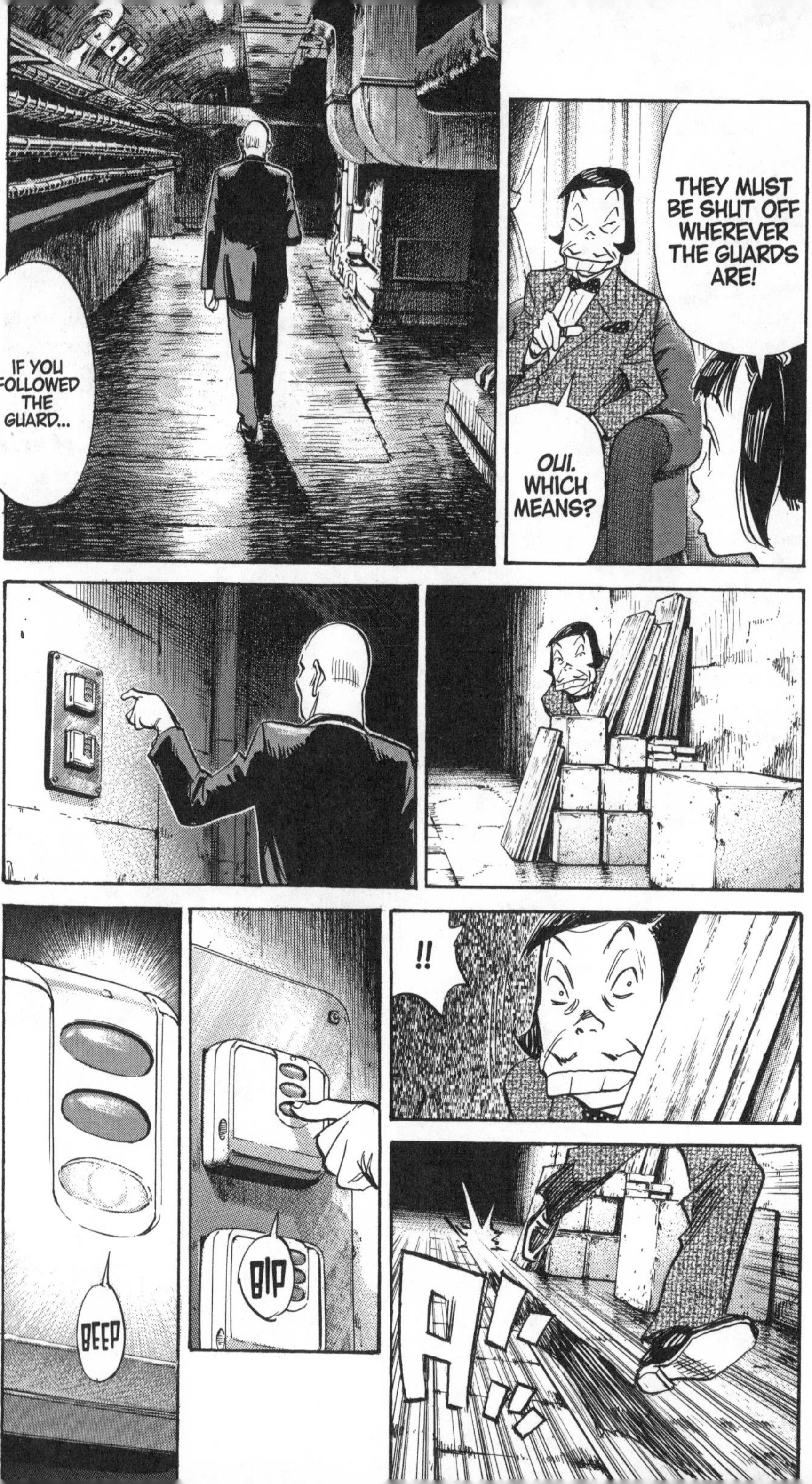
THEY MUST BE SHUT OFF WHEREVER THE GUARDS ARE!
OUI. WHICH MEANS?
IF YOU FOLLOWED THE GUARD...
!!
A!!
BIP
BEEP

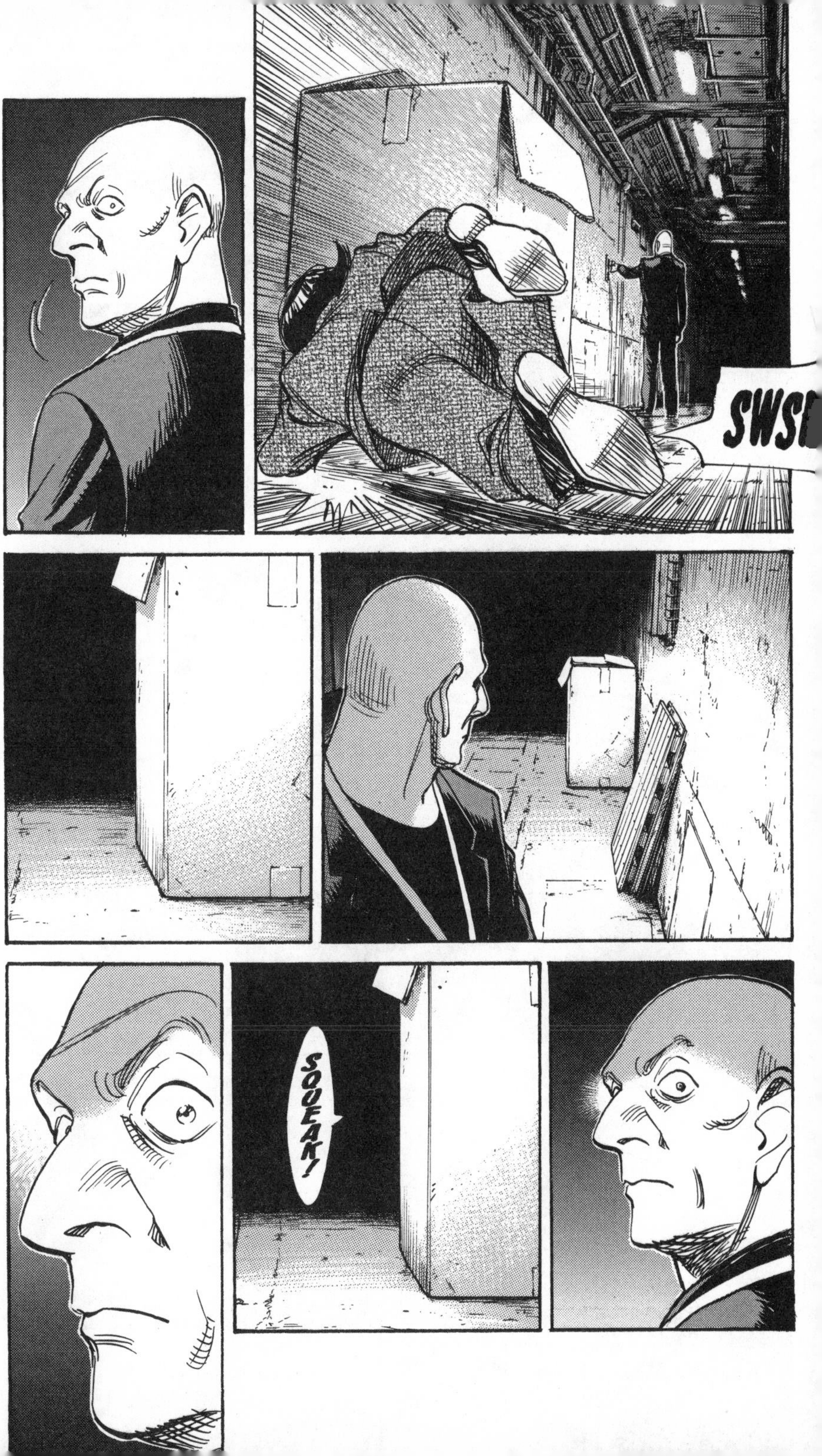
SWSH
SQUEAK!

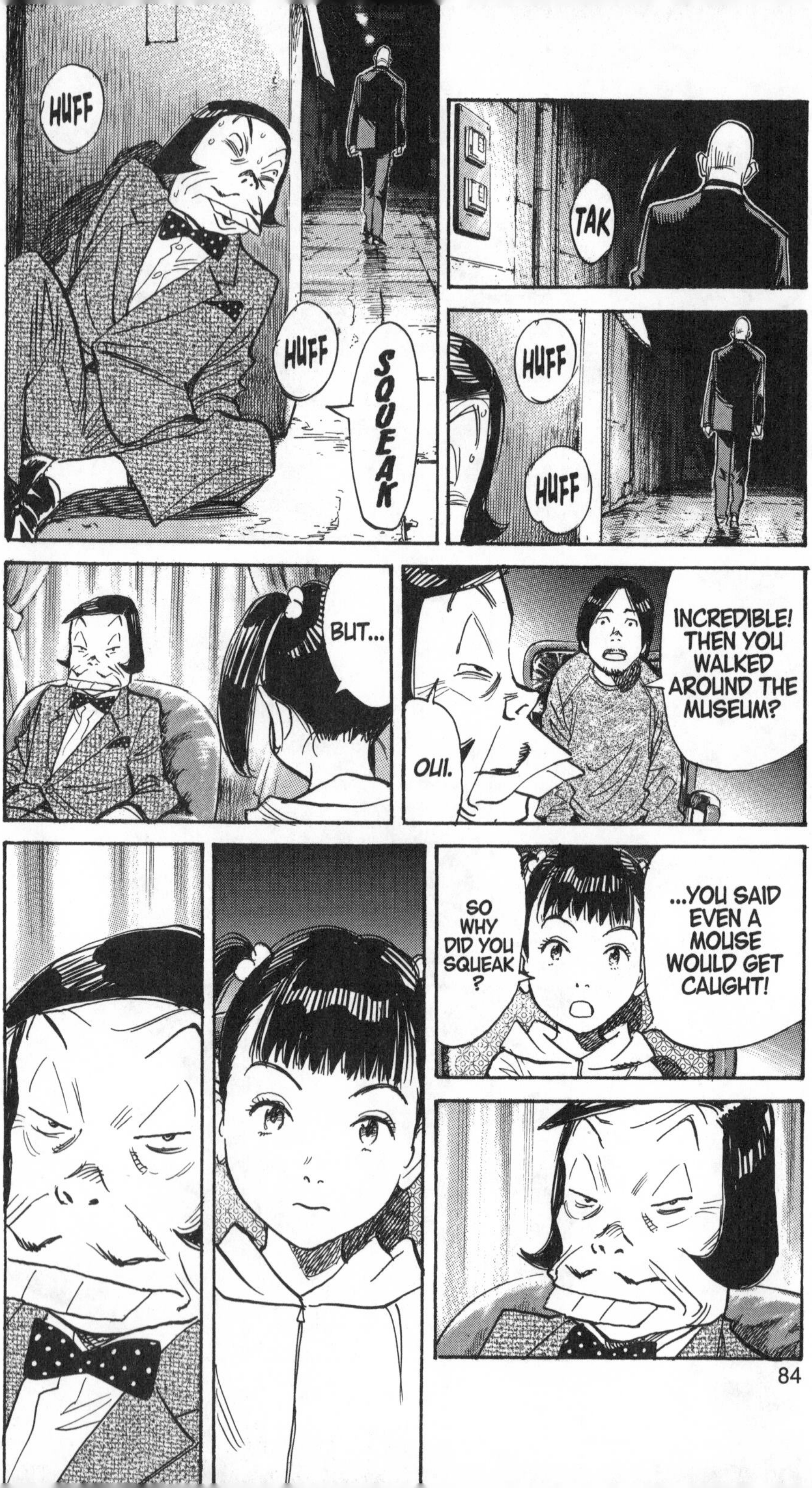
TAK
HUFF
HUFF
HUFF
HUFF
SQUEAK
INCREDIBLE! THEN YOU WALKED AROUND THE MUSEUM?
OUI.
BUT...
...YOU SAID EVEN A MOUSE WOULD GET CAUGHT!
SO WHY DID YOU SQUEAK?

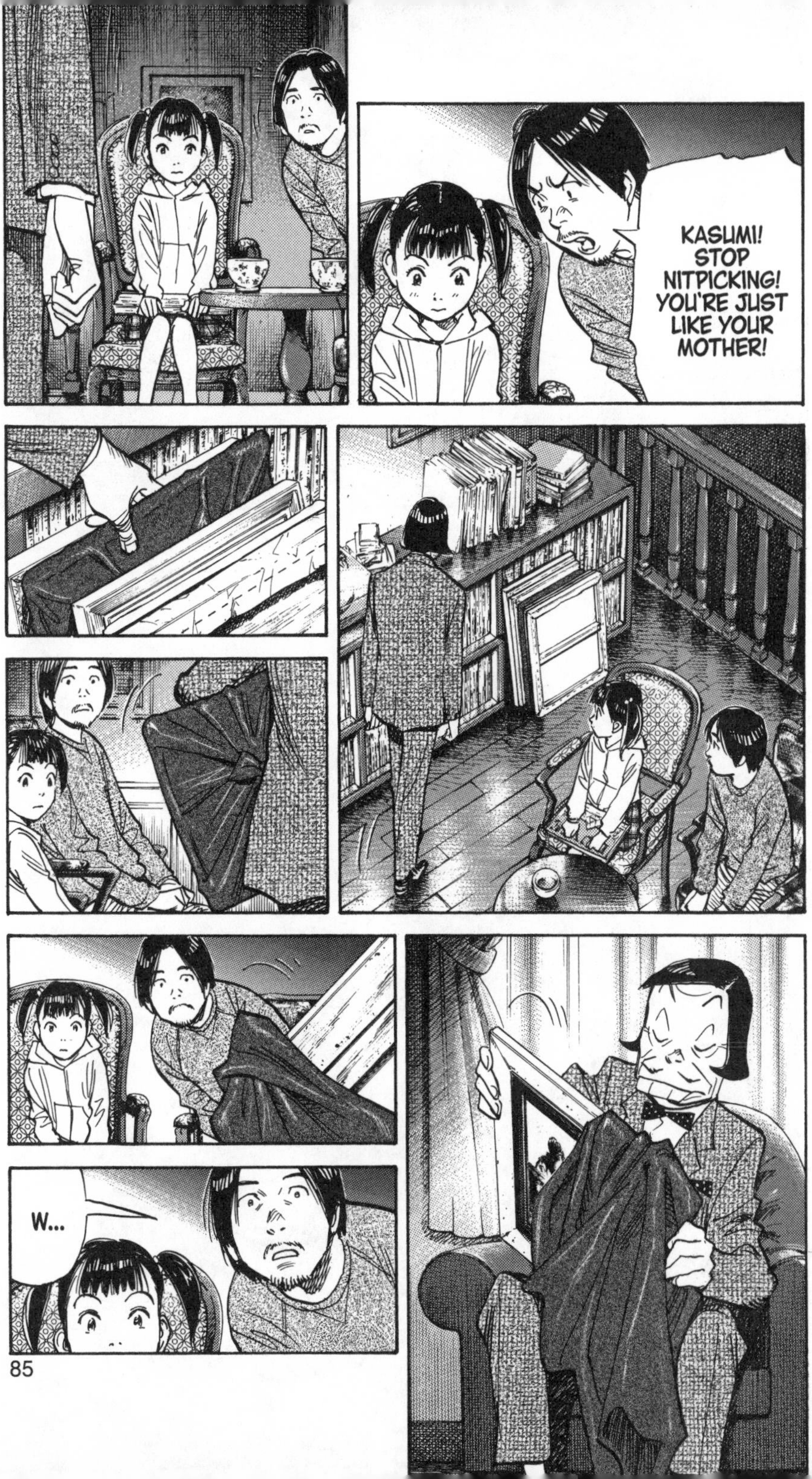
KASUMI! STOP NITPICKING! YOU'RE JUST LIKE YOUR MOTHER!
W...

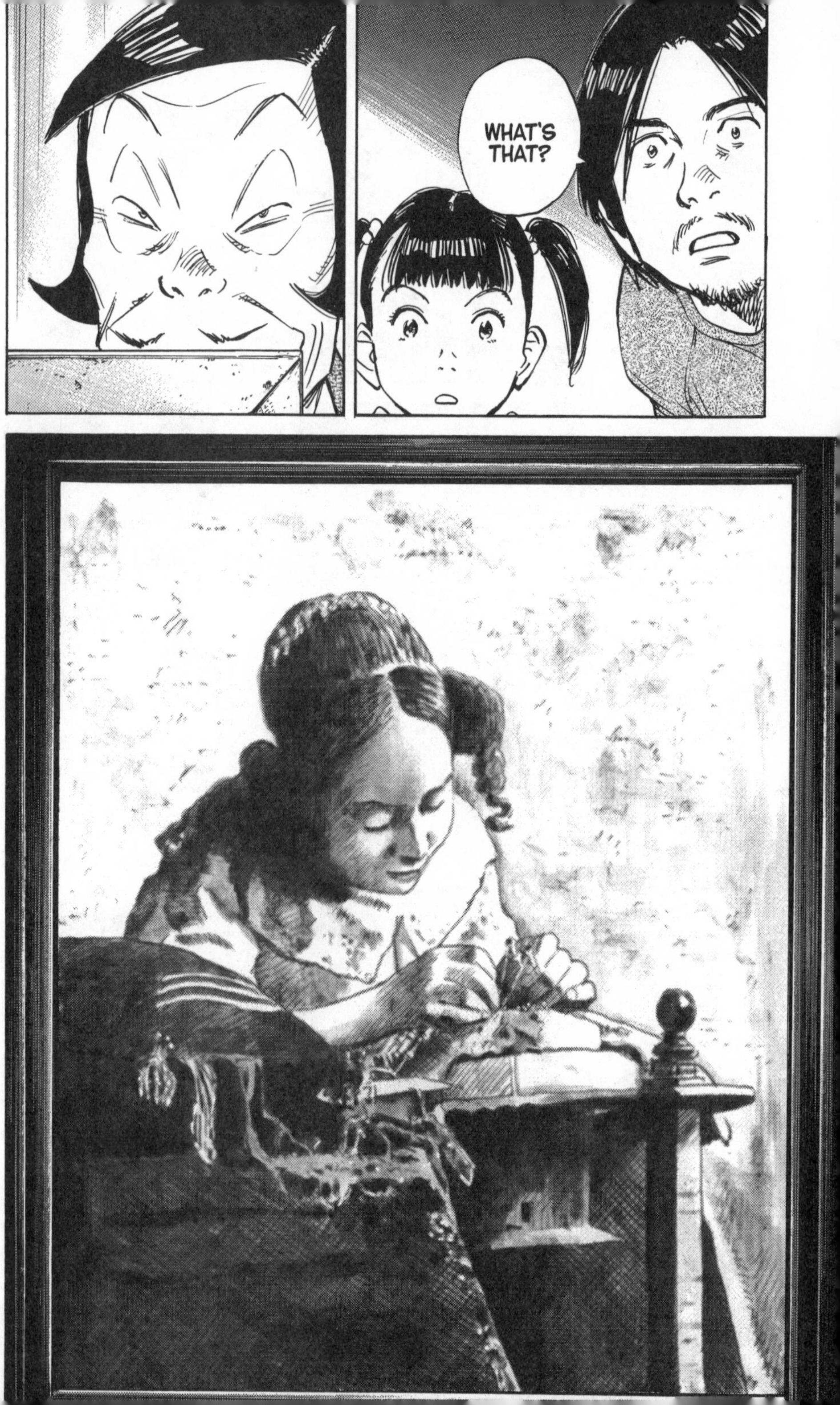
WHAT'S THAT?

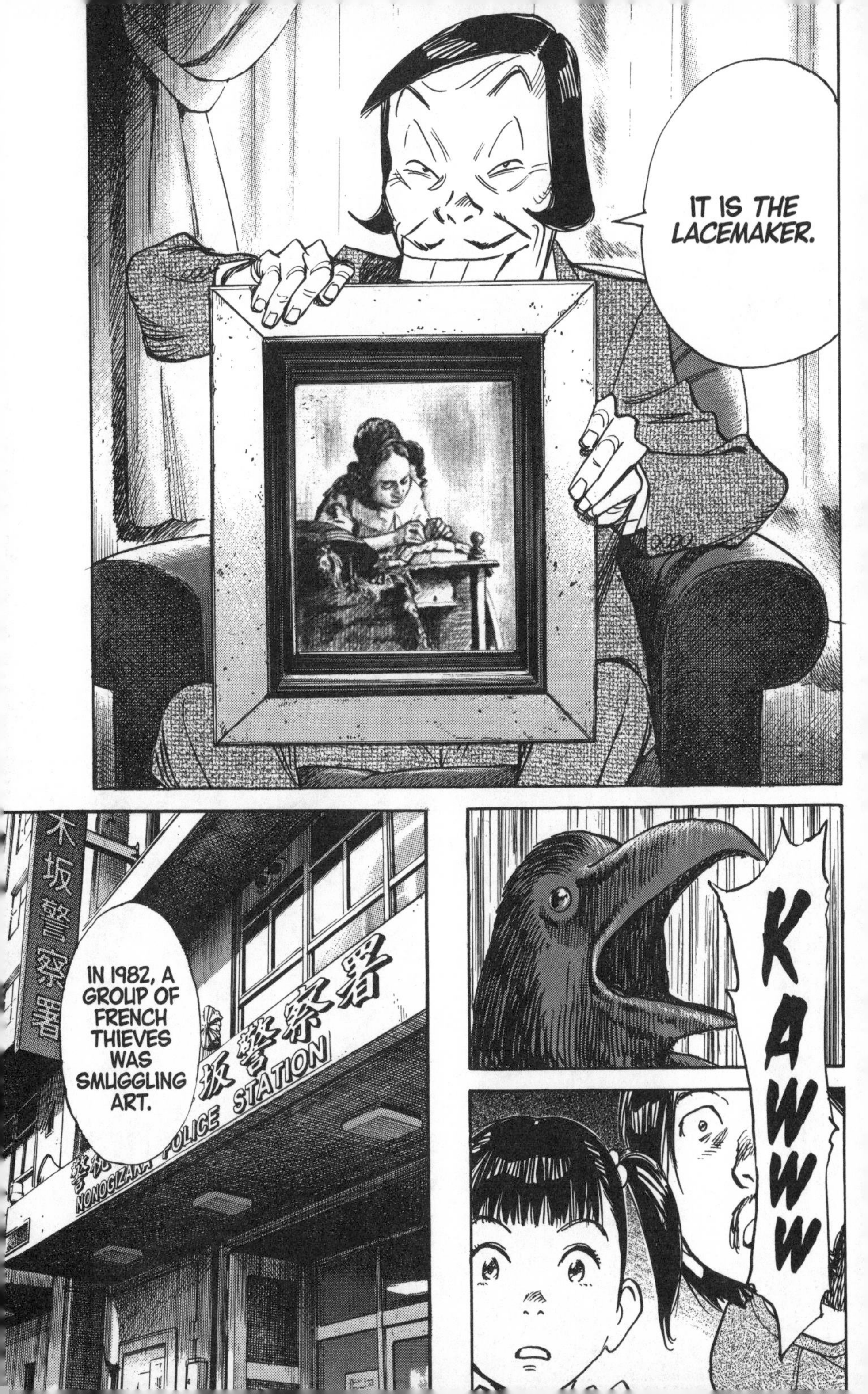
IT IS THE LACEMAKER.
KAWWW
IN 1982, A GROUP OF FRENCH THIEVES WAS SMUGGLING ART.
NONOGIZAKA POLICE STATION

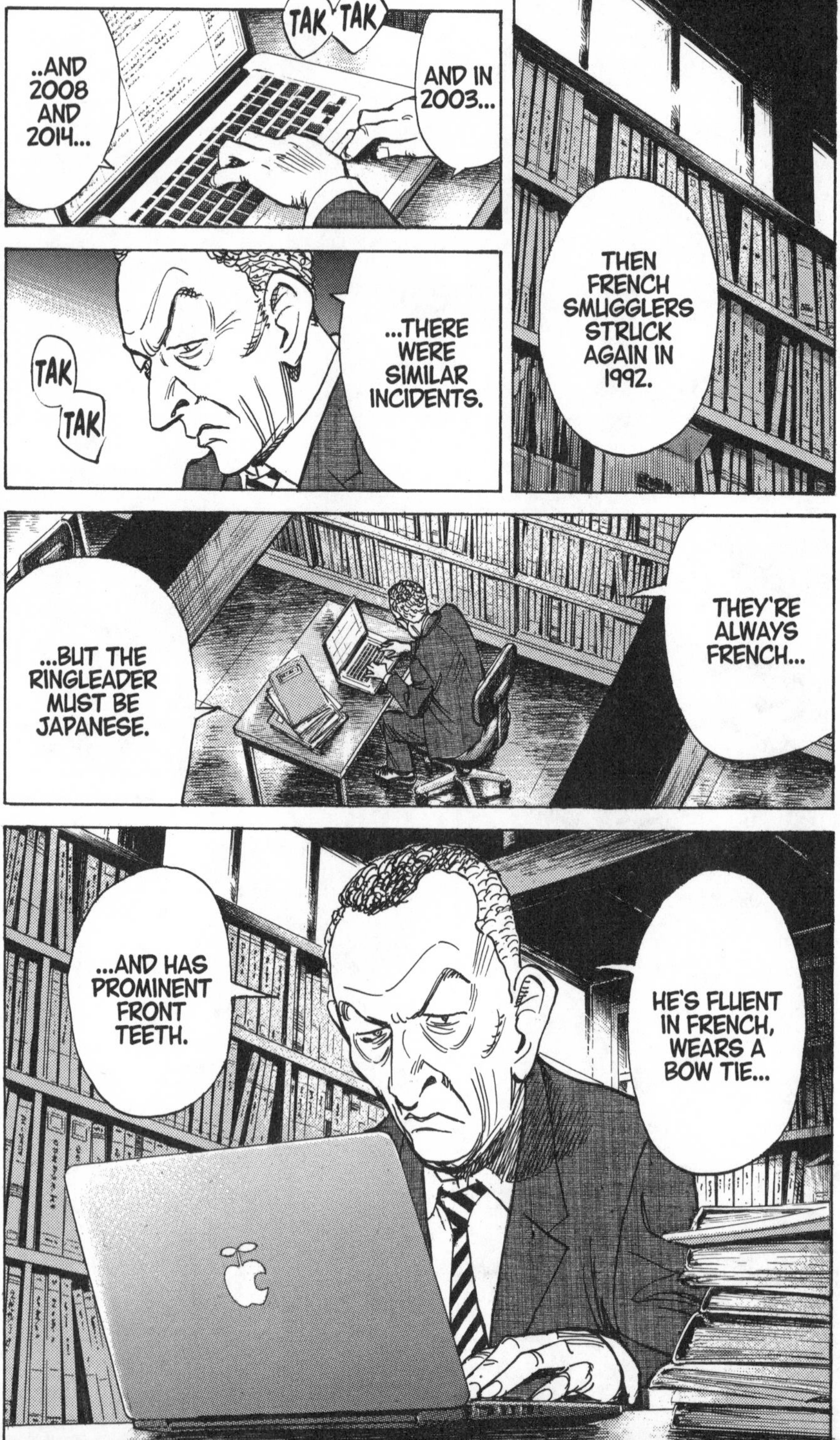
THEN FRENCH SMUGGLERS STRUCK AGAIN IN 1992.
TAK TAK
AND IN 2003...
..AND 2008 AND 2014...
...THERE WERE SIMILAR INCIDENTS.
TAK
TAK
THEY'RE ALWAYS FRENCH...
...BUT THE RINGLEADER MUST BE JAPANESE.
HE'S FLUENT IN FRENCH, WEARS A BOW TIE...
...AND HAS PROMINENT FRONT TEETH.

4ème Sheeh! Round Stone

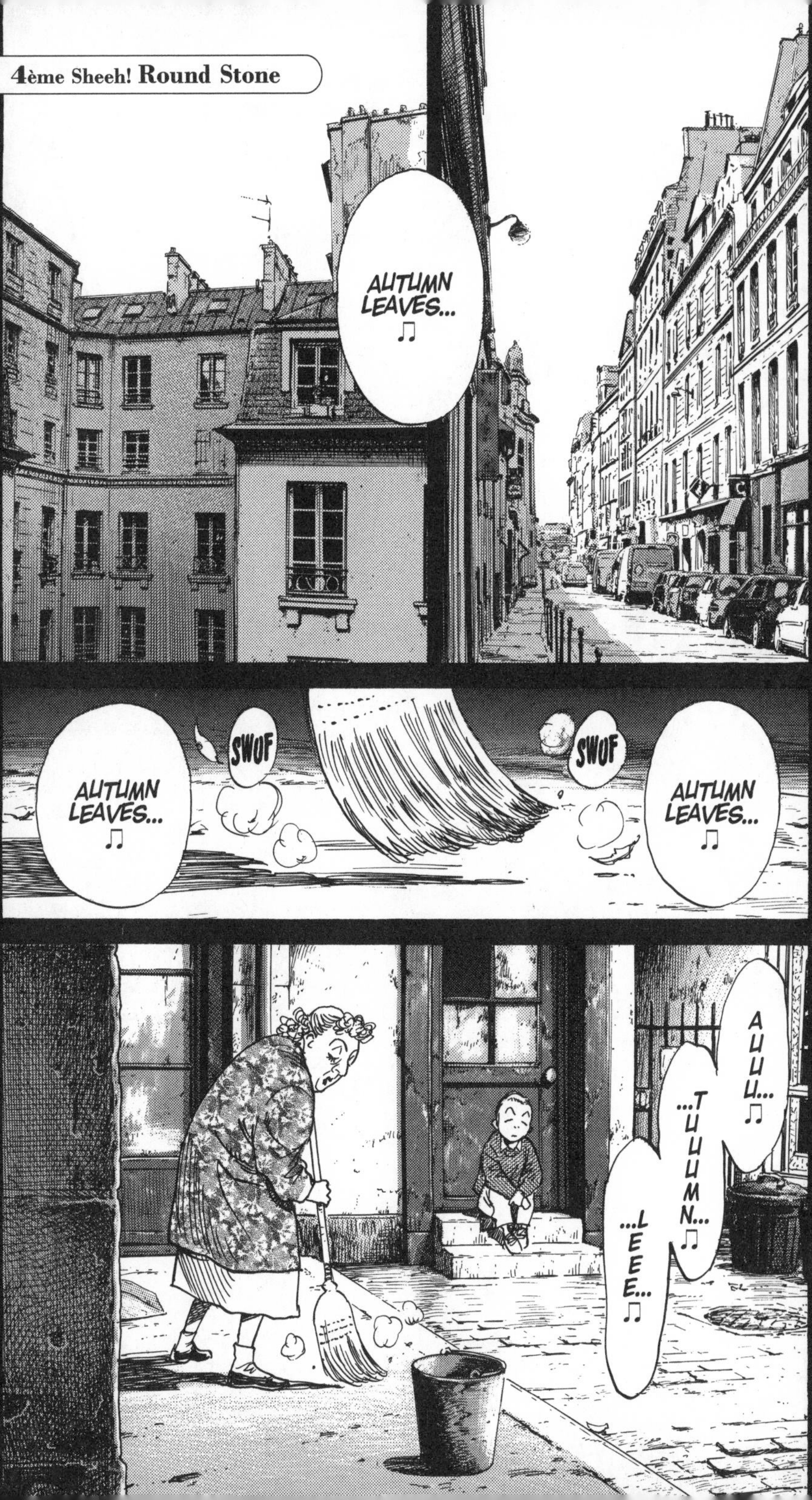
AUTUMN LEAVES... ♫
AUTUMN LEAVES... ♫
SWOF
SWOF
AUTUMN LEAVES... ♫
AUUU... ♫
...TUUUMN... ♫
...LEEE... ♫

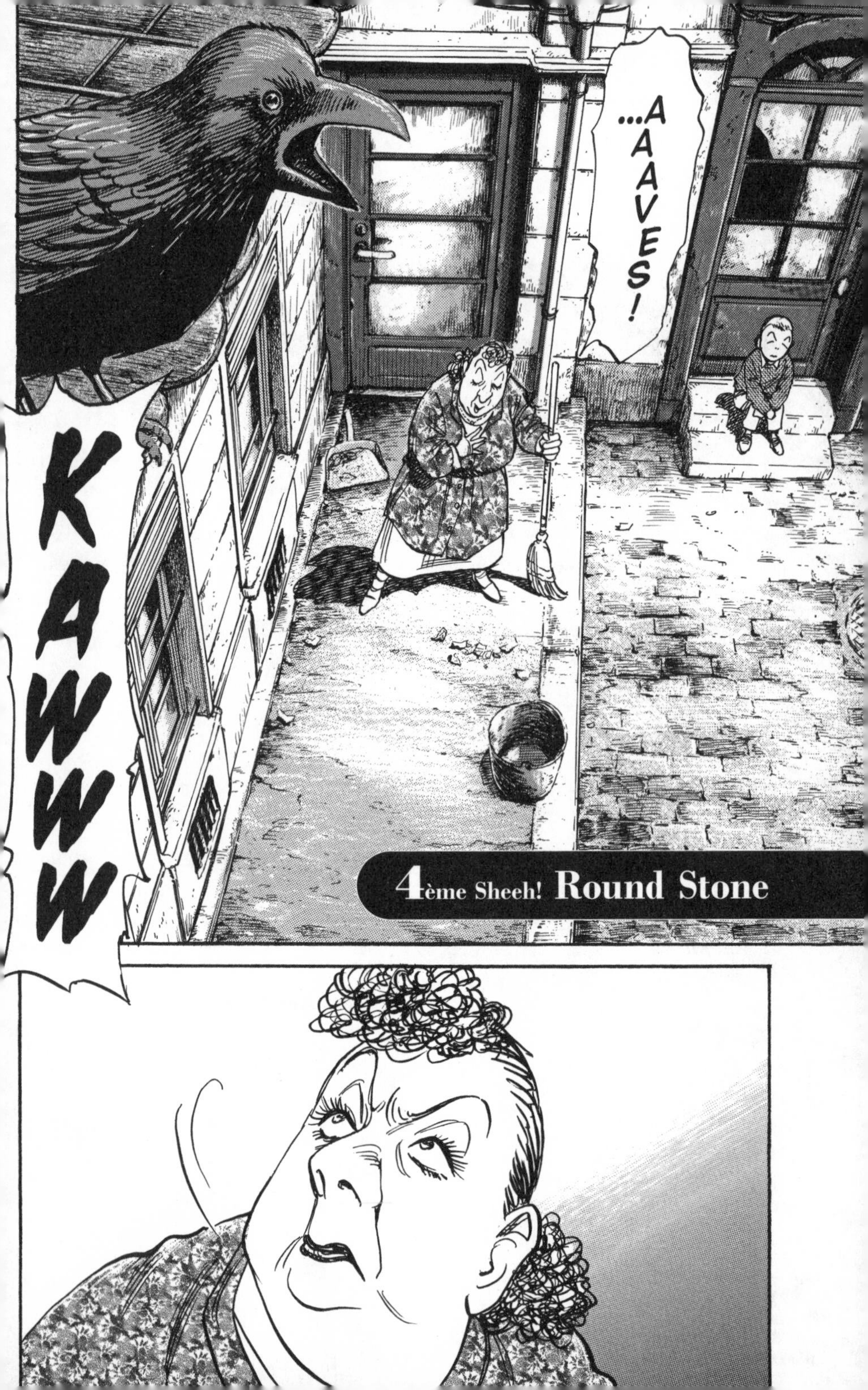
...AAAAVES!
KAWWW
4ème Sheeh! Round Stone

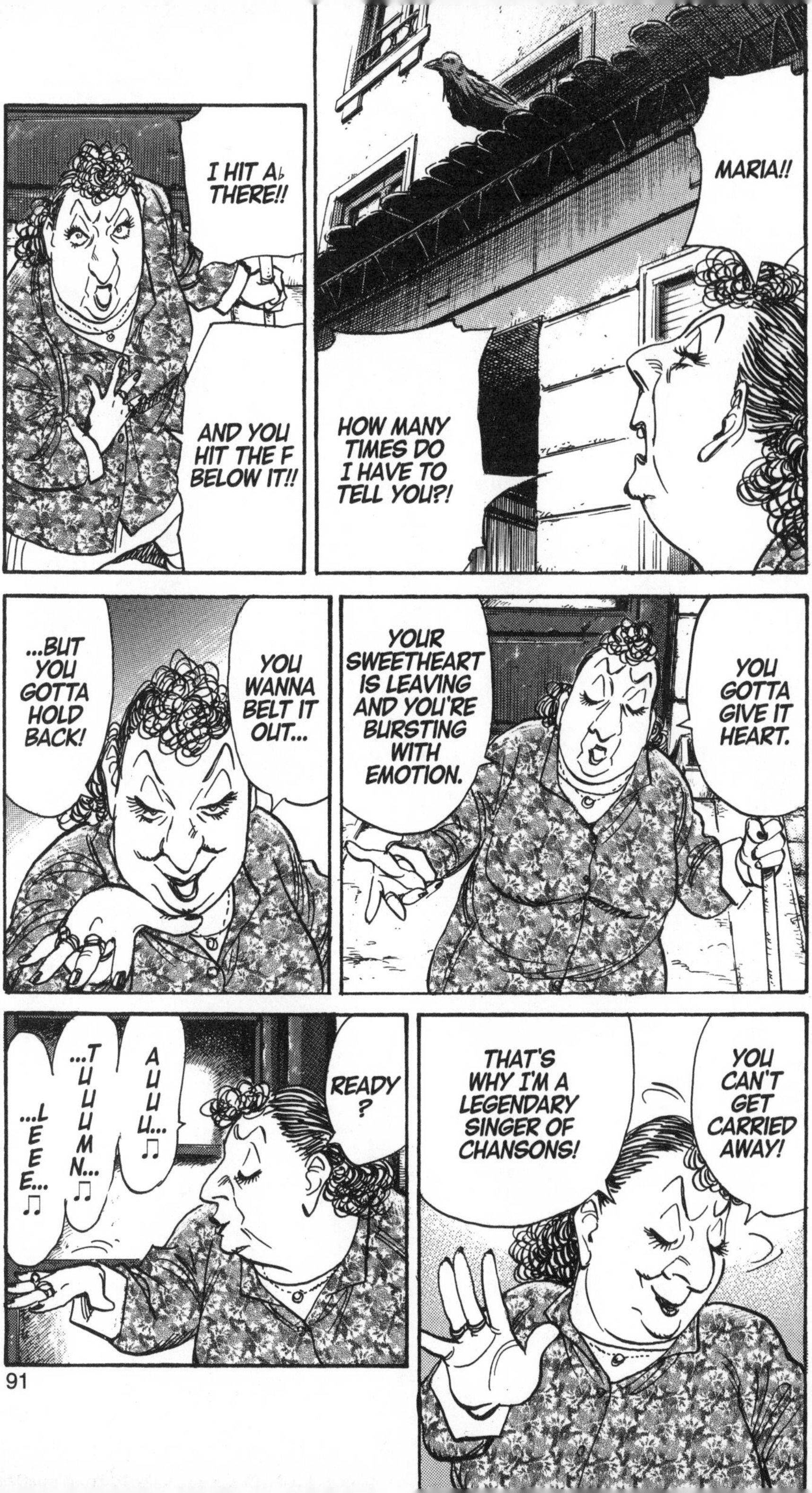
MARIA!!
HOW MANY TIMES DO I HAVE TO TELL YOU?!
I HIT A♭ THERE!!
AND YOU HIT THE F BELOW IT!!
YOU GOTTA GIVE IT HEART.
YOUR SWEETHEART IS LEAVING AND YOU'RE BURSTING WITH EMOTION.
YOU WANNA BELT IT OUT...
...BUT YOU GOTTA HOLD BACK!
YOU CAN'T GET CARRIED AWAY!
THAT'S WHY I'M A LEGENDARY SINGER OF CHANSONS!
READY?
AUUU...♫
...TUUUMN...♫
...LEEEE...♫

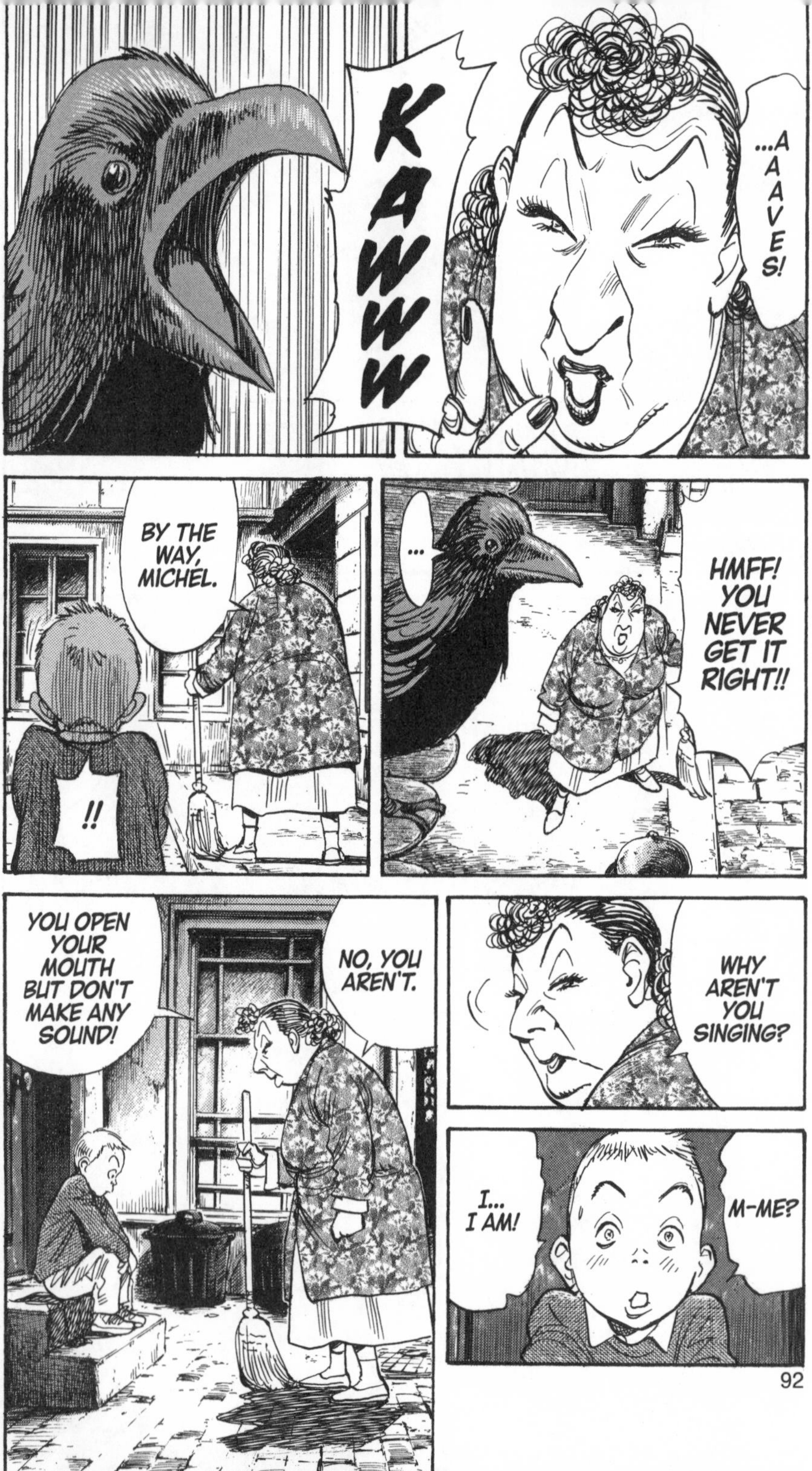
...AAAAVES!
KAWWW
HMFF! YOU NEVER GET IT RIGHT!!
...
BY THE WAY, MICHEL.
!!
WHY AREN'T YOU SINGING?
M-ME?
I... I AM!
NO, YOU AREN'T.
YOU OPEN YOUR MOUTH BUT DON'T MAKE ANY SOUND!

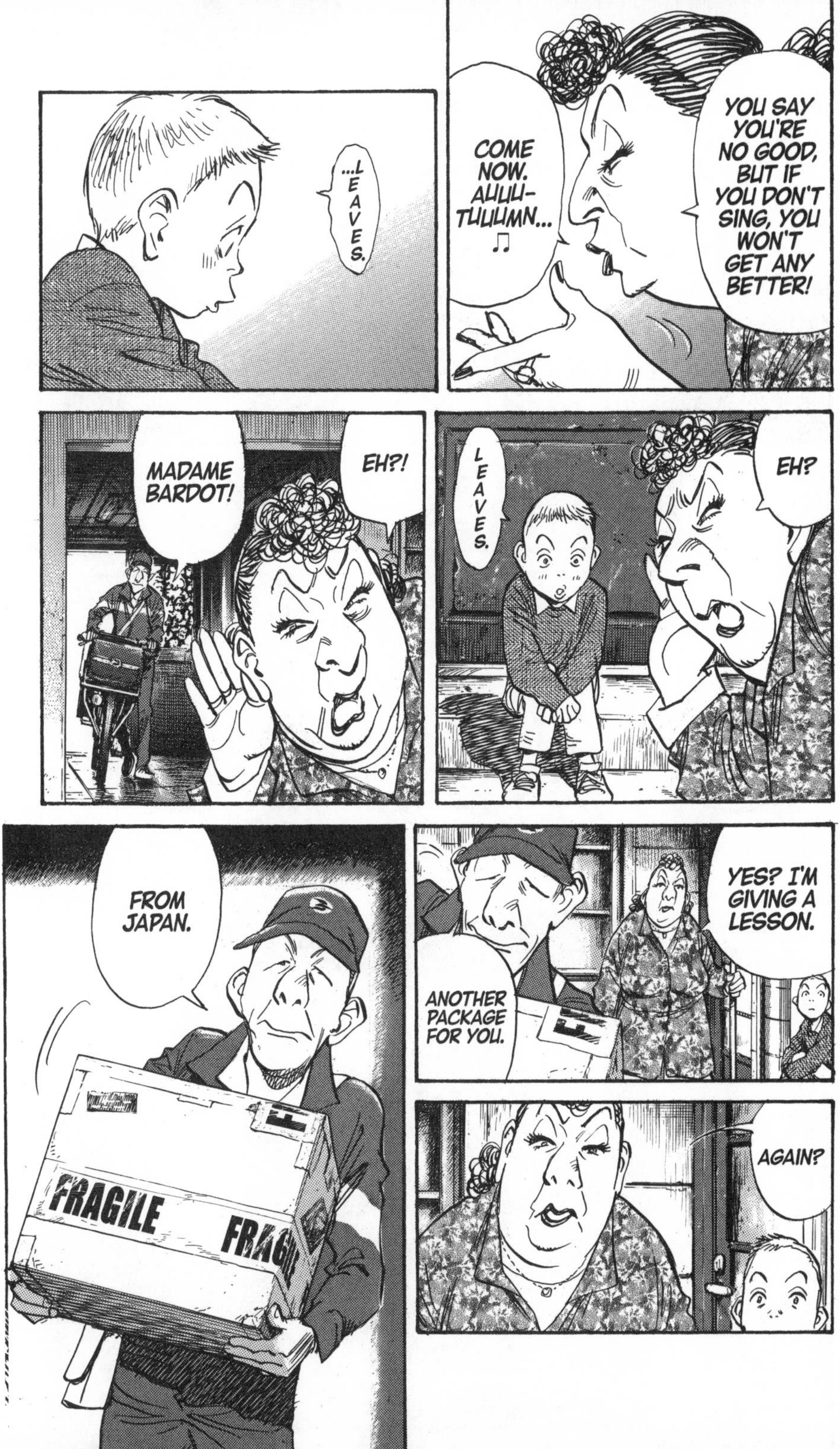
YOU SAY YOU'RE NO GOOD, BUT IF YOU DON'T SING, YOU WON'T GET ANY BETTER!
COME NOW. AUUU-TUUUMN... ♫
...LEAVES.
EH?
LEAVES.
EH?!
MADAME BARDOT!
YES? I'M GIVING A LESSON.
ANOTHER PACKAGE FOR YOU.
AGAIN?
FROM JAPAN.
FRAGILE
FRAGILE

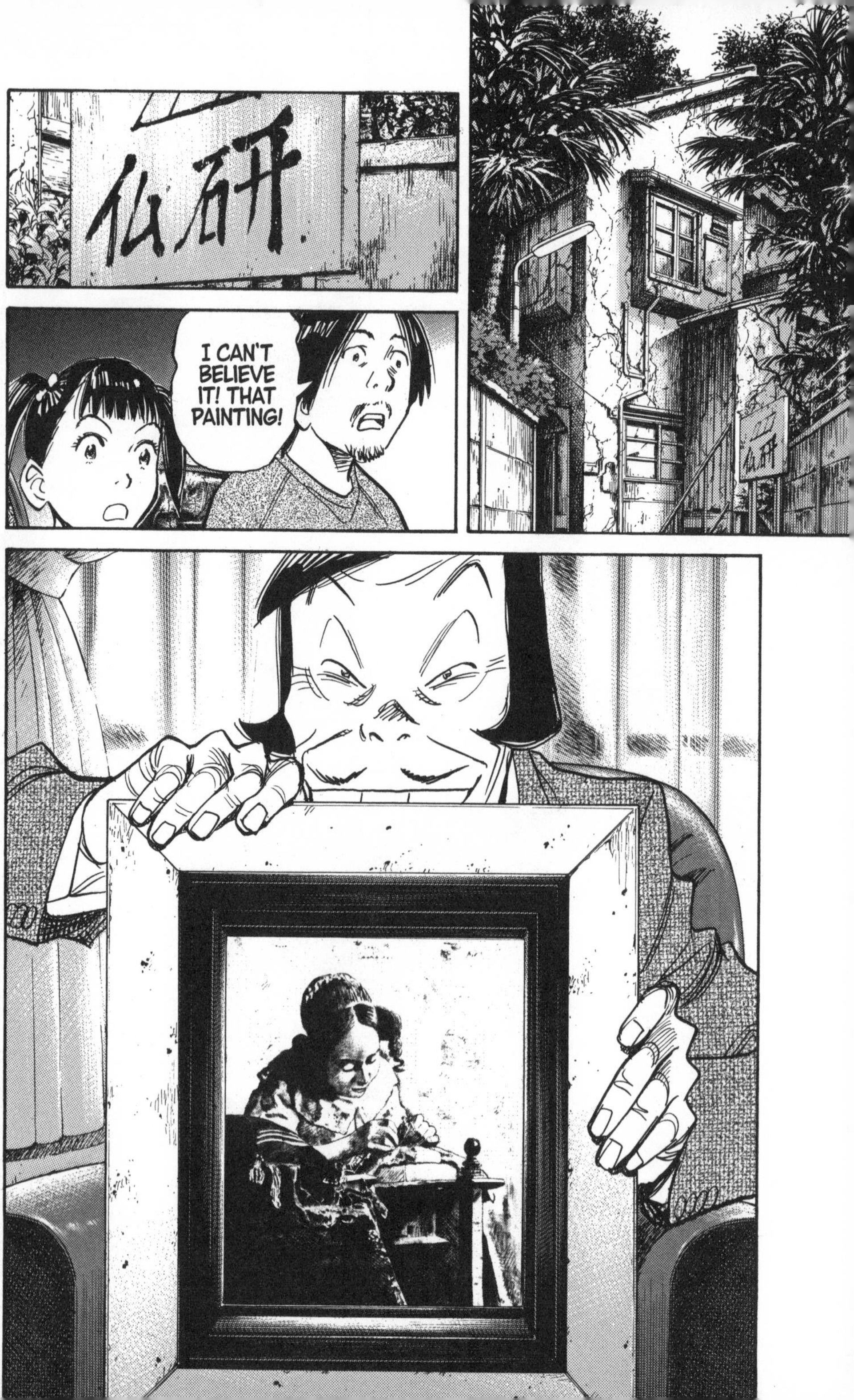
仏研
仏研
I CAN'T BELIEVE IT! THAT PAINTING!

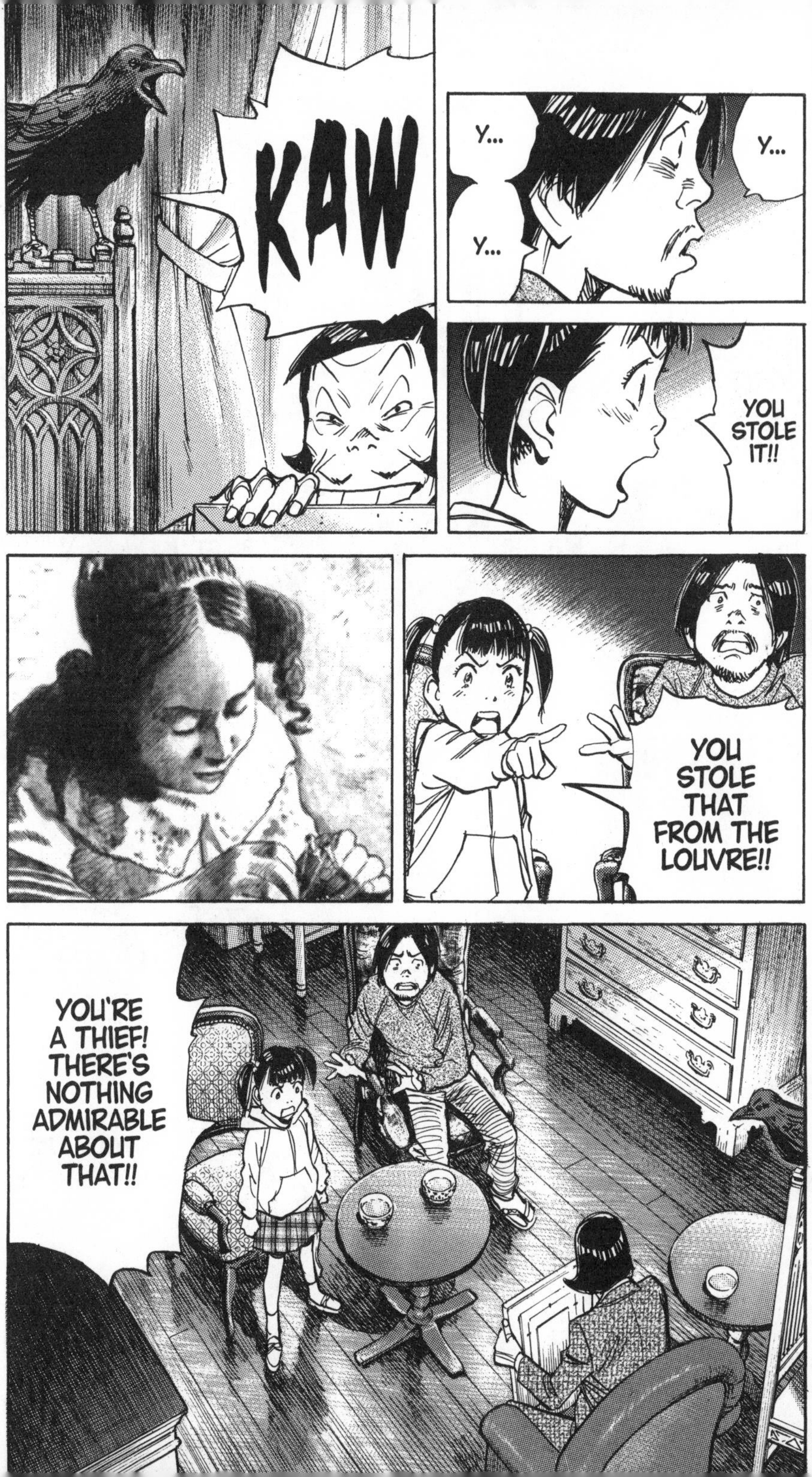
Y...
Y...
Y...
YOU STOLE IT!!
KAW
YOU STOLE THAT FROM THE LOUVRE!!
YOU'RE A THIEF! THERE'S NOTHING ADMIRABLE ABOUT THAT!!

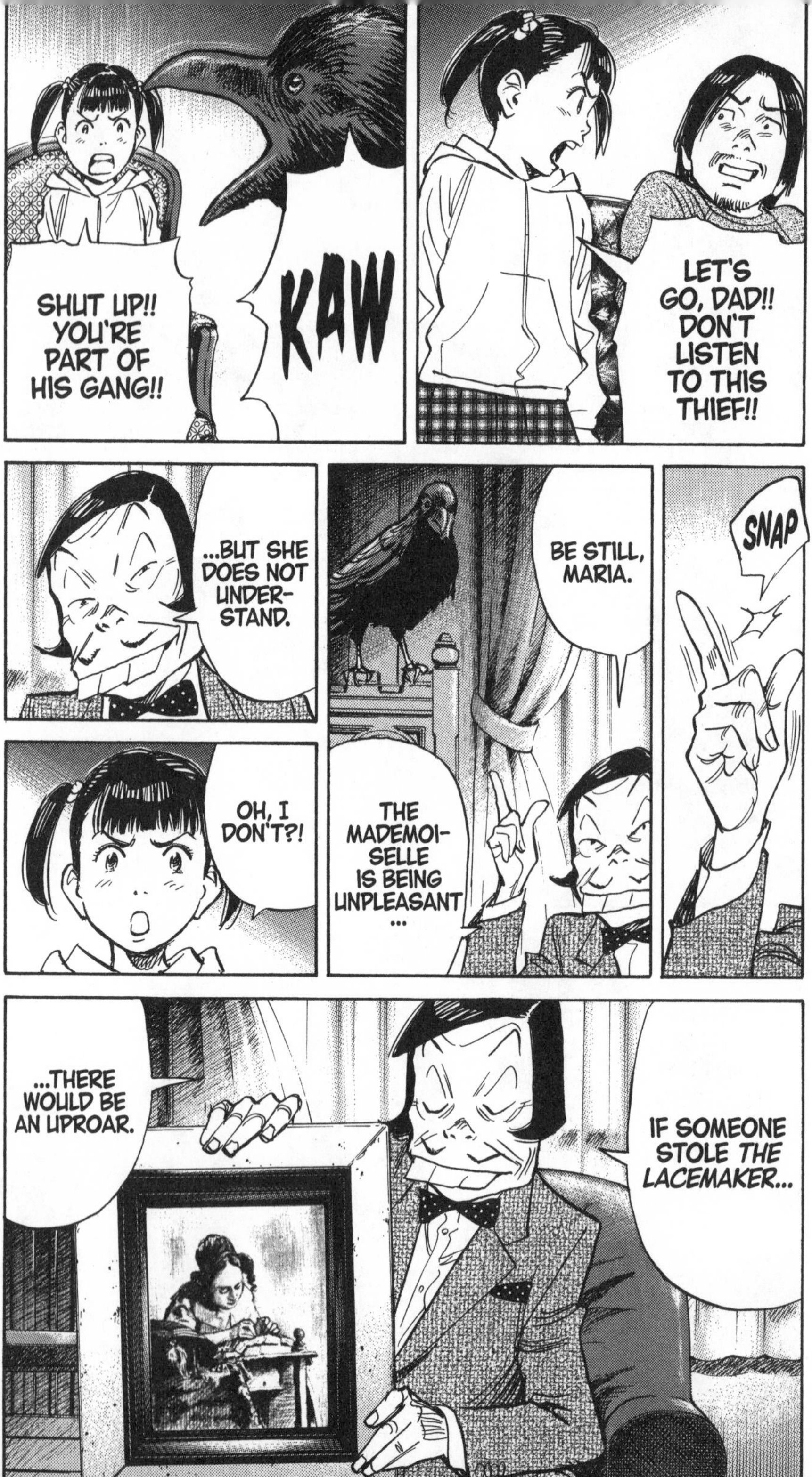
LET'S GO, DAD!! DON'T LISTEN TO THIS THIEF!!
KAW
SHUT UP!! YOU'RE PART OF HIS GANG!!
SNAP
BE STILL, MARIA.
THE MADEMOISELLE IS BEING UNPLEASANT...
...BUT SHE DOES NOT UNDERSTAND.
OH, I DON'T?!
IF SOMEONE STOLE THE LACEMAKER...
...THERE WOULD BE AN UPROAR.

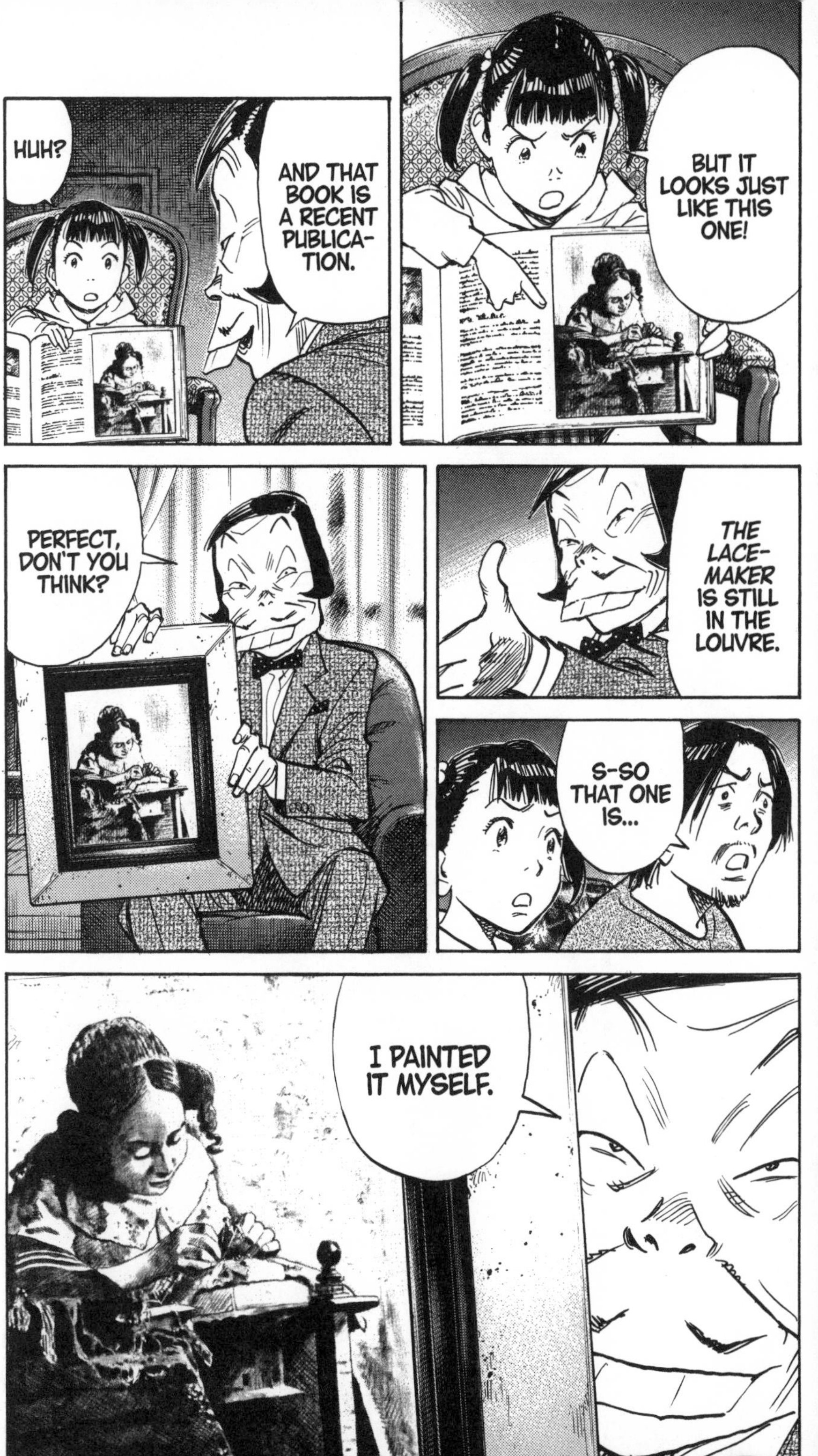
BUT IT LOOKS JUST LIKE THIS ONE!
AND THAT BOOK IS A RECENT PUBLICATION.
HUH?
THE LACE-MAKER IS STILL IN THE LOUVRE.
S-SO THAT ONE IS...
PERFECT, DON'T YOU THINK?
I PAINTED IT MYSELF.

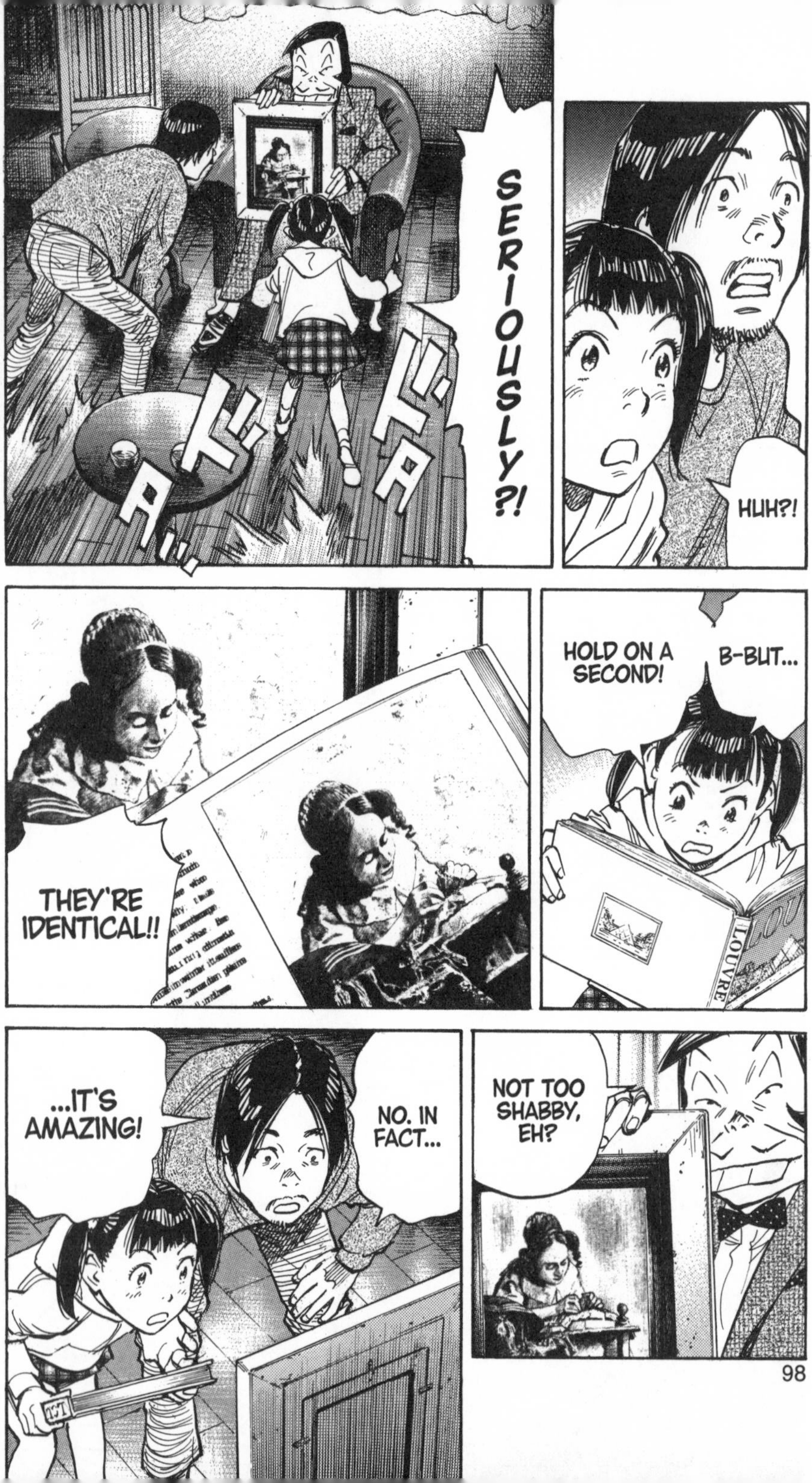
HUH?!
SERIOUSLY?!
B-BUT...
HOLD ON A SECOND!
THEY'RE IDENTICAL!!
NOT TOO SHABBY, EH?
NO. IN FACT...
...IT'S AMAZING!

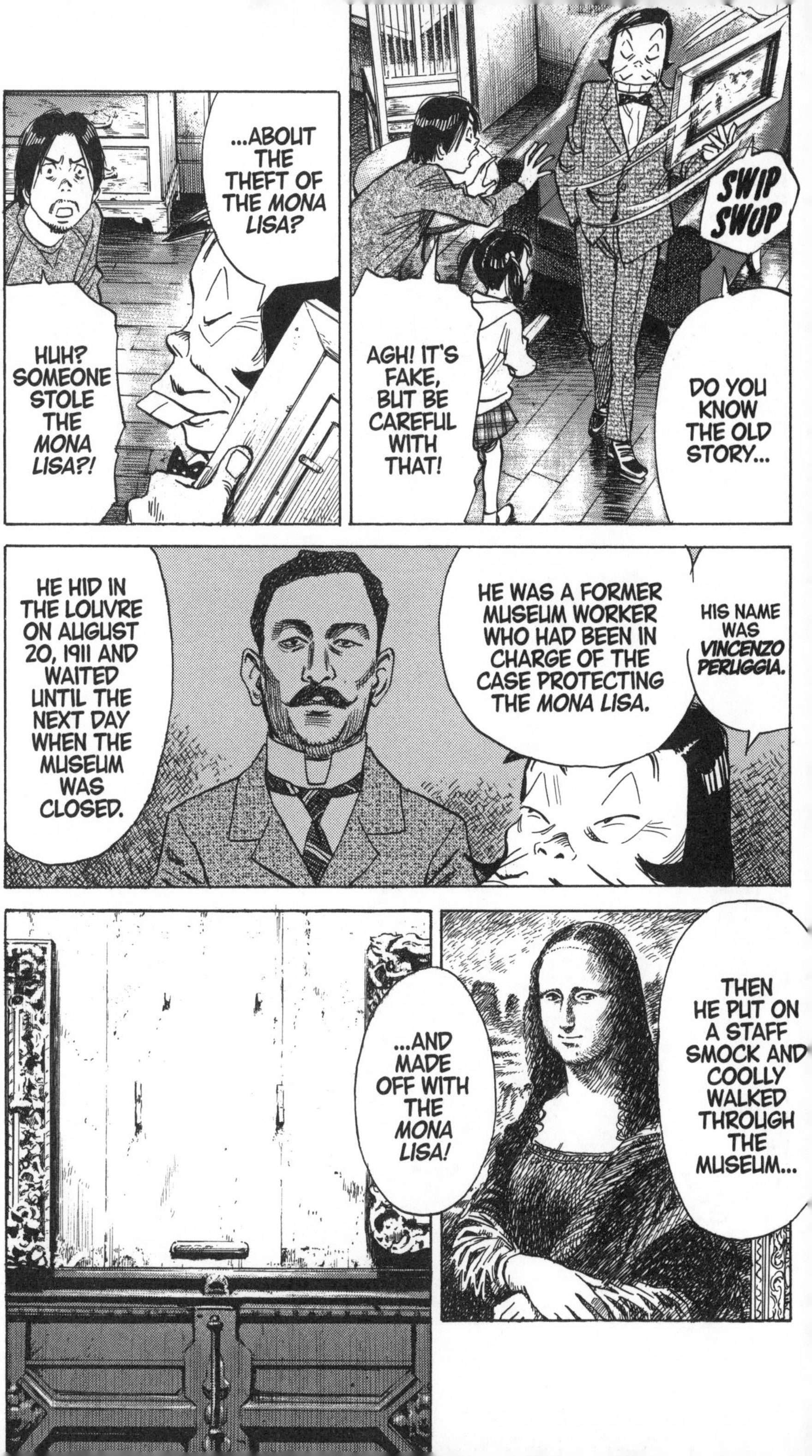

SWIP SWOP
DO YOU KNOW THE OLD STORY...
AGH! IT'S FAKE, BUT BE CAREFUL WITH THAT!
...ABOUT THE THEFT OF THE *MONA LISA*?
HUH? SOMEONE STOLE THE *MONA LISA*?!
HIS NAME WAS *VINCENZO PERUGGIA*.
HE WAS A FORMER MUSEUM WORKER WHO HAD BEEN IN CHARGE OF THE CASE PROTECTING THE *MONA LISA*.
HE HID IN THE LOUVRE ON AUGUST 20, 1911 AND WAITED UNTIL THE NEXT DAY WHEN THE MUSEUM WAS CLOSED.
THEN HE PUT ON A STAFF SMOCK AND COOLLY WALKED THROUGH THE MUSEUM...
...AND MADE OFF WITH THE *MONA LISA*!

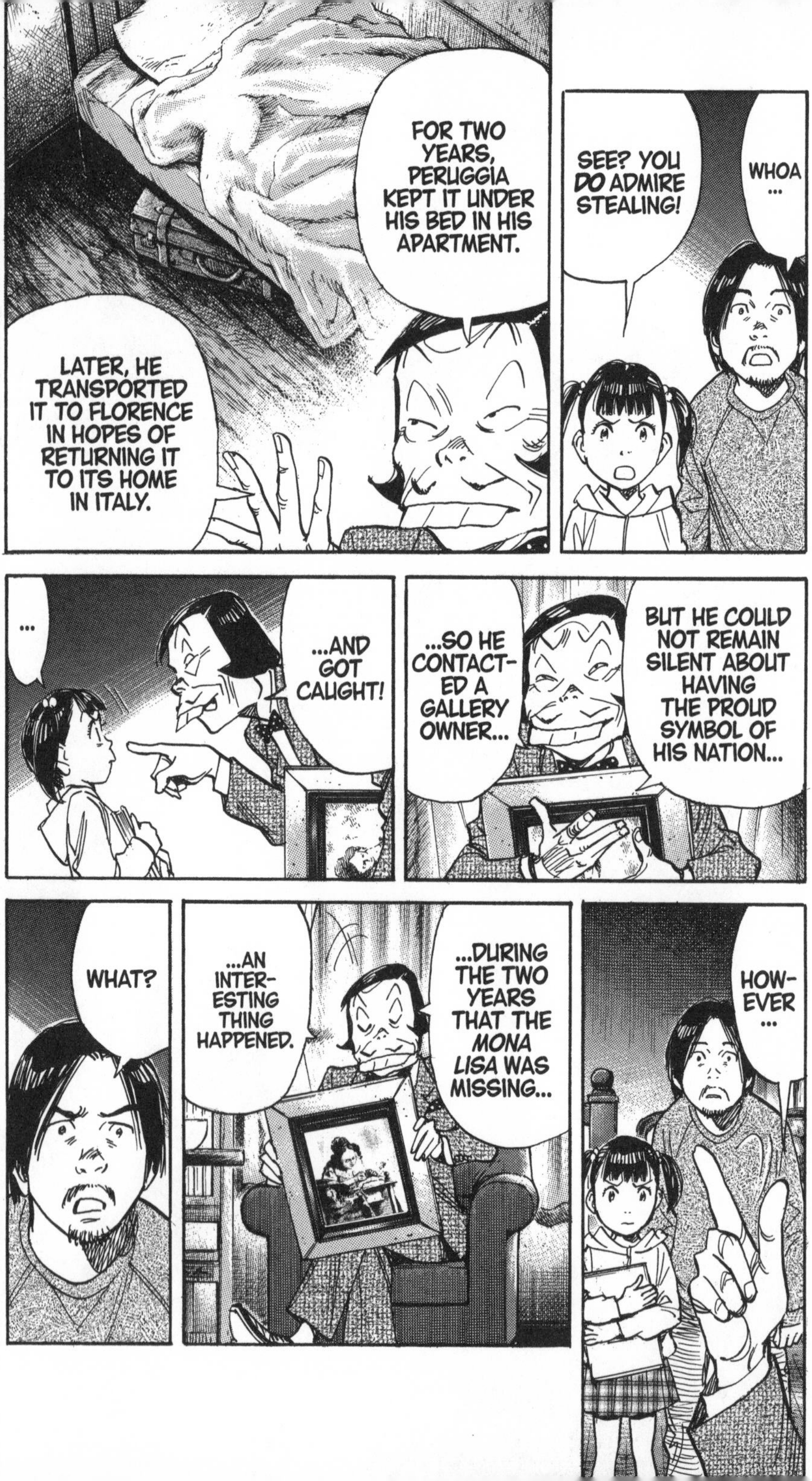
WHOA ...
SEE? YOU DO ADMIRE STEALING!
FOR TWO YEARS, PERUGGIA KEPT IT UNDER HIS BED IN HIS APARTMENT.
LATER, HE TRANSPORTED IT TO FLORENCE IN HOPES OF RETURNING IT TO ITS HOME IN ITALY.
BUT HE COULD NOT REMAIN SILENT ABOUT HAVING THE PROUD SYMBOL OF HIS NATION...
...SO HE CONTACTED A GALLERY OWNER...
...AND GOT CAUGHT!
...
HOWEVER ...
...DURING THE TWO YEARS THAT THE MONA LISA WAS MISSING...
...AN INTERESTING THING HAPPENED.
WHAT?

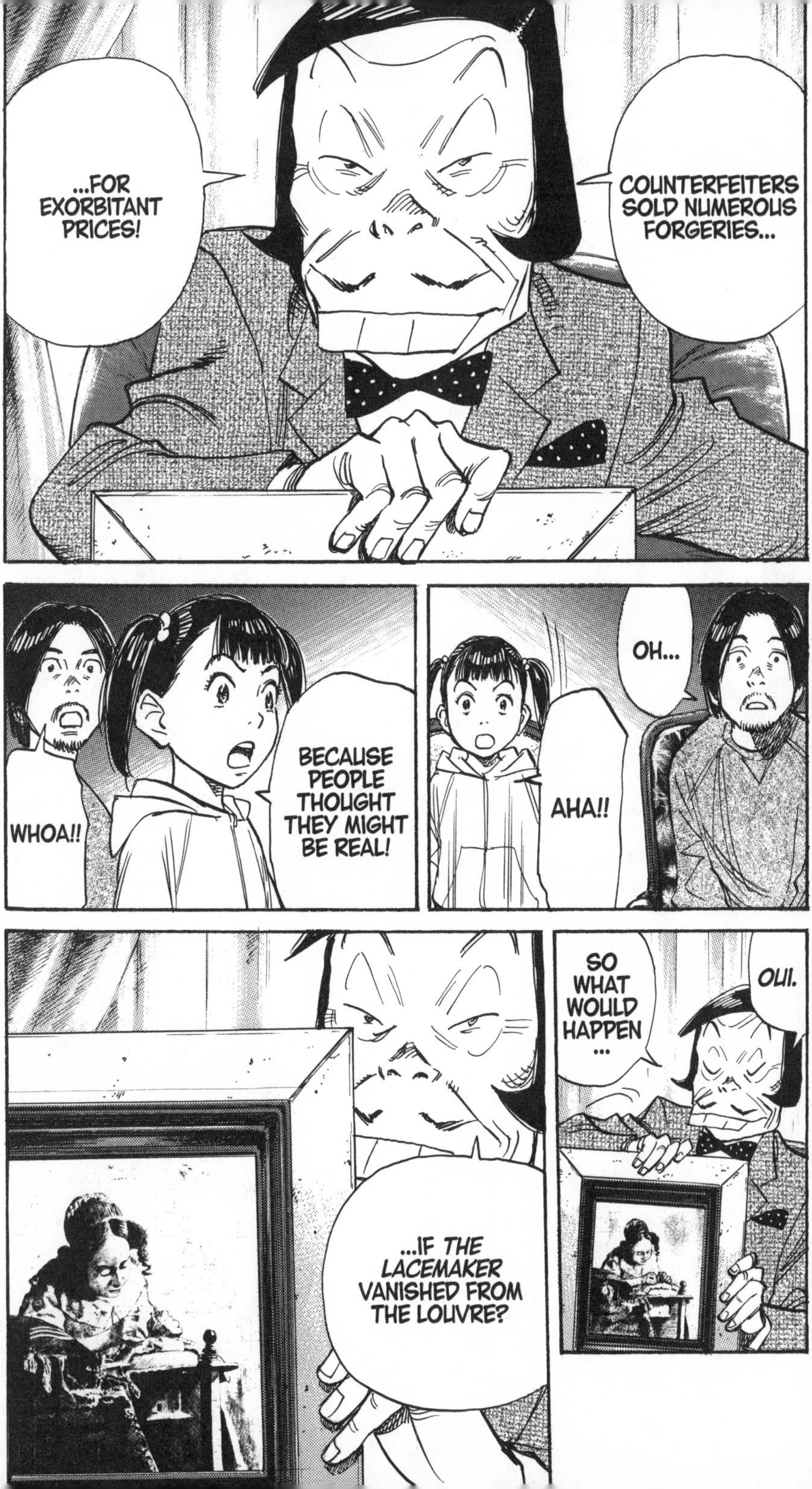
COUNTERFEITERS SOLD NUMEROUS FORGERIES...
...FOR EXORBITANT PRICES!
OH...
AHA!!
BECAUSE PEOPLE THOUGHT THEY MIGHT BE REAL!
WHOA!!
OUI.
SO WHAT WOULD HAPPEN ...
...IF *THE LACEMAKER* VANISHED FROM THE LOUVRE?

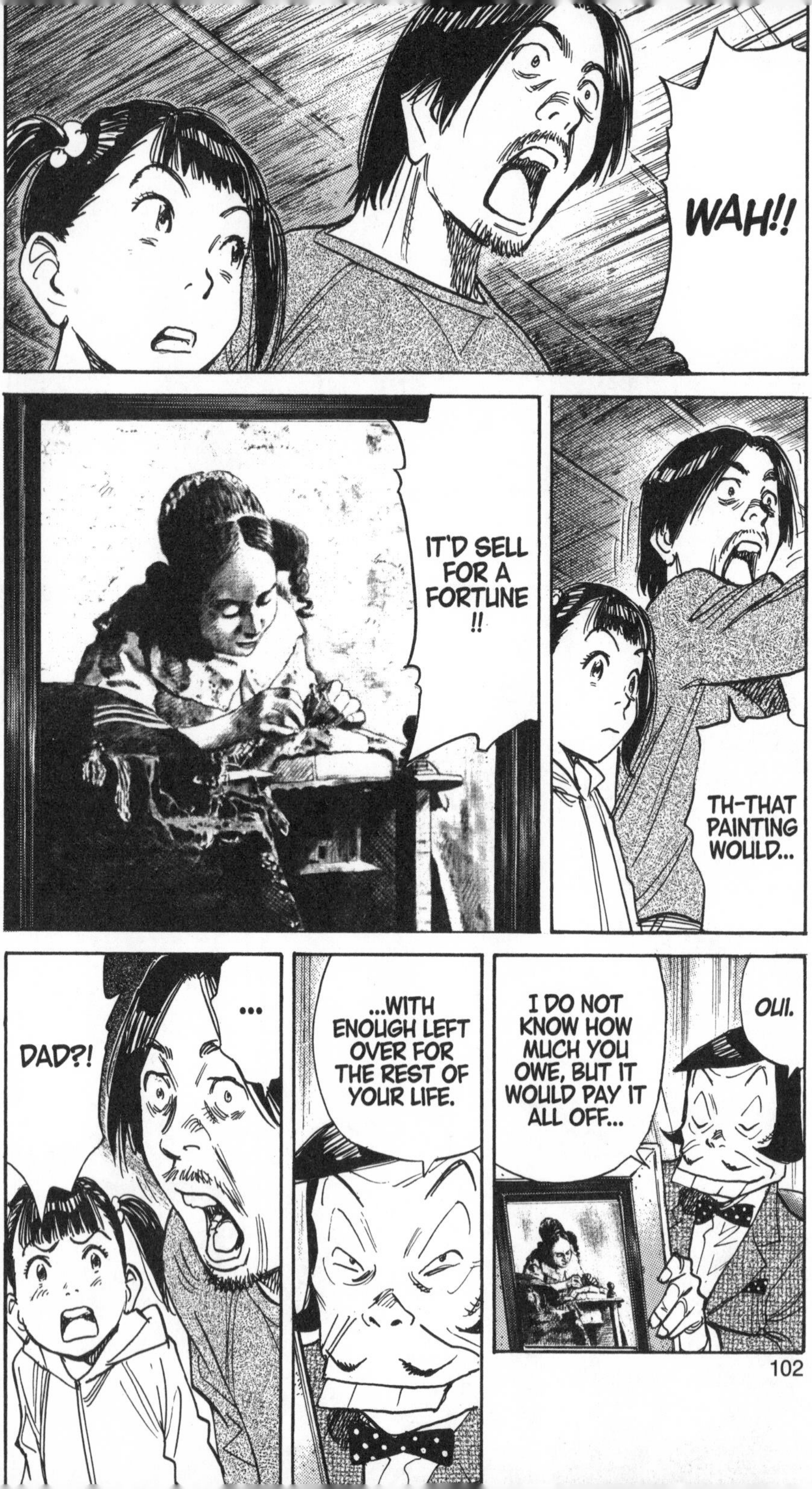
WAH!!
TH-THAT PAINTING WOULD...
IT'D SELL FOR A FORTUNE !!
OUI.
I DO NOT KNOW HOW MUCH YOU OWE, BUT IT WOULD PAY IT ALL OFF...
...WITH ENOUGH LEFT OVER FOR THE REST OF YOUR LIFE.
...
DAD?!

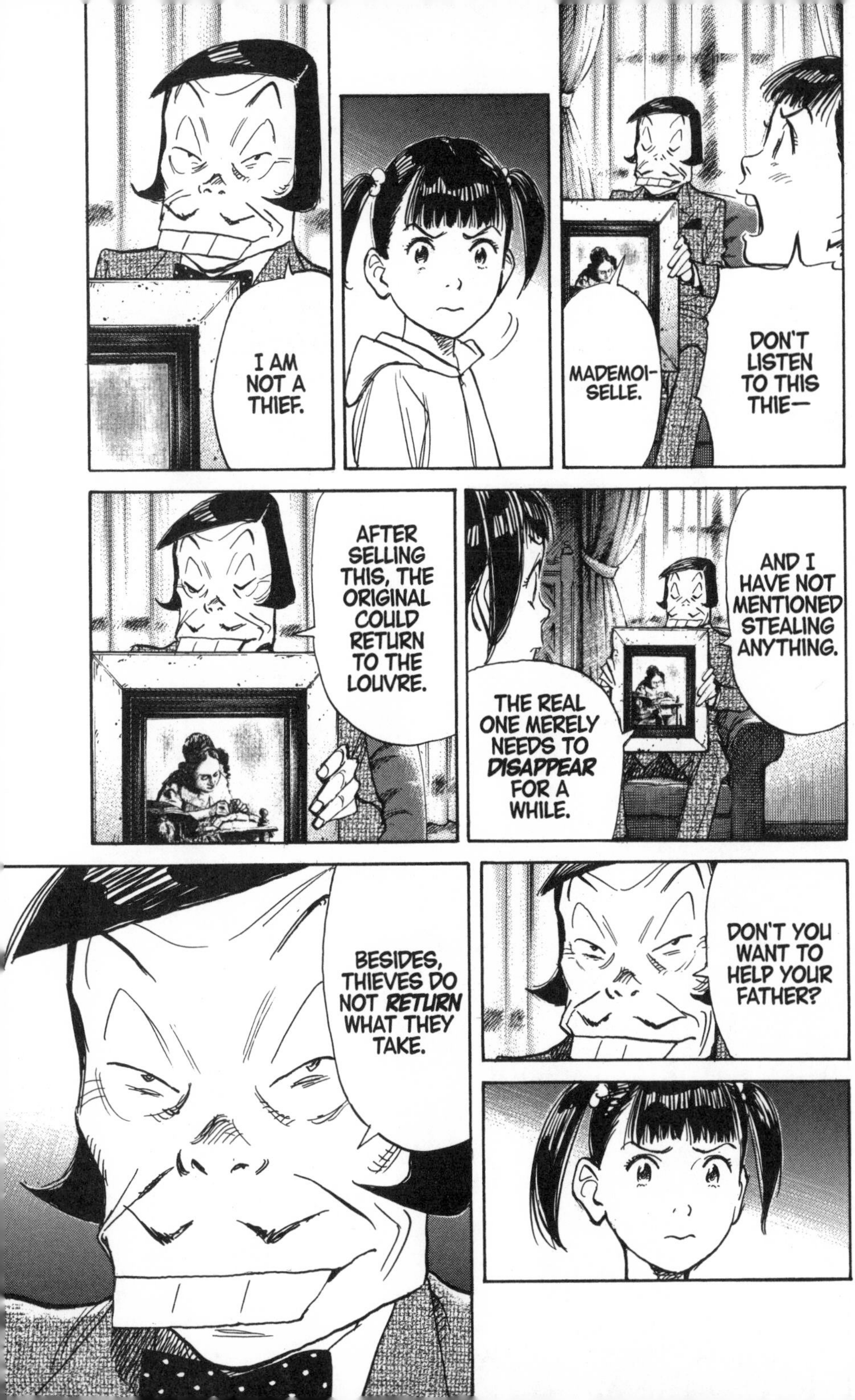
DON'T LISTEN TO THIS THIE—
MADEMOI-SELLE.
I AM NOT A THIEF.
AND I HAVE NOT MENTIONED STEALING ANYTHING.
THE REAL ONE MERELY NEEDS TO *DISAPPEAR* FOR A WHILE.
AFTER SELLING THIS, THE ORIGINAL COULD RETURN TO THE LOUVRE.
DON'T YOU WANT TO HELP YOUR FATHER?
BESIDES, THIEVES DO NOT *RETURN* WHAT THEY TAKE.

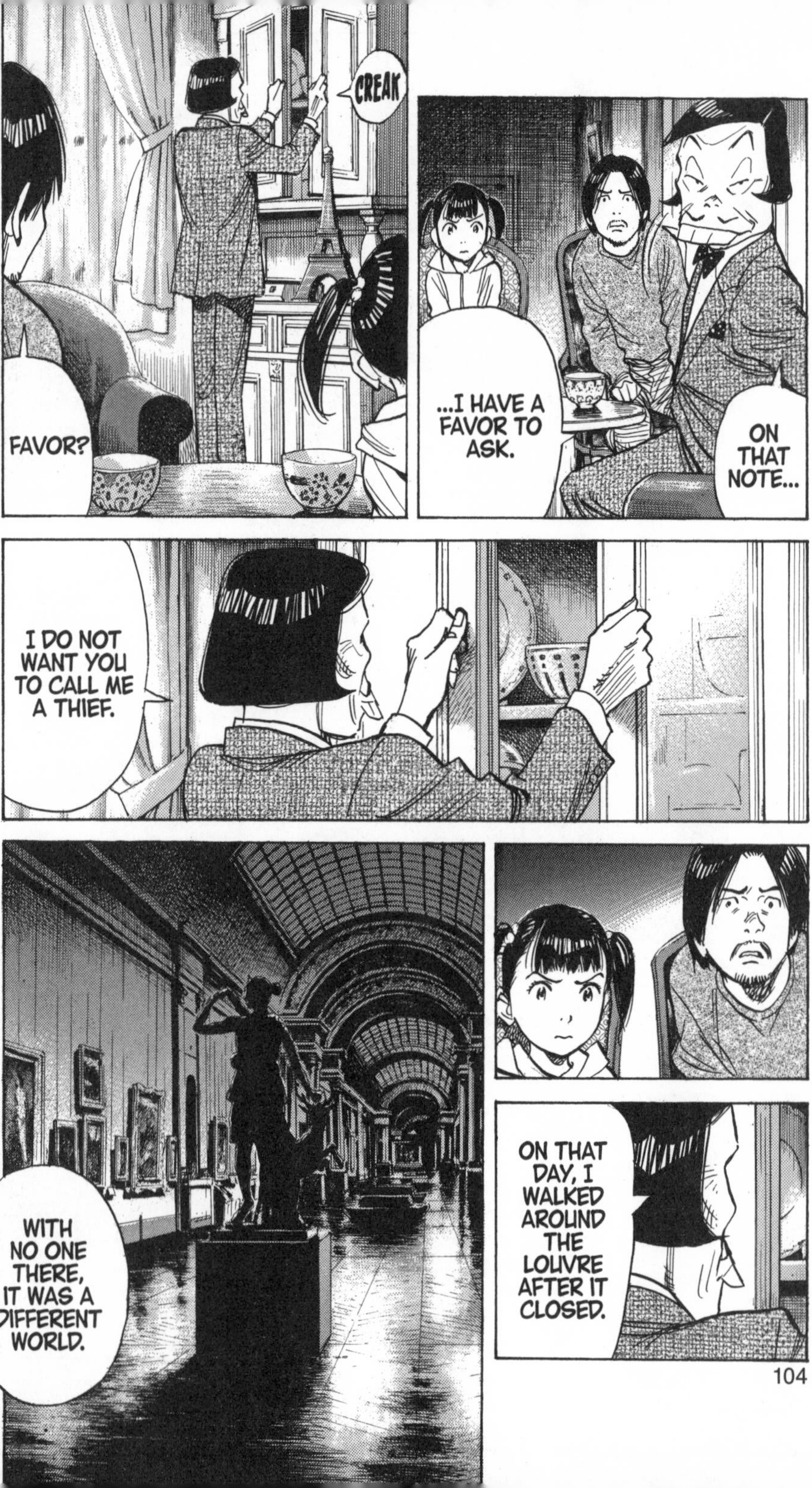
ON THAT NOTE...
...I HAVE A FAVOR TO ASK.
CREAK
FAVOR?
I DO NOT WANT YOU TO CALL ME A THIEF.
ON THAT DAY, I WALKED AROUND THE LOUVRE AFTER IT CLOSED.
WITH NO ONE THERE, IT WAS A DIFFERENT WORLD.

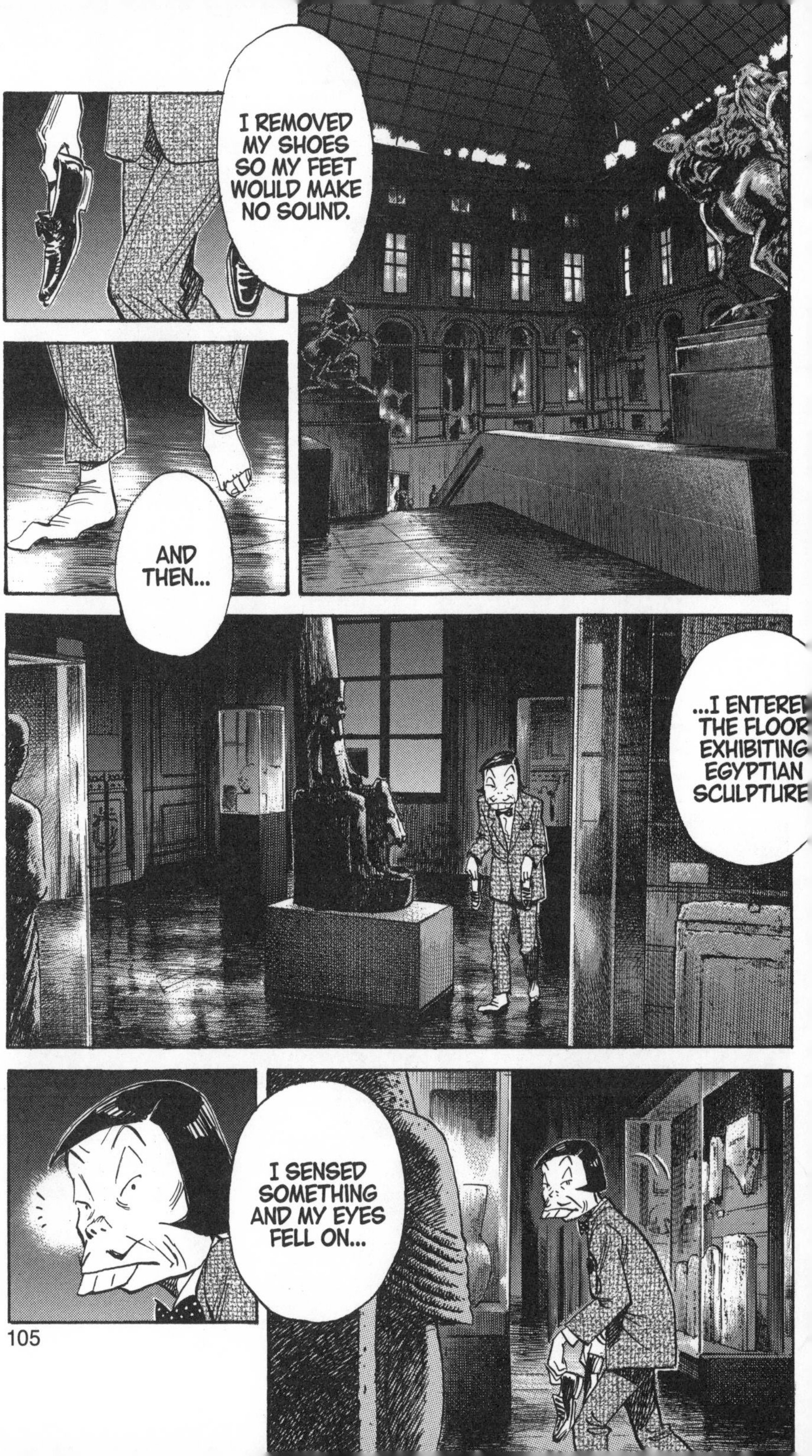
I REMOVED MY SHOES SO MY FEET WOULD MAKE NO SOUND.
AND THEN...
...I ENTERED THE FLOOR EXHIBITING EGYPTIAN SCULPTURE
I SENSED SOMETHING AND MY EYES FELL ON...

...A STATUE OF A MAN AND WOMAN.

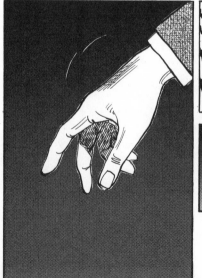

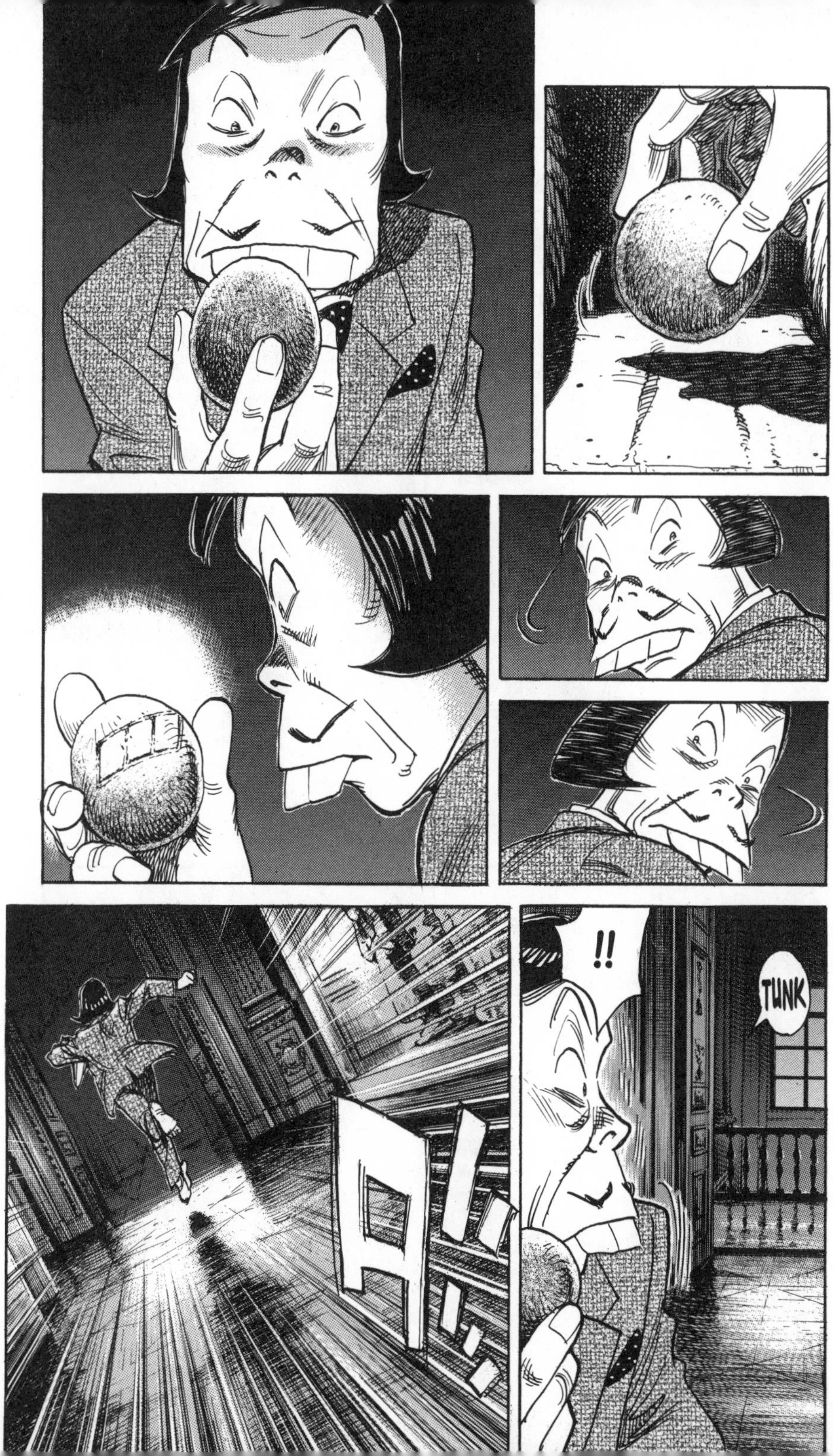
TUNK
!!

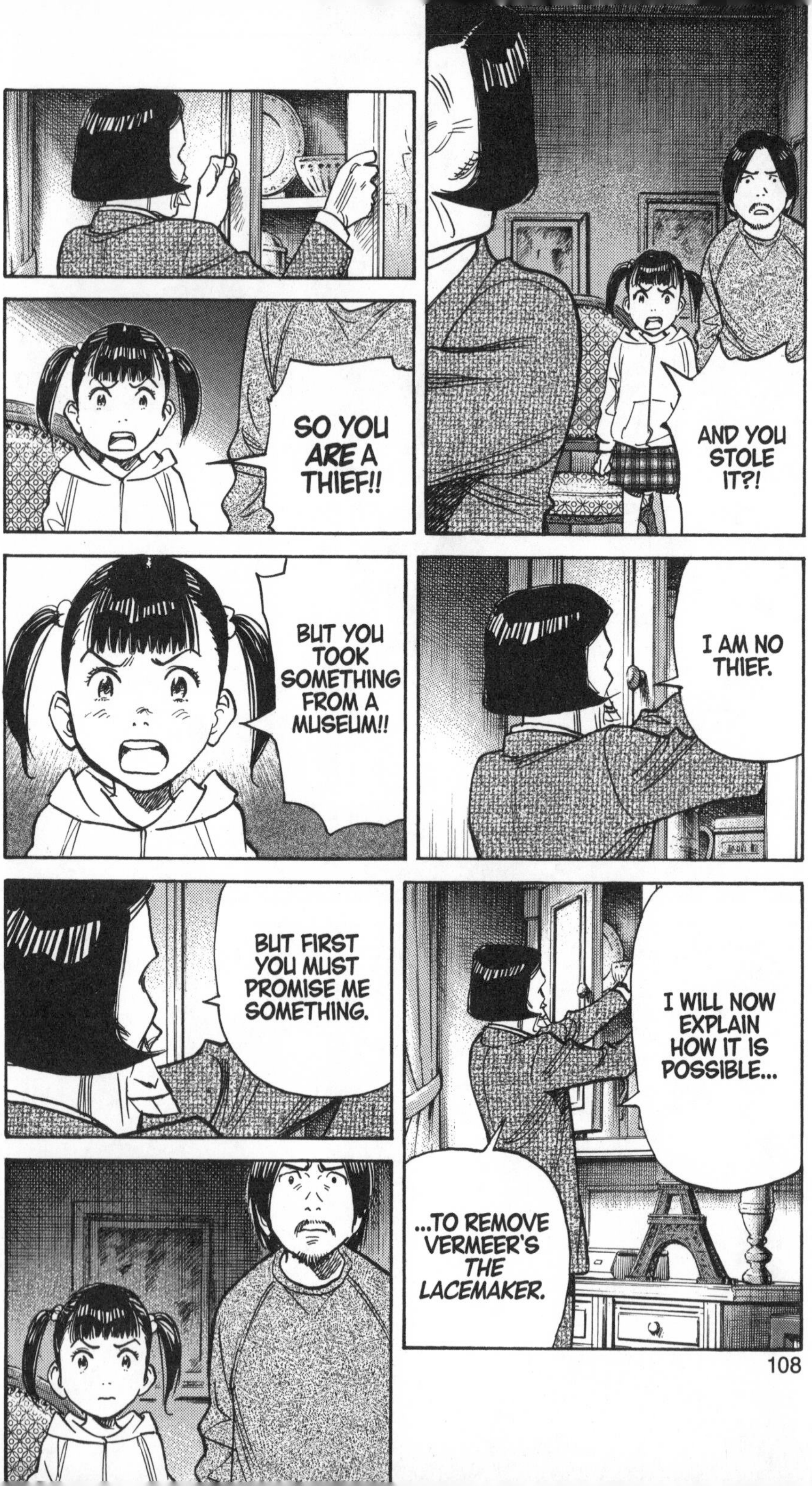
AND YOU STOLE IT?!
SO YOU *ARE* A THIEF!!
I AM NO THIEF.
BUT YOU TOOK SOMETHING FROM A MUSEUM!!
I WILL NOW EXPLAIN HOW IT IS POSSIBLE...
...TO REMOVE VERMEER'S *THE LACEMAKER.*
BUT FIRST YOU MUST PROMISE ME SOMETHING.

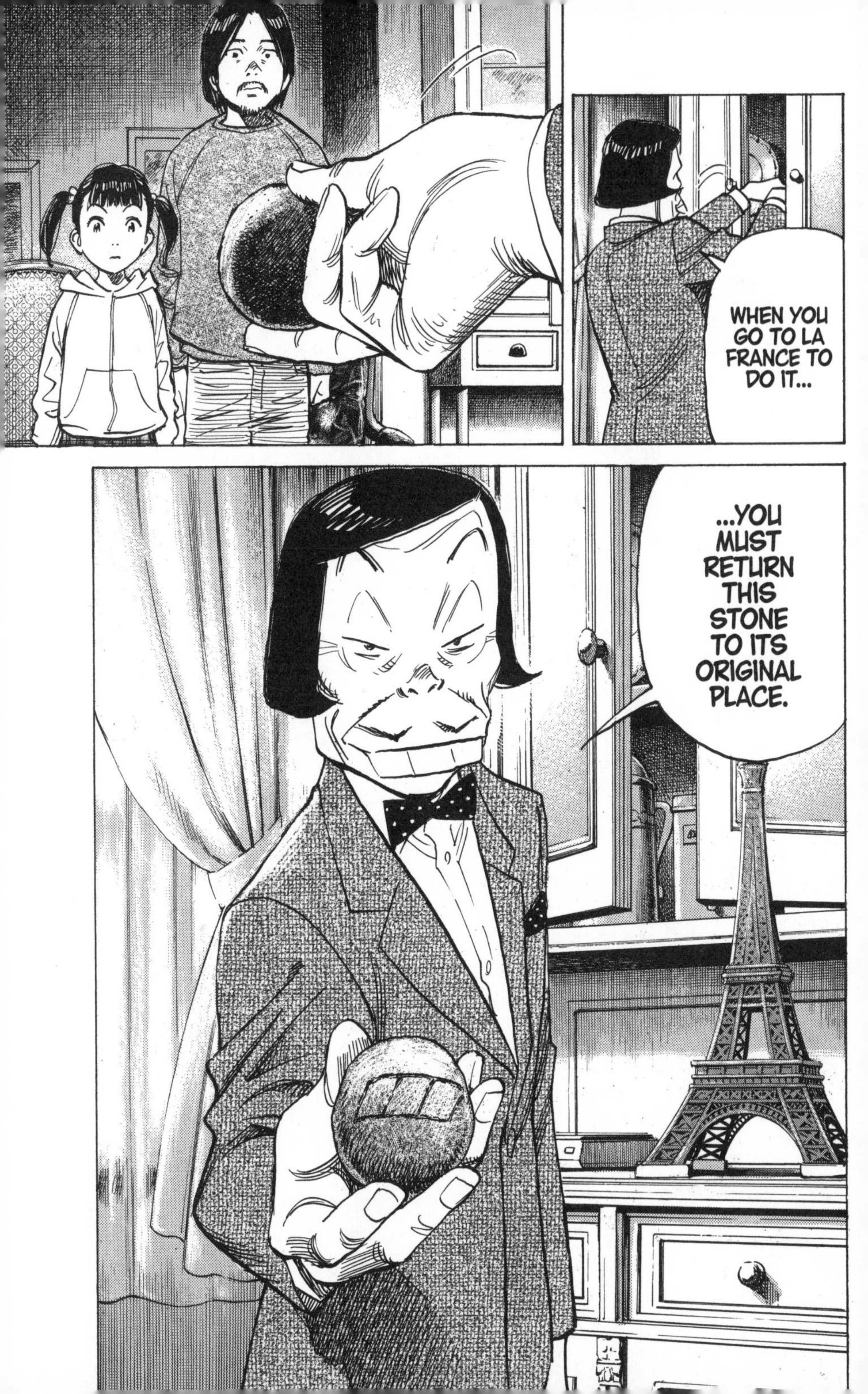
WHEN YOU GO TO LA FRANCE TO DO IT...
...YOU MUST RETURN THIS STONE TO ITS ORIGINAL PLACE.

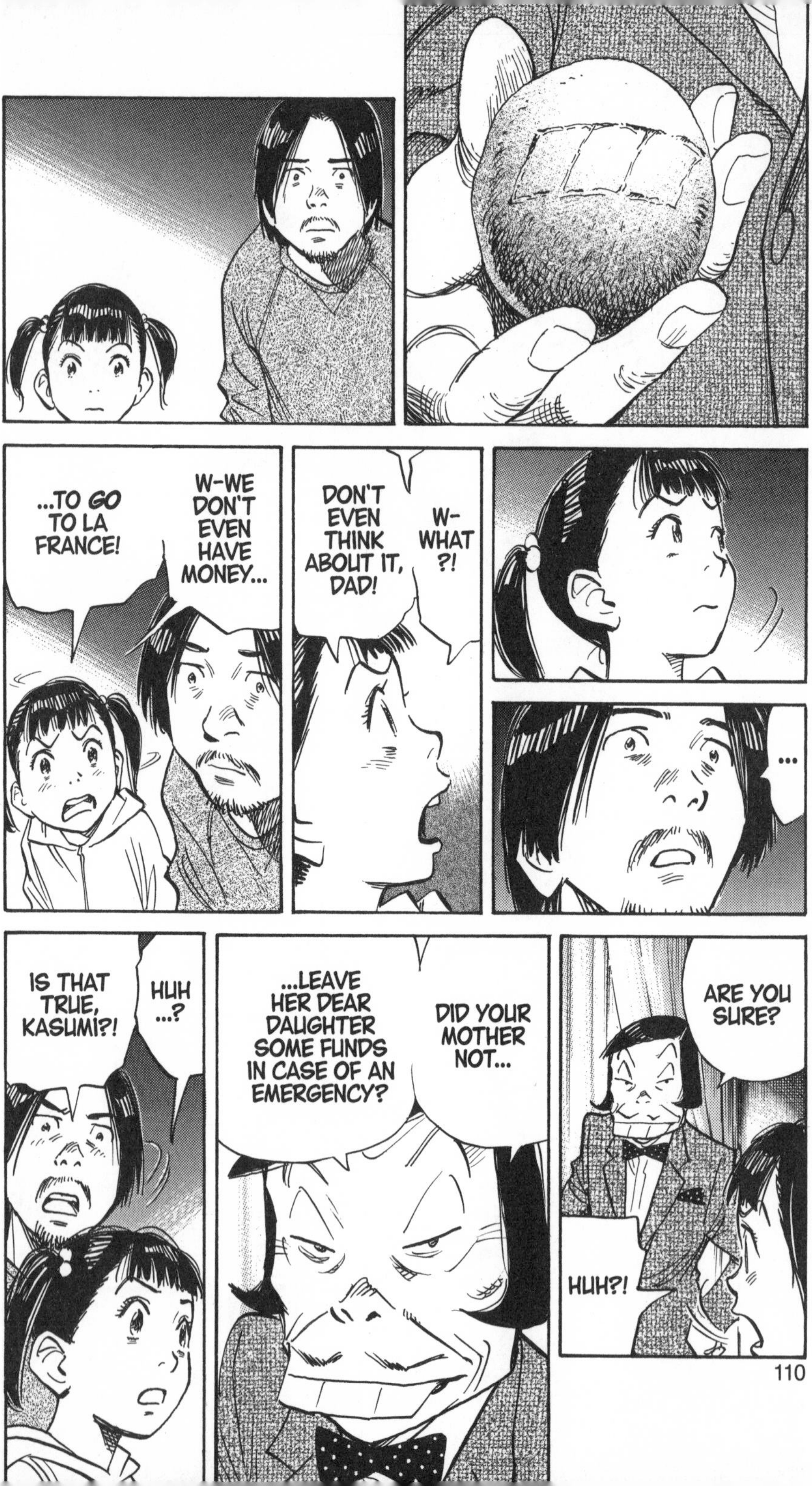
...
W-WHAT?!
DON'T EVEN THINK ABOUT IT, DAD!
W-WE DON'T EVEN HAVE MONEY...
...TO GO TO LA FRANCE!
ARE YOU SURE?
HUH?!
DID YOUR MOTHER NOT...
...LEAVE HER DEAR DAUGHTER SOME FUNDS IN CASE OF AN EMERGENCY?
HUH...?
IS THAT TRUE, KASUMI?!

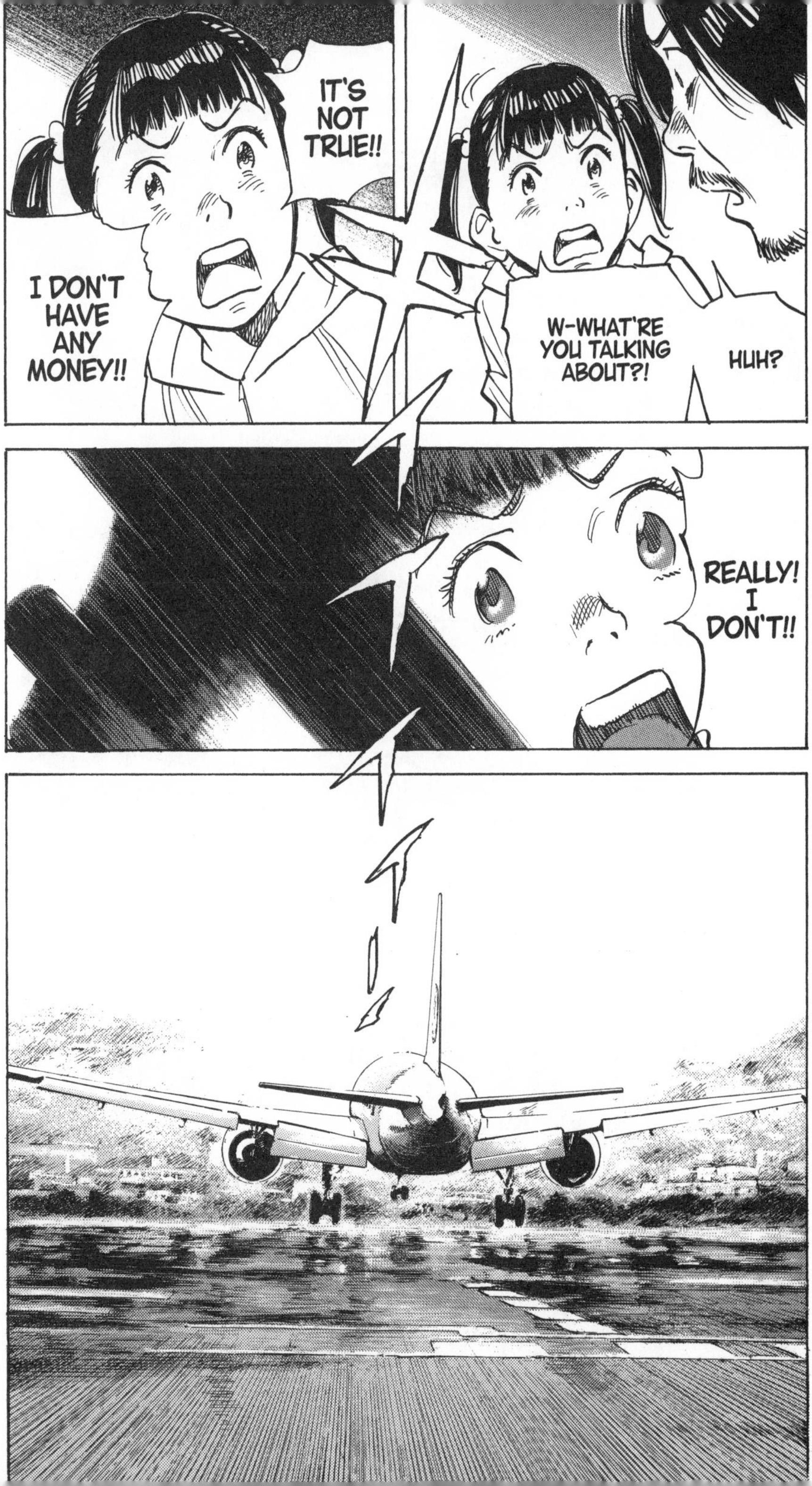
HUH?
W-WHAT'RE YOU TALKING ABOUT?!
IT'S NOT TRUE!!
I DON'T HAVE ANY MONEY!!
REALLY! I DON'T!!

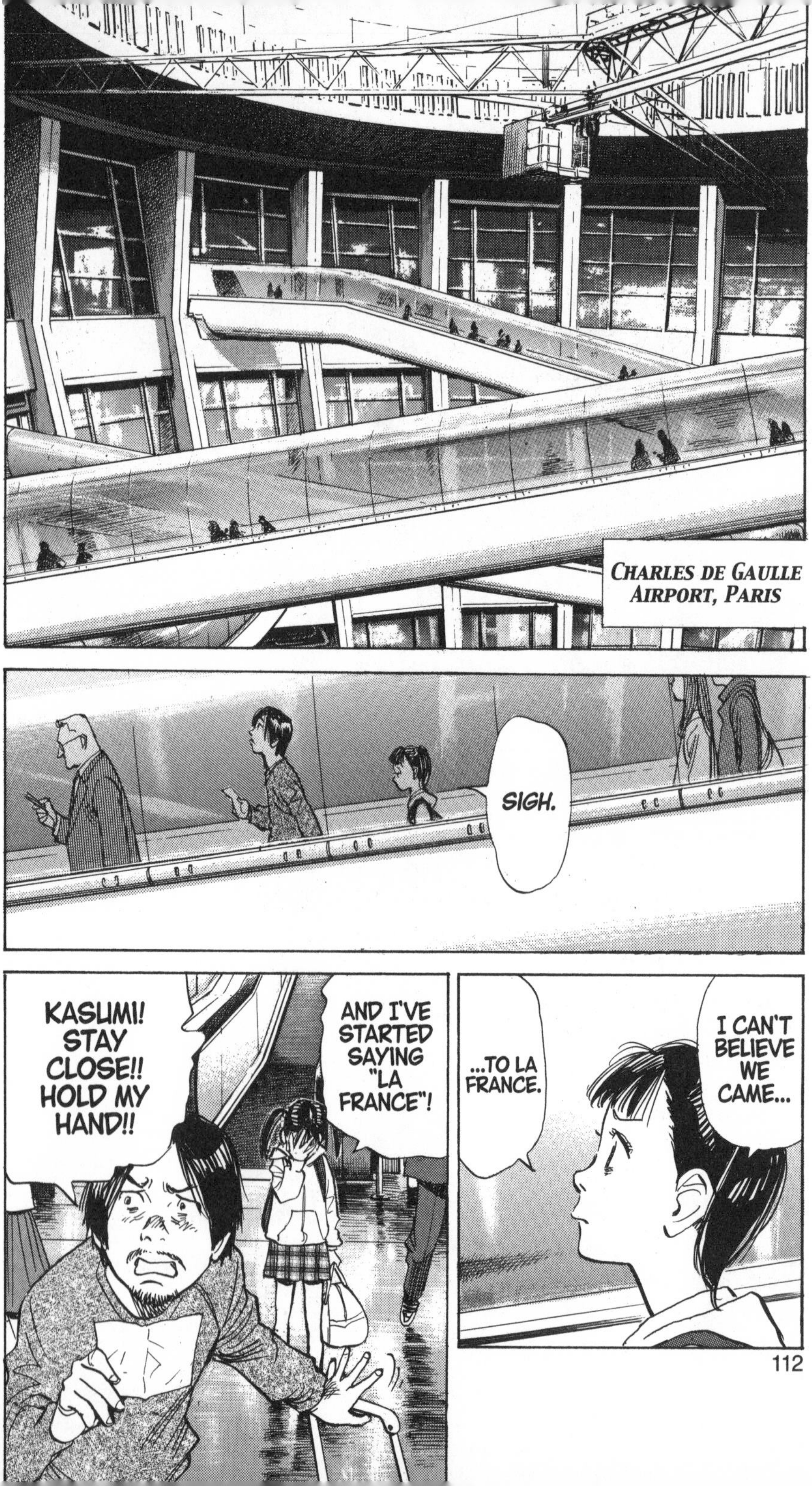
CHARLES DE GAULLE AIRPORT, PARIS
SIGH.
I CAN'T BELIEVE WE CAME...
...TO LA FRANCE.
AND I'VE STARTED SAYING "LA FRANCE"!
KASUMI! STAY CLOSE!! HOLD MY HAND!!

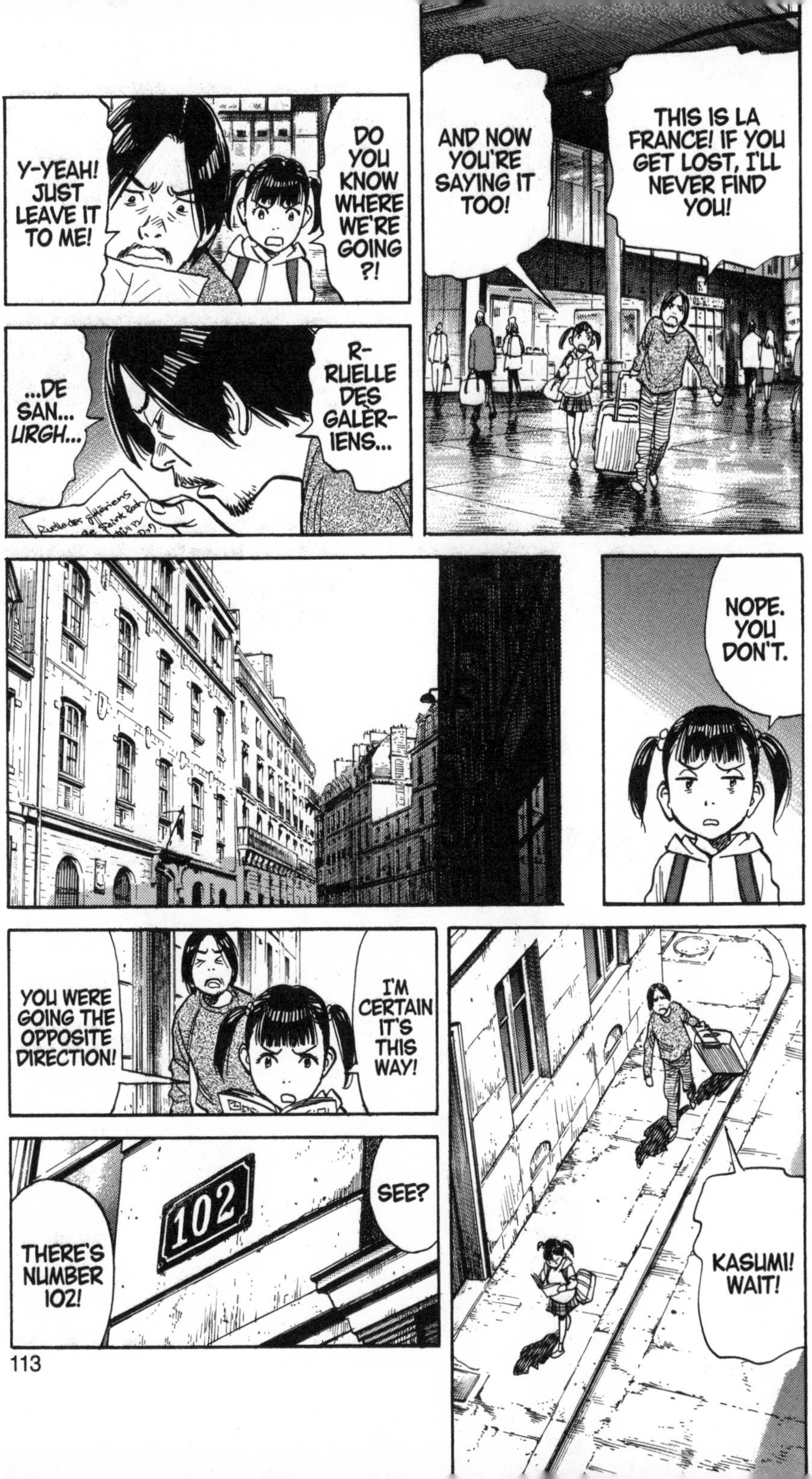
THIS IS LA FRANCE! IF YOU GET LOST, I'LL NEVER FIND YOU!
AND NOW YOU'RE SAYING IT TOO!
DO YOU KNOW WHERE WE'RE GOING?!
Y-YEAH! JUST LEAVE IT TO ME!
R-RUELLE DES GALÈRIENS...
...DE SAN... URGH...
NOPE. YOU DON'T.
KASUMI! WAIT!
I'M CERTAIN IT'S THIS WAY!
YOU WERE GOING THE OPPOSITE DIRECTION!
SEE?
102
THERE'S NUMBER 102!

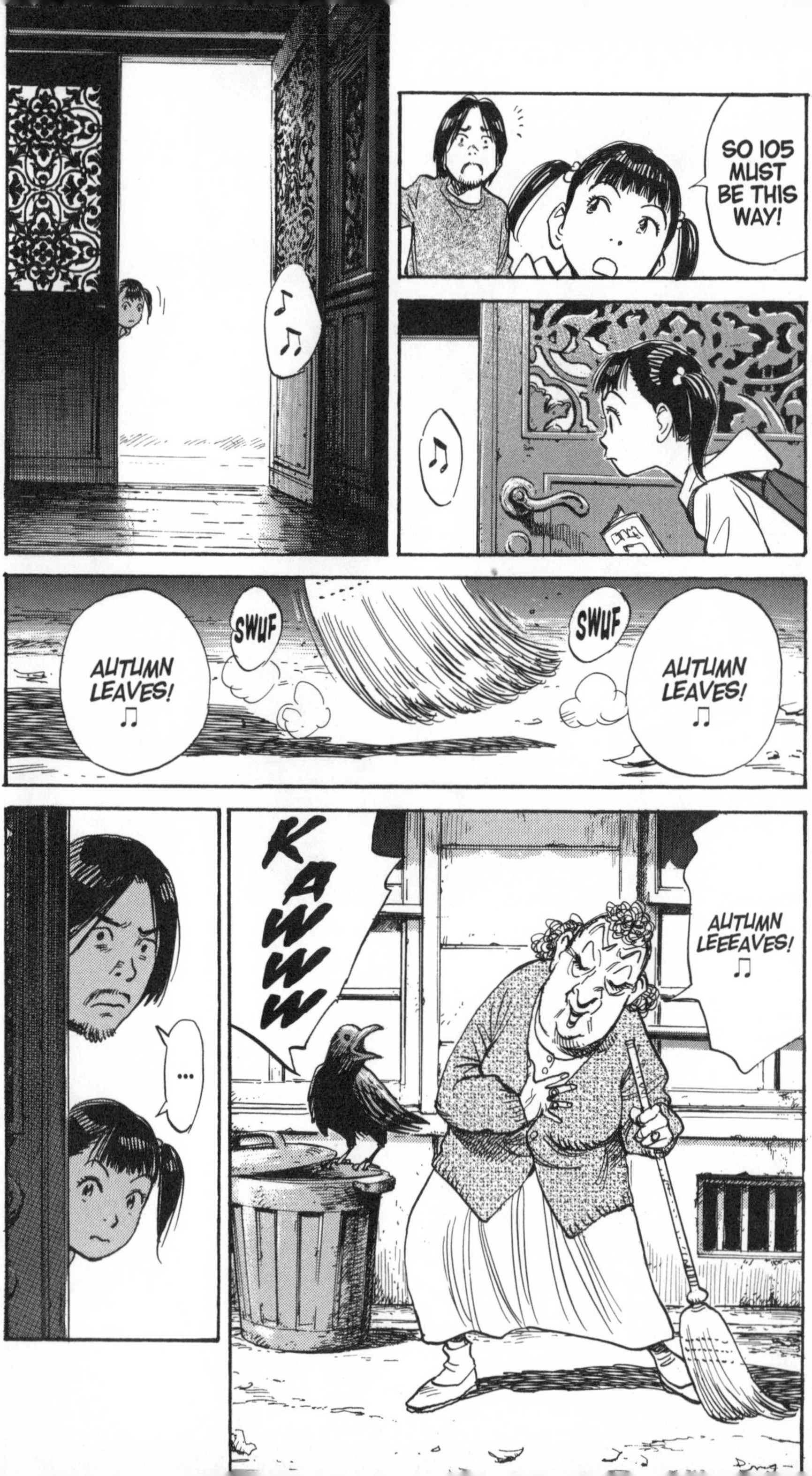
SO 105 MUST BE THIS WAY!
♫
♪ ♫
SWUF
AUTUMN LEAVES! ♫
SWUF
AUTUMN LEAVES! ♫
AUTUMN LEEEAVES! ♫
KAWWW
...

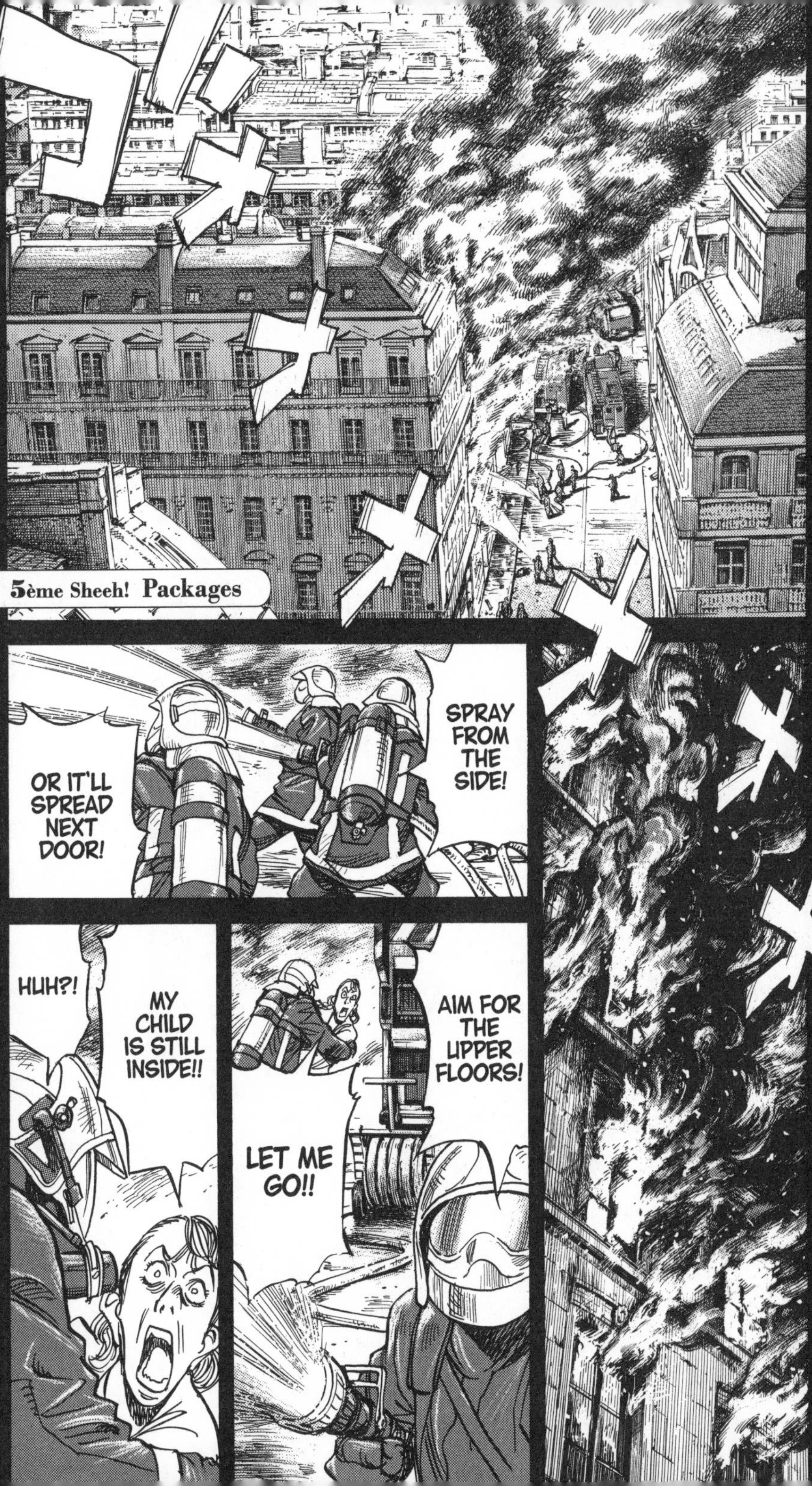
5ème Sheeh! Packages
SPRAY FROM THE SIDE!
OR IT'LL SPREAD NEXT DOOR!
AIM FOR THE UPPER FLOORS!
LET ME GO!!
MY CHILD IS STILL INSIDE!!
HUH?!

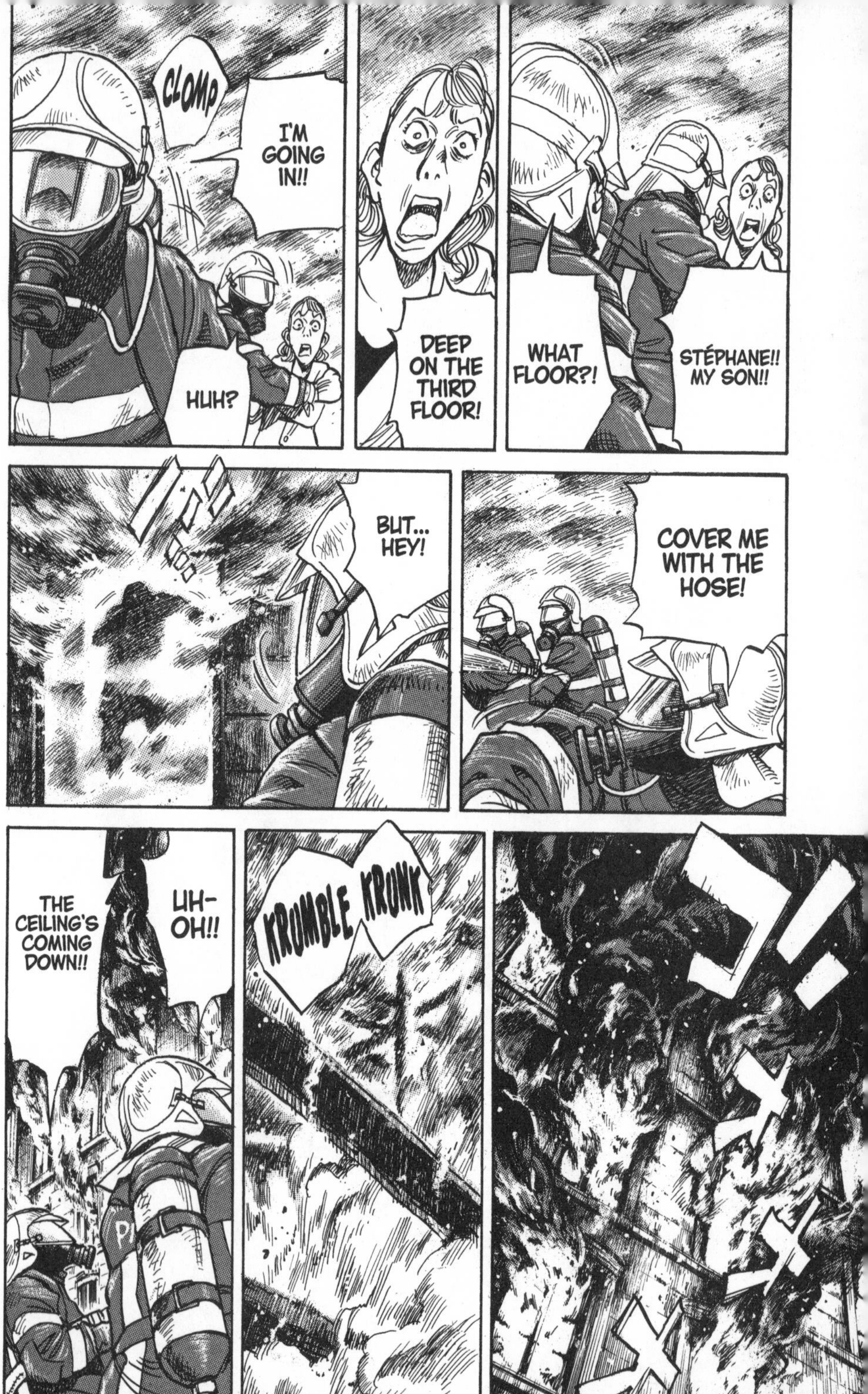
STÉPHANE!! MY SON!!
WHAT FLOOR?!
DEEP ON THE THIRD FLOOR!
CLOMP
I'M GOING IN!!
HUH?
COVER ME WITH THE HOSE!
BUT... HEY!
KRUNK
KRUMBLE
UH-OH!!
THE CEILING'S COMING DOWN!!

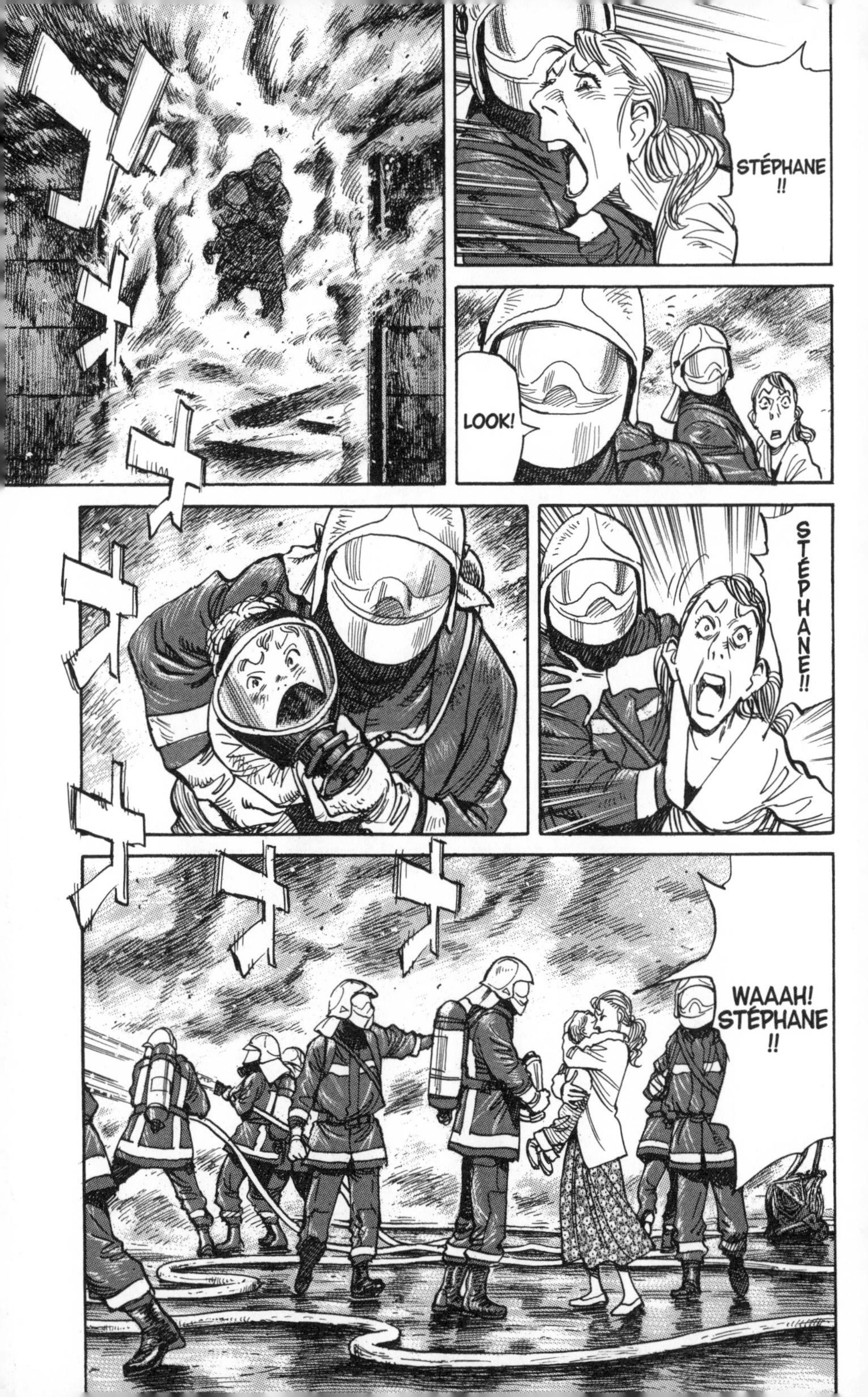
STÉPHANE!!
LOOK!
STÉPHANE!!
WAAAH! STÉPHANE!!

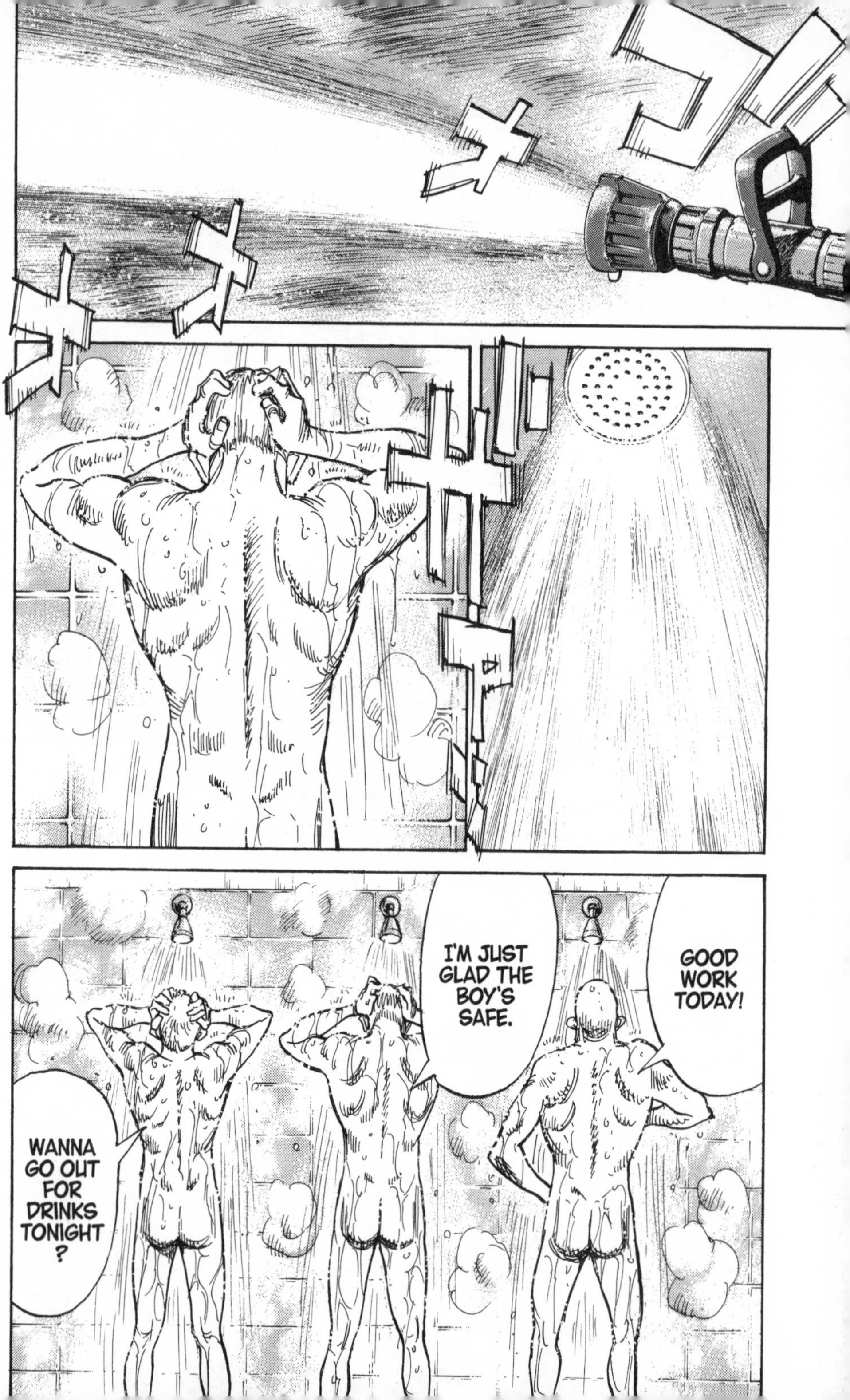
GOOD WORK TODAY!
I'M JUST GLAD THE BOY'S SAFE.
WANNA GO OUT FOR DRINKS TONIGHT?

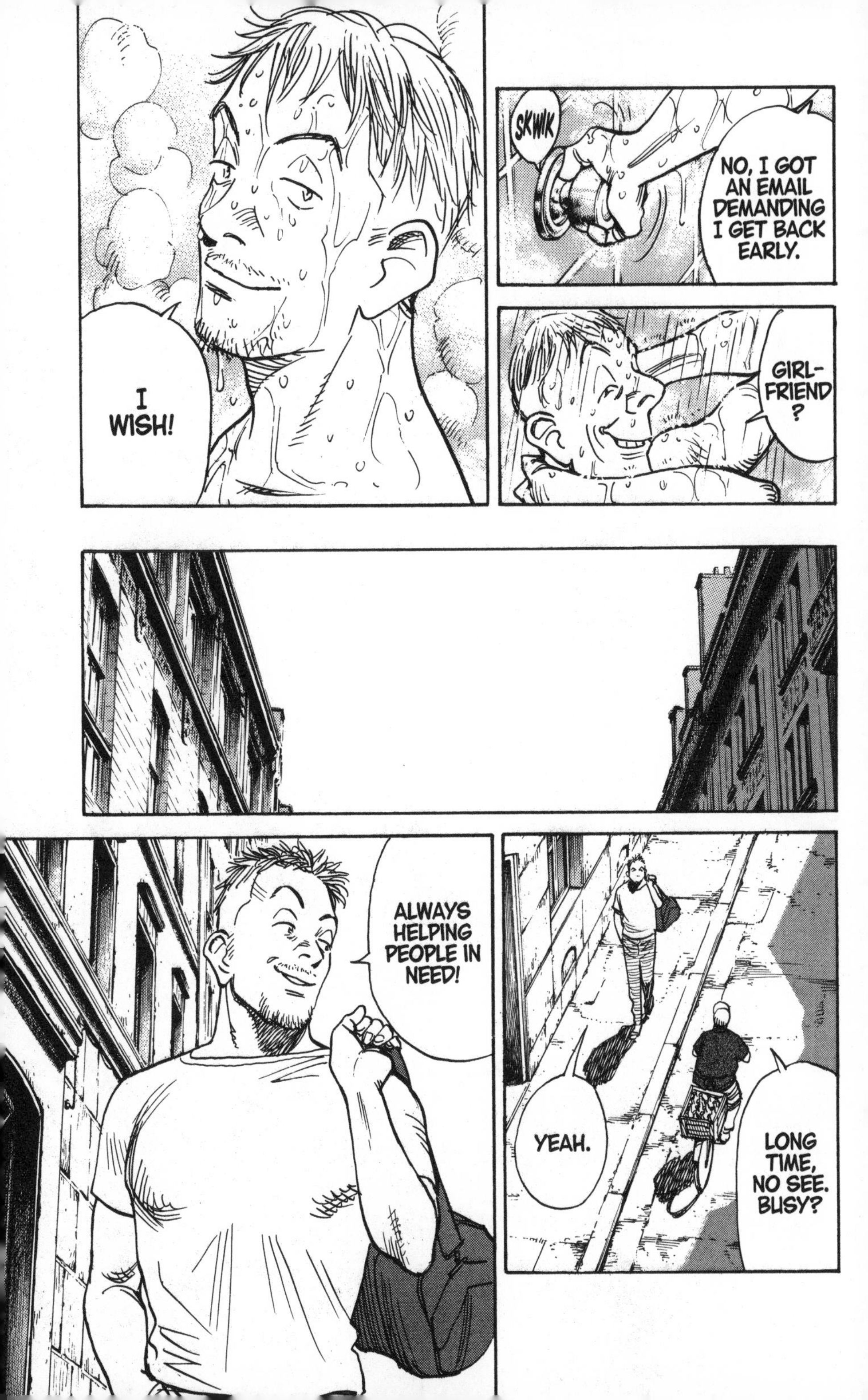
NO, I GOT AN EMAIL DEMANDING I GET BACK EARLY.
SKWIK
GIRL-FRIEND?
I WISH!
LONG TIME, NO SEE. BUSY?
YEAH.
ALWAYS HELPING PEOPLE IN NEED!

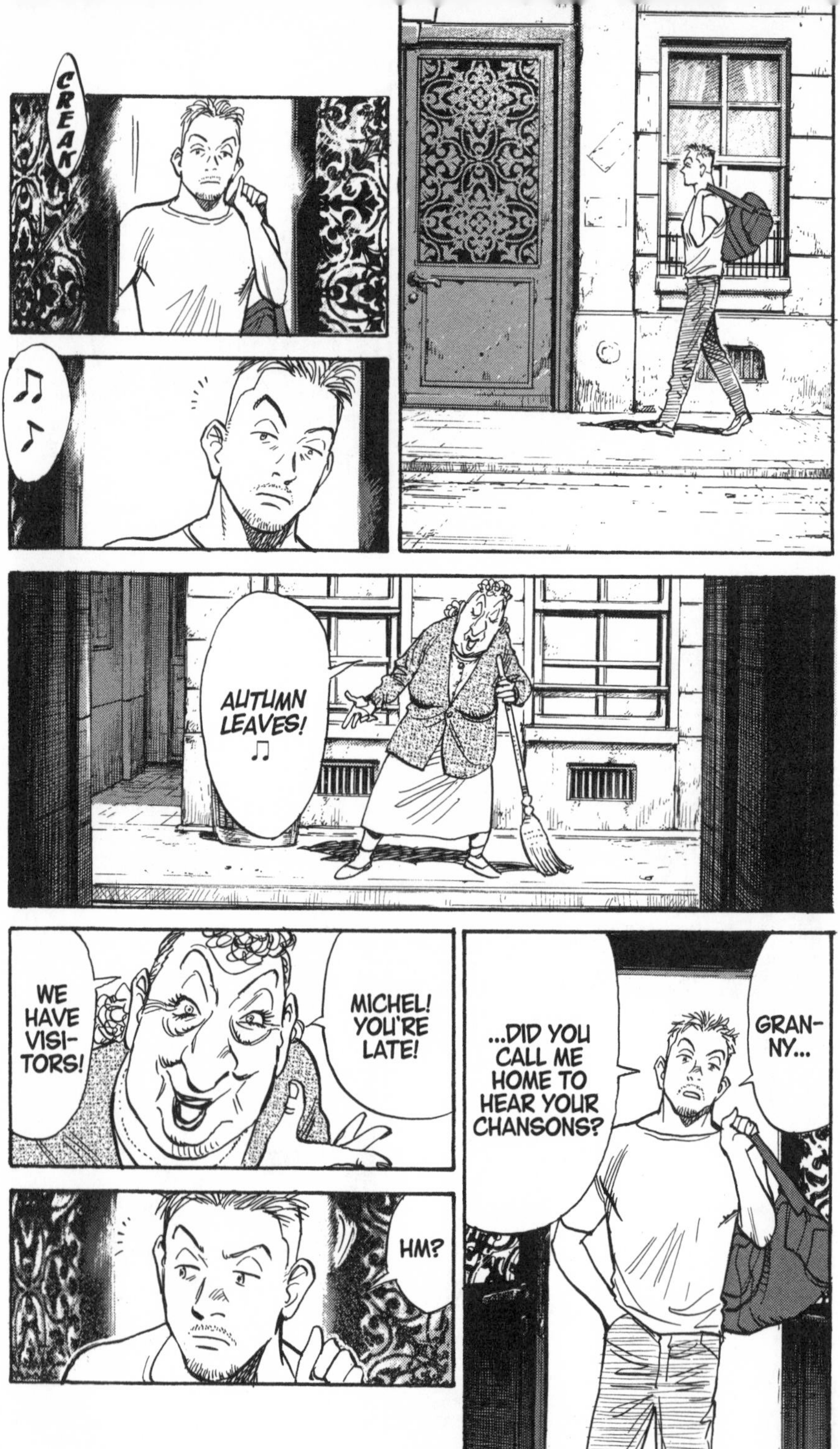
CREAK
♫ ♪
AUTUMN LEAVES! ♫
GRAN-NY...
...DID YOU CALL ME HOME TO HEAR YOUR CHANSONS?
MICHEL! YOU'RE LATE!
WE HAVE VISI-TORS!
HM?

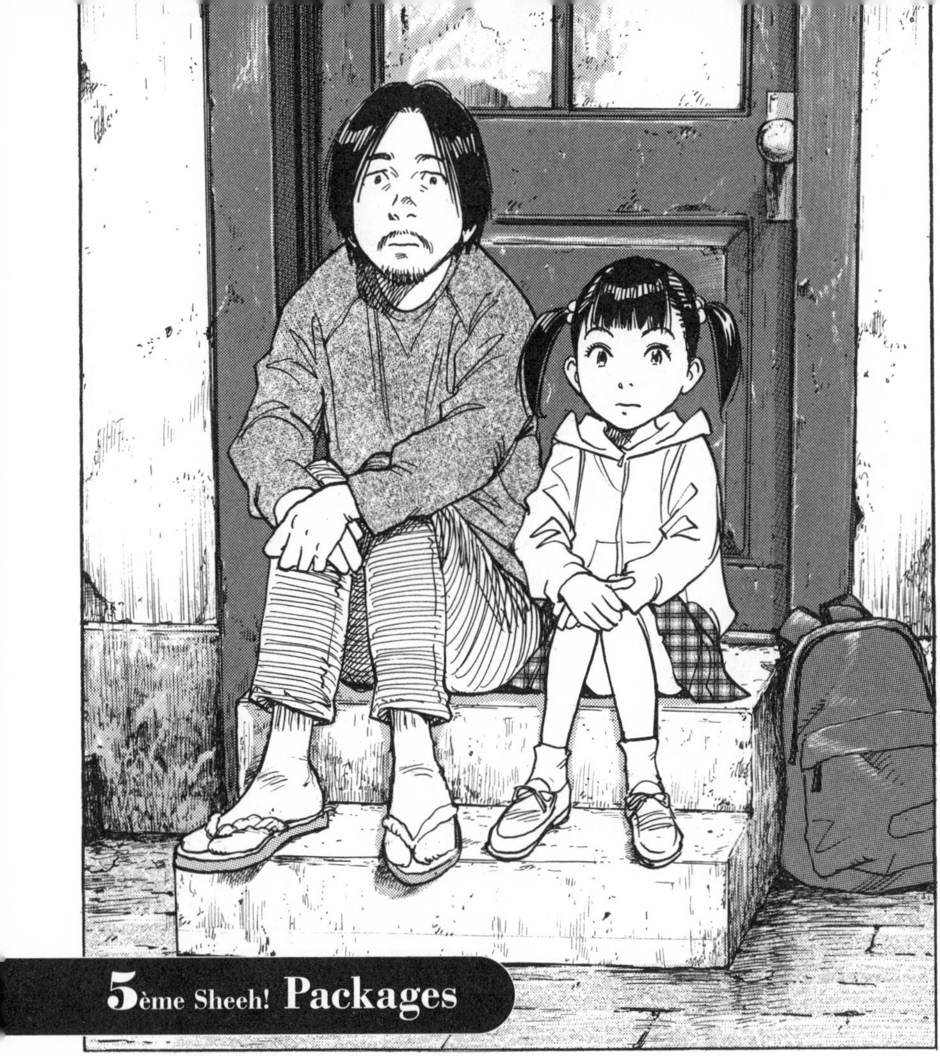
5ème Sheeh! Packages

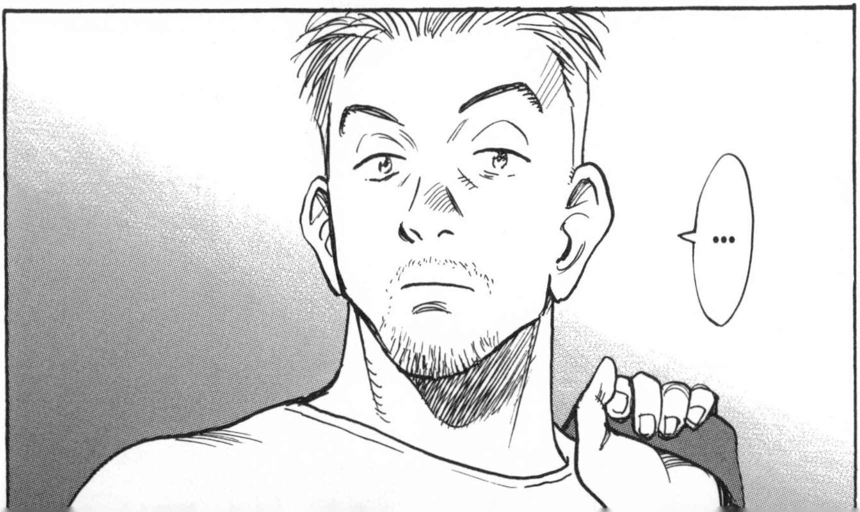
...

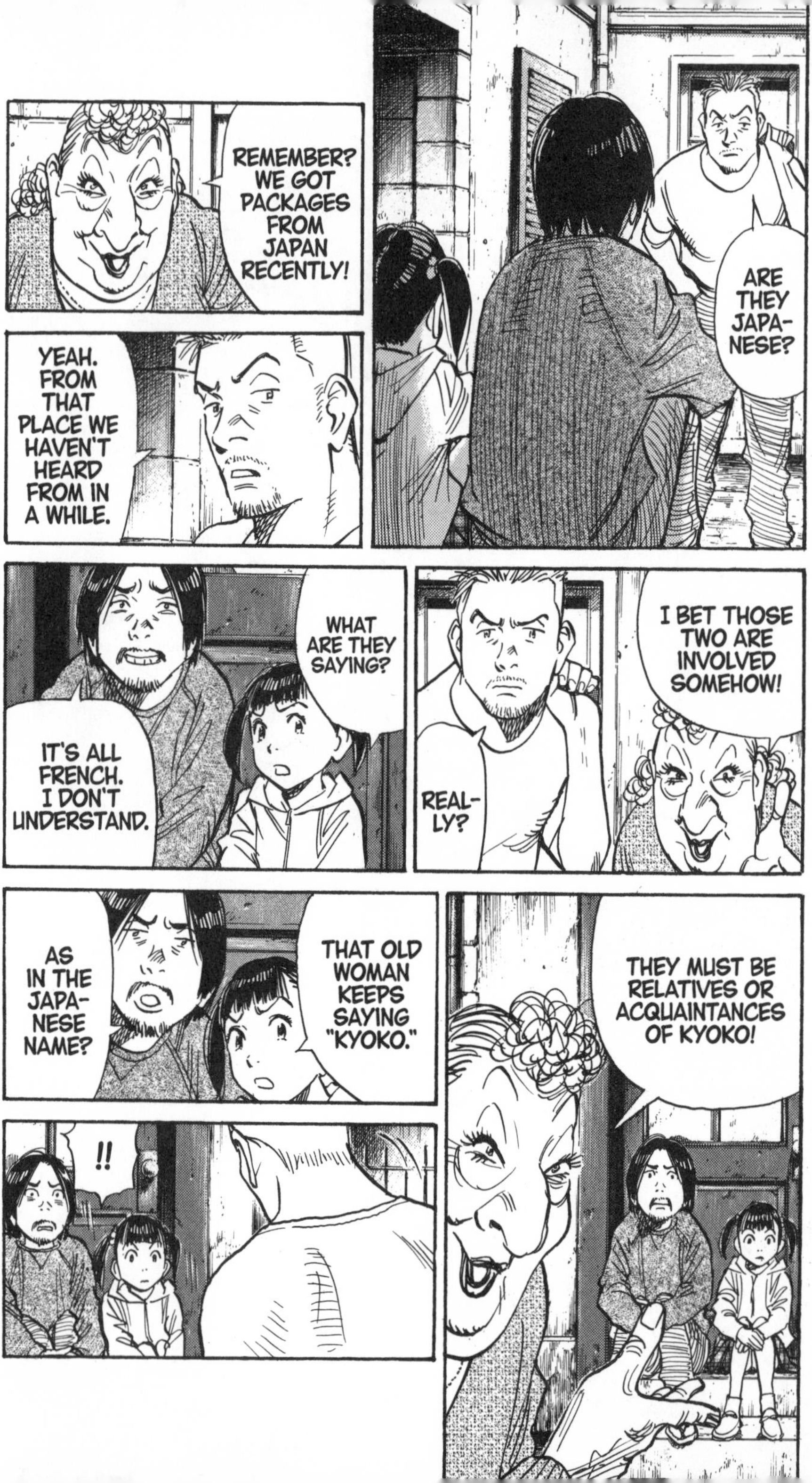
ARE THEY JAPANESE?
REMEMBER? WE GOT PACKAGES FROM JAPAN RECENTLY!
YEAH. FROM THAT PLACE WE HAVEN'T HEARD FROM IN A WHILE.
I BET THOSE TWO ARE INVOLVED SOMEHOW!
REALLY?
WHAT ARE THEY SAYING?
IT'S ALL FRENCH. I DON'T UNDERSTAND.
THEY MUST BE RELATIVES OR ACQUAINTANCES OF KYOKO!
THAT OLD WOMAN KEEPS SAYING "KYOKO."
AS IN THE JAPANESE NAME?
!!

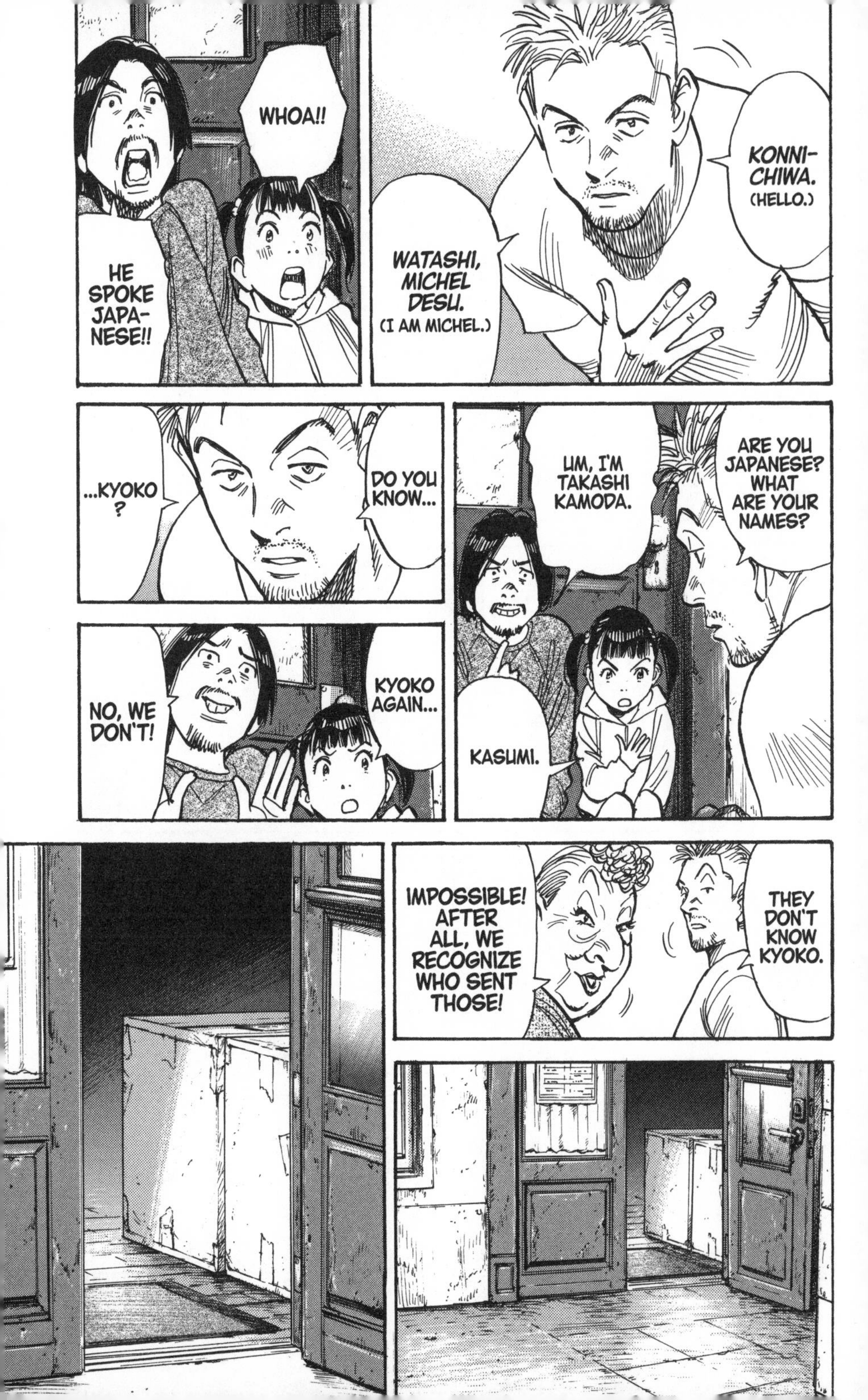
KONNI-CHIWA. (HELLO.)
WATASHI, MICHEL DESU. (I AM MICHEL.)
WHOA!!
HE SPOKE JAPA-NESE!!
ARE YOU JAPANESE? WHAT ARE YOUR NAMES?
UM, I'M TAKASHI KAMODA.
KASUMI.
DO YOU KNOW...
...KYOKO?
KYOKO AGAIN...
NO, WE DON'T!
THEY DON'T KNOW KYOKO.
IMPOSSIBLE! AFTER ALL, WE RECOGNIZE WHO SENT THOSE!

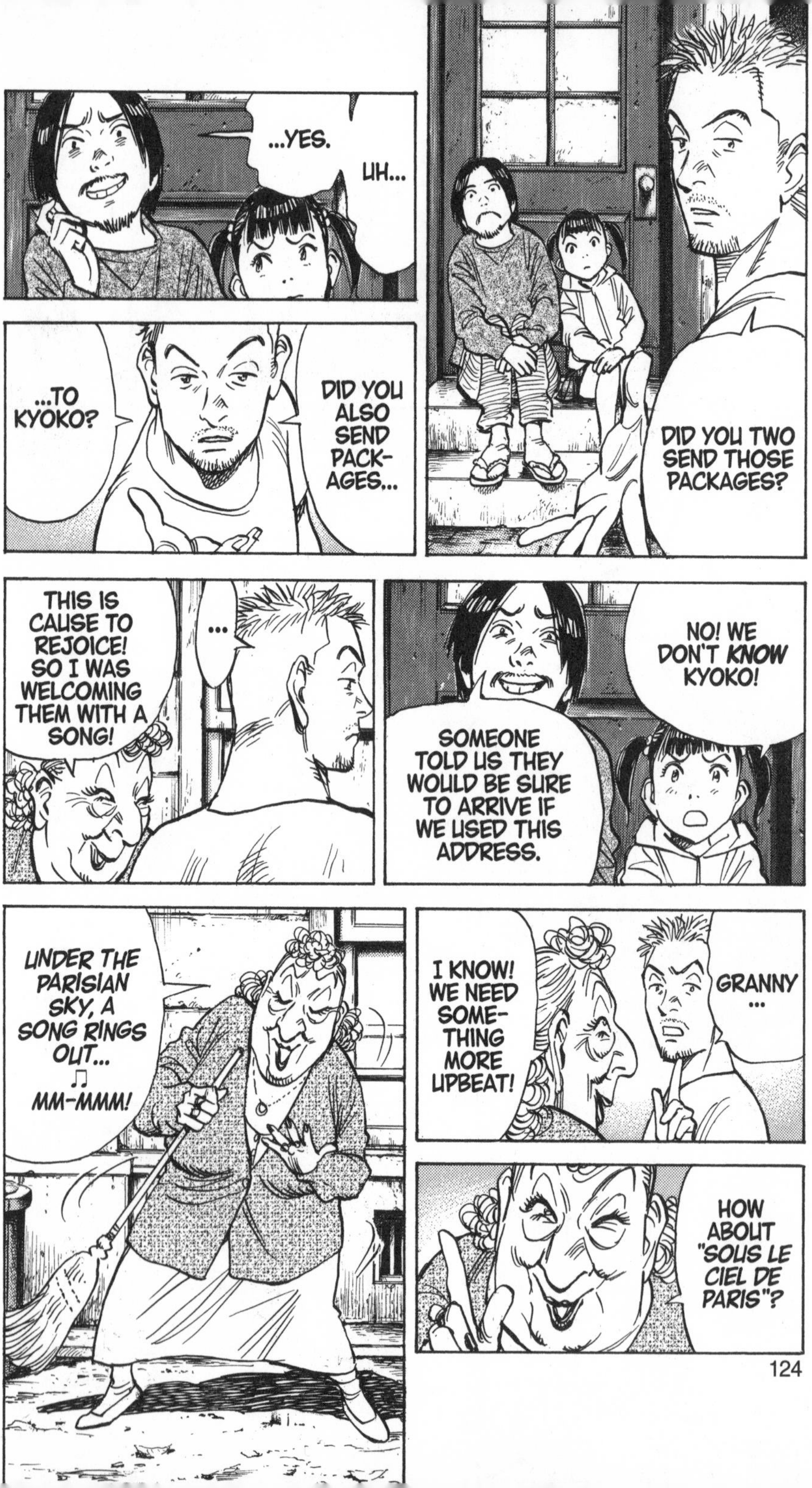
DID YOU TWO SEND THOSE PACKAGES?
UH...
...YES.
DID YOU ALSO SEND PACKAGES...
...TO KYOKO?
NO! WE DON'T *KNOW* KYOKO!
SOMEONE TOLD US THEY WOULD BE SURE TO ARRIVE IF WE USED THIS ADDRESS.
...
THIS IS CAUSE TO REJOICE! SO I WAS WELCOMING THEM WITH A SONG!
GRANNY...
I KNOW! WE NEED SOMETHING MORE UPBEAT!
HOW ABOUT "SOUS LE CIEL DE PARIS"?
UNDER THE PARISIAN SKY, A SONG RINGS OUT... ♫ MM-MMM!

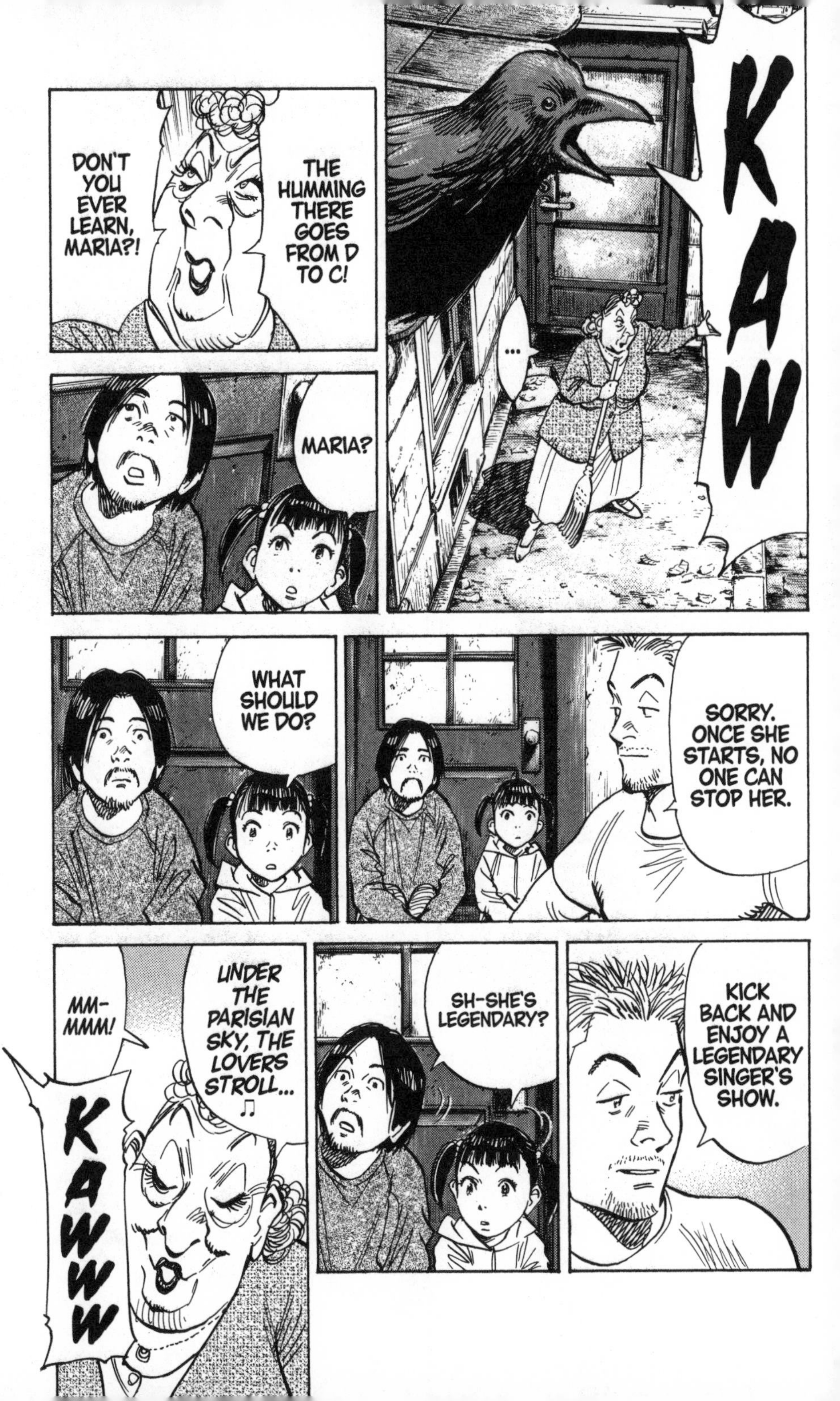
KAW
...
THE HUMMING THERE GOES FROM D TO C!
DON'T YOU EVER LEARN, MARIA?!
MARIA?
SORRY. ONCE SHE STARTS, NO ONE CAN STOP HER.
WHAT SHOULD WE DO?
KICK BACK AND ENJOY A LEGENDARY SINGER'S SHOW.
SH-SHE'S LEGENDARY?
UNDER THE PARISIAN SKY, THE LOVERS STROLL... ♫
MM-MMM!
KAWWW

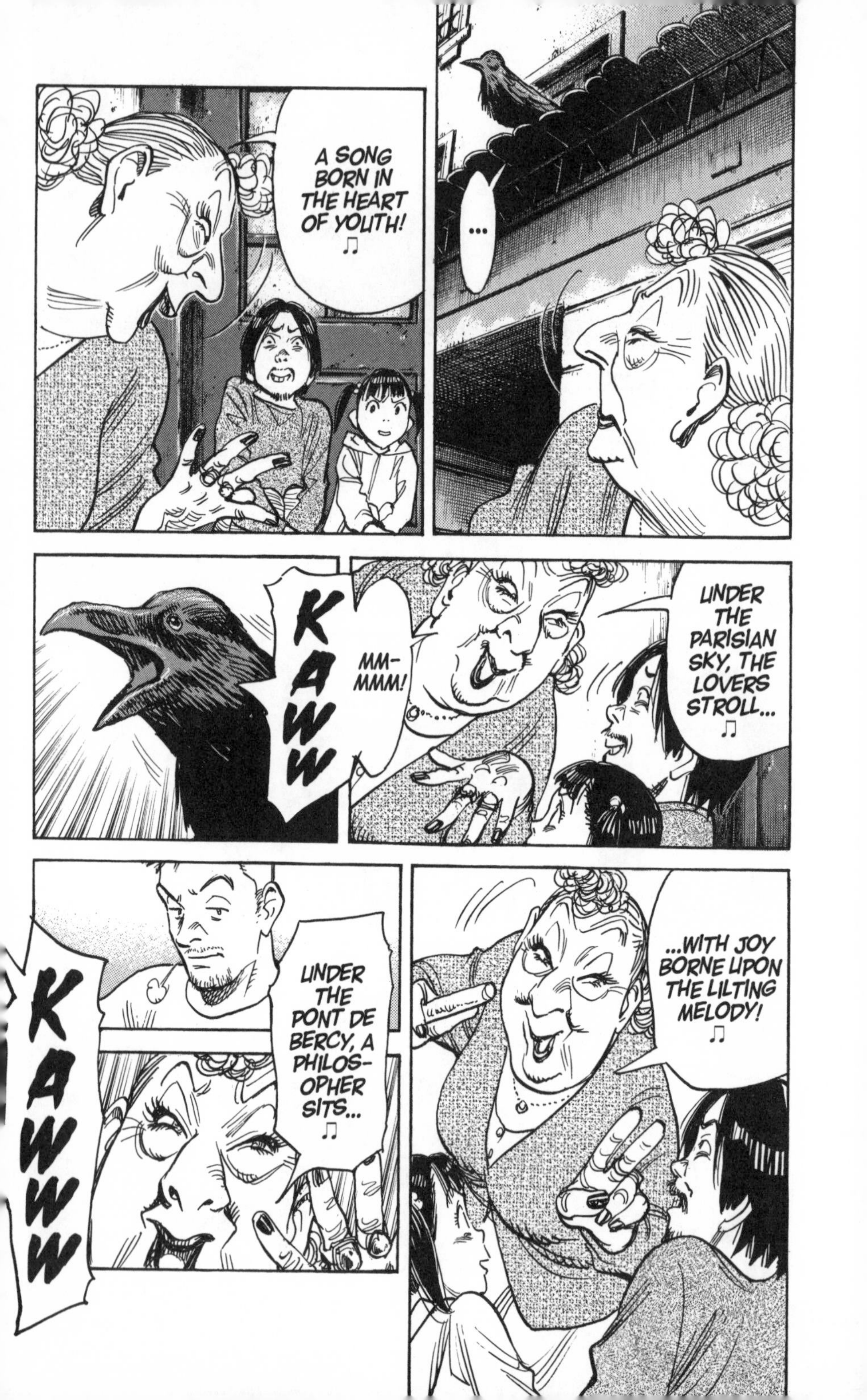
...
A SONG BORN IN THE HEART OF YOUTH! ♫
UNDER THE PARISIAN SKY, THE LOVERS STROLL... ♫
MM-MMM!
KAWW
...WITH JOY BORNE UPON THE LILTING MELODY! ♫
UNDER THE PONT DE BERCY, A PHILOSOPHER SITS... ♫
KAWWW

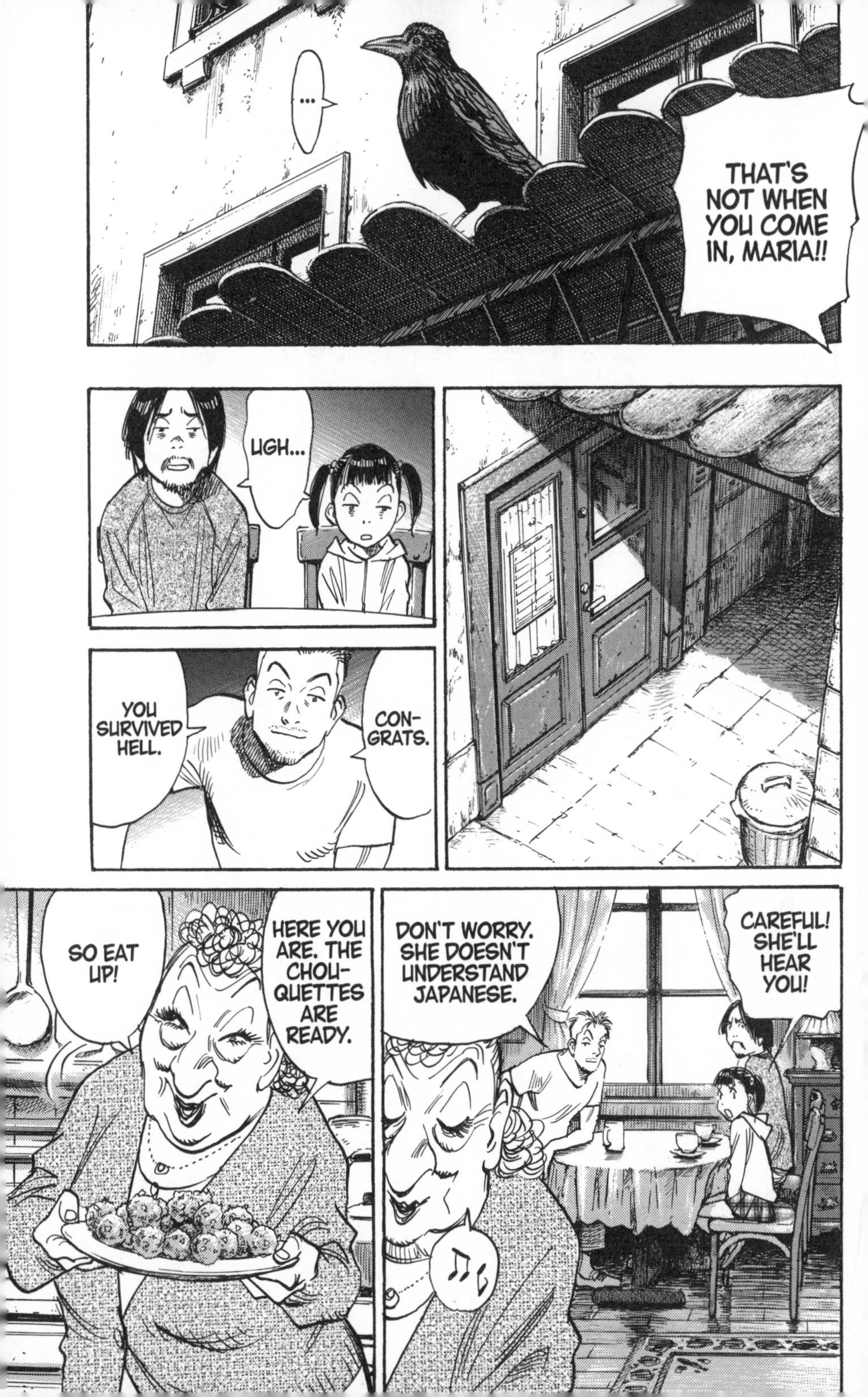
THAT'S NOT WHEN YOU COME IN, MARIA!!
...
UGH...
CON-GRATS.
YOU SURVIVED HELL.
CAREFUL! SHE'LL HEAR YOU!
DON'T WORRY. SHE DOESN'T UNDERSTAND JAPANESE.
HERE YOU ARE. THE CHOU-QUETTES ARE READY.
SO EAT UP!

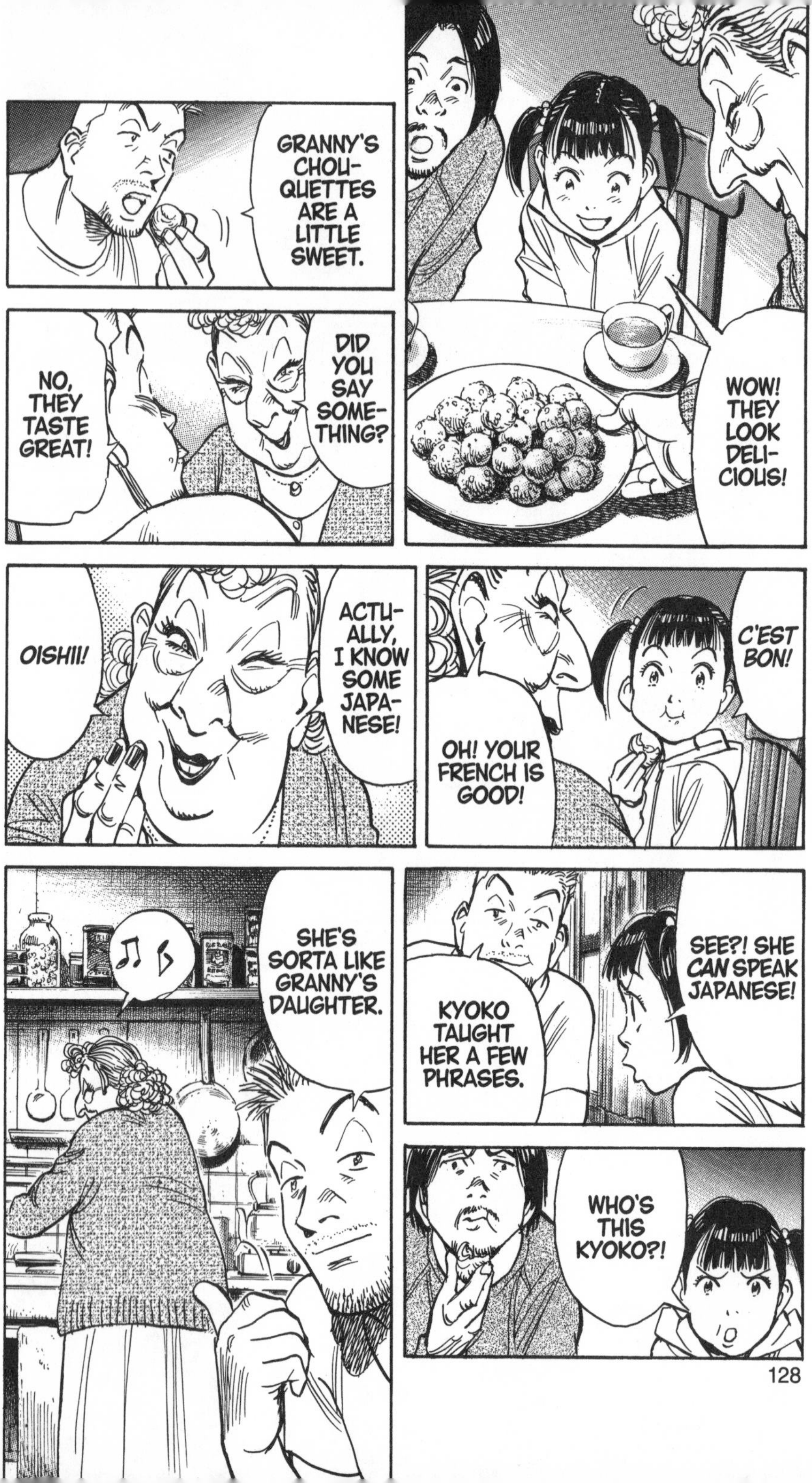
WOW! THEY LOOK DELICIOUS!
GRANNY'S CHOUQUETTES ARE A LITTLE SWEET.
DID YOU SAY SOMETHING?
NO, THEY TASTE GREAT!
C'EST BON!
OH! YOUR FRENCH IS GOOD!
ACTUALLY, I KNOW SOME JAPANESE!
OISHII!
SEE?! SHE CAN SPEAK JAPANESE!
KYOKO TAUGHT HER A FEW PHRASES.
WHO'S THIS KYOKO?!
SHE'S SORTA LIKE GRANNY'S DAUGHTER.

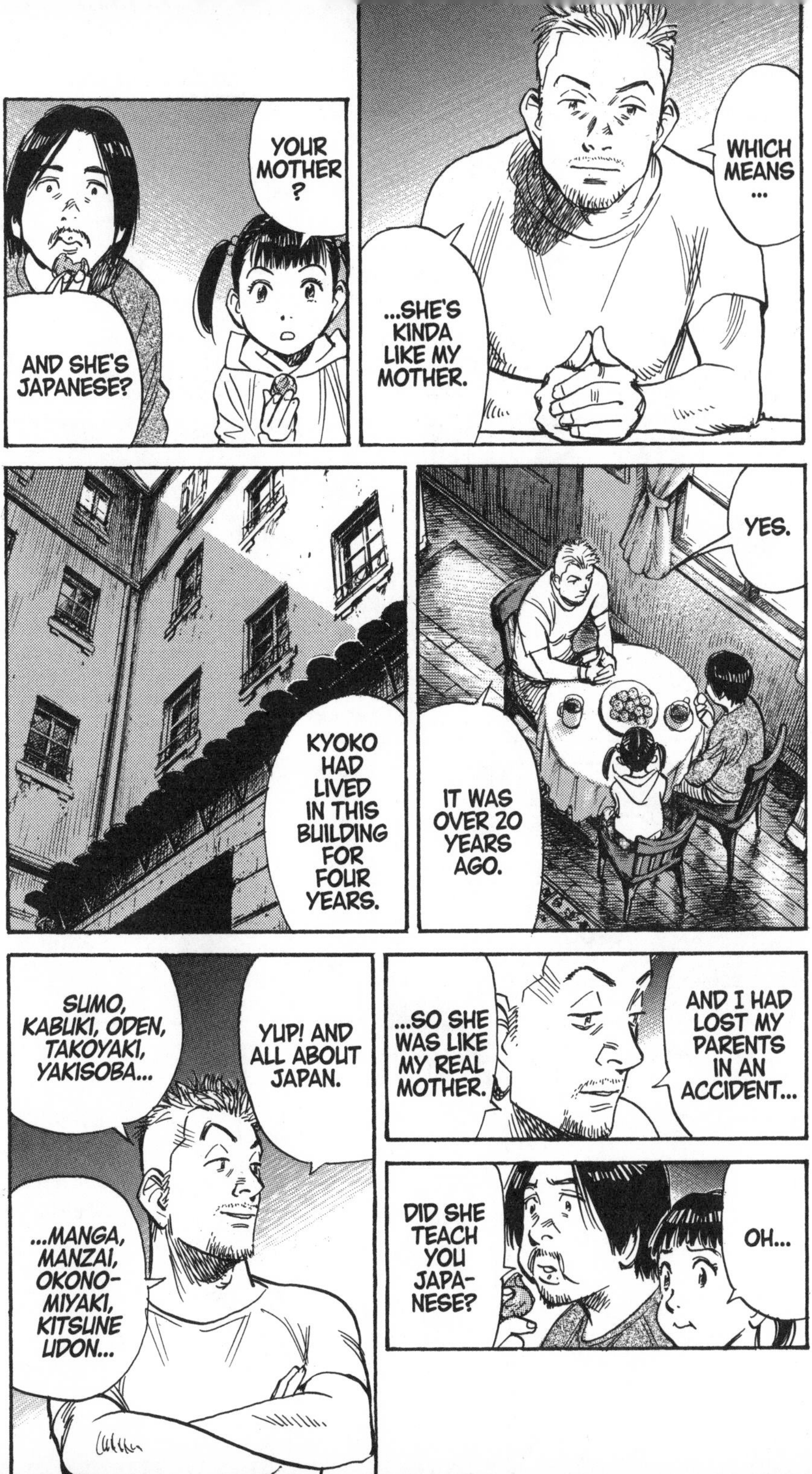
WHICH MEANS...
...SHE'S KINDA LIKE MY MOTHER.
YOUR MOTHER?
AND SHE'S JAPANESE?
YES.
IT WAS OVER 20 YEARS AGO.
KYOKO HAD LIVED IN THIS BUILDING FOR FOUR YEARS.
AND I HAD LOST MY PARENTS IN AN ACCIDENT...
...SO SHE WAS LIKE MY REAL MOTHER.
OH...
DID SHE TEACH YOU JAPA-NESE?
YUP! AND ALL ABOUT JAPAN.
SUMO, KABUKI, ODEN, TAKOYAKI, YAKISOBA...
...MANGA, MANZAI, OKONO-MIYAKI, KITSUNE UDON...

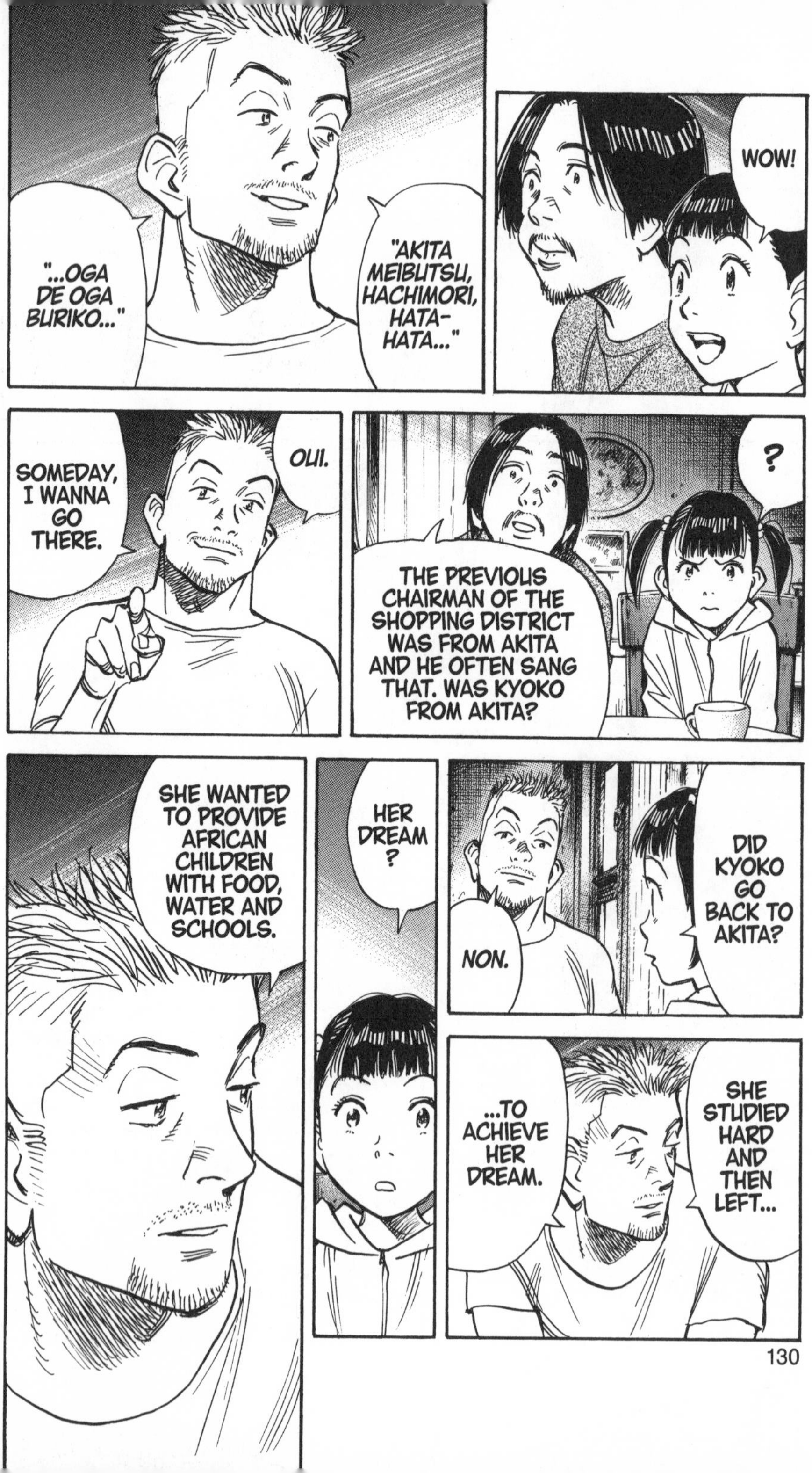
WOW!
"AKITA MEIBUTSU, HACHIMORI, HATA-HATA..."
"...OGA DE OGA BURIKO..."
?
THE PREVIOUS CHAIRMAN OF THE SHOPPING DISTRICT WAS FROM AKITA AND HE OFTEN SANG THAT. WAS KYOKO FROM AKITA?
OUI.
SOMEDAY, I WANNA GO THERE.
DID KYOKO GO BACK TO AKITA?
NON.
SHE STUDIED HARD AND THEN LEFT...
...TO ACHIEVE HER DREAM.
HER DREAM?
SHE WANTED TO PROVIDE AFRICAN CHILDREN WITH FOOD, WATER AND SCHOOLS.

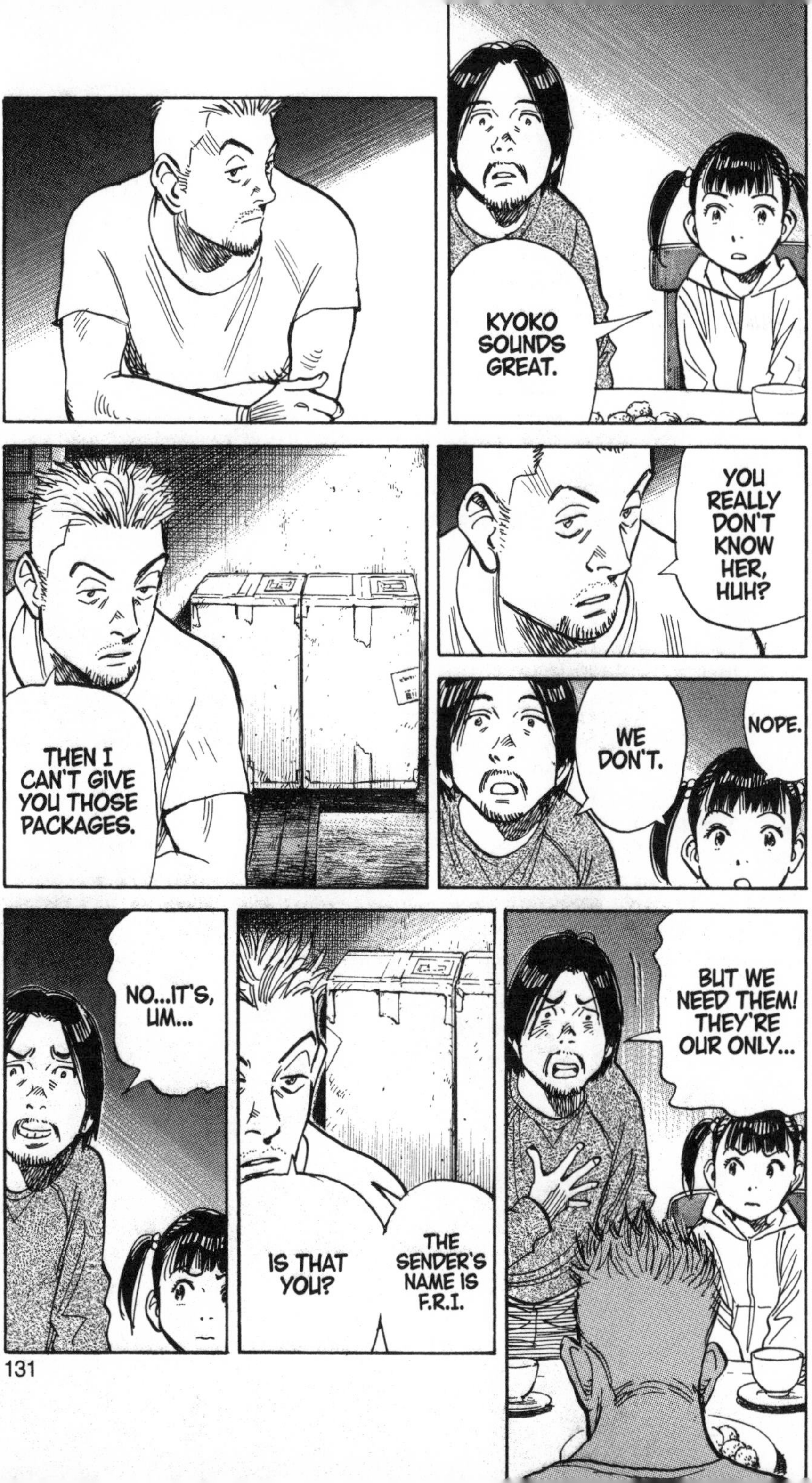
KYOKO SOUNDS GREAT.
YOU REALLY DON'T KNOW HER, HUH?
NOPE.
WE DON'T.
THEN I CAN'T GIVE YOU THOSE PACKAGES.
BUT WE NEED THEM! THEY'RE OUR ONLY...
THE SENDER'S NAME IS F.R.I.
IS THAT YOU?
NO...IT'S, UM...

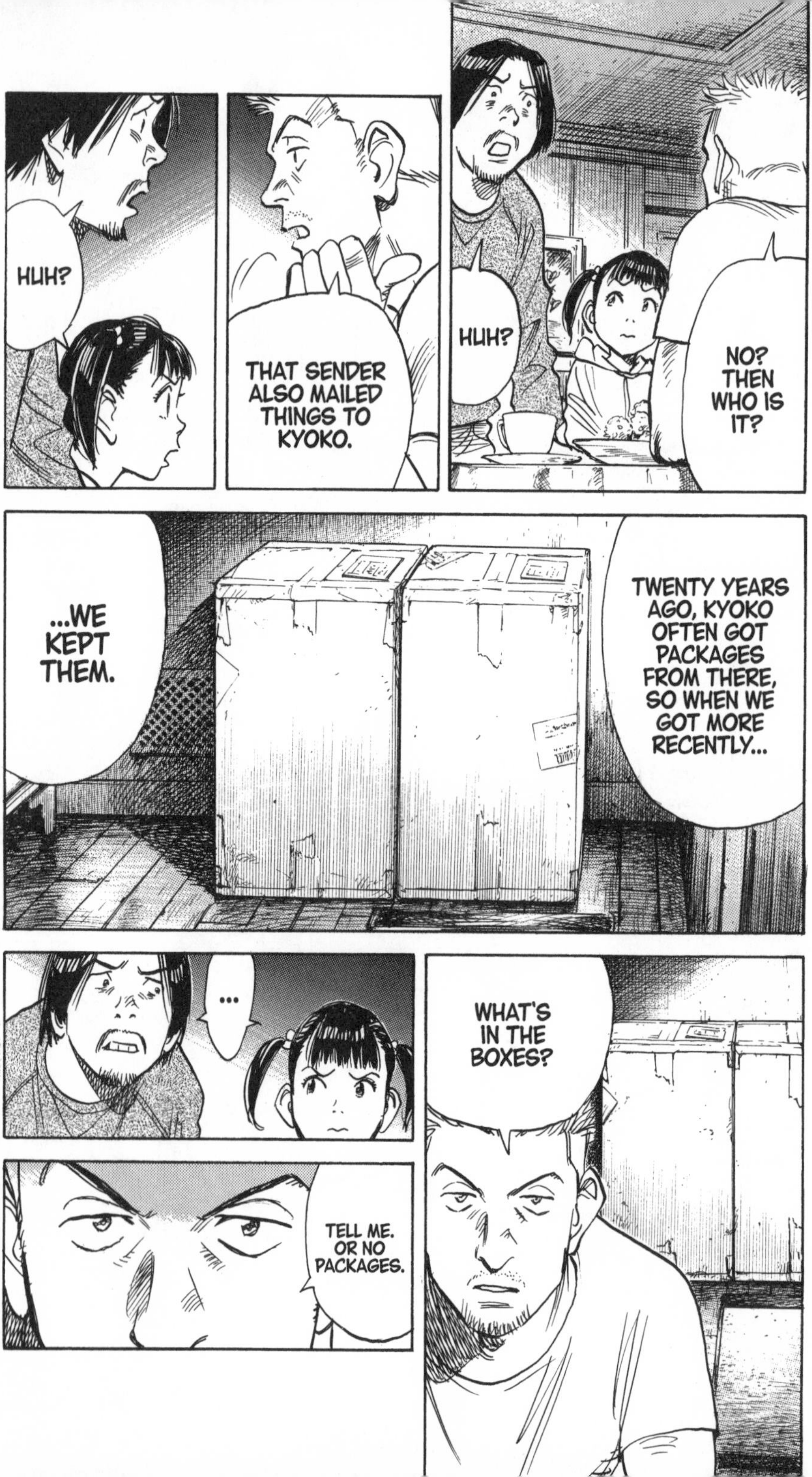
NO? THEN WHO IS IT?
HUH?
THAT SENDER ALSO MAILED THINGS TO KYOKO.
HUH?
TWENTY YEARS AGO, KYOKO OFTEN GOT PACKAGES FROM THERE, SO WHEN WE GOT MORE RECENTLY...
...WE KEPT THEM.
WHAT'S IN THE BOXES?
...
TELL ME. OR NO PACKAGES.

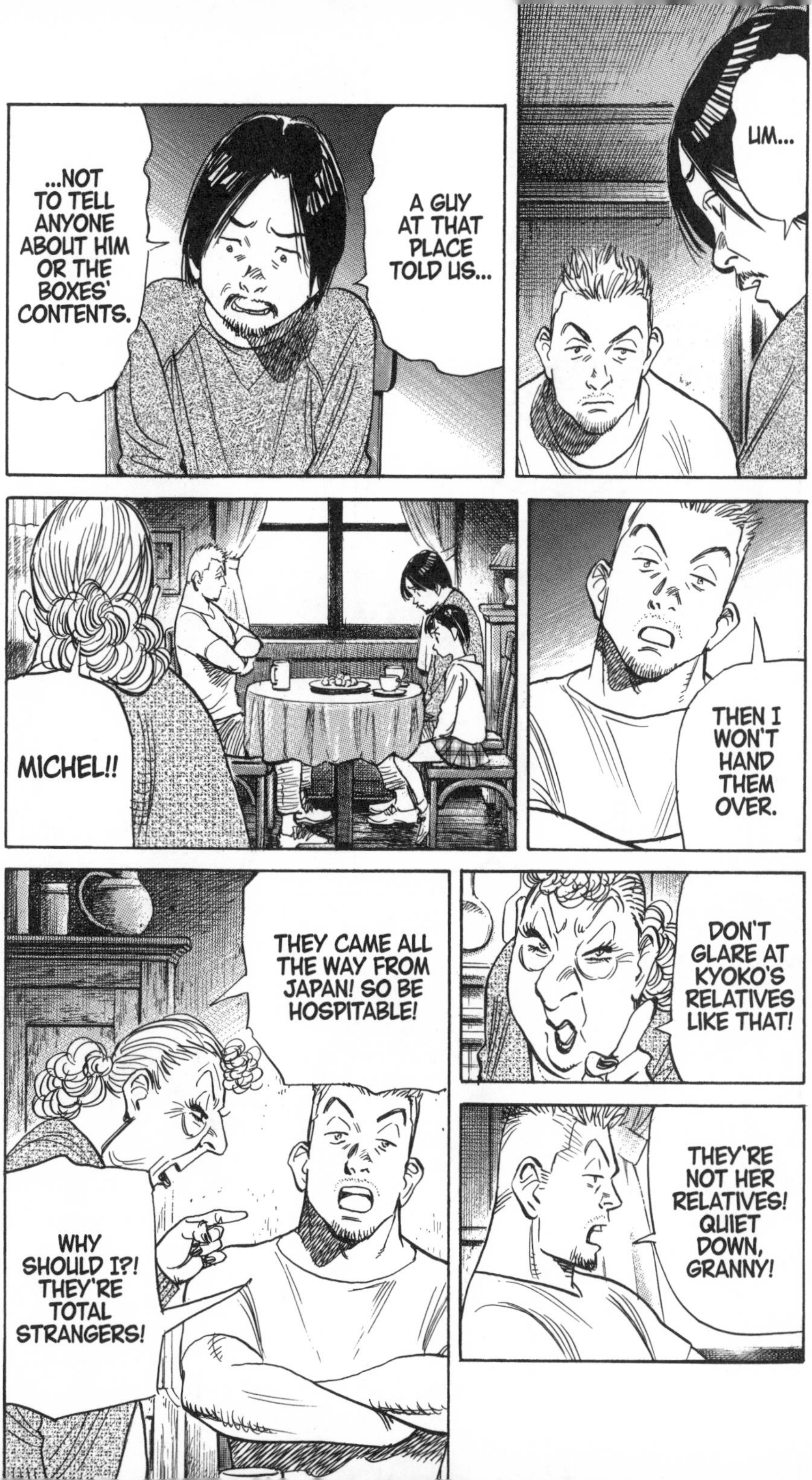
UM...
A GUY AT THAT PLACE TOLD US...
...NOT TO TELL ANYONE ABOUT HIM OR THE BOXES' CONTENTS.
THEN I WON'T HAND THEM OVER.
MICHEL!!
DON'T GLARE AT KYOKO'S RELATIVES LIKE THAT!
THEY'RE NOT HER RELATIVES! QUIET DOWN, GRANNY!
THEY CAME ALL THE WAY FROM JAPAN! SO BE HOSPITABLE!
WHY SHOULD I?! THEY'RE TOTAL STRANGERS!

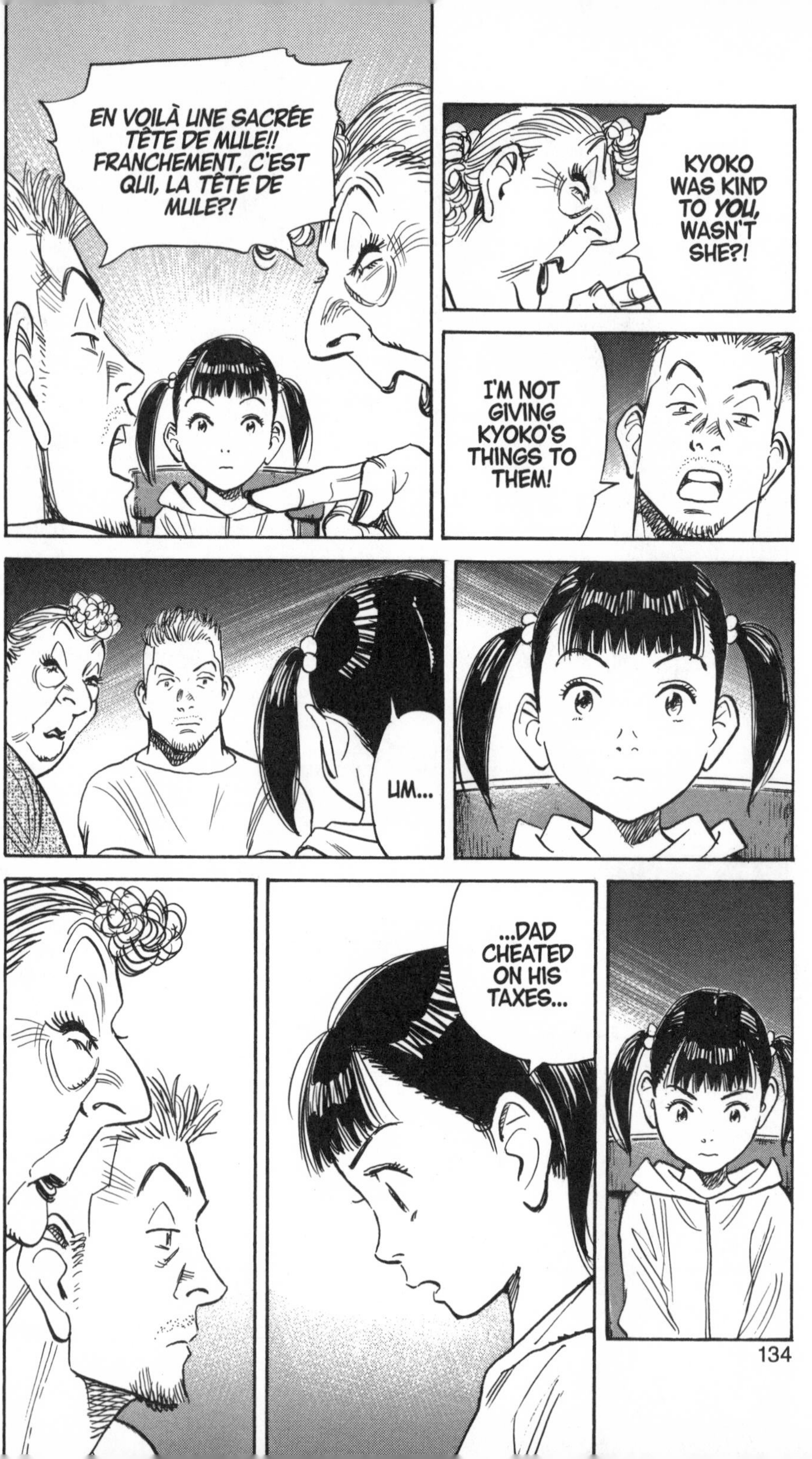
KYOKO WAS KIND TO *YOU*, WASN'T SHE?!
I'M NOT GIVING KYOKO'S THINGS TO THEM!
EN VOILÀ UNE SACRÉE TÊTE DE MULE!! FRANCHEMENT, C'EST QUI, LA TÊTE DE MULE?!
UM...
...DAD CHEATED ON HIS TAXES...

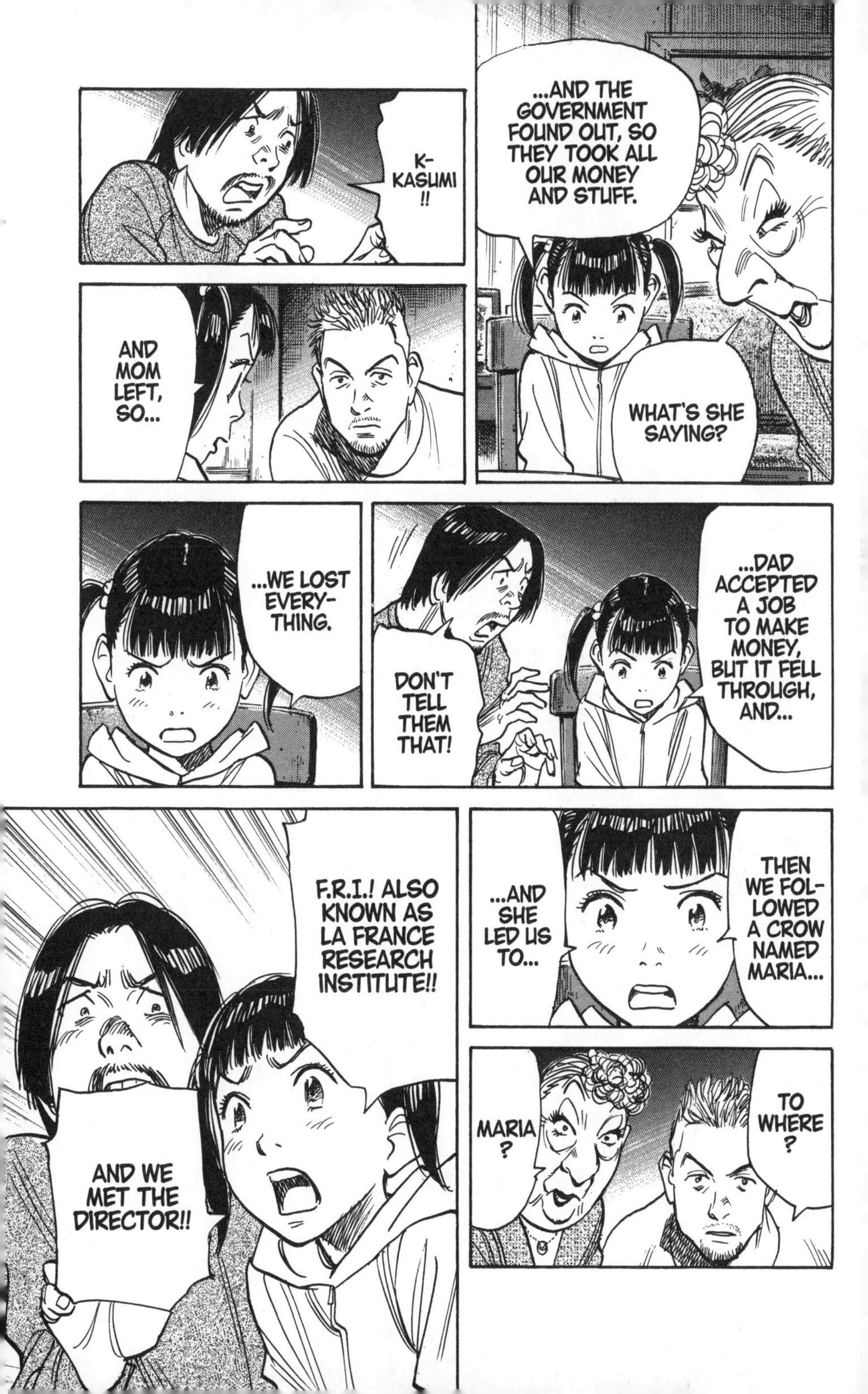
...AND THE GOVERNMENT FOUND OUT, SO THEY TOOK ALL OUR MONEY AND STUFF.
WHAT'S SHE SAYING?
K-KASUMI !!
AND MOM LEFT, SO...
...DAD ACCEPTED A JOB TO MAKE MONEY, BUT IT FELL THROUGH, AND...
DON'T TELL THEM THAT!
...WE LOST EVERY-THING.
THEN WE FOL-LOWED A CROW NAMED MARIA...
...AND SHE LED US TO...
TO WHERE ?
MARIA ?
F.R.I.! ALSO KNOWN AS LA FRANCE RESEARCH INSTITUTE!!
AND WE MET THE DIRECTOR!!

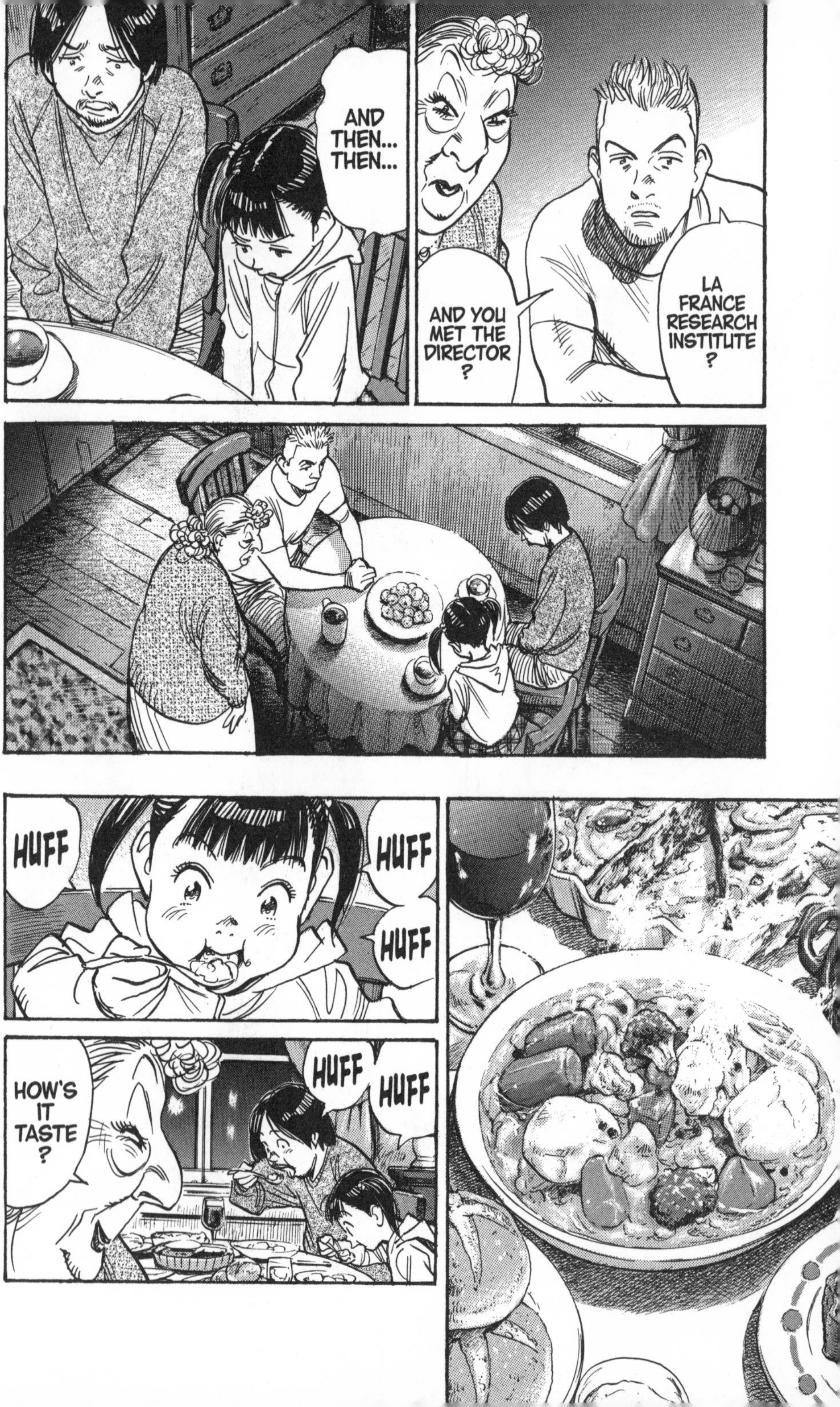
LA FRANCE RESEARCH INSTITUTE ?
AND YOU MET THE DIRECTOR ?
AND THEN... THEN...
HUFF
HUFF
HUFF
HUFF
HUFF
HOW'S IT TASTE ?

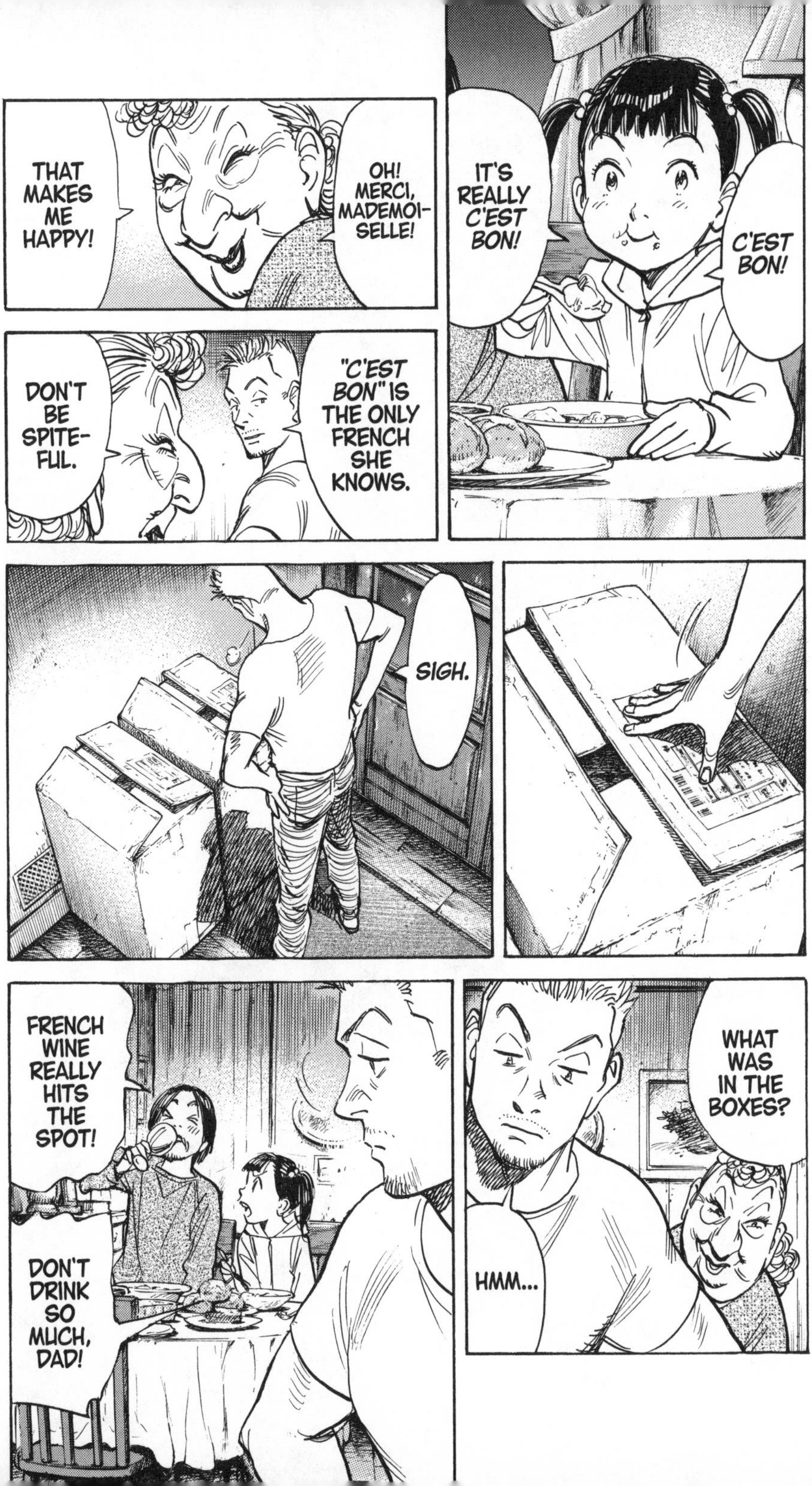
C'EST BON!
IT'S REALLY C'EST BON!
OH! MERCI, MADEMOI-SELLE!
THAT MAKES ME HAPPY!
"C'EST BON" IS THE ONLY FRENCH SHE KNOWS.
DON'T BE SPITE-FUL.
SIGH.
WHAT WAS IN THE BOXES?
HMM...
FRENCH WINE REALLY HITS THE SPOT!
DON'T DRINK SO MUCH, DAD!

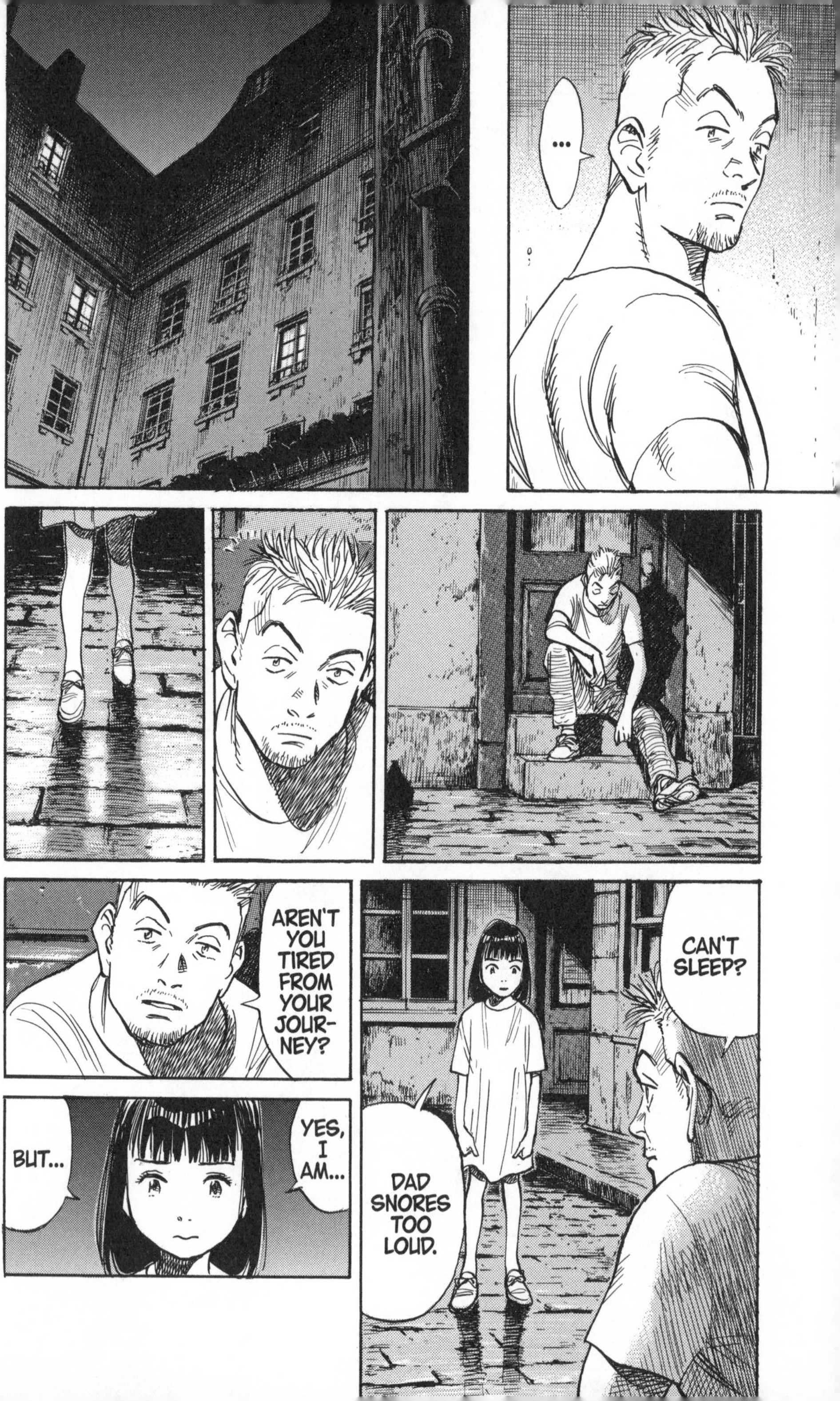
...
CAN'T SLEEP?
AREN'T YOU TIRED FROM YOUR JOURNEY?
YES, I AM...
BUT...
DAD SNORES TOO LOUD.

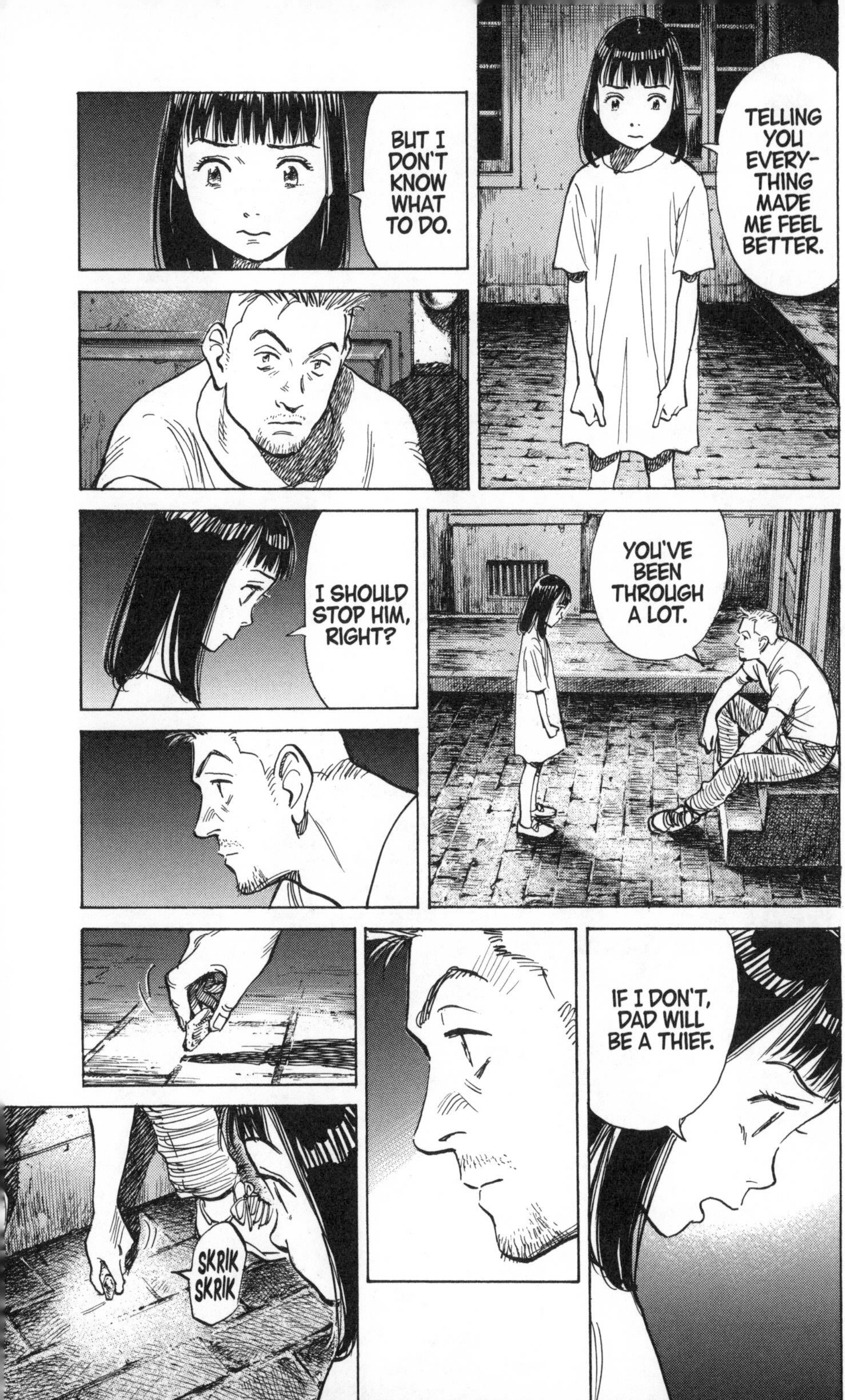
TELLING YOU EVERYTHING MADE ME FEEL BETTER.
BUT I DON'T KNOW WHAT TO DO.
YOU'VE BEEN THROUGH A LOT.
I SHOULD STOP HIM, RIGHT?
IF I DON'T, DAD WILL BE A THIEF.
SKRIK SKRIK

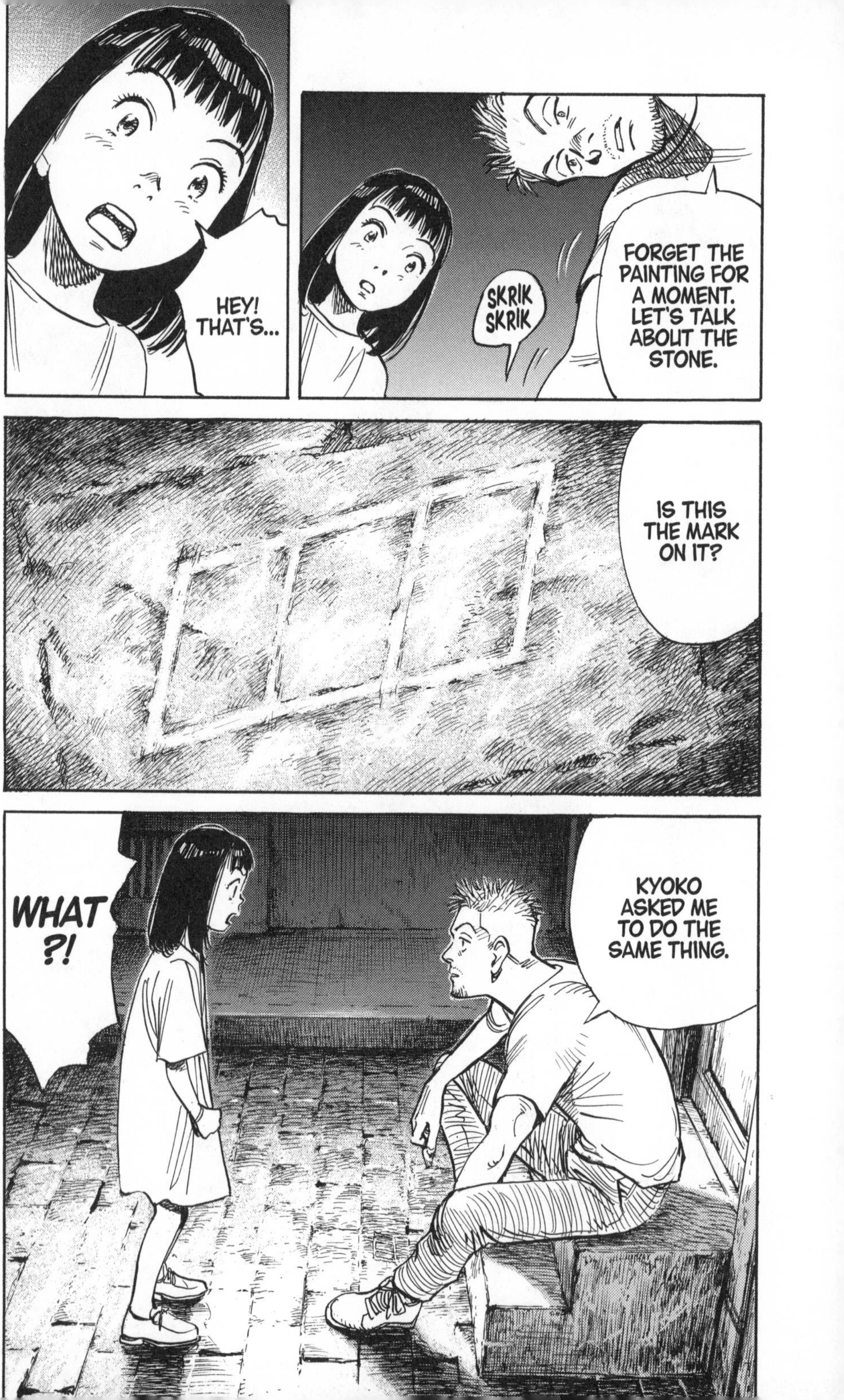
FORGET THE PAINTING FOR A MOMENT. LET'S TALK ABOUT THE STONE.
SKRIK SKRIK
HEY! THAT'S...
IS THIS THE MARK ON IT?
KYOKO ASKED ME TO DO THE SAME THING.
WHAT?!

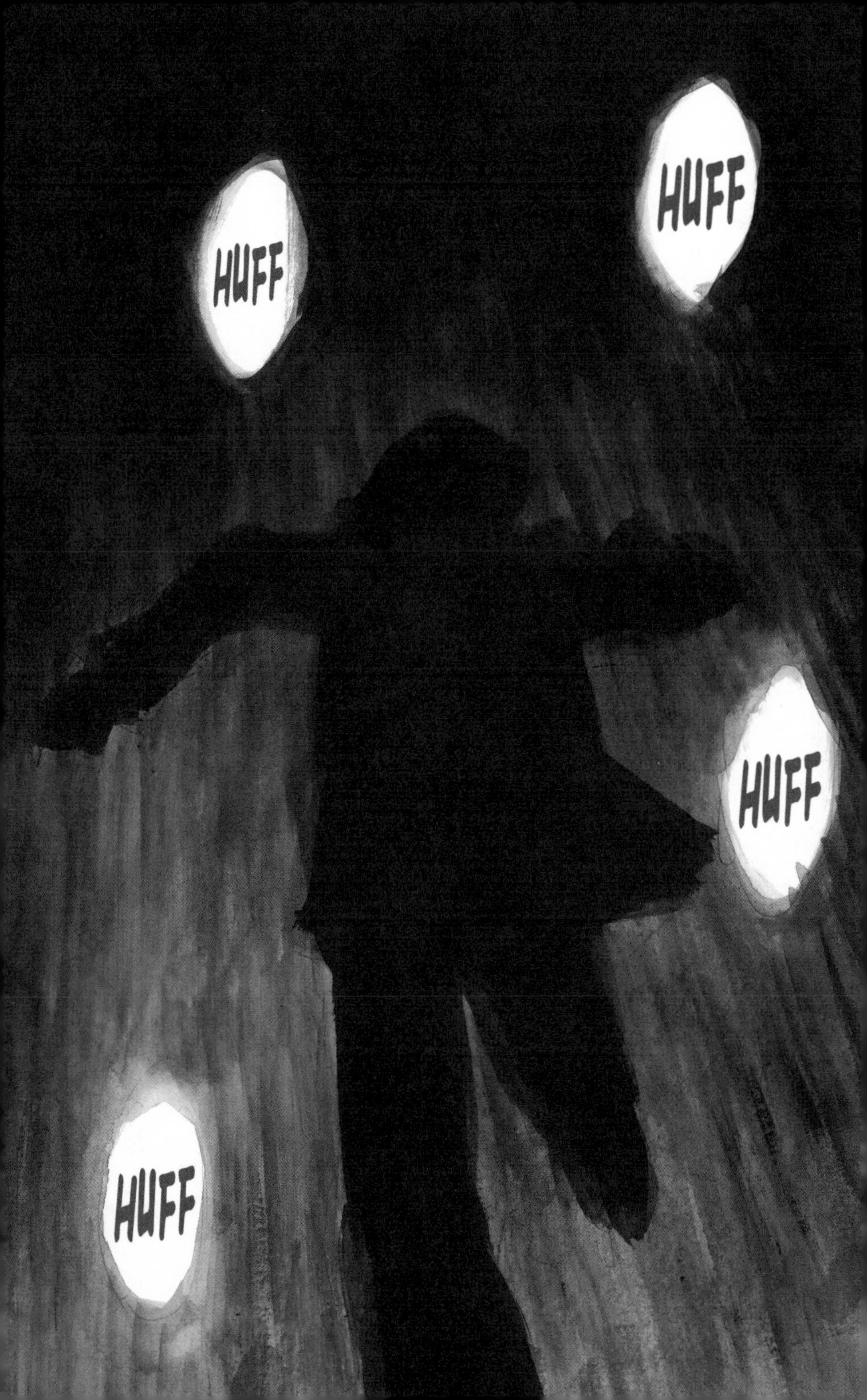
HUFF
HUFF
HUFF
HUFF

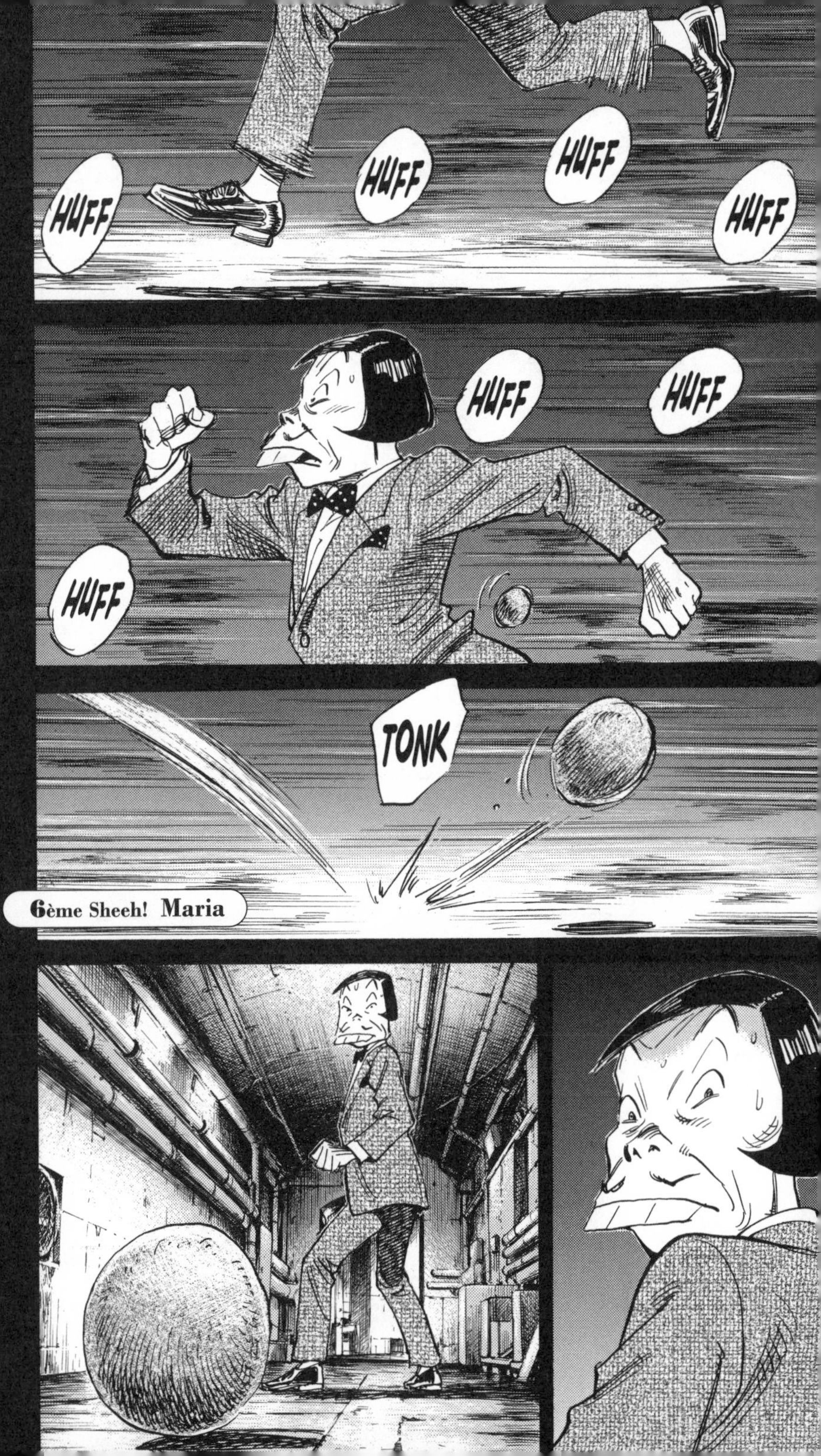
HUFF
HUFF
HUFF
HUFF
HUFF
HUFF
HUFF
TONK
6ème Sheeh! Maria

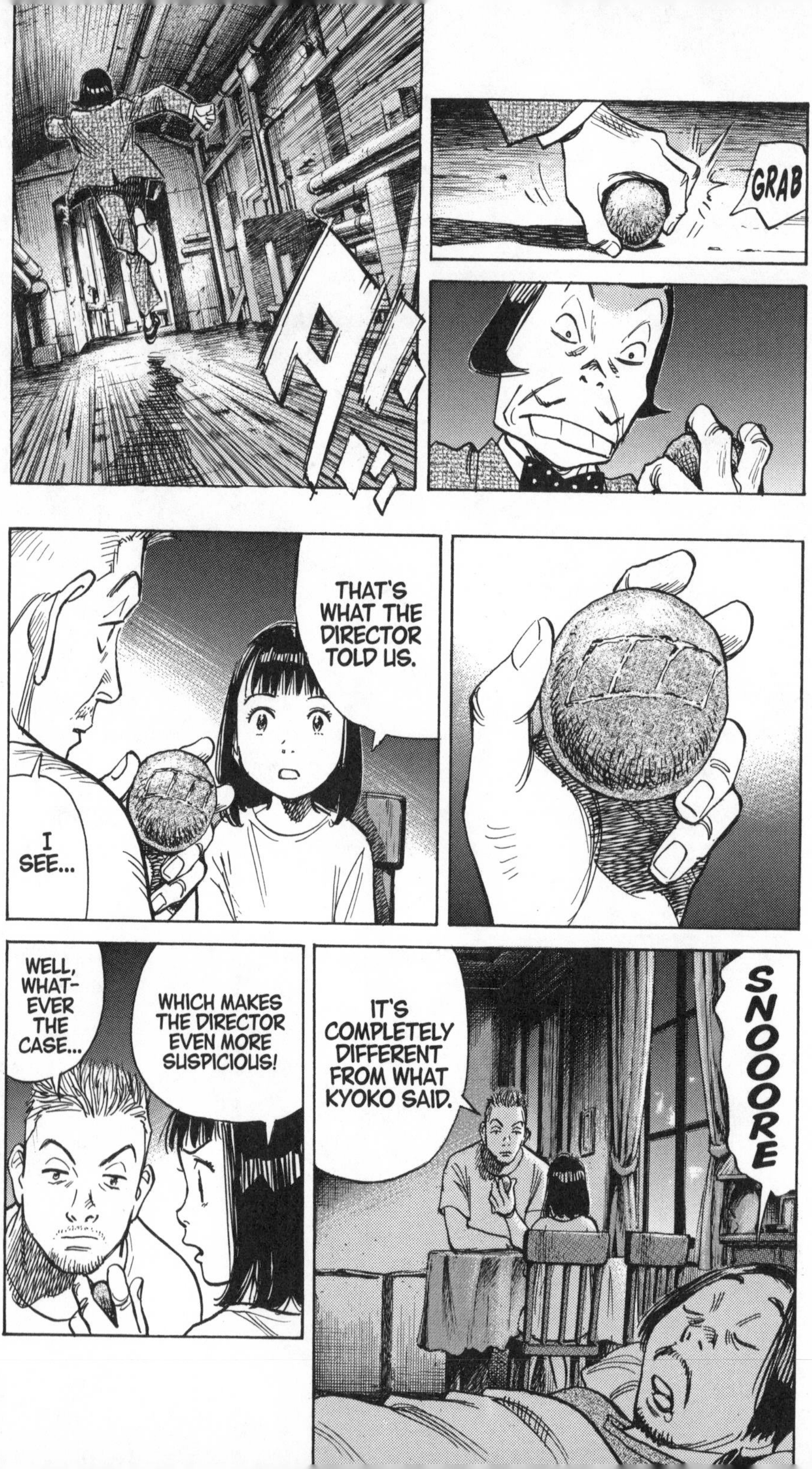
GRAB
THAT'S WHAT THE DIRECTOR TOLD US.
I SEE...
SNOOORE
IT'S COMPLETELY DIFFERENT FROM WHAT KYOKO SAID.
WHICH MAKES THE DIRECTOR EVEN MORE SUSPICIOUS!
WELL, WHATEVER THE CASE...

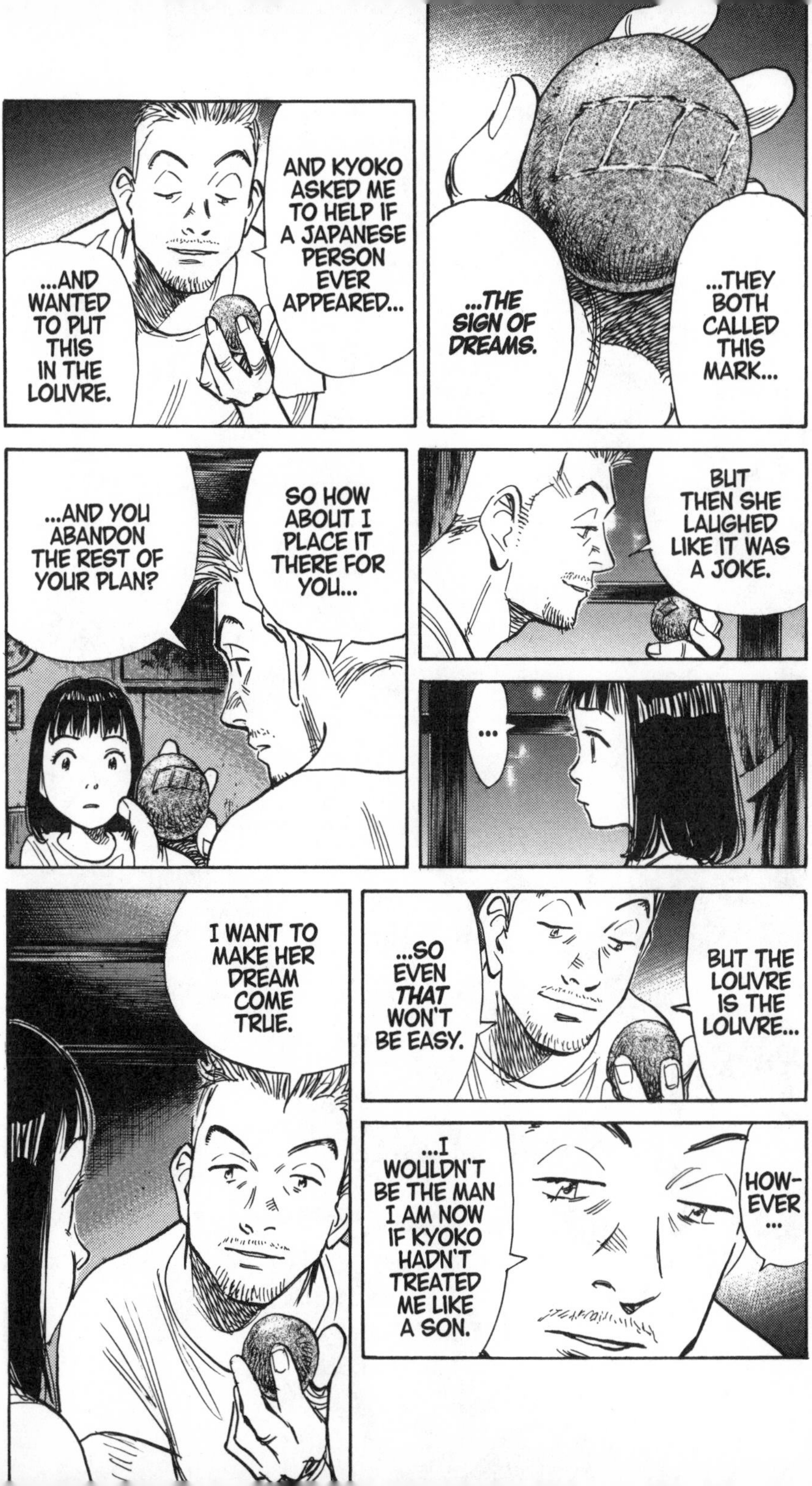
...THEY BOTH CALLED THIS MARK...
...THE SIGN OF DREAMS.
AND KYOKO ASKED ME TO HELP IF A JAPANESE PERSON EVER APPEARED...
...AND WANTED TO PUT THIS IN THE LOUVRE.
BUT THEN SHE LAUGHED LIKE IT WAS A JOKE.
...
SO HOW ABOUT I PLACE IT THERE FOR YOU...
...AND YOU ABANDON THE REST OF YOUR PLAN?
BUT THE LOUVRE IS THE LOUVRE...
...SO EVEN *THAT* WON'T BE EASY.
HOW-EVER...
...I WOULDN'T BE THE MAN I AM NOW IF KYOKO HADN'T TREATED ME LIKE A SON.
I WANT TO MAKE HER DREAM COME TRUE.

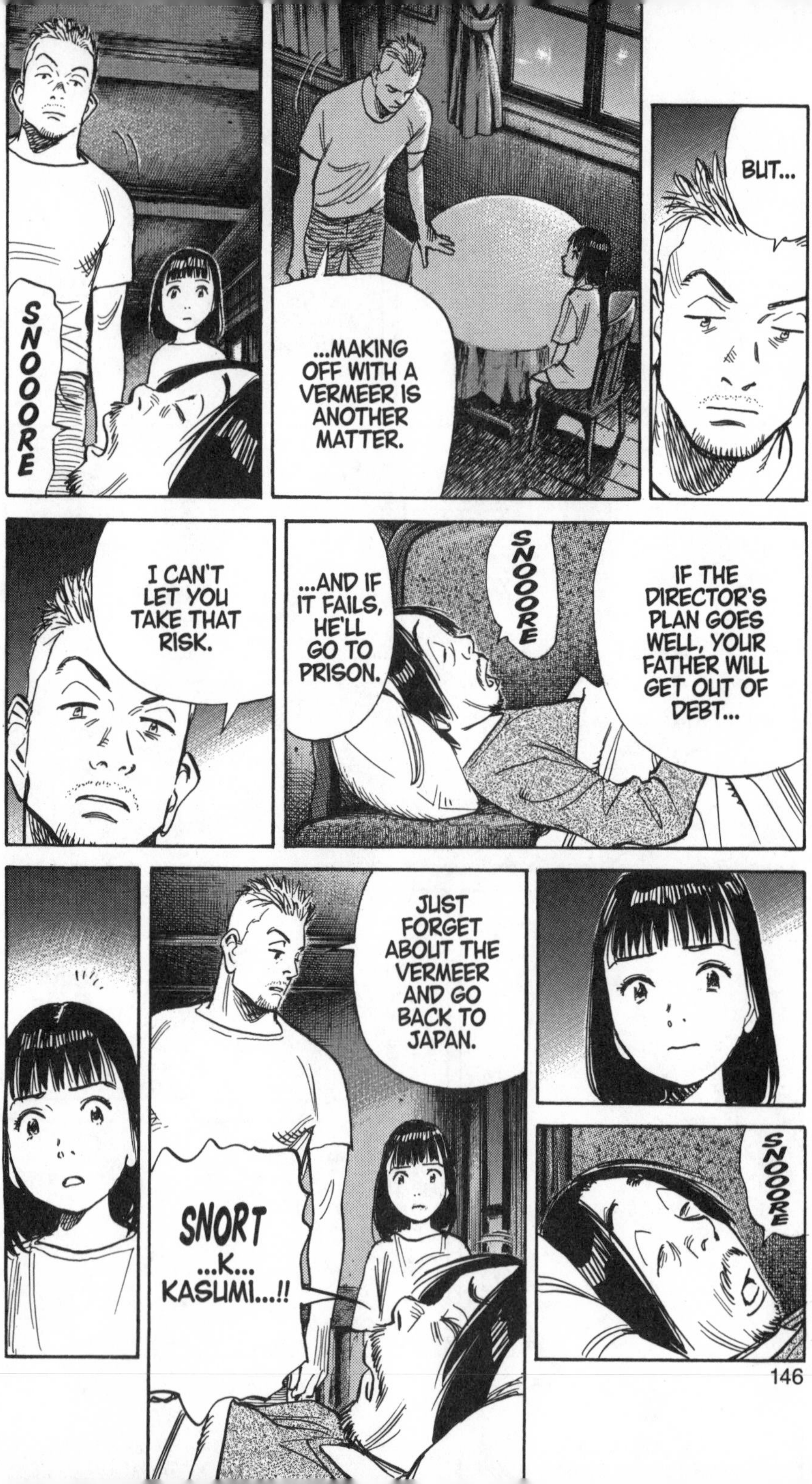
BUT...
...MAKING OFF WITH A VERMEER IS ANOTHER MATTER.
SNOOORE
IF THE DIRECTOR'S PLAN GOES WELL, YOUR FATHER WILL GET OUT OF DEBT...
SNOOORE
...AND IF IT FAILS, HE'LL GO TO PRISON.
I CAN'T LET YOU TAKE THAT RISK.
SNOOORE
JUST FORGET ABOUT THE VERMEER AND GO BACK TO JAPAN.
SNORT
...K... KASUMI...!!

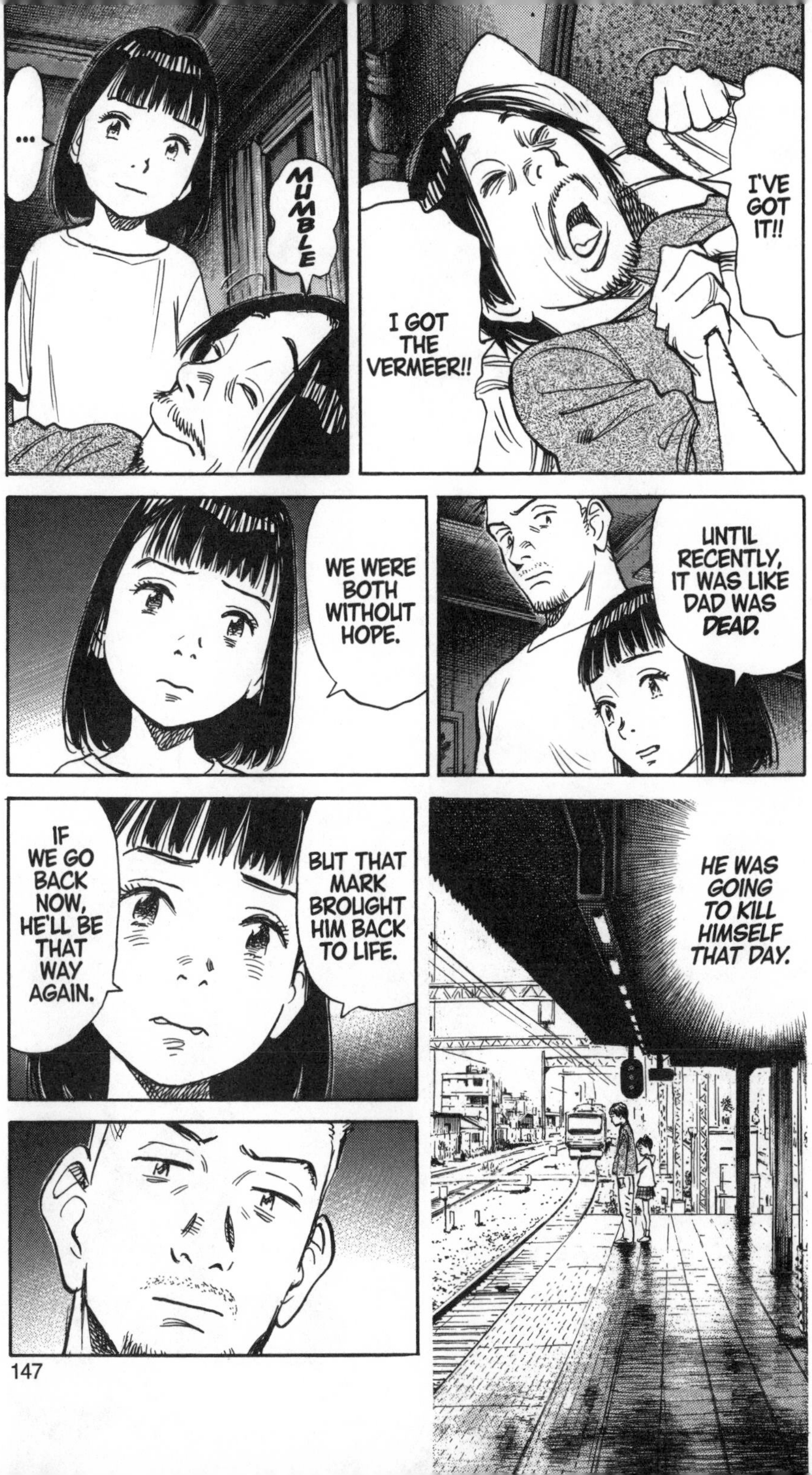
I'VE GOT IT!!
I GOT THE VERMEER!!
MUMBLE
...
UNTIL RECENTLY, IT WAS LIKE DAD WAS DEAD.
WE WERE BOTH WITHOUT HOPE.
HE WAS GOING TO KILL HIMSELF THAT DAY.
BUT THAT MARK BROUGHT HIM BACK TO LIFE.
IF WE GO BACK NOW, HE'LL BE THAT WAY AGAIN.

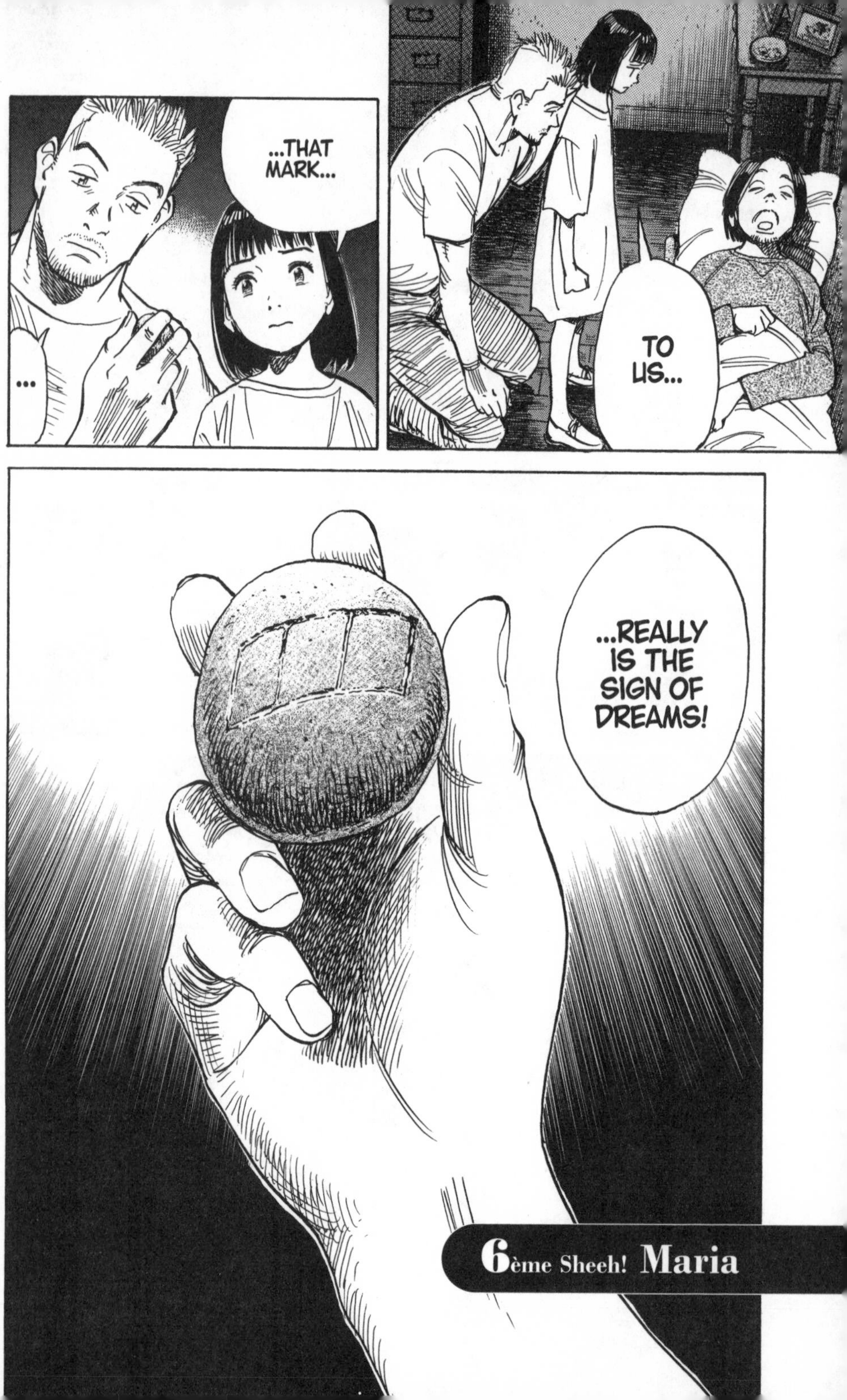
TO US...
...THAT MARK...
...
...REALLY IS THE SIGN OF DREAMS!
6ème Sheeh! Maria

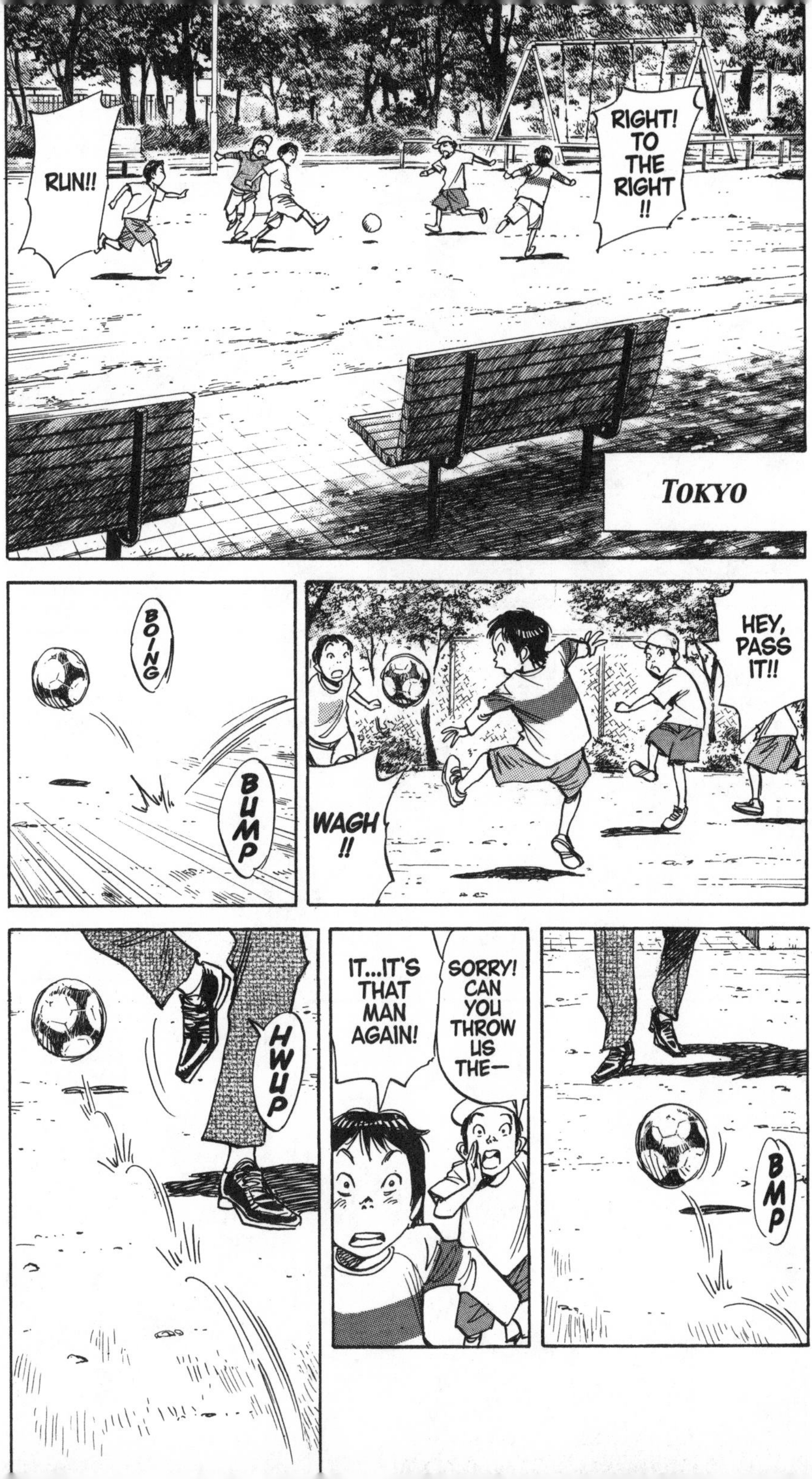
RIGHT! TO THE RIGHT!!
RUN!!
TOKYO
HEY, PASS IT!!
WAGH!!
BOING
BUMP
BMP
SORRY! CAN YOU THROW US THE—
IT...IT'S THAT MAN AGAIN!
HWUP

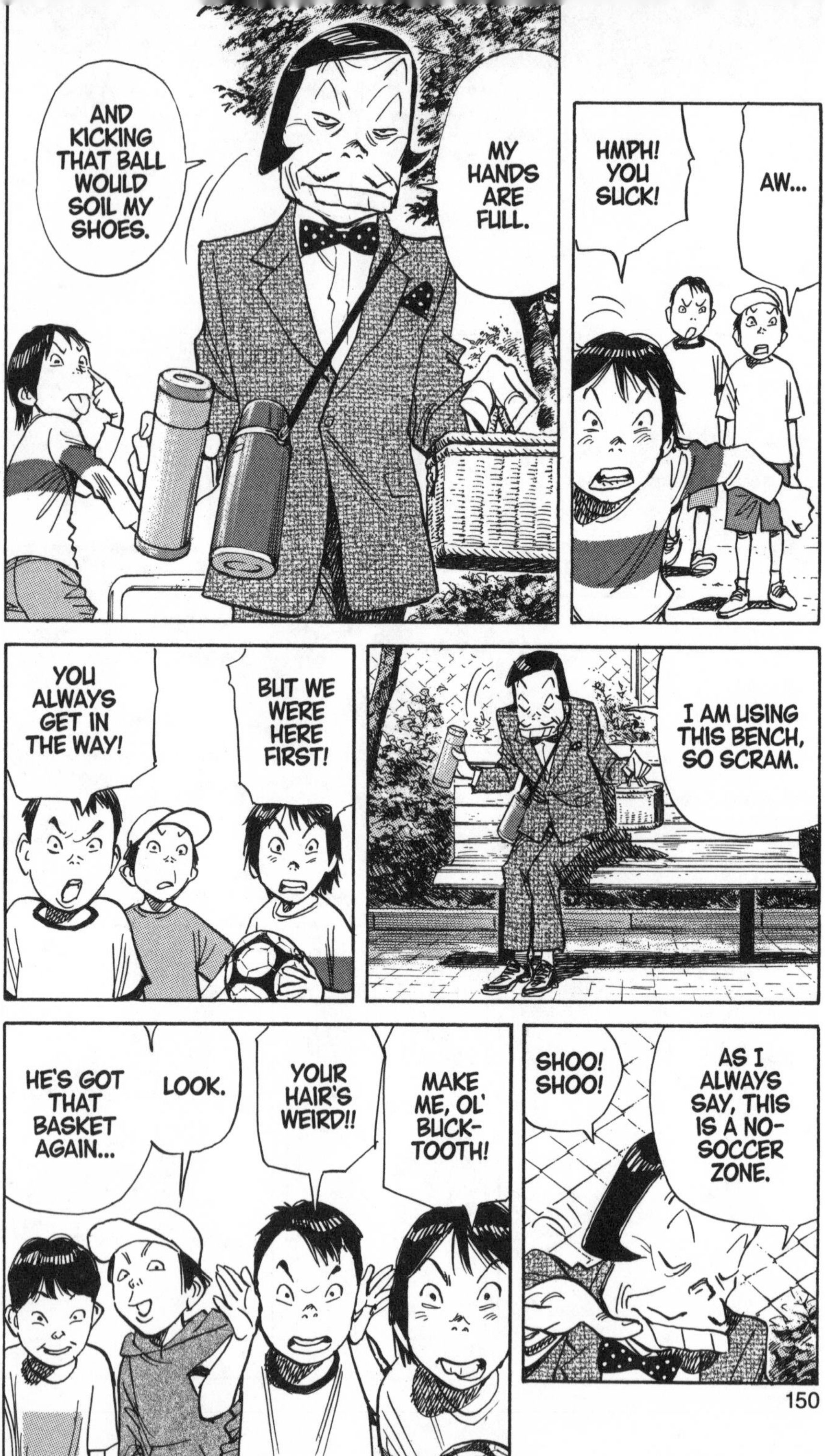
AW...
HMPH! YOU SUCK!
MY HANDS ARE FULL.
AND KICKING THAT BALL WOULD SOIL MY SHOES.
I AM USING THIS BENCH, SO SCRAM.
BUT WE WERE HERE FIRST!
YOU ALWAYS GET IN THE WAY!
AS I ALWAYS SAY, THIS IS A NO-SOCCER ZONE.
SHOO! SHOO!
MAKE ME, OL' BUCK-TOOTH!
YOUR HAIR'S WEIRD!!
LOOK.
HE'S GOT THAT BASKET AGAIN...

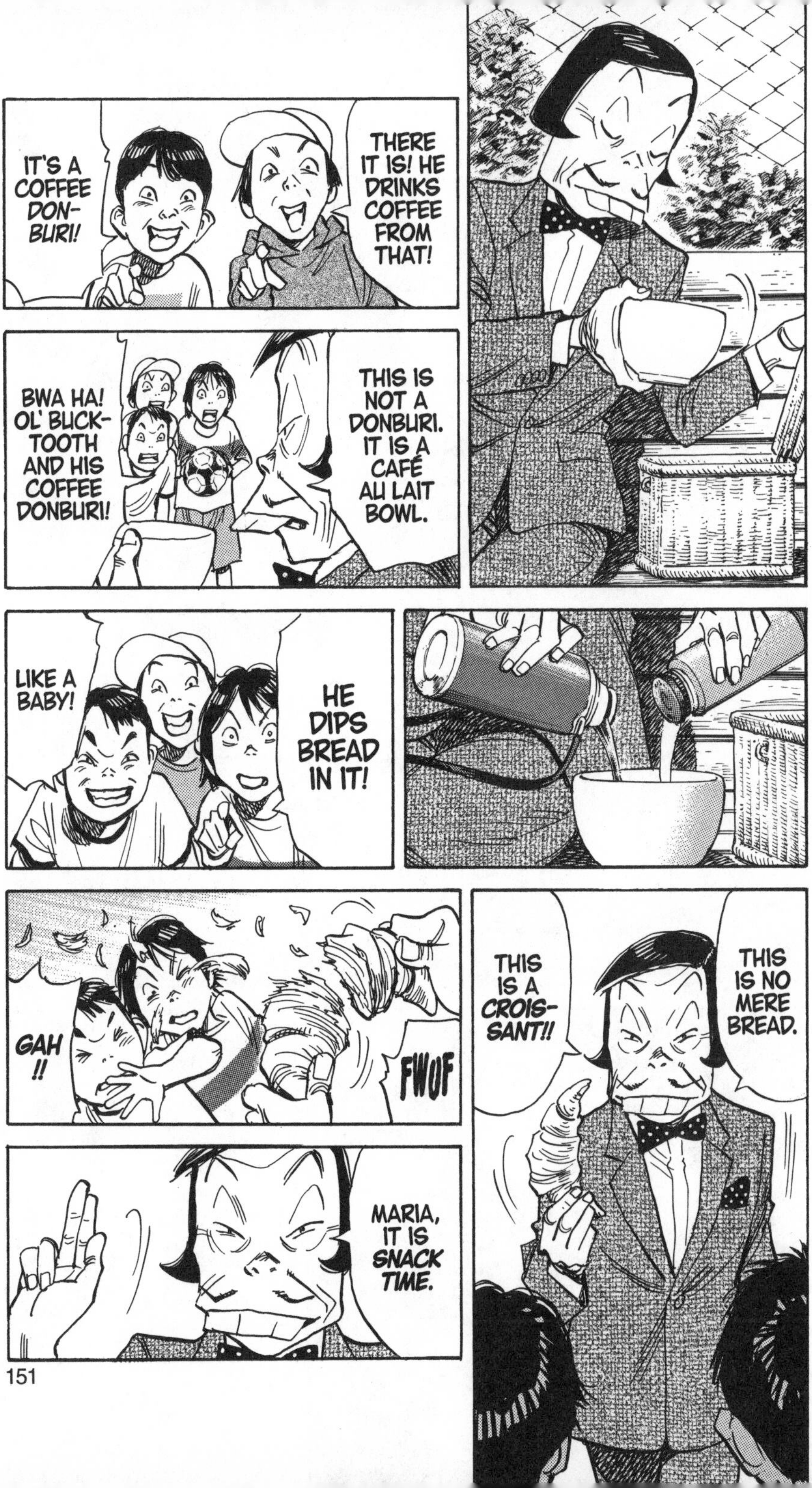
THERE IT IS! HE DRINKS COFFEE FROM THAT!
IT'S A COFFEE DON-BURI!
THIS IS NOT A DONBURI. IT IS A CAFÉ AU LAIT BOWL.
BWA HA! OL' BUCK-TOOTH AND HIS COFFEE DONBURI!
HE DIPS BREAD IN IT!
LIKE A BABY!
THIS IS NO MERE BREAD.
THIS IS A CROIS-SANT!!
FWUF
GAH !!
MARIA, IT IS SNACK TIME.

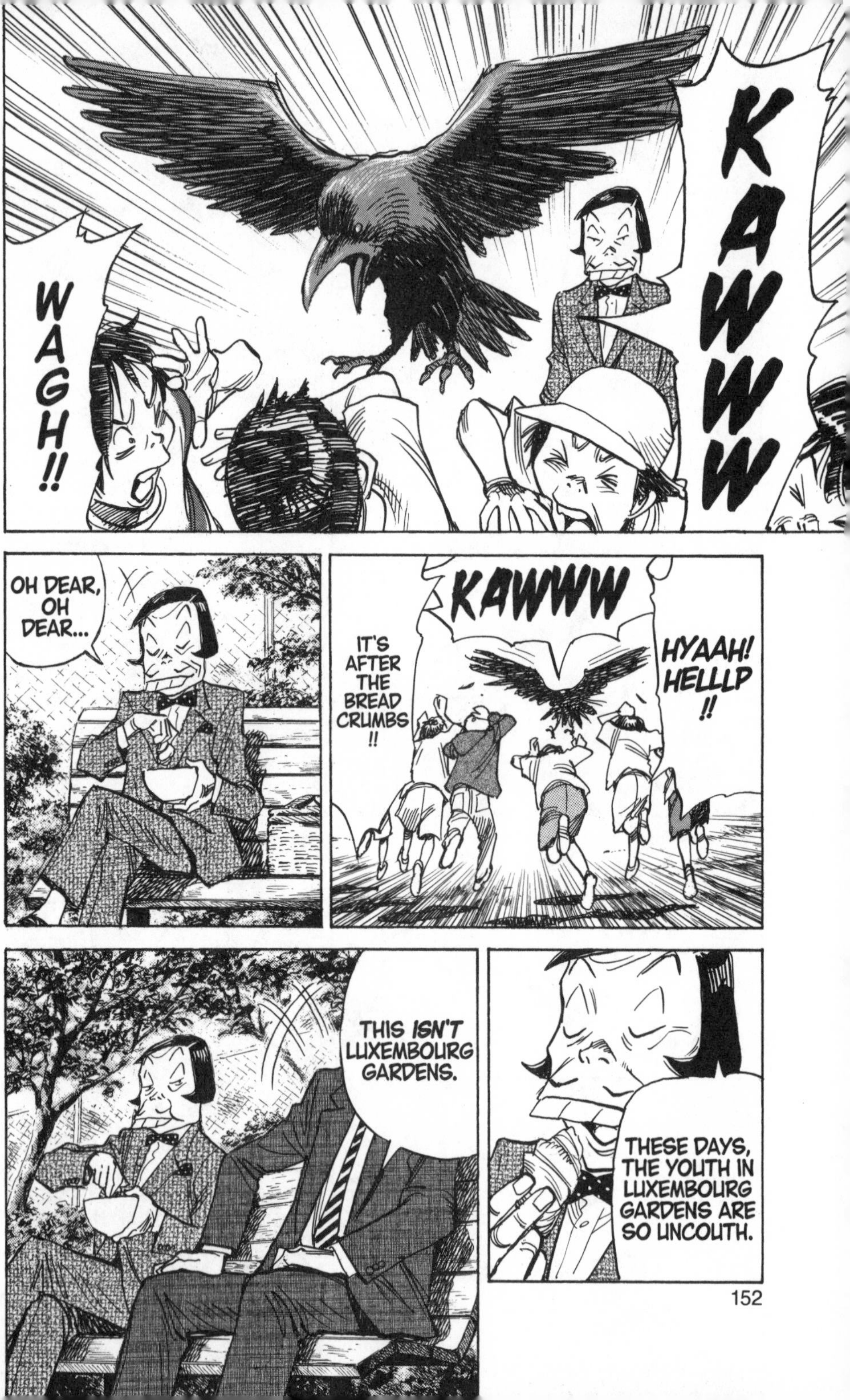
KAWWWW
WAGH!!
KAWWW
HYAAH! HELLLP!!
IT'S AFTER THE BREAD CRUMBS!!
OH DEAR, OH DEAR...
THESE DAYS, THE YOUTH IN LUXEMBOURG GARDENS ARE SO UNCOUTH.
THIS *ISN'T* LUXEMBOURG GARDENS.

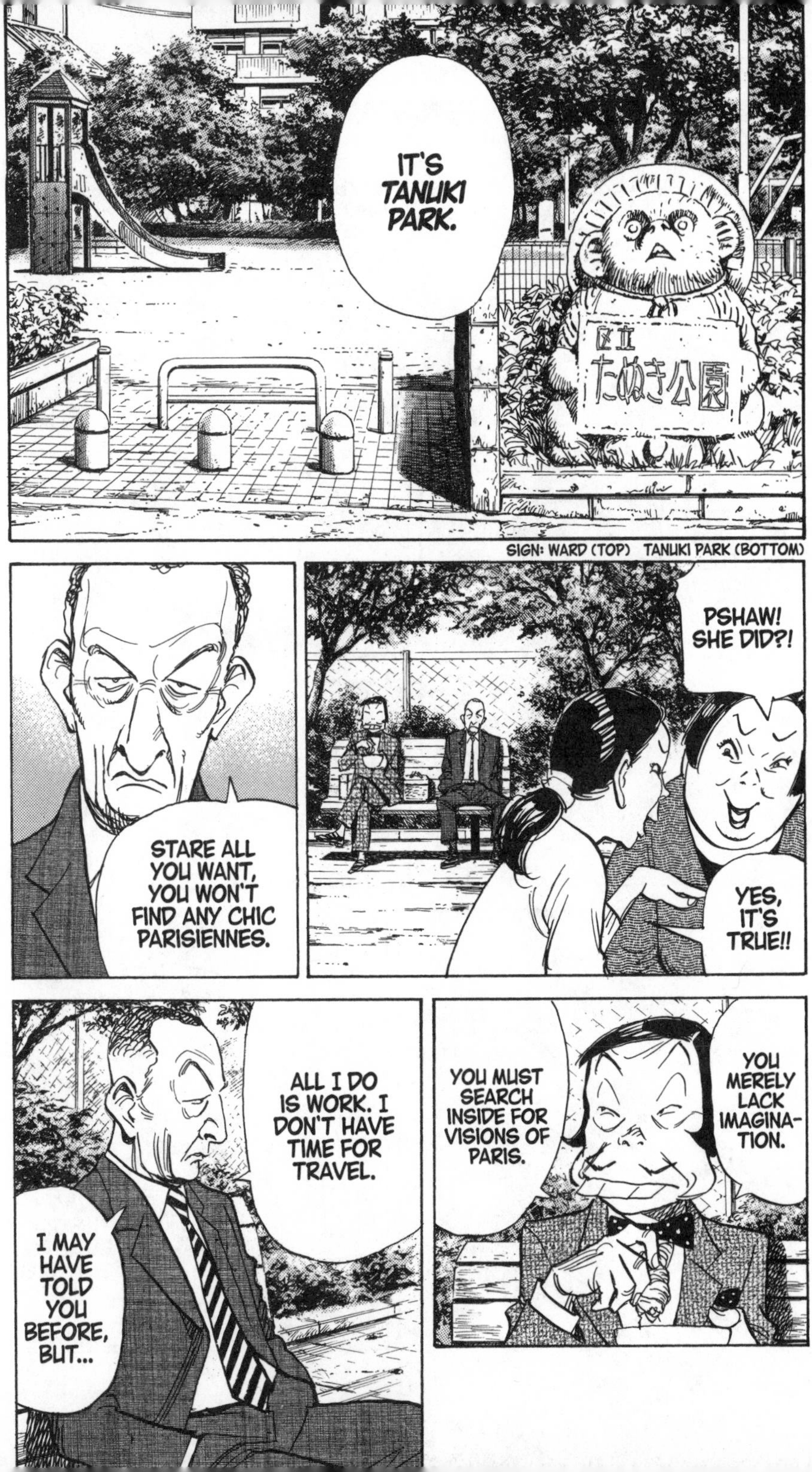
IT'S TANUKI PARK.
区立
たぬき公園
SIGN: WARD (TOP) TANUKI PARK (BOTTOM)
PSHAW! SHE DID?!
YES, IT'S TRUE!!
STARE ALL YOU WANT, YOU WON'T FIND ANY CHIC PARISIENNES.
YOU MERELY LACK IMAGINA-TION.
YOU MUST SEARCH INSIDE FOR VISIONS OF PARIS.
ALL I DO IS WORK. I DON'T HAVE TIME FOR TRAVEL.
I MAY HAVE TOLD YOU BEFORE, BUT...

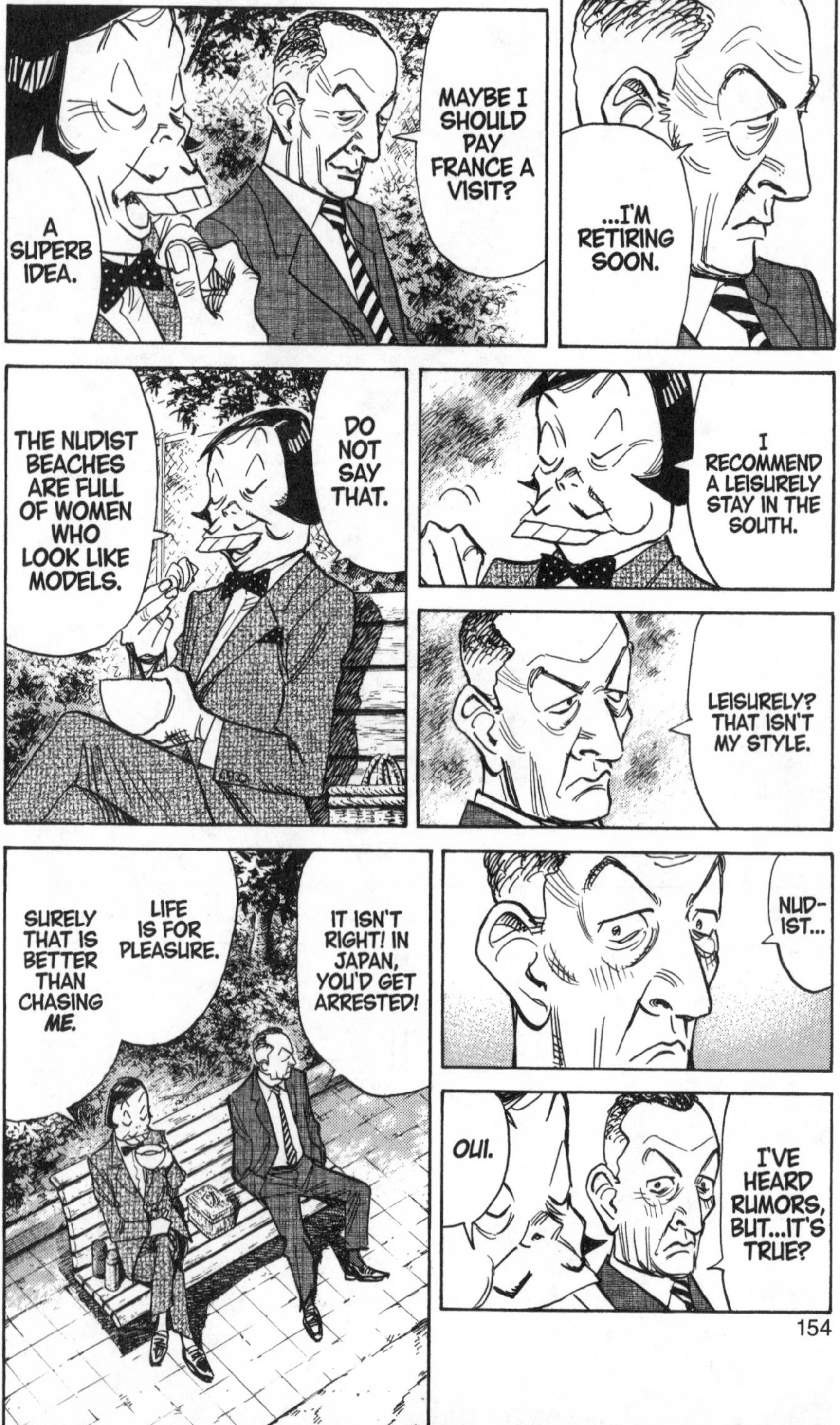
...I'M RETIRING SOON.
MAYBE I SHOULD PAY FRANCE A VISIT?
A SUPERB IDEA.
I RECOMMEND A LEISURELY STAY IN THE SOUTH.
LEISURELY? THAT ISN'T MY STYLE.
DO NOT SAY THAT.
THE NUDIST BEACHES ARE FULL OF WOMEN WHO LOOK LIKE MODELS.
NUD-IST...
I'VE HEARD RUMORS, BUT...IT'S TRUE?
OUI.
IT ISN'T RIGHT! IN JAPAN, YOU'D GET ARRESTED!
LIFE IS FOR PLEASURE.
SURELY THAT IS BETTER THAN CHASING *ME*.

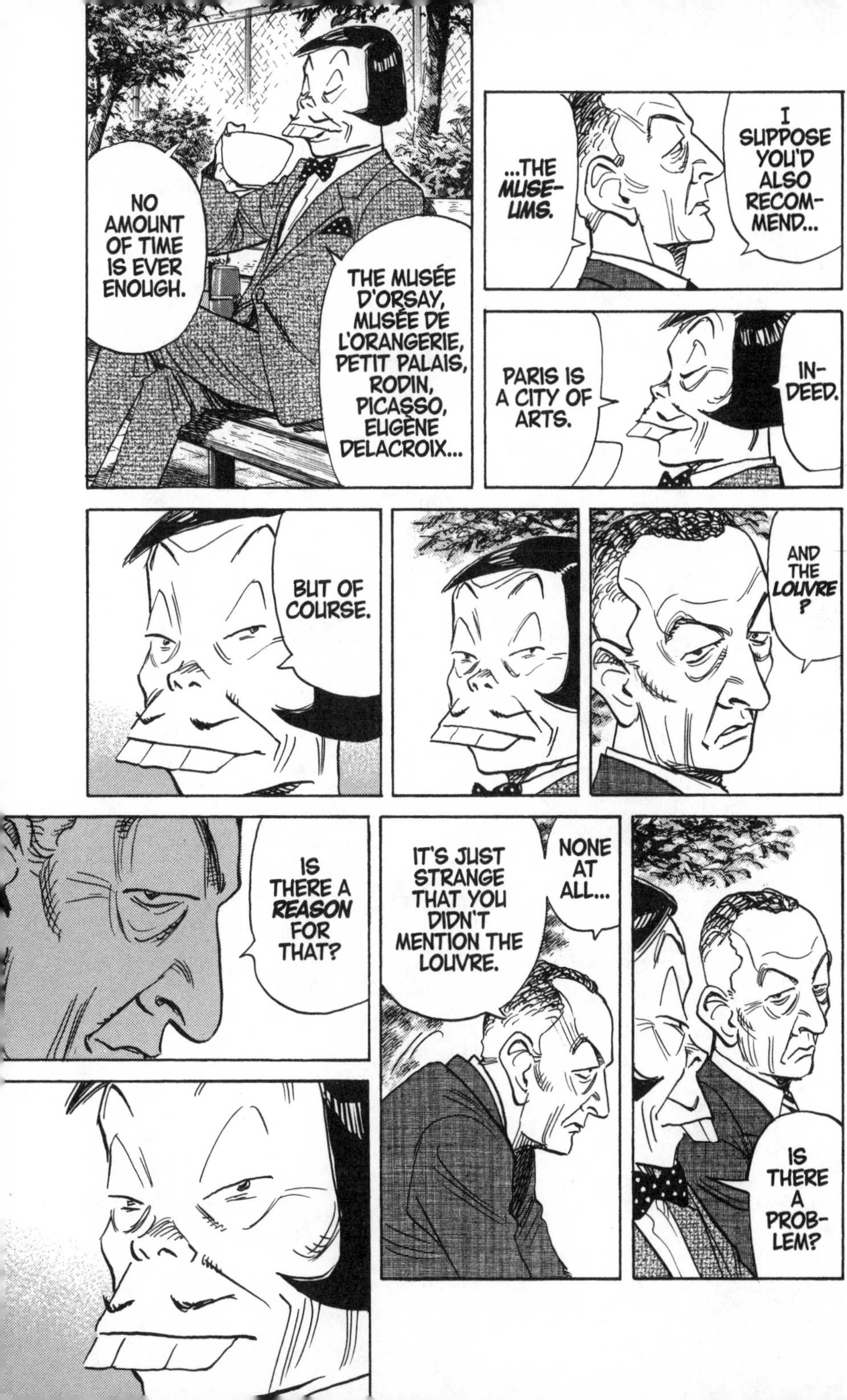
I SUPPOSE YOU'D ALSO RECOMMEND...
...THE *MUSEUMS.*
INDEED.
PARIS IS A CITY OF ARTS.
THE MUSÉE D'ORSAY, MUSÉE DE L'ORANGERIE, PETIT PALAIS, RODIN, PICASSO, EUGÈNE DELACROIX...
NO AMOUNT OF TIME IS EVER ENOUGH.
AND THE *LOUVRE*?
BUT OF COURSE.
IS THERE A PROBLEM?
NONE AT ALL...
IT'S JUST STRANGE THAT YOU DIDN'T MENTION THE LOUVRE.
IS THERE A *REASON* FOR THAT?

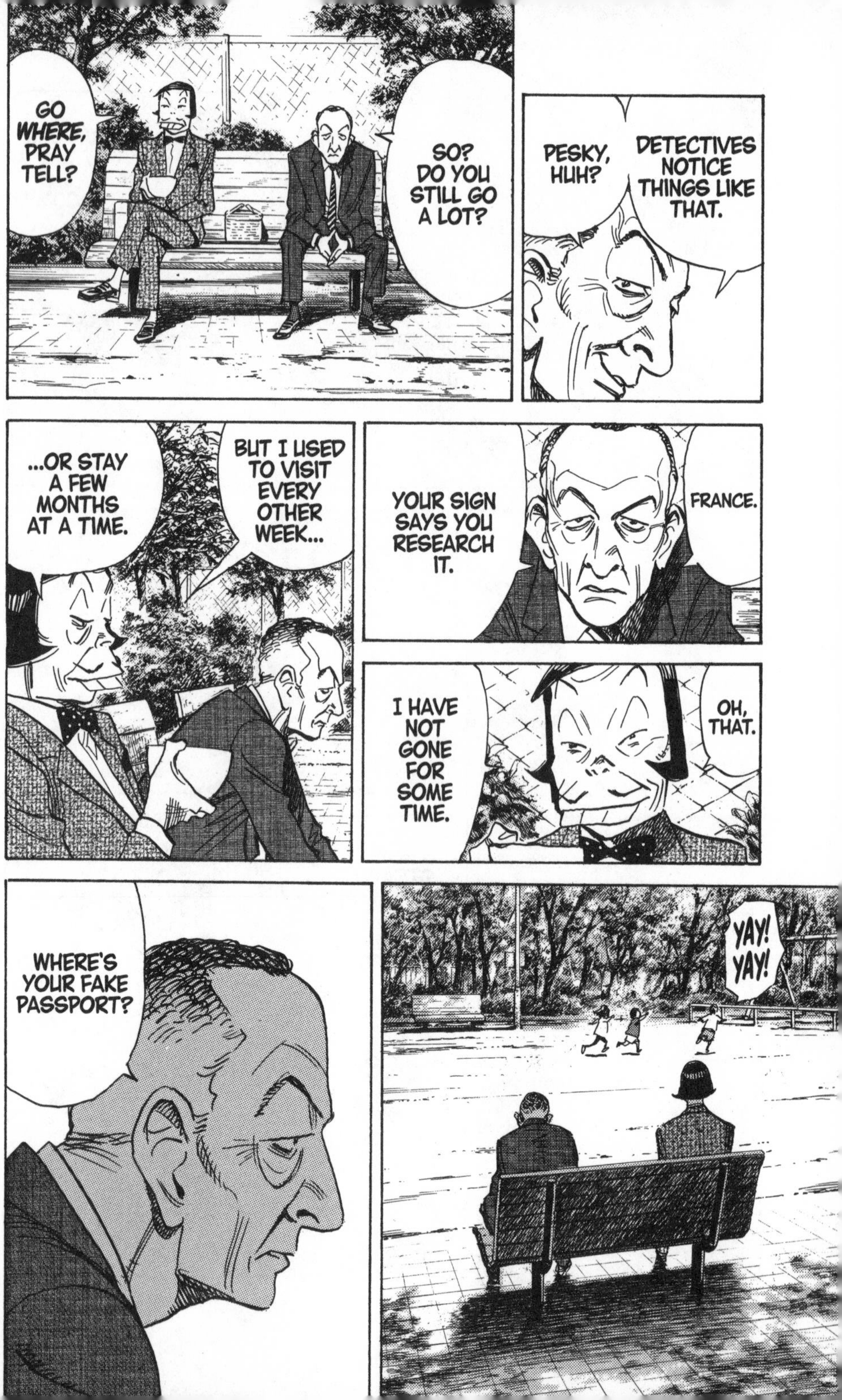
DETECTIVES NOTICE THINGS LIKE THAT.
PESKY, HUH?
SO? DO YOU STILL GO A LOT?
GO WHERE, PRAY TELL?
FRANCE.
YOUR SIGN SAYS YOU RESEARCH IT.
OH, THAT.
I HAVE NOT GONE FOR SOME TIME.
BUT I USED TO VISIT EVERY OTHER WEEK...
...OR STAY A FEW MONTHS AT A TIME.
YAY! YAY!
WHERE'S YOUR FAKE PASSPORT?

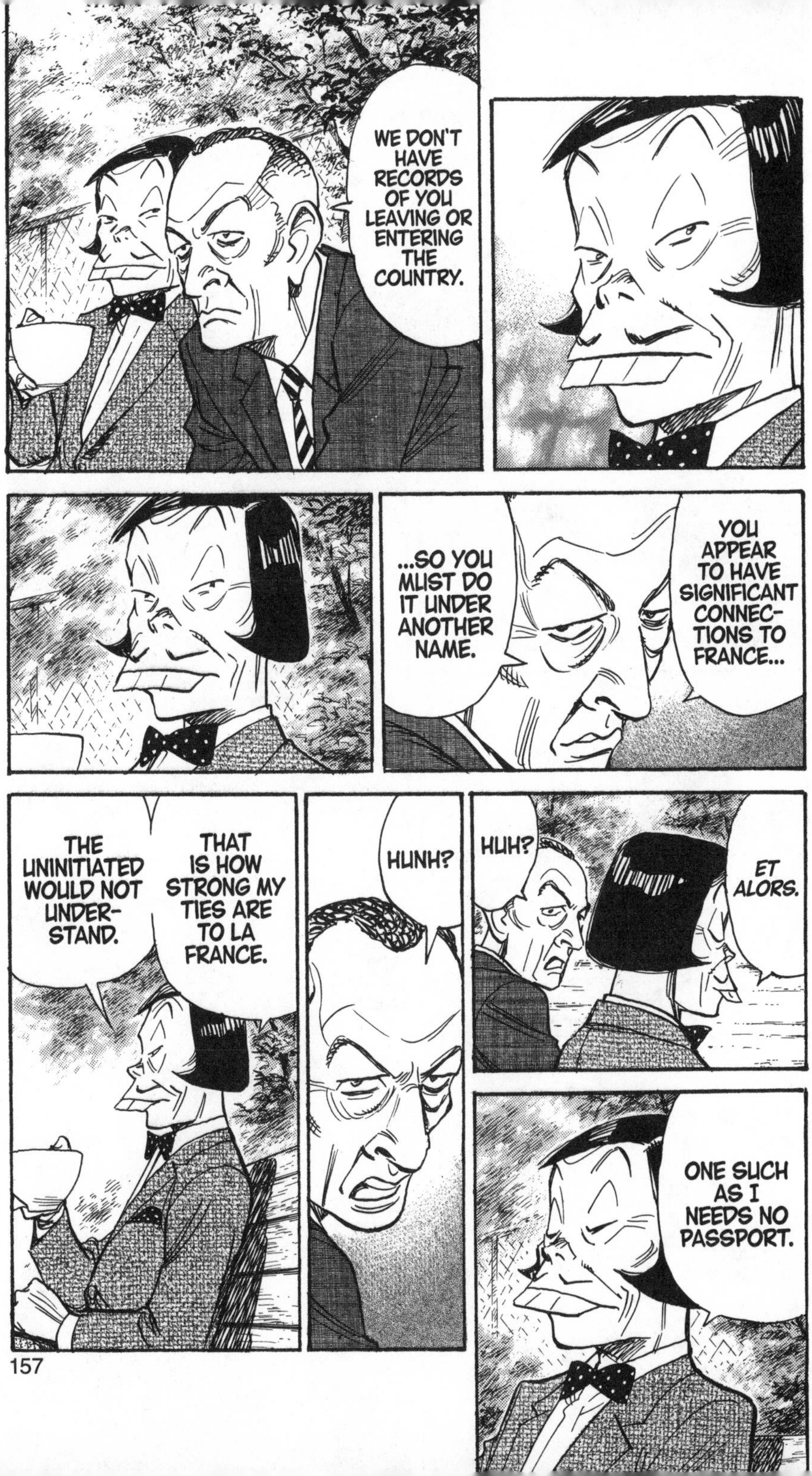
WE DON'T HAVE RECORDS OF YOU LEAVING OR ENTERING THE COUNTRY.
YOU APPEAR TO HAVE SIGNIFICANT CONNEC-TIONS TO FRANCE...
...SO YOU MUST DO IT UNDER ANOTHER NAME.
ET ALORS.
HUH?
ONE SUCH AS I NEEDS NO PASSPORT.
HUNH?
THAT IS HOW STRONG MY TIES ARE TO LA FRANCE.
THE UNINITIATED WOULD NOT UNDER-STAND.

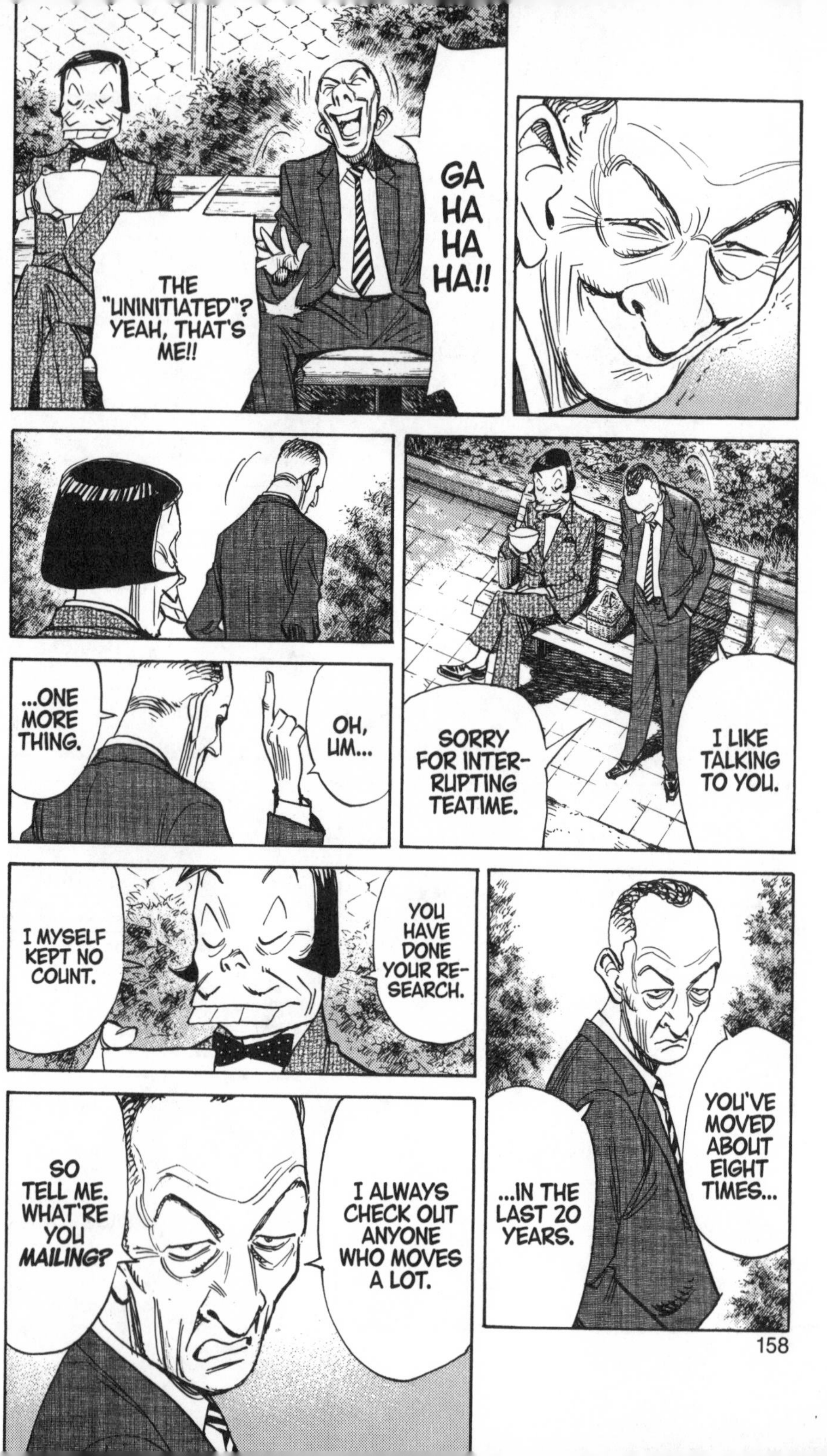
GA HA HA HA!!
THE "UNINITIATED"? YEAH, THAT'S ME!!
I LIKE TALKING TO YOU.
SORRY FOR INTER-RUPTING TEATIME.
OH, UM...
...ONE MORE THING.
YOU'VE MOVED ABOUT EIGHT TIMES...
...IN THE LAST 20 YEARS.
YOU HAVE DONE YOUR RE-SEARCH.
I MYSELF KEPT NO COUNT.
I ALWAYS CHECK OUT ANYONE WHO MOVES A LOT.
SO TELL ME. WHAT'RE YOU *MAILING?*

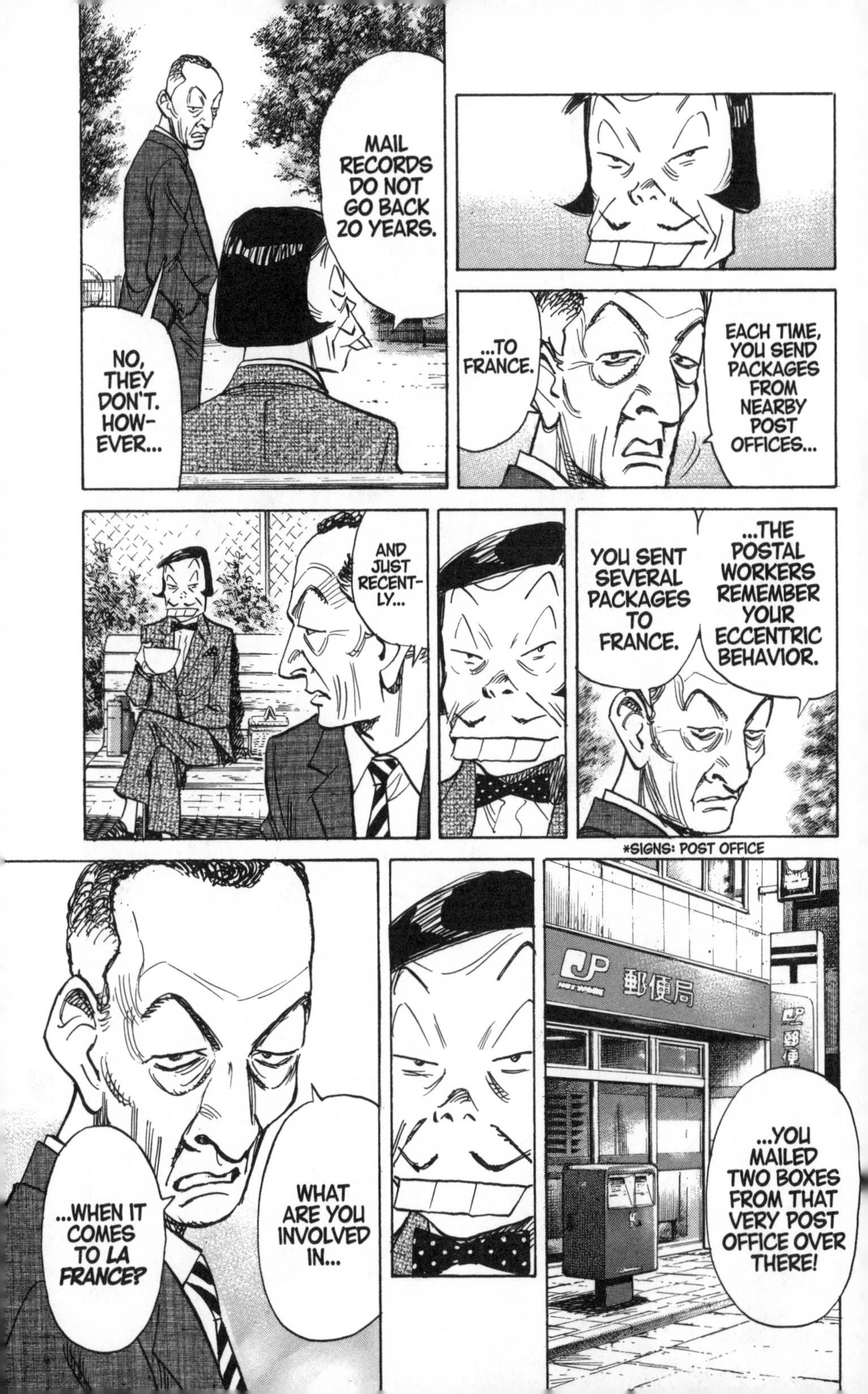
EACH TIME, YOU SEND PACKAGES FROM NEARBY POST OFFICES...
...TO FRANCE.
MAIL RECORDS DO NOT GO BACK 20 YEARS.
NO, THEY DON'T. HOW-EVER...
...THE POSTAL WORKERS REMEMBER YOUR ECCENTRIC BEHAVIOR.
YOU SENT SEVERAL PACKAGES TO FRANCE.
AND JUST RECENT-LY...
*SIGNS: POST OFFICE
JP
郵便局
...YOU MAILED TWO BOXES FROM THAT VERY POST OFFICE OVER THERE!
WHAT ARE YOU INVOLVED IN...
...WHEN IT COMES TO LA FRANCE?

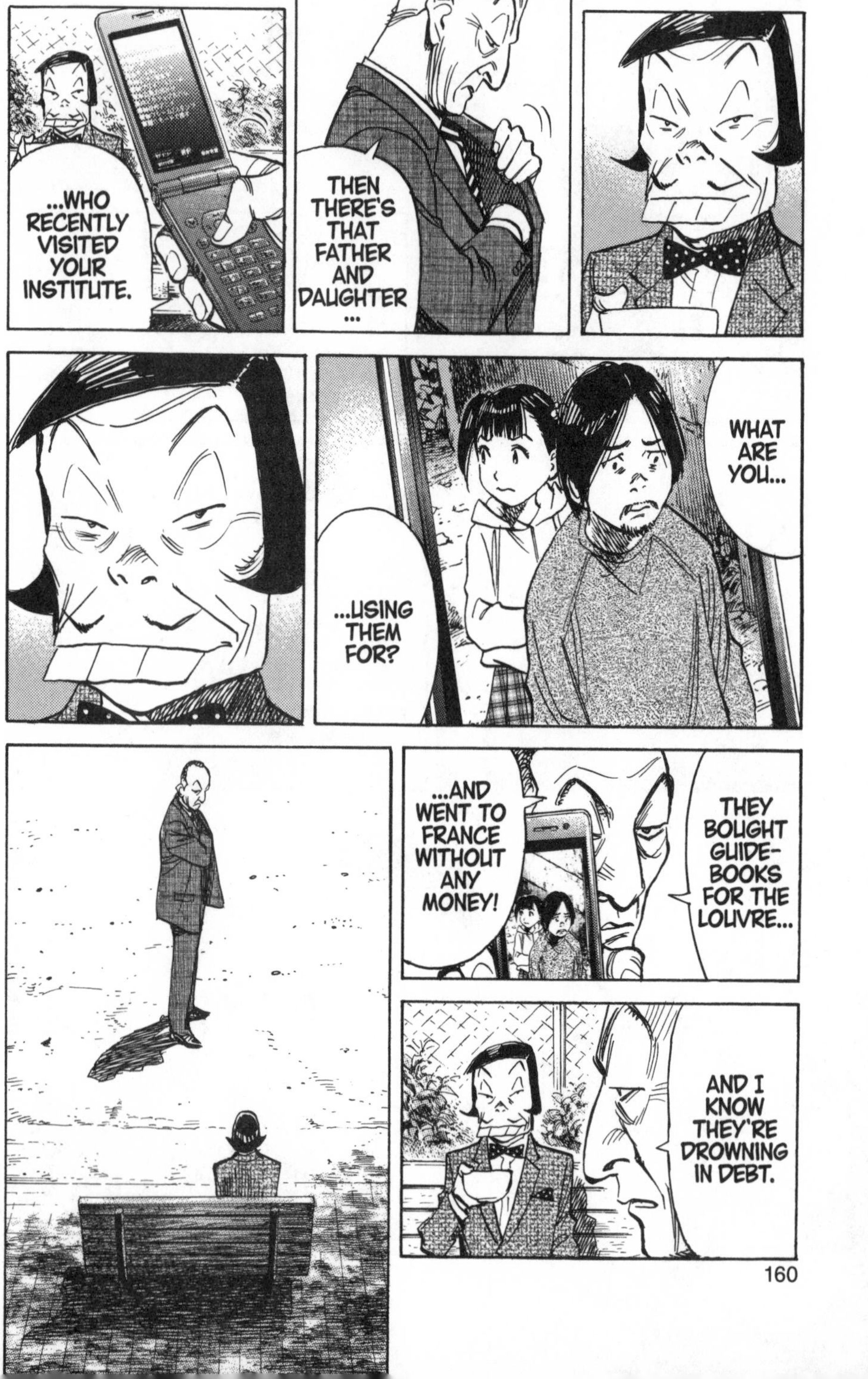
THEN THERE'S THAT FATHER AND DAUGHTER...
...WHO RECENTLY VISITED YOUR INSTITUTE.
WHAT ARE YOU...
...USING THEM FOR?
THEY BOUGHT GUIDE-BOOKS FOR THE LOUVRE...
...AND WENT TO FRANCE WITHOUT ANY MONEY!
AND I KNOW THEY'RE DROWNING IN DEBT.

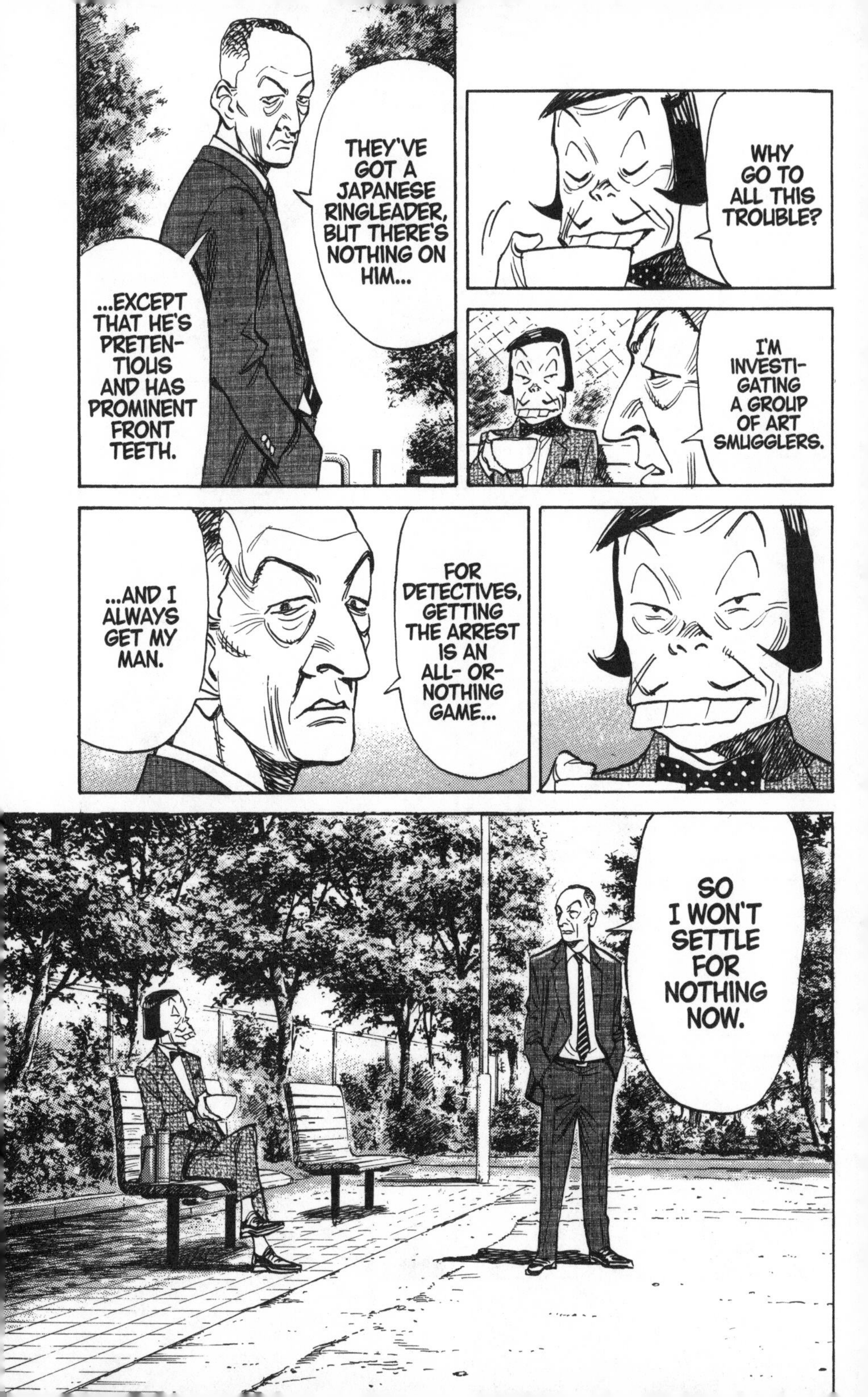
WHY GO TO ALL THIS TROUBLE?
I'M INVESTI-GATING A GROUP OF ART SMUGGLERS.
THEY'VE GOT A JAPANESE RINGLEADER, BUT THERE'S NOTHING ON HIM...
...EXCEPT THAT HE'S PRETEN-TIOUS AND HAS PROMINENT FRONT TEETH.
FOR DETECTIVES, GETTING THE ARREST IS AN ALL- OR- NOTHING GAME...
...AND I ALWAYS GET MY MAN.
SO I WON'T SETTLE FOR NOTHING NOW.

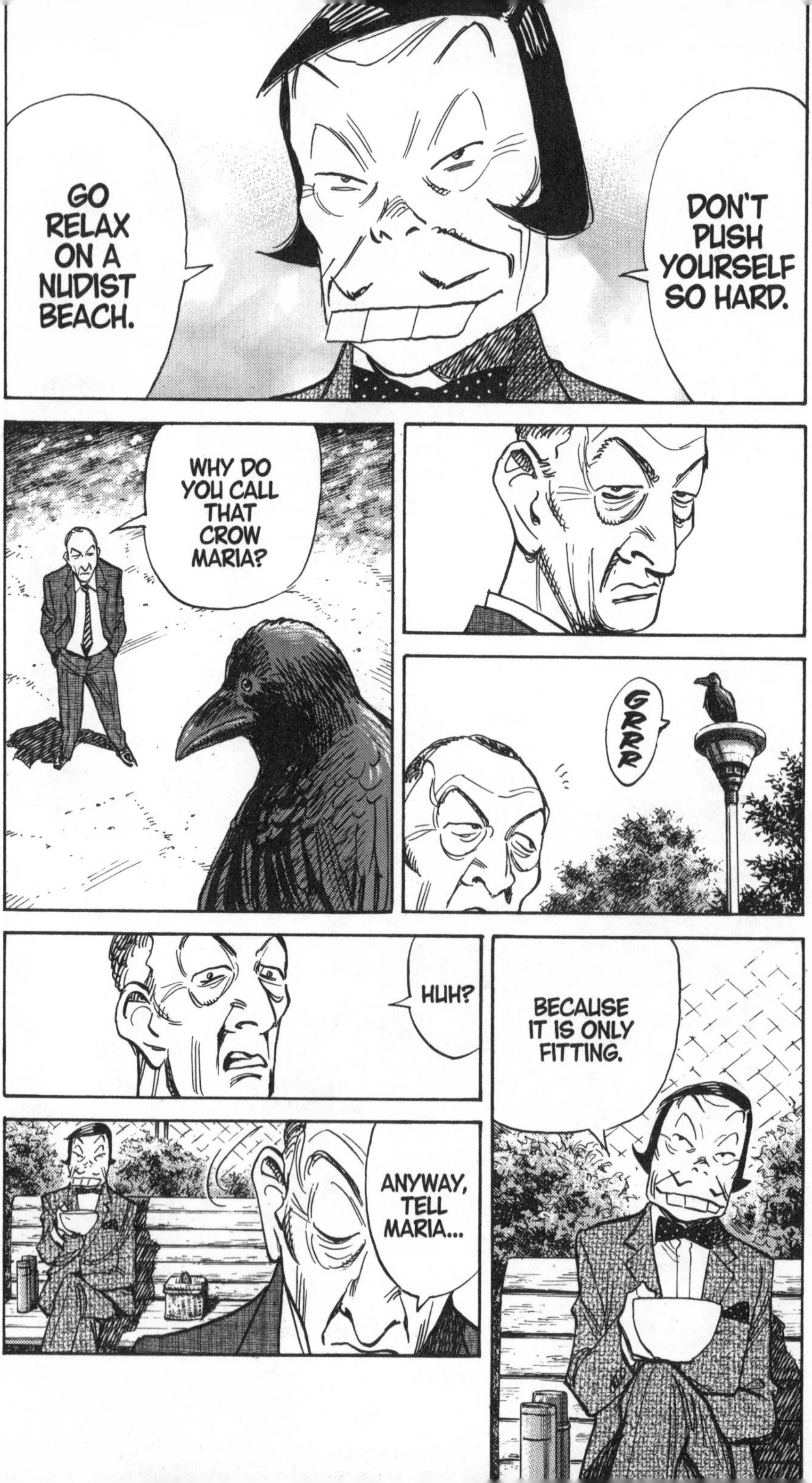
DON'T PUSH YOURSELF SO HARD.
GO RELAX ON A NUDIST BEACH.
GRRR
WHY DO YOU CALL THAT CROW MARIA?
BECAUSE IT IS ONLY FITTING.
HUH?
ANYWAY, TELL MARIA...

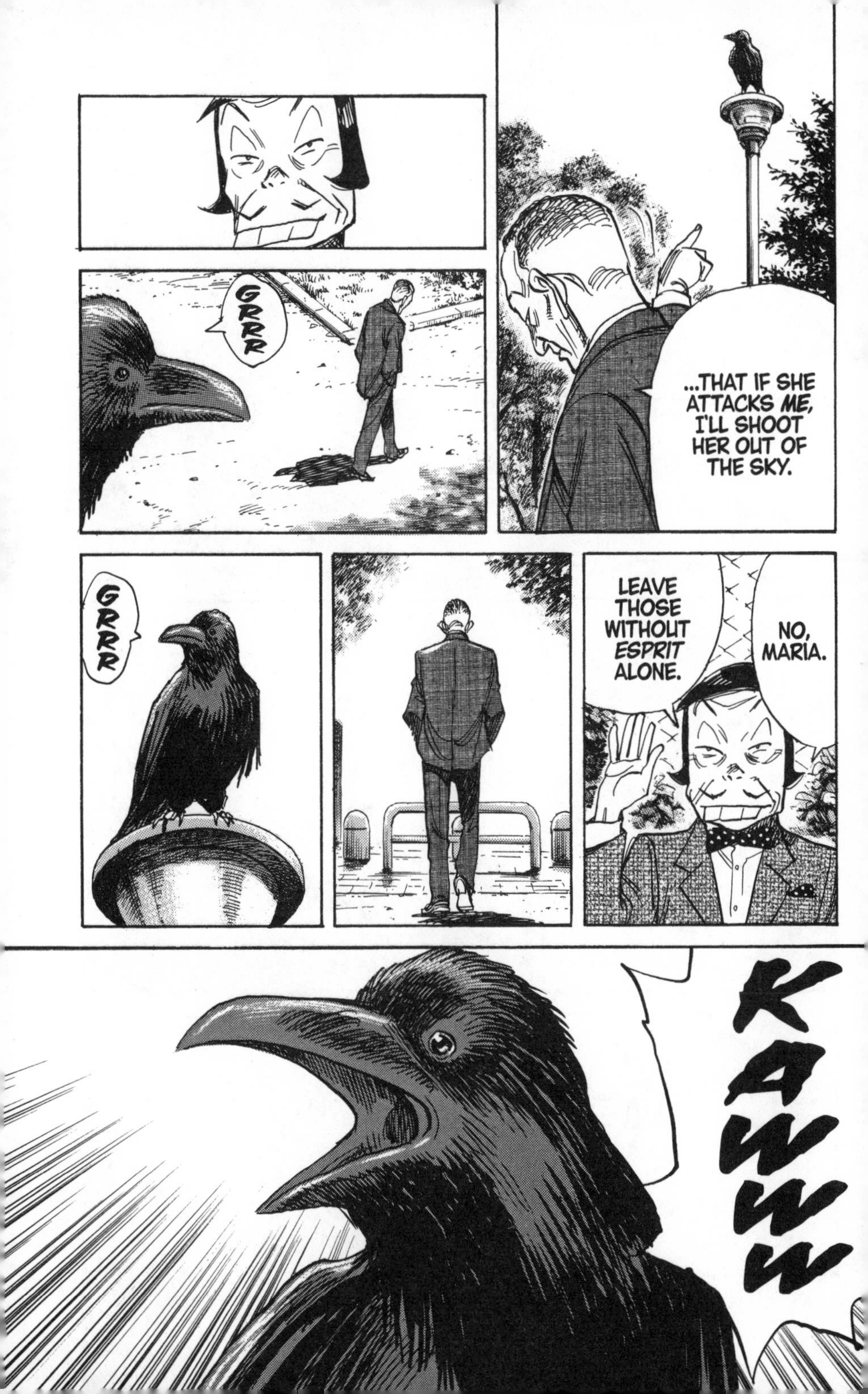
...THAT IF SHE ATTACKS *ME*, I'LL SHOOT HER OUT OF THE SKY.
GRRR
NO, MARIA.
LEAVE THOSE WITHOUT ESPRIT ALONE.
GRRR
KAWWW

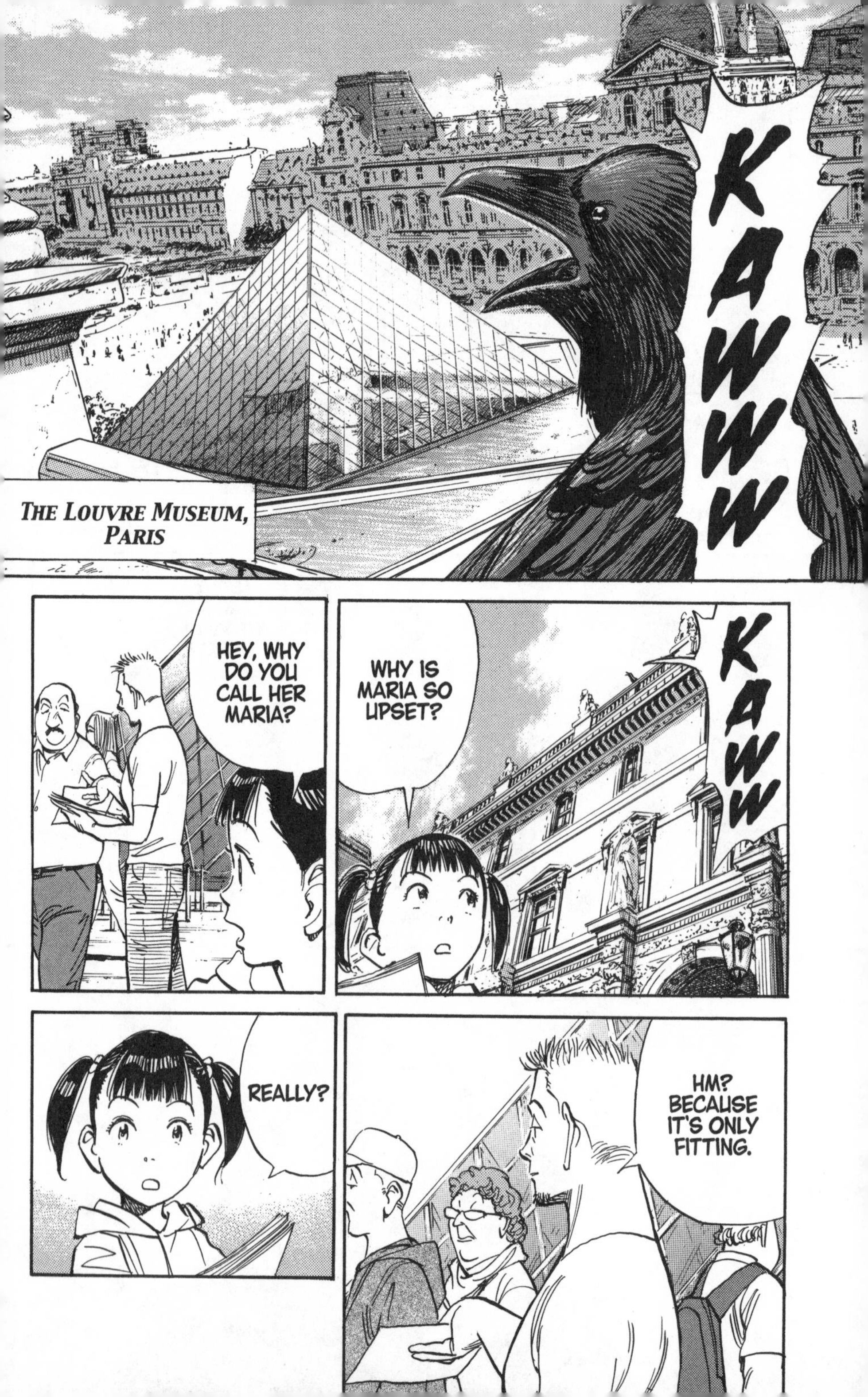
KAWWW
THE LOUVRE MUSEUM, PARIS
KAWW
WHY IS MARIA SO UPSET?
HEY, WHY DO YOU CALL HER MARIA?
HM? BECAUSE IT'S ONLY FITTING.
REALLY?

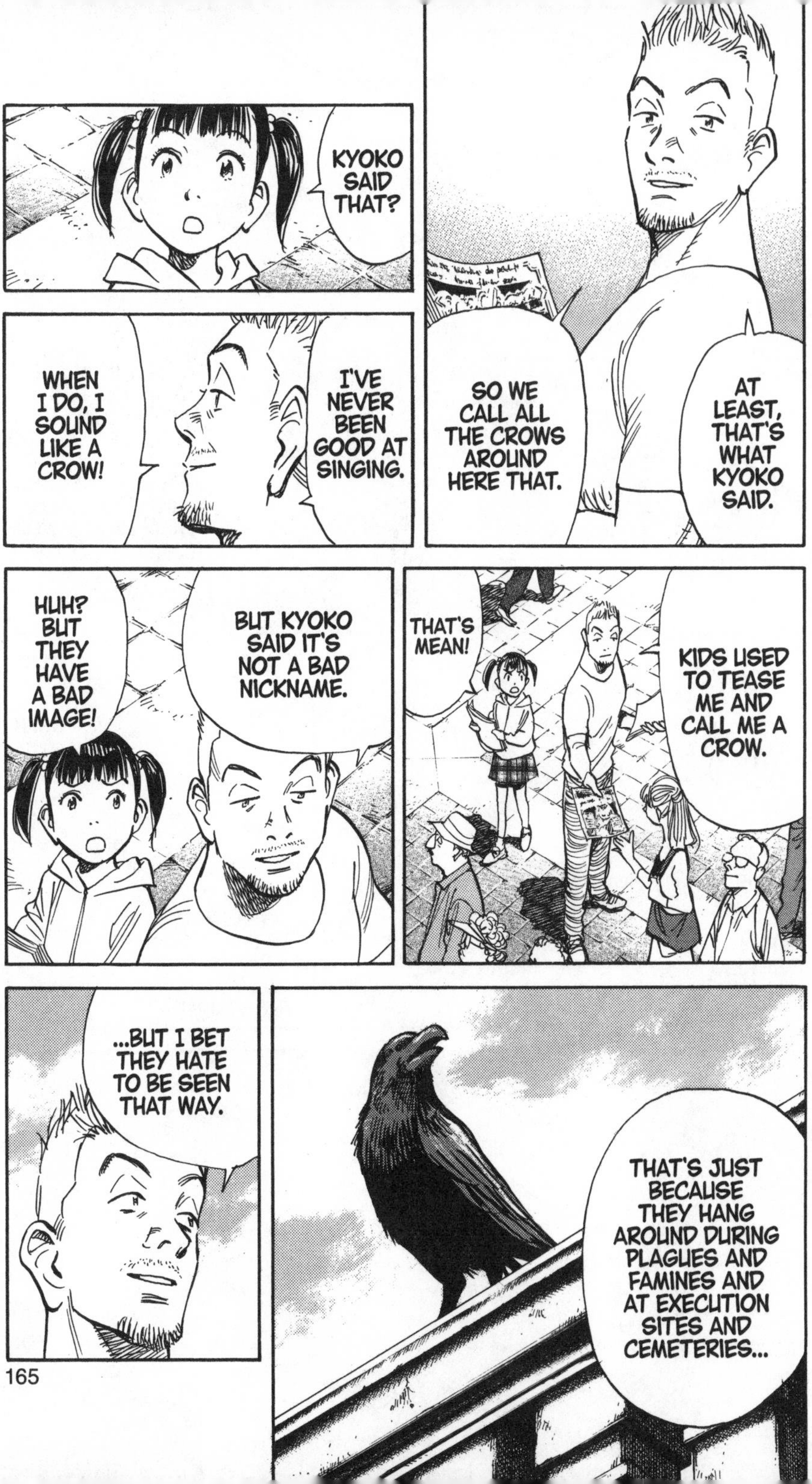
AT LEAST, THAT'S WHAT KYOKO SAID.
SO WE CALL ALL THE CROWS AROUND HERE THAT.
KYOKO SAID THAT?
I'VE NEVER BEEN GOOD AT SINGING.
WHEN I DO, I SOUND LIKE A CROW!
KIDS USED TO TEASE ME AND CALL ME A CROW.
THAT'S MEAN!
BUT KYOKO SAID IT'S NOT A BAD NICKNAME.
HUH? BUT THEY HAVE A BAD IMAGE!
THAT'S JUST BECAUSE THEY HANG AROUND DURING PLAGUES AND FAMINES AND AT EXECUTION SITES AND CEMETERIES...
...BUT I BET THEY HATE TO BE SEEN THAT WAY.

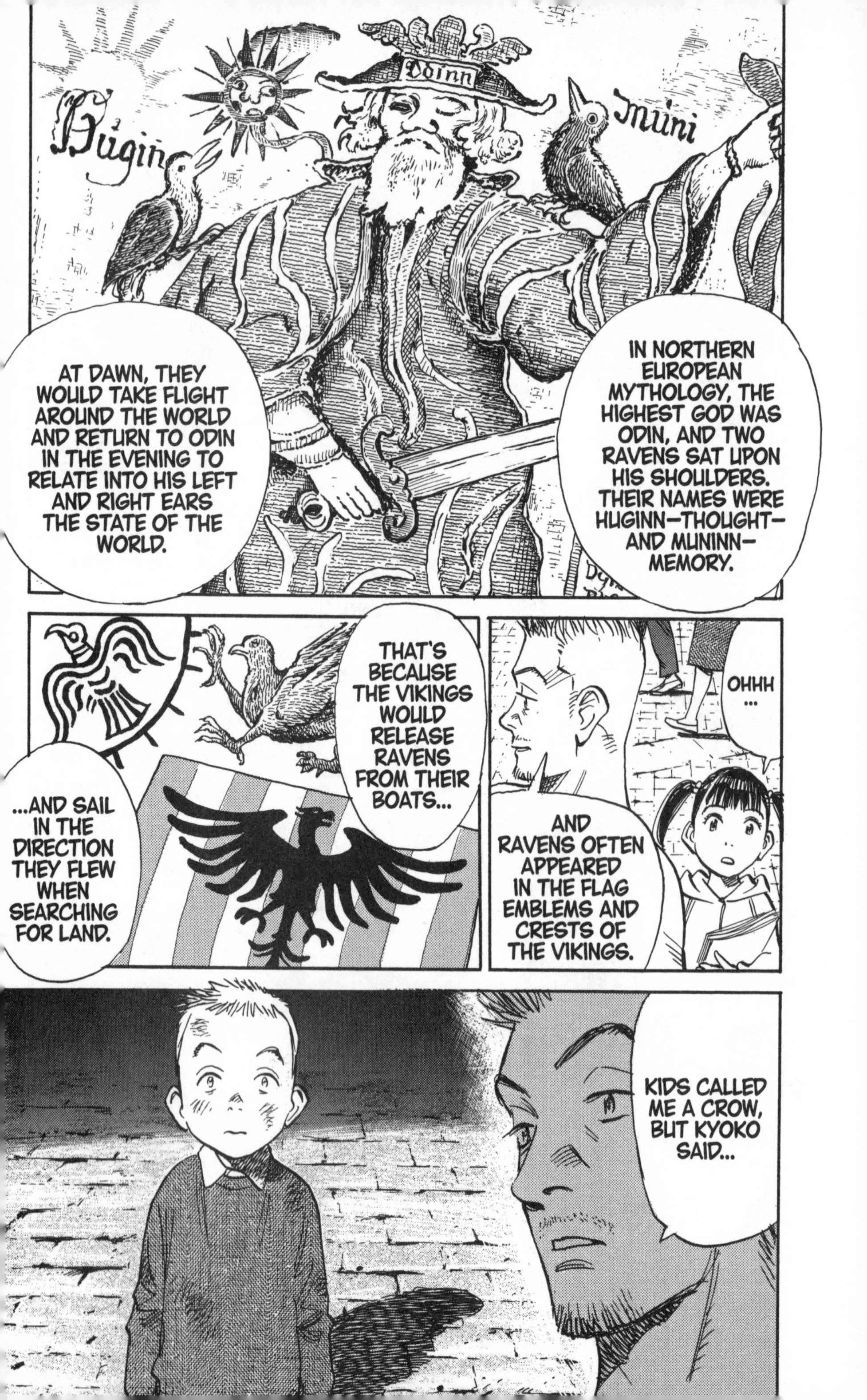
Odinn
Hugin
Muni
IN NORTHERN EUROPEAN MYTHOLOGY, THE HIGHEST GOD WAS ODIN, AND TWO RAVENS SAT UPON HIS SHOULDERS. THEIR NAMES WERE HUGINN—THOUGHT—AND MUNINN—MEMORY.
AT DAWN, THEY WOULD TAKE FLIGHT AROUND THE WORLD AND RETURN TO ODIN IN THE EVENING TO RELATE INTO HIS LEFT AND RIGHT EARS THE STATE OF THE WORLD.
OHHH ...
AND RAVENS OFTEN APPEARED IN THE FLAG EMBLEMS AND CRESTS OF THE VIKINGS.
THAT'S BECAUSE THE VIKINGS WOULD RELEASE RAVENS FROM THEIR BOATS...
...AND SAIL IN THE DIRECTION THEY FLEW WHEN SEARCHING FOR LAND.
KIDS CALLED ME A CROW, BUT KYOKO SAID...

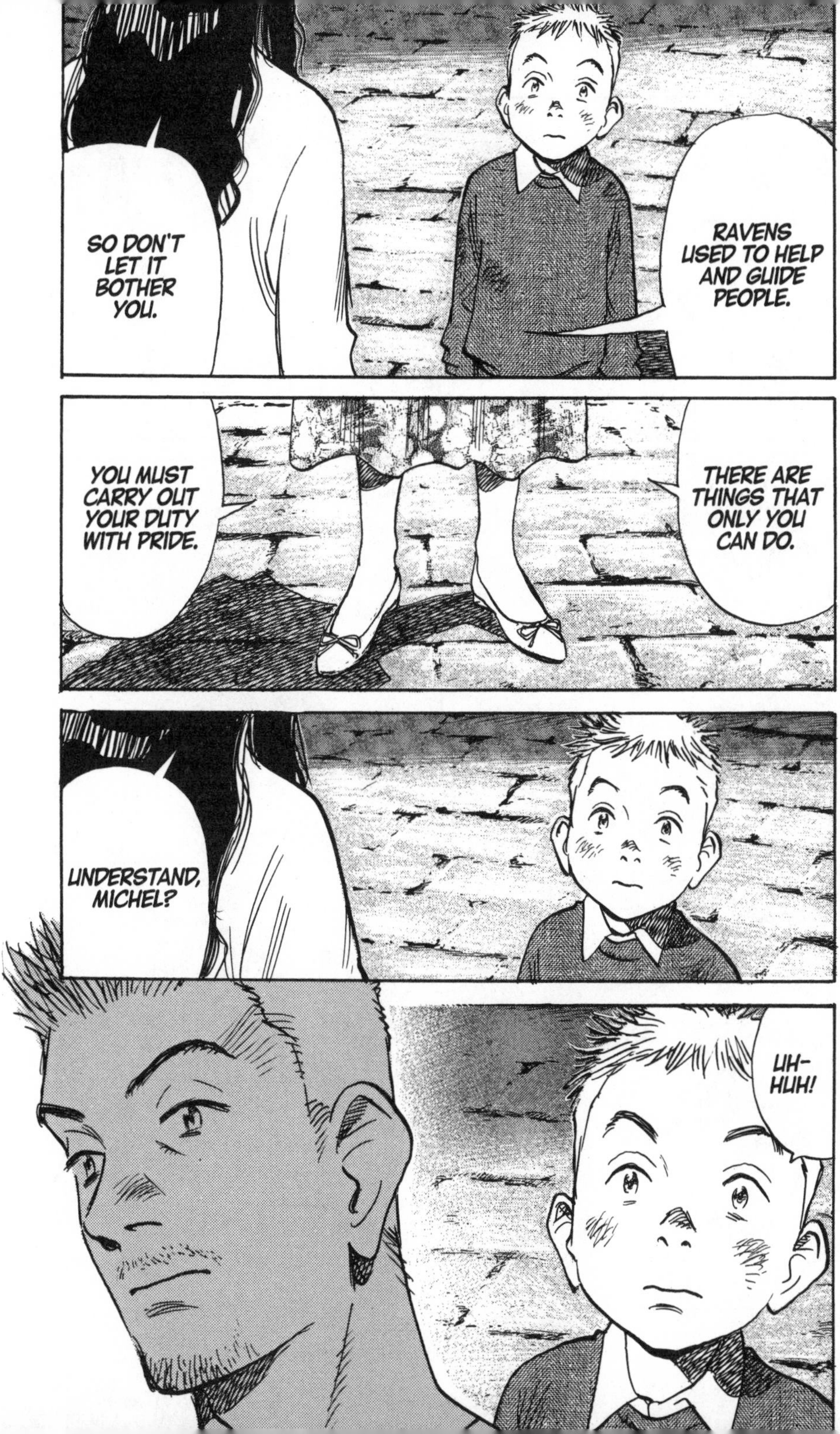
RAVENS USED TO HELP AND GUIDE PEOPLE.
SO DON'T LET IT BOTHER YOU.
THERE ARE THINGS THAT ONLY YOU CAN DO.
YOU MUST CARRY OUT YOUR DUTY WITH PRIDE.
UNDERSTAND, MICHEL?
UH-HUH!

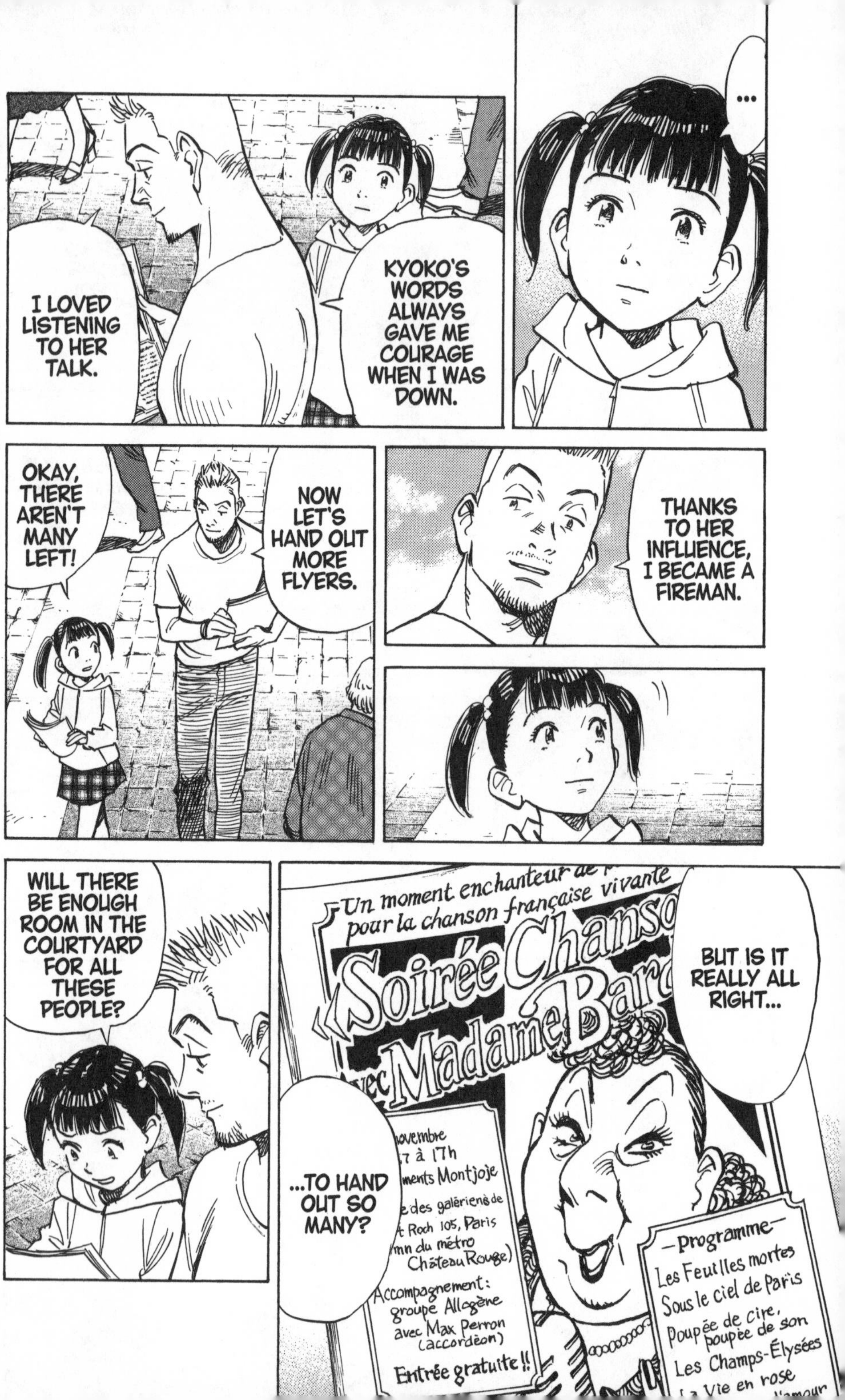
...
KYOKO'S WORDS ALWAYS GAVE ME COURAGE WHEN I WAS DOWN.
I LOVED LISTENING TO HER TALK.
THANKS TO HER INFLUENCE, I BECAME A FIREMAN.
NOW LET'S HAND OUT MORE FLYERS.
OKAY, THERE AREN'T MANY LEFT!
BUT IS IT REALLY ALL RIGHT...
...TO HAND OUT SO MANY?
Un moment enchanteur de
pour la chanson française vivante
Soirée Chanso
Madame Bar
novembre
à 17h
ments Montjoje
des galériens de
Roch 105, Paris
mn du métro
Château Rouge)
Accompagnement:
groupe Allogène
avec Max Perron
(accordéon)
Entrée gratuite !!
Programme
Les Feuilles mortes
Sous le ciel de Paris
Poupée de cire, poupée de son
Les Champs-Élysées
La Vie en rose
WILL THERE BE ENOUGH ROOM IN THE COURTYARD FOR ALL THESE PEOPLE?

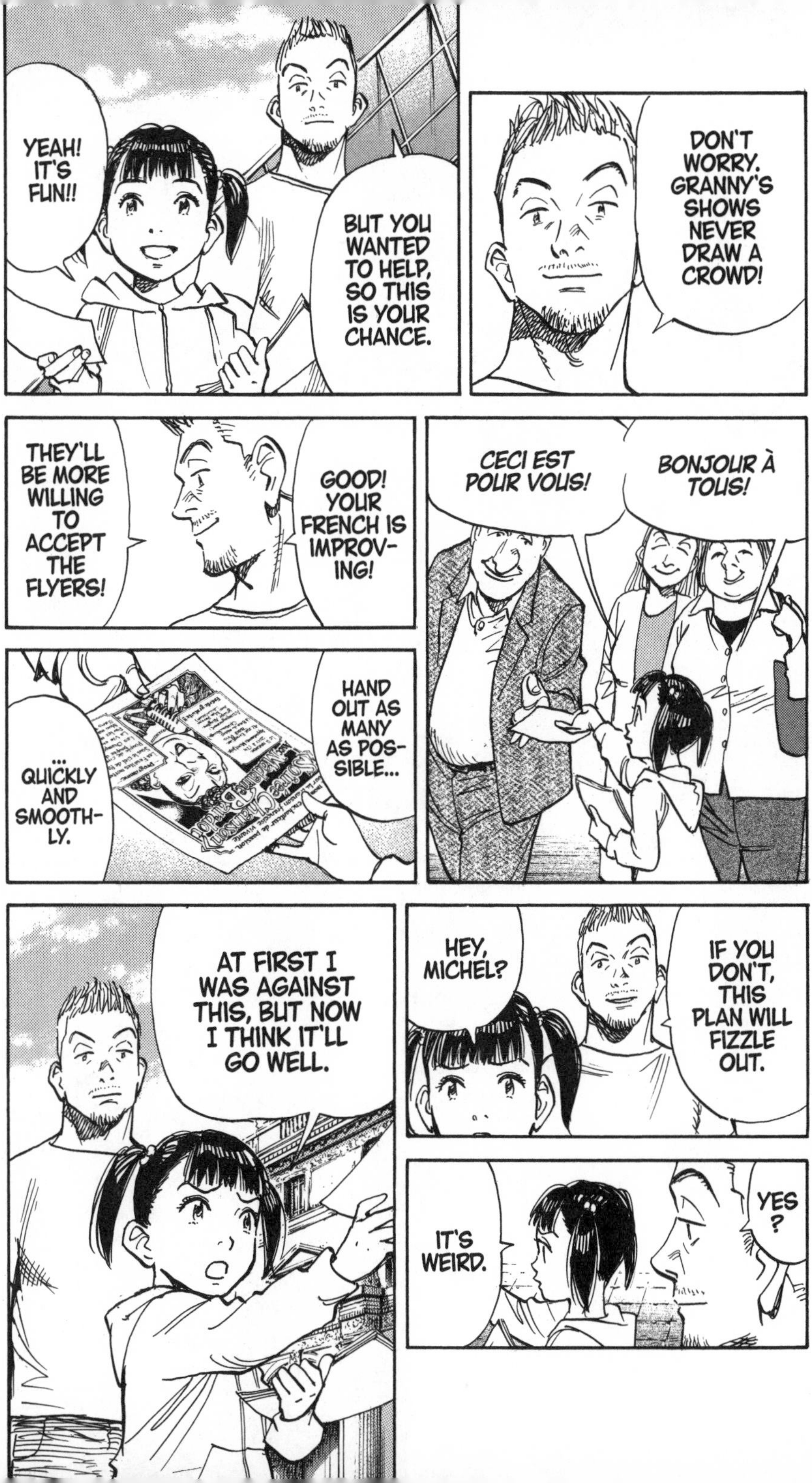
DON'T WORRY. GRANNY'S SHOWS NEVER DRAW A CROWD!
BUT YOU WANTED TO HELP, SO THIS IS YOUR CHANCE.
YEAH! IT'S FUN!!
BONJOUR À TOUS!
CECI EST POUR VOUS!
GOOD! YOUR FRENCH IS IMPROV-ING!
THEY'LL BE MORE WILLING TO ACCEPT THE FLYERS!
HAND OUT AS MANY AS POS-SIBLE...
...QUICKLY AND SMOOTH-LY.
IF YOU DON'T, THIS PLAN WILL FIZZLE OUT.
HEY, MICHEL?
YES?
IT'S WEIRD.
AT FIRST I WAS AGAINST THIS, BUT NOW I THINK IT'LL GO WELL.

IT'S LIKE THE DIRECTOR IS CONTROLLING EVERYTHING FROM AFAR.

...BUT MY DAD.

NO ONE WOULD LISTEN TO SUCH A SHADY GUY...

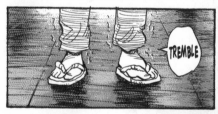

TREMBLE

TREMBLE

TREMBLE

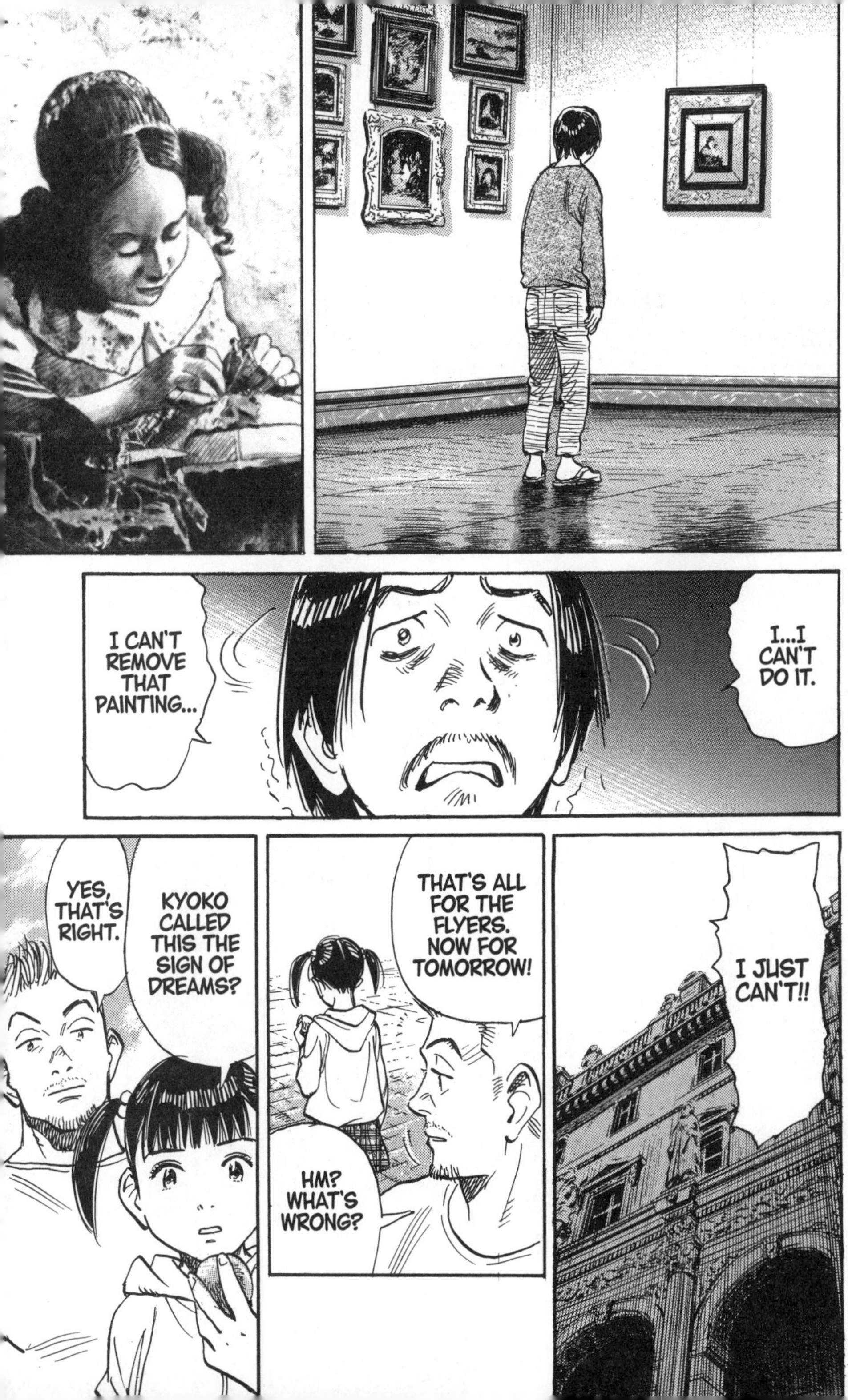
I...I CAN'T DO IT.
I CAN'T REMOVE THAT PAINTING...
I JUST CAN'T!!
THAT'S ALL FOR THE FLYERS. NOW FOR TOMORROW!
HM? WHAT'S WRONG?
KYOKO CALLED THIS THE SIGN OF DREAMS?
YES, THAT'S RIGHT.

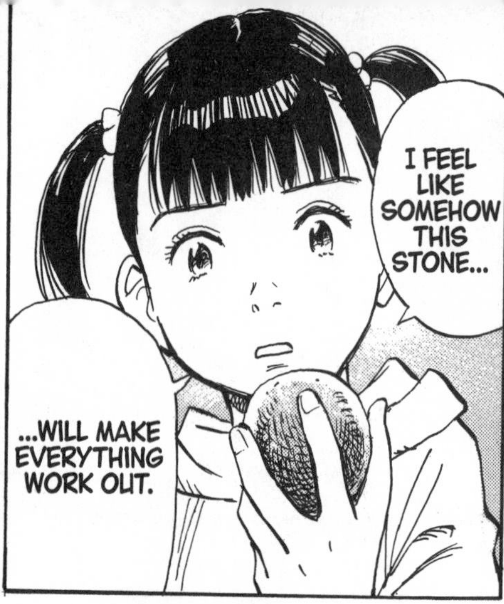
I FEEL LIKE SOMEHOW THIS STONE...
...WILL MAKE EVERYTHING WORK OUT.
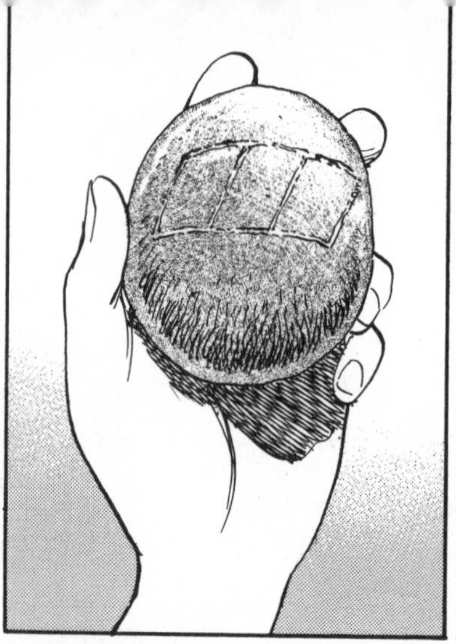
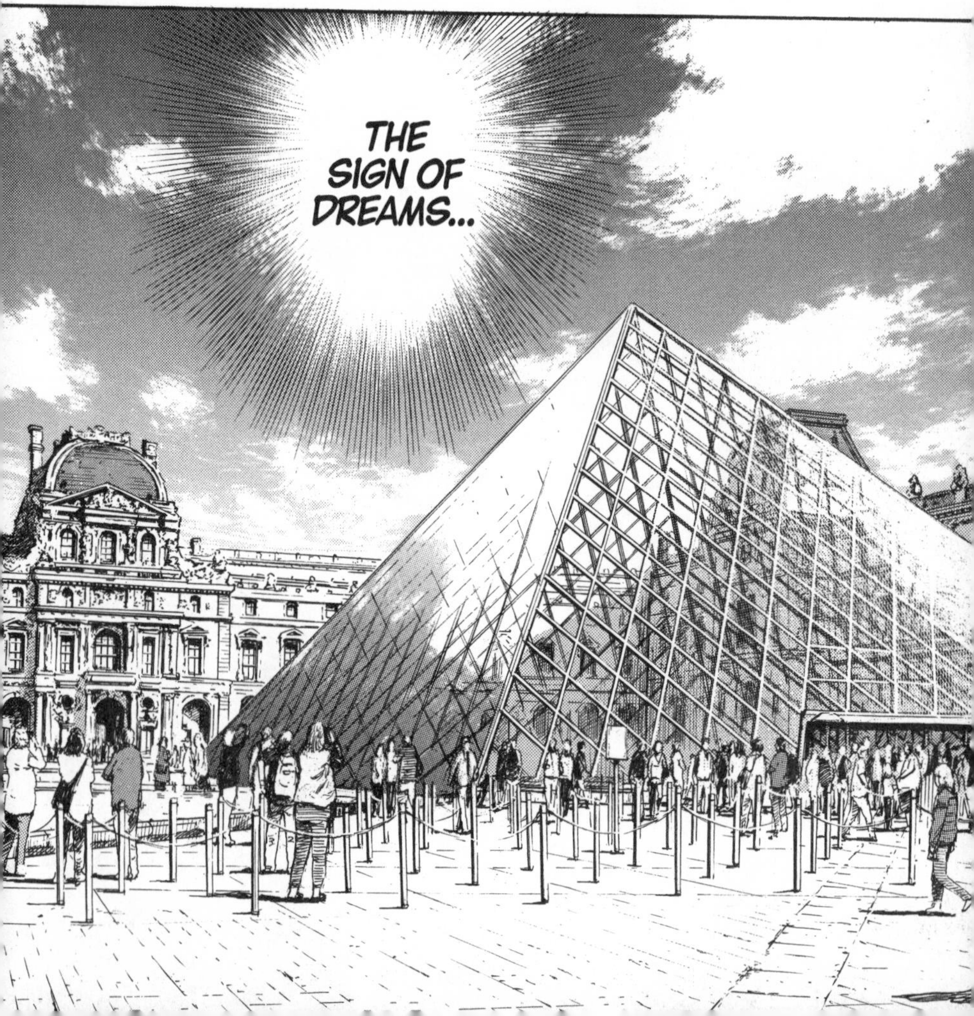
THE SIGN OF DREAMS...

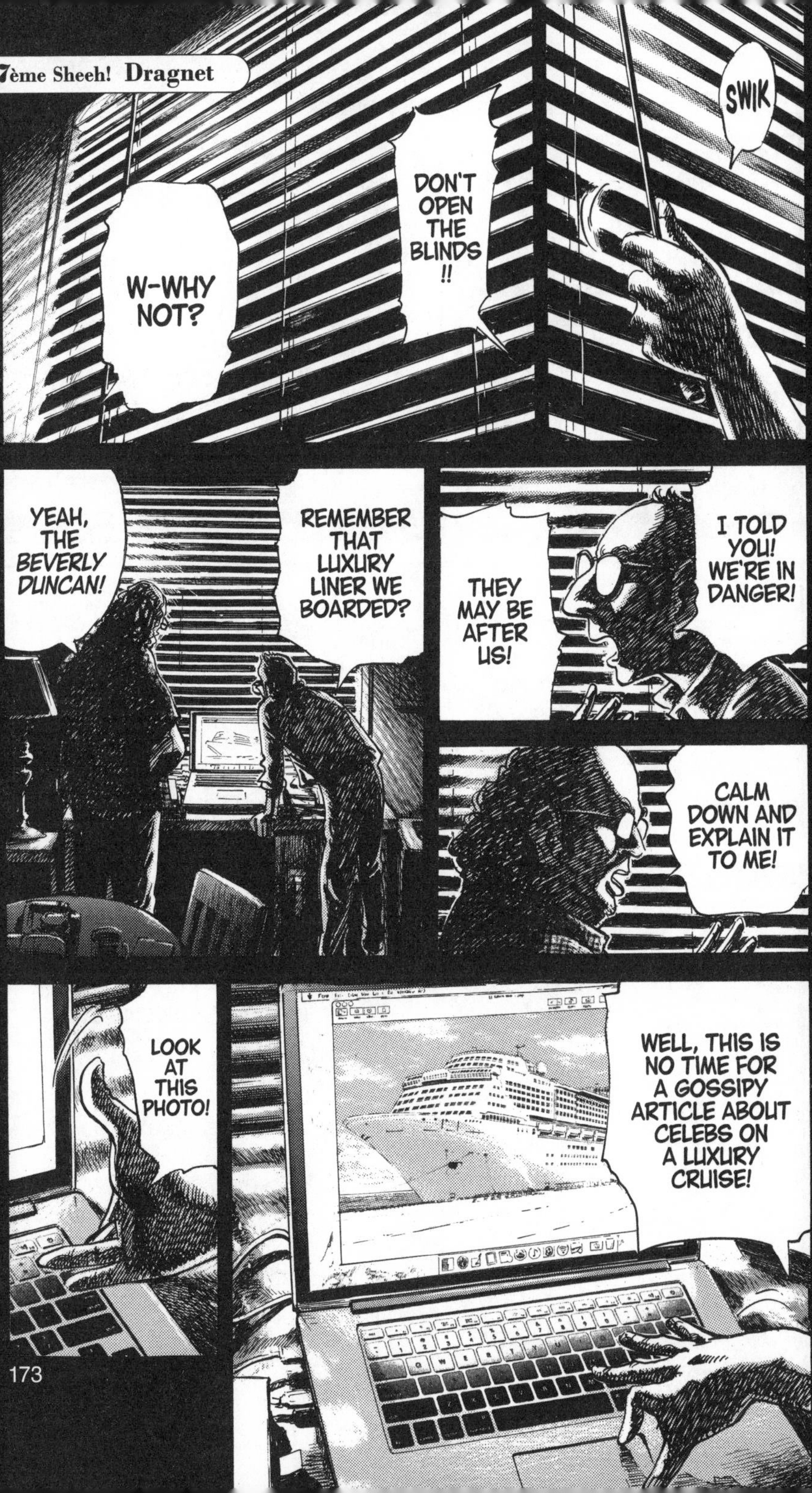
SWIK
DON'T OPEN THE BLINDS!!
W-WHY NOT?
I TOLD YOU! WE'RE IN DANGER!
THEY MAY BE AFTER US!
CALM DOWN AND EXPLAIN IT TO ME!
REMEMBER THAT LUXURY LINER WE BOARDED?
YEAH, THE BEVERLY DUNCAN!
WELL, THIS IS NO TIME FOR A GOSSIPY ARTICLE ABOUT CELEBS ON A LUXURY CRUISE!
LOOK AT THIS PHOTO!

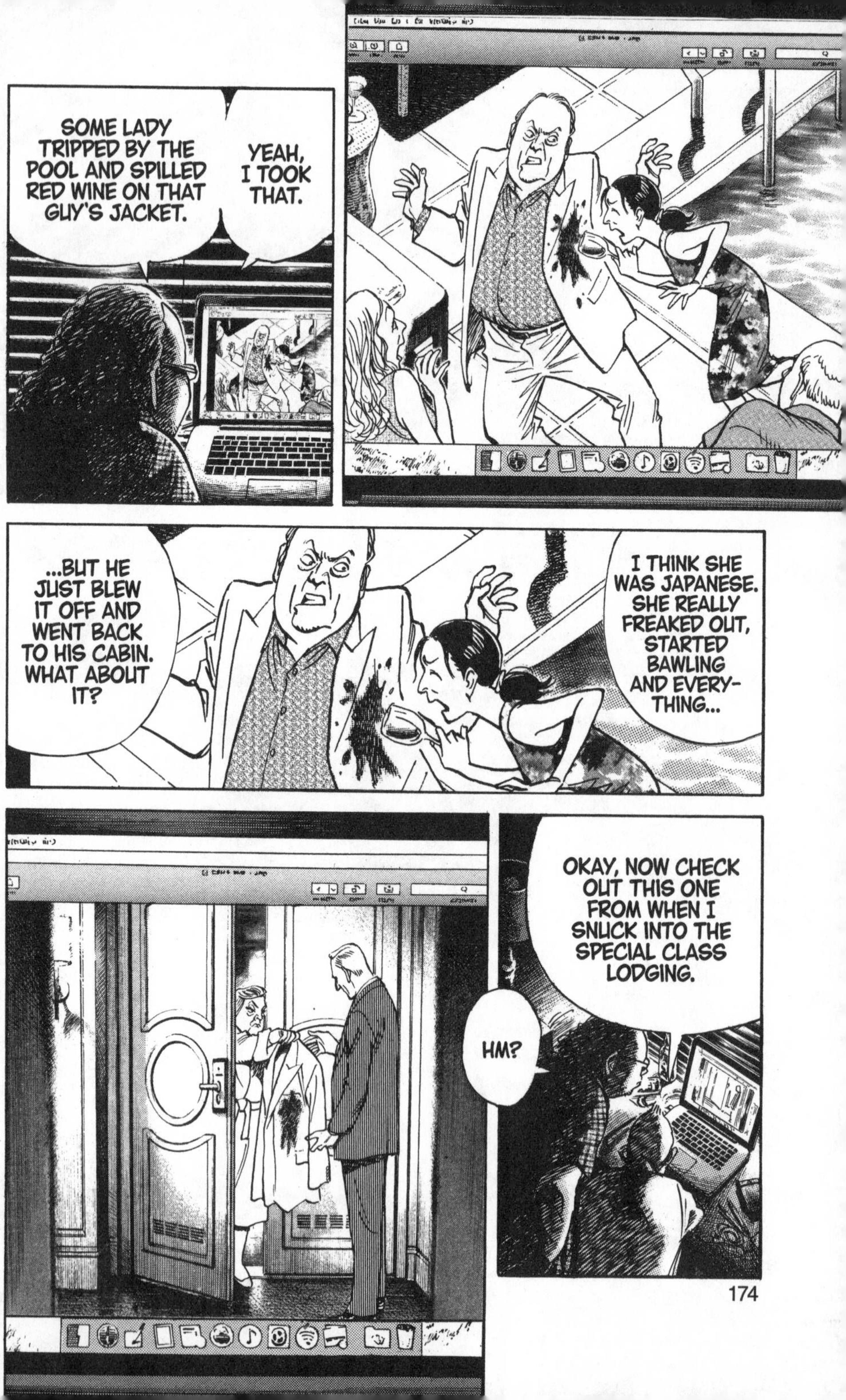
YEAH, I TOOK THAT.
SOME LADY TRIPPED BY THE POOL AND SPILLED RED WINE ON THAT GUY'S JACKET.
I THINK SHE WAS JAPANESE. SHE REALLY FREAKED OUT, STARTED BAWLING AND EVERY-THING...
...BUT HE JUST BLEW IT OFF AND WENT BACK TO HIS CABIN. WHAT ABOUT IT?
OKAY, NOW CHECK OUT THIS ONE FROM WHEN I SNUCK INTO THE SPECIAL CLASS LODGING.
HM?

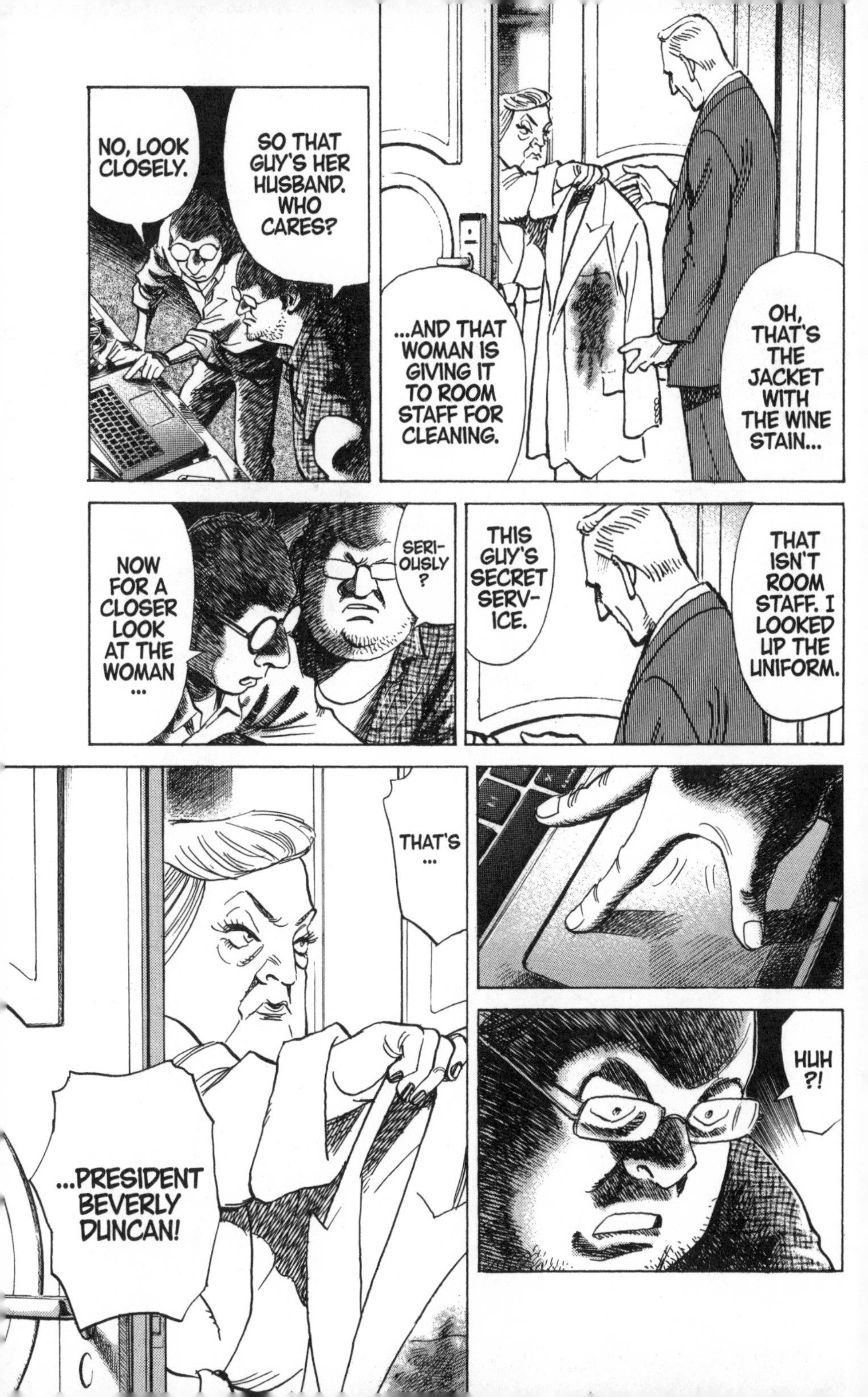
OH, THAT'S THE JACKET WITH THE WINE STAIN...
...AND THAT WOMAN IS GIVING IT TO ROOM STAFF FOR CLEANING.
SO THAT GUY'S HER HUSBAND. WHO CARES?
NO, LOOK CLOSELY.
THAT ISN'T ROOM STAFF. I LOOKED UP THE UNIFORM.
THIS GUY'S SECRET SERV-ICE.
SERI-OUSLY?
NOW FOR A CLOSER LOOK AT THE WOMAN...
HUH?!
THAT'S...
...PRESIDENT BEVERLY DUNCAN!

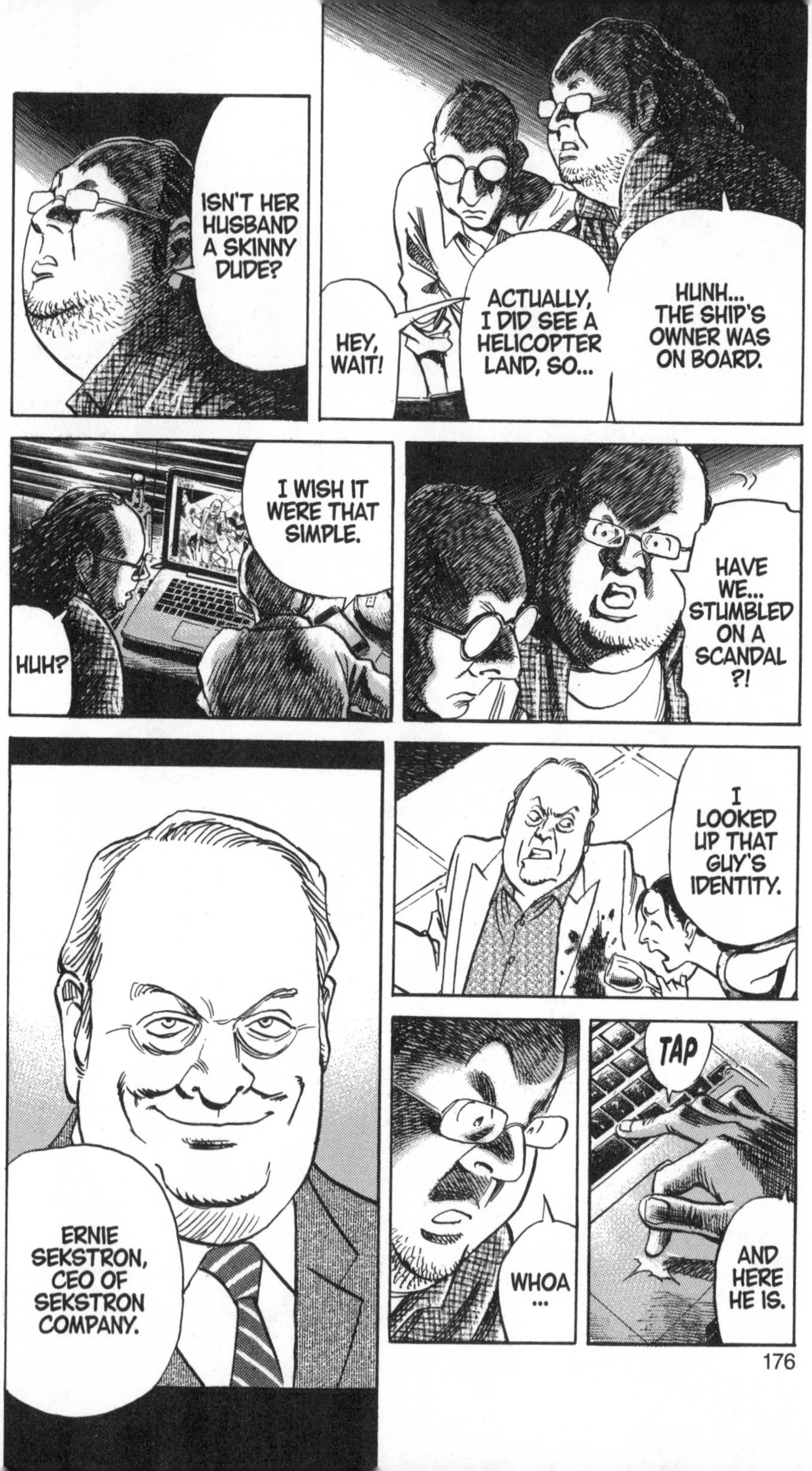
HUNH... THE SHIP'S OWNER WAS ON BOARD.
ACTUALLY, I DID SEE A HELICOPTER LAND, SO...
HEY, WAIT!
ISN'T HER HUSBAND A SKINNY DUDE?
HAVE WE... STUMBLED ON A SCANDAL ?!
I WISH IT WERE THAT SIMPLE.
HUH?
I LOOKED UP THAT GUY'S IDENTITY.
TAP
AND HERE HE IS.
WHOA ...
ERNIE SEKSTRON, CEO OF SEKSTRON COMPANY.

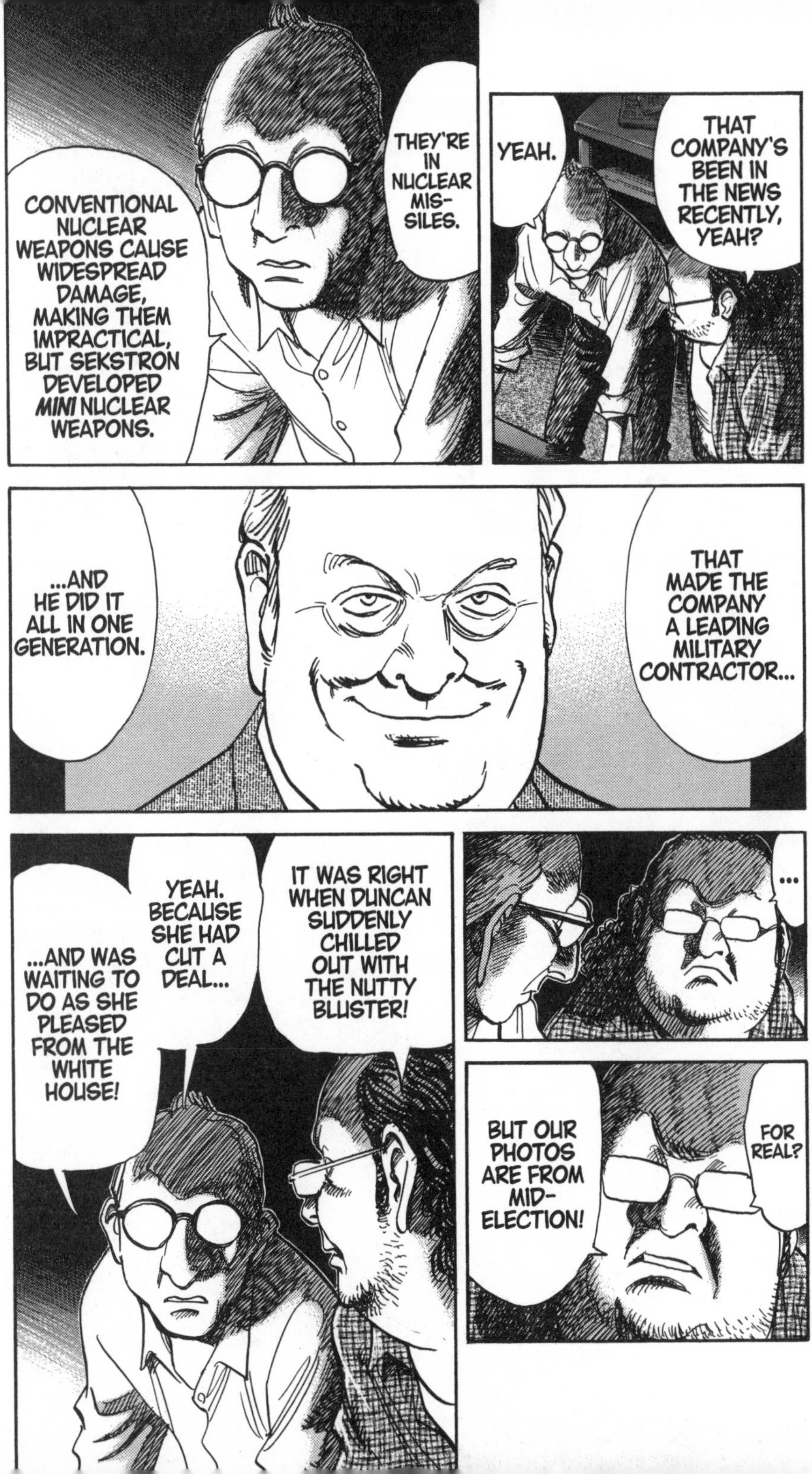
THAT COMPANY'S BEEN IN THE NEWS RECENTLY, YEAH?
YEAH.
THEY'RE IN NUCLEAR MIS-SILES.
CONVENTIONAL NUCLEAR WEAPONS CAUSE WIDESPREAD DAMAGE, MAKING THEM IMPRACTICAL, BUT SEKSTRON DEVELOPED *MINI* NUCLEAR WEAPONS.
THAT MADE THE COMPANY A LEADING MILITARY CONTRACTOR...
...AND HE DID IT ALL IN ONE GENERATION.
...
FOR REAL?
BUT OUR PHOTOS ARE FROM MID-ELECTION!
IT WAS RIGHT WHEN DUNCAN SUDDENLY CHILLED OUT WITH THE NUTTY BLUSTER!
YEAH. BECAUSE SHE HAD CUT A DEAL...
...AND WAS WAITING TO DO AS SHE PLEASED FROM THE WHITE HOUSE!

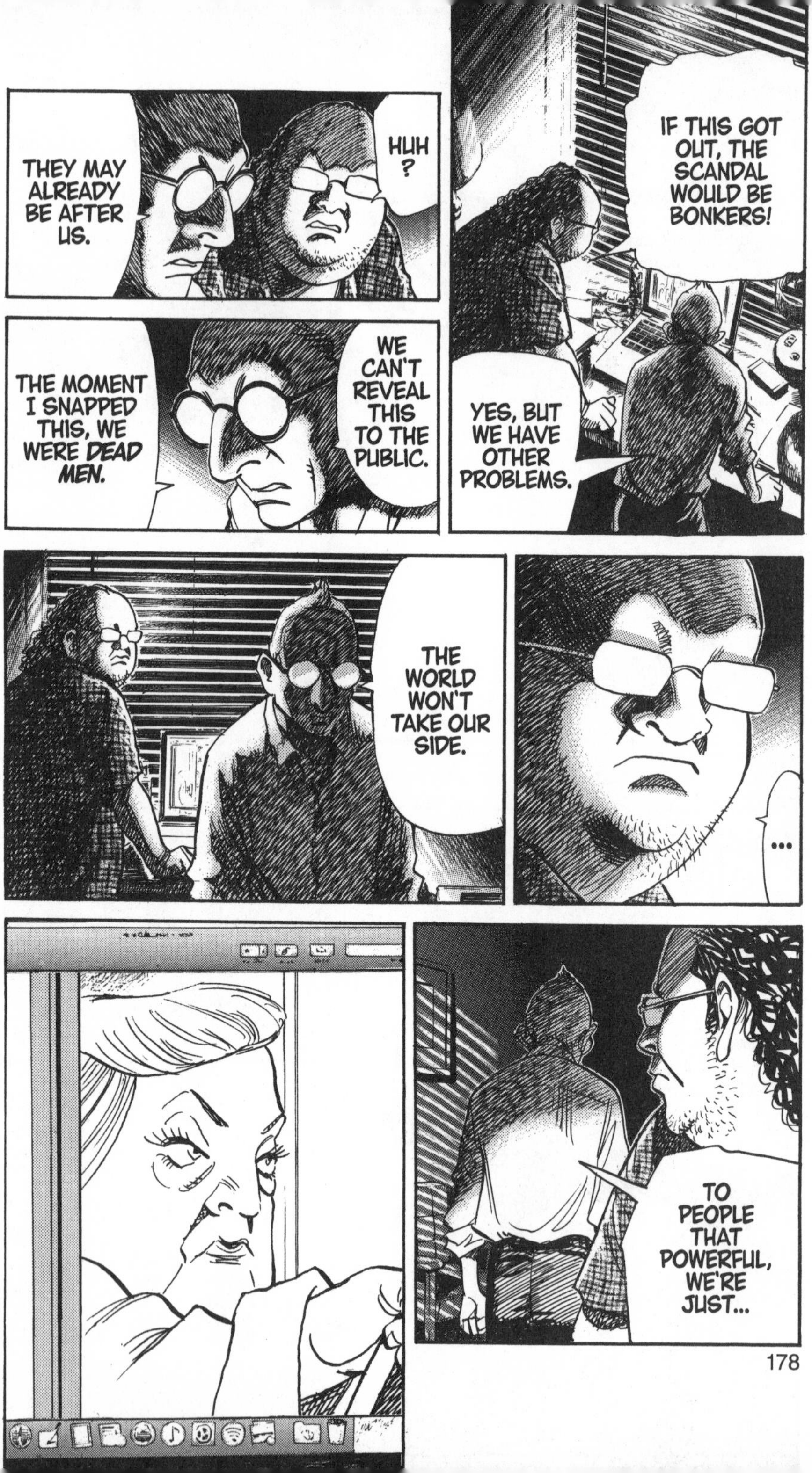
IF THIS GOT OUT, THE SCANDAL WOULD BE BONKERS!
YES, BUT WE HAVE OTHER PROBLEMS.
HUH?
THEY MAY ALREADY BE AFTER US.
WE CAN'T REVEAL THIS TO THE PUBLIC.
THE MOMENT I SNAPPED THIS, WE WERE *DEAD MEN.*
...
THE WORLD WON'T TAKE OUR SIDE.
TO PEOPLE THAT POWERFUL, WE'RE JUST...

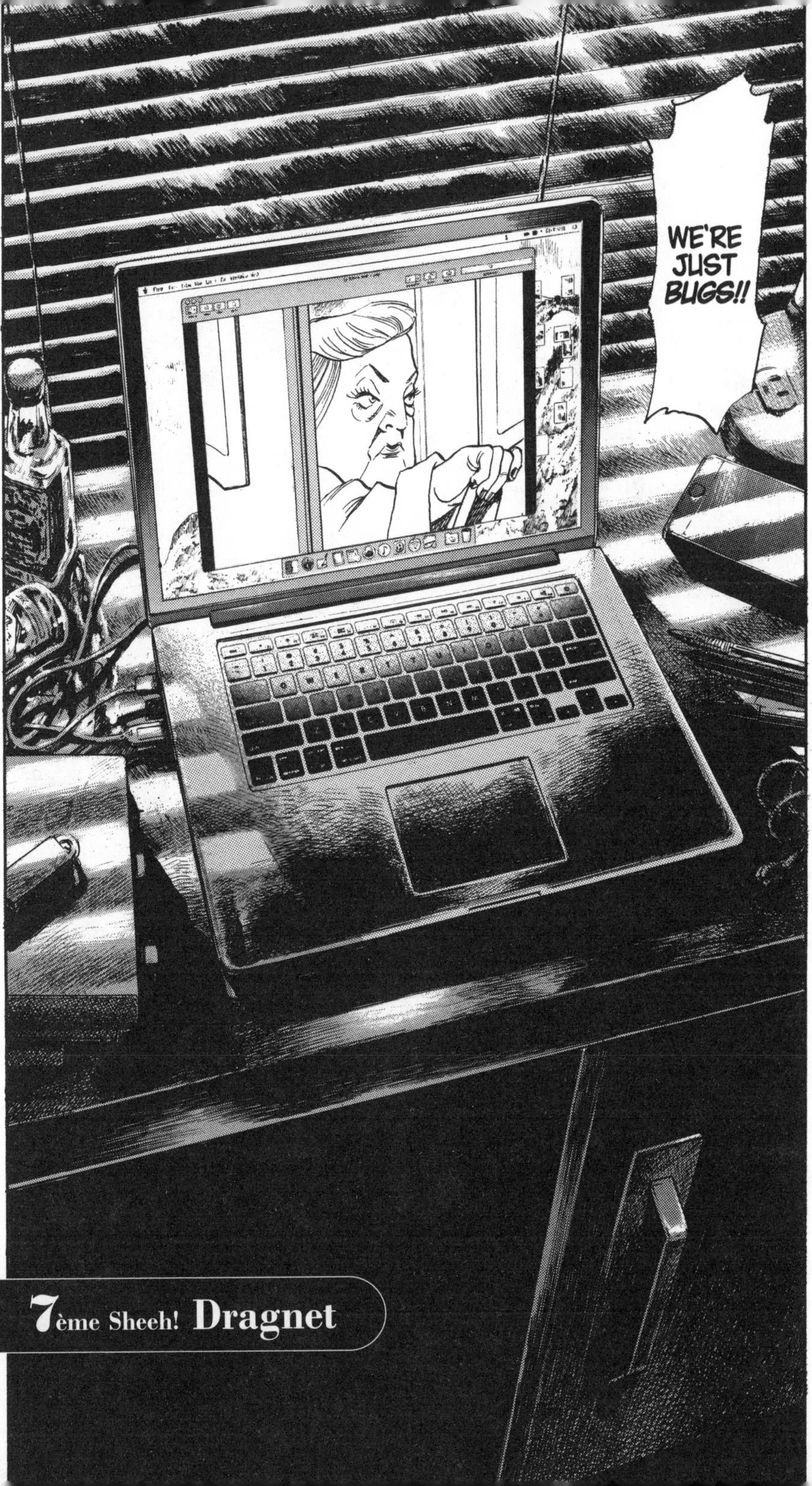
WE'RE JUST BUGS!!

7ème Sheeh! Dragnet

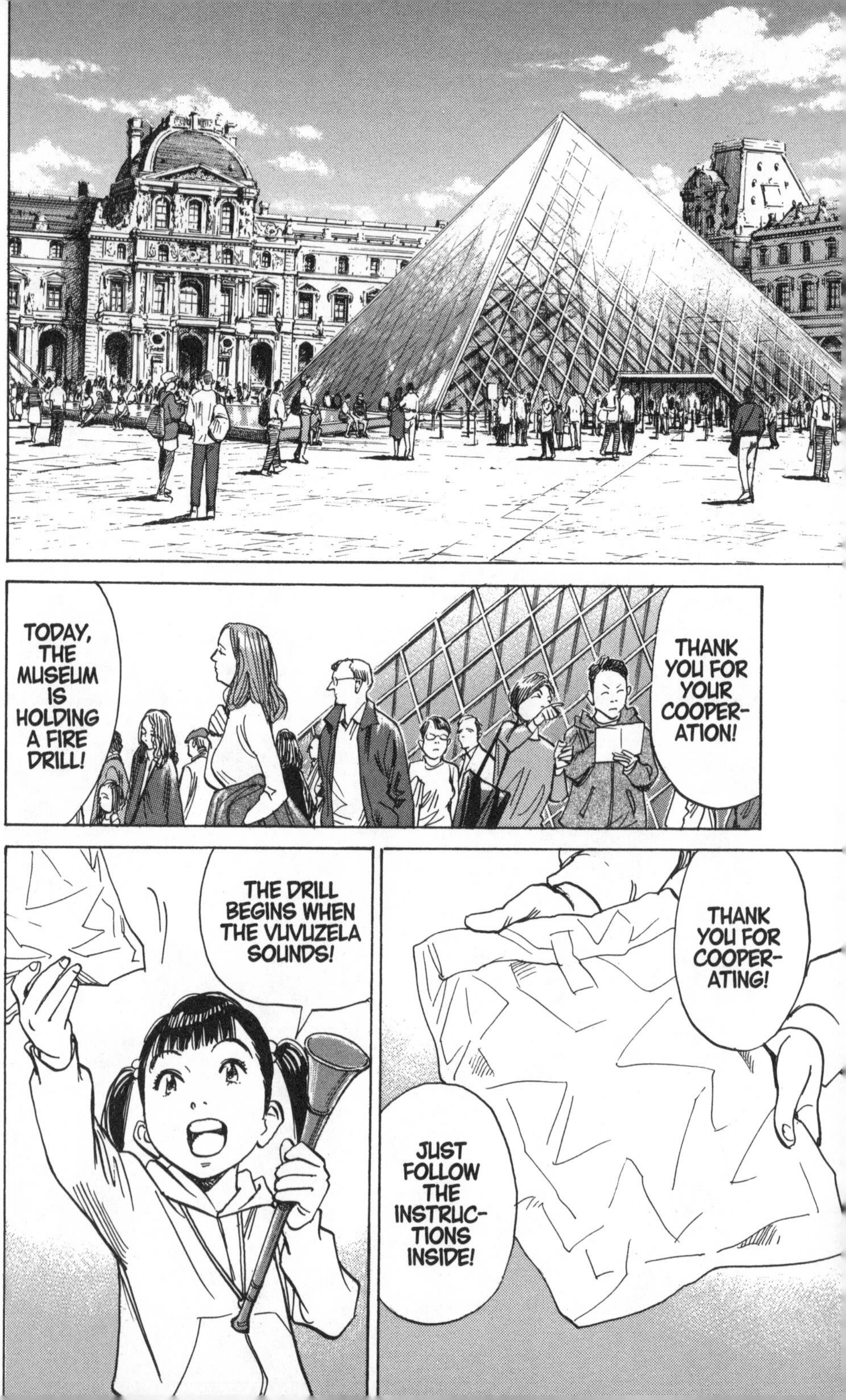
THANK YOU FOR YOUR COOPER-ATION!
TODAY, THE MUSEUM IS HOLDING A FIRE DRILL!
THANK YOU FOR COOPER-ATING!
JUST FOLLOW THE INSTRUC-TIONS INSIDE!
THE DRILL BEGINS WHEN THE VUVUZELA SOUNDS!

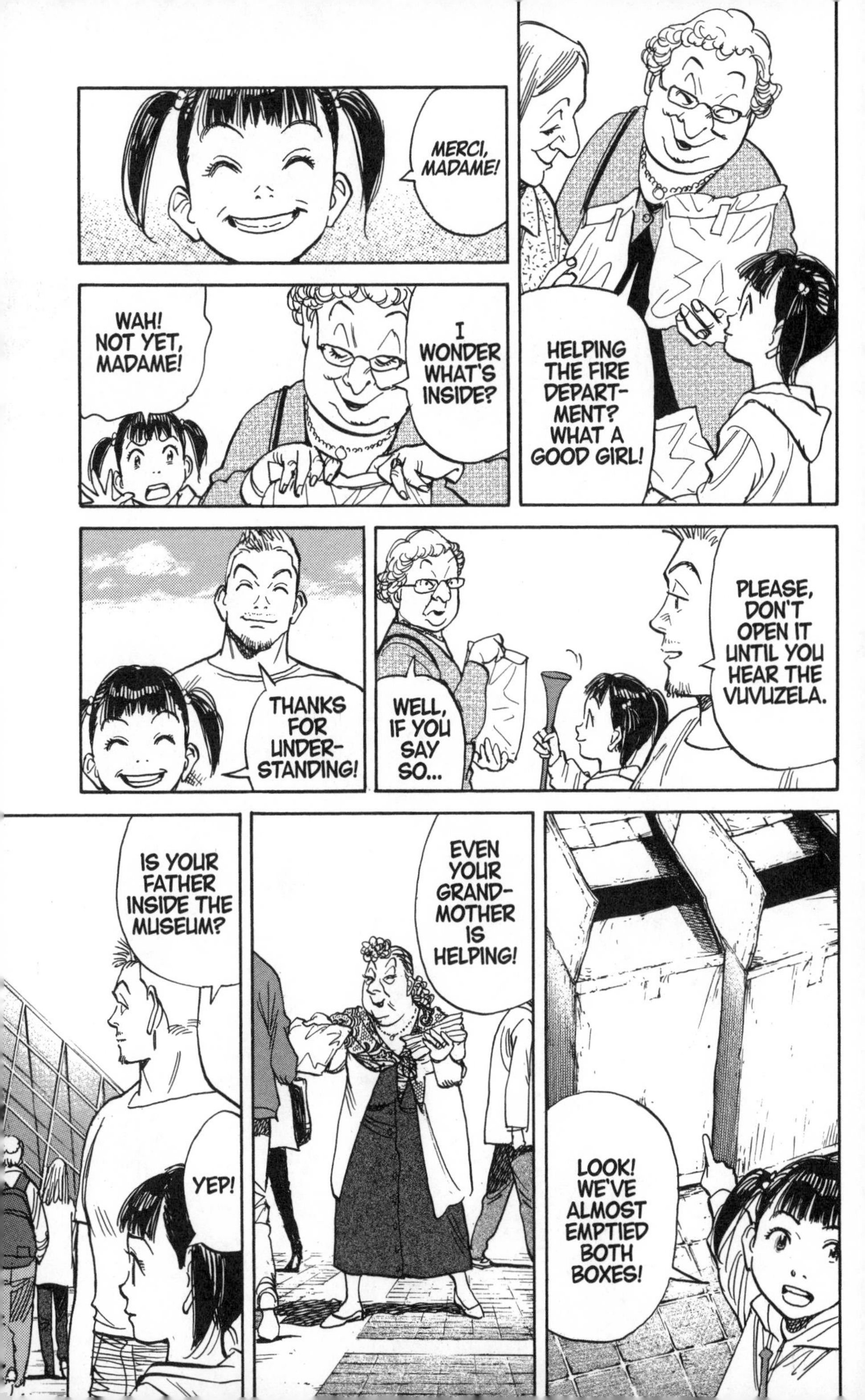
HELPING THE FIRE DEPARTMENT? WHAT A GOOD GIRL!
MERCI, MADAME!
I WONDER WHAT'S INSIDE?
WAH! NOT YET, MADAME!
PLEASE, DON'T OPEN IT UNTIL YOU HEAR THE VUVUZELA.
WELL, IF YOU SAY SO...
THANKS FOR UNDER-STANDING!
LOOK! WE'VE ALMOST EMPTIED BOTH BOXES!
EVEN YOUR GRAND-MOTHER IS HELPING!
IS YOUR FATHER INSIDE THE MUSEUM?
YEP!

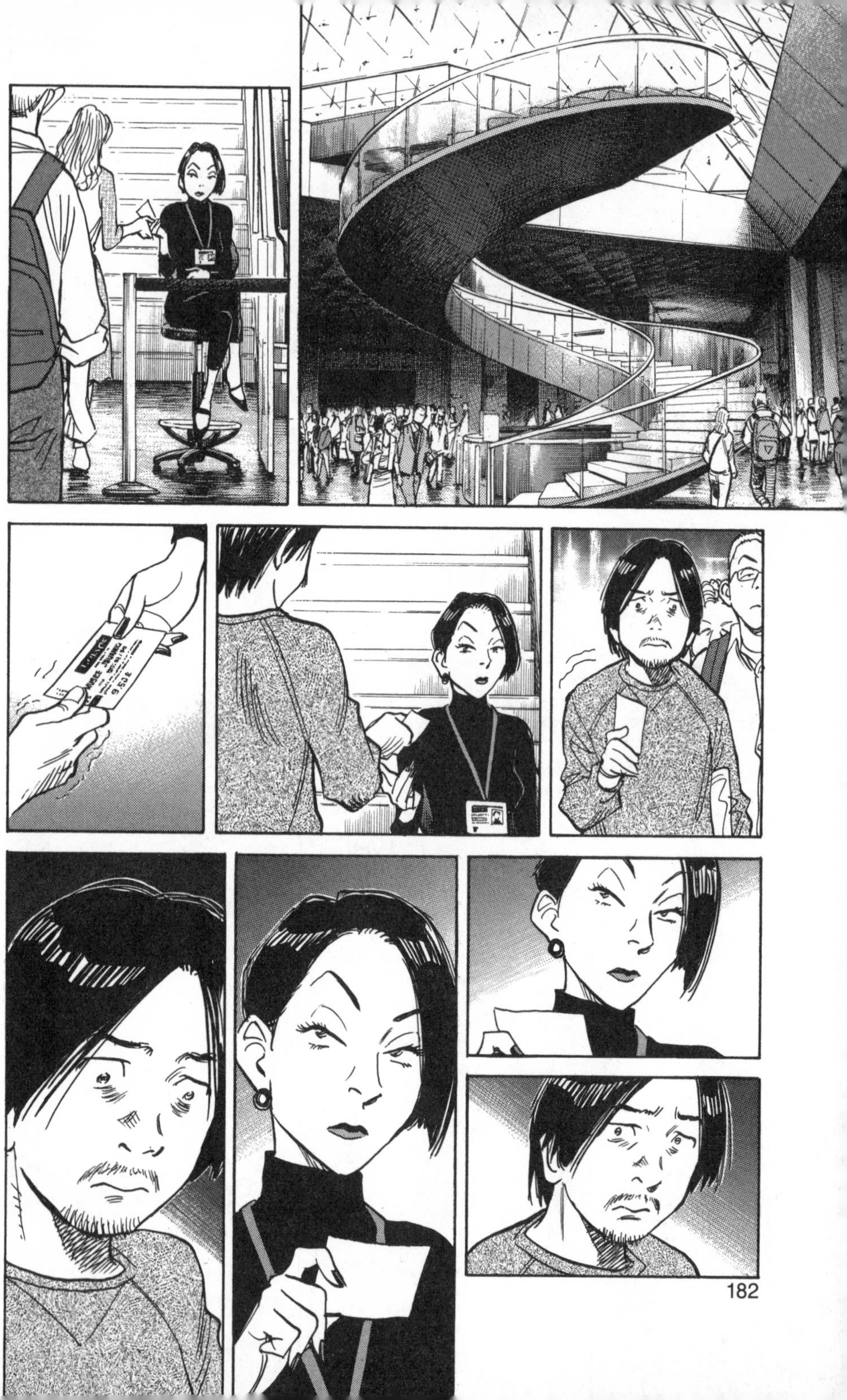

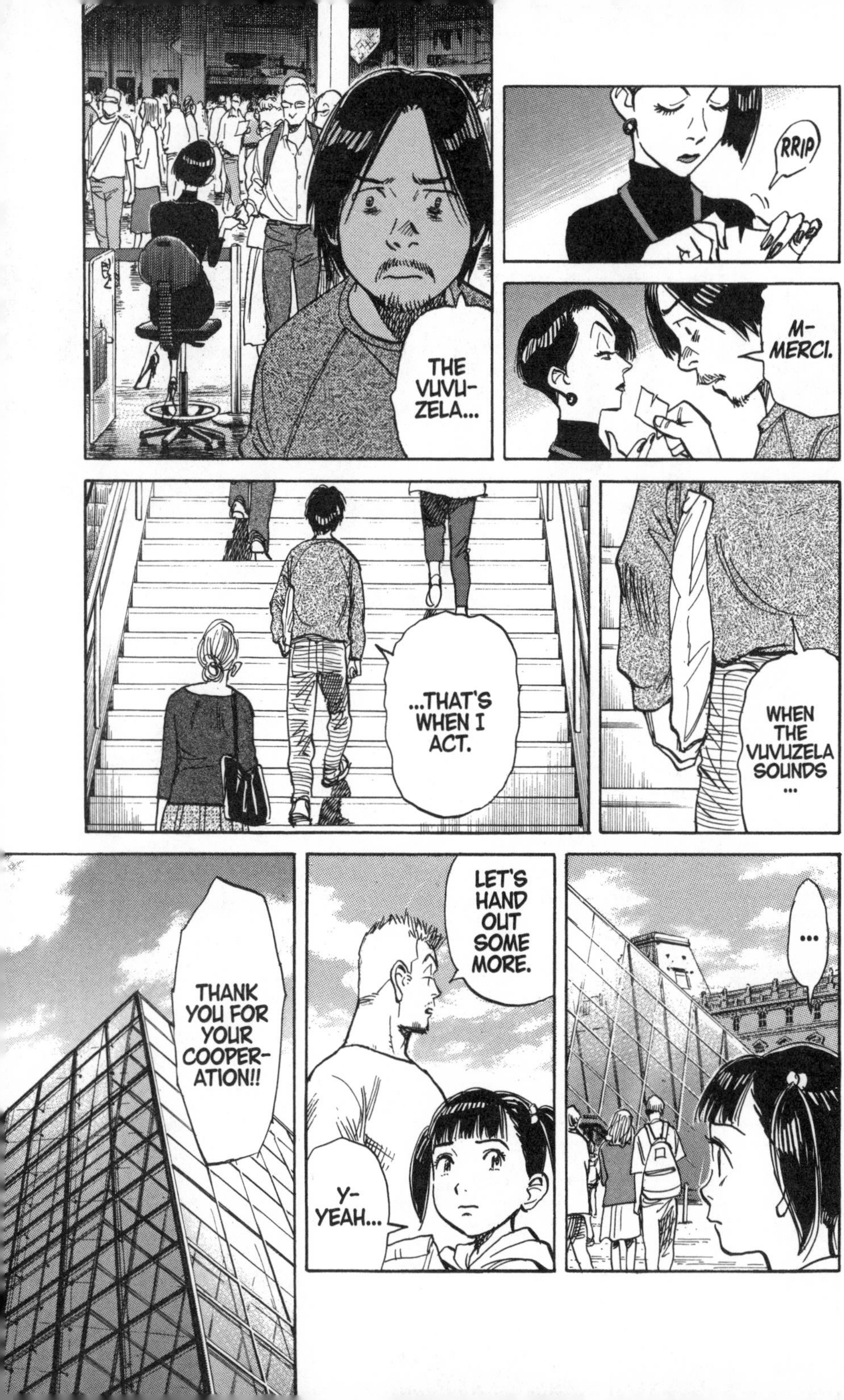
RRIP
M-MERCI.
THE VUVUZELA...
WHEN THE VUVUZELA SOUNDS ...
...THAT'S WHEN I ACT.
...
LET'S HAND OUT SOME MORE.
Y-YEAH...
THANK YOU FOR YOUR COOPERATION!!

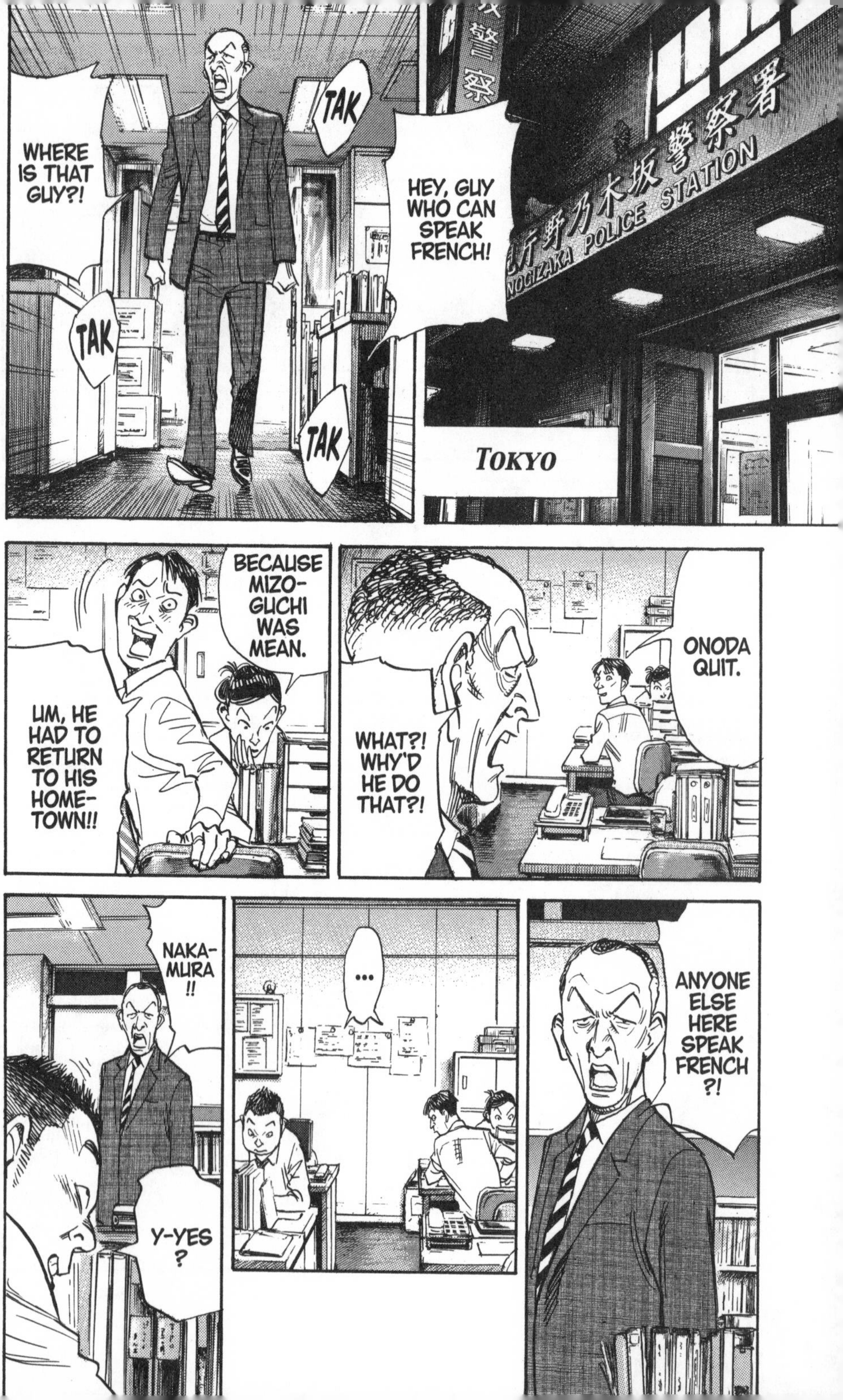
警察
庁野乃木坂警察署
NOGIZAKA POLICE STATION
TOKYO
HEY, GUY WHO CAN SPEAK FRENCH!
TAK
WHERE IS THAT GUY?!
TAK
TAK
ONODA QUIT.
WHAT?! WHY'D HE DO THAT?!
BECAUSE MIZO-GUCHI WAS MEAN.
UM, HE HAD TO RETURN TO HIS HOME-TOWN!!
ANYONE ELSE HERE SPEAK FRENCH?!
...
NAKA-MURA!!
Y-YES?

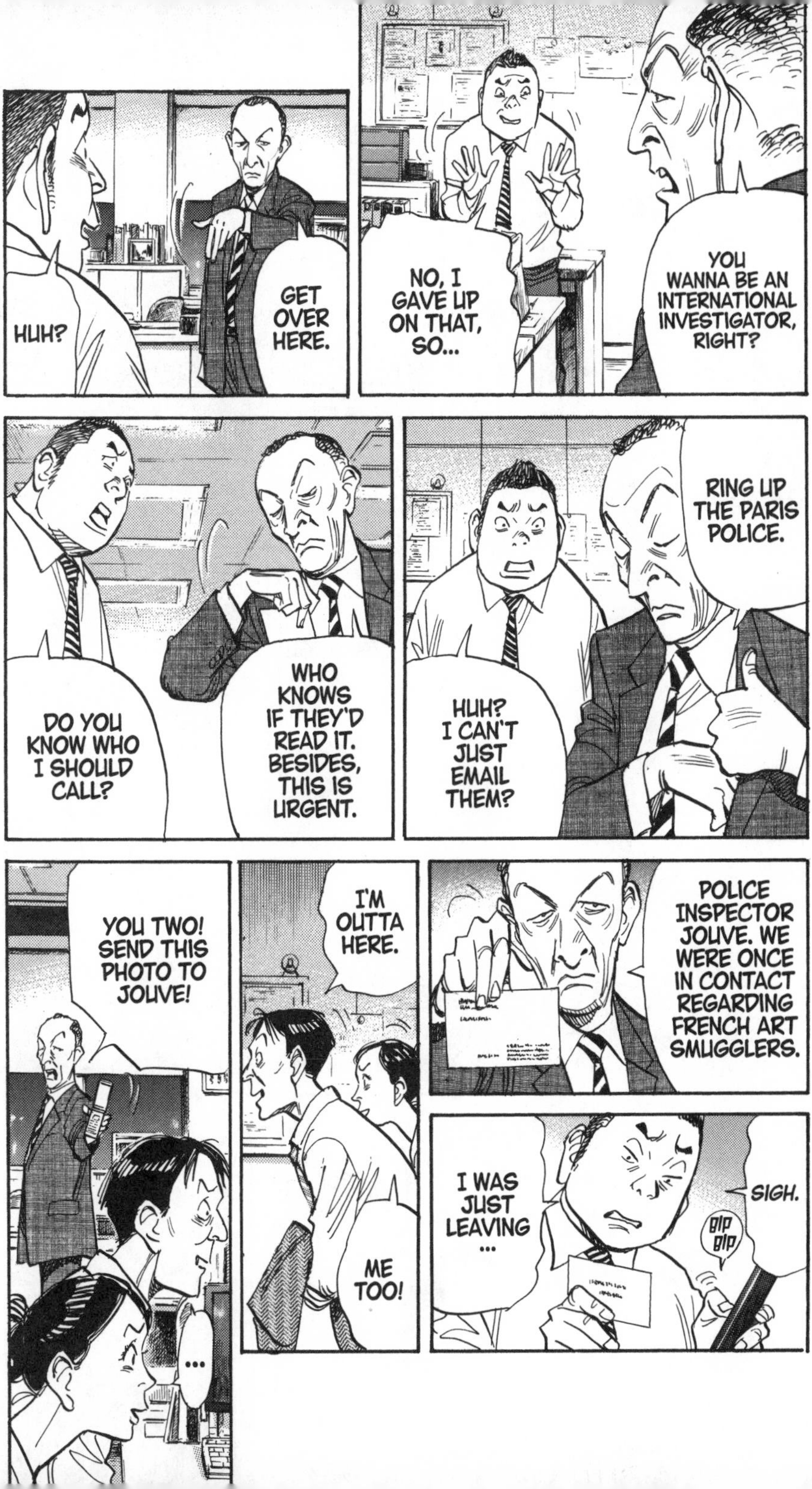
YOU WANNA BE AN INTERNATIONAL INVESTIGATOR, RIGHT?
NO, I GAVE UP ON THAT, SO...
GET OVER HERE.
HUH?
RING UP THE PARIS POLICE.
HUH? I CAN'T JUST EMAIL THEM?
WHO KNOWS IF THEY'D READ IT. BESIDES, THIS IS URGENT.
DO YOU KNOW WHO I SHOULD CALL?
POLICE INSPECTOR JOUVE. WE WERE ONCE IN CONTACT REGARDING FRENCH ART SMUGGLERS.
SIGH.
BLIP BLIP
I WAS JUST LEAVING...
I'M OUTTA HERE.
ME TOO!
YOU TWO! SEND THIS PHOTO TO JOUVE!
...

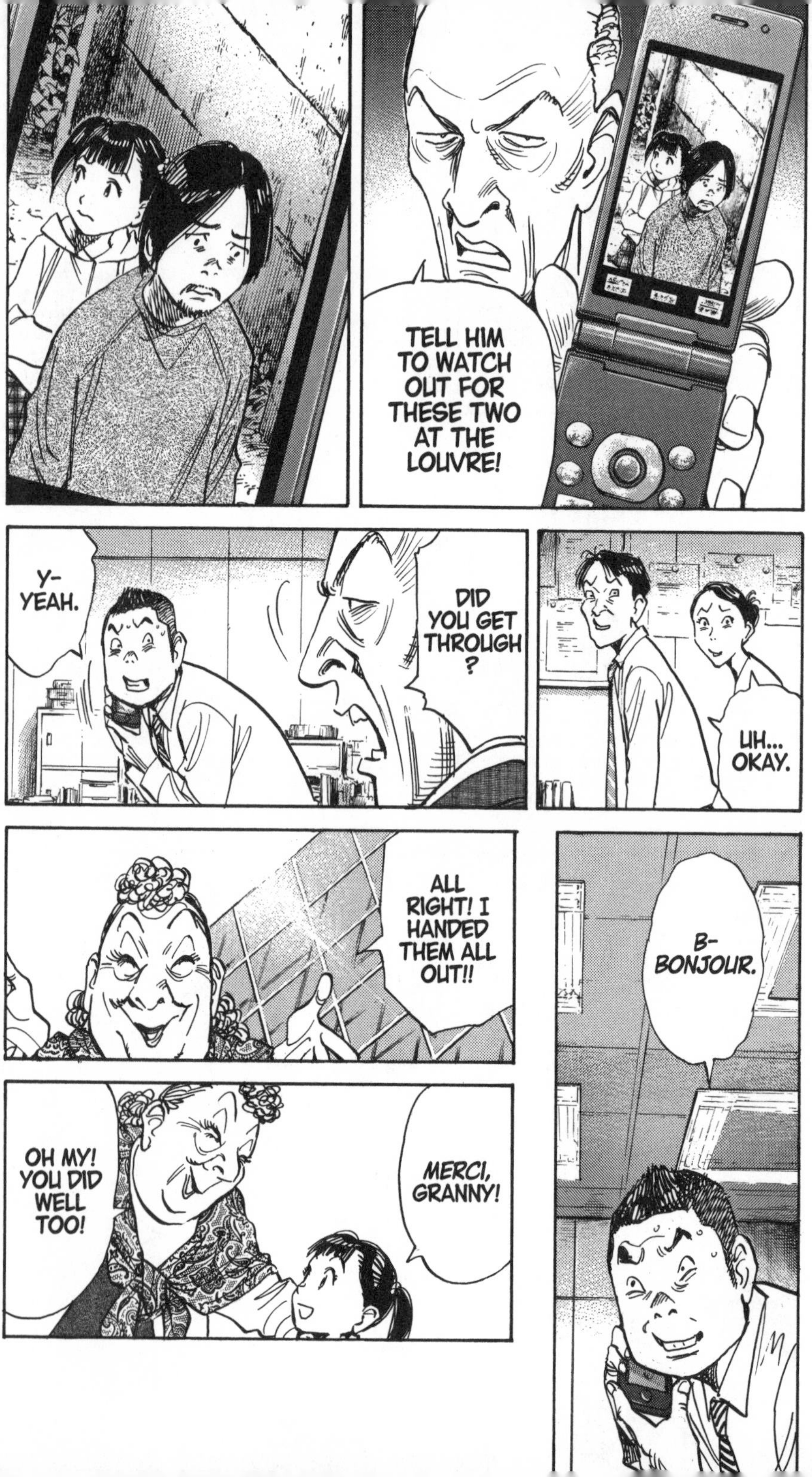
TELL HIM TO WATCH OUT FOR THESE TWO AT THE LOUVRE!
UH... OKAY.
DID YOU GET THROUGH?
Y-YEAH.
B-BONJOUR.
ALL RIGHT! I HANDED THEM ALL OUT!!
MERCI, GRANNY!
OH MY! YOU DID WELL TOO!

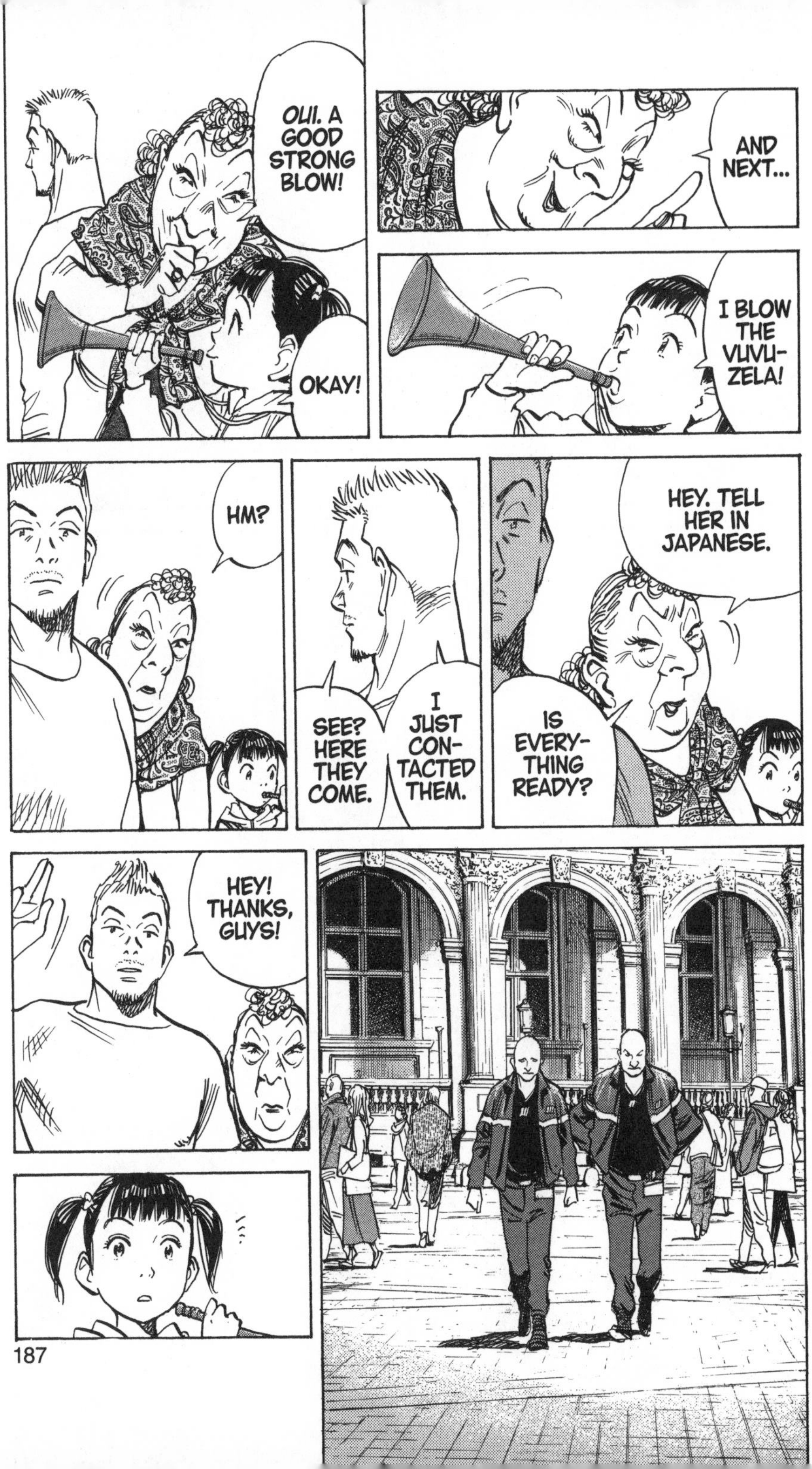
AND NEXT...
I BLOW THE VUVU-ZELA!
OUI. A GOOD STRONG BLOW!
OKAY!
HEY. TELL HER IN JAPANESE.
IS EVERY-THING READY?
I JUST CON-TACTED THEM.
SEE? HERE THEY COME.
HM?
HEY! THANKS, GUYS!

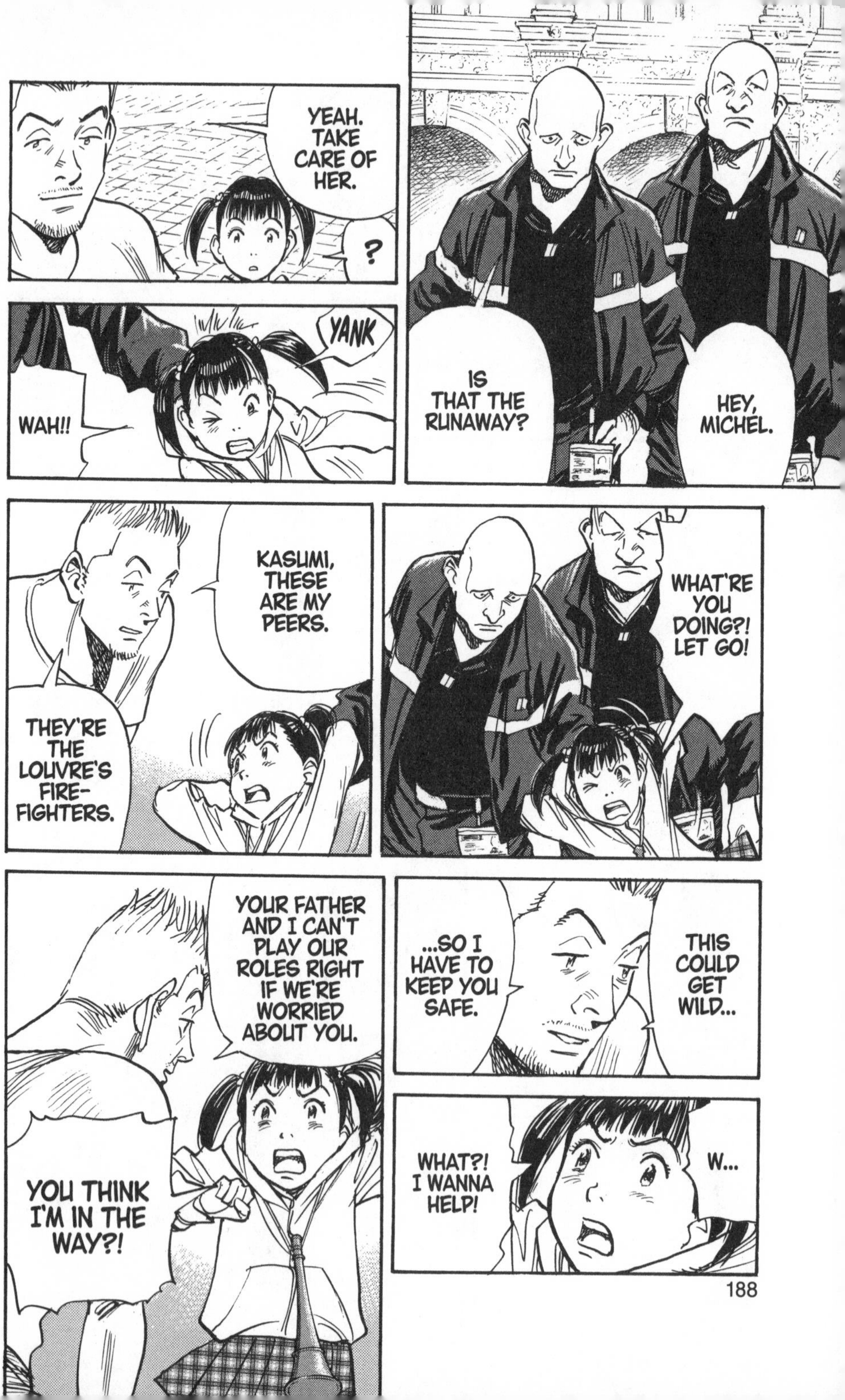
HEY, MICHEL.
IS THAT THE RUNAWAY?
YEAH. TAKE CARE OF HER.
?
YANK
WAH!!
WHAT'RE YOU DOING?! LET GO!
KASUMI, THESE ARE MY PEERS.
THEY'RE THE LOUVRE'S FIRE-FIGHTERS.
THIS COULD GET WILD...
...SO I HAVE TO KEEP YOU SAFE.
W...
WHAT?! I WANNA HELP!
YOUR FATHER AND I CAN'T PLAY OUR ROLES RIGHT IF WE'RE WORRIED ABOUT YOU.
YOU THINK I'M IN THE WAY?!

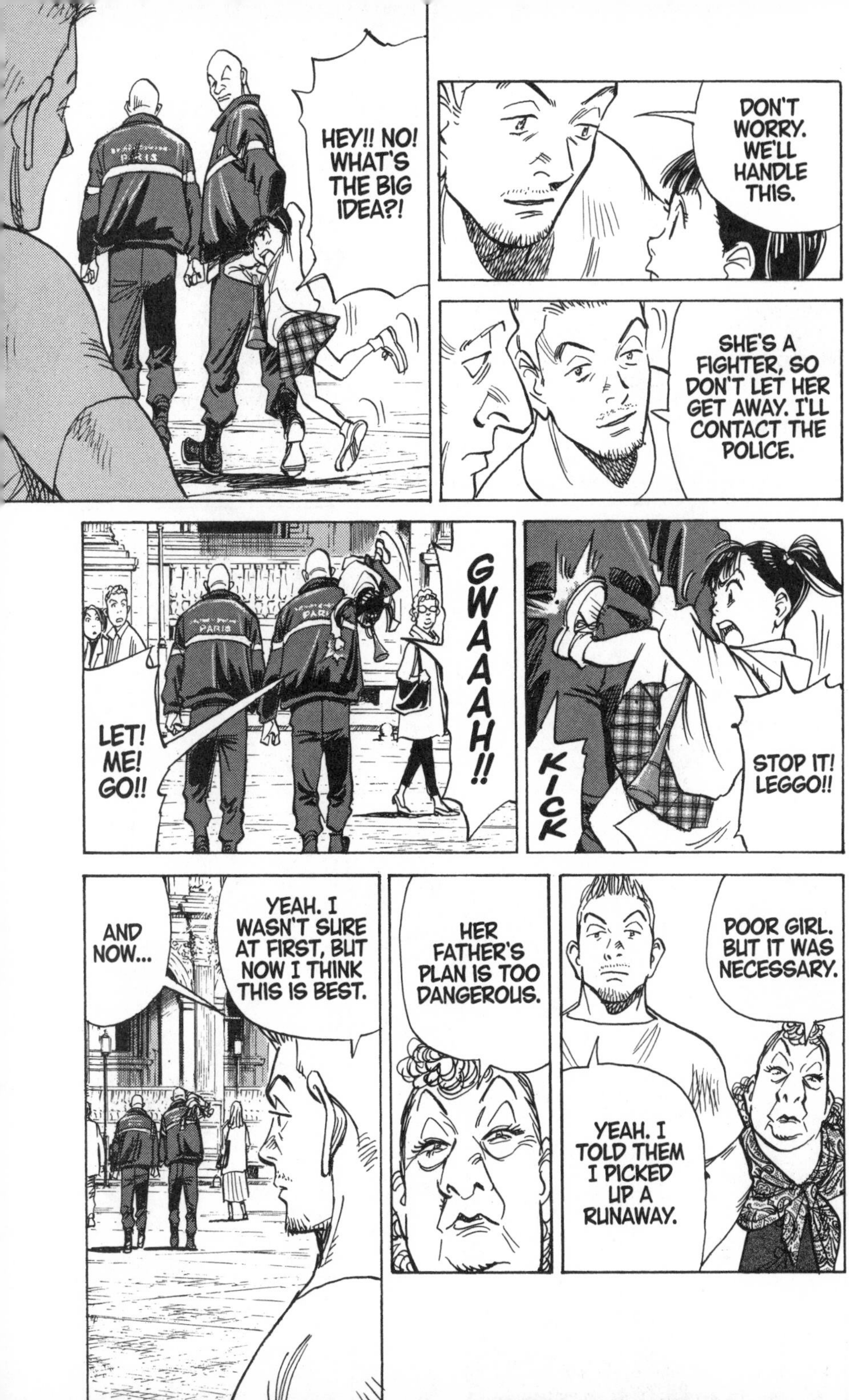
DON'T WORRY. WE'LL HANDLE THIS.
SHE'S A FIGHTER, SO DON'T LET HER GET AWAY. I'LL CONTACT THE POLICE.
HEY!! NO! WHAT'S THE BIG IDEA?!
STOP IT! LEGGO!!
KICK
GWAAAAH!!
LET! ME! GO!!
POOR GIRL. BUT IT WAS NECESSARY.
YEAH. I TOLD THEM I PICKED UP A RUNAWAY.
HER FATHER'S PLAN IS TOO DANGEROUS.
YEAH. I WASN'T SURE AT FIRST, BUT NOW I THINK THIS IS BEST.
AND NOW...

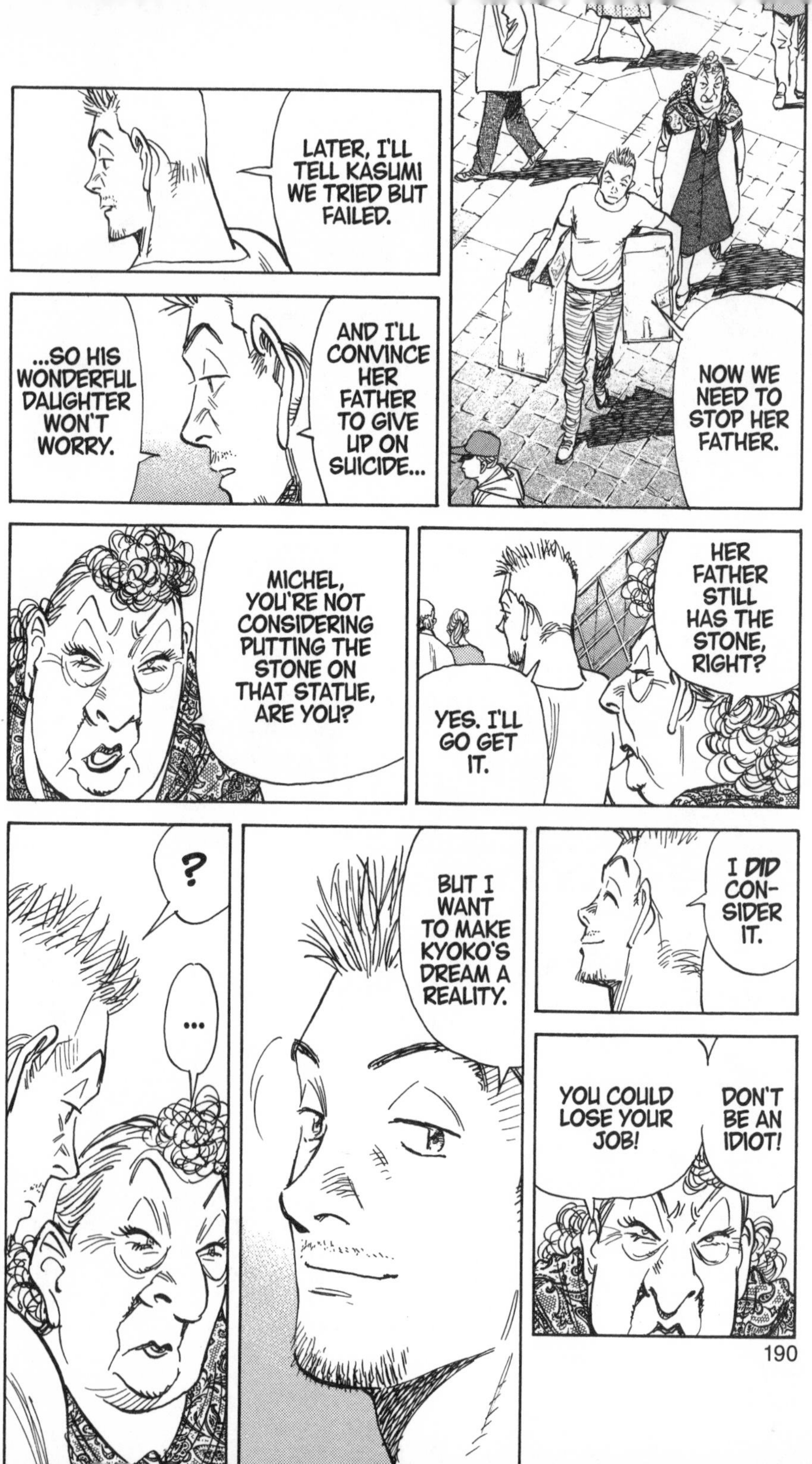
NOW WE NEED TO STOP HER FATHER.
LATER, I'LL TELL KASUMI WE TRIED BUT FAILED.
AND I'LL CONVINCE HER FATHER TO GIVE UP ON SUICIDE...
...SO HIS WONDERFUL DAUGHTER WON'T WORRY.
HER FATHER STILL HAS THE STONE, RIGHT?
YES. I'LL GO GET IT.
MICHEL, YOU'RE NOT CONSIDERING PUTTING THE STONE ON THAT STATUE, ARE YOU?
I *DID* CON-SIDER IT.
DON'T BE AN IDIOT!
YOU COULD LOSE YOUR JOB!
BUT I WANT TO MAKE KYOKO'S DREAM A REALITY.
?
...

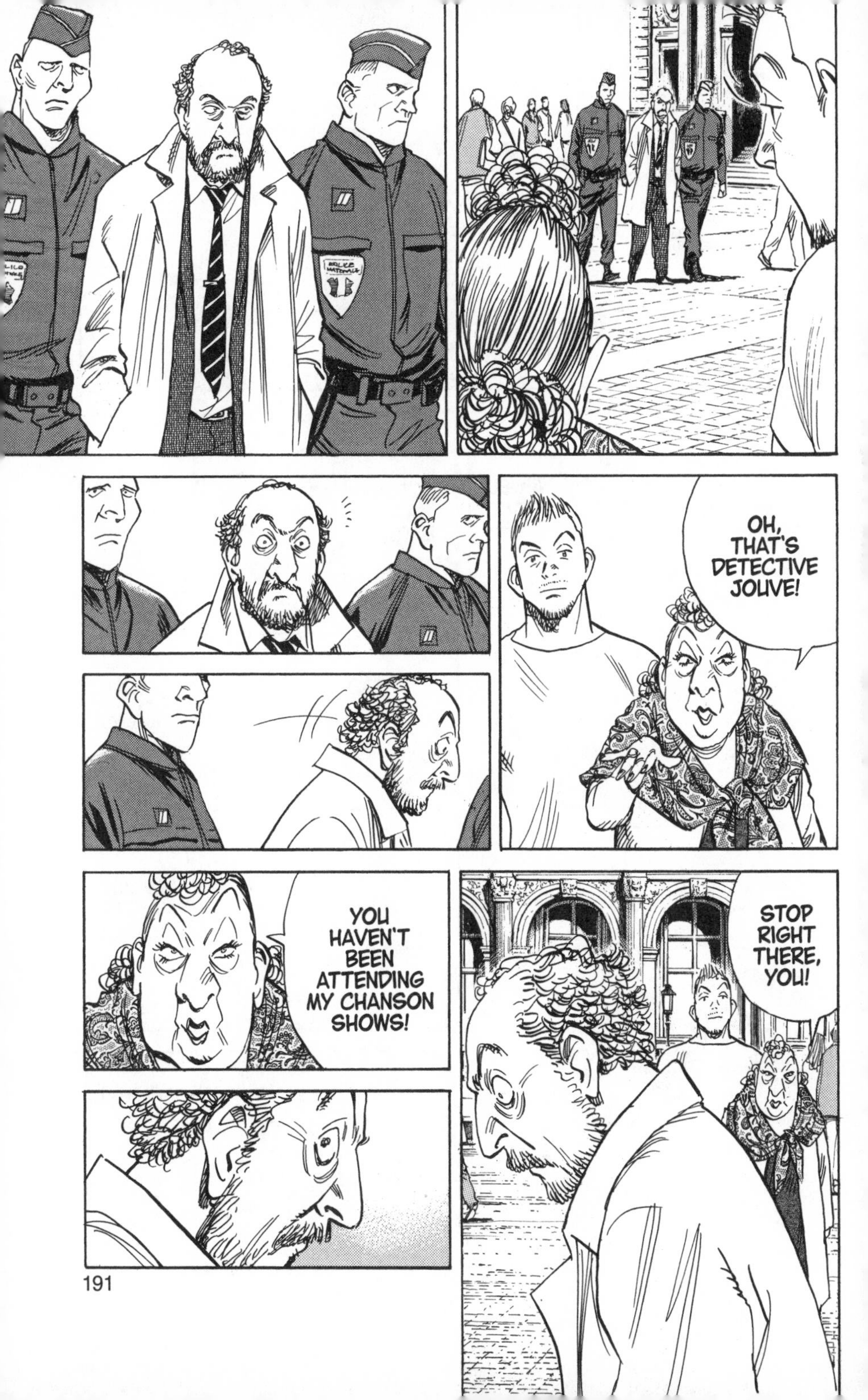
OH, THAT'S DETECTIVE JOUVE!
STOP RIGHT THERE, YOU!
YOU HAVEN'T BEEN ATTENDING MY CHANSON SHOWS!

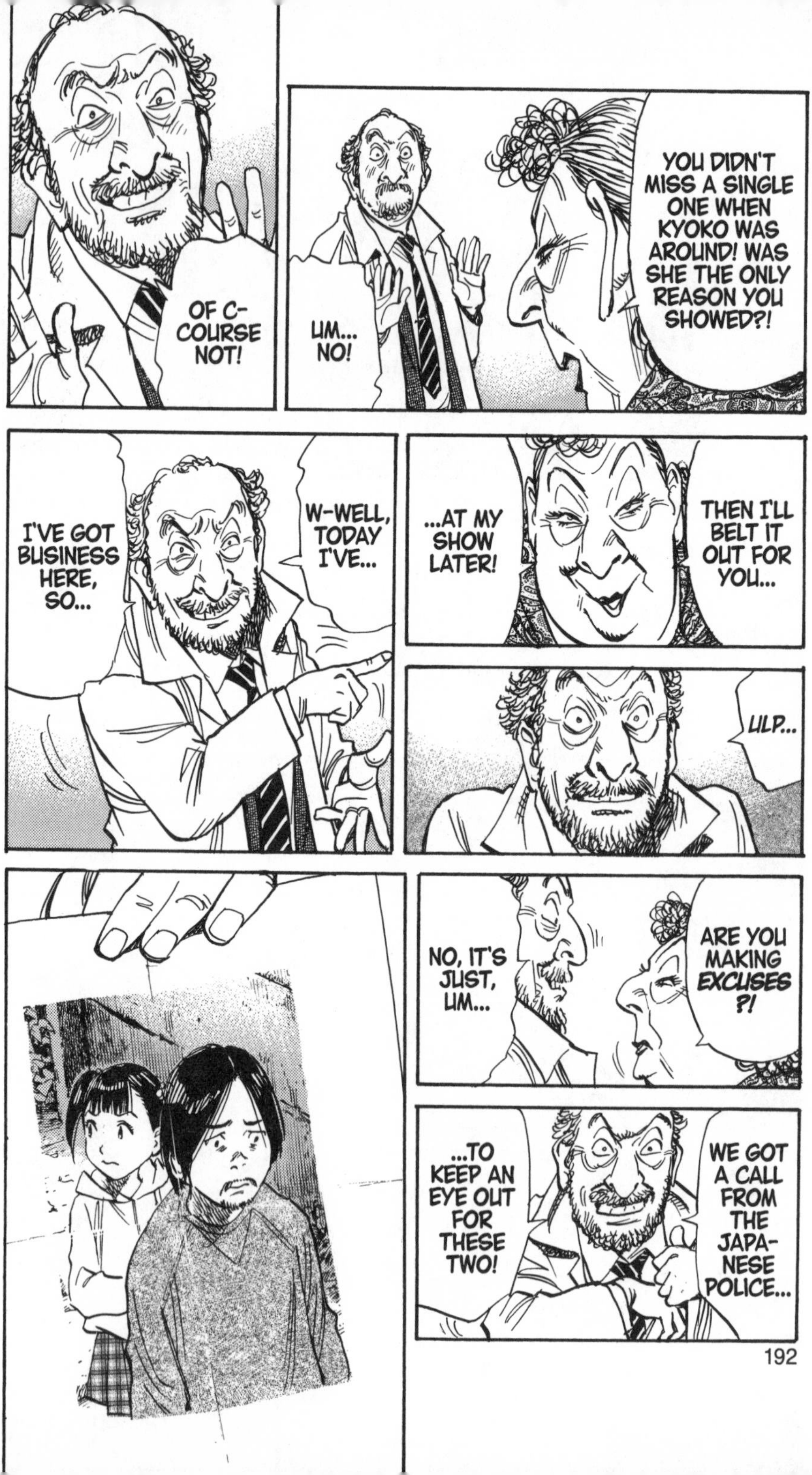
YOU DIDN'T MISS A SINGLE ONE WHEN KYOKO WAS AROUND! WAS SHE THE ONLY REASON YOU SHOWED?!
UM... NO!
OF C-COURSE NOT!
THEN I'LL BELT IT OUT FOR YOU...
...AT MY SHOW LATER!
ULP...
W-WELL, TODAY I'VE...
I'VE GOT BUSINESS HERE, SO...
ARE YOU MAKING *EXCUSES*?!
NO, IT'S JUST, UM...
WE GOT A CALL FROM THE JAPA-NESE POLICE...
...TO KEEP AN EYE OUT FOR THESE TWO!

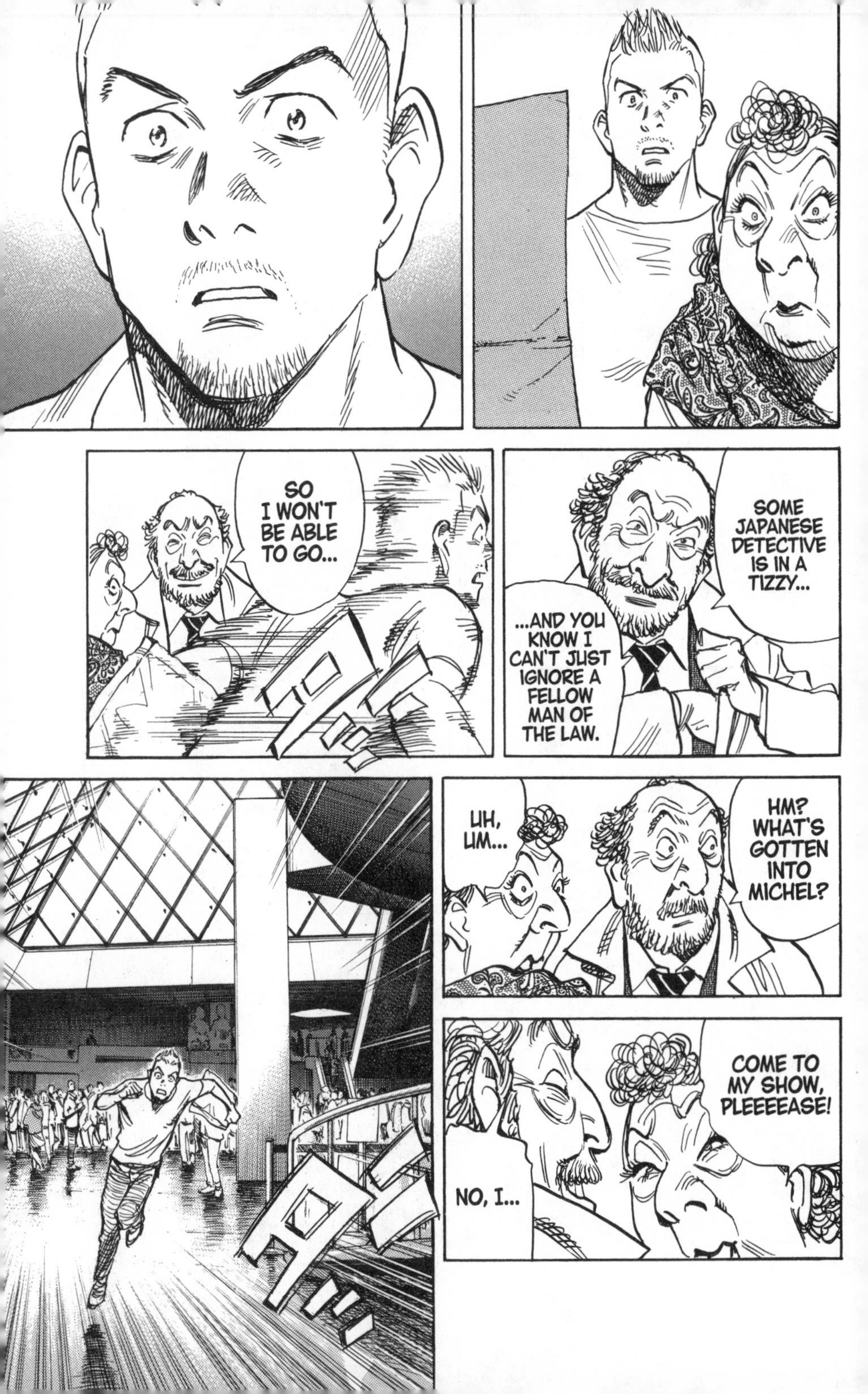
SOME JAPANESE DETECTIVE IS IN A TIZZY...
...AND YOU KNOW I CAN'T JUST IGNORE A FELLOW MAN OF THE LAW.
SO I WON'T BE ABLE TO GO...
HM? WHAT'S GOTTEN INTO MICHEL?
UH, UM...
COME TO MY SHOW, PLEEEEASE!
NO, I...

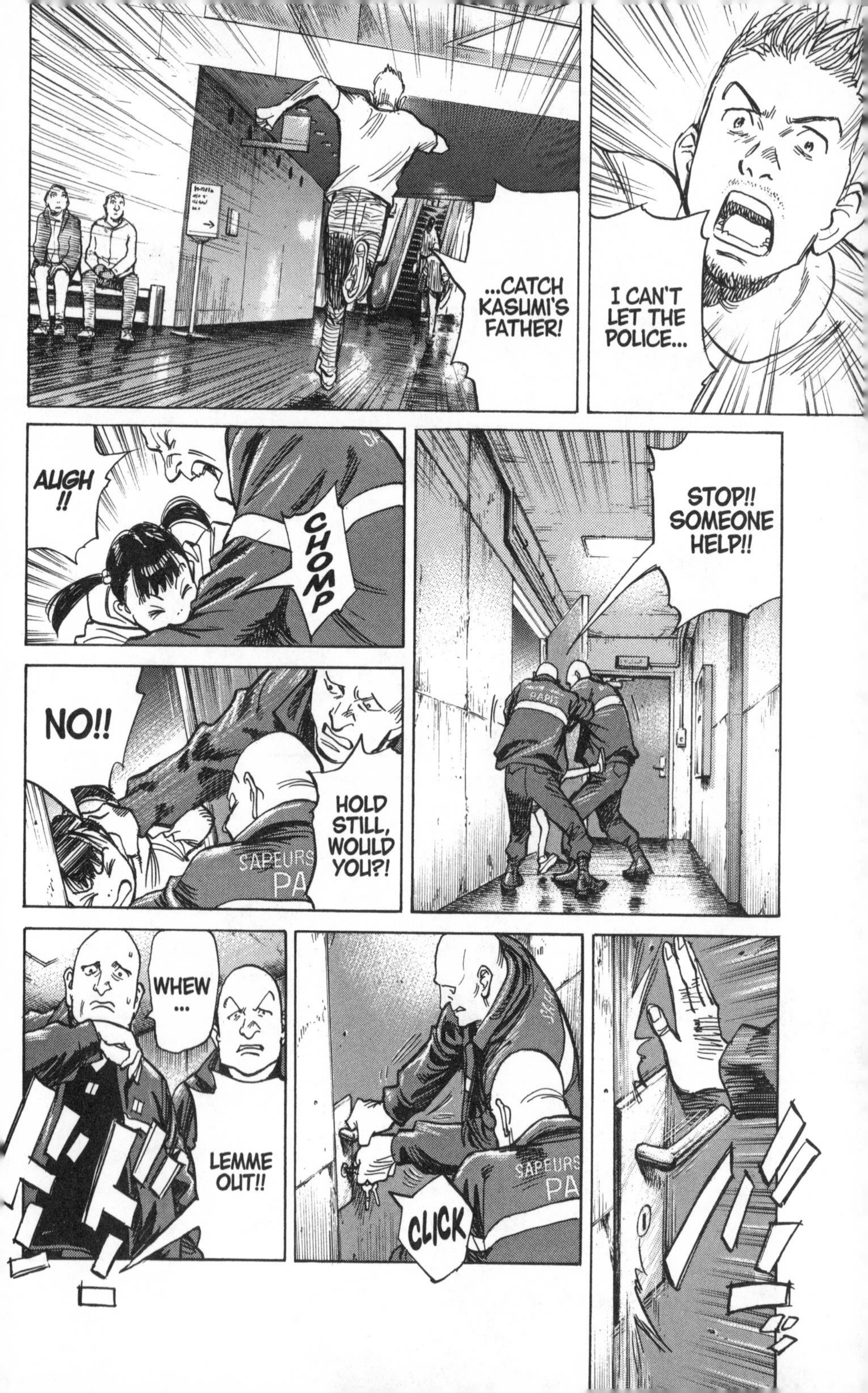
I CAN'T LET THE POLICE...
...CATCH KASUMI'S FATHER!
STOP!! SOMEONE HELP!!
AUGH !!
CHOMP
NO!!
HOLD STILL, WOULD YOU?!
CLICK
WHEW ...
LEMME OUT!!

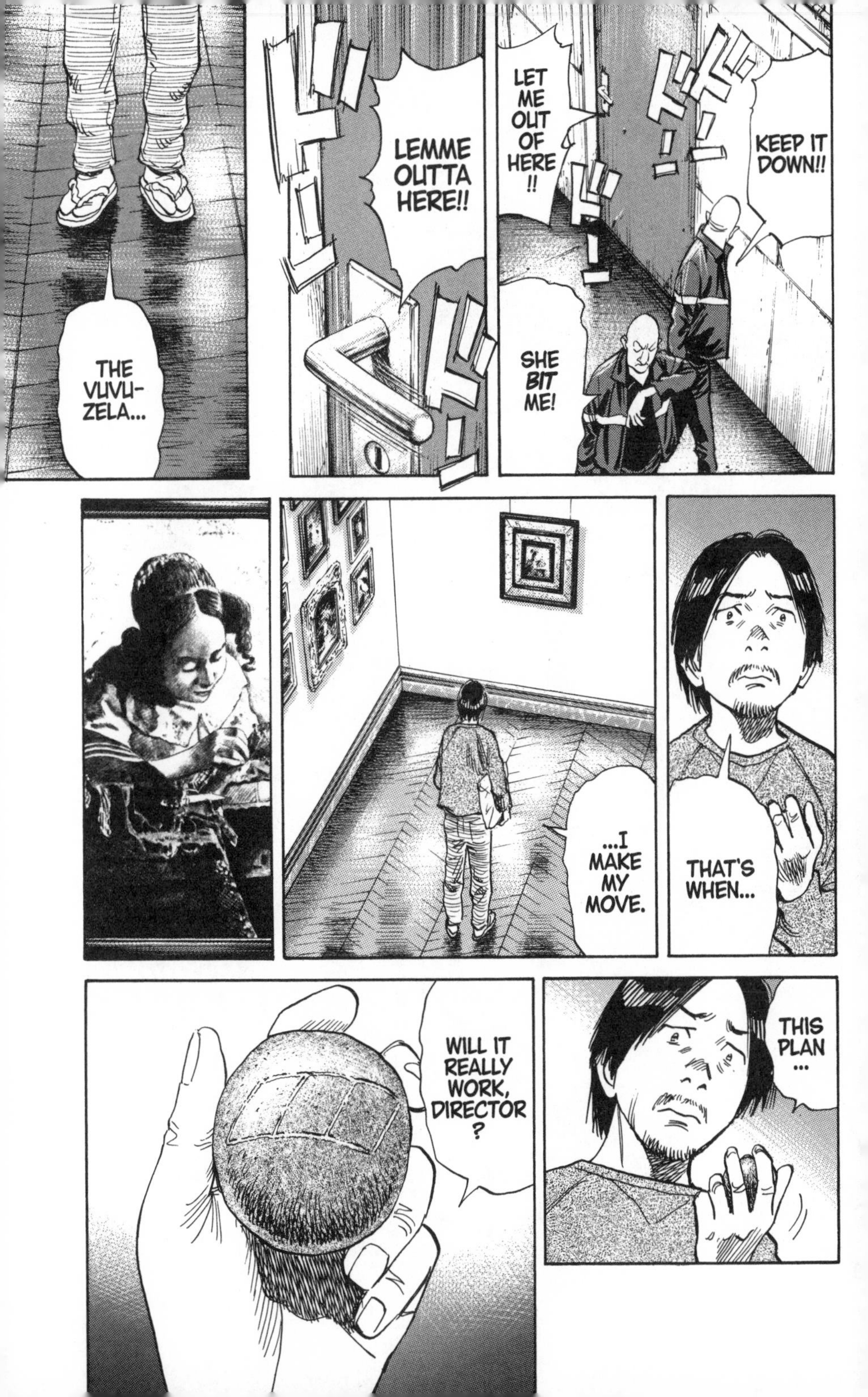
KEEP IT DOWN!!
LET ME OUT OF HERE !!
SHE BIT ME!
LEMME OUTTA HERE!!
THE VUVU-ZELA...
THAT'S WHEN...
...I MAKE MY MOVE.
THIS PLAN ...
WILL IT REALLY WORK, DIRECTOR ?

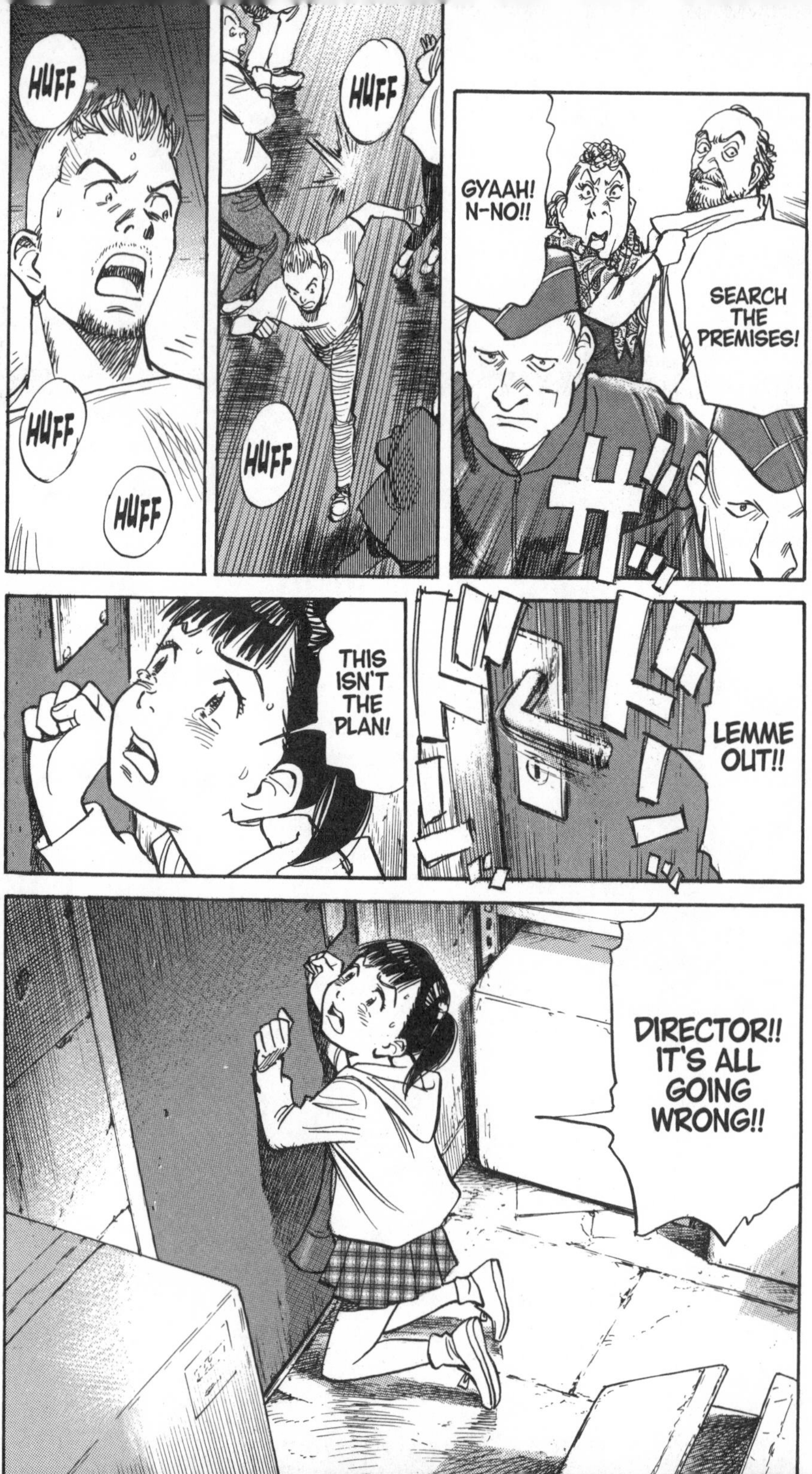
GYAAH! N-NO!!
SEARCH THE PREMISES!
HUFF
HUFF
HUFF
HUFF
HUFF
LEMME OUT!!
THIS ISN'T THE PLAN!
DIRECTOR!! IT'S ALL GOING WRONG!!

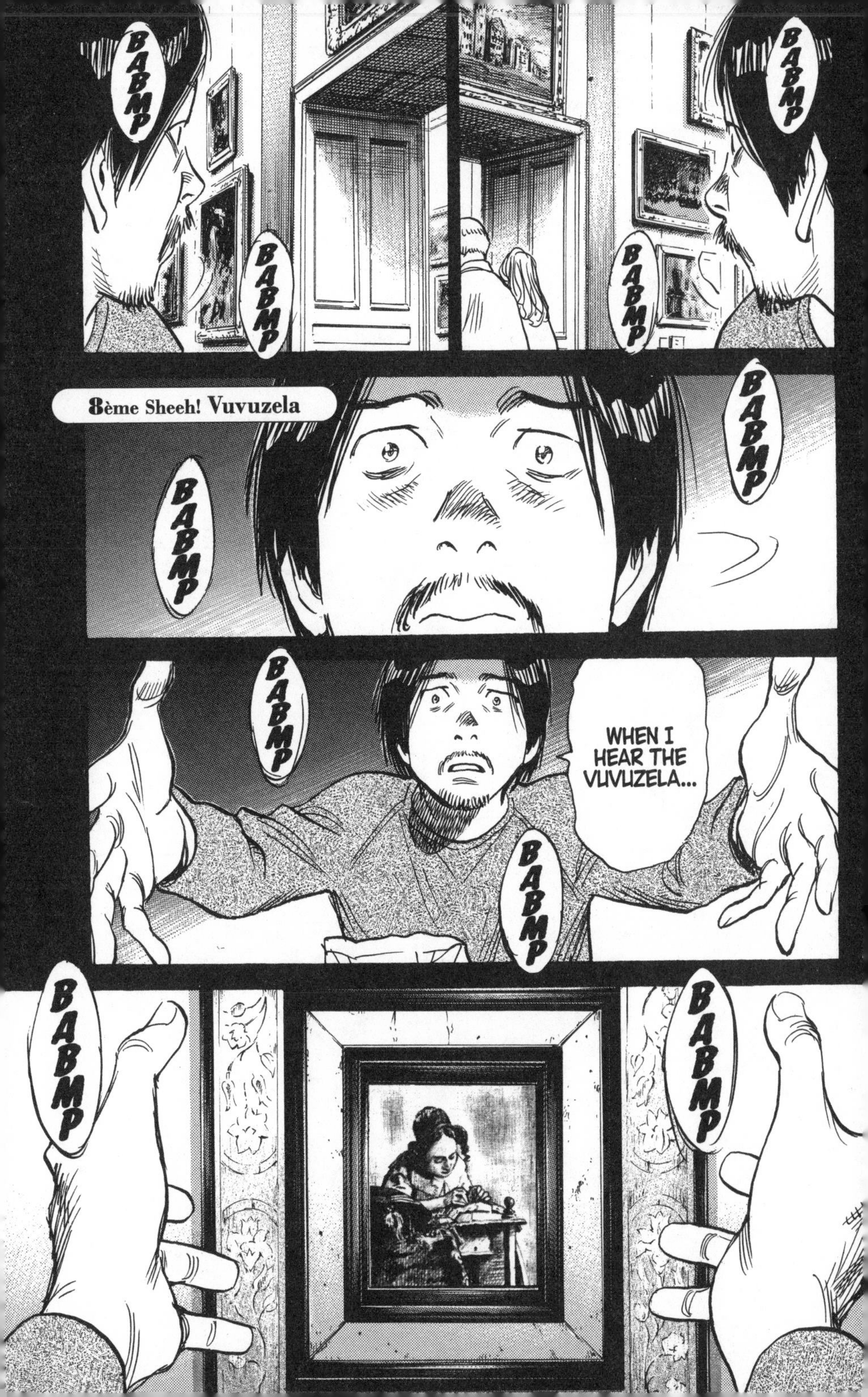
BABMP
BABMP
BABMP
BABMP
BABMP
8ème Sheeh! Vuvuzela
BABMP
WHEN I HEAR THE VUVUZELA...
BABMP
BABMP
BABMP
BABMP

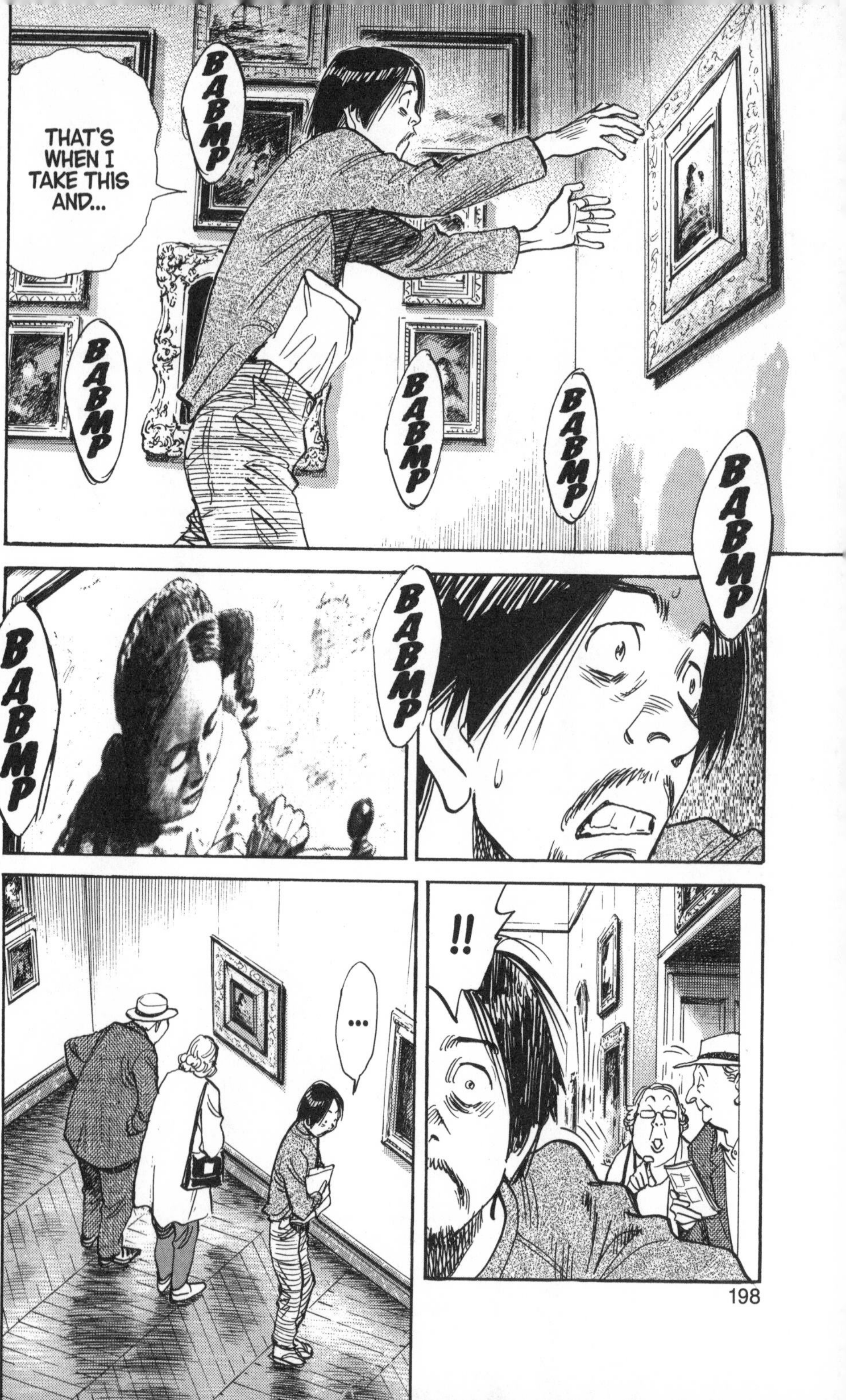
THAT'S WHEN I TAKE THIS AND...
BABMP
BABMP
BABMP
BABMP
BABMP
BABMP
BABMP
!!
...

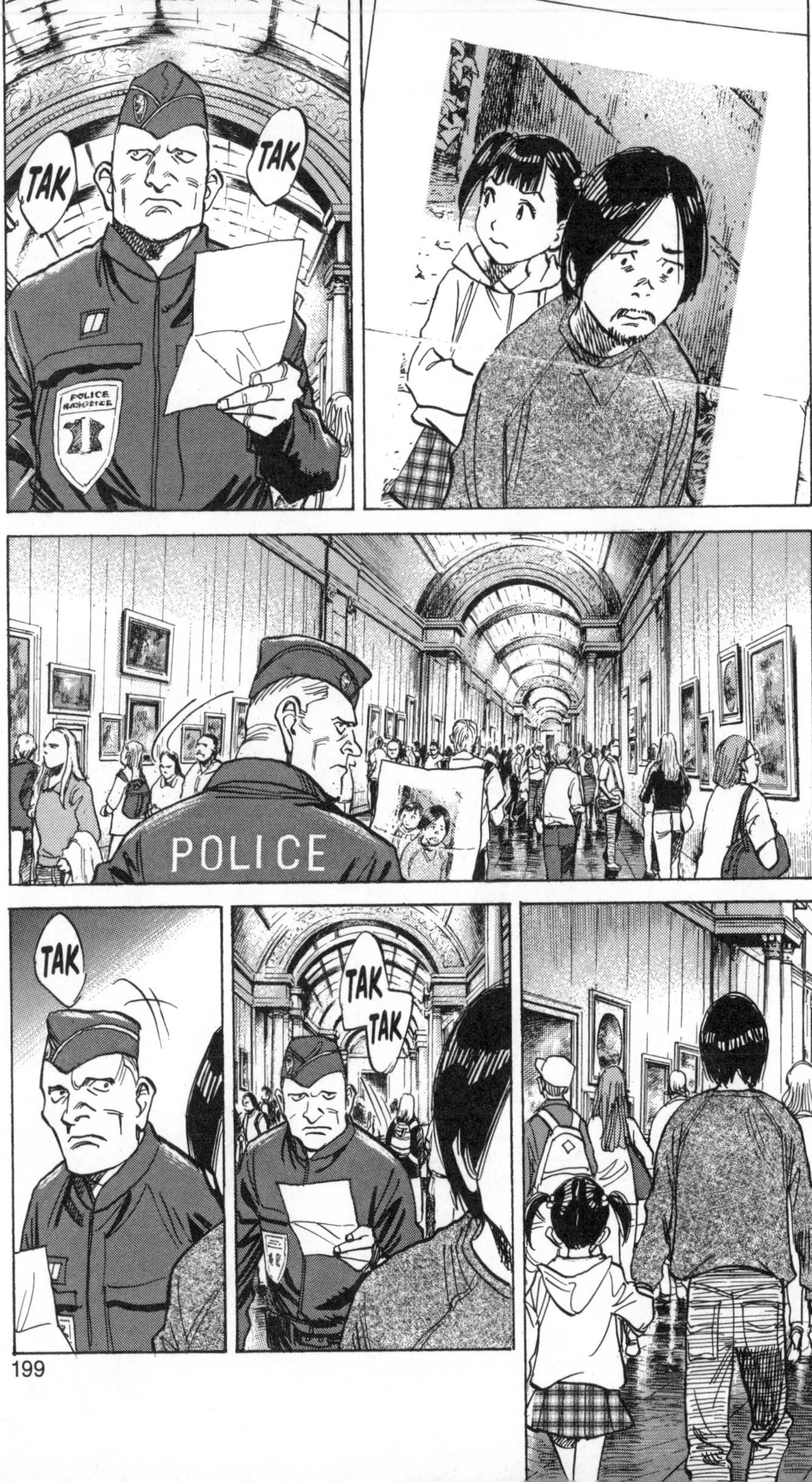
TAK
TAK
POLICE
TAK
TAK
TAK

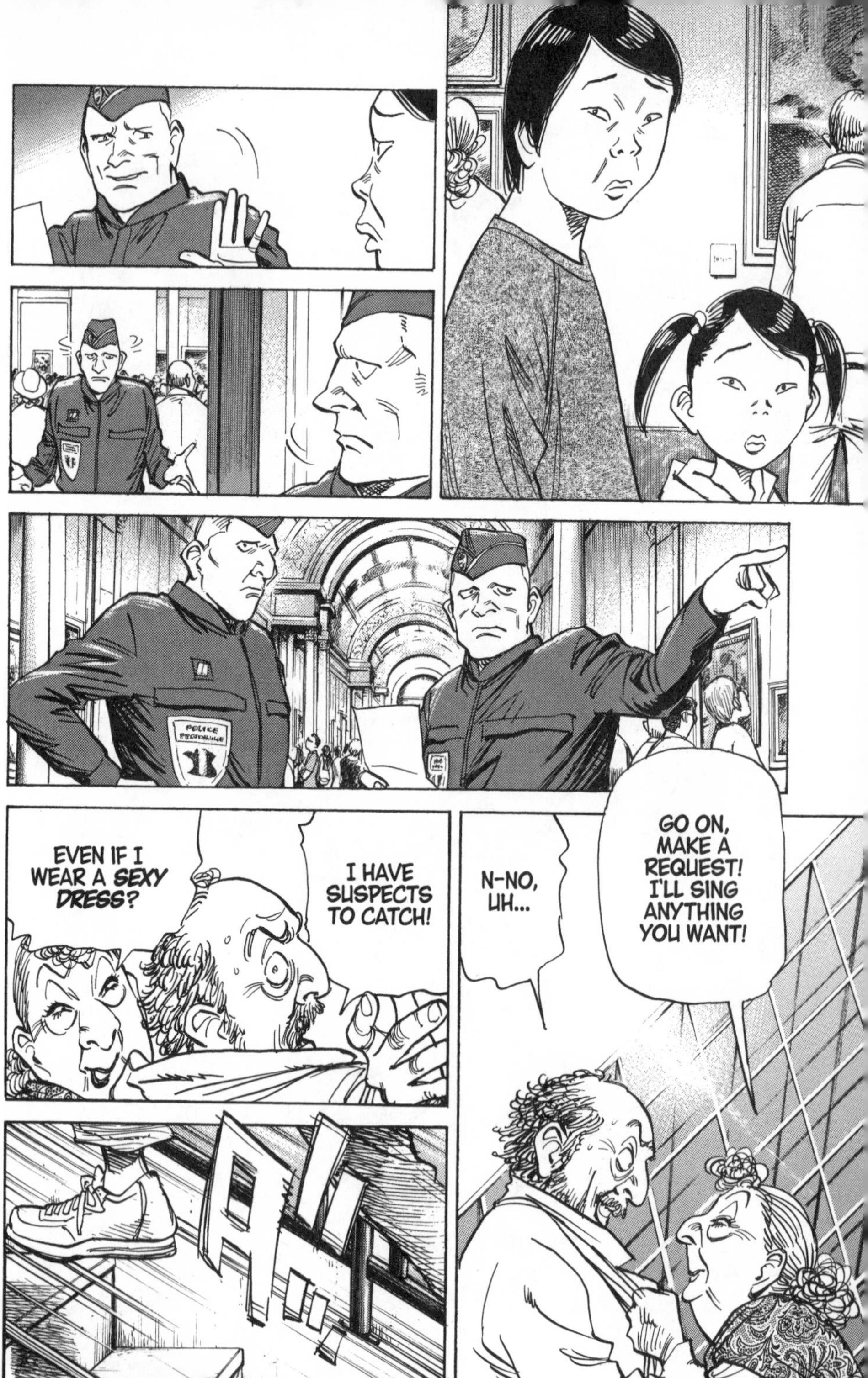
GO ON, MAKE A REQUEST! I'LL SING ANYTHING YOU WANT!
N-NO, UH...
I HAVE SUSPECTS TO CATCH!
EVEN IF I WEAR A *SEXY DRESS*?

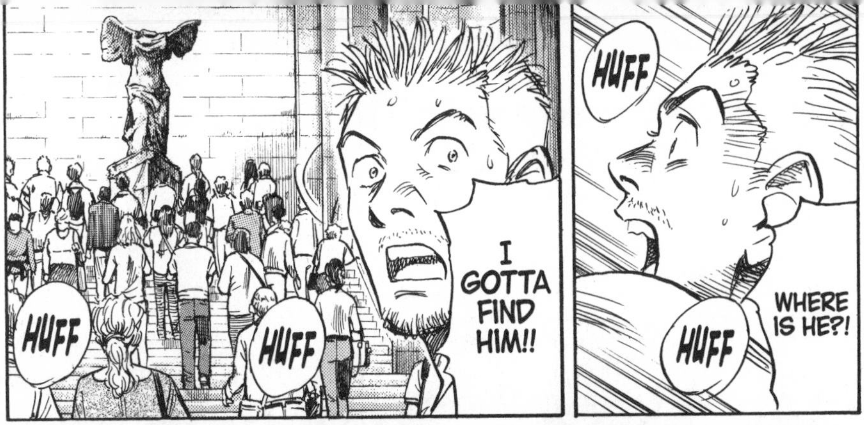
HUFF
WHERE IS HE?!
HUFF
I GOTTA FIND HIM!!
HUFF
HUFF

8ème Sheeh! Vuvuzela

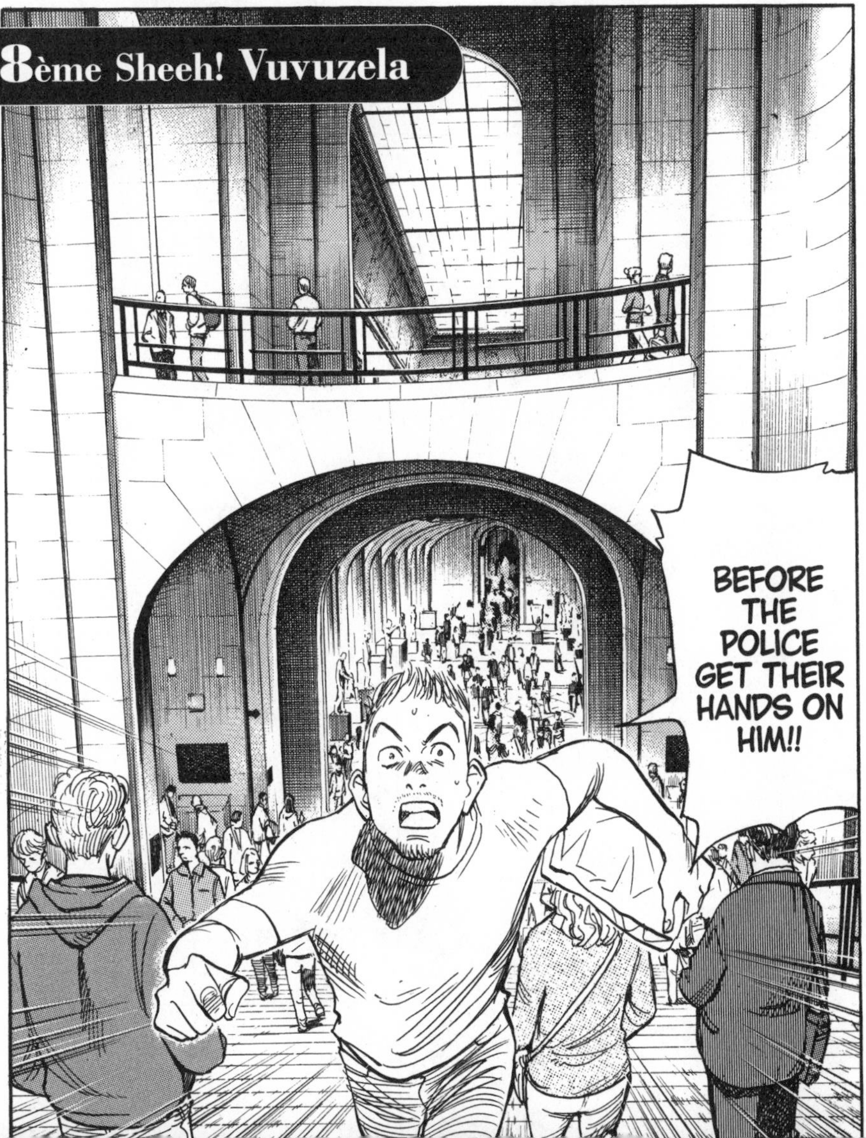
BEFORE THE POLICE GET THEIR HANDS ON HIM!!

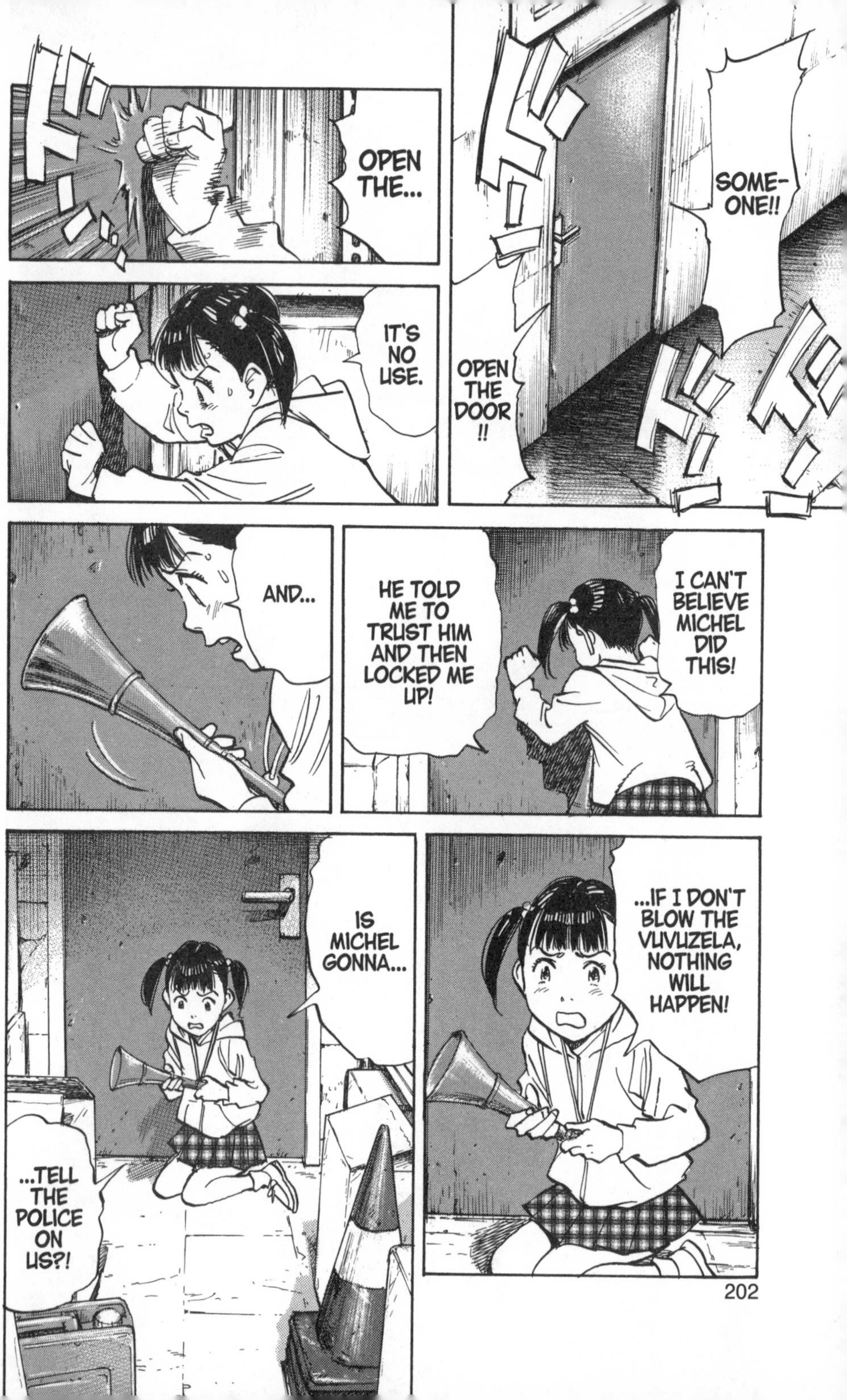
SOME-ONE!!
OPEN THE...
OPEN THE DOOR!!
IT'S NO USE.
I CAN'T BELIEVE MICHEL DID THIS!
HE TOLD ME TO TRUST HIM AND THEN LOCKED ME UP!
AND...
...IF I DON'T BLOW THE VUVUZELA, NOTHING WILL HAPPEN!
IS MICHEL GONNA...
...TELL THE POLICE ON US?!

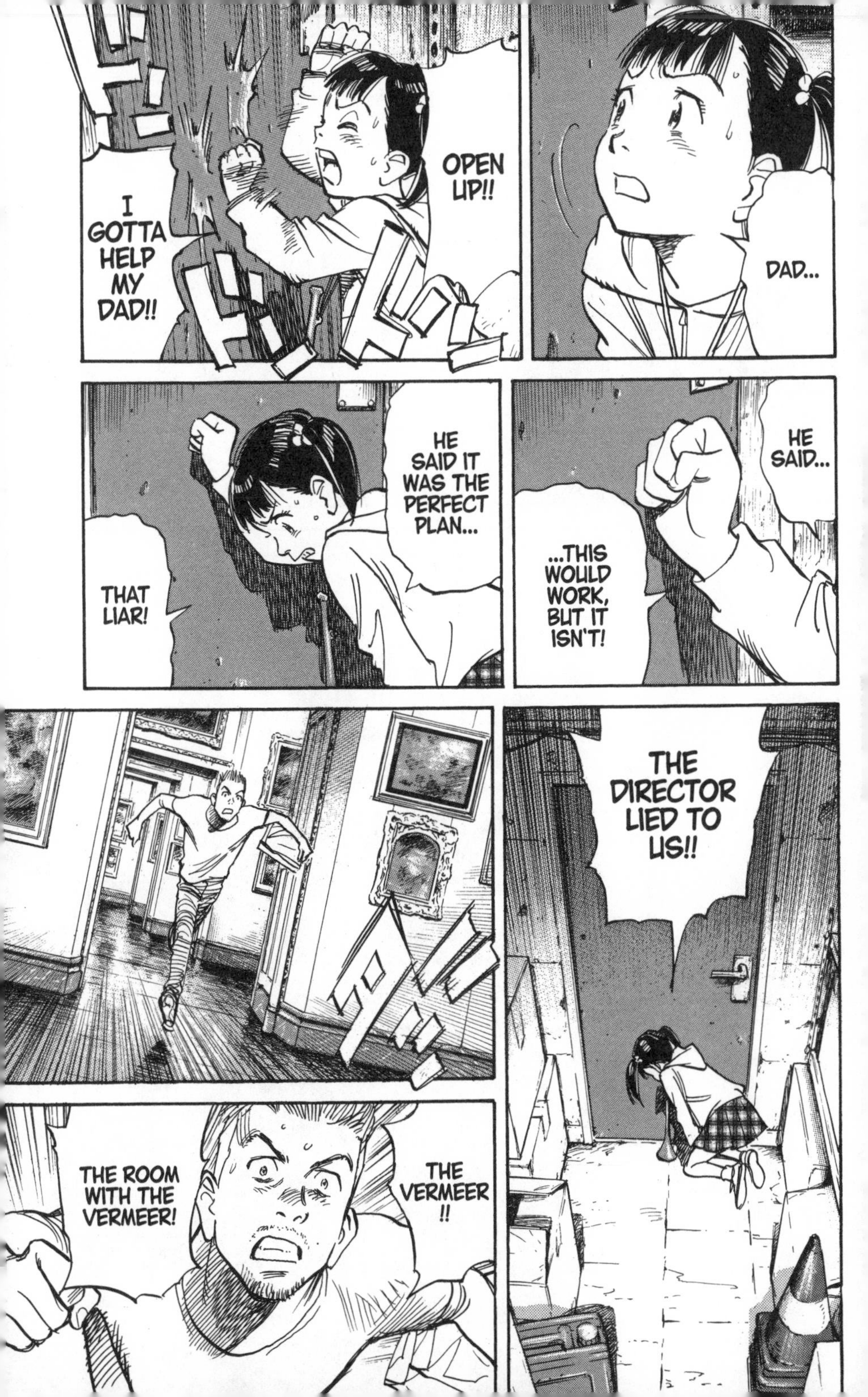
DAD...
OPEN UP!!
I GOTTA HELP MY DAD!!
HE SAID...
...THIS WOULD WORK, BUT IT ISN'T!
HE SAID IT WAS THE PERFECT PLAN...
THAT LIAR!
THE DIRECTOR LIED TO US!!
THE VERMEER !!
THE ROOM WITH THE VERMEER!

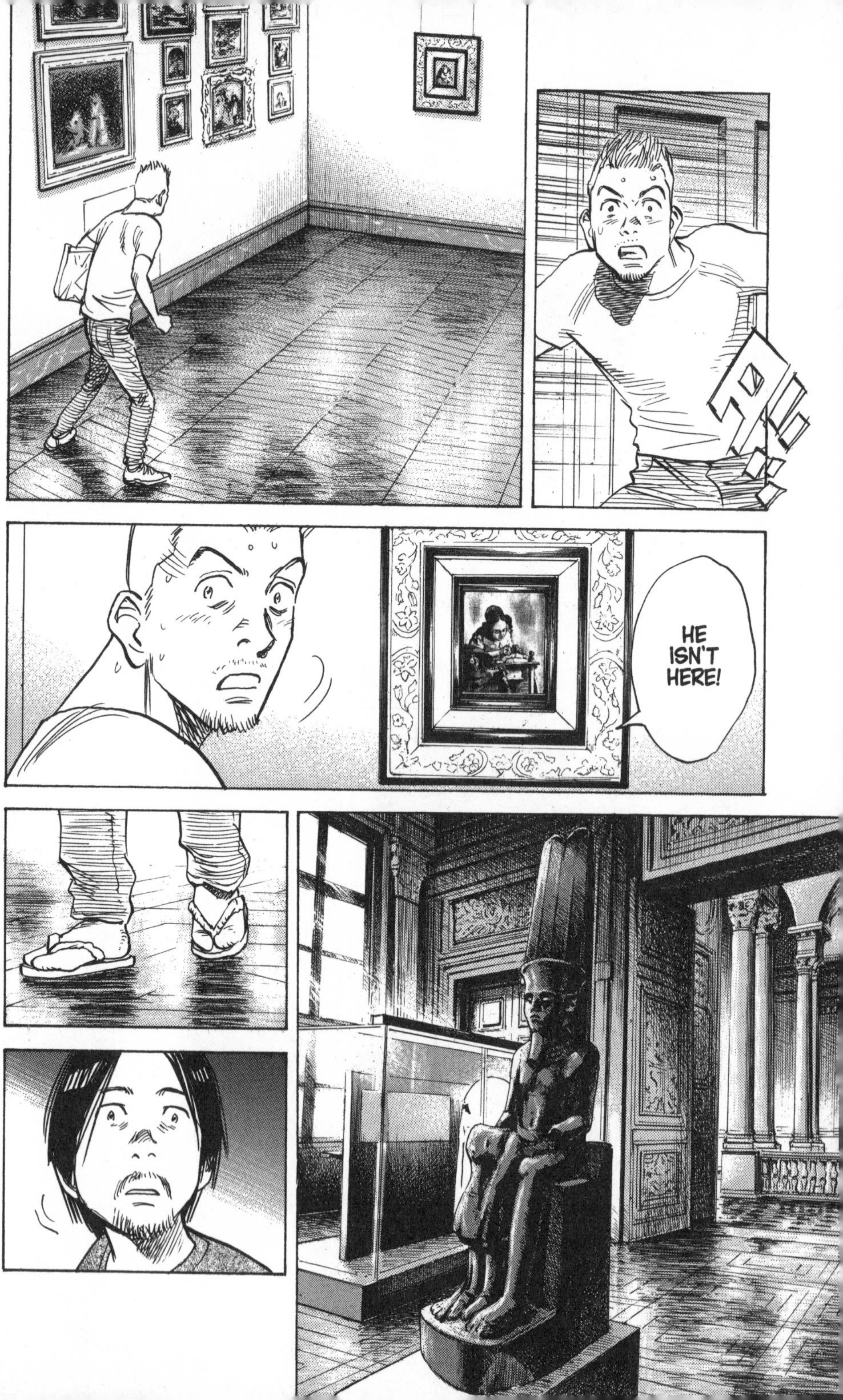
HE ISN'T HERE!

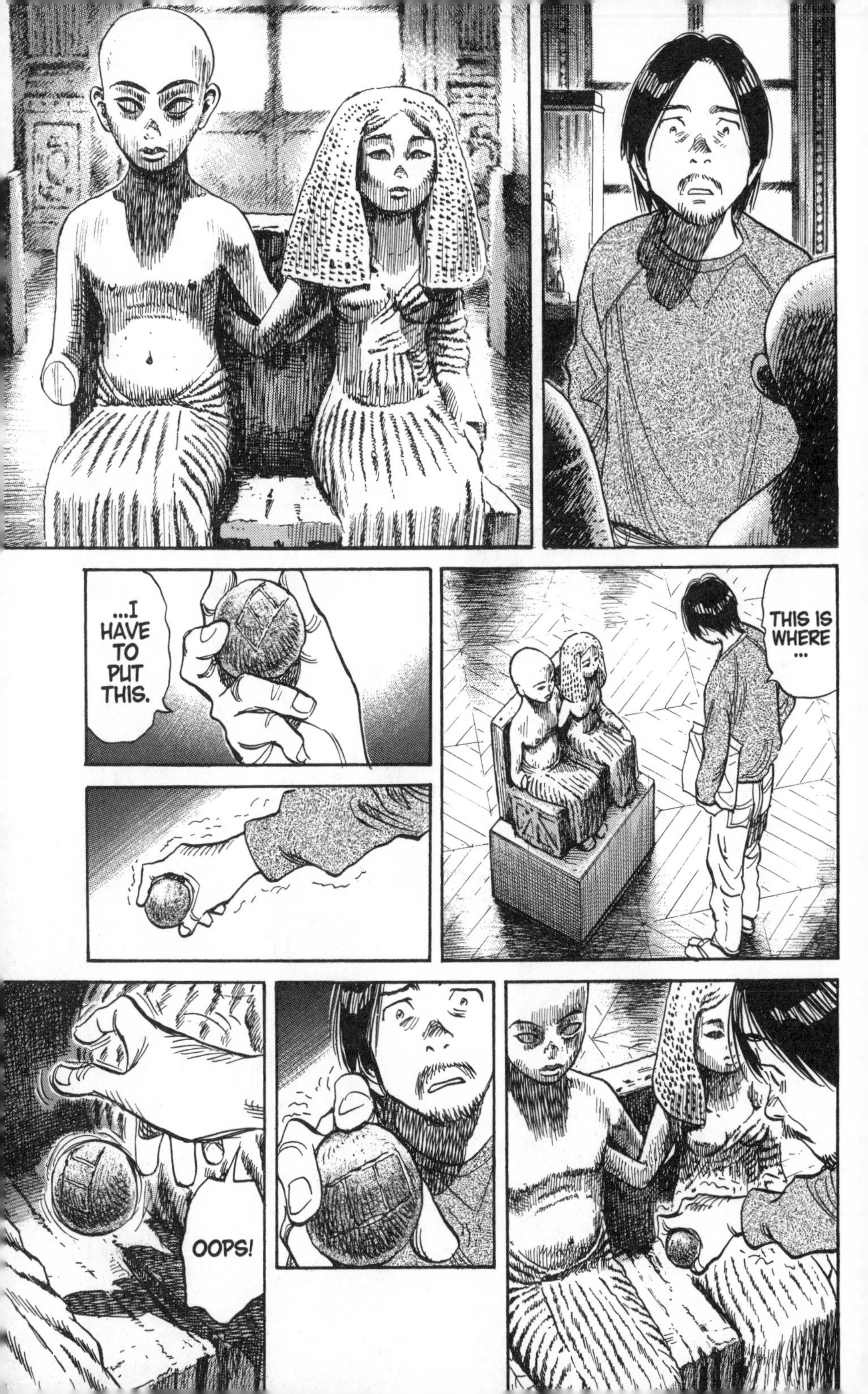
THIS IS WHERE ...
...I HAVE TO PUT THIS.
OOPS!

GAAAH!!

ROLLL

W-W-WHOA NO!!

BOUNCE

CLONK

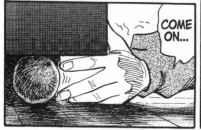

UMPH!

AGH...!

COME ON...

ROLLL

TAK

TAK

MY HAND WON'T REACH...

TAK

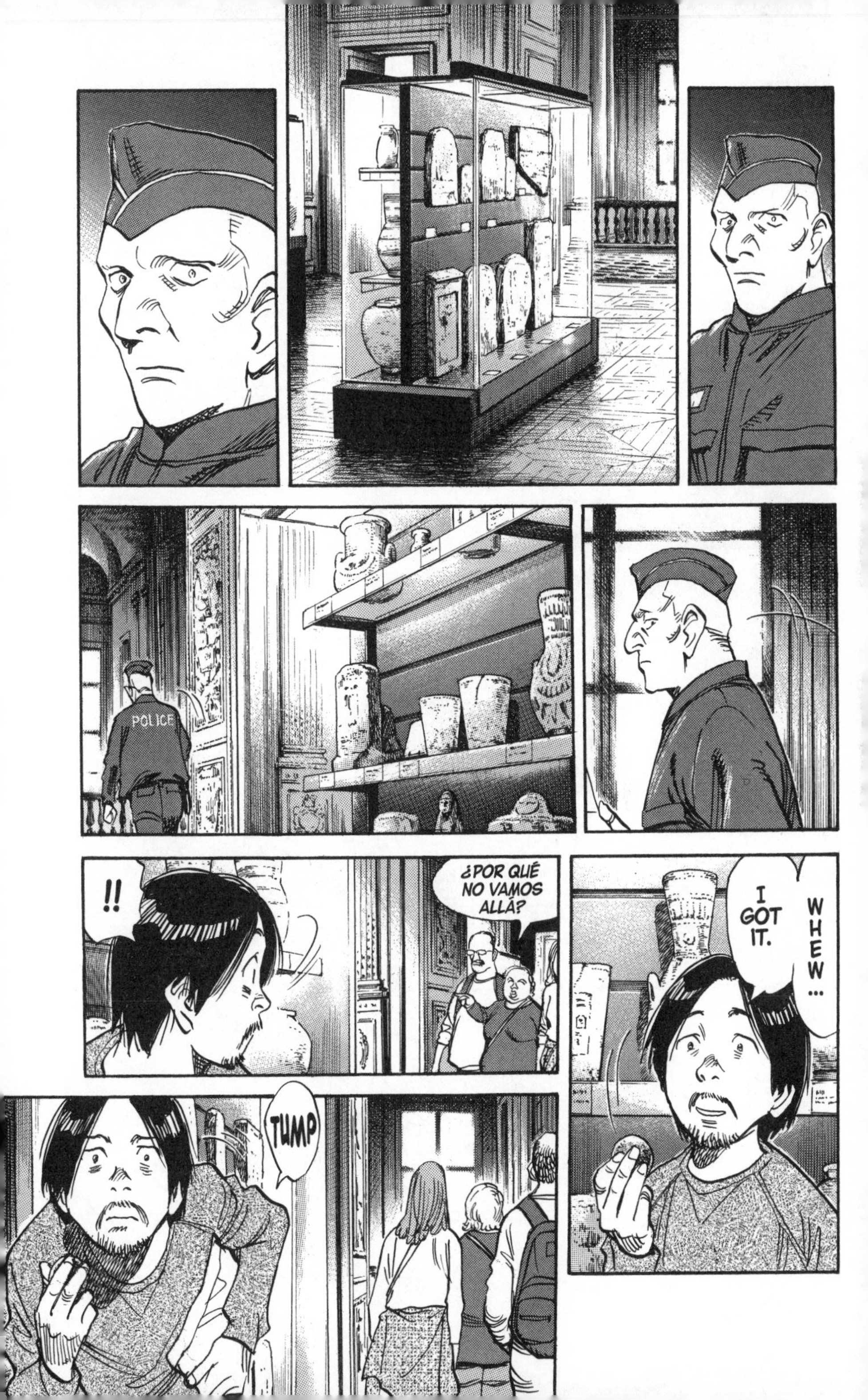
POLICE
I GOT IT.
WHEW...
¿POR QUÉ NO VAMOS ALLÁ?
!!
TUMP

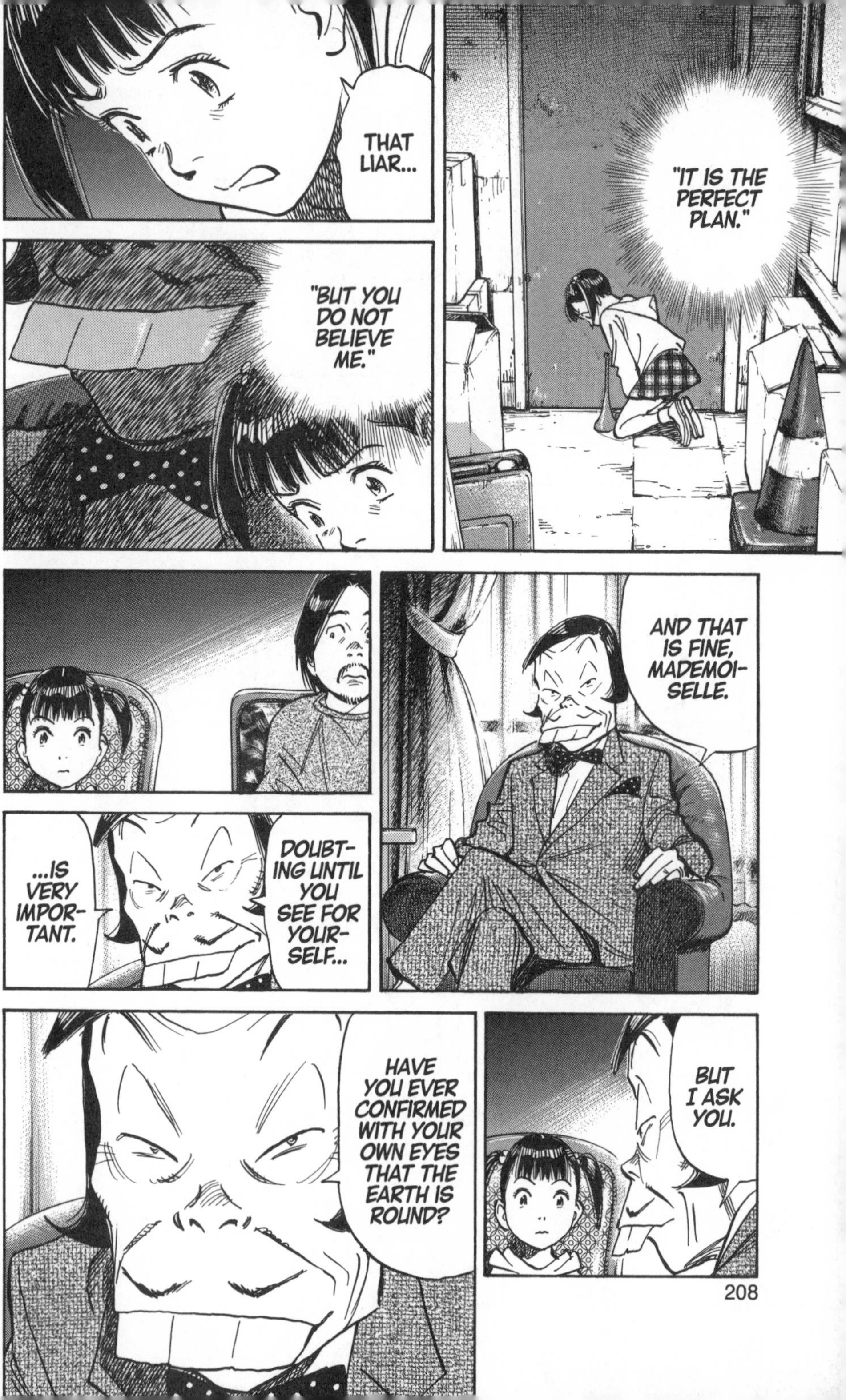
"IT IS THE PERFECT PLAN."
THAT LIAR...
"BUT YOU DO NOT BELIEVE ME."
AND THAT IS FINE, MADEMOISELLE.
DOUBTING UNTIL YOU SEE FOR YOURSELF...
...IS VERY IMPORTANT.
BUT I ASK YOU.
HAVE YOU EVER CONFIRMED WITH YOUR OWN EYES THAT THE EARTH IS ROUND?

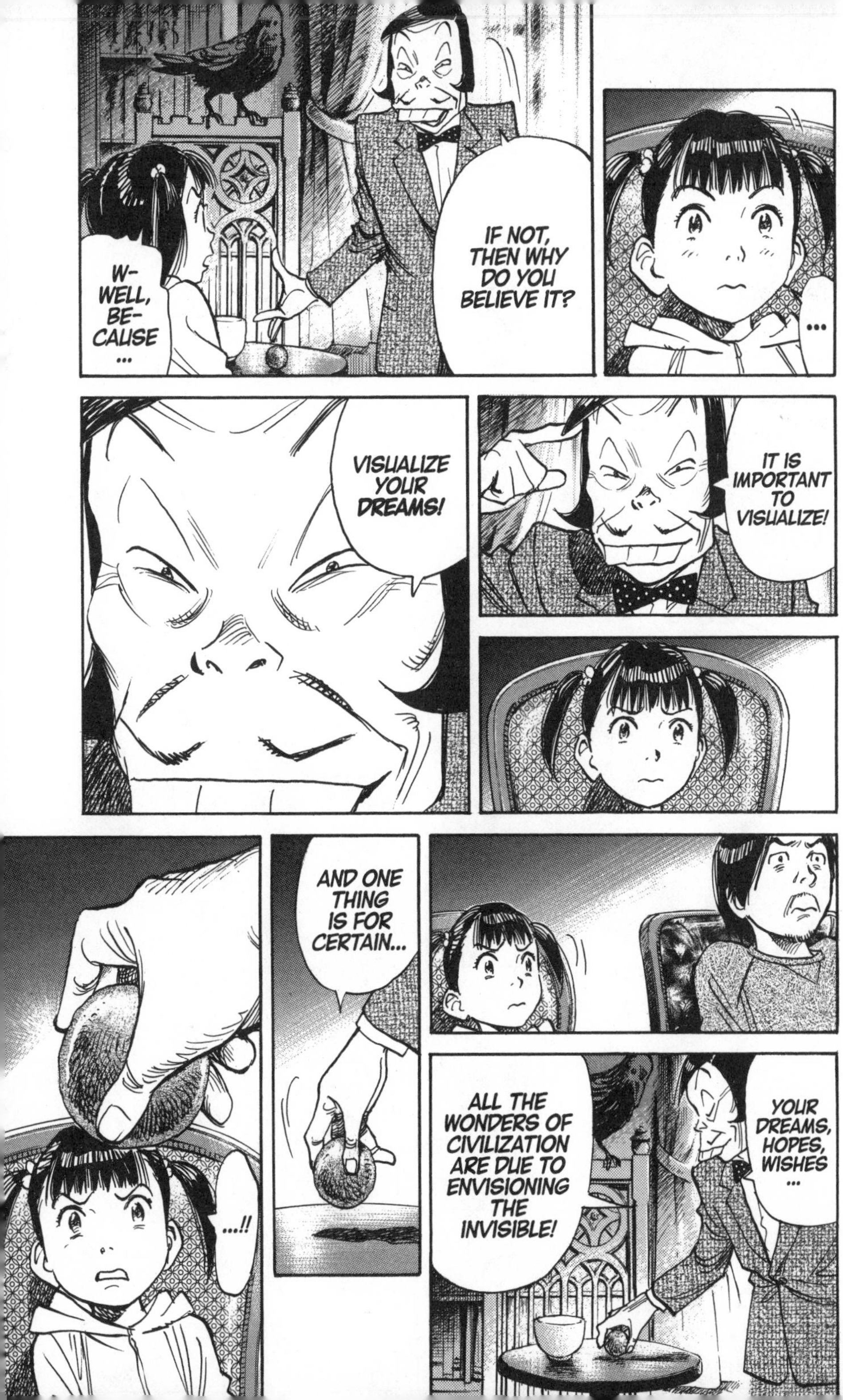
...
IF NOT, THEN WHY DO YOU BELIEVE IT?
W-WELL, BE-CAUSE...
IT IS IMPORTANT TO VISUALIZE!
VISUALIZE YOUR DREAMS!
YOUR DREAMS, HOPES, WISHES...
ALL THE WONDERS OF CIVILIZATION ARE DUE TO ENVISIONING THE INVISIBLE!
AND ONE THING IS FOR CERTAIN...
...!!

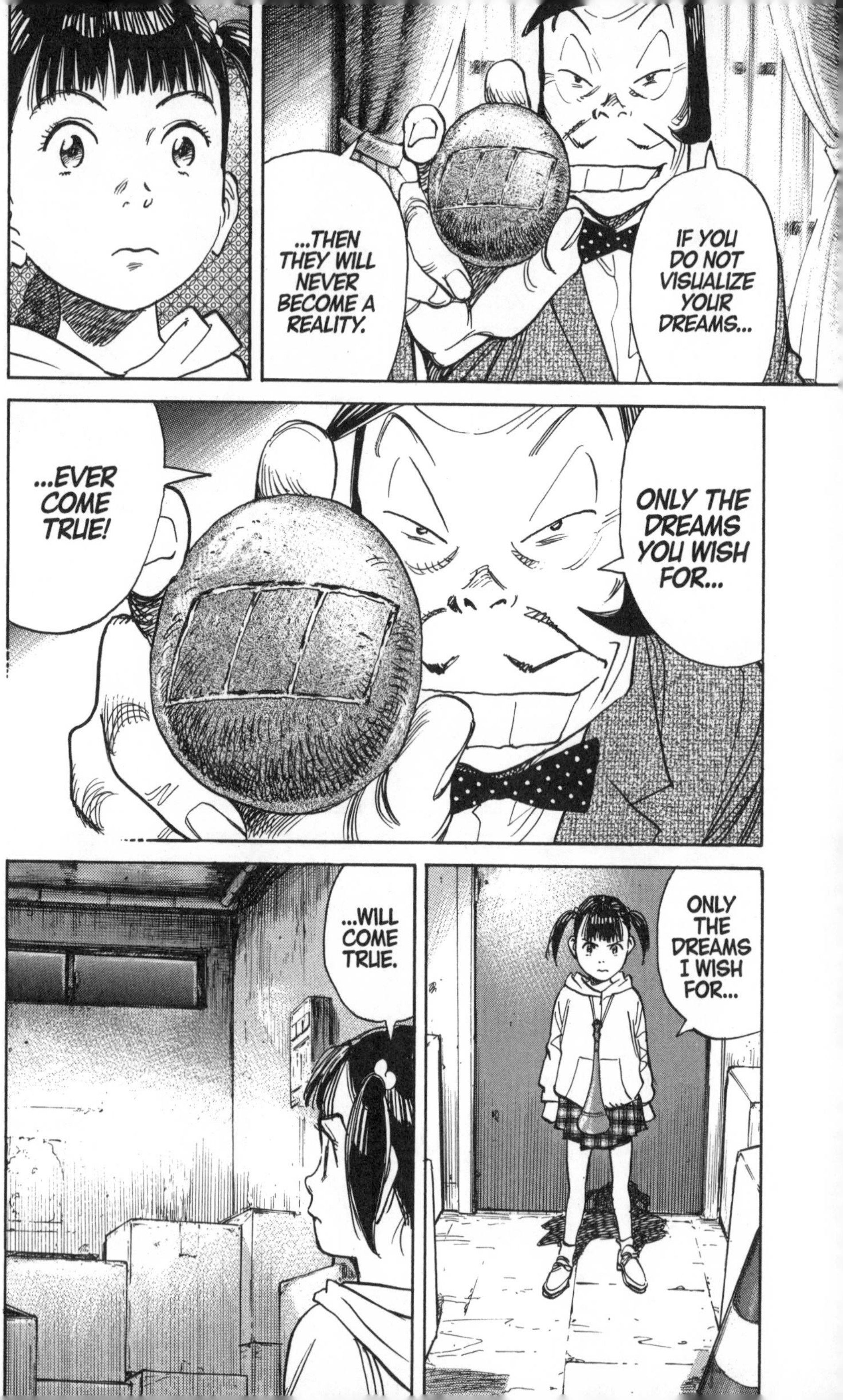
IF YOU DO NOT VISUALIZE YOUR DREAMS...
...THEN THEY WILL NEVER BECOME A REALITY.
ONLY THE DREAMS YOU WISH FOR...
...EVER COME TRUE!
ONLY THE DREAMS I WISH FOR...
...WILL COME TRUE.

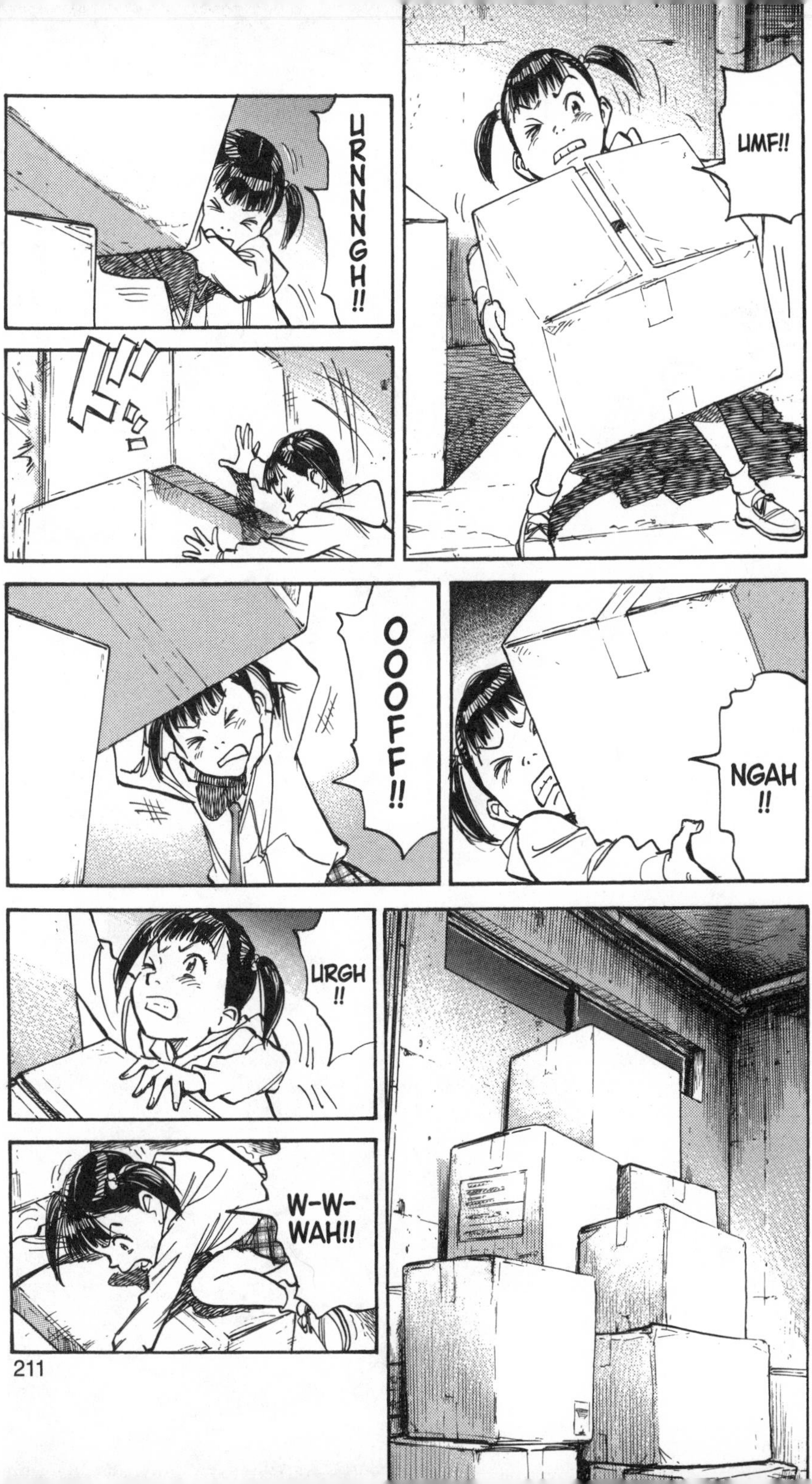
UMF!!
URNNNGH!!
NGAH!!
OOOFF!!
URGH!!
W-W-WAH!!

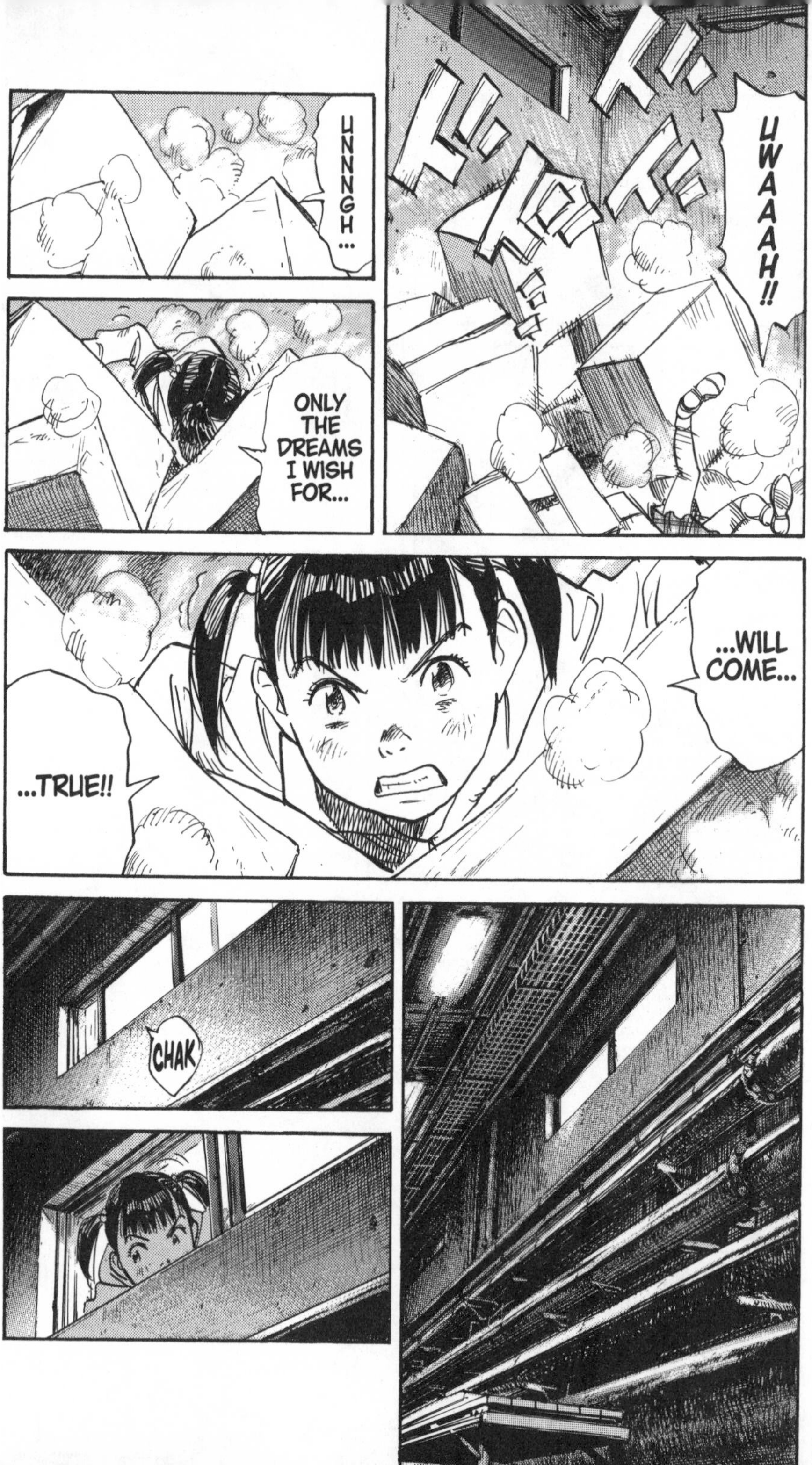
UWAAAAH!!
UNNNGH...
ONLY THE DREAMS I WISH FOR...
...WILL COME...
...TRUE!!
CHAK

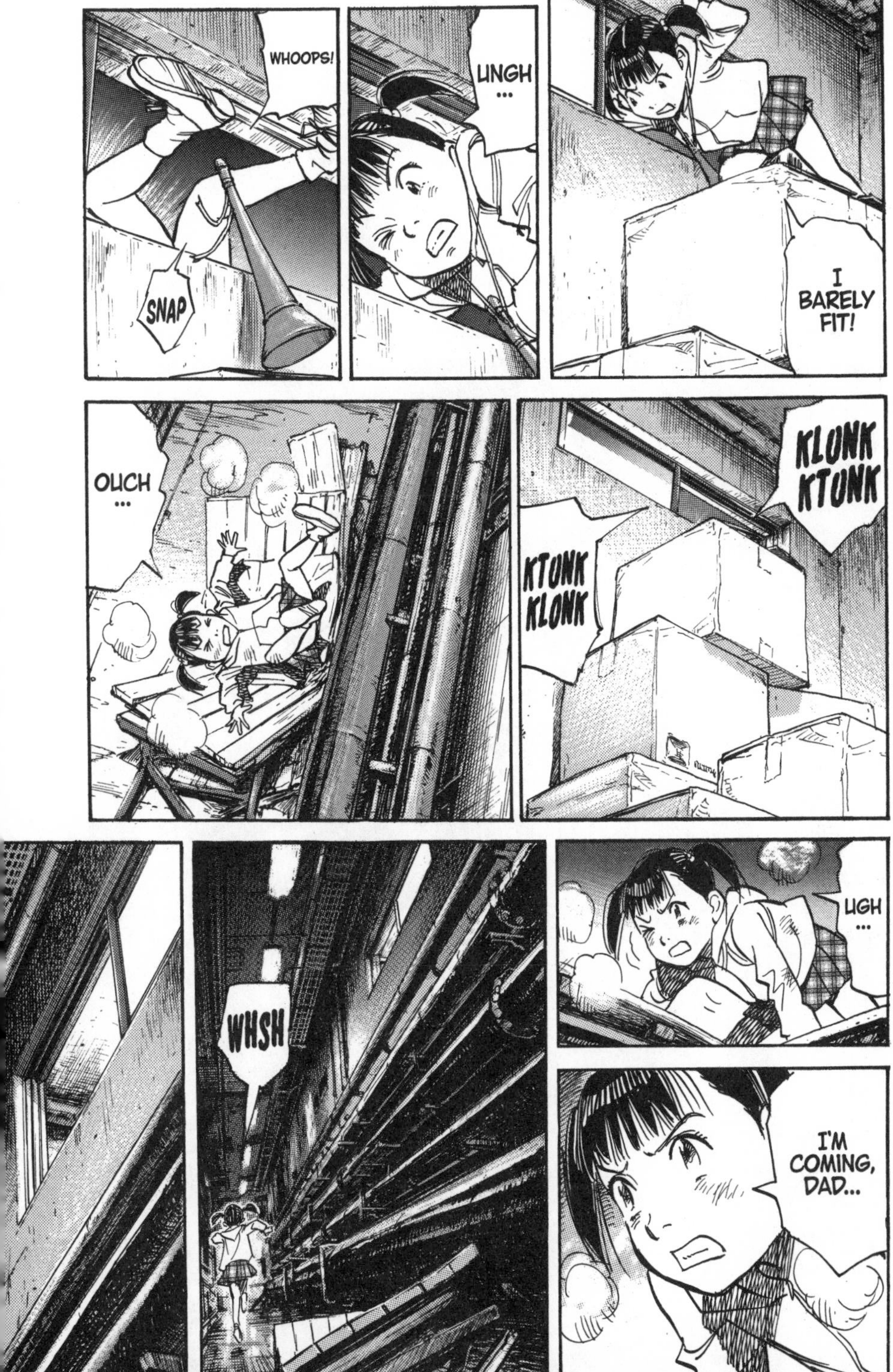
I BARELY FIT!
UNGH ...
WHOOPS!
SNAP
KLUNK KTUNK
KTUNK KLONK
OUCH ...
UGH ...
I'M COMING, DAD...
WHSH

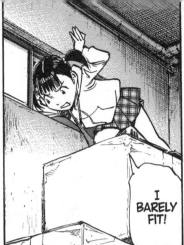

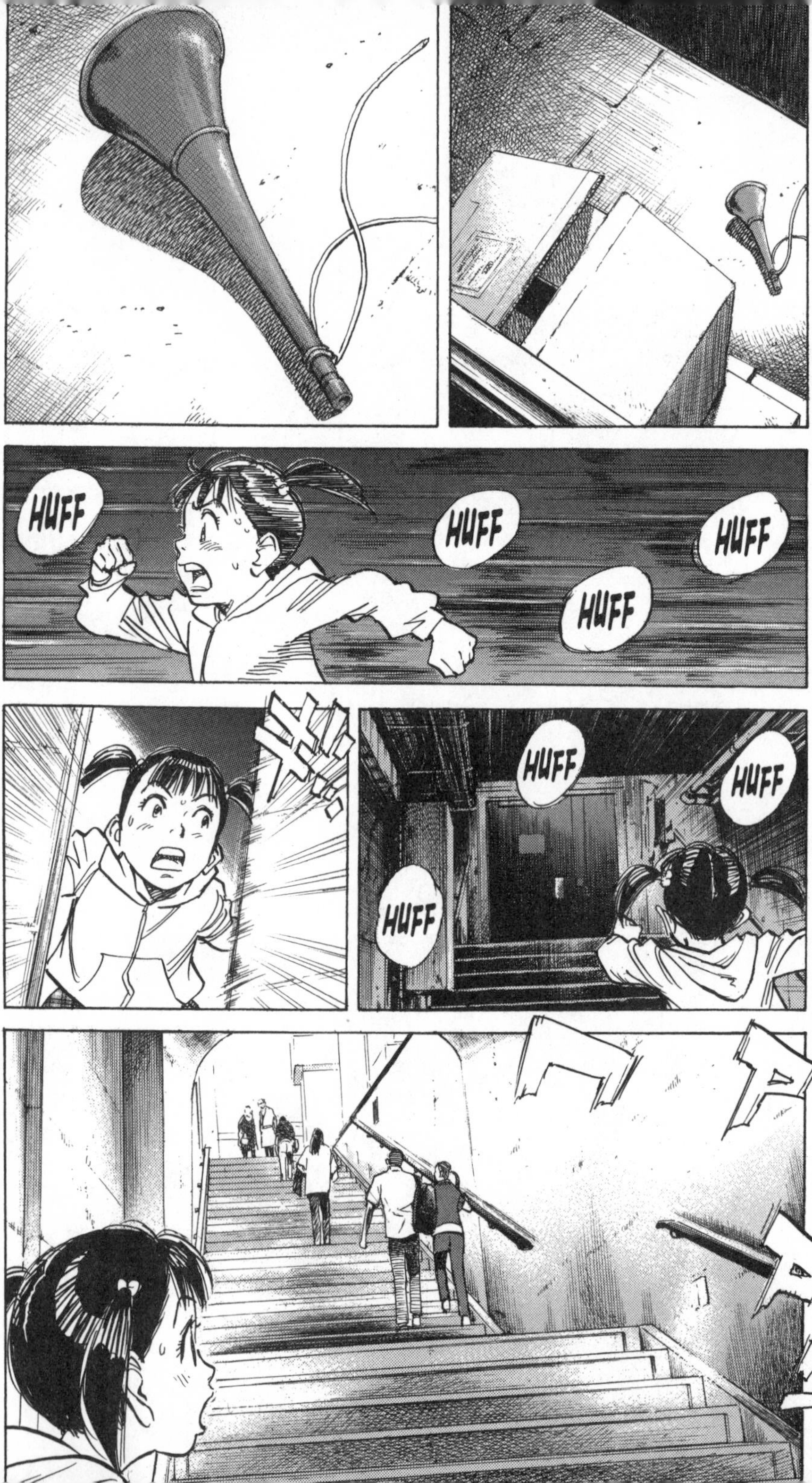
HUFF
HUFF
HUFF
HUFF
HUFF
HUFF
HUFF

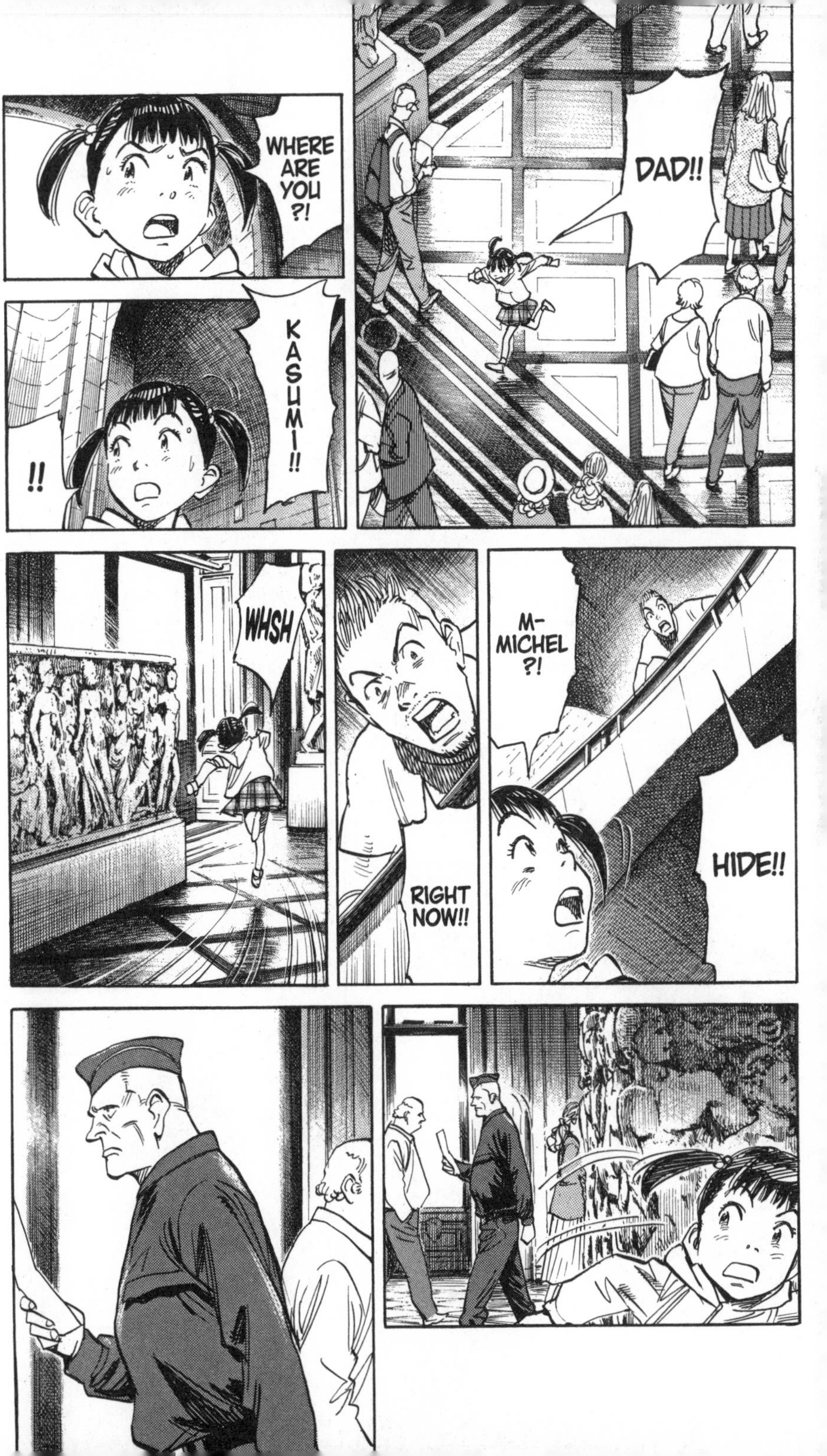
DAD!!
WHERE ARE YOU ?!
KASUMI!!
!!
M-MICHEL ?!
HIDE!!
RIGHT NOW!!
WHSH

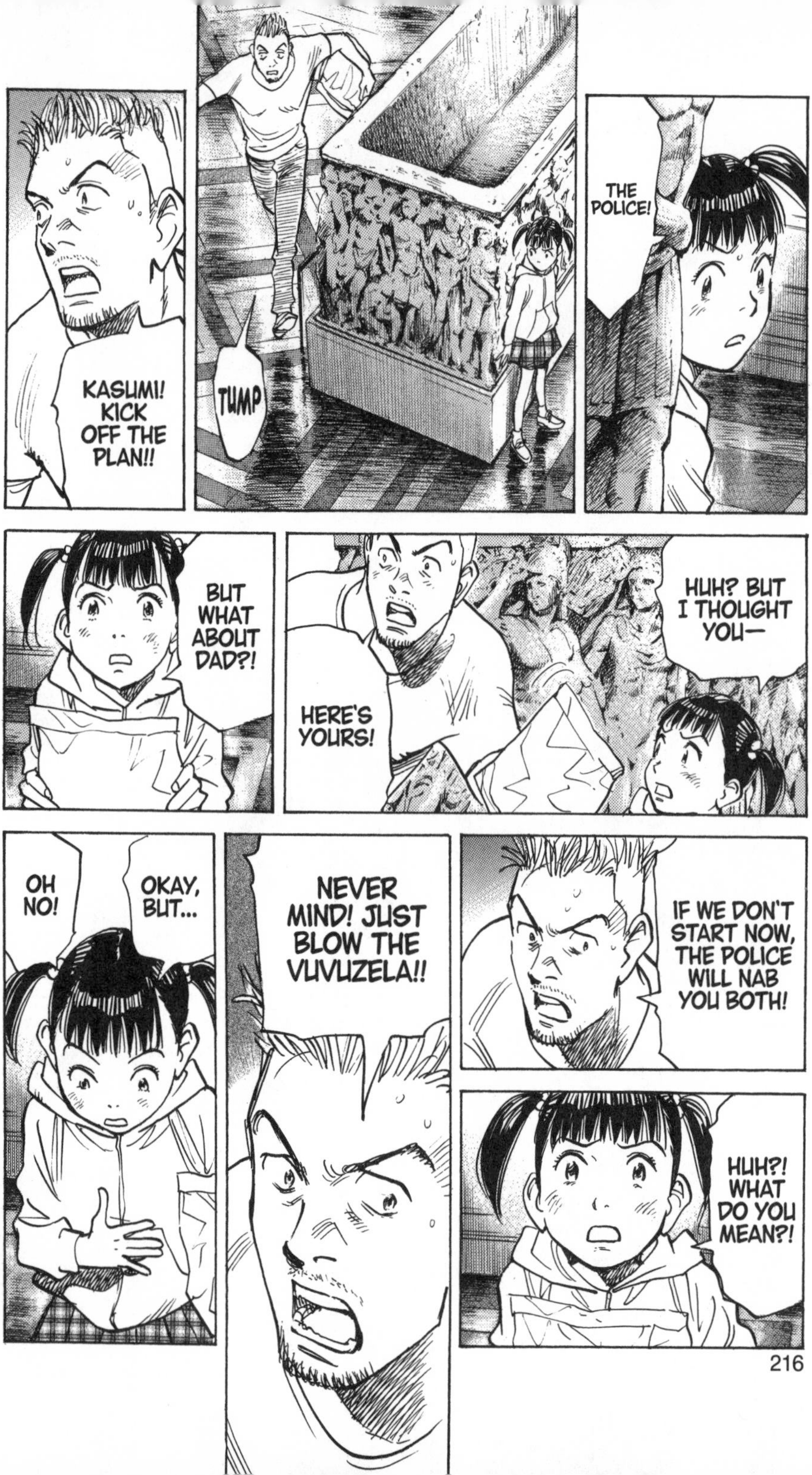
THE POLICE!
TUMP
KASUMI! KICK OFF THE PLAN!!
HUH? BUT I THOUGHT YOU—
HERE'S YOURS!
BUT WHAT ABOUT DAD?!
IF WE DON'T START NOW, THE POLICE WILL NAB YOU BOTH!
HUH?! WHAT DO YOU MEAN?!
NEVER MIND! JUST BLOW THE VUVUZELA!!
OKAY, BUT...
OH NO!

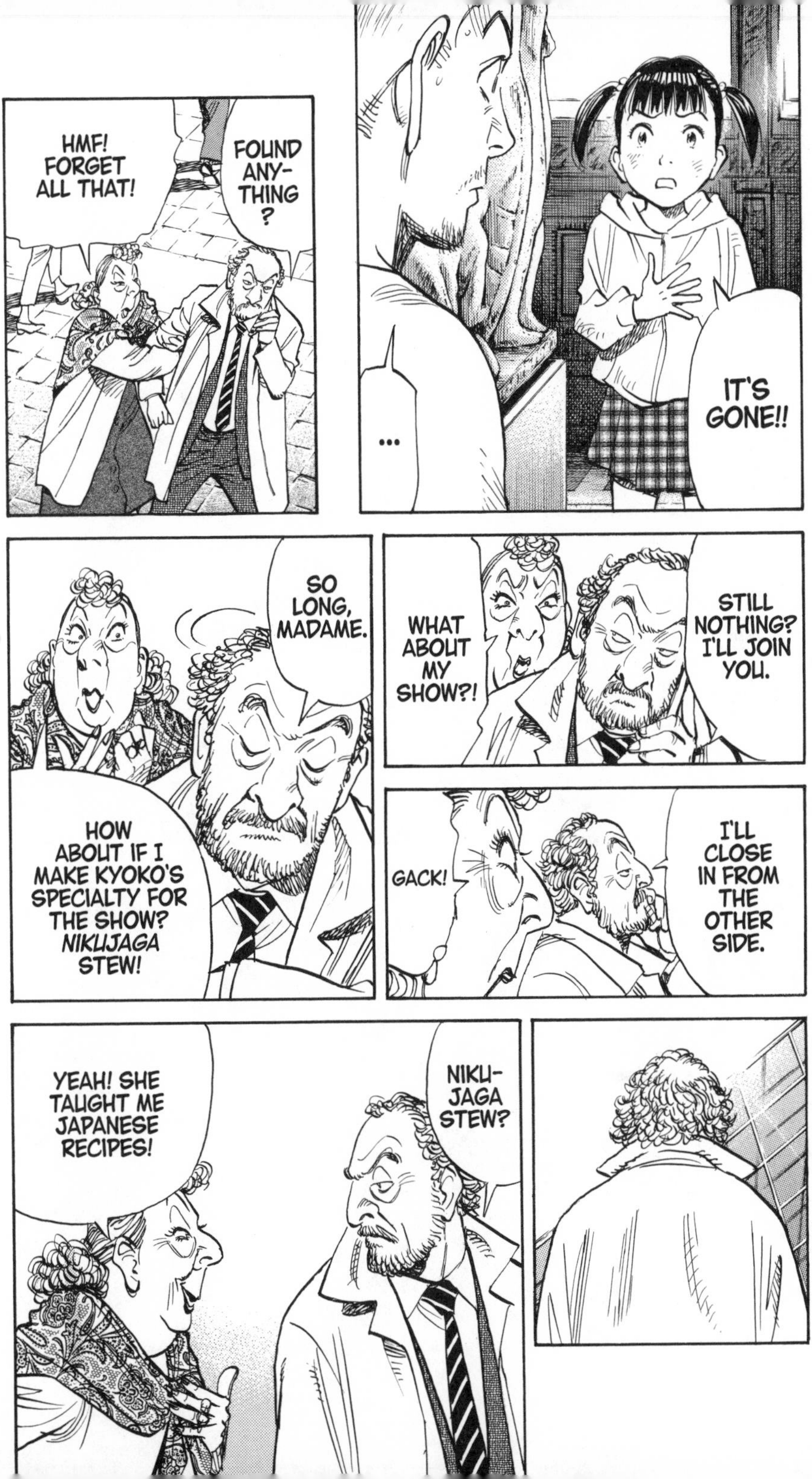
IT'S GONE!!
...
FOUND ANY-THING?
HMF! FORGET ALL THAT!
STILL NOTHING? I'LL JOIN YOU.
WHAT ABOUT MY SHOW?!
I'LL CLOSE IN FROM THE OTHER SIDE.
GACK!
SO LONG, MADAME.
HOW ABOUT IF I MAKE KYOKO'S SPECIALTY FOR THE SHOW? NIKUJAGA STEW!
NIKU-JAGA STEW?
YEAH! SHE TAUGHT ME JAPANESE RECIPES!

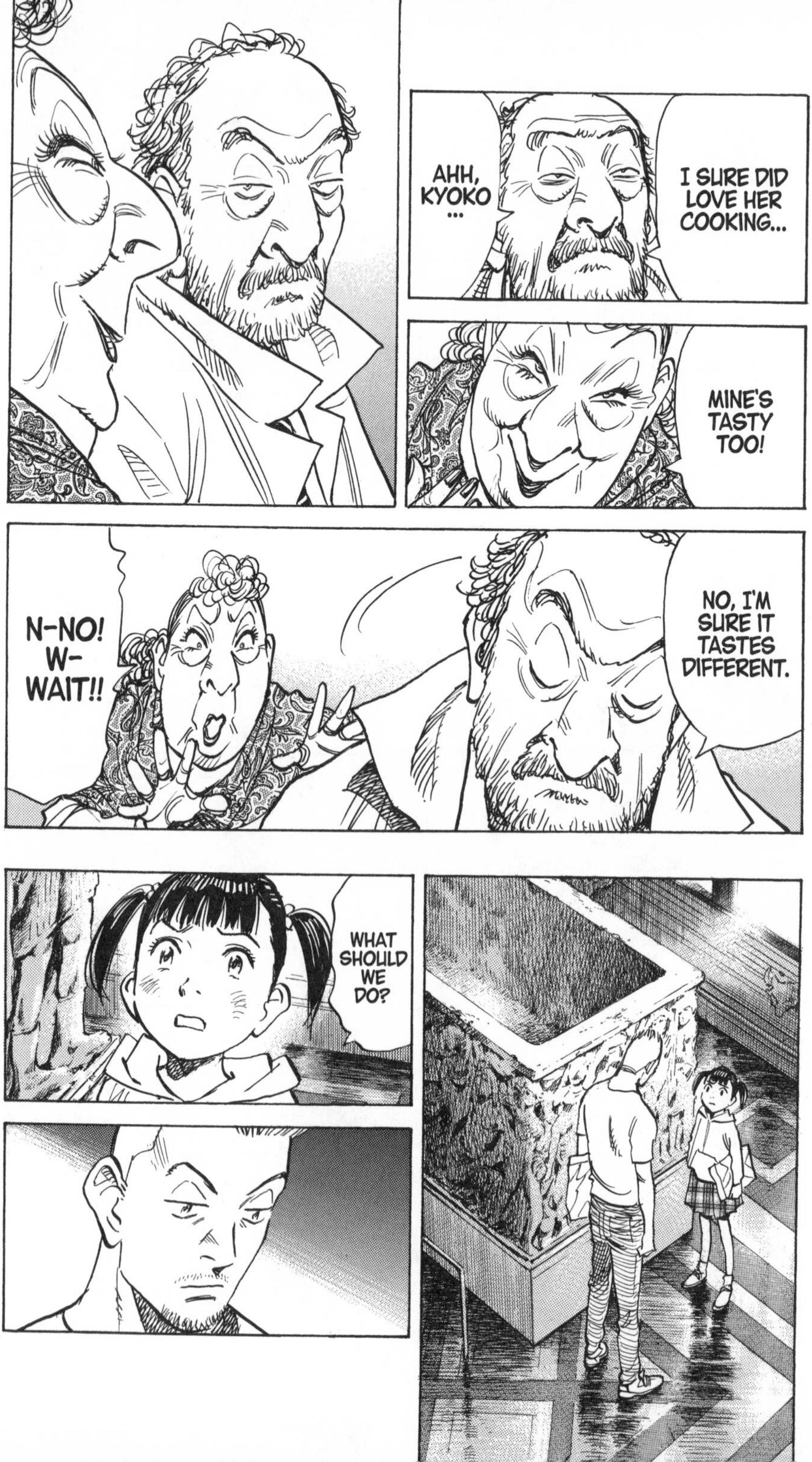
I SURE DID LOVE HER COOKING...
AHH, KYOKO ...
MINE'S TASTY TOO!
NO, I'M SURE IT TASTES DIFFERENT.
N-NO! W-WAIT!!
WHAT SHOULD WE DO?

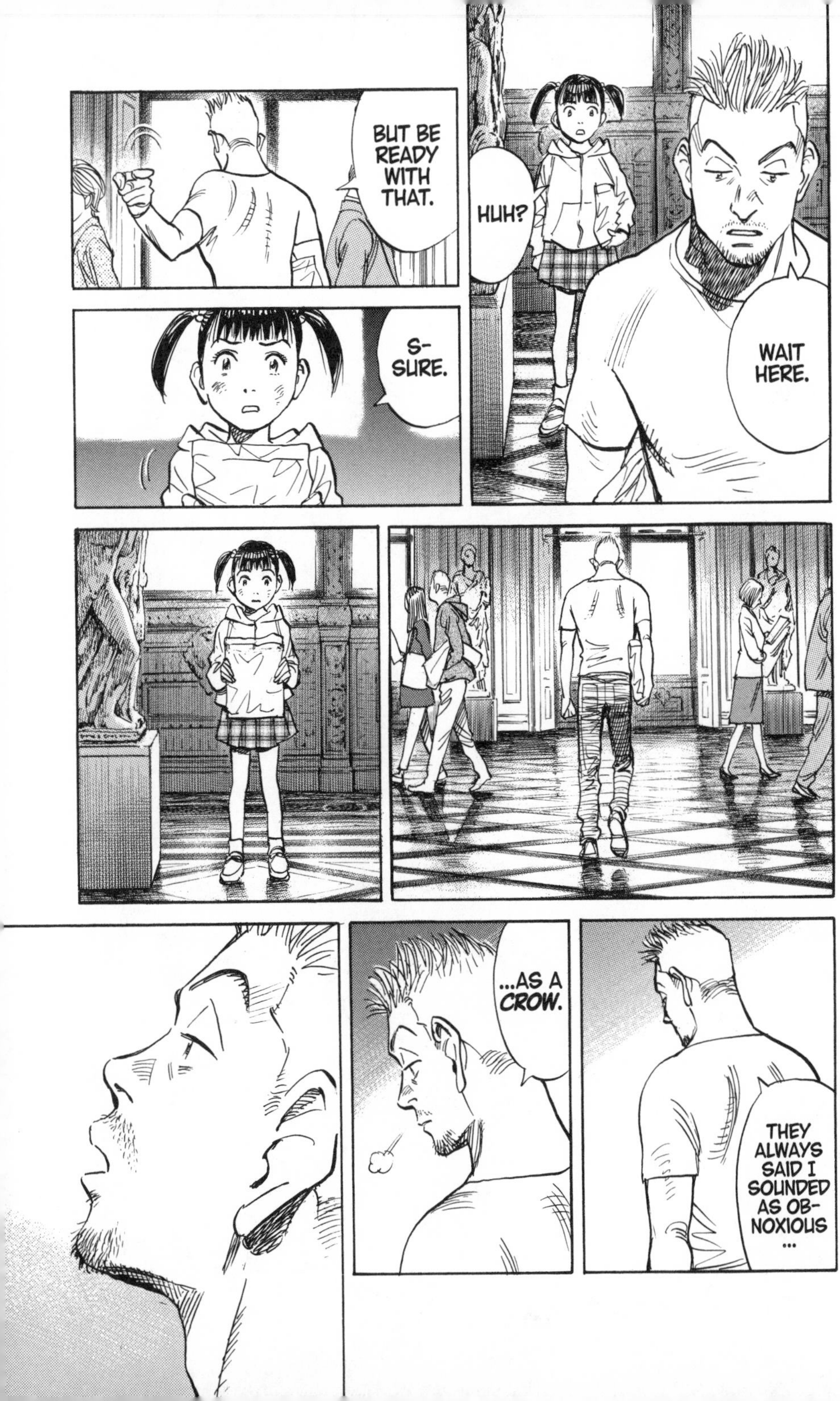
WAIT HERE.
HUH?
BUT BE READY WITH THAT.
S-SURE.
THEY ALWAYS SAID I SOUNDED AS OB-NOXIOUS...
...AS A CROW.

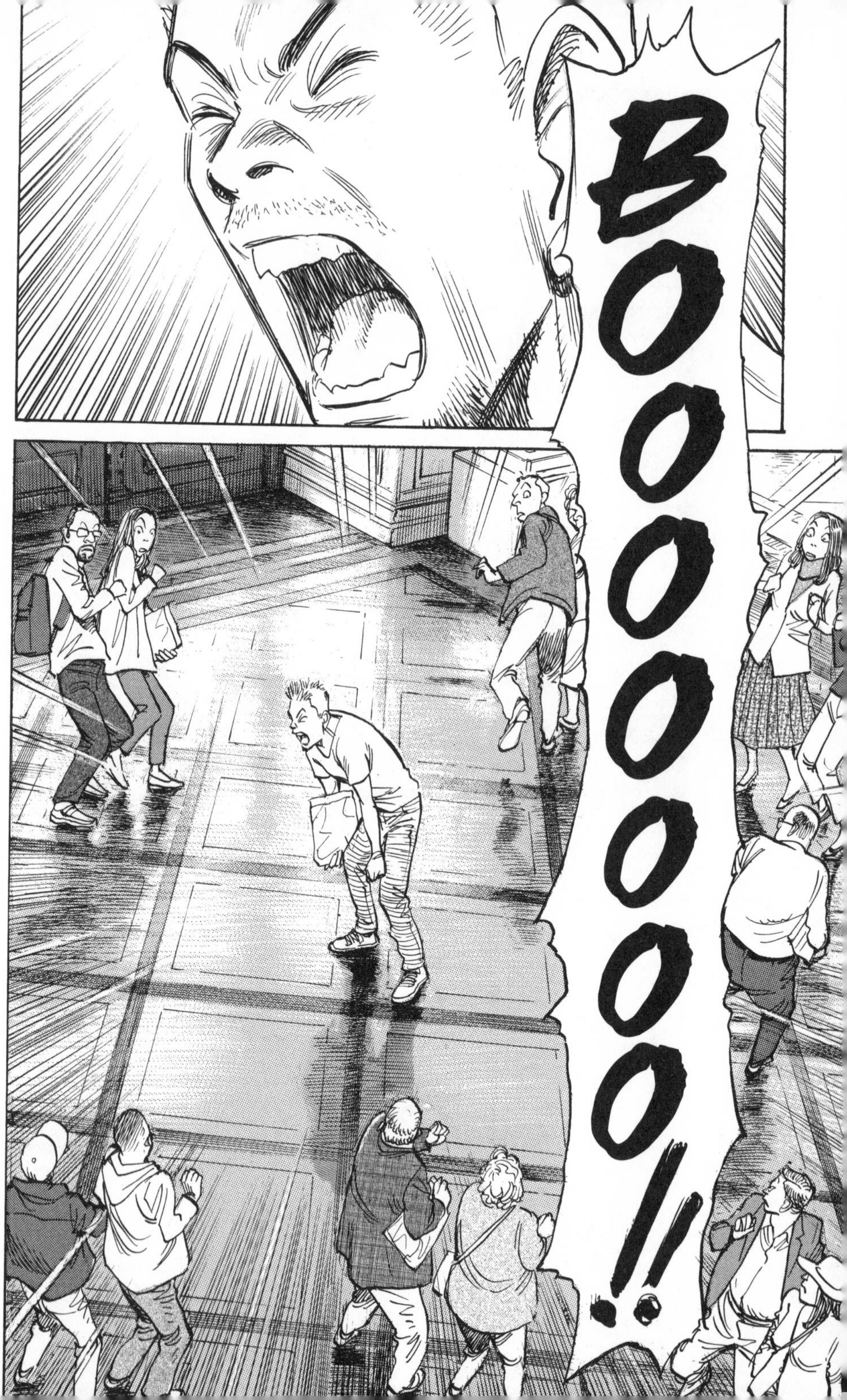
BOOOOOOO!!

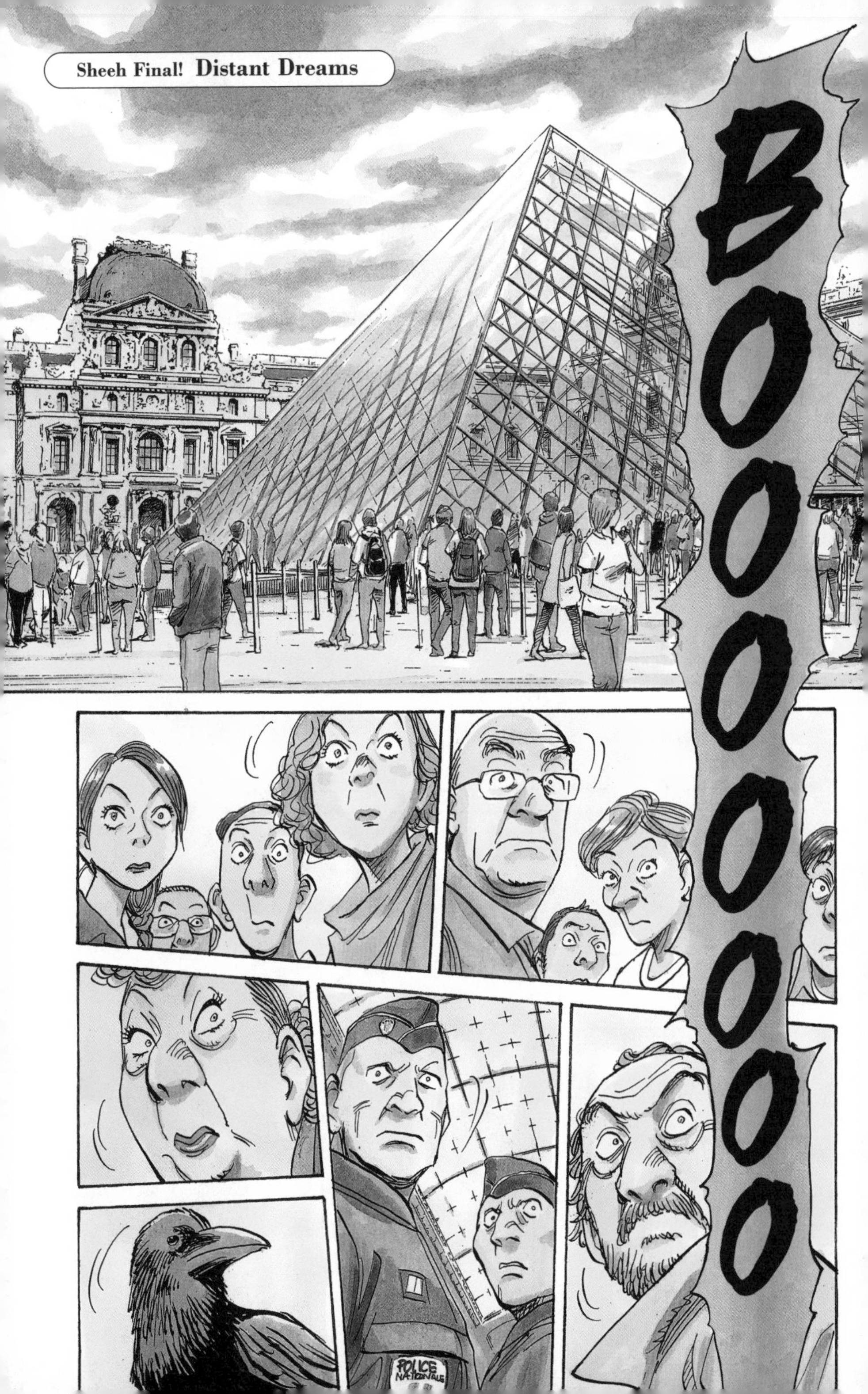
Sheeh Final! Distant Dreams
BOOOOOOOOOOO
POLICE NATIONALE

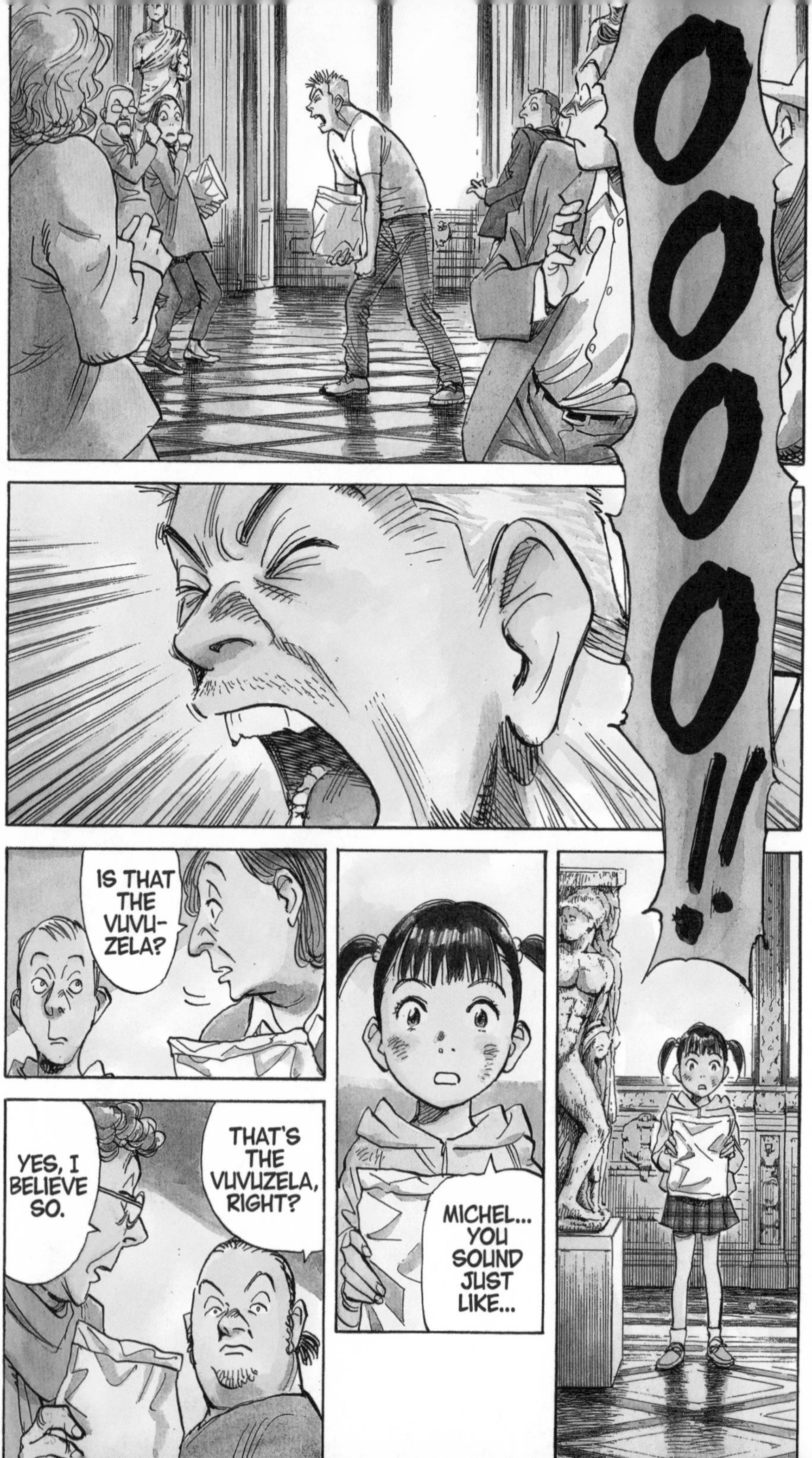
OOOOOO!!
MICHEL... YOU SOUND JUST LIKE...
IS THAT THE VUVUZELA?
THAT'S THE VUVUZELA, RIGHT?
YES, I BELIEVE SO.

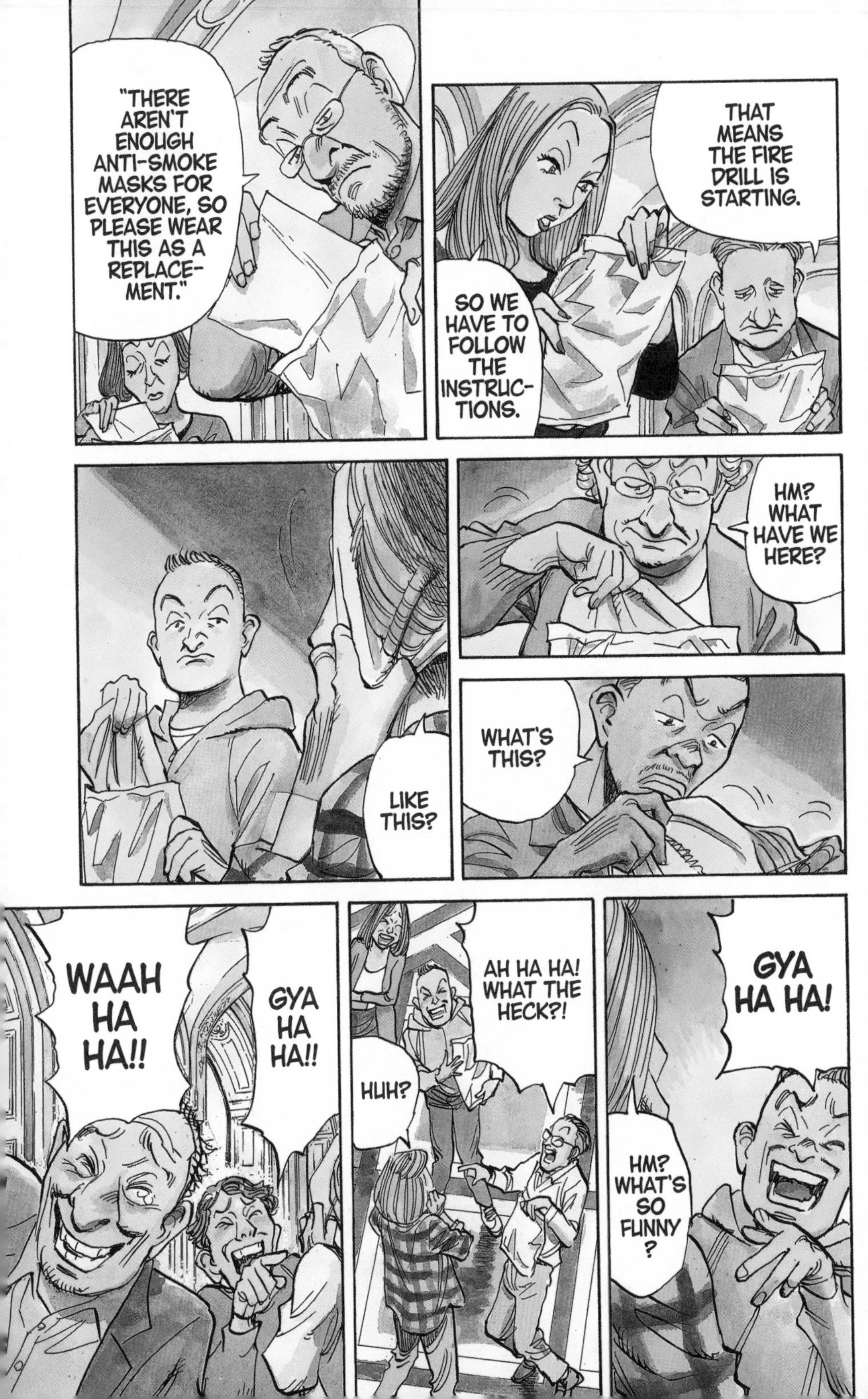
THAT MEANS THE FIRE DRILL IS STARTING.
SO WE HAVE TO FOLLOW THE INSTRUCTIONS.
"THERE AREN'T ENOUGH ANTI-SMOKE MASKS FOR EVERYONE, SO PLEASE WEAR THIS AS A REPLACEMENT."
HM? WHAT HAVE WE HERE?
WHAT'S THIS?
LIKE THIS?
GYA HA HA!
HM? WHAT'S SO FUNNY?
AH HA HA! WHAT THE HECK?!
HUH?
GYA HA HA!!
WAAH HA HA!!

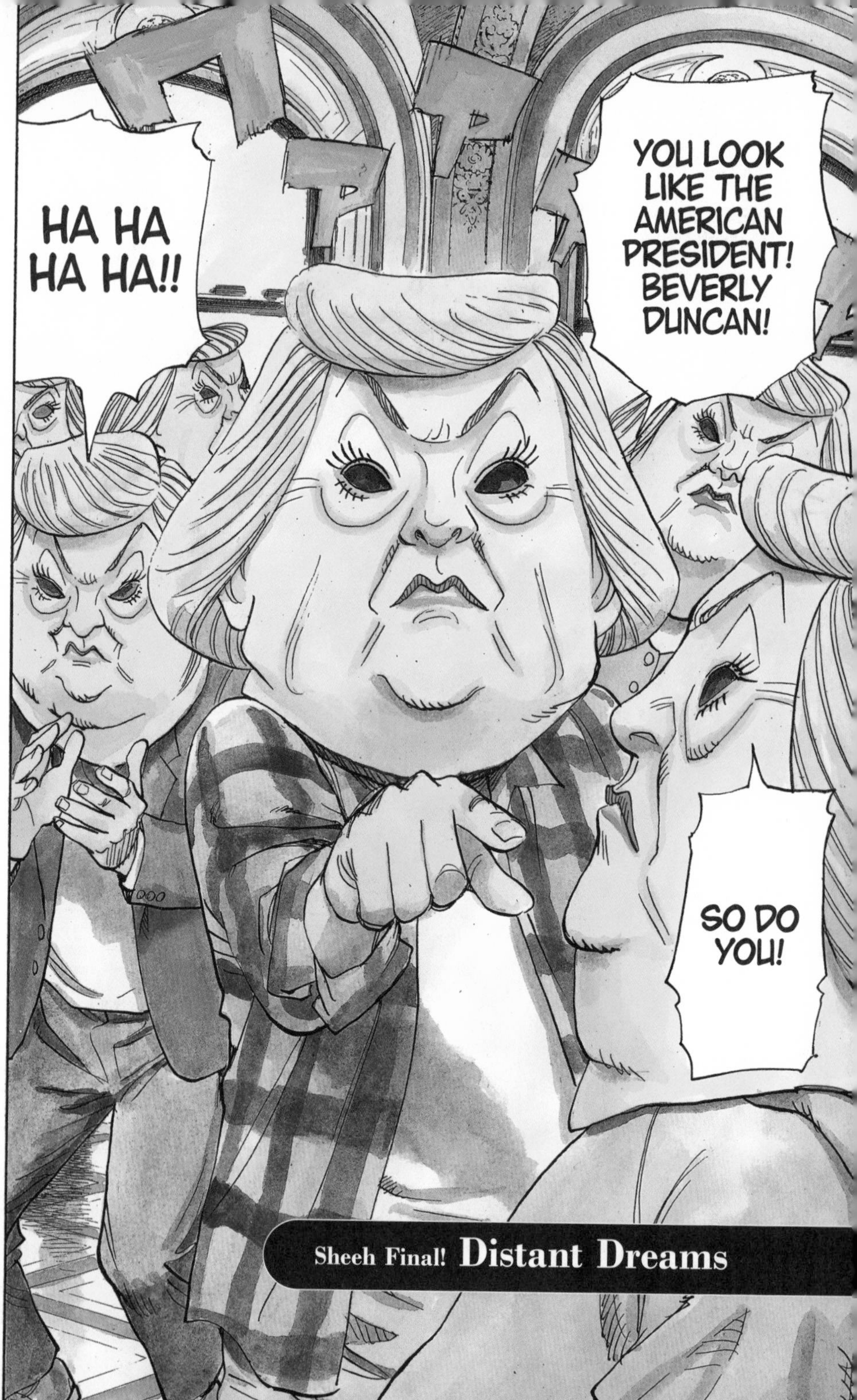
YOU LOOK LIKE THE AMERICAN PRESIDENT! BEVERLY DUNCAN!
HA HA HA HA!!
SO DO YOU!
Sheeh Final! Distant Dreams

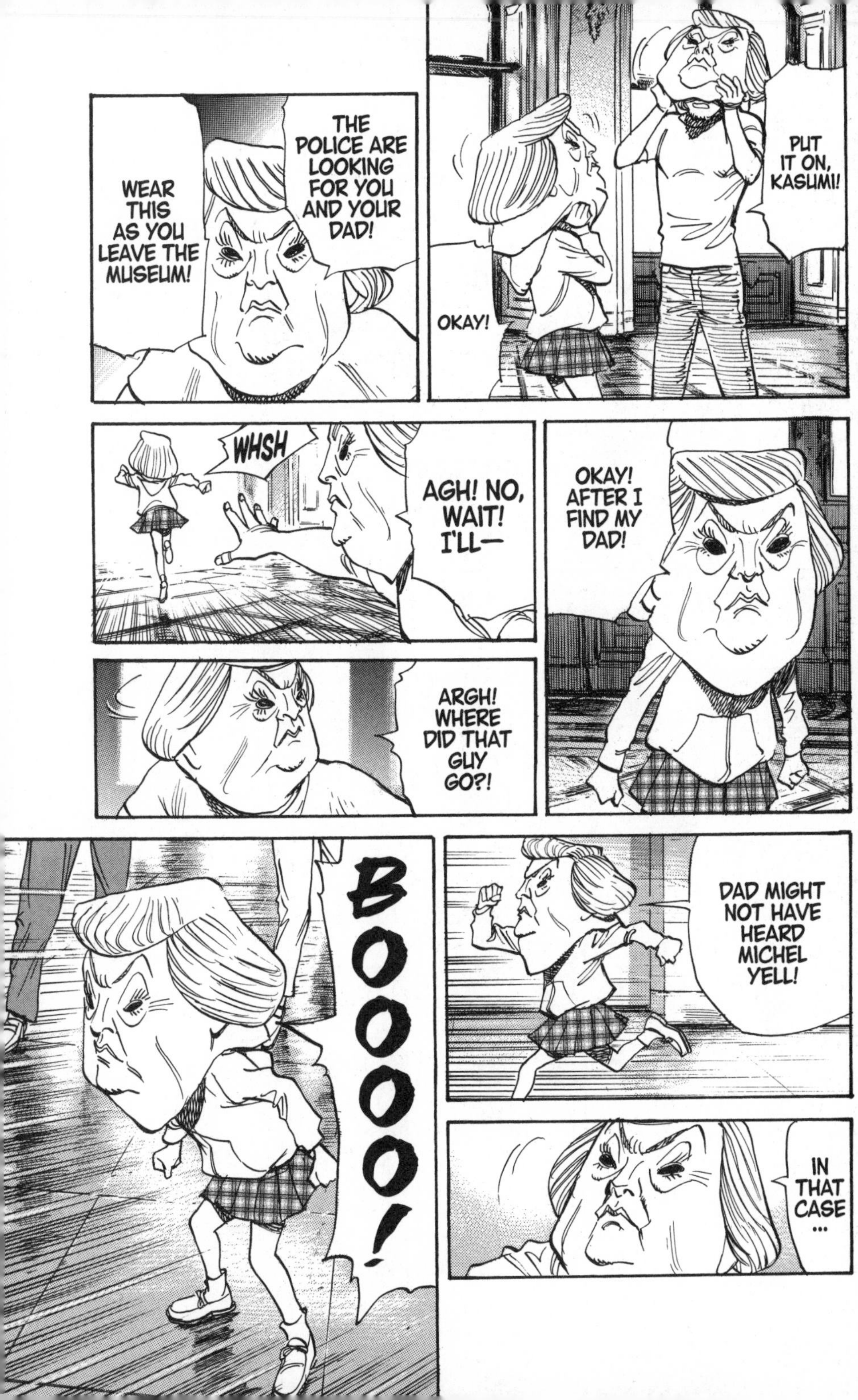
PUT IT ON, KASUMI!
OKAY!
THE POLICE ARE LOOKING FOR YOU AND YOUR DAD!
WEAR THIS AS YOU LEAVE THE MUSEUM!
OKAY! AFTER I FIND MY DAD!
AGH! NO, WAIT! I'LL—
WHSH
ARGH! WHERE DID THAT GUY GO?!
DAD MIGHT NOT HAVE HEARD MICHEL YELL!
IN THAT CASE ...
BOOOO!

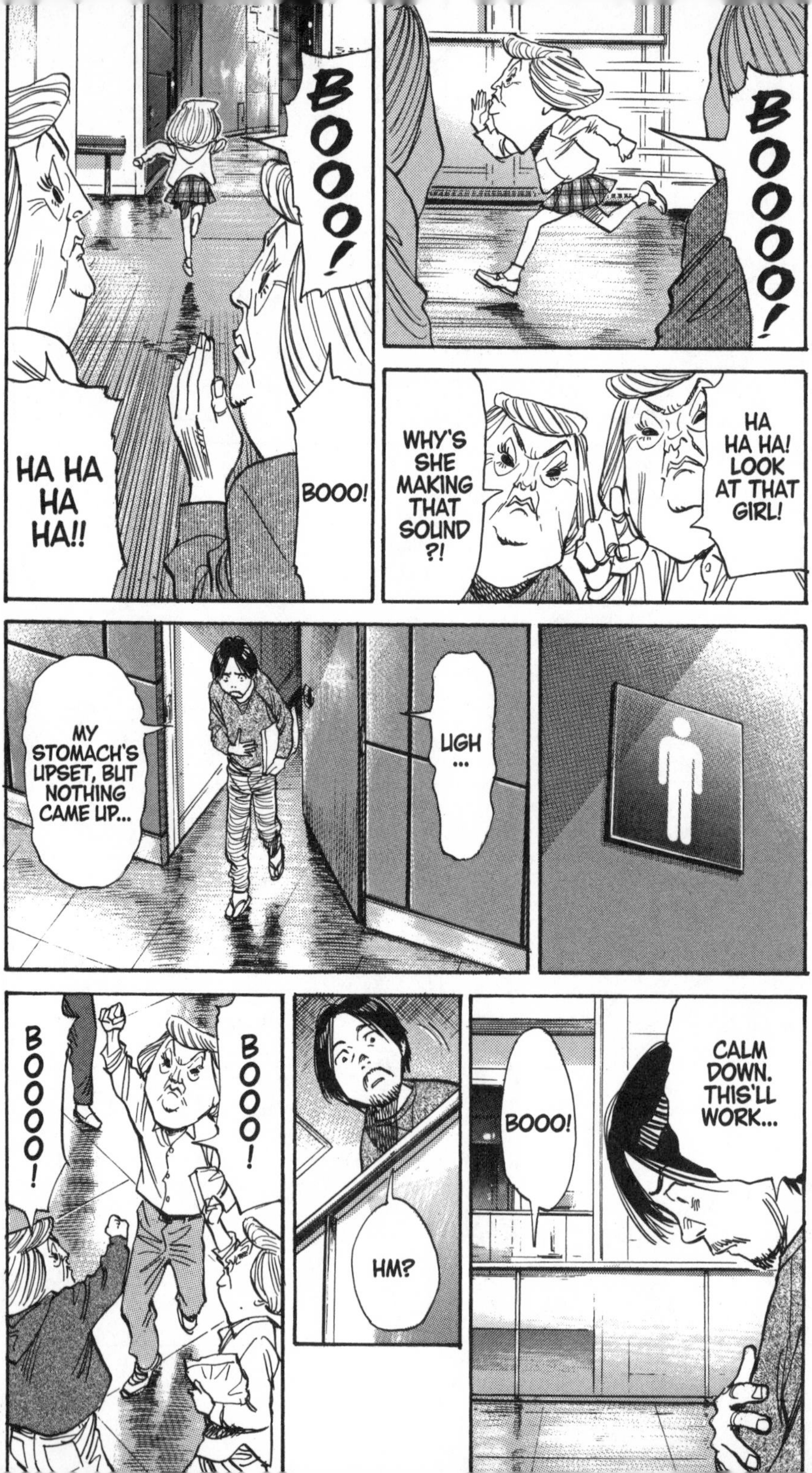
BOOOOO!
HA HA HA! LOOK AT THAT GIRL!
WHY'S SHE MAKING THAT SOUND?!
BOOOO!
BOOO!
HA HA HA HA!!
UGH...
MY STOMACH'S UPSET, BUT NOTHING CAME UP...
CALM DOWN. THIS'LL WORK...
BOOO!
HM?
BOOO!
BOOOOO!

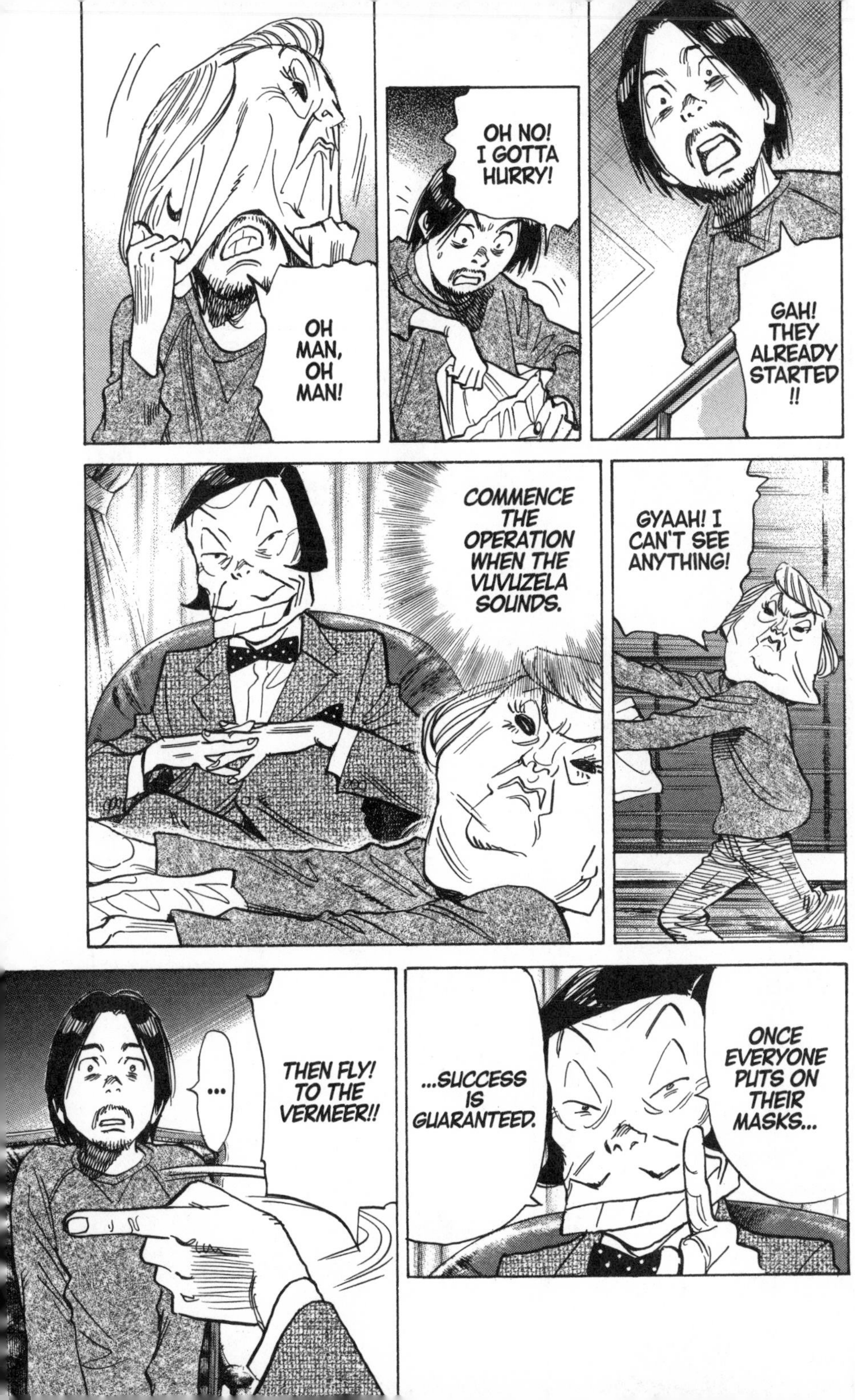
GAH! THEY ALREADY STARTED!!
OH NO! I GOTTA HURRY!
OH MAN, OH MAN!
GYAAH! I CAN'T SEE ANYTHING!
COMMENCE THE OPERATION WHEN THE VUVUZELA SOUNDS.
ONCE EVERYONE PUTS ON THEIR MASKS...
...SUCCESS IS GUARANTEED.
THEN FLY! TO THE VERMEER!!
...

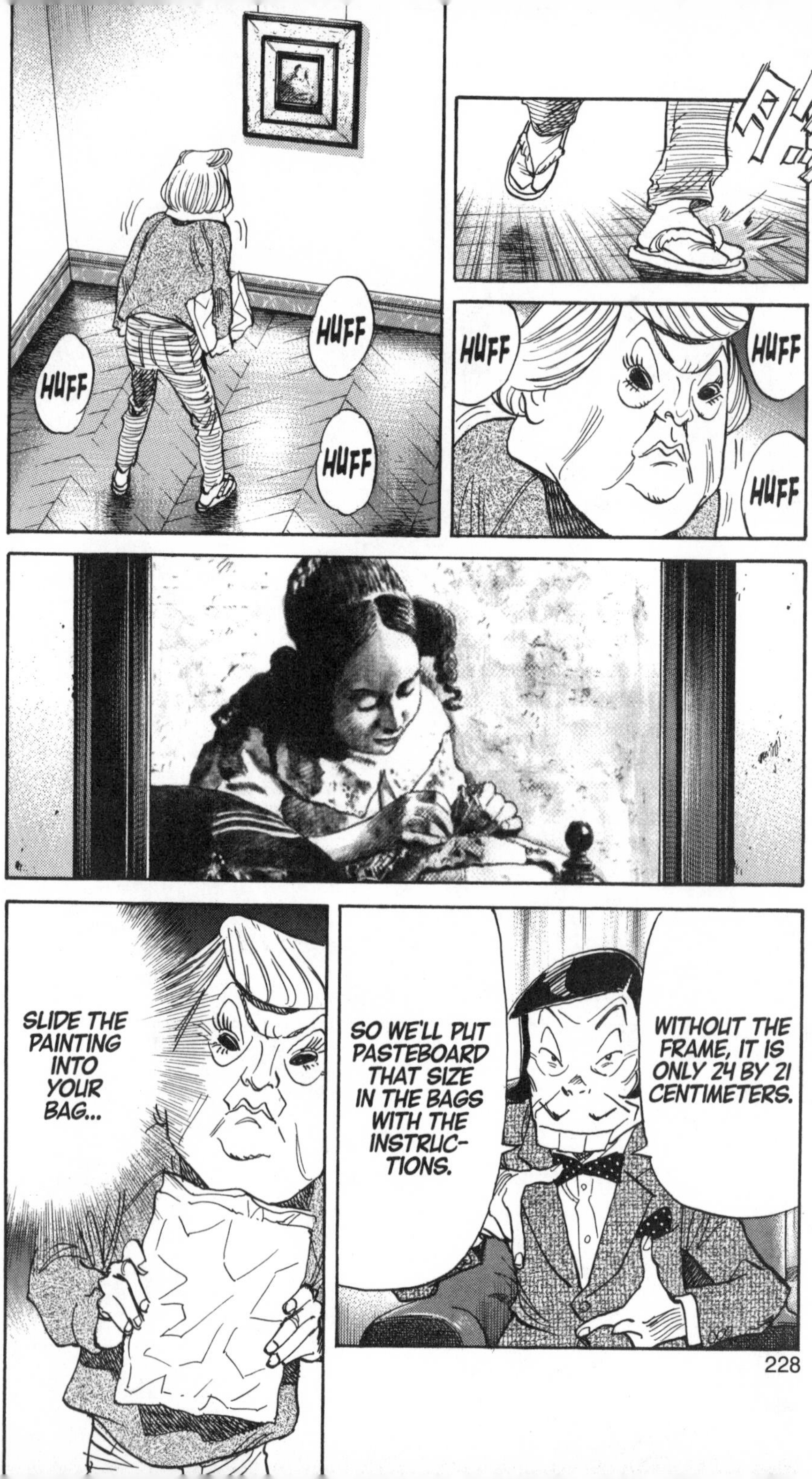
HUFF
HUFF
HUFF
HUFF
HUFF
HUFF
WITHOUT THE FRAME, IT IS ONLY 24 BY 21 CENTIMETERS.
SO WE'LL PUT PASTEBOARD THAT SIZE IN THE BAGS WITH THE INSTRUC-TIONS.
SLIDE THE PAINTING INTO YOUR BAG...

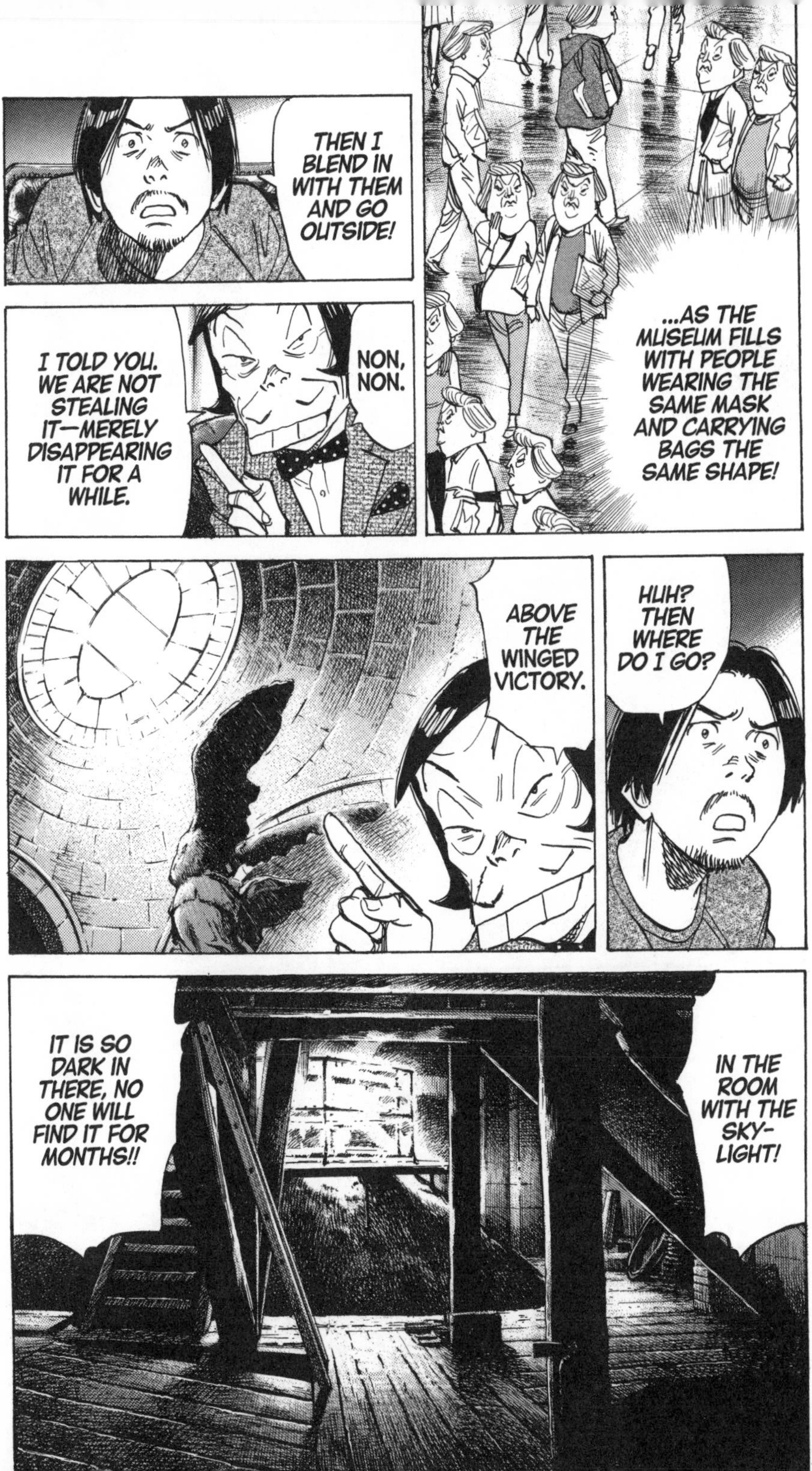
...AS THE MUSEUM FILLS WITH PEOPLE WEARING THE SAME MASK AND CARRYING BAGS THE SAME SHAPE!
THEN I BLEND IN WITH THEM AND GO OUTSIDE!
NON, NON.
I TOLD YOU. WE ARE NOT STEALING IT—MERELY DISAPPEARING IT FOR A WHILE.
HUH? THEN WHERE DO I GO?
ABOVE THE WINGED VICTORY.
IN THE ROOM WITH THE SKY-LIGHT!
IT IS SO DARK IN THERE, NO ONE WILL FIND IT FOR MONTHS!!

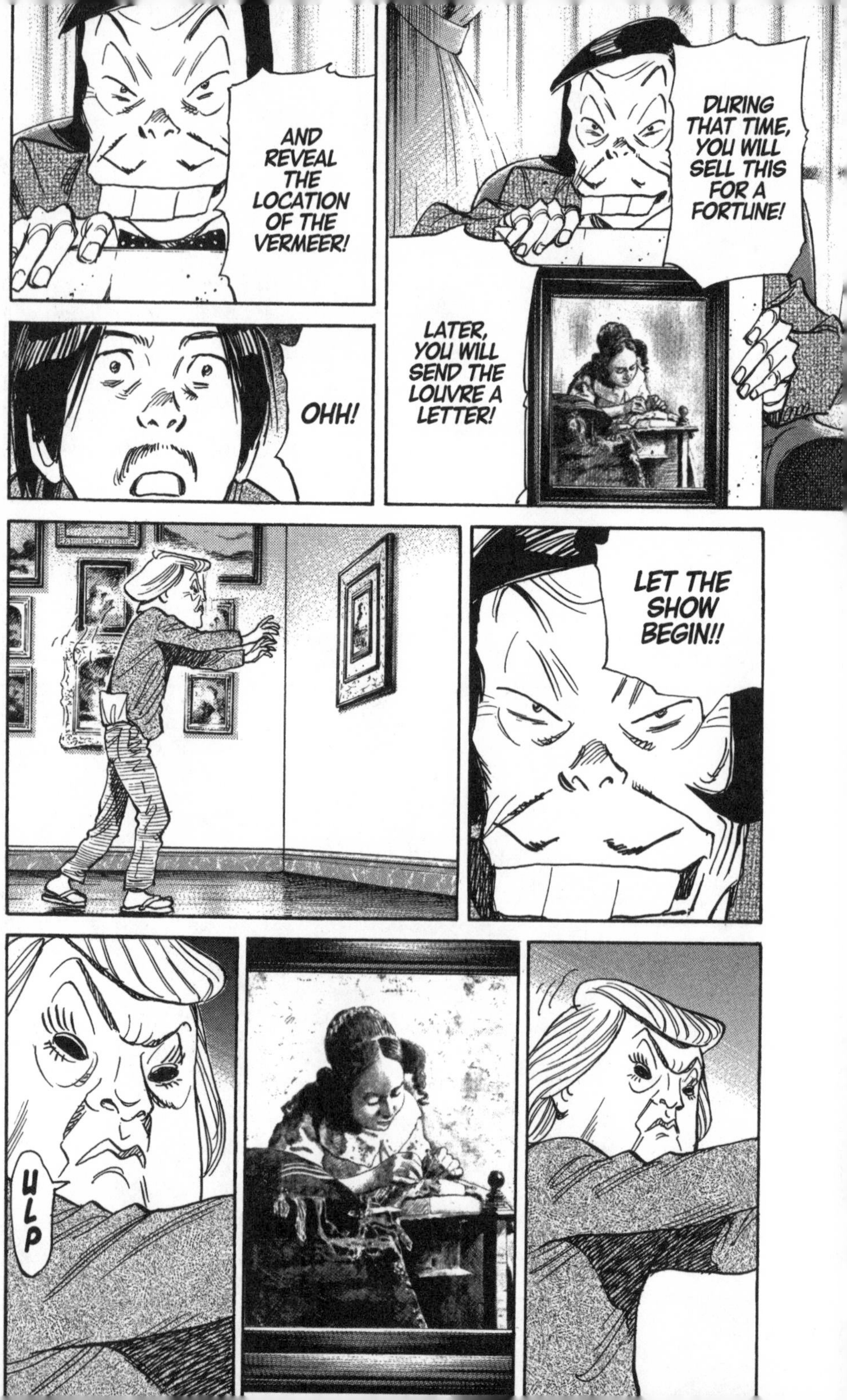
DURING THAT TIME, YOU WILL SELL THIS FOR A FORTUNE!
LATER, YOU WILL SEND THE LOUVRE A LETTER!
AND REVEAL THE LOCATION OF THE VERMEER!
OHH!
LET THE SHOW BEGIN!!
ULP

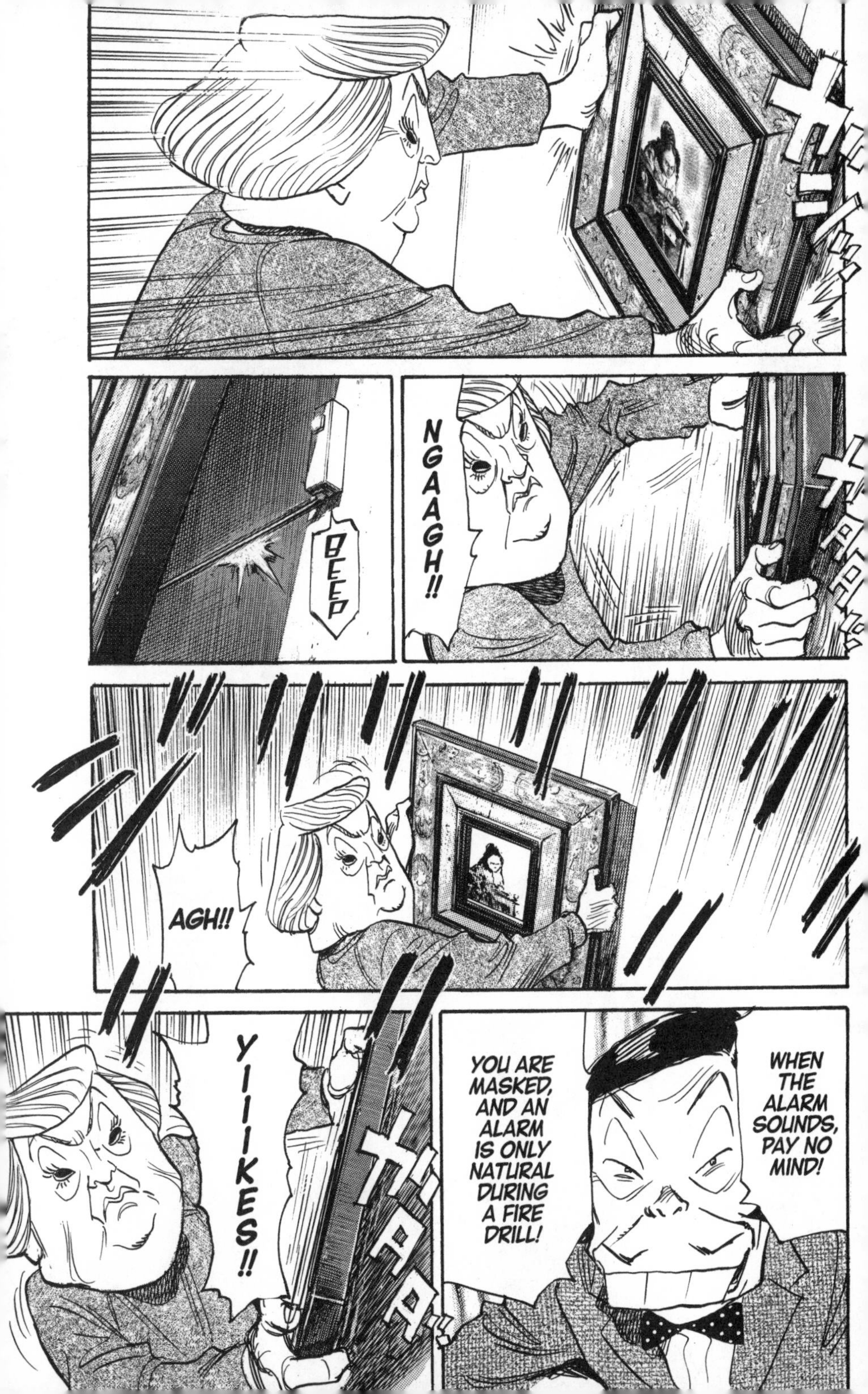
NGAAAGH!!
BEEP
AGH!!
WHEN THE ALARM SOUNDS, PAY NO MIND!
YOU ARE MASKED, AND AN ALARM IS ONLY NATURAL DURING A FIRE DRILL!
YIIIIKES!!

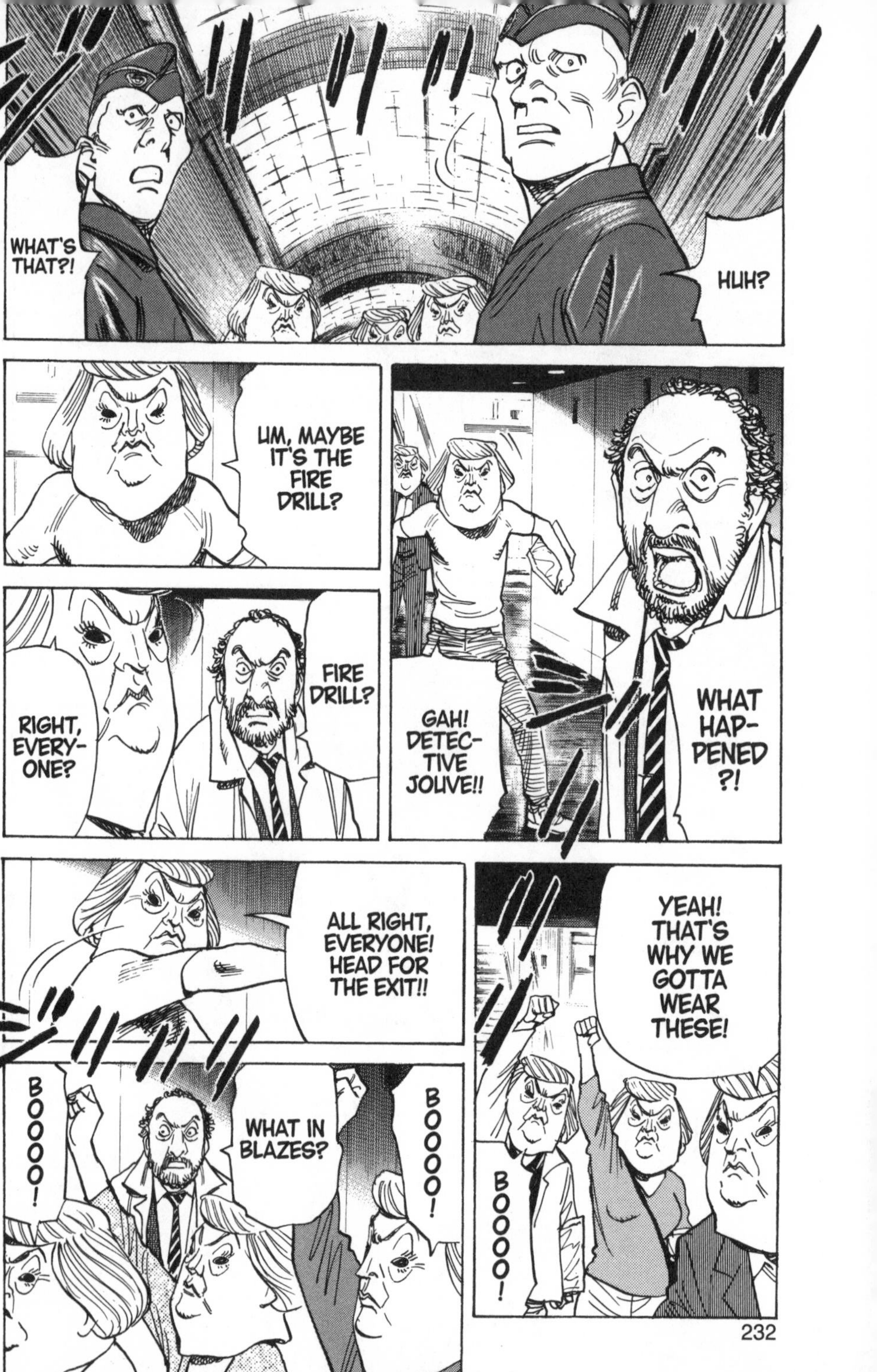
HUH?
WHAT'S THAT?!
WHAT HAPPENED?!
GAH! DETECTIVE JOUVE!!
UM, MAYBE IT'S THE FIRE DRILL?
FIRE DRILL?
RIGHT, EVERYONE?
YEAH! THAT'S WHY WE GOTTA WEAR THESE!
BOOOOO!
ALL RIGHT, EVERYONE! HEAD FOR THE EXIT!!
BOOOOO!
WHAT IN BLAZES?
BOOOOO!

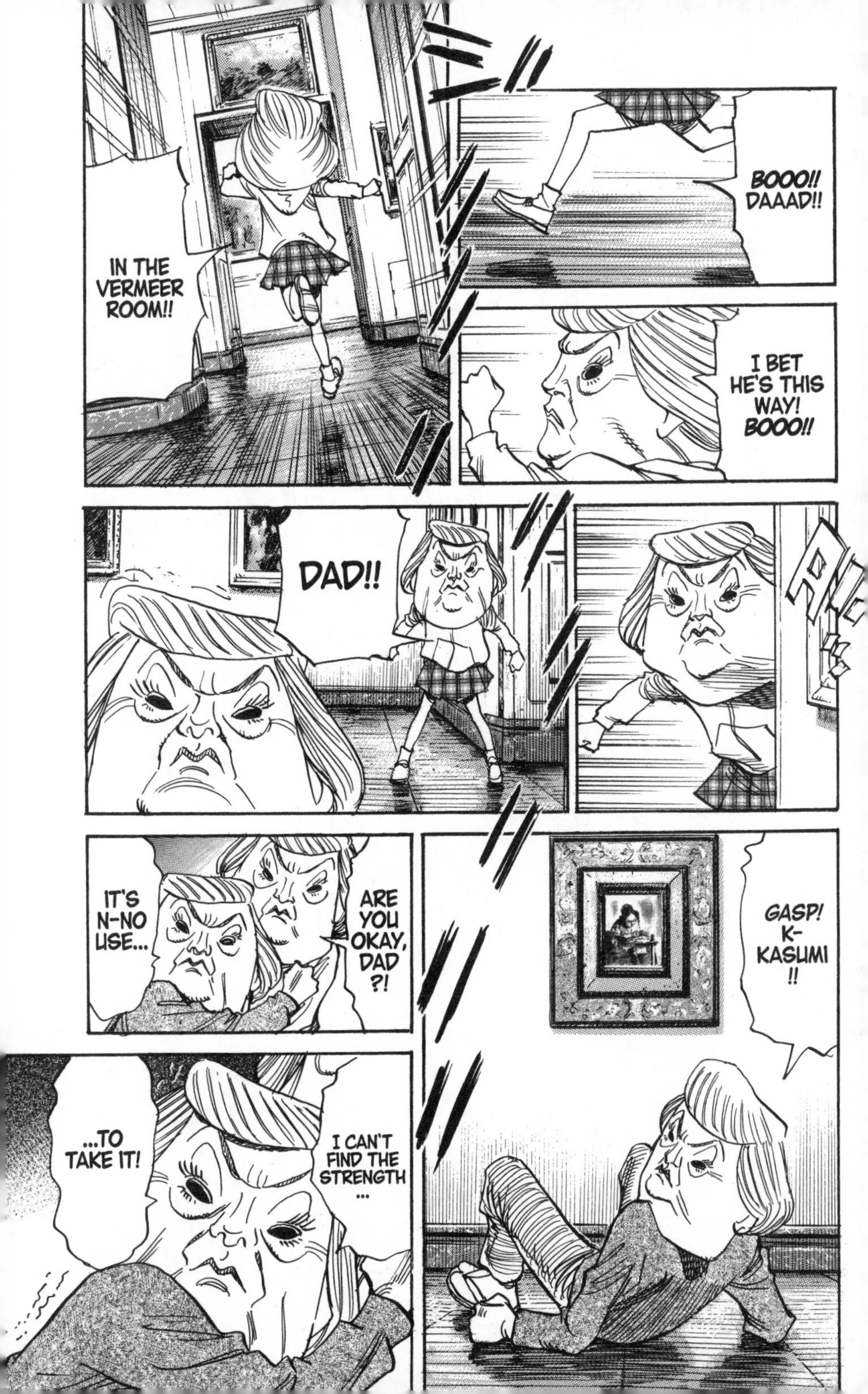
BOOO!! DAAAD!!
I BET HE'S THIS WAY! BOOO!!
IN THE VERMEER ROOM!!
DAD!!
GASP! K-KASUMI!!
ARE YOU OKAY, DAD?!
IT'S N-NO USE...
I CAN'T FIND THE STRENGTH...
...TO TAKE IT!

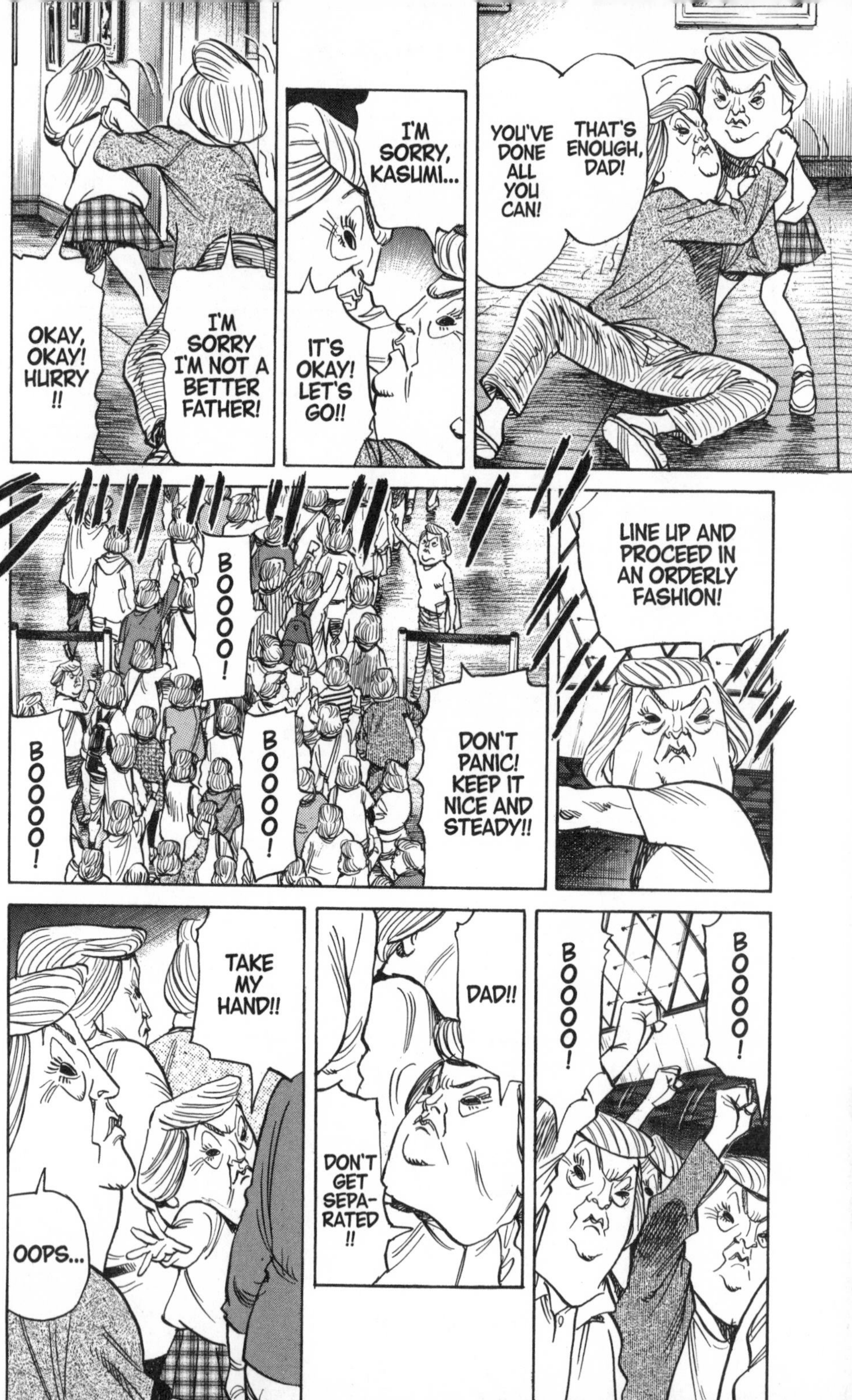
THAT'S ENOUGH, DAD!
YOU'VE DONE ALL YOU CAN!
I'M SORRY, KASUMI...
IT'S OKAY! LET'S GO!!
I'M SORRY I'M NOT A BETTER FATHER!
OKAY, OKAY! HURRY!!
LINE UP AND PROCEED IN AN ORDERLY FASHION!
DON'T PANIC! KEEP IT NICE AND STEADY!!
BOOOOO!
BOOOOO!
BOOOOO!
BOOOOO!
BOOOOO!
DAD!!
DON'T GET SEPA-RATED!!
TAKE MY HAND!!
OOPS...

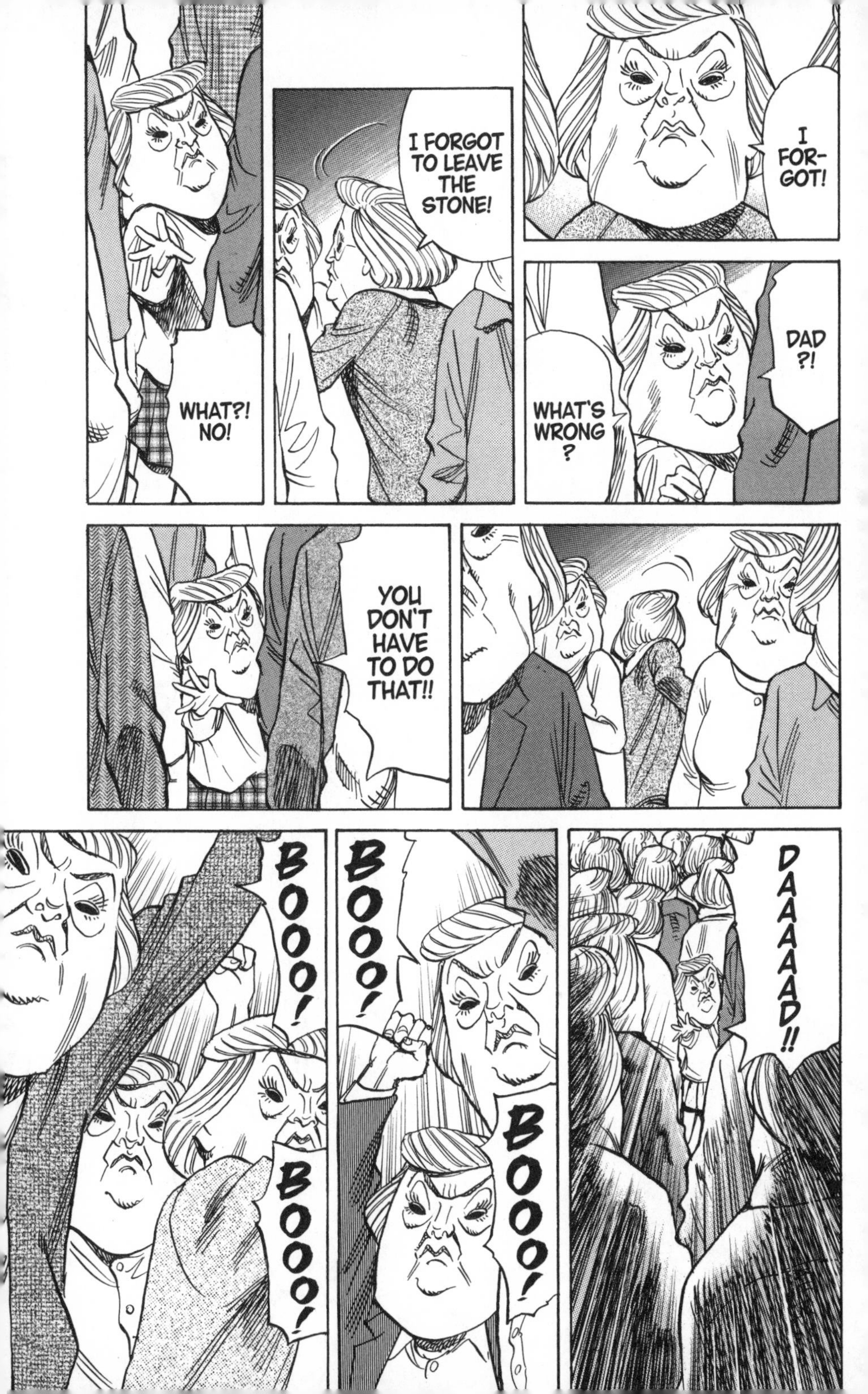
I FOR- GOT!
DAD?!
WHAT'S WRONG?
I FORGOT TO LEAVE THE STONE!
WHAT?! NO!
YOU DON'T HAVE TO DO THAT!!
DAAAAAD!!
BOOOO!
BOOOO!
BOOOO!
BOOOO!

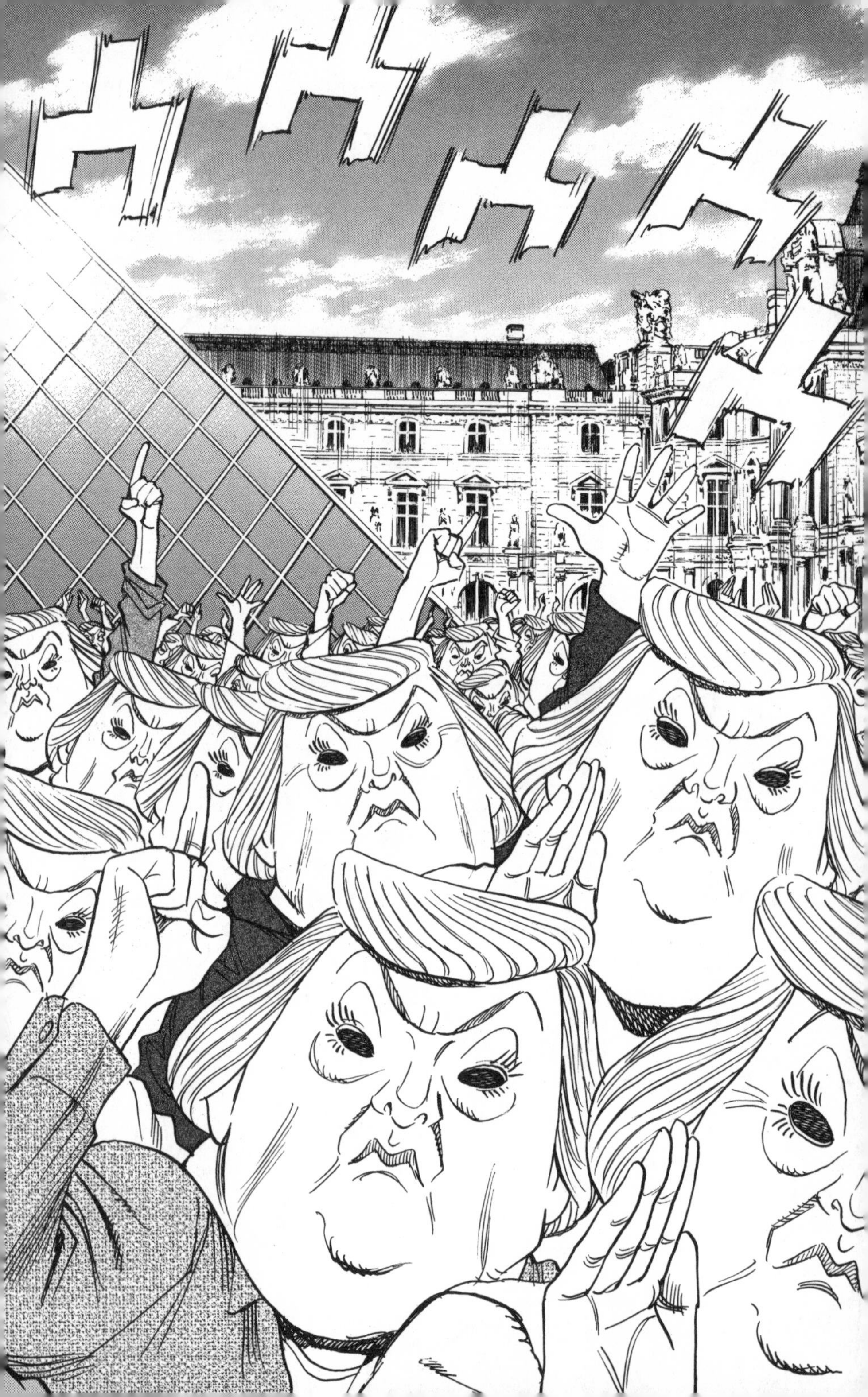

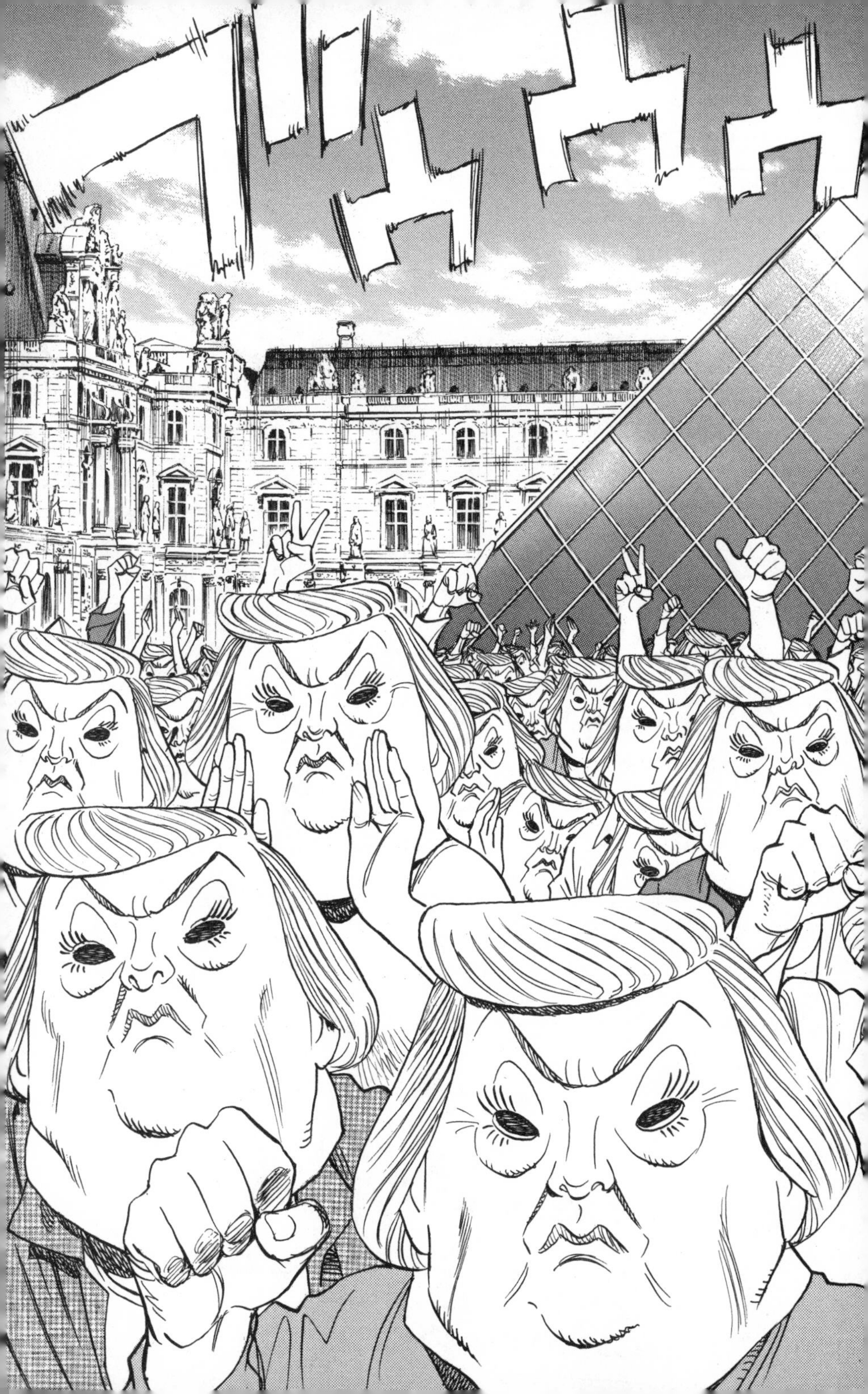
ヷウウウ

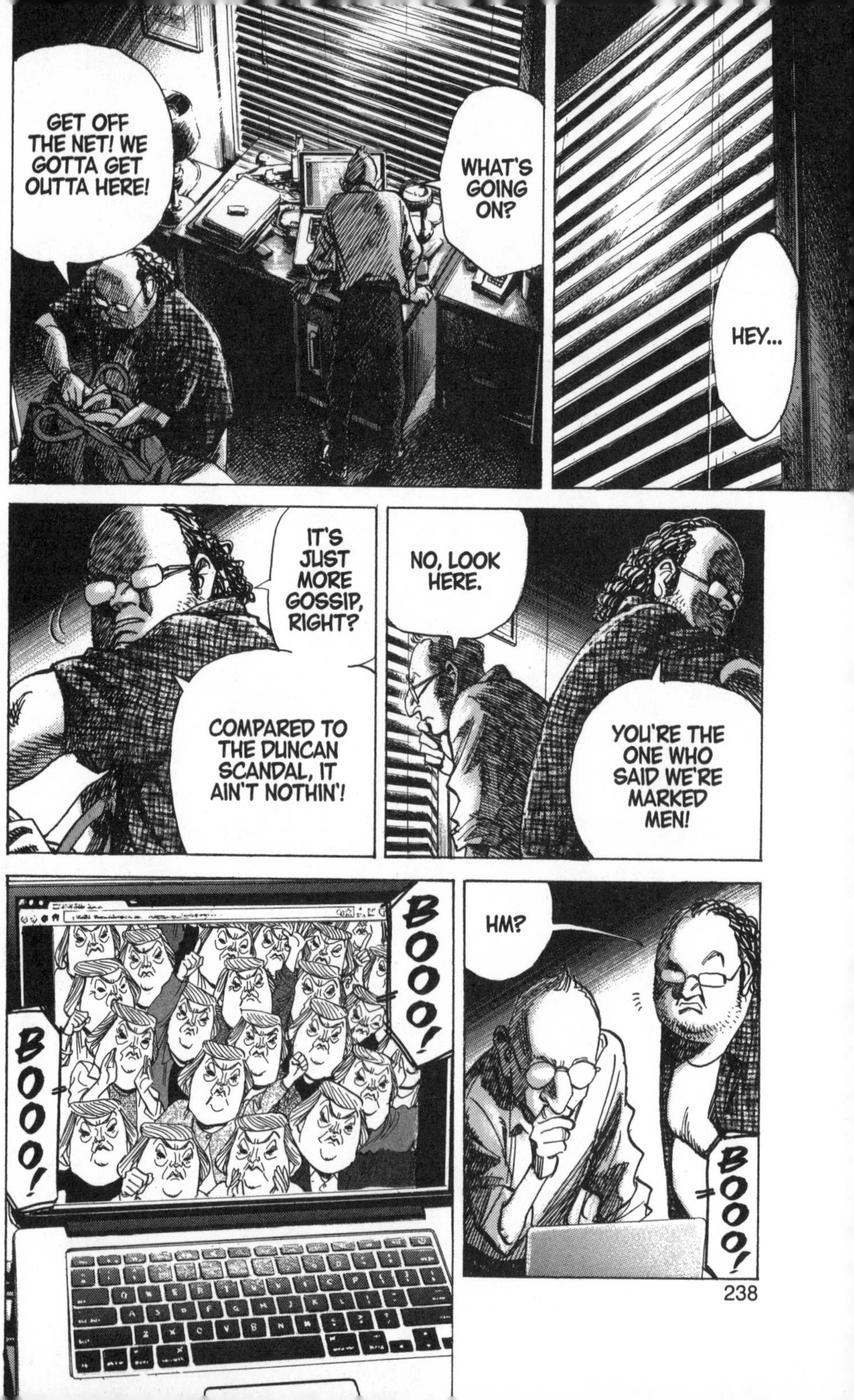
HEY...
WHAT'S GOING ON?
GET OFF THE NET! WE GOTTA GET OUTTA HERE!
NO, LOOK HERE.
YOU'RE THE ONE WHO SAID WE'RE MARKED MEN!
IT'S JUST MORE GOSSIP, RIGHT?
COMPARED TO THE DUNCAN SCANDAL, IT AIN'T NOTHIN'!
HM?
BOOOO!
BOOOO!
BOOOO!

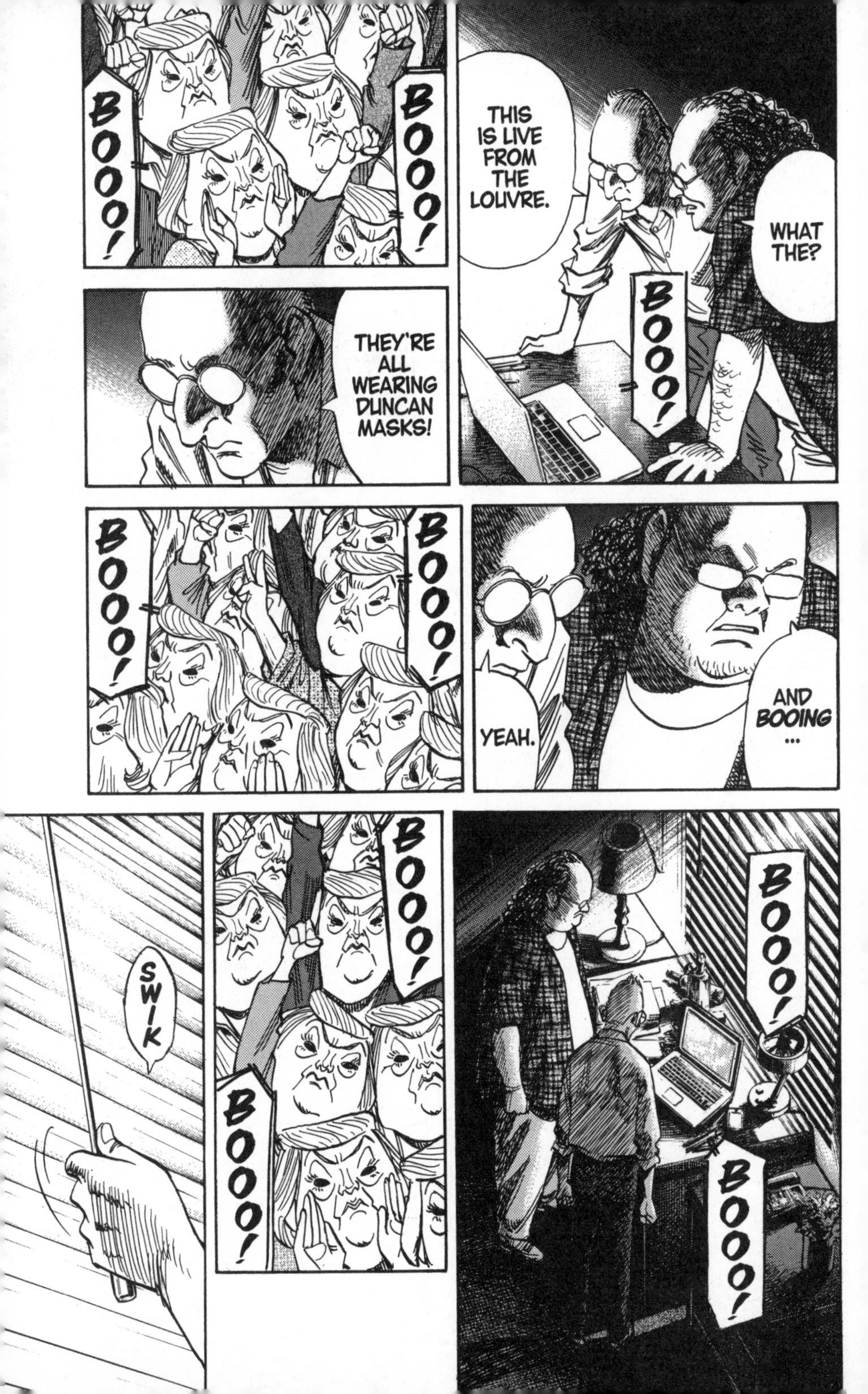

THIS IS LIVE FROM THE LOUVRE.
WHAT THE?
BOOOO!
BOOOO!
BOOOO!
THEY'RE ALL WEARING DUNCAN MASKS!
AND BOOING ...
YEAH.
BOOOO!
BOOOO!
BOOOO!
BOOOO!
BOOOO!
BOOOO!
SWIK

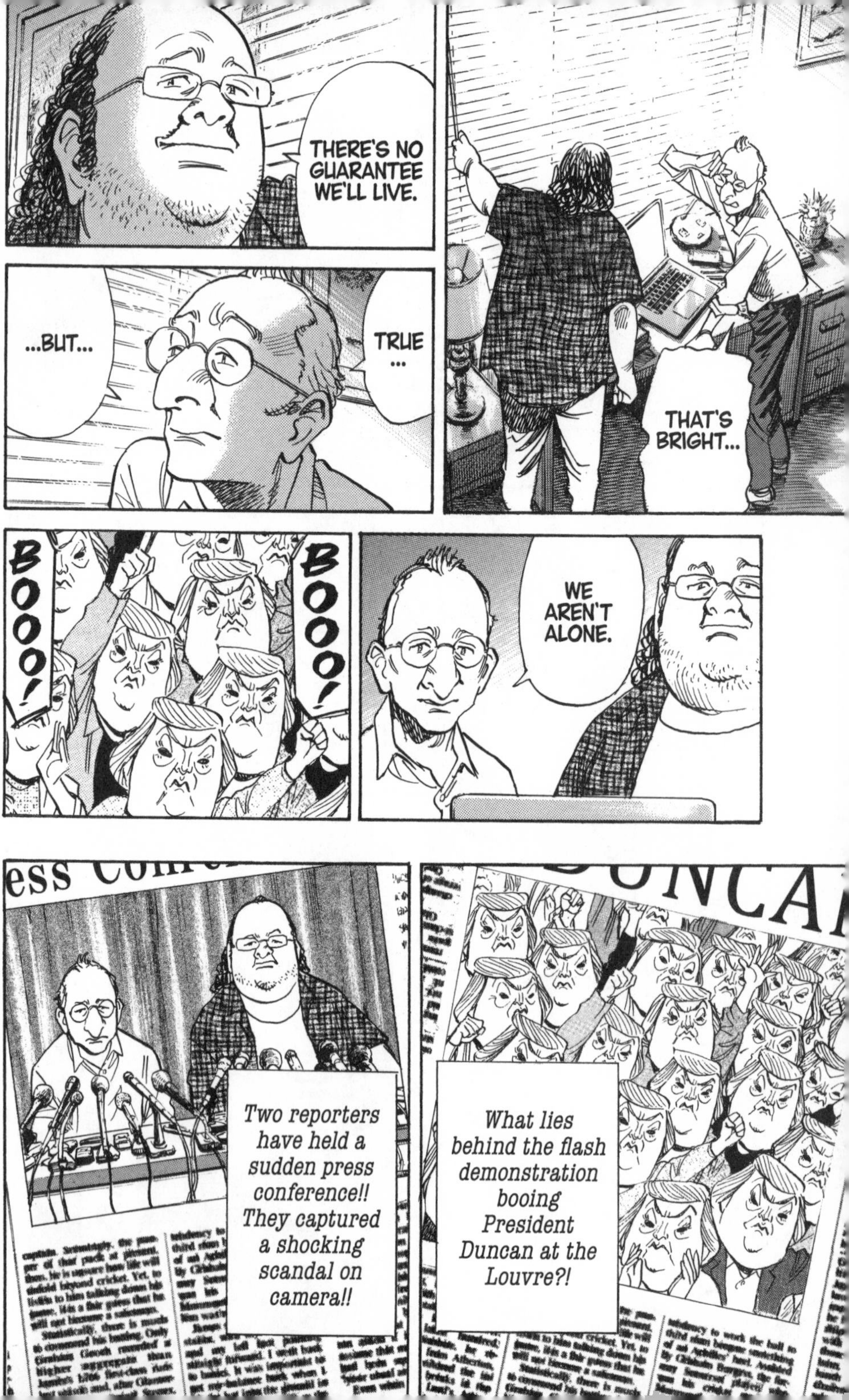
THAT'S BRIGHT...
THERE'S NO GUARANTEE WE'LL LIVE.
TRUE ...
...BUT...
WE AREN'T ALONE.
BOOOO!
BOOOO!
What lies behind the flash demonstration booing President Duncan at the Louvre?!
Two reporters have held a sudden press conference!! They captured a shocking scandal on camera!!

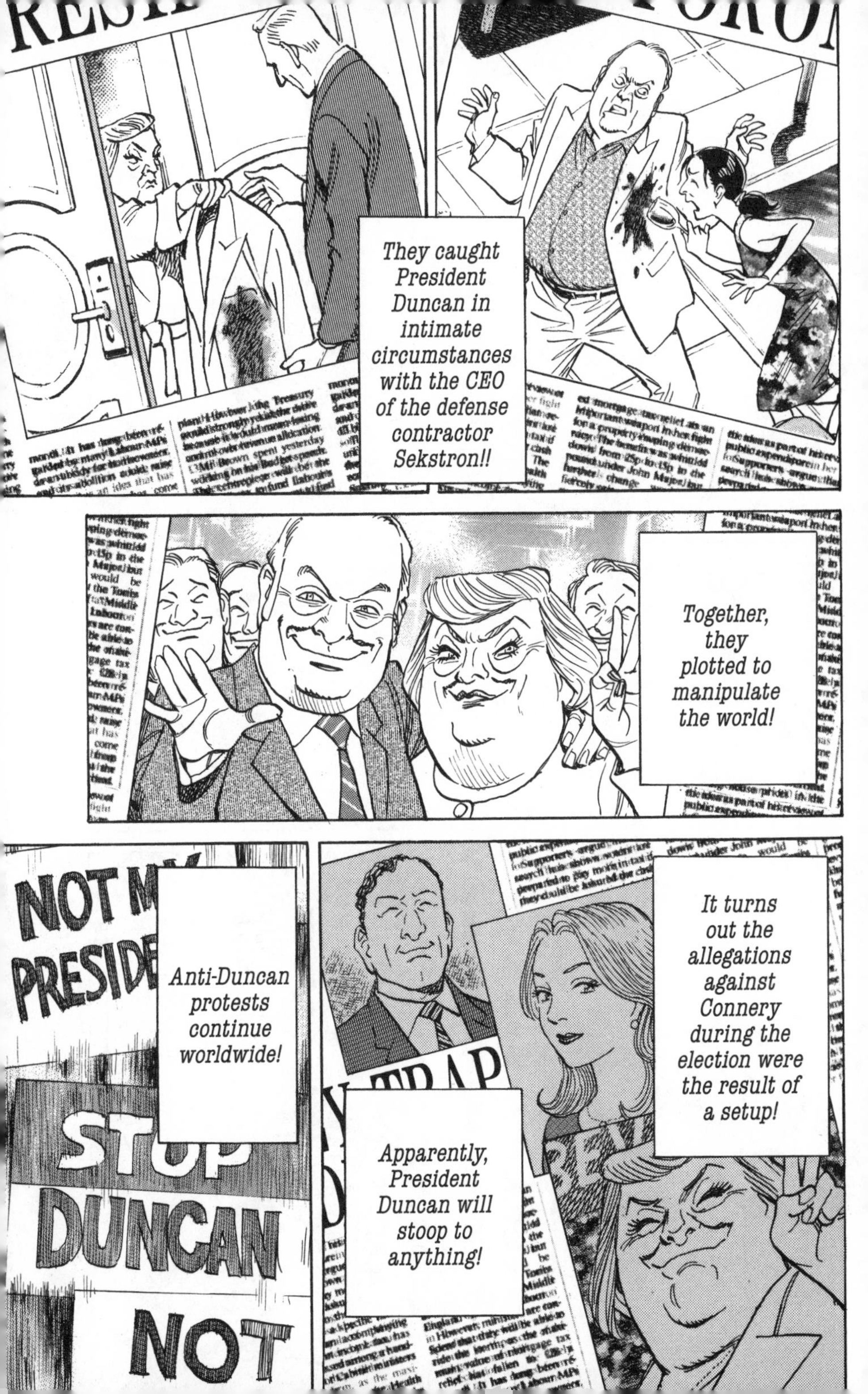

They caught President Duncan in intimate circumstances with the CEO of the defense contractor Sekstron!!
Together, they plotted to manipulate the world!
It turns out the allegations against Connery during the election were the result of a setup!
Apparently, President Duncan will stoop to anything!
Anti-Duncan protests continue worldwide!
STOP DUNCAN
NOT

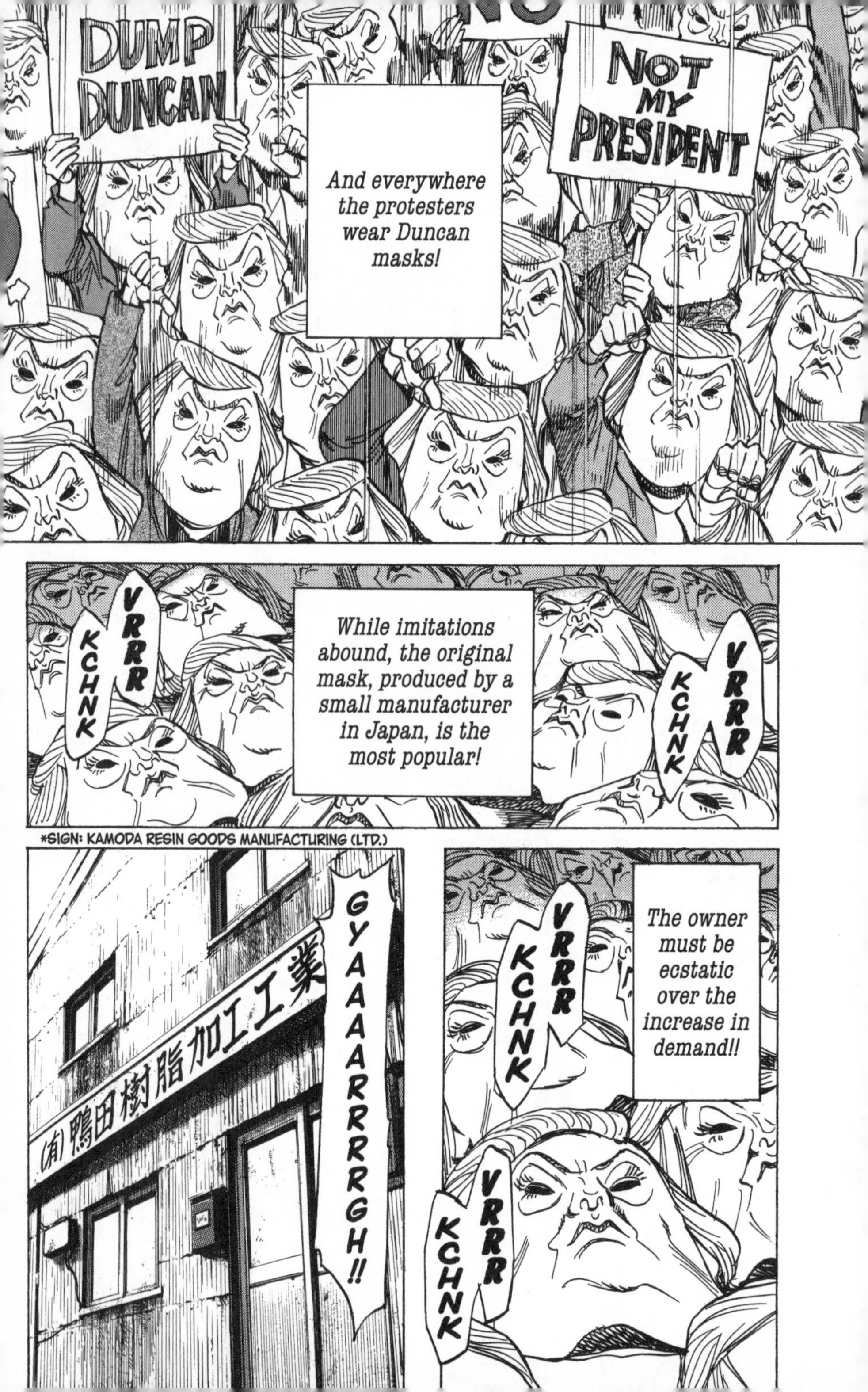
NOT MY PRESIDENT
And everywhere the protesters wear Duncan masks!
DUMP DUNCAN
VRRR
KCHNK
While imitations abound, the original mask, produced by a small manufacturer in Japan, is the most popular!
VRRR
KCHNK
The owner must be ecstatic over the increase in demand!!
VRRR
KCHNK
VRRR
KCHNK
GYAAAARRRRRGH!!
*SIGN: KAMODA RESIN GOODS MANUFACTURING (LTD.)
(有)鴨田樹脂加工業

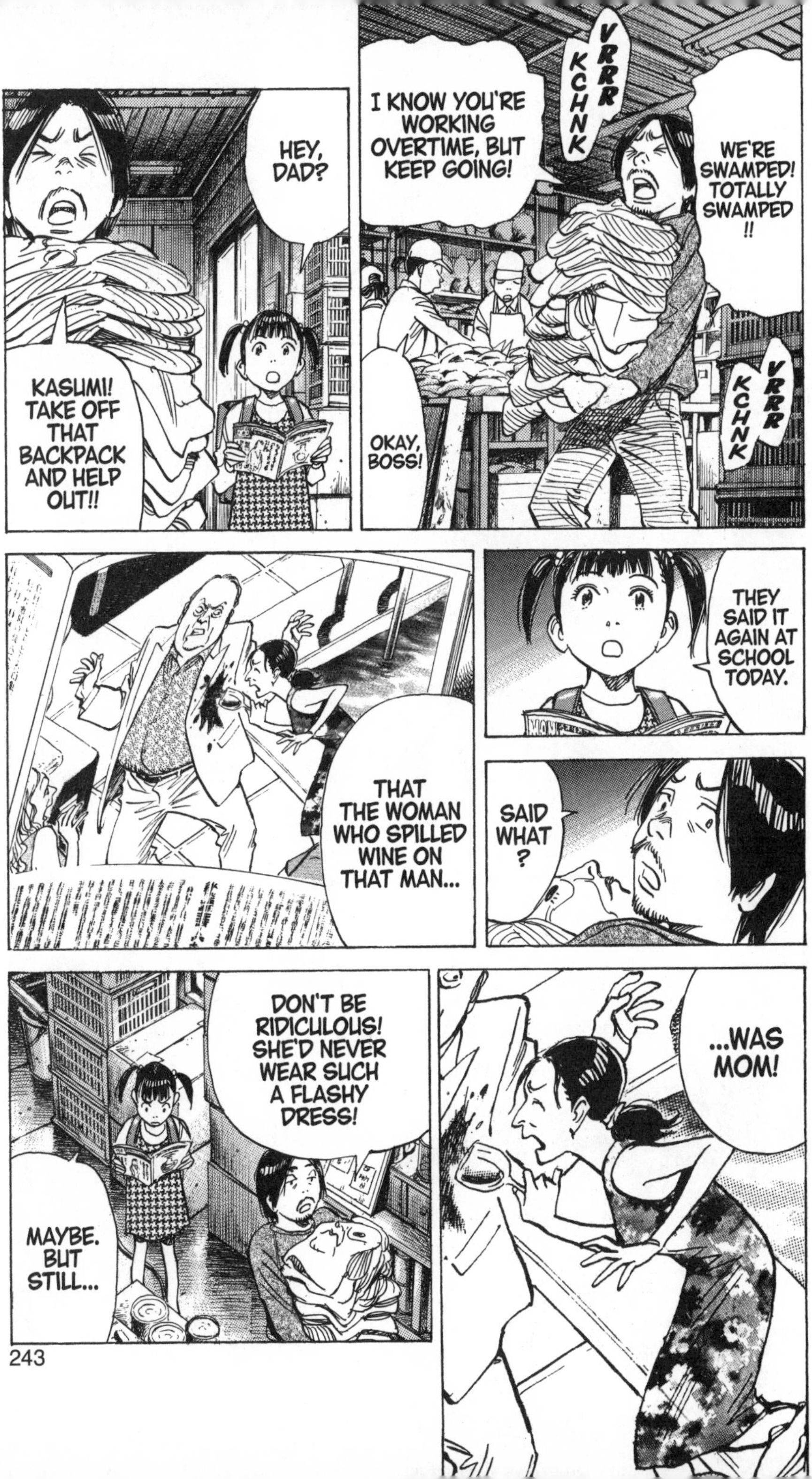
VRRR KCHNK
WE'RE SWAMPED! TOTALLY SWAMPED!!
I KNOW YOU'RE WORKING OVERTIME, BUT KEEP GOING!
VRRR KCHNK
OKAY, BOSS!
HEY, DAD?
KASUMI! TAKE OFF THAT BACKPACK AND HELP OUT!!
THEY SAID IT AGAIN AT SCHOOL TODAY.
SAID WHAT?
THAT THE WOMAN WHO SPILLED WINE ON THAT MAN...
...WAS MOM!
DON'T BE RIDICULOUS! SHE'D NEVER WEAR SUCH A FLASHY DRESS!
MAYBE. BUT STILL...

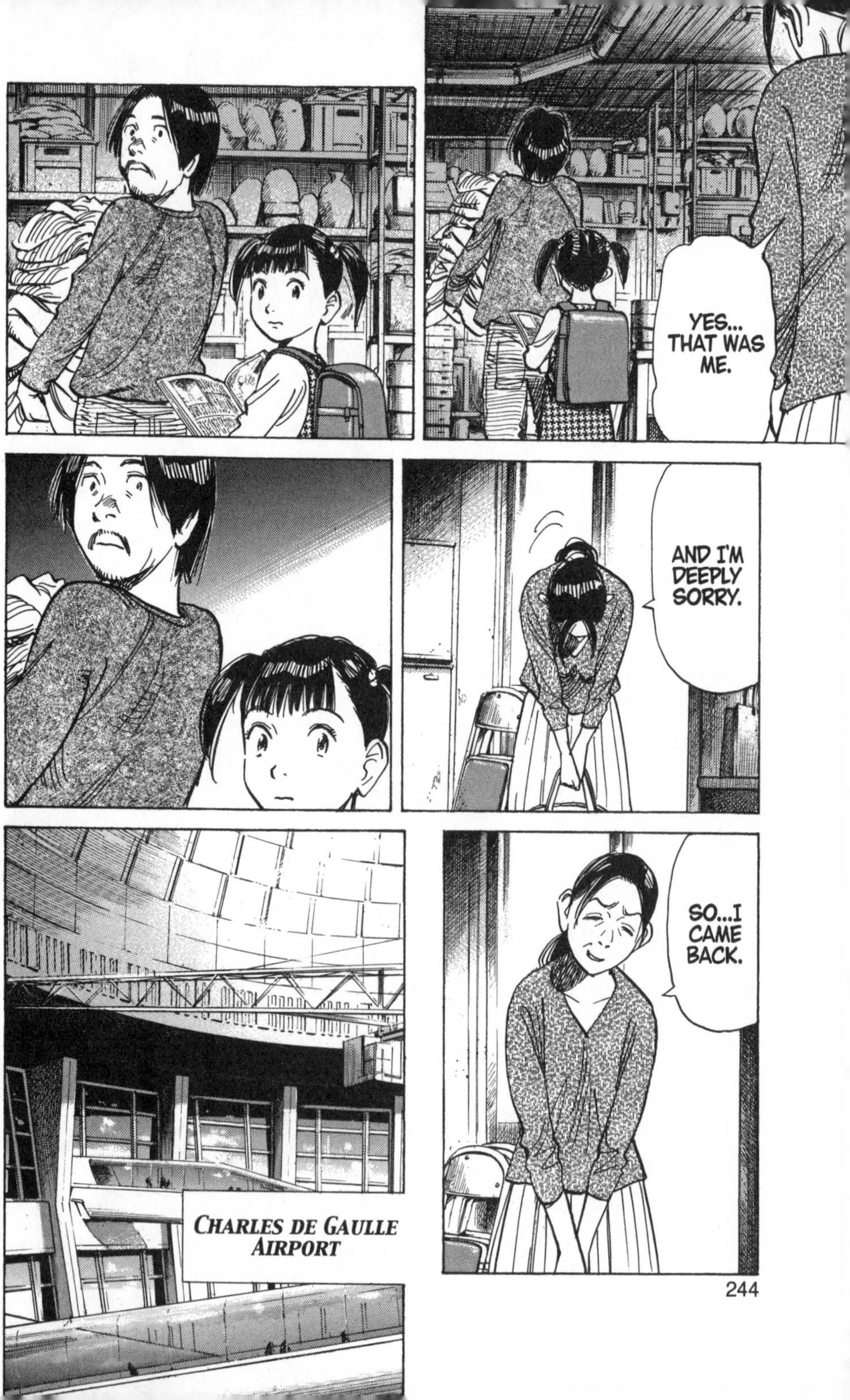
YES... THAT WAS ME.
AND I'M DEEPLY SORRY.
SO...I CAME BACK.
CHARLES DE GAULLE AIRPORT

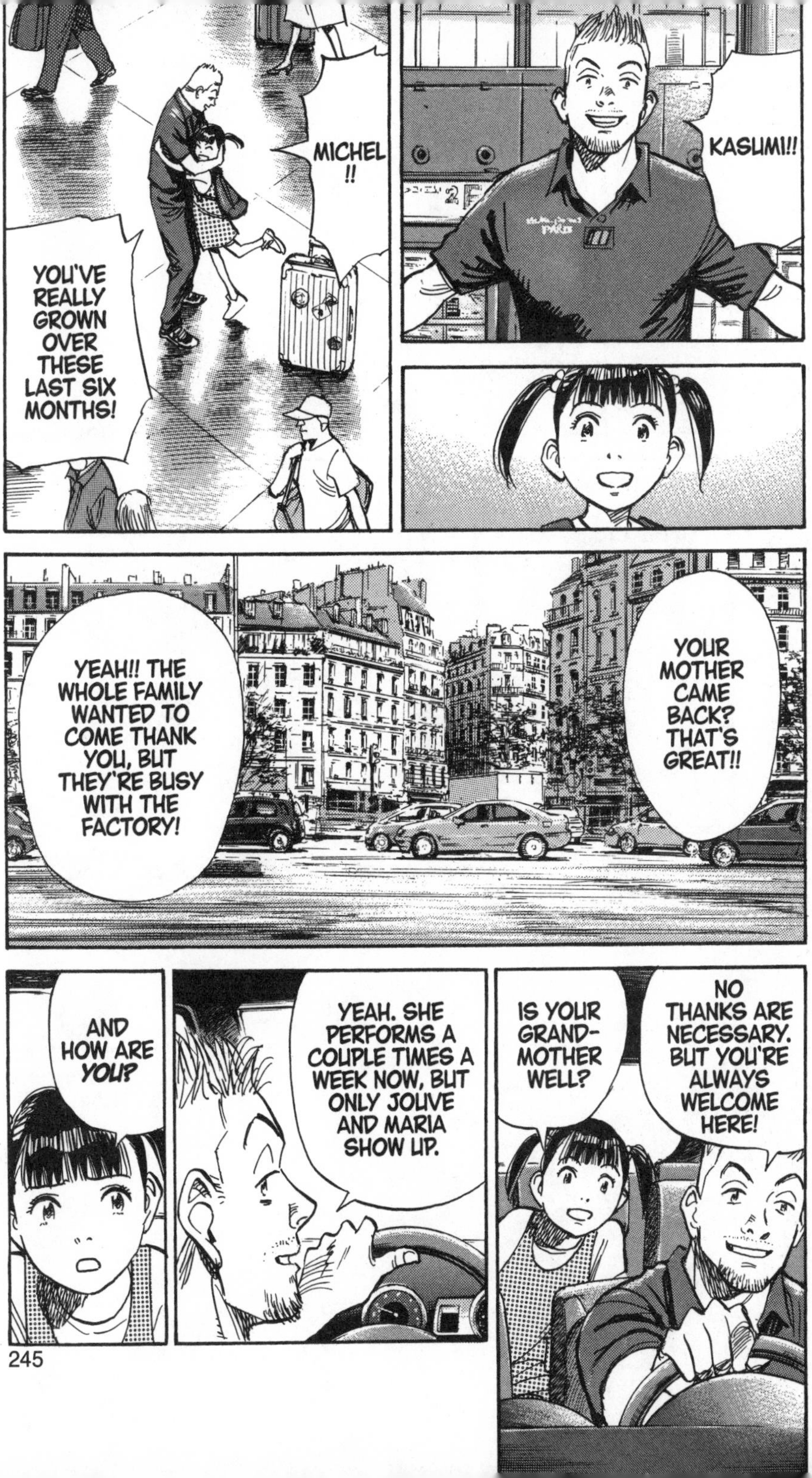
KASUMI!!
MICHEL !!
YOU'VE REALLY GROWN OVER THESE LAST SIX MONTHS!
YOUR MOTHER CAME BACK? THAT'S GREAT!!
YEAH!! THE WHOLE FAMILY WANTED TO COME THANK YOU, BUT THEY'RE BUSY WITH THE FACTORY!
NO THANKS ARE NECESSARY. BUT YOU'RE ALWAYS WELCOME HERE!
IS YOUR GRAND-MOTHER WELL?
YEAH. SHE PERFORMS A COUPLE TIMES A WEEK NOW, BUT ONLY JOLIVE AND MARIA SHOW UP.
AND HOW ARE *YOU*?

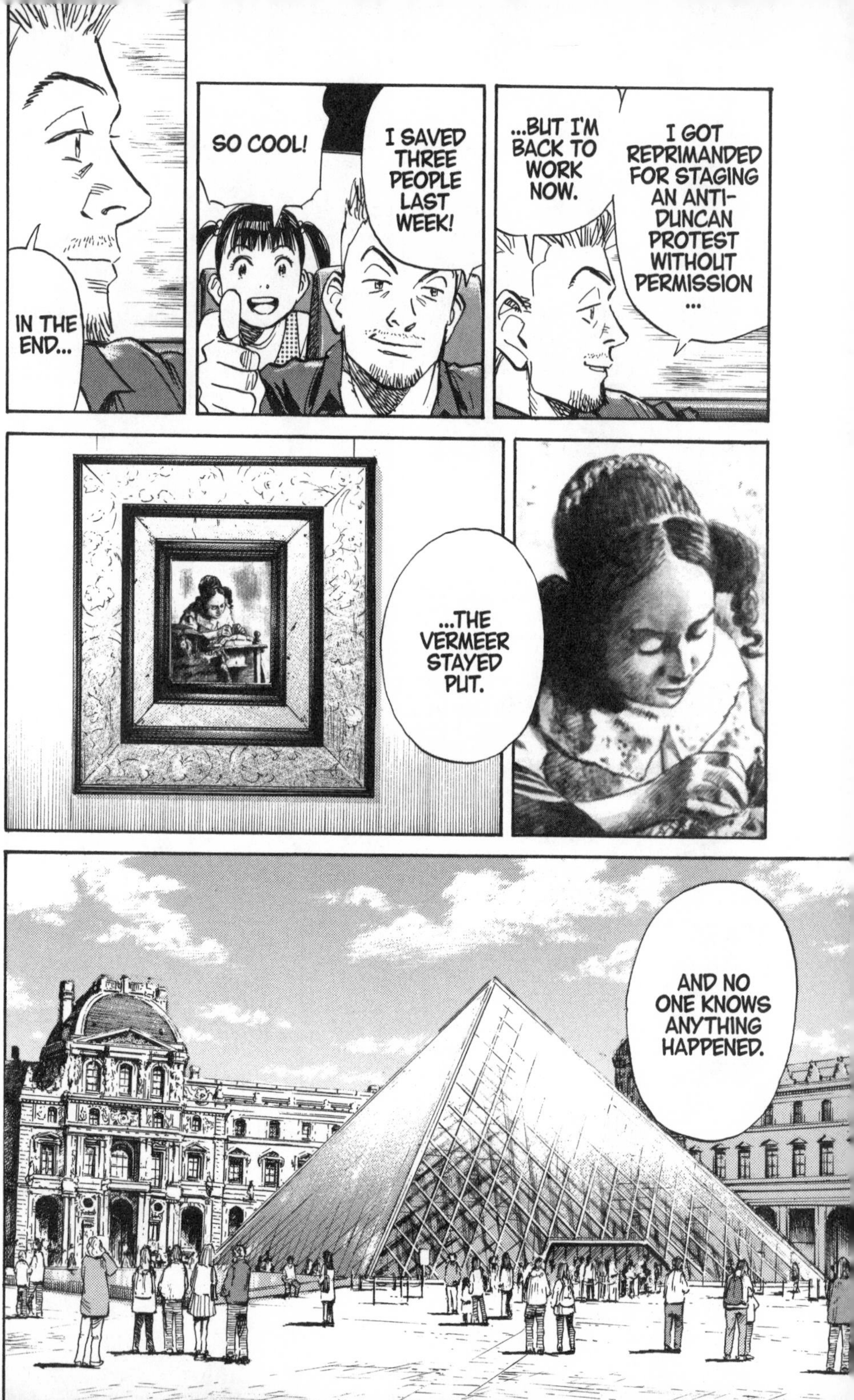
I GOT REPRIMANDED FOR STAGING AN ANTI-DUNCAN PROTEST WITHOUT PERMISSION ...
...BUT I'M BACK TO WORK NOW.
I SAVED THREE PEOPLE LAST WEEK!
SO COOL!
IN THE END...
...THE VERMEER STAYED PUT.
AND NO ONE KNOWS ANYTHING HAPPENED.

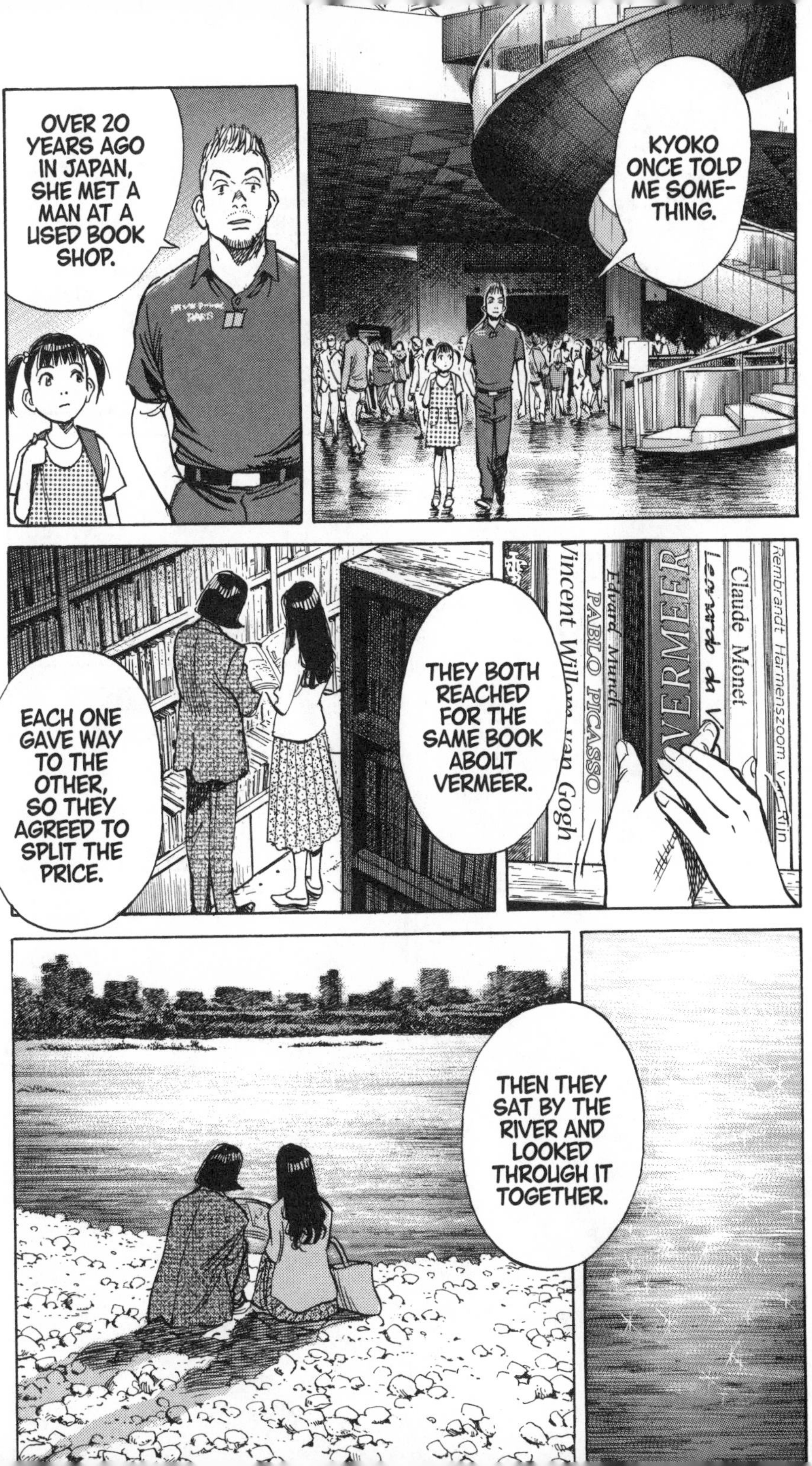
KYOKO ONCE TOLD ME SOME-THING.
OVER 20 YEARS AGO IN JAPAN, SHE MET A MAN AT A USED BOOK SHOP.
Rembrandt Harmenszoom
Claude Monet
VERMEER
Edvard Munch
PABLO PICASSO
THEY BOTH REACHED FOR THE SAME BOOK ABOUT VERMEER.
EACH ONE GAVE WAY TO THE OTHER, SO THEY AGREED TO SPLIT THE PRICE.
THEN THEY SAT BY THE RIVER AND LOOKED THROUGH IT TOGETHER.

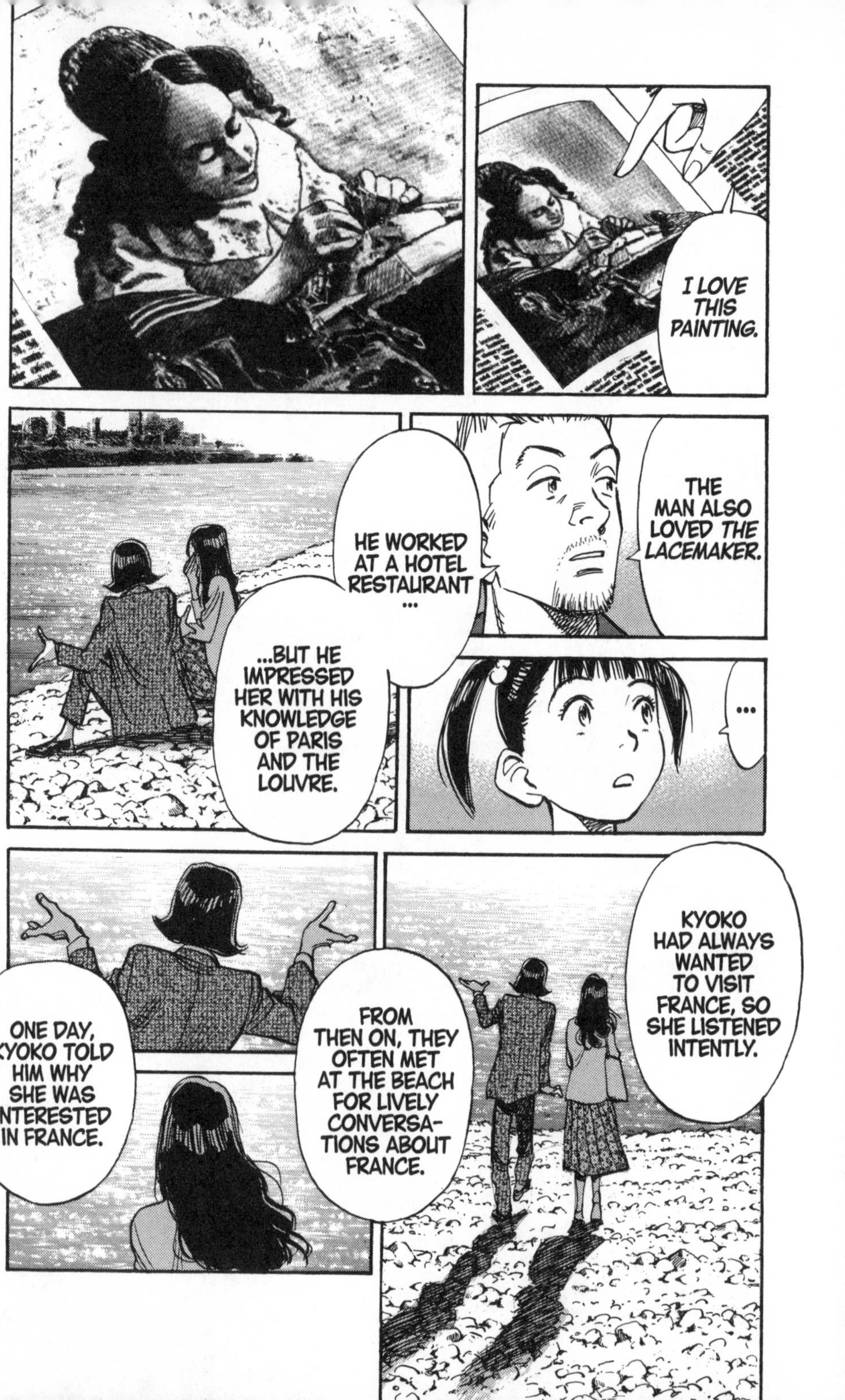
I LOVE THIS PAINTING.
THE MAN ALSO LOVED THE LACEMAKER.
HE WORKED AT A HOTEL RESTAURANT...
...
...BUT HE IMPRESSED HER WITH HIS KNOWLEDGE OF PARIS AND THE LOUVRE.
KYOKO HAD ALWAYS WANTED TO VISIT FRANCE, SO SHE LISTENED INTENTLY.
FROM THEN ON, THEY OFTEN MET AT THE BEACH FOR LIVELY CONVERSA-TIONS ABOUT FRANCE.
ONE DAY, KYOKO TOLD HIM WHY SHE WAS INTERESTED IN FRANCE.

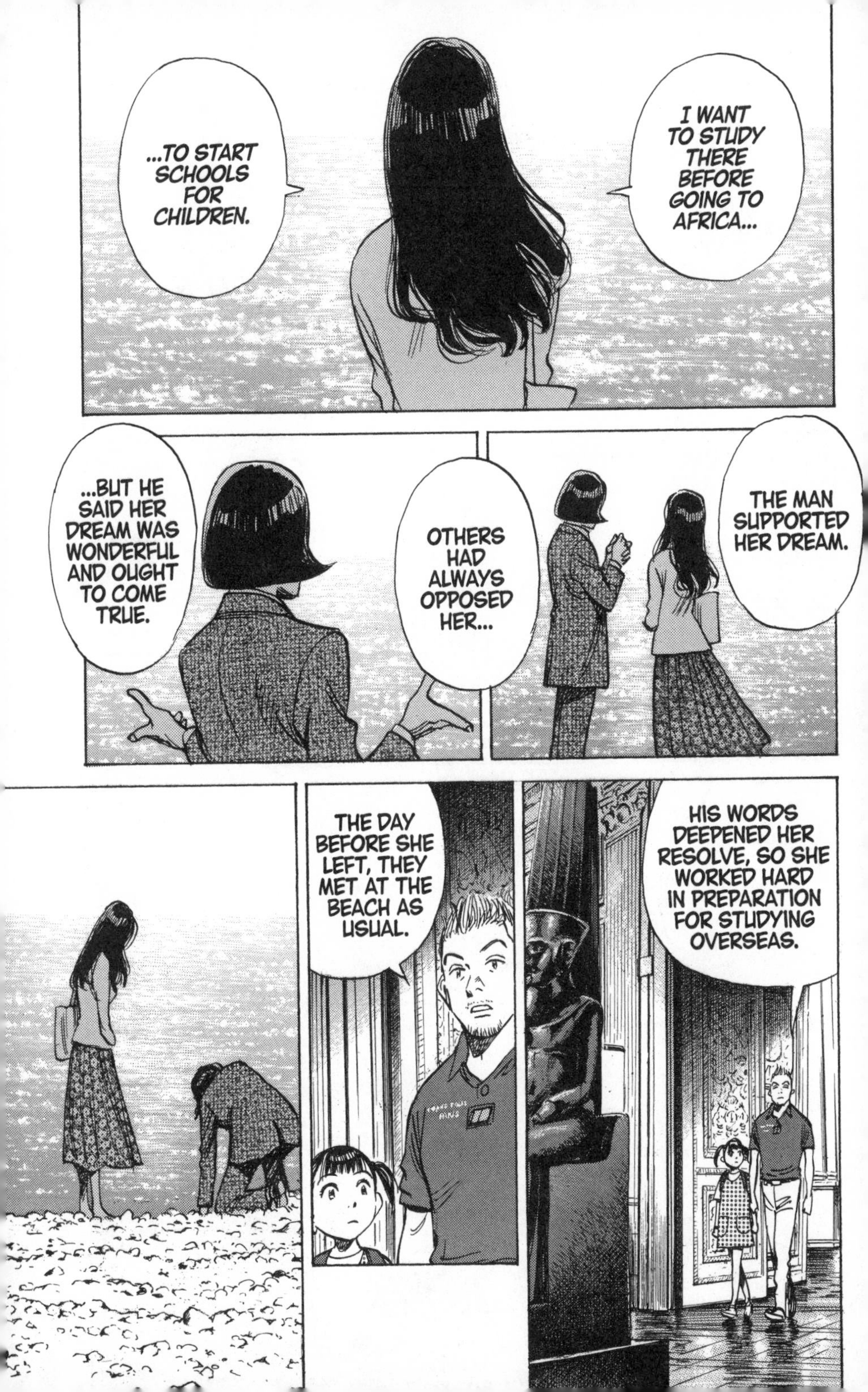
I WANT TO STUDY THERE BEFORE GOING TO AFRICA...
...TO START SCHOOLS FOR CHILDREN.
THE MAN SUPPORTED HER DREAM.
OTHERS HAD ALWAYS OPPOSED HER...
...BUT HE SAID HER DREAM WAS WONDERFUL AND OUGHT TO COME TRUE.
HIS WORDS DEEPENED HER RESOLVE, SO SHE WORKED HARD IN PREPARATION FOR STUDYING OVERSEAS.
THE DAY BEFORE SHE LEFT, THEY MET AT THE BEACH AS USUAL.

THE MAN PICKED UP A ROUND STONE...

...AND USED A KEY TO CARVE SOMETHING INTO IT.

GRND GRND

GRND GRND

IT WAS A SIGN OF THEIR MEETING...

...AND REPRESENTED THE FULFILLMENT OF DREAMS.

HOLD OUT YOUR HAND.

HM?

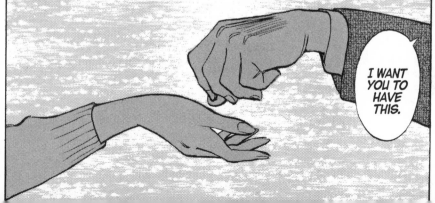

I WANT YOU TO HAVE THIS.

NO.
YOU SHOULD BRING THIS TO FRANCE.
WHAT?
...
THERE IS ONE DREAM I WANT TO COME TRUE MORE THAN ANY OTHER.
I WANT THIS SIGN OF OUR RELATIONSHIP...
...TO ADORN THE LOUVRE.

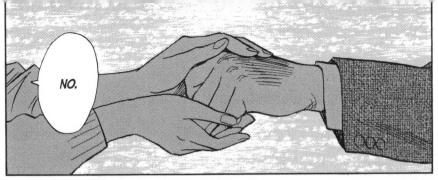

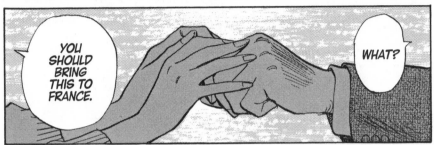

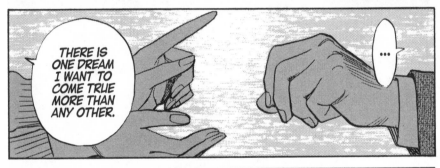

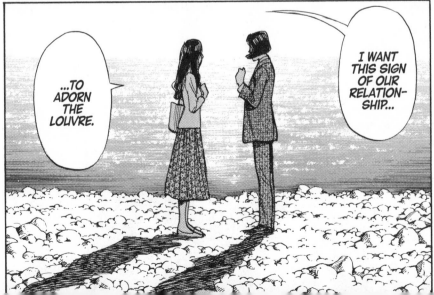

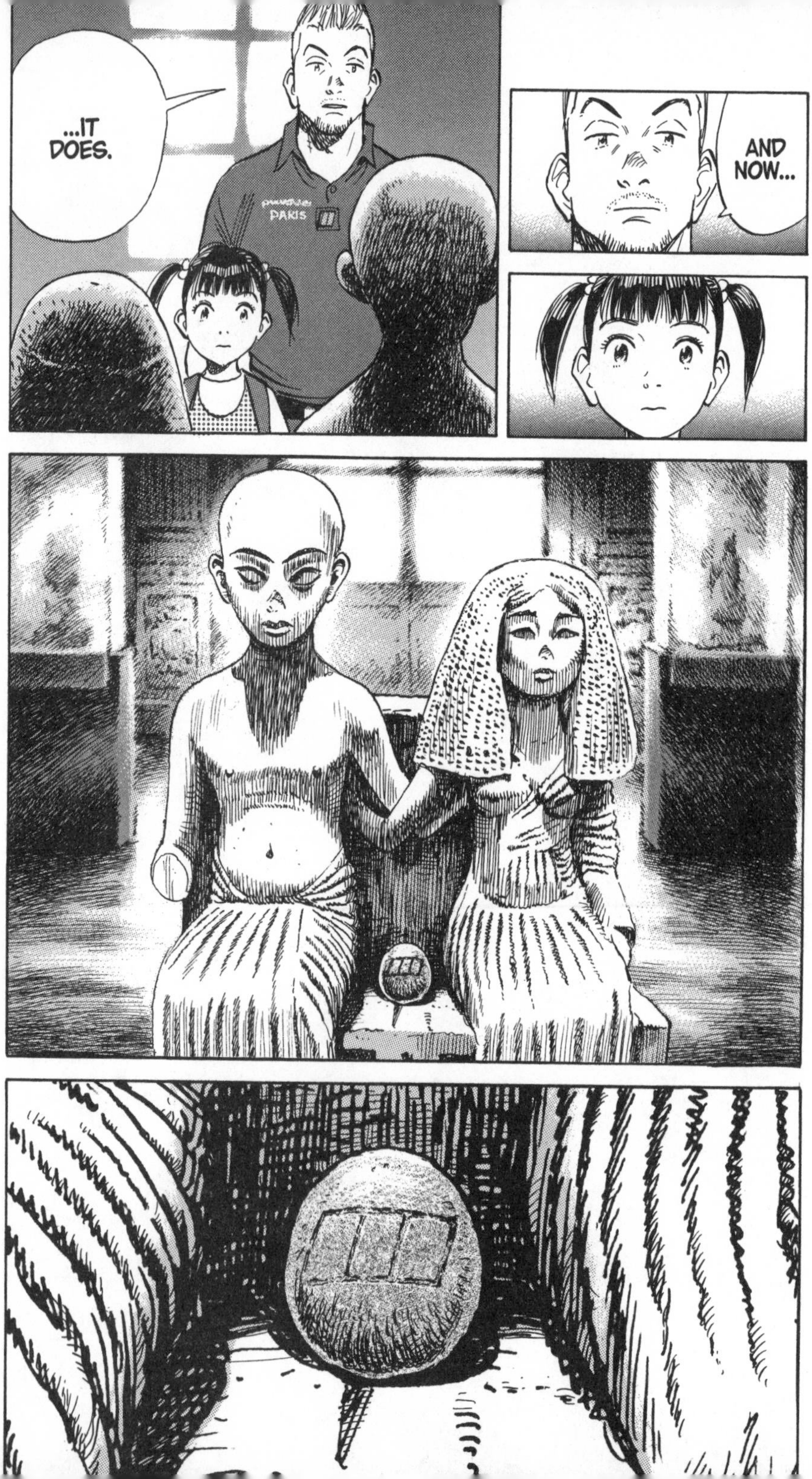

AND NOW...
...IT DOES.

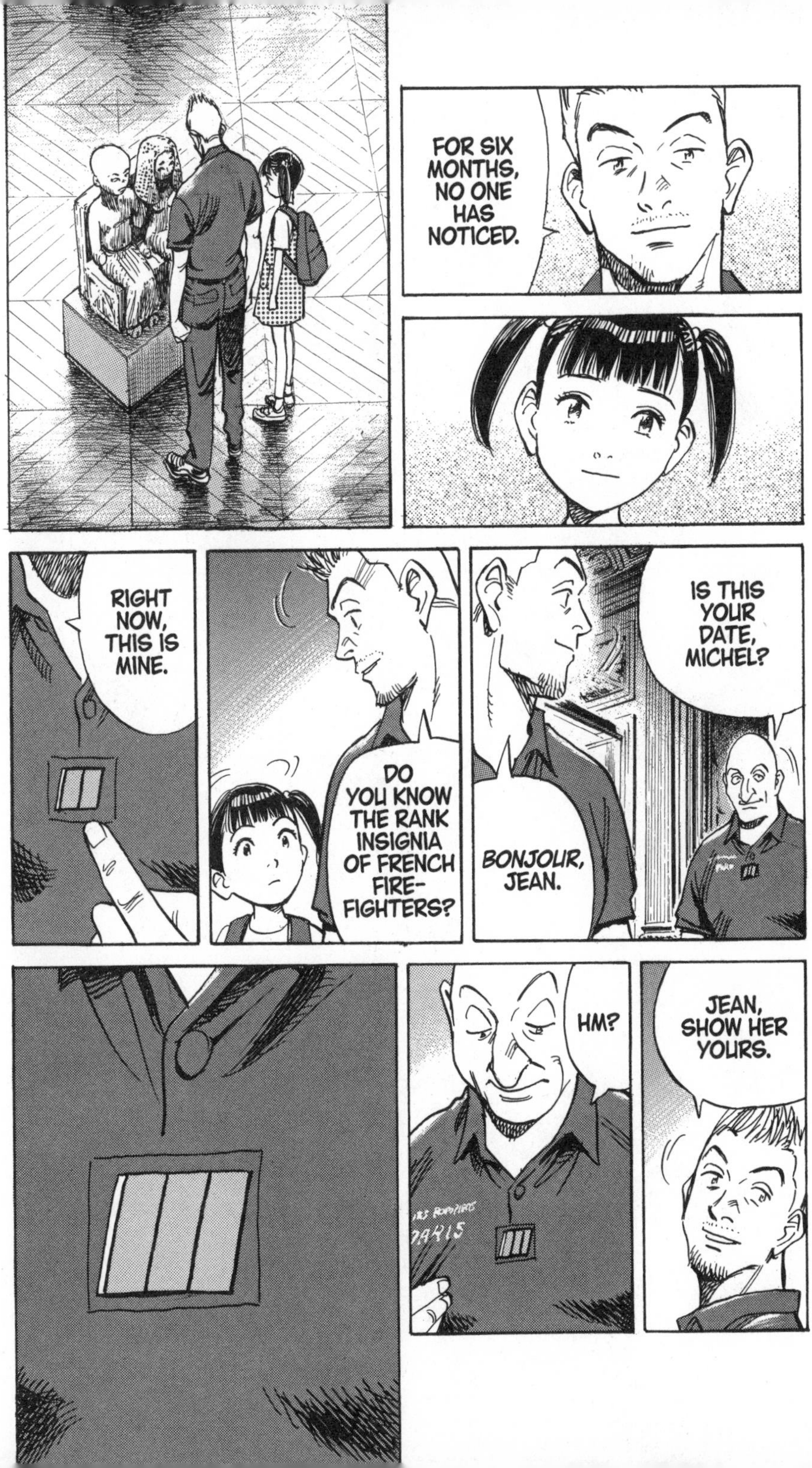
FOR SIX MONTHS, NO ONE HAS NOTICED.
IS THIS YOUR DATE, MICHEL?
BONJOUR, JEAN.
DO YOU KNOW THE RANK INSIGNIA OF FRENCH FIRE-FIGHTERS?
RIGHT NOW, THIS IS MINE.
JEAN, SHOW HER YOURS.
HM?

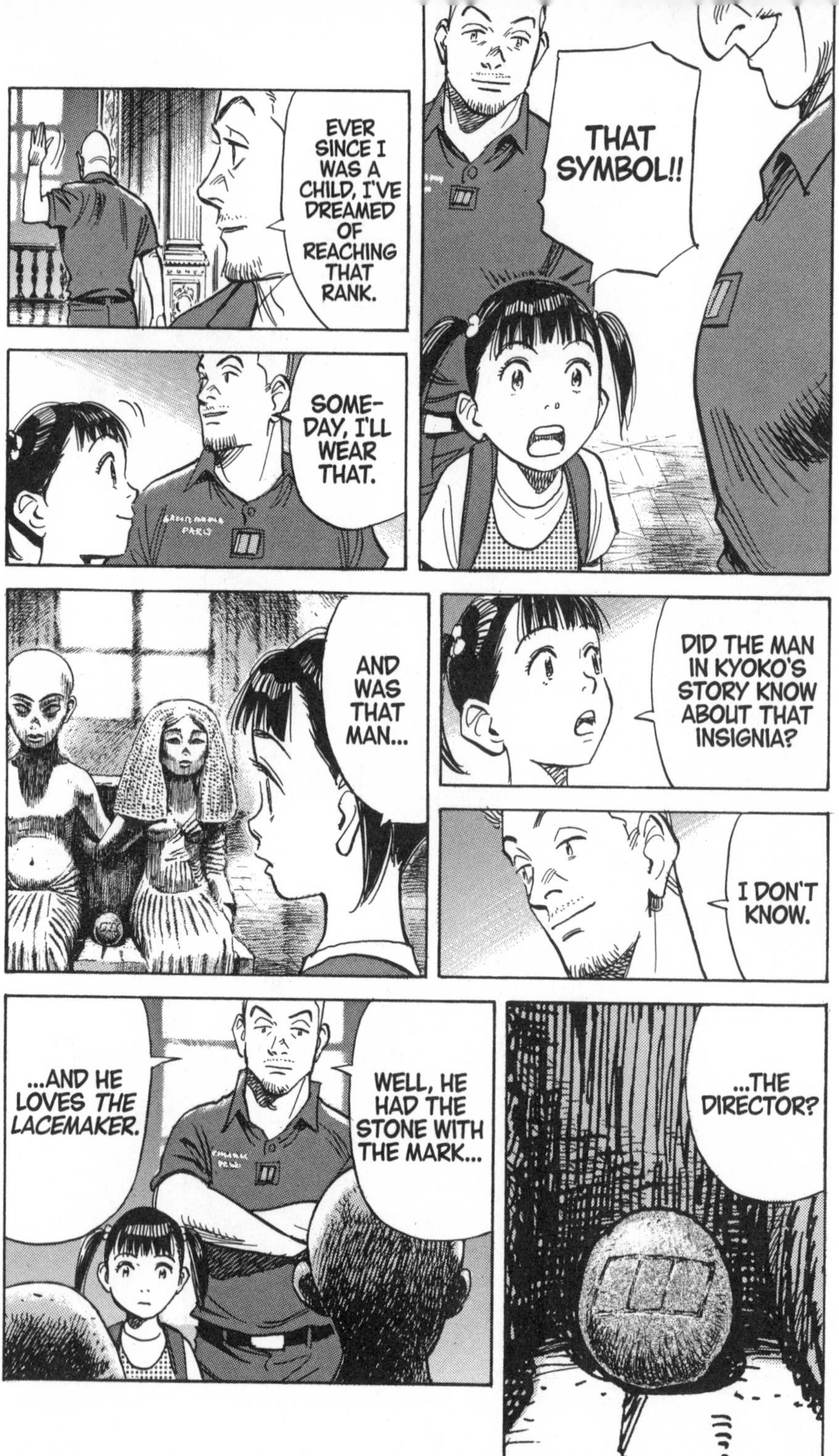
THAT SYMBOL!!
EVER SINCE I WAS A CHILD, I'VE DREAMED OF REACHING THAT RANK.
SOME-DAY, I'LL WEAR THAT.
DID THE MAN IN KYOKO'S STORY KNOW ABOUT THAT INSIGNIA?
I DON'T KNOW.
AND WAS THAT MAN...
...THE DIRECTOR?
WELL, HE HAD THE STONE WITH THE MARK...
...AND HE LOVES THE LACEMAKER.

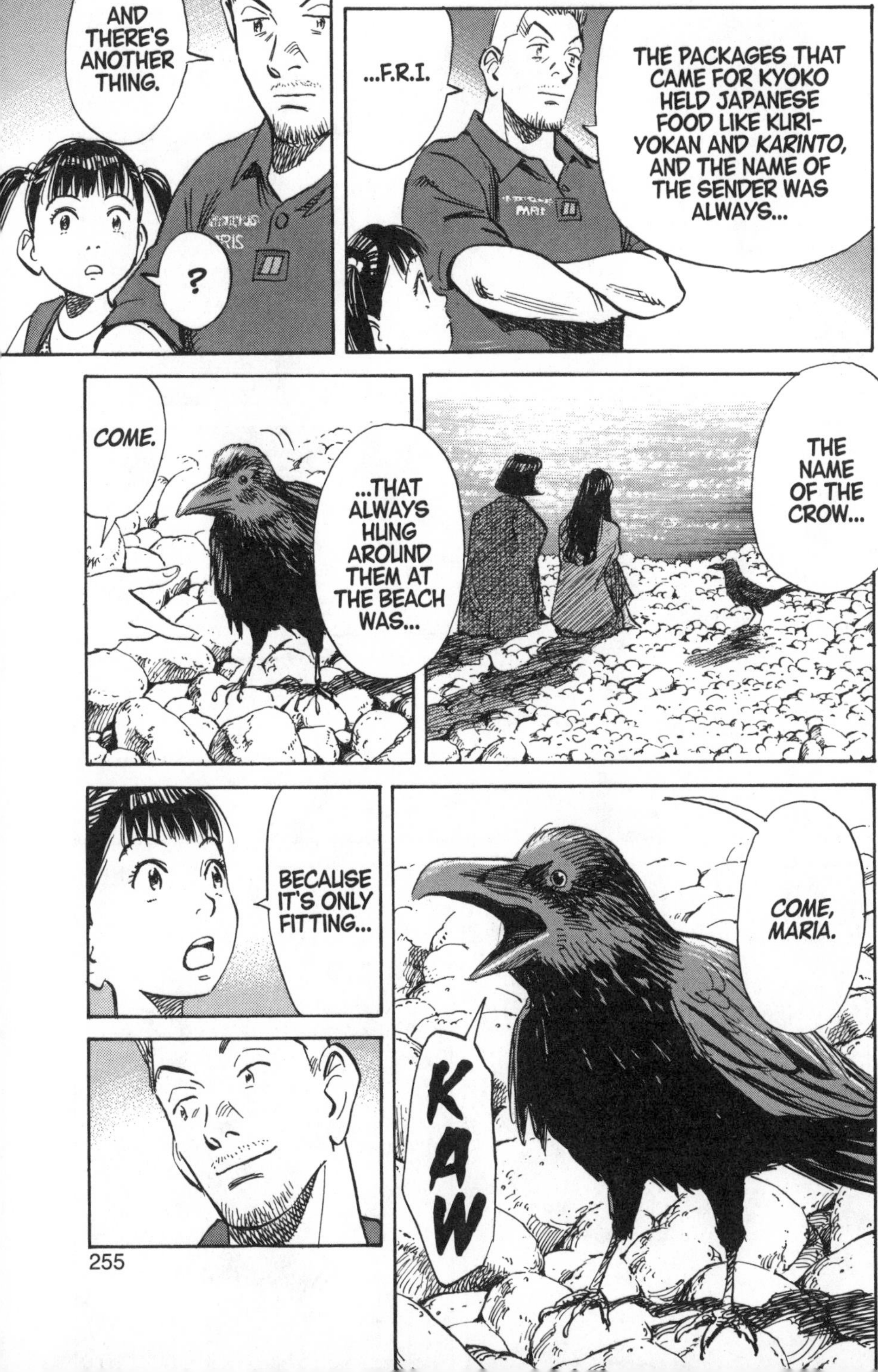

THE PACKAGES THAT CAME FOR KYOKO HELD JAPANESE FOOD LIKE KURI-YOKAN AND *KARINTO*, AND THE NAME OF THE SENDER WAS ALWAYS...
...F.R.I.
AND THERE'S ANOTHER THING.
?
THE NAME OF THE CROW...
...THAT ALWAYS HUNG AROUND THEM AT THE BEACH WAS...
COME.
COME, MARIA.
KAW
BECAUSE IT'S ONLY FITTING...

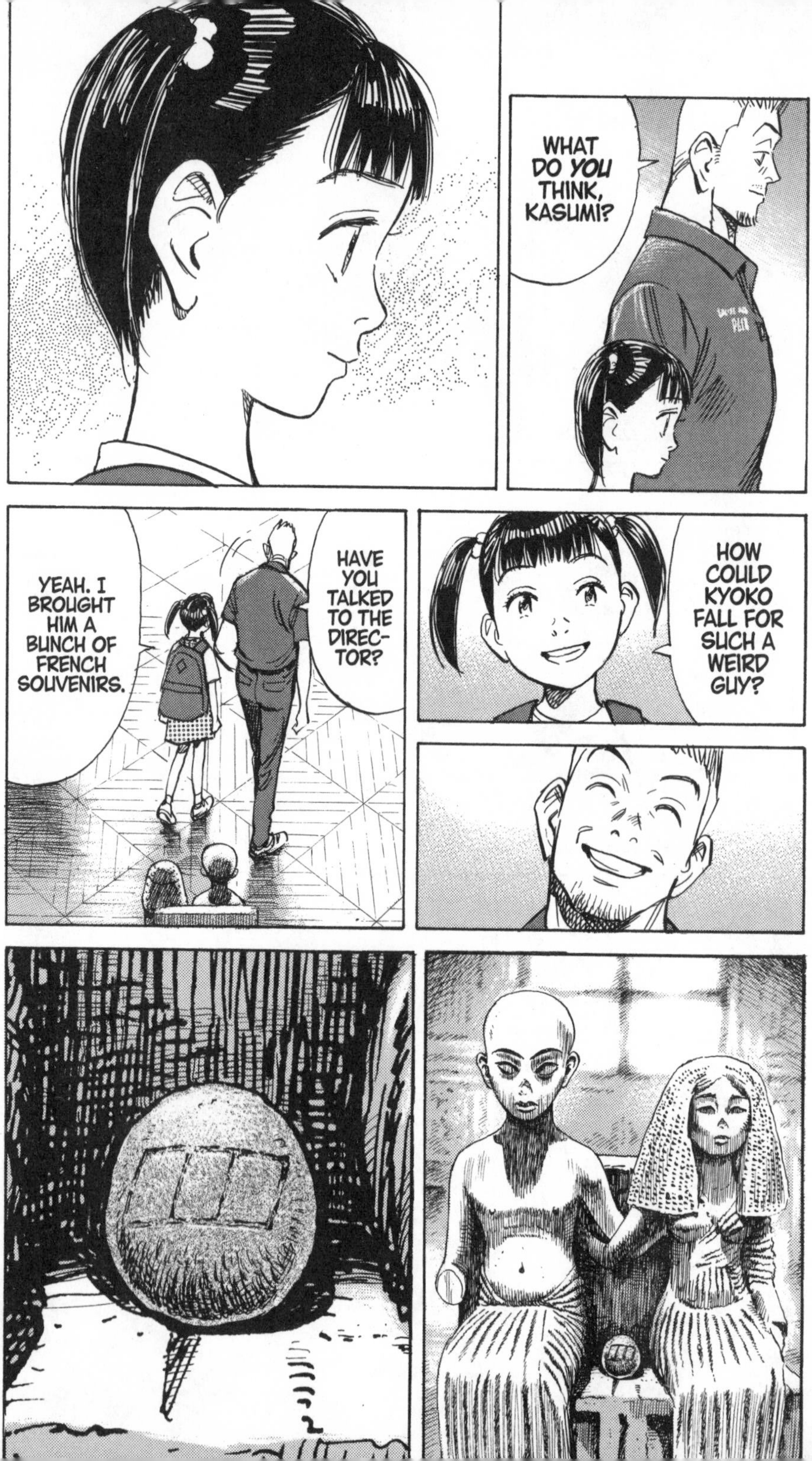
WHAT DO YOU THINK, KASUMI?
HOW COULD KYOKO FALL FOR SUCH A WEIRD GUY?
HAVE YOU TALKED TO THE DIRECTOR?
YEAH. I BROUGHT HIM A BUNCH OF FRENCH SOUVENIRS.

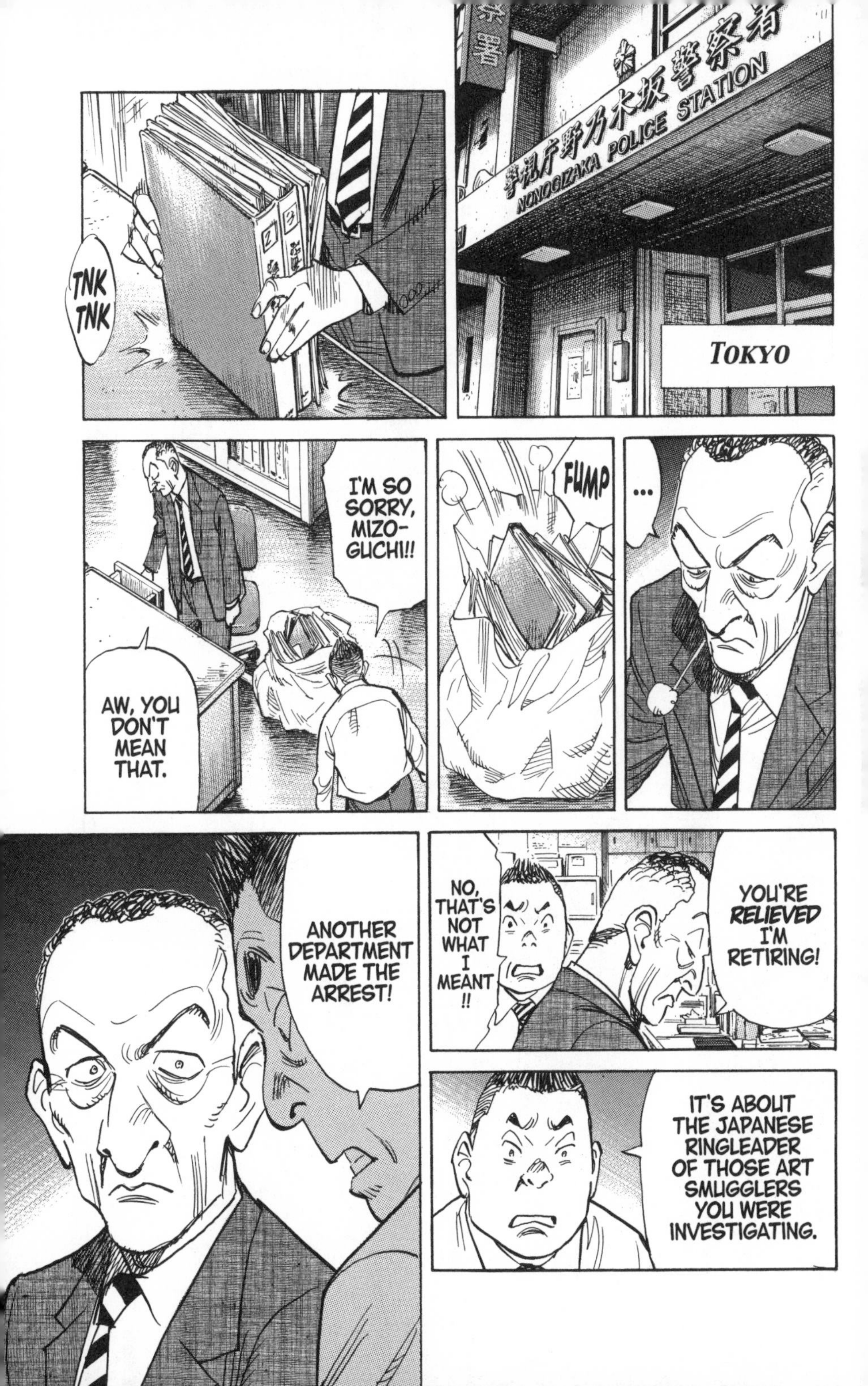
NONOGIZAKA POLICE STATION
TOKYO
TNK TNK
...
FUMP
I'M SO SORRY, MIZOGUCHI!!
AW, YOU DON'T MEAN THAT.
YOU'RE RELIEVED I'M RETIRING!
NO, THAT'S NOT WHAT I MEANT!!
IT'S ABOUT THE JAPANESE RINGLEADER OF THOSE ART SMUGGLERS YOU WERE INVESTIGATING.
ANOTHER DEPARTMENT MADE THE ARREST!

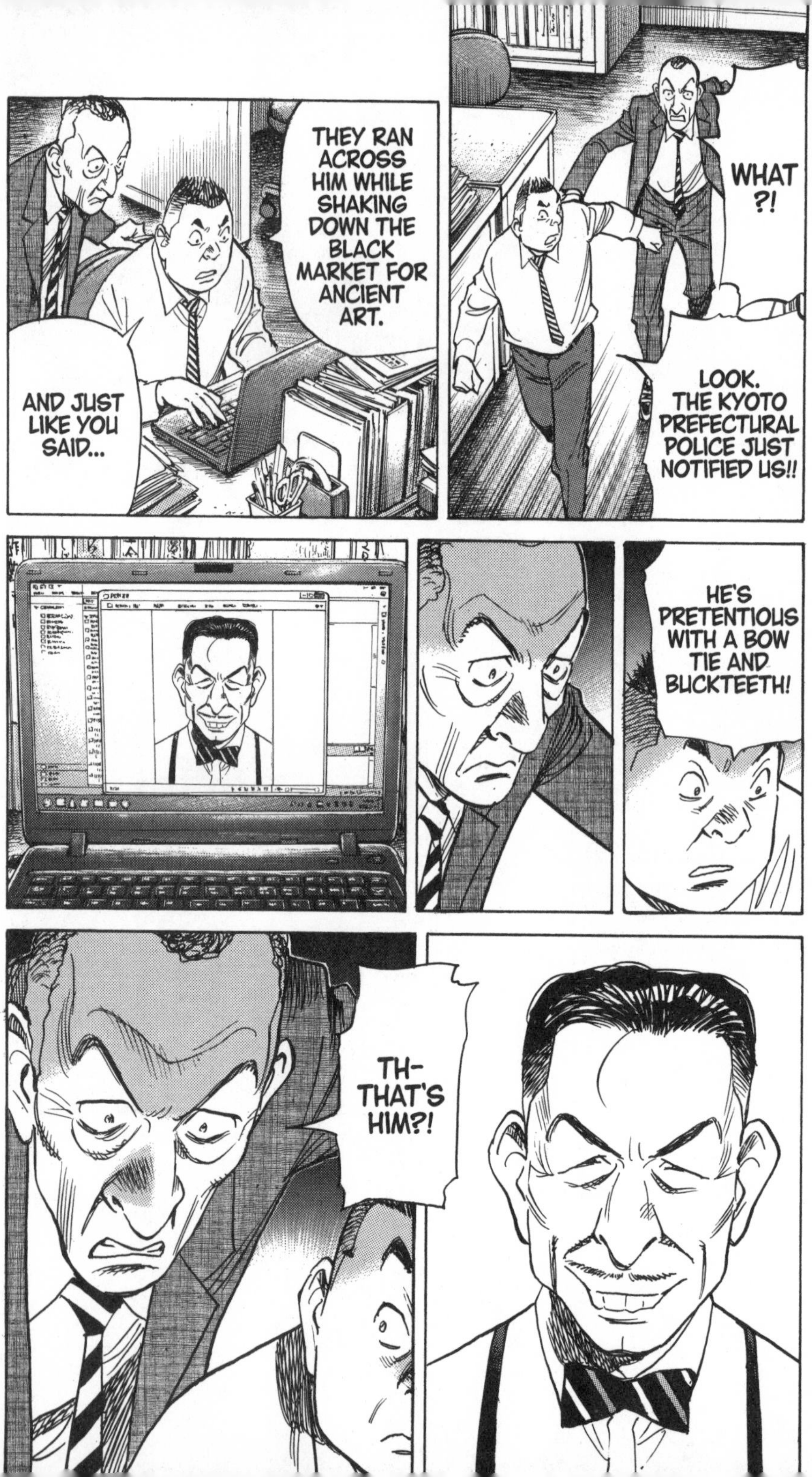
WHAT?!
LOOK. THE KYOTO PREFECTURAL POLICE JUST NOTIFIED US!!
THEY RAN ACROSS HIM WHILE SHAKING DOWN THE BLACK MARKET FOR ANCIENT ART.
AND JUST LIKE YOU SAID...
HE'S PRETENTIOUS WITH A BOW TIE AND BUCKTEETH!
TH- THAT'S HIM?!

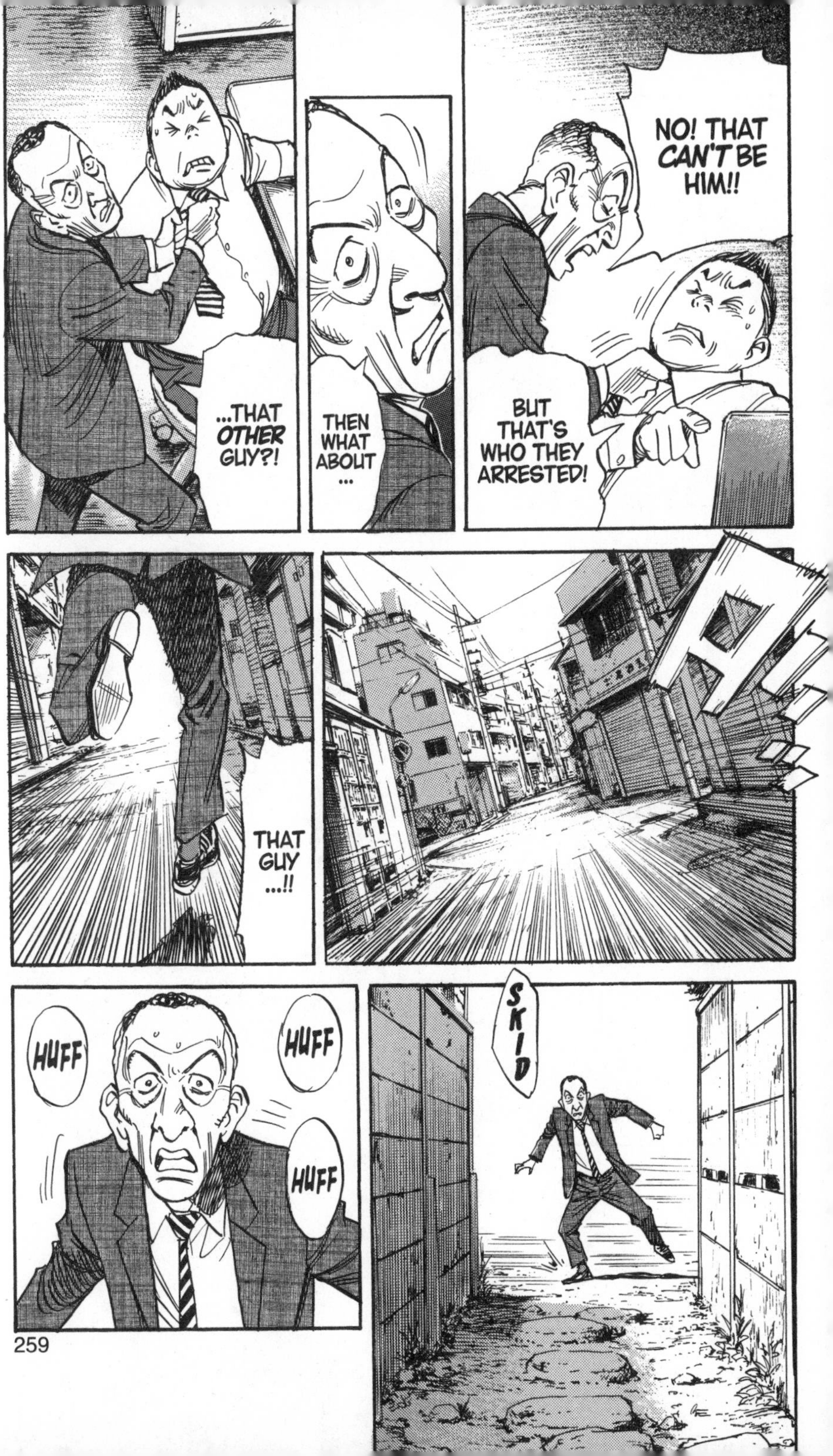
NO! THAT CAN'T BE HIM!!
BUT THAT'S WHO THEY ARRESTED!
THEN WHAT ABOUT ...
...THAT OTHER GUY?!
THAT GUY ...!!
SKID
HUFF
HUFF
HUFF

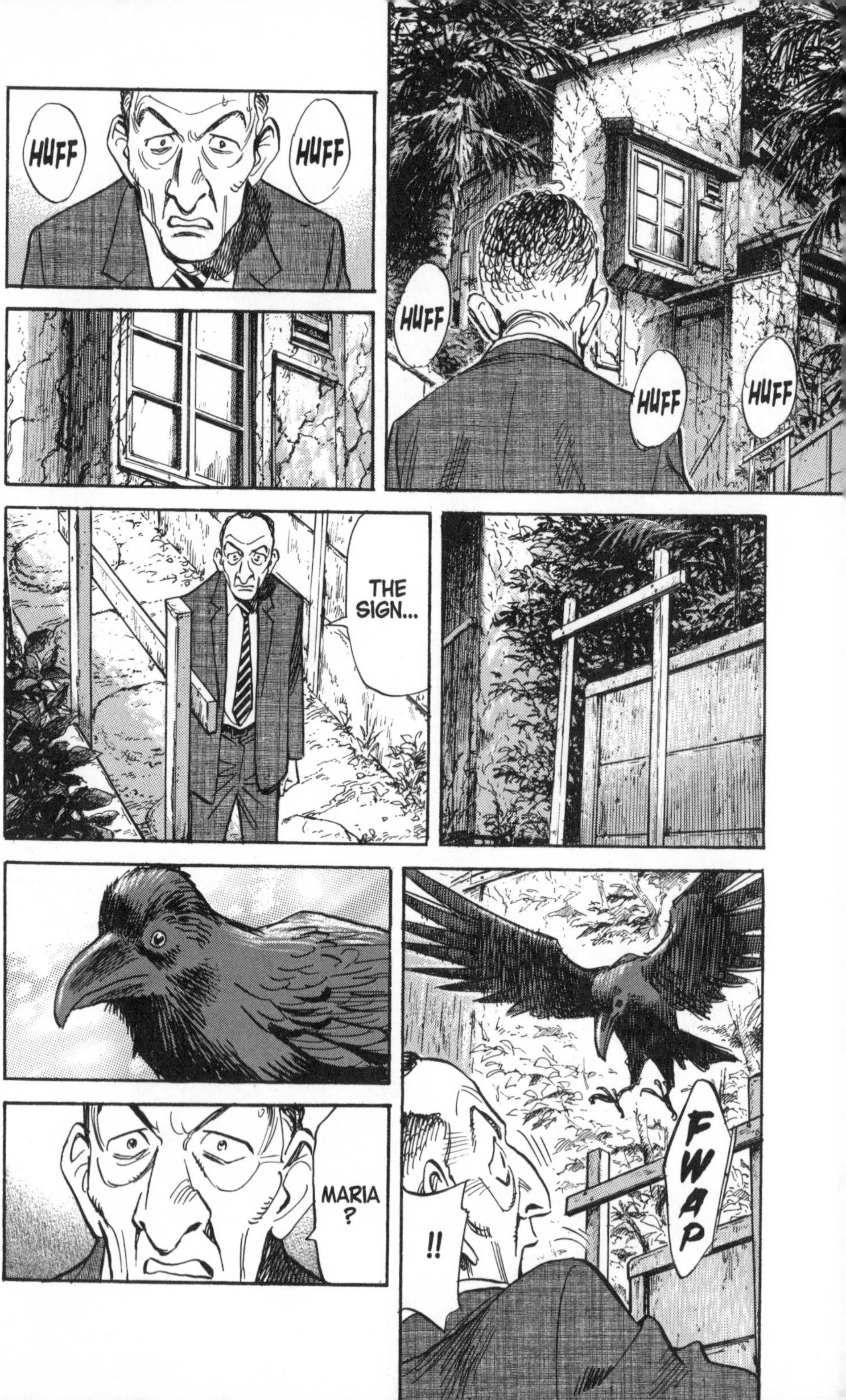
HUFF
HUFF
HUFF
HUFF
HUFF
THE SIGN...
FWAP
!!
MARIA ?

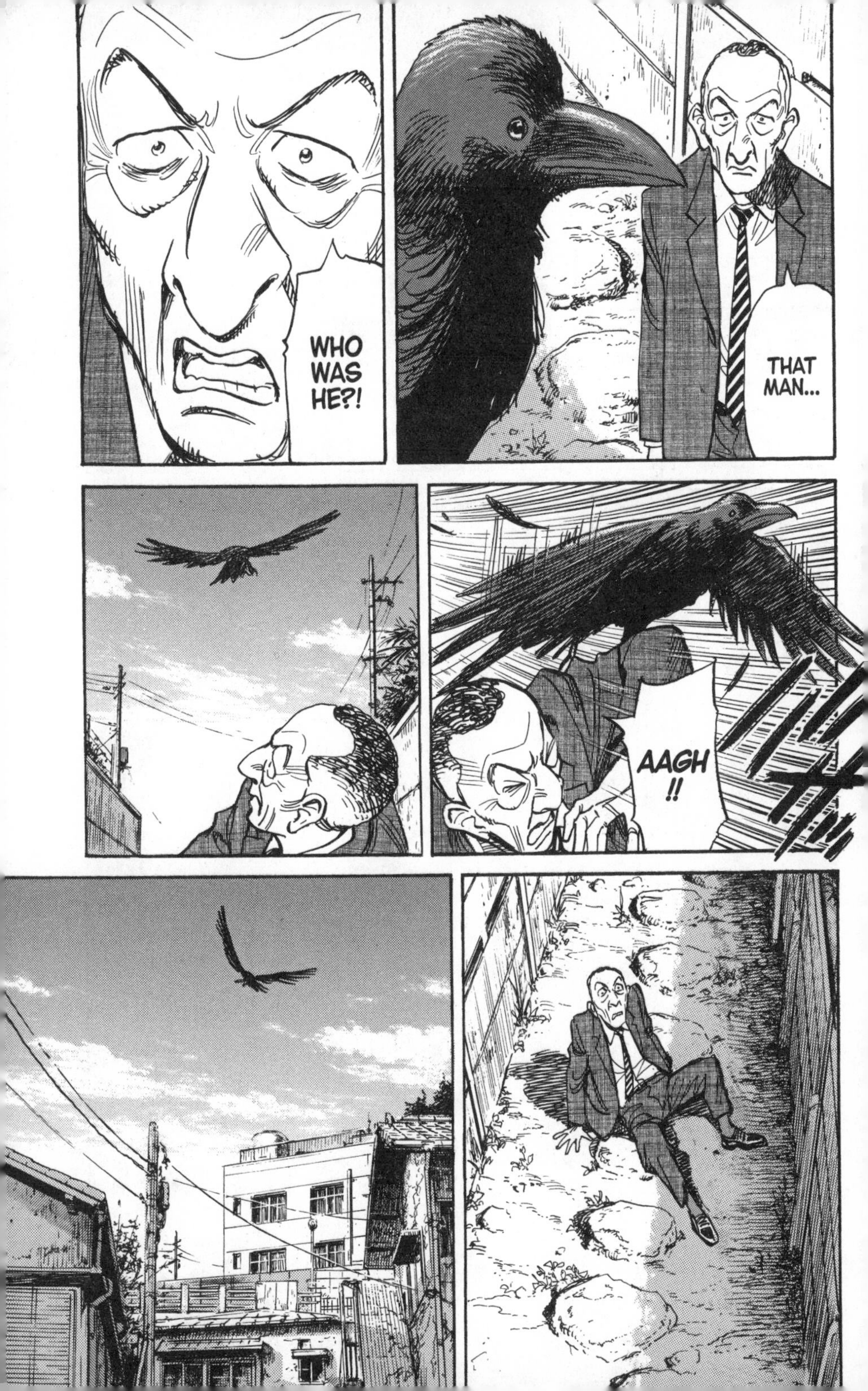
THAT MAN...
WHO WAS HE?!
AAGH !!

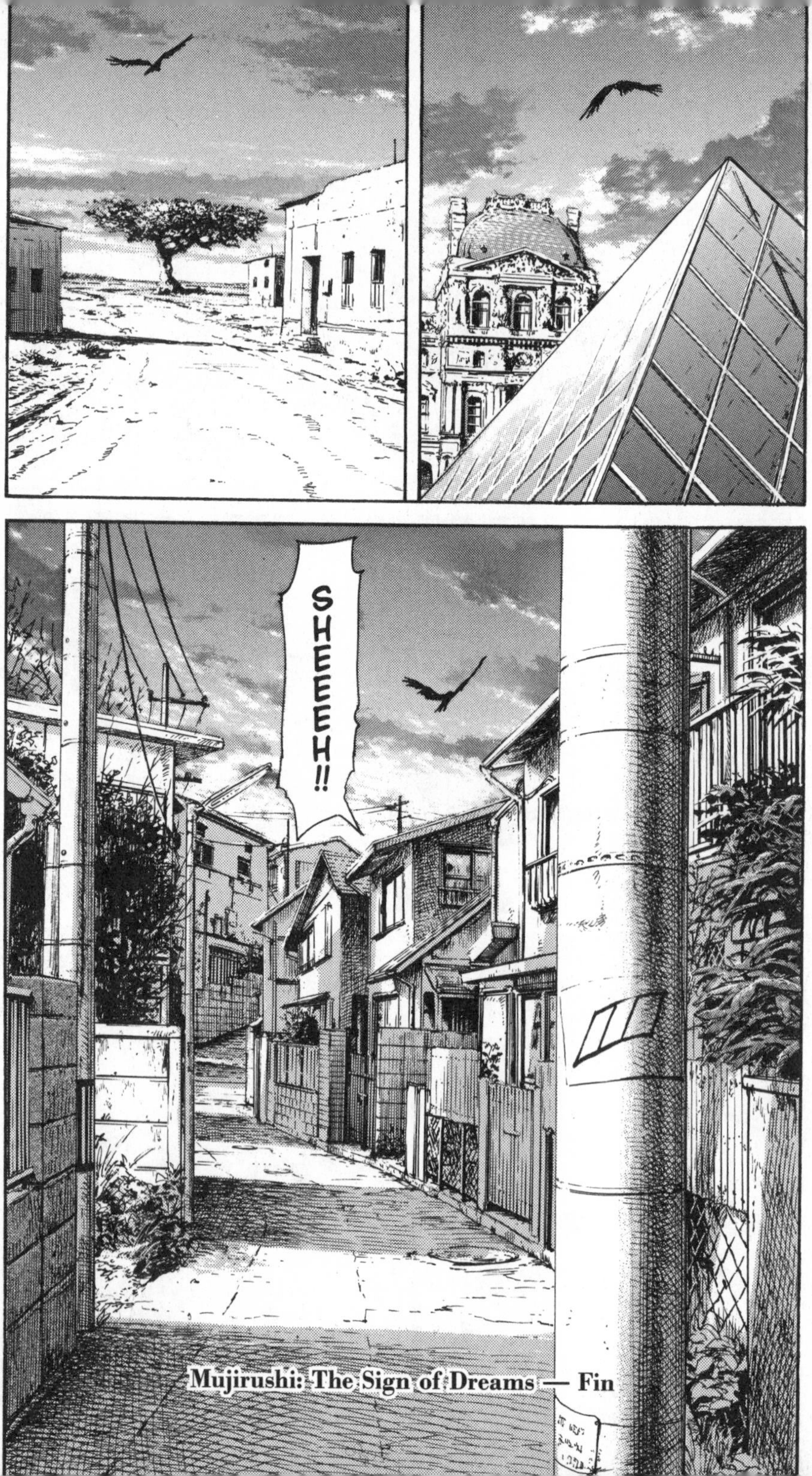
SHEEEEH!!
Mujirushi: The Sign of Dreams — Fin

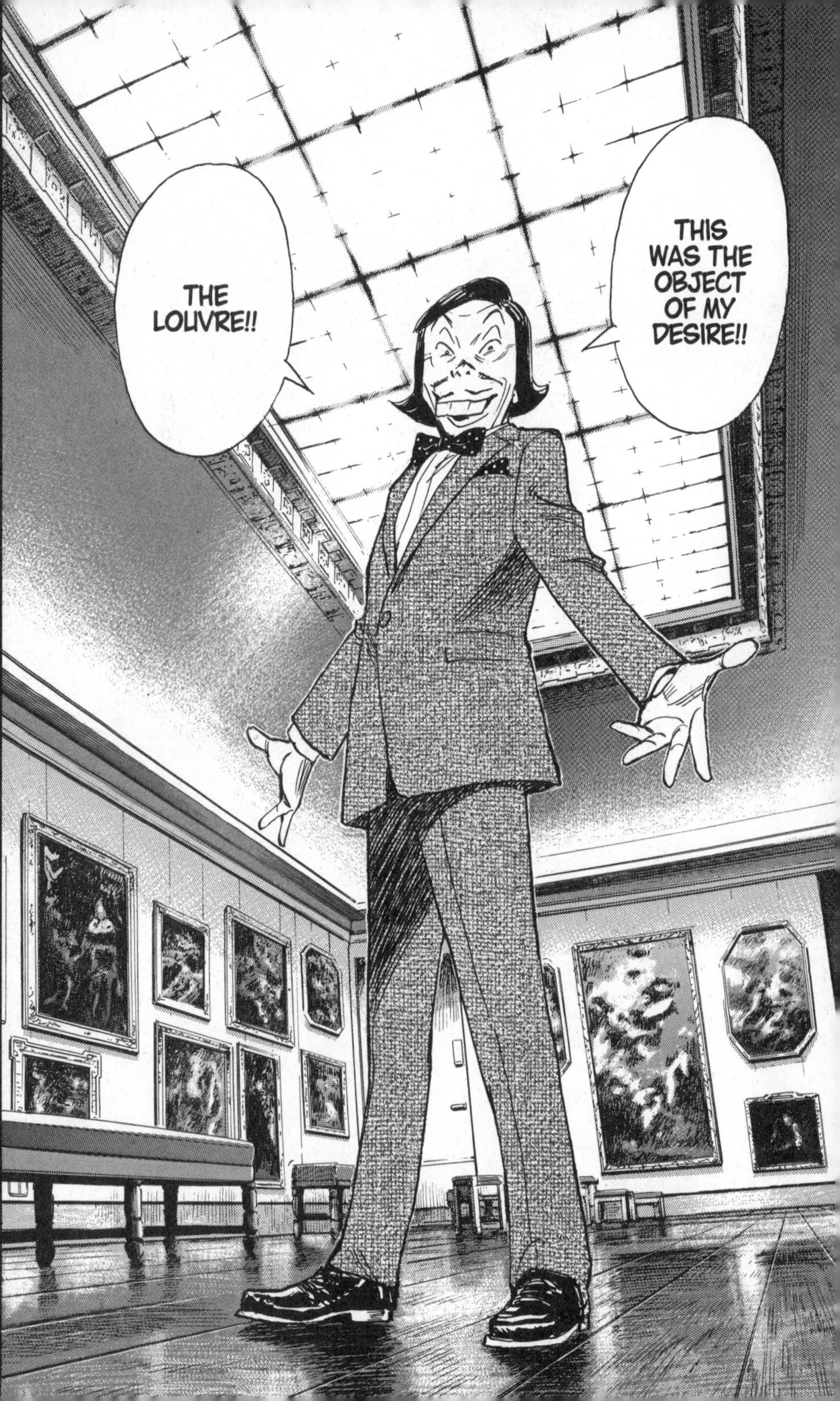
THIS WAS THE OBJECT OF MY DESIRE!!
THE LOUVRE!!

66

Iyami from Fujio Akatsuka's *Osomatsu-kun*
appears in this manga. Iyami's popularity
and influence was so great that in the mid-
'60s in Japan, whenever children took a
picture they did his iconic "Sheeh" pose.

But children weren't the only ones inspired
by Iyami. Godzilla once struck the pose
in a movie, and when the Beatles visited
Japan, John Lennon and Paul McCartney
even joined in on the fun.

99

SPOKEN BY
NAOKI URASAWA

193.7 - hwoosh (da: running)

194.6 - hwam (ban: slamming door)

194.8 - bam bam (don don: hitting door)

195.1 - bam bam bam (don don don: hitting door)

195.2 - bam bam (don don: hitting door)

196.1 - tromp (za: footsteps)

196.4 - bam bam (don don: hitting door)

200.7 - fwsh (da: running)

202.1 - bam bam bam (don don don: hitting door)

202.2 - bam (don: hitting door)

203.2 - bam bam (don don: hitting door)

203.6 - whsh (da: running)

204.1 - whsh (da: running)

211.3 - fump (do: placing box)

212.1 - fadump bumpbmp (dodododo: falling)

214.5 - crik (gi: door creaking

214.6 - waaah (waaan: crowd talking)

228.1 - ftap (da: footstep)

231.1 - gshak (gashi: grabbing painting)

231.2 - katak (gatata: removing painting)

231.4 - vriiiiing (jiririririririririri: alarm)

231.6 - clatter (gatata: shaking)

232.1 - vriiing (jiririririri: alarm)

232.2-7 - vriiing vriiing (jiririri jiririri: alarm)

233.1-6 - vriiiiiiing (jiririririririri: alarm)

233.4 - whsh (da: running)

234.4-5 - vriiiiiiiing (jiririririririririri: alarm)

236-237.1 - booooooooo (buuuuuuuuu: shouting)

259.4 - whoosh (da: running)

261.3 - fwap (basa: wings flapping)

Sound Effects Glossary

The sound effects in this edition of *Mujirushi: The Sign of Dreams* have been preserved in their original Japanese format. To avoid additional lettering cluttering up the panels, a list of the sound effects (FX) is provided here.

Each FX is listed by page and panel number, so for example **6.3** would mean the FX is on **page 6** in **panel 3**.

3.6 – grab (ga: grasping)

4.1 – whsh (da: running)

11.2 – rattle rattle rattle rattle (gara gara gara gara: balls rattling)

11.7 – hurray (waaaa: cheering)

18.2 – swap (ban: slapping)

22.2 – bwonk (paa: train horn)

22.3 – vroosh (gaaaa: train passing)

26.4 – fwap (basasa: wings flapping)

60.1 – fwup (ba: raising paper)

60.3 – tromp tromp (doka doka: footsteps)

74.3 – bump (don: colliding)

74.4 – flup (ba: spilling wallet)

82.6 – whsh (da: running)

98.2 – tatump tump (dota dota: footsteps)

107.7 – whoosh (da: running)

111.1-4 – vreee (kiiiiin: airplane)

115.1-2 – gwooosh (gooooooo: flames)

116.5 – fwsh (ba: running)

116.6 – gwooosh (goooo: flames)

117.3-6 – gwooosh (gooooooo: flames)

118.1 – gwoosh (goooo: fire hose)

118.2-3 – spwaah (zaa: shower)

143.3 – whoosh (da: running)

193.4 – whoosh (da: running)

Completed around 1669–1670, Johannes Vermeer's *The Lacemaker* joined the Louvre's Dutch paintings collection in 1870. The smallest of the few paintings completed by the Dutch Golden Age artist, *The Lacemaker* continues Vermeer's study of everyday domestic life.

PAGE 91:
A *chanson* is a type of lyric-driven, often nonreligious French folk song, originating anytime from the Middle Ages to the present day across a variety of styles.

PAGE 127:
Chouquettes are a type of French choux pastry, similar to a cream puff, topped with pearl sugar.

PAGE 130:
At the end of page 129, Michel lists all the things that Kyoko taught him about Japan, beginning with common words like *sumo* and *kabuki*. But it's on this page that he begins to list uncommon words, such as *Akita meibutsu* (Akita's famous products), *Hachimori Hatahata* (hachimori butterfish) and *Oga de Oga buriko* (Oga yellowtail). These words come from a folk song called "Akita Ondo" (literally the "Akita Marching Song") that originated in Japan's Akita prefecture. Since these are not common words in Japan, Kasumi is understandably confused.

PAGE 162:
When Mizoguchi asks why the crow is called Maria, the Director replies that it's "only fitting." However, the literal translation of his reply is, "Because it's *karasu* (crow), it must be Maria." The idea is that the two naturally go together. This is due to a play on words. The Japanese word for crow, *karasu*, is written in the same way as the last name of renowned opera singer Maria Callas in Japanese.

PAGE 217:
Nikujaga is a common winter dish in Japan made by stewing meat, potatoes and onions in a sweet soy sauce.

Translation Notes

PAGE 42:
There's a reason the Director looks so familiar. He's the longtime side character and antagonist Iyami in the popular *Osomatsu* media franchise. Much like his portrayal here, the Iyami seen in *Osomatsu* is a Francophile and a con artist, who claims to be from France. Though there's no proof of him having ever been there.

PAGE 51:
Anne Pingeot, born May 13, 1943, wasn't just former president of France Francois Mitterand's mistress. As an art historian, she is an expert on 19th-century French sculpture. She even worked as a curator for the sculpture departments at both the Louvre and Musée d'Orsay.

PAGE 56:
Okame, or *otafuku,* are a type of Japanese mask. *Okame* literally translates to "tortoise," a symbol of longevity in Japan, and *otafuku* to "much good fortune." The mask, the feminine half of the traditional Japanese *kyogen* (comic theater) pair, depicts an always-smiling, full-cheeked Japanese woman said to bring good fortune to any man she marries.

PAGE 63:
Baltan is an alien race from Planet Baltan featured prominently in the *Ultraman* franchise.

PAGE 64:
Sylvie Vartan is a Bulgarian-French singer and actress best known for the songs she recorded during the yé-yé craze, a Beatles-influenced pop style that took Southern Europe by storm in the early 1960s.

PAGE 66:
Kuri-yokan is the chestnut variety of *yokan,* a jellied Japanese dessert made with red bean paste.

夢 MUJIRUSHI 印
The Sign of Dreams
VIZ SIGNATURE EDITION

STORY & ART BY **NAOKI URASAWA**

TRANSLATION & ADAPTATION **John Werry**
TOUCH-UP ART & LETTERING **Steve Dutro**
DESIGN **Alice Lewis**
EDITOR **Karla Clark**

MUJIRUSHI
by Naoki URASAWA
© 2018 Naoki URASAWA/N WOOD STUDIO

All rights reserved.
Original Japanese edition published by SHOGAKUKAN.
English translation rights in the United States of America, Canada, the United Kingdom, Ireland,
Australia and New Zealand arranged with SHOGAKUKAN.

Cooperation / Fujio Production Ltd.
©Fujio Akatsuka
Special Cooperation / Musée du Louvre

©Musée du Louvre

Kazuo UMINO, Isao YOSHIMURA + Bay Bridge Studios

Autumn Leaves
English lyric by Johnny Mercer
French lyric by Jacques Prevert
Music by Joseph Kosma
(c) 1947, 1950 (Renewed) ENOCH ET CIE
Sole Selling Agent for U.S. and Canada: MORLEY MUSIC CO., by agreement with ENOCH ET CIE
All Rights Reserved
Reprinted by Permission of Hal Leonard LLC

Under Paris Skies (Sous Le Ciel De Paris)
English Words by Kim Gannon
French Words by Jean Drejac
Music by Hubert Giraud
Copyright (c) 1951, 1953, 1956 (Renewed) by Editions Choudens
All Rights for the U.S. and Canada Controlled by Music Sales Corporation (ASCAP)
International Copyright Secured   All Rights Reserved
Reprinted by Permission of Hal Leonard LLC

Printed in Canada

Published by VIZ Media, LLC
P.O. Box 77010
San Francisco, CA 94107

10 9 8 7 6 5 4 3 2 1
First printing, July 2020

VIZ MEDIA
viz.com

VIZ SIGNATURE

vizsignature.com